CONTRACT LAW

PRINCIPLES AND CONTEXT

Contract Law: Principles and Context presents the development of contract law through a considered selection of cases that are both authoritative and used as factual examples to explain the law.

The text introduces readers to the nature and range of contracts, the process for making a contract, rights and duties, adjustments to contracts, vitiating factors and unfair conduct, ending contracts, and remedies and restitution. The text considers the historical development of contracts through case law and legislation, then takes the reader to particular issues with contracts as they might arise in real life and navigates a legal pathway through them.

Written in a clear and engaging style, *Contract Law* provides a fresh, topical and accessible account of the Australian law of contract, and is an invaluable resource for contract law students and practitioners.

Andrew Stewart is the John Bray Professor of Law at the University of Adelaide and works as a consultant with the national law firm Piper Alderman.

Warren Swain is Professor of Law and Deputy Dean in the Faculty of Law at the University of Auckland.

Karen Fairweather is a Senior Lecturer in the Faculty of Law at the University of Auckland.

CONTRACT LAW

PRINCIPLES AND CONTEXT

Andrew Stewart
Warren Swain
Karen Fairweather

CAMBRIDGE
UNIVERSITY PRESS

CAMBRIDGE
UNIVERSITY PRESS

University Printing House, Cambridge CB2 8BS, United Kingdom

One Liberty Plaza, 20th Floor, New York, NY 10006, USA

477 Williamstown Road, Port Melbourne, VIC 3207, Australia

314–321, 3rd Floor, Plot 3, Splendor Forum, Jasola District Centre, New Delhi – 110025, India

79 Anson Road, #06–04/06, Singapore 079906

Cambridge University Press is part of the University of Cambridge.

It furthers the University's mission by disseminating knowledge in the pursuit of education, learning and research at the highest international levels of excellence.

www.cambridge.org
Information on this title: www.cambridge.org/9781107687486

First published 2019

Cover designed by Anne-Marie Reeves
Typeset by SPi Global
Printed in China by C & C Offset Printing Co. Ltd, April 2019

A catalogue record for this publication is available from the British Library

A catalogue record for this book is available from the National Library of Australia

ISBN 978-1-107-68748-6 Paperback

CONTENTS

PREFACE

It is hard to think of a more foundational legal subject than contract law. Most forms of legal practice involve advising on issues or disputes involving contracts – which is precisely why it is a compulsory area of study in any law degree (and often business degrees as well). But more than that, contracts are central to modern life. For most of us, they provide a framework for earning a living, operating a bank account, accessing the internet, buying daily essentials, and so much more besides.

For all three of us, thinking, writing, talking and advising about this fundamental topic has been a central part of our academic and professional lives. The urge to write this book was born out of a belief that it was possible to produce a relatively concise and practically focused account of the Australian law of contract, and at the same time explore the critical issues in the field that so fascinate us as teachers and scholars. Our aim has been to write a high quality, topical and accessible book that provides insights into current controversies and a wealth of further references for those who wish to dig deeper. It is a work that, we hope, is firmly grounded in the law, practice and policy issues of today, while still explaining the historical evolution of the subject. The text incorporates developments up to September 2018, although a few later references are also included.

There are always many people to thank on a project of this scale. We have received research assistance and feedback from a number of colleagues and students, including (in alphabetical order) Ryan Catterwell, Jordan Curtis, John Eldridge, Daniel Gambitsis, Mark Giancaspro, Ross Grantham, Philip Rocconi, Shauna Roeger, Jessica Viven-Wilksch and Alex Wawryk. We are also grateful for the helpful comments provided by the anonymous reviewers engaged by the publisher to look over our draft chapters. Nina Sharpe was instrumental in commissioning the book, while Lucy Russell has shown wonderful patience in shepherding it through to completion and been an unfailing source of both encouragement and support. We have also appreciated Ellie Gleeson's expert editing, and Jodie Fitzsimmons' help in getting the book to press. But, most of all, we would like to thank our nearest and dearest, who as always have had to put up with some distracted and frantic authors!

Andrew Stewart
Warren Swain
Karen Fairweather
December 2018

TABLE
OF CASES

TABLE OF STATUTES

ACKNOWLEDGEMENTS

We are grateful to the following individuals and organisations for permission to use their material in *Contract Law*.

Extract from A. Stewart and R. Owens *Experience or Exploitation? The Nature, Prevalence and Regulation of Unpaid Work Experience, Internships and Trial Periods in Australia*. Fair Work Ombudsman, Melbourne, 2013. © Fair Work Ombudsman www.fairwork.gov.au.

Extracts from *Legione v Hateley* (1983) 152 CLR 406; *Trident General Insurance Co Ltd v McNiece Bros Pty Ltd* (1988) 165 CLR 107: Reproduced with permission of Thomson Reuters (Professional) Australia Limited, legal.thomsonreuters.com.au.

Extracts from the National Credit Code (NCC): © Australian Securities and Investments Commission. Reproduced with permission. The National Credit Code is a schedule to the *National Consumer Credit Protection Act 2009*, which is administered by the Australian Securities and Investments Commission (ASIC). The current version is available at www.legislation.gov.au/Details/C2018C00302.

Every effort has been made to trace and acknowledge copyright. The publisher apologises for any accidental infringement and welcomes information that would redress this situation.

PART

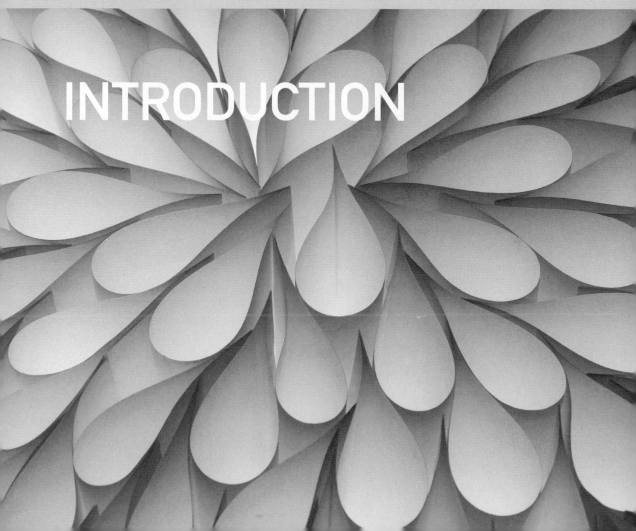

INTRODUCTION

1

SOME BASIC QUESTIONS

What is a contract?

1.01   The prevalence of contracts

We make contracts all the time, even if we don't realise or think about it; for instance, when we buy a cup of coffee, or get on a bus or train, or use a commercial car park. There is a tendency to think about contracts as written or printed documents.[1] Ask an employee if they have a contract, and they'll usually answer 'yes' only if they can remember signing some sort of formal agreement. But, in fact, *every* employee has a contract. Merely agreeing to work in return for wages constitutes a contract in the eyes of the law, even if all the arrangements were made verbally and there is little, if any, documentation of the terms of the job. The same is true for many other everyday transactions. If you buy something, or agree to pay money for a service (such as being transported somewhere, or having your property looked after), you are generally making a contract. Certain types of contract have to be recorded in writing to be legally enforceable; for example, an agreement to buy and sell land. But those types are very much the exception, not the rule: see **5.44**.

If contracts are important to individual consumers, they are absolutely central to the operation of any business. Most commercial enterprises will, at some point, acquire premises and/or a website, secure finance, open a bank account, purchase supplies, employ staff, insure against certain risks or losses – and, of course, agree to supply goods or services to their clients. Once again, all of those transactions involve contracts.

Contracts are not quite all-pervasive. There are some transactions that, for reasons explored below, the law does not recognise as involving a contract. And, in at least one major instance, Australian law has stopped treating a type of agreement as being contractual in nature: that being an arrangement to get married. It used to be possible to sue your fiancé(e) for 'breach of promise' if they failed to honour an engagement to marry, but that type of action was abolished in Australia by legislation in 1976.[2] In other respects, however, contracts are on the rise. In the government sector, for instance, many arrangements or relationships are now recognised as having a contractual basis – even if there remain important exceptions.[3]

1.02   A rough definition

So what then is a *contract*? The word can be used in many ways or contexts; consider, for example, the notion of a 'social contract' in political philosophy, or the 'psychological contract' that is said to lie at the heart of modern employment relations.[4] But in a book of this kind, we are using the term in its legal sense. Even then, it is hard to give an answer that is both accurate and concise. A rough definition would be this: an *agreement* between two or more *parties*, involving one or more *promises* that are *given for something in return*, and that the parties *intend to be legally enforceable*.

---

1   See eg Wilkinson-Ryan & Hoffman 2015, presenting empirical evidence that most individuals associate contracts with some kind of *formalised* agreement.
2   See *Marriage Act 1961* (Cth) s 111A, inserted by the *Marriage Amendment Act 1976* (Cth).
3   See Seddon 2018: ch 1; and see further **5.07**.
4   See eg Rousseau 1762; Rousseau 1995. It is a striking coincidence that the authors of leading works in these very different fields should happen to share the same surname!

More is said about the requirements for contract formation in Chapter 5. But for now, three elements of this definition are worth exploring in a little more detail: the concept of being a 'party' to a contract; the significance of legal enforceability and how we know when it is intended; and the requirement that a contract involve some kind of exchange.

1.03   The parties to a contract

The term *party* will be used a lot in this book, generally to mean a person who has made a contract with someone else. The 'person' concerned may be an individual, or an artificial entity (such as a corporation or a state) that the law treats as if it were a person. Corporations or governments can enter into legally binding agreements, even though they necessarily have to act through the agency of human beings.[5]

In practice, the vast majority of contracts are made between two parties (buyer and seller, landlord and tenant, employer and employee, etc). Most of the book is written on that assumption; for instance, by referring to 'both parties', 'the other party', and so on. But it is certainly possible to make a contract with more than two parties, as Chapter 8 will explain. That chapter also explores the legal position of a *third party*. Confusingly, this term generally denotes a person who is *not* a party to a particular contract, but who is affected by it or connected to it in some way. As will be seen, the general rule in Australia is that a third party cannot enforce a contract, nor can it be enforced against them. This is true even if the parties to the contract intended to confer a benefit or an obligation on that person. This principle is known as the doctrine of *privity of contract*.

To take a simple example, suppose a manufacturer makes a batch of electrical goods and sells them to a distributor. The distributor sells some of them to a retailer. The retailer sells one of these items (say, a toaster) to you. What we have here is a chain of contracts, with different parties to each. If the toaster doesn't work, you may be able to sue the retailer for *breach of contract* (that is, for failing to comply with a contractual obligation), for reasons explained in Chapter 9. But you, the consumer, cannot sue the manufacturer on that basis, because, in this case, you are not party (or 'privy') to any contract with that business.[6] This is not to say you have no remedy at all. You may, for example, be able to sue the manufacturer for committing the *tort* (a civil wrong) of negligence, or for breaching Part 3–5 of the Australian Consumer Law (ACL).[7] But there can be no claim under the law of contract.

1.04   The intention for an agreement to be legally enforceable

Not all agreements are contracts. For example, if two friends agree to meet for dinner, that is just a social arrangement. It would be absurd to suppose that if one didn't show up, the other could take them to court and sue for breach of contract. It would be understood that the arrangement was not one that was *intended* to carry legal consequences.

---

5   As to the power of an agent to enter into a contract on behalf of their 'principal', see further **8.04**.
6   But compare the famous case of *Carlill v Carbolic Smoke Ball* (1893), where a contract *was* found to exist between a manufacturer and a consumer: see **5.06**.
7   See Luntz et al 2017: 427–31, 847–56. As to the ACL, see **1.15**.

Contracts are a form of private law-making. Many laws are imposed by the state, in the form of prohibitions and commandments. Depending on how they are framed, these norms of conduct may be enforced either through the criminal justice system (where the state itself pursues sanctions against a law-breaker), or through civil proceedings (where one member of society asks a court to impose remedies against another).[8] But our legal system also allows citizens and organisations to voluntarily assume obligations that can be enforced by the state's legal apparatus. There are a number of ways in which this can happen. For example, one or more persons may create a *trust* – an arrangement that requires specified property to be held by one person and dealt with for the benefit of another: see **8.14**. But the most common way in which legal obligations are privately created is through the making of a contract. As the High Court of Australia put it in *Australian Woollen Mills v Commonwealth* (1954) at 457: 'It is of the essence of contract, regarded as a class of obligations, that there is a voluntary assumption of a legally enforceable duty.'[9]

So how do we know whether, in making an agreement, the parties do in fact intend that a failure to comply with the agreement may lead to a civil action for breach of contract? What if the issue was never discussed? In theory, this might present a problem; but in practice it generally doesn't. This is because an intention for an agreement to be enforceable can often be inferred, simply from the nature of the transaction. If you agree to buy, sell or hire something, or to work in return for some form of payment, it can be assumed that you and the other party intended the arrangement to be legally binding, unless there is something in your dealings to suggest otherwise. Conversely, if you make some kind of arrangement with a family member or friend, especially of a non-commercial kind, the courts are less likely to identify an intention to make a contract (or an *intention to create legal relations*, as it is often put). More is said about this in Chapter 5.

If there is a problem with intention that tends to crop up in practice, it is in determining *at what point* the parties have formulated an agreement they intend to be legally binding. It is not uncommon for parties to arrive at a tentative or preliminary agreement, while contemplating either some further process of negotiation, or the need for some condition to be satisfied, before the arrangement is finalised. The status and enforceability of such preliminary agreements is considered in Chapter 6.

It is also important to understand that contractual intention is usually assessed *objectively*. A court does not usually ask what the parties actually or *subjectively* intended. Rather, the question is what a reasonable person would believe they had in mind: see **5.02–5.03**, **10.02**.

1.05   Contract as exchange

In some legal systems, a promise to do something may become legally enforceable even if it is *gratuitous* – that is, given with no expectation or insistence that the *promisor* (the person making the promise) will receive anything in return from the *promisee* (the person to whom it

---

8   The line between criminal and civil liability has been significantly blurred in recent years by the rise of regulatory regimes that allow government agencies to seek what are described as civil remedies (including monetary fines) for breaches of statutory requirements: see eg *Commonwealth v Director, Fair Work Building Industry Inspectorate* (2015); and see further **3.16**.

9   For analysis of what it means to speak of a contract as a *voluntary* act, see Robertson 2005.

is made). For example, under the 'civil law' systems that predominate in Europe, it is generally sufficient that the reason (*causa*) for making the promise is a serious or significant one.[10]

Under Australian law, by contrast, a gratuitous promise cannot be the basis for a contract. This is one of the many principles that we inherited from the English common law: that a contract must involve (or, as it is sometimes said, be 'supported by') *consideration*. In this context, 'consideration' is a technical term that packs a lot of legal meaning into a single word. It denotes a requirement of bargain or exchange – or as the Latin phrase puts it, *quid pro quo*. What one party is promising to do must be in return for something that the other party is doing or promising to do. So, if you promise to give someone a car, that is just a gift, a gratuitous promise. But if you promise to give someone a car *in return* for them promising to give you some money, that element of reciprocity satisfies the requirement of consideration: you have made a contract of sale. That is true even if nothing has yet been done to fulfil those promises. An exchange of commitments is sufficient.

The doctrine of consideration also requires that what each party is doing or promising to do must have 'value'. Normally, that requirement is easily satisfied – especially as the law does not generally require that what is given represent fair or 'adequate' value. So in the example just given, both the car and the promised sum of money will be treated as 'good consideration' – even if the sum in question represents far less than the car might be worth to other purchasers. But, as will be explained in Chapter 5, there are also some highly technical rules as to what constitutes 'valuable consideration'. Some commitments are treated as 'insufficient' to constitute good consideration; for instance, promising to do something that you are already obliged to do.

While the requirement of consideration means that gratuitous promises cannot be legally enforced, there are at least two important exceptions. The first is that any promise will be rendered enforceable, even in the absence of consideration, if it is expressed in a formal document known as a *deed*: see **5.47**. The second stems from the operation of a doctrine known as *estoppel*. In some cases at least, as Chapter 7 will explain, this may allow a promisee to go to court and hold a promisor to their commitment, where the promisee has relied on the promise to their detriment.

1.06 Bilateral and unilateral contracts

The overwhelming majority of contracts are *bilateral* in nature; that is, they involve each party promising to do something for the other.[11] A vendor promises to deliver goods or hand over the title to land, in return for the purchaser agreeing to pay for the property they are acquiring. A landlord agrees to give temporary possession of land or premises, in exchange for the tenant undertaking to pay rent. An employee promises to provide their labour, on the

---

10   As to the distinction between *causa* and the common law notion of 'consideration' discussed below, see eg Lorenzen 1919. Interestingly, a recent package of reforms intended to modernise French contract law has abolished the *causa* requirement: see *Ordinance No 2016–131*; and for background, see Rowan 2017: 816–18.

11   Some judges use the term 'synallagmatic' in preference to bilateral: see eg *Hong Kong Fir Shipping v Kawasaki Kisen Kaisha* (1962) at 65. But compare *Simic v New South Wales Land and Housing* (2016) at [16], [36], highlighting the term's origin in civil law systems to refer to a particular type of what common lawyers would call a 'bilateral contract'.

basis that the employer will pay them for their work. In each of these and many other similar cases, there is generally a moment (no matter how brief) where the parties' agreement is wholly *executory*; that is, they have exchanged promises, but are yet to fulfil them. To put it another way, when a bilateral contract is made, both parties typically assume an obligation to do something they have not yet done.

With a small minority of contracts, however, the obligation is only ever on one side: these are called *unilateral* contracts. One party promises to do something, if the other party satisfies some condition that they *may* fulfil, but are not *bound* to fulfil. The classic example is a reward. You promise someone a sum of money if they supply you with certain information (say, the whereabouts of your missing cat, or the identity of someone who has committed a criminal offence), which they may or may not be able to do, and are not promising to do. If the promisee fails to supply the information, you cannot sue them for breach of contract. Indeed there *is* no contract – unless and until the promisee performs the act you have requested. If they do so, that provides the consideration for your executory promise and you now become obliged to fulfil it. But at no point is the promisee under any obligation to perform. More is said about unilateral contracts and some of the legal issues they raise in Chapter 5. But it is worth emphasising that in practice they are very much the exception rather than the rule.

Why should promises be enforced?

1.07   Moral explanations

In Chapter 2 we briefly survey some of the large body of literature on the theoretical underpinnings of contract law. Some of that literature seeks to explain the enforceability of contracts by reference to what are essentially *moral* considerations. These include the *ethical imperative* to keep a promise, a recognition that the parties to a transaction have *consented* to the imposition of legal obligations, or the need to protect a person whose *reliance* on a promise being kept has caused them to act in a particular way.

The problem with many of these theories, however, is their limited descriptive force – they struggle to explain some of the rules of modern contract law. They have also, for the most part, been developed well after the 'classical' period in the nineteenth century when, as described below, many of those rules crystallised into something like their current form. The key lawmakers of that period may conceivably have had a fully formed set of ideas that underlay the principles they were helping to formulate. But if they did, it was rare for them to be mentioned or explained.[12]

1.08   A practical perspective: security, specification and risk allocation

At the risk of being accused of oversimplification, it seems to us that the main reason that what we now describe as 'contractual' promises are considered to be legally enforceable is a simple one. If they were not, the trade in property, services and credit that has

---

12   See further **2.05** concerning the influences on, and limitations of, 'classical' contract theory.

become central to modern societies would, if not break down entirely, at least have to operate in a very different fashion.[13]

Contracts arguably perform at least three key functions in relation to commercial dealings. The first is to *secure supply*; that is, to bolster the expectation that what one party has promised, the other will in fact receive. One of the most influential modern writers on contract law, Hugh Collins, notes that some markets have been shown to function effectively even without state enforcement. And even where there is a legal apparatus available to enforce promises, the trust that one party places in the other to fulfil their commitments may play at least as important a role in inducing transactions as the sanctions notionally available in the event of non-performance. Furthermore, non-legal sanctions (such as the threat of refusing to transact in the future, or of inflicting reputational damage) are in practice used far more commonly than litigation.[14] All these points may be accepted. Yet it is still hard to believe that individuals and organisations could or would deal with one another in the same way without at least an *assumption* that their contracts could, if necessary, be legally enforced. This is a point that obviously takes on greater significance in relation to certain types of market, such as banking and financial services. The same applies to transactions involving large sums of money or between parties with low levels of trust.

A second function is to *specify* what has and has not been agreed. A failure to do this in relation to what are considered the 'essential' terms for a given type of transaction may render an agreement unenforceable, on the basis that it is 'incomplete': see **5.36**, **5.38**. As noted there, however, courts are often willing to imply terms to fill what would otherwise be significant gaps in what has been agreed.

A third important function of contracts is to *manage risk*. Besides stipulating any benefits to be conferred or tasks undertaken, the parties may agree on how certain eventualities are to be handled. These may relate to the parties themselves (such as a failure to meet a specified standard of performance, or a desire to vary or end the arrangement), or to matters outside their control (such as the unavailability of key supplies or finance, or a change in market conditions). The use of 'exemption clauses' to exempt or limit a party's liability for breach of contract or other wrongdoing is merely one example of such explicit risk allocation. Some transactions are indeed entered into with the primary purpose of managing a particular risk, such as an insurance contract or a contract of guarantee. Each of these types of arrangement are discussed in Chapter 11.

The fact that we are presenting here what might be seen as an *economic* explanation for the making and enforcement of contracts does not mean that we accept everything that has been written by way of economic analysis of contract law. For one thing, much of that writing is normative rather than positive: it is concerned with what the law *ought* to provide, as opposed to explaining or justifying its current rules. For another, as we note in **2.17**, there are very different strands of economic thinking at work in this literature, some more persuasive than others.

---

13   See eg Goddard 2000: 125–7, discussing the practicalities of not having an enforceable law of contract in Bangladesh. This is not to suggest that the rules of modern contract law should necessarily strive or be adapted to promote commercial needs: see **2.04**.

14   See Collins 1999: ch 5; and see further **2.04**. See also the discussion of 'self-help' remedies in **3.02–3.04**.

How and when did contract law develop?

1.09   The nature and origins of the common law

The modern law of contract in Australia, as in other countries colonised by the British (including the United States, India, Canada and New Zealand), is based on a set of principles that have their origins in the English common law. The term *common law* can have many different meanings: see *PGA v R* (2012) at [20]–[25]. But it is used here in the sense of a flexible body of rules formulated and developed by judges. Dating back to the twelfth century, and originally based on local customs, the English common law crystallised over a period of centuries into a set of recognised principles that could be applied to resolve legal disputes.[15] Although parliament came to be recognised as having the superior power to make laws, the common law could still fill the many gaps left by statutes and regulations.

Under the doctrine of precedent or *stare decisis* ('let the decision stand'), a court was expected to respect and 'apply' any previous decision by an earlier court that dealt with the same circumstances. This practice was facilitated by the publication of 'law reports' that summarised the facts of selected cases and reproduced all or part of the judgments given to decide them. In theory, once a common law rule was formulated by one judge, it was fixed for all time. In practice, however, a later judge might choose to 'distinguish' an earlier ruling, on the basis that it dealt with circumstances that were materially different. Some judges might overlook (deliberately or otherwise) a particular precedent, leading to conflicting 'authorities'. As the English courts became organised into hierarchies, it became more common for the 'superior' courts to have to resolve such conflicts. In this way the common law gradually evolved, with existing principles being qualified, refined and (occasionally) discarded as new decisions were given. It is now universally recognised that judges are at liberty to make new law as part of this process, within the constraints imposed by the doctrine of precedent: see eg *O'Toole v Charles David* (1990) at 267; *Commonwealth Bank v Barker* (2014) at [19]. But debate remains fierce as to how willing they should be to correct 'defects' in the law, and what factors should properly influence their decision-making.[16]

Unlike the civil codes that came to predominate in continental Europe, and that owed their origin to Roman law, the common law is by definition not set out in any authoritative document. Instead, it has to be gleaned or distilled from countless judicial rulings. In practice, many key principles are relatively uncontentious. But nevertheless, any attempts to 'state' the common law – including in a book like this one – necessarily involve informed guesswork. They are no more than predictions about how the authors expect a court to determine a case, based on what has gone before.[17]

---

15   For the best short overview of the history of the English common law, see Baker 2002: ch 2.

16   As to the debates over the respective merits of 'formalism' on the one hand, and 'pragmatism' or 'contextualism' on the other, see eg Thomas 2005: chs 3, 12; and see further **2.14**.

17   The extent to which courts are willing to have regard to the opinions of scholars (whether academic or otherwise), as expressed in textbooks or journal articles, differs from country to country, and from period to period: see the various articles in vol 29 no 1 of the *University of Queensland Law Journal* (2010). As to the particular status enjoyed in the US by the American Law Institute's *Restatements*, see **2.12**.

1.10   Development of the English law of contract

In Anglo-Saxon times, which ran from the fifth century to the arrival of the Normans in 1066, contracts required either swearing an oath or making an agreement and depositing a pledge in order to secure performance. A new law of contract began to emerge in the twelfth century.[18] Any structure was derived from the 'forms of action' then used in the courts: covenant, debt and trespass. Each action had its own distinct rules. In the thirteenth century, the action of covenant had the potential to develop into a catch-all action. The core of the claim was that an agreement had been entered into and was either not performed or mis-performed, with damages (an award of compensation) the standard remedy. But once use of a deed to record the agreement became mandatory in the early fourteenth century, covenant withered.[19]

Where a deed was used, the action of debt on a bond was an attractive option, especially for straightforward loan transactions. The name of the action was taken from the *bond*, which was a sealed instrument under which one person acknowledged that they were in debt to another. With the invention of the conditional bond, the action for debt became more flexible. Suppose A wanted B to build a house. B agreed to pay A £20, subject to a condition that the bond would be void if the house were built as agreed. This helped to secure performance and fixed a sum payable in the event of breach. The onus lay on B to show that they had performed. Failure to do so made them liable for £20, with very few defences available. In these circumstances, it is unsurprising that debt on a bond was the dominant contract action for many centuries.

Informal contracts were less easy to enforce. The action of debt on a contract was limited by the fact that although no deed was required, it could only be used in a claim for a fixed sum of money or goods. In the early Middle Ages, the actions of trespass, and trespass on the case, could be used in cases of contractual mis-performance and non-performance, because breaching an agreement was seen as a wrong (or what is now called a 'tort'). But during the thirteenth century, non-performance was excluded on the basis that 'not doing is no trespass'. This left gaps in the law relating to informal contracts in the important Royal Courts. Many such claims had to be litigated in the Local, Mercantile or even the Ecclesiastical Courts instead.

By the end of the fifteenth century, trespass on the case could once again be used for nonfeasance. From it, the action of *assumpsit* emerged. It took its name from the wording of the 'count' (ie the allegation in the claim): the defendant 'assumed and faithfully promised' to do something for the plaintiff. The count stressed that the obligation rested on a promise or contract. From around 1570, in order to bring assumpsit the plaintiff was also required to show that the promise was supported by good consideration. Consideration, as noted earlier, was based on the idea that the plaintiff had given something in exchange for the promise. Assumpsit was good at plugging gaps in the older remedies. It could be used for agreements for the sale of land and for services, and against executors where debt on a contract was unavailable. Plaintiffs also began to use assumpsit even where an action of debt could be brought, though some judges were still disinclined to allow this because there was an existing remedy. Matters came to a head in *Slade's Case* (1602), where a decision of all the judges

---

18   For a detailed account, see Ibbetson 1999.
19   For an account of this important development, see Baker 2012.

favoured allowing assumpsit even though debt was available. As a result, a general remedy for informal contracts was available once more.

The rise of assumpsit led to concerns that it was too easy to bring claims on verbal promises. The *Statute of Frauds 1677* (Imp) introduced a writing requirement for important agreements, such as those involving the sale of land or the sale of goods worth more than £10 (see **5.44**). Eighteenth century judges like Lord Mansfield sought to ensure that the law of contract better fitted with commercial expectations.[20] Mercantile practice was influential in helping to create the beginnings of the modern law of negotiable instruments (see **14.09**) and contracts of insurance. There matters rested until the rise of the so-called 'will' theory of contract in the nineteenth century (see **2.05**). By around 1870, under the influence of the great writers like Leake, Pollock and Anson, lawyers began to think in terms of a coherent and unified law of contract.[21] Their ideas formed the basis of the classical law of contract which, in a modified form, is still with us today.[22]

A key element of this model was, and is, the notion of *freedom of contract*. As Jessel MR famously put it in *Printing and Numerical Registering v Sampson* (1875) at 465:

> [I]f there is one thing which more than another public policy requires, it is that men [sic] of full age and competent understanding shall have the utmost liberty of contracting, and that their contracts when entered into freely and voluntarily shall be held sacred and shall be enforced by Courts of justice.

This type of statement emphasises both the importance of the law in facilitating the enforcement of contracts and the *autonomy* to be accorded to contracting parties in formulating their rights and obligations.

1.11   Australianising the common law

When the British colonists arrived in Australia in the late eighteenth and early nineteenth centuries, they brought with them both the English common law and any legislation (such as the *Statute of Frauds*) that could have general application, as opposed to being directed specifically to events or matters in Britain.[23] Once established, each of the colonies could pass legislation of their own, and their courts could, in theory, develop their own version of the common law. But in practice, the local judges tended to defer to the authority of the British courts, an attitude that persisted well past federation. For most of the twentieth century, Australian courts were generally content to treat British decisions as authoritative and there was little independent development of the common law. This changed in the 1970s and 1980s, as some of the remaining legal ties were cut with the UK (including the abolition of appeals to the London-based Privy Council). It was during this period in particular that the High Court of Australia began to assert a greater freedom to depart from British precedents, although earlier outbreaks of resistance can be identified.[24]

---

20   See Swain 2015a: 75–96. Lord Mansfield was described by a contemporary judge in *Lickbarrow v Mason* (1787) at 73 as 'the founder of the commercial law of this country'.
21   See Simpson 1975a; Waddams 2007; Swain 2015a: chs 8–9.
22   For an account of the foundations of the modern law, see Swain 2015a.
23   The formal date of 'reception' of these laws differs from colony to colony: see Castles 1982: chs 14–15.
24   See Mason 2004; Finn 2016.

In relation to the common law of contract, the years 1982 and 1983 saw a large number of cases reach the High Court, covering a wide range of contractual issues.[25] While few of the decisions could be regarded as particularly radical, the Court took the opportunity to put its own stamp on the law.[26] The next decade saw the Court develop the Australian common law in ways that departed from English precedents in key respects. A notable example was *Waltons Stores v Maher* (1988), concerning the doctrine of promissory estoppel (see **7.04– 7.06**). Since the mid-1990s, however, the Court has tended to adopt a narrower and more formalist approach to the development of the law. In the words of Paul Finn (2010: 47), it has displayed 'a marked preoccupation with doctrine and close doctrinal analysis not overtly influenced by policy considerations'.[27] But there has been no suggestion of any retreat from the commitment to a distinctively Australian approach. As French CJ put it, quoting one of his predecessors as Chief Justice of the High Court (Mason 1987 at 154), the value of English judgments today depends on 'the persuasive force of their reasoning': *Paciocco v ANZ Banking Group* (2016) at [8]. In that respect, they are given no greater status than those of other common law countries.

1.12   The growth in legislation

Early examples can be found in England of parliament intervening to regulate contracts (or, at least, what we would now regard as contractual dealings). In 1351, for instance, the *Statute of Labourers* introduced a set of rules to fix wages and govern the availability of workers in the wake of the Black Death. Before 1854, the rates of interest that could be charged on loan transactions were likewise regulated by the various statutes of usury.[28] The importance of the *Statute of Frauds 1677* in requiring certain common types of agreement to be in writing has already been noted. But it has been in the period since the late nineteenth century that statutory regulation of contracts has really taken off.

The preponderance of that regulation has been concerned with specific types of contracts. Sometimes, the purpose of legislating has simply been to 'codify' a body of principles already developed at common law. An important example of that was the *Sale of Goods Act 1893* (UK), which provided a model for similar statutes in force today in every Australian State and Territory.[29] But more commonly, legislation has been used to reform the law. For instance, the *Insurance Contracts Act 1984* (Cth) introduced important new requirements as to the way

---

25   To mention just a few, these included *Codelfa Construction v State Rail Authority* (1982) (see **9.21**, **15.05**); *Legione v Hateley* (1983) (see **7.07**, **16.24**); *Taylor v Johnson* (1983) (see **5.02**, **18.39**); and *Commercial Bank v Amadio* (1983) (see **20.04**).

26   As to the significance of this period, compared to what had gone before, see Carter & Stewart 1993. It is notable that the first entirely Australian contract law textbook did not appear until 1986, when the first edition of what is now Carter 2018 was published.

27   For a good example, see *Andrews v ANZ Banking Group* (2012), where the Court insisted on answering an important question about the modern rule against penalties (see **22.20**) by delivering what was essentially an essay on the treatment of bonds in the seventeenth and eighteenth centuries.

28   These restrictions were abolished by the *Usury Laws Repeal Act 1854* (UK).

29   See *Sale of Goods Act 1923* (NSW); *Goods Act 1958* (Vic); *Sale of Goods Act 1896* (Qld); *Sale of Goods Act 1895* (WA); *Sale of Goods Act 1895* (SA); *Sale of Goods Act 1896* (Tas); *Sale of Goods Act 1954* (ACT); *Sale of Goods Act 1972* (NT).

in which most insurance arrangements are documented and explained, and limited the capacity of insurers to escape liability.

This last measure illustrates what has become a very common theme with statutory incursions into contract law. The purpose for legislating has frequently been to temper the principle of freedom of contract – and more especially to protect what are perceived to be 'weaker' parties against the capacity of others to draft, perform or enforce contracts in ways that take advantage of their superior resources or bargaining power.[30] More is said about this in Chapter 2. For now, it suffices to note that tenants have been protected in their dealings with landlords, employees in the terms on which they agree to supply their labour, and – most generally – consumers in acquiring goods and services from businesses. That protection may take different forms, but often includes the imposition of minimum obligations on the stronger party which cannot be weakened or removed, even by agreement. Various examples of this approach are discussed in Chapter 9.

Historically, 'welfarist' regulation has been oriented towards individuals. But recent decades have seen the extension of similar protections to small(er) businesses in dealing with larger counterparts; for example, in the context of franchise arrangements or retail leases.[31] In the same way, prohibitions against misleading, oppressive or unfair conduct in commerce that might once have been intended to assist consumers have been interpreted or extended to cover dealings between businesses, as will be explained in Chapters 18–20.

The prohibitions just mentioned can be found in their current form in the ACL, a measure discussed in more detail in **1.15**. The ACL is a statutory regime that applies to a wide range of consumer and commercial contracts. A further example in this category is provided by the laws in each State and Territory that regulate conveyancing and other dealings in property.[32] While most obviously concerned with agreements relating to land, these statutes also contain important provisions that can apply to any type of contract. This is the case, for example, in relation to the assignment or transfer of contractual rights (see **14.03**), or the effect of a stipulation that performance be completed by a set time (see **16.16**). Some jurisdictions have provisions on the enforceability of contracts for the benefit of a third party (see **8.18–8.20**). There are also many other instances of statutes regulating particular aspects of contractual dealings, such as agreements with children and young people (see **5.42**), or the effect of a contract being 'frustrated' (see **15.15–15.17**).

1.13   The internationalisation of contract law

International trade has been around for as long as humans have had boats. But that trade has steadily grown in significance over the centuries. In recent times, it has been boosted by the ease of electronic communication and the rise of 'global value chains' that spread the

---

30   See generally Atiyah 1979. As to the inequality in bargaining power that characterises a large proportion of contractual dealings, see **2.02**.

31   See eg *Competition and Consumer (Industry Codes—Franchising) Regulation 2014* (Cth); *Retail and Commercial Leases Act 1995* (SA). See also **9.18** and **20.21–20.32**, discussing the more general regulation of unfair contractual terms.

32   *Conveyancing Act 1919* (NSW); *Property Law Act 1958* (Vic); *Property Law Act 1974* (Qld); *Property Law Act 1969* (WA); *Law of Property Act 1936* (SA); *Conveyancing and Law of Property Act 1884* (Tas); *Civil Law (Property) Act 2006* (ACT); *Law of Property Act 2000* (NT).

production of goods and services over a number of countries.[33] Given the scope and significance today of global commerce, it is hardly surprising that there are pressures to standardise the rules that apply to both domestic and, more especially, international transactions.

At the most obvious level, when a contract involves parties and/or subject-matter located in different countries, there must be a process for determining whose laws apply and which nation's courts can or should assert jurisdiction over any dispute. The relevant rules here are those set by what is known as *private international law*. They also apply to resolve conflicts between the laws of different States and Territories in Australia,[34] though typically those differences tend to be less dramatic. As explained in Chapter 3, where the application of these rules to contractual disputes is briefly outlined, Australia has been slow to join the international trend to the standardisation of private international law, though there are signs that this may change.

Of course, if countries adjust their laws to minimise differences in the way they regulate contracts, this will in itself reduce the likelihood of conflicts and may lower transaction costs. The *harmonisation* of Australian contract law with that of other jurisdictions is a point to which we return in Chapter 2. For now, two broad points may be made.

The first is that, as a number of commentators have pointed out,[35] there has been little sign of Australian contract law taking on a more international focus. Nor is much attention typically given to the global dimensions of the subject in the courses or texts studied at law schools. As explained earlier, the 'Australianisation' of the common law applied in this country has seen significant divergences from its English counterpart, while there has been a corresponding decline in the degree of deference to British precedents. But this has not been offset by any great increase in the citation and application of cases from other common law jurisdictions.[36] High Court judges have indeed highlighted the need to 'subject [foreign rules] to inspection at the border to determine their adaptability to native soil': *Commonwealth Bank v Barker* (2014) at [18].

At a statutory level, there are certainly examples of international standards influencing or indeed being directly translated into domestic law.[37] For example, the *Civil Aviation (Carriers' Liability) Act 1959* (Cth) gives effect to a variety of international agreements, including the Montreal Convention,[38] concerning the carriage by air of passengers, baggage and cargo. Similarly, every State and Territory has legislation to implement the *United Nations Convention on the International Sale of Goods 1980*, otherwise known as the CISG or Vienna Convention.[39] This contains a detailed set of rules for regulating the international sale and purchase of

---

33   As to the prevalence and impact of global value chains, see eg World Bank Group 2017.

34   For completeness, it may be noted that any conflict between a federal and State or Territory law is invariably resolved in favour of the former, provided the federal law is valid. In the case of State laws, this flows from s 109 of the *Constitution*, and with Territory laws the doctrine of 'paramountcy': see Williams et al 2018: ch 11, 388–90.

35   See eg Finn 2010; Keyes 2014.

36   See Smyth 2008; although compare the more recent assessment in Spottiswood 2018.

37   Besides the examples below, see also the *Electronic Transactions Acts* noted in **2.10**, and the commercial arbitration legislation discussed in **3.09**.

38   Formally known as the *Convention for the Unification of Certain Rules for International Carriage by Air 1999*.

39   *Sale of Goods (Vienna Convention) Act 1986* (NSW); *Goods Act 1958* (Vic) Pt IV; *Sale of Goods (Vienna Convention) Act 1986* (Qld); *Sale of Goods (Vienna Convention) Act 1986* (WA); *Sale of Goods (Vienna Convention) Act 1986* (SA); *Sale of Goods (Vienna Convention) Act 1987* (Tas); *Sale of Goods (Vienna Convention) Act 1987* (ACT); *Sale of Goods (Vienna Convention) Act 1987* (NT).

most types of goods, other than those acquired for personal, family or household use. It applies where the parties are located in countries that have each adopted the CISG, or where the law of such a country otherwise applies.[40] More is said about this instrument as a possible basis for harmonising or developing Australian contract law in the next chapter. But it is worth emphasising just how few legal practitioners seem to know about it. When they do, they often draft provisions to exclude its application, something expressly permitted by article 6.[41]

The second point is that Australia's 'isolationism' is all the more notable when set against the emergence of what some are calling a new 'law merchant' (*lex mercatoria*), or transnational law of commerce.[42] It is generally possible for those involved in international contracts not just to select a particular set of rules, but to have them applied in the event of a dispute by an arbitrator of the parties' choosing: see **3.09**, **3.23**. English law remains a very popular choice in this regard.[43] But it is also now possible to select a privately formulated set of rules, such as the Principles of International Commercial Contracts promulgated by the International Institute for the Unification of Private Law (UNIDROIT).[44] This restatement has been influenced, as with other such exercises, by the CISG. Again, we return to its significance in Chapter 2, in the context of an abortive attempt by the federal government in 2011–2012 to initiate a rethink of Australian contract law.

What are the sources of contract law?

1.14   Statutory rules

As already mentioned, there are many statutes that regulate contractual dealings, either directly or indirectly. Besides the vast array of rules that impact on the conduct of any business or enterprise, the indirect category includes the laws discussed in Chapter 3 that empower courts or other persons to resolve civil disputes. In a few instances – generally involving large infrastructure projects or mining ventures – a statute may even incorporate the terms of a particular contract.[45]

Under the Australian federal system, the Commonwealth can only legislate on matters specified in the *Constitution*. Contract law is not one of those subjects, at least in any general sense. Nor, unlike some other countries, does the *Constitution* impose any norms or values that directly shape contractual rules.[46] Some of the Commonwealth's enumerated powers permit the regulation of transactions of a certain type, or in a particular industry; as, for example, with banking or insurance, at least when not carried on by the States (*Constitution* ss 51(xiii), (xiv)). Trade and commerce that involves parties located in more than one State or

---

40   Australia and most of its major trading partners have ratified the CISG, though not India or the UK.
41   See Spagnolo 2009.
42   See eg Berger 2010; Robertson 2011, 2012. On the historical misconceptions about *lex mercatoria* which have influenced modern advocates of the idea, see Donahue 2004.
43   See eg Vogenauer 2013.
44   The UNIDROIT Principles were first published in 1994, then updated in 2004, 2010 and 2016: see www.unidroit.org/instruments/commercial-contracts/unidroit-principles-2016. For commentary on the 2010 version, see Vogenauer 2015.
45   As to the status and effect of such statutory agreements, see Seddon 2018: 128–36.
46   Compare the examples discussed in Cherednychenko 2004.

outside Australia can be governed by federal laws (s 51(i)). So can anything happening in, or with a sufficient connection to, one of the Territories (s 122). In recent times, the power in s 51(xx) to legislate on trading, financial or foreign corporations has been interpreted by the High Court to permit the regulation of the 'activities' or 'relationships' of those bodies: see *New South Wales v Commonwealth* (2006) at [178]. The power over 'postal, telegraphic, telephonic, and other like services' (s 51(v)) likewise allows federal rules on transactions that involve the post, telephone or internet. The Commonwealth can also use the 'external affairs' power (s 51 (xxix)) to legislate on matters outside Australia or of international concern; for example when the nation has agreed to abide by some form of international treaty or standard.[47]

These various powers have been used to create a number of federal statutes that regulate contracts. The most significant of these is the *Competition and Consumer Act 2010* (Cth), originally enacted as the *Trade Practices Act 1974* (Cth). In practical terms, it covers most forms of commerce, but not quite all. A business or consumer transaction occurring within a single State and to which neither party is a corporation or a Commonwealth agency will typically fall outside its scope, except for any communications involving the internet, phone or post. To cover those exceptions, complementary State legislation is needed. This has been done in relation to the ACL, which is discussed separately below.

There has been a notable shift in recent decades to national or harmonised regulation of commerce, under the aegis of the Council of Australian Governments. This has sometimes been achieved by the States referring legislative powers to the Commonwealth under s 51(xxxvii) of the *Constitution*, to create or support federal laws such as the *National Consumer Credit Protection Act 2009* (Cth) or the *Fair Work Act 2009* (Cth). The latter uses State referrals to help regulate all private sector employment relationships, other than in Western Australia.[48] In other instances, the States have agreed to legislate in identical or at least substantially similar terms. Examples include statutes on the enforceability of agreements to resolve commercial disputes by arbitration (see **3.09**), or the acceptability of electronic forms of storage and communication (see **2.10**).

Nevertheless, there are still many types of contract regulation that are left to the States and Territories. Besides the examples given earlier of statutes on the sale of goods or dealings in land, other common transactions typically subject to local regulation include those involving building, passenger transport and gambling.

1.15   The Australian Consumer Law

Prior to 2011, consumer transactions were regulated by a combination of federal, State and Territory laws that were similar, but far from identical. Following a recommendation by the Productivity Commission (2008) for the creation of uniform consumer protection laws, the ACL was enacted as Schedule 2 to the *Competition and Consumer Act 2010* (Cth).[49]

---

47   See eg *International Arbitration Act 1974* (Cth), discussed in **3.09**.
48   Even in WA, most employees are still covered by this Act, because their employers are trading or financial corporations, or Commonwealth agencies: see Stewart et al 2016: ch 6.
49   See *Trade Practices Amendment (Australian Consumer Law) Act (No 2) 2010* (Cth). Although the bulk of the ACL took effect from 1 January 2011, the provisions on unfair terms commenced earlier, as a result of separate legislation: see **20.21**.

As a federal law, the scope of the ACL's application is largely dictated by s 131 of the 2010 Act, which refers to conduct or contraventions by trading, financial or foreign corporations. But the effect of the complex 'extension' provisions in ss 5 and 6 of the 2010 Act is that the ACL can also (among other things) apply to conduct by natural persons and other entities in relation to interstate or overseas trade, or in a Territory, or when using postal or telecommunications services. These various provisions reflect the mix of constitutional powers mentioned above. To the extent there are any remaining gaps in coverage, they are filled by laws in each State and Territory. These adopt the ACL and apply it to any form of trading conduct, whether by corporations or otherwise.[50]

Whether the ACL applies as a federal, State or Territory law, the obligations it imposes are generally the same. But the distinction does matter for certain purposes. For example, it is only the Australian Competition and Consumer Commission (ACCC) that has the authority to commence certain proceedings under the federal version. And it is the Federal Court or Federal Circuit Court that must hear proceedings brought by either the ACCC or a private litigant under the ACL as a federal law, rather than a State court.[51]

The ACL contains rules that are broadly similar in effect to those in other comparable countries.[52] But it has a number of curious features that belie its title. As already noted, some of its key prohibitions apply to *any* conduct in trade or commerce, with no requirement for a consumer to be involved or affected. And when its provisions *are* limited to the treatment of consumers, or to consumer contracts, there is no standard definition of those terms. Different meanings apply for different purposes, some going well beyond the ordinary conception to protect even the largest of businesses.[53]

A review of the ACL was completed in 2017.[54] As a result, two sets of amendments have been passed to increase the penalties for breaches of the ACL and to make other changes to its provisions.[55] Some of these changes are discussed in later chapters.

1.16   The common law

Whatever the position may once have been, the High Court has insisted in recent years that there is a single common law of Australia: see eg *Lipohar v R* (1999) at [43]–[59]. It has also indicated that each 'intermediate' court of appeal (such as the Full Federal Court or Victorian Court of Appeal) should generally follow any other such court's ruling on the common law, unless persuaded it is plainly wrong: *Farah Constructions v Say-Dee* (2007) at [135]. In theory,

---

50   See *Fair Trading Act 1987* (NSW) Pt 3; *Australian Consumer Law and Fair Trading Act 2012* (Vic) Ch 2; *Fair Trading Act 1989* (Qld) Pts 3, 3A, 3B; *Fair Trading Act 2010* (WA) Pt 3; *Fair Trading Act 1987* (SA) Pt 3; *Australian Consumer Law (Tasmania) 2010* (Tas) Pt 2; *Fair Trading (Australian Consumer Law) Act 1992* (ACT) Pt 2; *Consumer Affairs and Fair Trading Act 1990* (NT) Pt 4.

51   ACL s 2 (definition of 'regulator'); *Competition and Consumer Act 2010* (Cth) ss 138–138B. For further discussion of the scope and application of the ACL, see Corones 2013: ch 3.

52   See Corones et al 2016.

53   Compare, for example, the definitions used for the 'consumer guarantees' (see **9.29**) and the controls on unfair terms (see **20.24**); and see further Carter 2010.

54   See CAANZ 2017.

55   See *Treasury Laws Amendment (2018 Measures No 3) Act 2018* (Cth); *Treasury Laws Amendment (Australian Consumer Law Review) Act 2018* (Cth).

this should reduce disagreements and make it easier to determine what the common law position is on any given issue. But the reality is very different.

It is not often that there are clear divisions of opinion between Australian jurisdictions. Instead, the divisions tend to exist between different judges, both beyond and *within* a single jurisdiction. In New South Wales alone, for example, there are multiple views on the vexed question of whether Australia does or should recognise a general contractual duty of good faith and fair dealing: see **12.21**. The difficulties, both for students and lawyers seeking to advise their clients, are exacerbated by two other factors. One is the willingness of many modern judges to embark on detailed reviews of the authorities (precedents) on any given issue, to the point where some judgments read more like journal articles.[56] Combined with the ease of internet access to just about every decision, whether formally reported or not, the result is a proliferation of judicial observations, lending potential support to many different arguments or positions.

The second and more serious problem is the lack of leadership displayed by the High Court in recent decades.[57] As mentioned earlier, opinions will inevitably differ as to how creative judges should be in seeking to 'develop' the law. But at the very least, we should surely expect those at the apex of the court system to issue rulings that improve the clarity and consistency of the law they are administering. All too often, however, High Court decisions have either failed to resolve uncertainties in the common law, or created unnecessary problems. Many examples could be given, but two obvious illustrations involve the circumstances in which 'extrinsic' evidence can be used to help interpret a written contract (see **10.07–10.11**) and the rule against 'penal' provisions (see **22.19–22.24**).

All this would not matter so much if the common law played only a minor part in regulating contracts. It is true, as Mark Leeming (2013: 1002) has pointed out, that statutes play a 'central' and often 'under-appreciated' role:

> Most of what is actually occurring in the legal system is the construction and application of statutes. A great deal of what is simplistically described as 'common law' is the historical product of, or response to, statutes. And much of the contemporaneous 'development' in the day-to-day workings of courts in fact involves a process of harmonisation informed by statutory norms. Even when a court decides *not* to alter the law, the role of statutes can be influential.

Yet despite the fact that common law principles must yield to the superior force of legislation, they still have important gaps to fill. Even the highly detailed statutes that regulate the likes of employment and insurance assume the continued operation of common law rules as to the formation and termination of contracts, the implication and interpretation of terms, the remedies available for breach of contract, and so on. Sometimes too, common law rules are given direct effect by a statute, as with the prohibition on unconscionable conduct in s 20 of the ACL: see **20.13**.

More generally, even where legislation is being applied, it is not unusual for it to be interpreted by reference to established norms and values of the common law – even though

---

56   Together with a tendency to summarise almost every piece of evidence, the result has been an extraordinary growth in the average length of judgments: see eg Waye 2009.

57   See Stewart 2012: 79–87.

this may not always be explicitly acknowledged.[58] To be sure, it has become accepted that the influence flows the other way as well. For example, it may be appropriate to take account of statutory provisions in adjusting or developing the common law, at least where there is a 'consistent pattern of legislative policy': see eg *Esso v Commissioner of Taxation* (1999) at [23]–[24]. Furthermore, common law principles should not be applied in such a way as to contradict or defeat the purposes of a statutory regime. This approach is evident in the cases discussed in Chapter 21, dealing with the effect of statutory breaches on the enforcement of rights under or connected to a contract. The High Court has, in this context, emphasised the desirability of 'coherence' in the law: see eg *Equuscorp v Haxton* (2012) at [23].[59] There has also been at least one recent instance of the court refusing to countenance an innovation in the common law widely accepted in other countries, because of a belief that it involved 'complex policy considerations' more appropriate for a legislature to address: see *Commonwealth Bank v Barker* (2014), discussed in **9.26**.[60] Nevertheless, the common law remains a significant, not to say vibrant, source of contractual rights and obligations, notwithstanding the continual encroachment of legislation.

1.17 Equity

In its popular sense, *equity* is generally taken to mean equality or fairness. But to a lawyer, and as used in this book, it means a subset of the common law that has its roots in the decisions of the English Court of Chancery.[61] Set up to handle petitions for justice directed to the Chancellor (or, originally, the King), the court came to develop new principles and procedures for granting redress, especially in circumstances where the common law principles applied in other courts would unfairly deny relief. A key element became that of 'conscience'. As Lord Ellesmere put it in the *Earl of Oxford's Case* (1615) at 7: 'The office of the Chancellor is to correct men's [sic] consciences for fraud, breach of trust, wrongs and oppressions of what nature soever they be.'[62]

Before going on, a brief note on terminology is required. The term 'common law', as used so far in this chapter, has generally denoted any kind of judge-made law or non-statutory law. In that sense, it *includes* equity. But when speaking of equity and the common law having differing rules or approaches, we are starting to use 'common law' in a different way, as meaning the rules originally developed and administered by certain courts other than Chancery, such as Exchequer or King's Bench. So 'common law' can mean either *all* judge-made law, or just one part of it. It would clearly be preferable to have a different term for this subset, but the language is too well-entrenched now to change. The key to avoiding confusion is to pay attention to the context. If, as in the paragraphs that follow, a contrast is being drawn between common law and equitable principles, then 'common law' is being used to mean the subset of judge-made law that is not equity.

---

58   For an example from case law on the statutory prohibition on misleading and deceptive conduct in trade and commerce, see **18.25**.
59   See further Bant 2015; Grantham & Jensen 2016; Fell 2018.
60   As to the broader question here of the respective law-making roles of parliaments and the courts, see the various views discussed in Golding 2016.
61   See generally Loughlan 2003; Dal Pont 2015a: 1–31.
62   See further Parkinson 2003.

As a result of the *Supreme Court of Judicature Acts* of 1873 and 1875, the Court of Chancery was abolished and the administration of common law and equity was 'fused'. The English courts could generally from this point apply both common law and equitable principles. Some irreconcilable conflicts between the two bodies of law were settled by statutory provisions, some of which survive today: see eg **16.16**, discussing requirements for performance of a contract by a set time. But otherwise equity and the common law were left to operate in tandem.

The Australian colonies (and later, States) did not have an equivalent to the Court of Chancery. But their Supreme Courts did, to varying degrees, have separate procedures or divisions for equitable matters. The separate administration of common law and equity persisted into the twentieth century – and in the case of New South Wales, as late as the 1970s.[63] Even today, the New South Wales Supreme Court has an Equity Division, with a separate Chief Judge, although this handles a wider range of matters than purely equitable claims.

Space here does not permit a full summary of the many concepts and principles that are distinctive to equity. Some are briefly explained later in the book, such as the nature of a *fiduciary* obligation (see **12.16**). But for now, two particular aspects can be highlighted. The first is that in various situations a court may be asked, in the name of equity, to restrain a party from *unconscionably* (or as some say, *unconscientiously*) seeking to assert a right they would otherwise have. The doctrines of promissory estoppel (see **7.04**), relief against forfeiture (see **16.24**) and unconscionable bargains (see **20.03**) each illustrate this. The second is that some of the *remedies* that a court may grant either to enforce, adjust or annul contractual (or other) rights are considered to be equitable in nature. Examples in this category include orders for specific performance, rectification or rescission. As will be explained in Chapter 3, and in more detail in later parts of the book, these remedies differ from some of their common law counterparts (such as the actions for debt or damages) in being available only at the *discretion* of the court.

What distinguishes the brand of equity now administered in the Australian courts from that in other countries is the continuing emphasis on the special and different nature of equitable principles. This view has been nurtured over the years in pockets of the legal fraternity, especially at the 'equity bar' in New South Wales, many of whose leading lights have gone on to senior judicial roles. The creative use of equitable doctrines and remedies can be seen in most of the key High Court decisions of the 1980s that, as noted in **1.11**, put an Australian stamp on the law of contract. But there has also been resistance to what is pejoratively termed the 'fusion fallacy' – the idea that the Judicature Acts and the equivalent reforms they inspired in Australia represented anything more than administrative changes to the court system. At its most narrow and intemperate, this view has seen the excoriation of any judge or commentator who dares to suggest that the separate waters of common law and equity might over time be commingled.[64] It can be seen, for instance, in the High Court's thoroughly unhelpful decision in *Andrews v ANZ Banking Group* (2012) to undo more than a century of development and

---

63 See *Supreme Court Act 1970* (NSW); *Law Reform (Law and Equity) Act 1972* (NSW).
64 See especially Heydon et al 2015: 47–61. This is the latest edition of a book which, since its original publication in 1975, has encapsulated both the best and worst of the modern Australian approach to equity.

revive the ancient equitable basis for the rule against penalties: see **22.20**. It has also created confusion over the proper basis for certain 'restitutionary' remedies: see **24.12**.

1.18 International law

Mention has already been made of the existence of international instruments such as the Vienna Convention, which may be a source of rules for domestic contract law. But this cannot happen in any direct sense. In Australia, the ratification of a treaty by the federal government may create obligations under international law, as between the nations involved. But unlike the position in some other countries, the ratification does not have any effect in domestic law, unless or until the instrument concerned is expressly given such effect by legislation: see *Minister for Immigration v Teoh* (1995) at 286–7.[65]

Whether or not an international instrument has been given legislative effect, it is still open to an Australian court to refer to it in resolving a question of statutory interpretation, or indeed in refining or developing the common law. But while examples of this can be found,[66] consistently with what was said earlier about Australian isolationism, they tend to be the exception rather than the rule.

1.19 Soft law

The concept of regulation extends much more widely than legally enforceable rules, just as there are many more 'regulatory actors' than the state.[67] The term *soft law* is sometimes used to capture the idea of rules and principles that do not have direct legal effect, but which are nonetheless intended to influence behaviour. For example, companies or trading associations may develop standard forms or codes of practice for contracting, either at a domestic or transnational level, that influence the formation or content of agreements within an industry or sector, or that provide mechanisms for resolving disputes.[68] Governments too can use soft law to influence transactions; for example, through procurement rules that require organisations to comply with certain standards if they wish to be eligible to supply goods or services to government agencies or be involved in government-funded projects.[69]

What are the boundaries of contract law?

1.20 Contract law and other legal categories

In recent decades, academic lawyers have become interested in the way that private law is ordered, or what is sometimes called 'legal taxonomy'. One motivation is a desire to develop

---

65   See further Williams et al 2018: 974–9.
66   See eg *Koompahtoo Local Aboriginal Land Council v Sanpine* (2007) at [108]; *Franklins v Metcash* (2009) at [8]–[9].
67   See generally Baldwin et al 2012: 2–3; Black 2002; Freiberg 2017.
68   See eg Menting 2017. To take just one example, see Howell 2015, discussing the Australian Banking Association's Code of Banking Practice (see **11.13**) and its interaction with the statutory regulation of financial services.
69   See eg Howe 2006, discussing the use of this technique to set or influence employment conditions.

'restitution' as a third legal category within a broader 'law of obligations', alongside contract and tort.[70] This is said to cover or explain various situations in which a person may be obliged to return or pay for benefits they have obtained at someone else's expense. In some of those circumstances, what used to be known as 'quasi-contractual' actions were available. That category has been abandoned. But there remains some disagreement about the true doctrinal justification for the law of restitution, even though it is now generally accepted as quite separate from contract law: see **24.01**.

It is no doubt desirable for private law to be well ordered. But there remains something highly artificial about drawing hard lines between contract and other legal categories.[71] The law of contract does not exist in isolation. As already noted, equitable doctrines have had a profound impact on the law of contract in Australia. Some contracts also have a dual character. Both a lease and a freehold covenant (a promise made by the owner of land concerning its use) are created by a contract. Under the doctrine of privity, contracts generally only bind the parties to the agreement. Yet, because a lease and freehold covenant generate proprietary as well as contractual rights, they are capable of binding third parties: see **8.21**.

Despite the history of the law of contract, modern lawyers are accustomed to think of a contract as the product of an agreement. Tort liability, in contrast, is seen as something that is imposed by the law rather than by the parties. But the two bodies of law are not as distinct as this may suggest. Tort and contract enjoy a close relationship. As noted at **1.10**, the law of contract developed in part through the actions of trespass and trespass on the case, which we would now see as actions in tort. There is even a long established tort of inducing a breach of contract.[72] Once it was accepted that it was possible to sue in the tort of negligence to recover 'pure economic loss' (that is, financial loss unconnected to physical injuries or property damage), the boundary between contract and tort became more fluid. In the same way that damages for breach of contract reflect economic losses flowing from the breach, as discussed in Chapter 23, so damages in negligence might be awarded for economic losses flowing from the breach of a duty of care.[73] These developments have opened the way for concurrent liability when the same facts might potentially give rise to a claim in both contract and tort. Australian law does not generally prevent a plaintiff from having or making that choice: see *Astley v Austrust* (1999), noted in **23.19**. Concurrent liability will, for example, occur where there is a negligent or deceitful misstatement which is incorporated as a term of a contract: see **18.03**. Tort law has also been used to fill gaps in situations which are close to a contract, but where a key element of contractual liability is missing: see eg *Hill v Van Erp* (1997), discussed in **8.15**.

But despite the artificiality of distinguishing between contract and tort (or equity, or property, or restitution, etc), there are practical reasons for continuing to do just that. The sheer volume of the rules and principles that govern all these areas make them difficult to cover in a single book, or to teach or study in a single course, other than at a very general level. Besides, generations of lawyers have become used to thinking about and practising the law by reference to these categories. Although this book has some distinctive features and emphases,

---

70   Particularly in the important scholarship of Peter Birks: see eg Birks 1989, 2005.
71   See Burrows 1998 for a discussion of the division of the law of obligations.
72   See eg *Lumley v Gye* (1853); Deakin 2011: 773–82; and see further **3.18**.
73   See Luntz et al 2017: ch 16.

it adopts what is in the end a fairly conventional view of what to cover, what to omit and what to mention only in passing, in providing an account of 'the law of contract'.

A law of contract or a law of contracts?

1.21   Is there a general law of contract?

It should be evident from what has already been said that different rules apply to different types of contract.[74] This is not just a function of the many statutory regimes that target particular industries or transactions. Even under the common law, there are principles or exceptions that are specific to certain contracts; for example, in the context of privity of contract (see **8.08**) or the doctrine of frustration (see **15.13**). Seemingly general rules can produce very different results when applied to particular categories of agreement; for instance, with the concept of 'essential terms' (see **5.36**, **5.38**), the implication of terms by law (see **9.25**), or the discretion to award specific performance (see **22.03**).

Nevertheless, there remains a core of common law principles that can still be said to comprise a law of contract – even if their application may vary in different contexts. It is those principles, together with some of the generally (or at least widely) applicable provisions in the ACL and the various property law statutes, that are the principal focus of this book. We refer in many instances, even if only in passing, to special rules or regimes for particular contracts. This is not just because of their practical importance, but to avoid any impression that there are universal principles. But even so, our aim is the same as that of most contract law courses – to provide a general understanding of the topic, and a foundation for further and more detailed study or practice in relation to particular types of transaction.

How is this book organised?

1.22   Outlining the rest of the book

The remainder of this introductory part of the book canvasses a range of practical and theoretical perspectives on the nature and regulation of contracts (Chapter 2), before going on to outline the various ways in which contractual disputes may be resolved (Chapter 3). One of those ways involves initiating litigation and seeking a court order. The key remedies for *enforcing* a contract, seeking compensation (or *damages*) for breach of contract or obtaining *restitution* for benefits conferred under an ineffective or terminated contract are dealt with in more detail in Chapters 22–24, which together comprise Part VII.

Before then, Part II explores the processes for making a contact. Chapter 4 looks at the pre-contract phase, examining how agreements are negotiated, what (if any) information must be disclosed to the other party and whether any liability may be incurred if a contract fails to materialise. Chapter 5 outlines the various elements that must be satisfied for a valid contract to be formed, while as previously mentioned Chapter 6 explores the various risks and pitfalls of

---

74   As to the various ways in which contracts can be classified, see the taxonomy in Mouzas & Furmston 2013.

striking a 'preliminary' agreement. Chapter 7 explains the concept of estoppel, the equitable versions of which can be used to enforce certain promises even when they lack contractual force. Chapter 8 concludes the part by examining the doctrine of privity and the significance of being party to a contract.

In Part III, we turn to rights and duties under a contract. Chapter 9 explains how a stipulation may expressly or impliedly become a *term* of a contract, while also outlining some of the key obligations imposed on contracting parties by legislation such as the ACL. Following a discussion in Chapter 10 of the principles for interpreting or construing a contractual provision, Chapter 11 looks at ways in which contracts may be used either to limit or remove a person's liability for some form of wrongdoing, or to hold someone else responsible. Chapter 12 examines some of the rules for determining the standard, time and order of contractual performance, including the vexed question of whether, and to what extent, a party must perform in good faith.

Part IV concerns the adjustment of rights and obligations after a contract is made. It details the ways in which the rights and obligations under a contract can be *varied* (Chapter 13), or *transferred* to someone else (Chapter 14), before examining what happens if there is a major change of circumstances (Chapter 15). Part V goes on to look at the different ways in which a contract may be *terminated* (Chapter 16), before outlining the consequences of that happening (Chapter 17).

In Part VI, we look at various ways in which a person's conduct or state of mind may vitiate the formation of a contract, prevent it from being enforced, or breach certain prohibitions under the ACL or similar legislation. There are separate chapters on misinformation, including *misrepresentation* and *mistake* (Chapter 18); the use of *duress* or *undue influence* to procure a contract (Chapter 19); the common law and statutory rules on *unconscionable conduct* and *unfairness* (Chapter 20); and the circumstances in which a contractual or other claim may be defeated by reason of some form of *illegality* or contravention of *public policy* (Chapter 21).

Following Part VII on remedies, to which reference has already been made, we conclude with a glossary of some of the terms used in the text, and a bibliography of the secondary sources quoted throughout the book.

THEMES AND PERSPECTIVES

2.01   Introduction

This chapter outlines some of the more important ideas and developments explored in the voluminous literature about contracts and their regulation. In a book of this type and size, it is impossible to do justice to that literature. But our aim is to give readers at least some sense of the diversity of topics, views and theories on offer, together with references to key sources.[1]

We start by examining two important practical features of contractual dealings: the fact that contracts are rarely the subject of negotiations between parties dealing with one another on a more or less equal footing; and the tendency for disputes to be resolved without reference to the formal rules and processes of contract law.

We go on to look at four trends concerning or affecting the regulation of contracts over the past two centuries. One is the introduction of regimes that seek to protect weaker parties – and the challenge to that objective posed by neoliberal approaches to governance and regulation. The second is the shift away from hard and fast rules that help promote certainty in the law, towards generalised principles and discretionary powers that aim to achieve 'just' outcomes in particular circumstances. The third is the growing use of information technology not just to facilitate communications between parties or the recording of concluded agreements, but to structure transactions or, indeed, whole markets. The fourth is the shift towards the codification of rules about contracts and/or the harmonisation of the laws that apply in different jurisdictions. Attempts to achieve these goals have been sporadic and incomplete in Australia, but more successful in other jurisdictions.

Finally, we review various theories or critical analyses that seek to explain or highlight certain aspects of contract law, or to suggest ways in which it could be reformed.

Contracts in practice: inequality of bargaining power

2.02   Power imbalances in contractual dealings

The typical description of a contract as an *agreement* or a *bargain* suggests the idea of a negotiated exchange. The reality is often very different. Contractual terms are often set out in a *standardised form*, with little if any scope for alteration or even discussion: see **4.04**. Indeed, an increasing number of contracts involve interactions not with a human being, but an *automated system* (such as a ticket machine or an online booking tool) with engineering or programming that does not permit any form of negotiation. What facilitates those practices is a more general feature of many contractual relationships: a profound *imbalance of power* between parties. This is not just evident in most consumer transactions, or in employment relationships, but in many transactions between businesses. The small company dealing with a big bank is often at just as much a disadvantage as any individual account-holder or bank employee.

It may be accepted, as Trebilcock (1976: 364–5) points out, that the main reason for having standardised and non-negotiable terms is to reduce transaction costs. Their existence does not

---

1   For much fuller overviews, see eg Seddon & Bigwood 2017: ch 28; Smith 2004.

of itself suggest a use (or abuse) of market power. The real question is whether the party who is forced to take or leave such terms has a 'workably competitive range of alternative sources' for whatever they are contracting to supply or acquire. The Productivity Commission (2015: 86) makes a similar point, noting that bargaining power necessarily 'depends on the relative costs to each party of failing to reach an agreement – primarily their capacity to hold out from entering into an arrangement, and their ability to seek alternatives'. In the case of the Australian banking industry, the 'striking asymmetry of power and information between bank and customer' is exacerbated by the lack of competitive pressures or any fear of enterprise failure. It allows banks to minimise risks, giving them 'only as much "skin in the game" in their dealings with customers as *the bank* chooses'.[2]

In practice, many parties either are not in a position to find an alternative to the transaction on offer or – which may be just as important – *perceive* that they have no alternative. Coupled with the lack of practice or skill in bargaining typically found in a society where 'haggling' over purchases is not a daily routine, and what economists call 'asymmetries' in the parties' access to relevant information, contracting parties rarely deal on equal terms.[3]

2.03   Responses to inequality

One of the most obvious ways in which contracting parties may seek to counter their lack of power is to take *collective action*. Longstanding examples of this include guilds or trade associations that seek to standardise terms of dealing in an industry, or establish a single body to make sales on behalf of a group of producers. However, any formal attempt to insist on negotiating with customers or suppliers on a collective rather than individual basis may run into legal problems. The common law doctrine of *restraint of trade* outlined in Chapter 21 presumptively invalidates agreements that limit a person's freedom to enter future transactions. Part IV of the *Competition and Consumer Act 2010* (Cth) also has specific prohibitions on cartels and other 'anti-competitive' arrangements: see **21.30**.

In some cases, legislation may specifically authorise collective bargaining. For example, it is inherently unlawful at common law for employees to form trade unions, or to act in combination to withdraw their labour through strikes and other types of 'industrial action'. But since the late nineteenth century, statutory regimes have sought to shield workers and unions from the criminal or civil liability to which they would otherwise be subject. Today, measures such as the *Fair Work Act 2009* (Cth) provide for 'enterprise agreements' with employers that set minimum wages and other conditions for specified types of work. Employees may also lawfully withdraw or threaten to withdraw their labour, at least when negotiating a new enterprise agreement.[4] For contractors who do not work as employees, however, or for other types of business (such as small producers), there are greater restrictions. Under the authorisation and notification provisions in Part VII of the *Competition and Consumer Act 2010* (Cth), the Australian Competition and Consumer Commission (ACCC) can allow parties to engage in

---

2   Royal Commission into Misconduct in the Banking Industry 2018: 269 (emphasis in original).

3   For a broader perspective on the concept of 'power' in contractual relations and a critical analysis of the approach typically taken by courts, see Barnhizer 2005.

4   See Stewart et al 2016: chs 3, 14, 25–27. Note also the exemption in s 51(2)(a) of the *Competition and Consumer Act 2010* (Cth).

collective bargaining of a type that might otherwise infringe the restrictive practices provisions in Part IV. But there is no institutional support for such bargaining, and it is hard to gain permission for boycotts or other forms of concerted pressure.[5]

Campaigns to persuade individual consumers to boycott particular products or businesses are less likely to encounter legal restraints. Indeed, s 45DD(3) of the *Competition and Consumer Act* specifically exempts boycotts from certain forms of liability under Part IV if their substantial purpose is environmental or consumer protection. Such campaigns are just a small part of what has become a much larger movement to help consumers make better choices or understand risks, or indeed to understand their legal rights. The advent of the internet and social media has radically increased the possibilities in this regard, both for advocacy groups such as Choice and businesses such as TripAdvisor that offer comparison services.

Both collective action and greater information can go only so far, however, in tackling entrenched inequalities of bargaining power. Another important response, therefore, has been the introduction of laws that seek to regulate contracting procedures, impose minimum conditions or prohibit harsh or one-sided terms. More said about such 'welfarist' reforms in **2.06**.

Contracts in practice: the (ir)relevance of contract law

2.04   How relevant is contract law?

A number of empirical studies have challenged the assumption that contracts are important in practice. In the most famous of these, Macaulay (1963) reported that manufacturing businesses in Wisconsin typically conducted transactions with only scant regard for the law. Little attempt was made to detail obligations, even when expensive purchases were being made. Adjustments to prices, times or quantity of supply were frequently sought and granted, even in circumstances where one of the parties might have insisted on sticking to the original terms. Disputes were typically resolved informally and with little regard to the parties' legal rights, with litigation tending to occur only when the parties' relationship had come to an end.[6]

Macaulay's findings have been replicated in later studies from other countries and industries.[7] They are consistent with the anecdotal experience of many people who have worked in commerce, or as legal advisers, although there are undoubtedly sectors or transactions where contracts tend to be more carefully planned. But even if many people in business make, vary and end agreements with little regard to the strict legal position, that does not mean contract law is unimportant. Even in sectors where informality reigns, there will be occasional disputes that are resolved either in court or by reference to some form of legal advice. And the influence of the law is necessarily felt whenever standard form contracts are used, given that these will usually have been prepared by (or with input from) lawyers.

---

5   See eg McCrystal 2009; although note this was written before the changes introduced by the *Competition and Consumer Amendment (Competition Policy Review) Act 2017* (Cth) Sch 9.

6   For more on Macaulay's work, see Braucher et al 2013.

7   See eg Beale & Dugdale 1975; Bernstein 1992.

As Collins (1999: ch 6) notes, we can analyse contractual behaviour from at least three frames of reference: the underlying relationship between the parties; the particular 'deal' that is being made; and the contract that gives legal effect to that deal. Even if the last of these tends to be the least important in practice, it is still likely to be invoked or relied upon where it is rational to do so.

The larger question is perhaps what these empirical studies, and the 'relational' analysis they have helped to spawn (see **2.16**), might tell us about whether modern contract law is properly suited to commercial transactions. It seems clear that some of the current rules could be improved; for example, by removing unnecessary barriers to modification: see **13.02**. But this is not to say that we should rewrite every rule of contract law to 'suit business'. Business people, as Gava (2006: 264) points out, tend to make use of contract law as a 'form of insurance', or as a 'last resort mechanism' when their preferred tools for resolving disputes are not available. From that perspective, the 'law is attractive only because of its formalist nature, not because of the specific nature or usefulness of particular doctrines'.[8]

From freedom of contract to welfarism

2.05   The classical approach

The foundations of modern contract law were developed in the nineteenth century. For the first time lawyers began to think in terms of a law of contract, rather than a law of contracts: see **1.10**. This unified body of doctrine is known as the *classical* model of contract law. It has proved to be enormously influential and enduring. Elements remain in place today.

English contract law at the time lacked a coherent structure. Once it was decided that one was needed, it had to be borrowed from the work of the French writer Robert Joseph Pothier.[9] At the heart of this new version of contract law was the idea that contracts were formed by a 'meeting of the minds' of the parties involved. This was the so-called *will theory* of contract. This made agreement and intention the central organising principles. But although the will theory might suggest that subjective agreement should be required, the law soon began to insist on an objective test of intention: see **5.02**.

The development of classical contract law during this period is easy to identify in retrospect, but the underlying reasons are complex and contested. It seems likely that one factor was an intellectual shift, with the evolution of new ways of thinking about contract law and the emergence of a body of contract literature. At the same time, it seems likely that economic changes also played a part, as well as reforms to the way that the common law operated, especially the diminished role of the civil jury.[10] The classical model placed strong emphasis on party autonomy and *freedom of contract*. In his classic work, *The Rise and Fall of Freedom of Contract*, Atiyah (1979) suggested that the prevailing political philosophy of laissez faire individualism was an important influence. According to Horwitz (1977: ch 6), this led contract

---

8   See further Gava 2013. But acknowledging the force of Gava's critique of 'instrumentalist' approaches does not in turn mean embracing his preference for 'strict legalism' in judicial decision-making: see eg Carrigan 2013.

9   See Evans 1806. For an early example of Pothier's influence, see Chitty 1834.

10   See Swain 2015a.

law in the nineteenth century to place less emphasis on the values of fairness than previously. But that draws the contrast too sharply. Although changes occurred, the law of contract in 1850 had more in common with the law in 1750 than Horwitz is prepared to recognise. In particular, the idea that courts placed much weight on fairness in any systematic way in earlier centuries does not withstand close scrutiny.[11]

2.06 Protective regulation

In the latter part of his book, Atiyah (1979) charted the erosion of the principle of freedom of contract during the twentieth century, as legislation was progressively introduced in the United Kingdom to protect weaker parties such as consumers, residential tenants and employees. It was a similar story in Australia and other developed countries. Such *welfarist regulation* operated in a range of ways. Some interventions were procedural in nature, requiring for instance that contract terms be properly documented or that certain matters be explained. Others were substantive, mandating some terms and prohibiting others. So, for instance, manufacturers and retailers could not exclude their responsibility for supplying goods of acceptable quality, employers were obliged to pay minimum wages, and the capacity of landlords to demand and retain rental bonds (deposits) was curtailed. Similar approaches were taken in relation to insurance and home building contracts, hire purchase agreements and, eventually, some purely commercial (business to business) transactions as well, such as commercial leases and franchise agreements. Today, as noted in **1.12**, there are few types of contract that are not subject to significant statutory regulation.

Over the past few decades, however, the scope and content of protective regulation have been challenged by the rise of *neoliberal* philosophies. In their modern form, these seek to reduce the degree of state control over both economic and social affairs and instead promote a greater role for competition and market forces. The embrace of such ideals has led to constant calls for 'deregulation' – or, more accurately, a reconfiguration of the balance between state and non-state regulation.[12] The successful push to privatise significant areas of government activity has certainly made contracts (and, in turn, contract law) more important; for example, in providing for the delivery of privatised services formerly the direct responsibility of governments.[13] Yet in Australia at least, those anxious to wind back consumer and employee protections have had few successes – and at least one spectacular failure, in the form of the Howard Government's 'Work Choices' reforms to labour legislation.[14] If anything, the scope and quantity of protective regulation have continued to grow, especially as the failure of market forces to constrain exploitative behaviour has been exposed. The introduction of a national mechanism to challenge unfair and one-sided contractual terms – first for consumers in 2010 and then for small businesses in 2016 – is just one of many examples: see **20.21– 20.22**. The case for maintaining and enhancing regulation has certainly been helped by revelations of unethical and sometimes unlawful behaviour in sectors such as financial

---

11   See Simpson 1979; Swain 2016.
12   See Freiberg 2017: 33–8.
13   See eg Daintith 1979; Vincent-Jones 2000.
14   As to those reforms, the backlash against which played a major role in the Liberal/National Coalition losing power at the 2007 federal election, see eg Murray 2006; Stewart et al 2016: 66–9.

services, or of 'wage theft' by employers. But it is also notable that even the Productivity Commission, which can generally be expected to favour market forces, has been willing in recent years to make an economic case for both consumer protection and employment standards.[15]

From doctrine to discretion

2.07   The value of certainty

Certainty is often prized as a value in contract (or, more broadly, commercial) law.[16] As Lord Mansfield put it in *Vallejo v Wheeler* (1774) at 153: 'In all mercantile transactions the great object should be certainty: and therefore, it is of more consequence that a rule should be certain, than whether the rule is established one way or the other.' Classical principles promoted certainty in at least two ways: through formal rules that purported to leave judges little *discretion* in their application; and the emphasis already mentioned on freedom of contract. The latter, for example, discouraged any search for fairness or distributive justice. So, for example, the doctrine of consideration required that each party promise or provide something of value – but there was no need for that to be an 'adequate' price for whatever was being offered in return. Consideration could be something of purely nominal value, yet still legally sufficient: see **5.31**.

2.08   The rise of conscience and (perhaps) good faith

Since the 1980s in Australia, the goal of certainty in contracting has been challenged by the rise or resuscitation of equitable doctrines such as promissory estoppel (see **7.04**), relief against forfeiture or penalties (see **16.24**, **22.20**), unilateral mistake (see **18.39**) and unconscionable bargains (see **20.03–20.04**). Each of these provide grounds for a court to refuse enforcement of what is otherwise a lawful contract – or, in the case of estoppel, to enforce a promise that is not binding under the ordinary rules of contract law. They all operate by reference to a standard – *good conscience*, or its negative form, *unconscionability* – that is necessarily ad hoc in its focus and that explicitly affords judges discretion as to the extent of their intervention.[17] As the High Court has stressed, the standard is applied by reference to 'well developed principles'. Nor is equitable intervention triggered merely because of 'an element of hardship or unfairness in the terms of the transaction in question, or in the manner of its performance': *Tanwar Enterprises v Cauchi* (2003) at [20], [26]; and see further **20.02**. Nevertheless, these doctrines have plainly created more uncertainty as to the enforceability of certain agreements or promises.

A further challenge is posed by the possible recognition of another potentially indeterminate standard: that of *good faith*. The uncertainty created here operates at two distinct levels: whether a general principle of good faith and fair dealing is or is not part of Australian law; and

---

15   See Productivity Commission 2008, 2015.
16   As to the different meanings that 'certainty' may have in this context, see Eldridge 2018a.
17   As to how the concept of conscience can or might be analysed by reference to broader concepts of justice and fairness, see Bigwood 2000.

if it is, what its application might mean in practice. The debate about this issue is canvassed in Chapter 12. For now, it suffices to say that the Australian judiciary seems irrevocably split not just over whether to recognise the principle, but what form it should take. Multiple views have been expressed on the matter, which plainly calls for resolution by the High Court. But it is unclear when a suitable case might reach the Court – and its past record does not inspire confidence that it would settle the issue, even if given the chance.

2.09   Statutory discretions

The rise of judicial discretion in determining whether to enforce contracts has not been limited to equitable doctrines, or the possible recognition of a duty of good faith. As part of the growing body of protective regulation to which reference has already been made, legislation has invested courts and tribunals with the power to review the fairness or reasonableness of particular terms. This has become an established feature of the regulation of exclusion or limitation clauses: see **11.09**. But as discussed in Chapter 20, there are now notable examples of more general powers to identify unfair terms. Sometimes, as with the provisions in the Australian Consumer Law (ACL), concerning consumer or small business contracts for the supply of goods, services or land, the power is limited to invalidating the offending term. But there are also examples of more dramatic statutory powers to modify or rewrite contracts so that they operate fairly: see **13.20**.

Other discretionary jurisdictions focus not on the fairness of a particular term, but on the exercise of a contractual power. One of the most commonly invoked is the Fair Work Commission's jurisdiction to review decisions by employers to terminate employment. Even if the employer has lawfully exercised a contractual right to dismiss an employee, the tribunal may be asked under Part 3–2 of the *Fair Work Act 2009* (Cth) to determine whether the termination was harsh, unjust or unreasonable. If it was, the employer may be ordered either to reinstate the worker, re-employ them in a different job, or pay up to six months' remuneration by way of compensation.

From paper to smart contracts: the rise of e-commerce

2.10   The challenge of digital technologies

The increasing use of computers and 'smart' devices in communications and commerce is posing challenges to the law of contract. Some, but by no means all, of these were addressed by the *Electronic Transactions Acts*, introduced in the late 1990s and early 2000s by the Commonwealth and all States and Territories.[18] Originally intended to give effect to UNCITRAL's Model Law on Electronic Commerce 1996, they were later modified to allow

---

18   *Electronic Transactions Act 1999* (Cth); *Electronic Transactions Act 2000* (NSW); *Electronic Transactions (Victoria) Act 2000* (Vic); *Electronic Transactions (Queensland) Act 2001* (Qld); *Electronic Transactions Act 2011* (WA); *Electronic Transactions Act 2000* (SA); *Electronic Transactions Act 2000* (Tas); *Electronic Transactions Act 2001* (ACT); *Electronic Transactions (Northern Territory) Act 2000* (NT).

Australia to ratify the *United Nations Convention on the Use of Electronic Communications in International Contracts 2005*.[19] Among other things, these statutes stipulate that a contract is not to be treated as invalid merely because one or more automated systems have been used to make it, without the involvement of a natural person.[20] They also provide that, at least as a general rule, electronic communications or storage may be used to satisfy any requirement that a contract be 'signed' or recorded in writing: see **5.45**. But they do not answer every question about the use of electronic technology. For example, it remains unclear whether clicking or tapping to indicate agreement to terms on an app or website *necessarily* means that those terms are contractually binding: see **9.05**.

As the use of digital technologies accelerates, more difficult issues may need to be addressed. *Blockchain*, for example, uses a 'peer-to-peer' network to create a 'distributed and tamper-proof database technology that can be used to store any type of data, including financial transactions'.[21] It has allowed digital currencies (or 'cryptocurrencies') such as Bitcoin to operate independently of any central bank. A blockchain can also store programs (commonly termed '*smart contracts*') which can autonomously verify whether specified conditions are met and then execute transactions. For example, a rental agreement might be automatically renewed, or a household device might be programmed to order certain supplies when they are found to be running low. Such arrangements can be accommodated within the framework of the existing law of contract – but not without raising some interesting questions.[22] More generally, the OECD has highlighted the problem of 'how to enforce law in the absence of any intermediary or how and to whom to impute legal liability for [wrongs] caused by blockchain-based systems'.[23] This is just part of a broader challenge to the enforcement of territorially-bounded laws in an era when technology allows trade to operate so readily across borders: see **3.24**.

Codification and harmonisation

2.11   A national contract law?

In 2011, the then federal Attorney-General, Robert McClelland, held out the prospect of creating 'a national set of laws governing contracts, to clarify discrepancies between the States and make it easier to do business across borders'. He talked of producing a 'draft contractual code' which would be 'bedded down' by mid-2012.[24] Unsurprisingly, this ambitious target was not met. A discussion paper was released in March 2012, calling for submissions on any 'costs, difficulties, inefficiencies or lost opportunities' experienced with the present law of contract, and on how (if at all) the law might be reformed to address those problems.[25] Workshops were subsequently held to discuss these issues with business and consumer groups, legal practitioners and academics. But there has been no public sign since then of any action on the

---

19   See eg *Electronic Transactions Amendment Act 2011* (Cth); and see Mik 2010.
20   See eg *Electronic Transactions Act 2000* (NSW) s 14C.
21   OECD 2017: 317.
22   See eg Giancaspro 2017a; Radin 2017.
23   OECD 2017: 13.
24   Bowers 2011.
25   Attorney-General's Department 2012.

proposal – although it did inspire a flurry of academic literature on the subject.[26] These writings have explored two related yet separate ideas, each of which also featured in the 2012 discussion paper. They are that Australian law should be *codified*; and that it should be *harmonised* – either to create greater uniformity within Australia, or to bring it more into alignment with the rules that apply in other countries.

2.12   Codifying contract law

Codification is generally understood to involve the process of drawing together the main legal rules that govern a particular subject and stating them in a comprehensive and coherent form. This may be done with one or more objectives in mind. These include simply *restating* the existing law in an authoritative form, *resolving uncertainties* or *filling gaps* in that law, or more substantially *reforming* it.[27]

There is nothing novel in the idea of codifying contract law.[28] The subject is a standard inclusion in the Civil Codes found throughout continental Europe, as well as Japan, while China adopted a single Contract Law in 1999. There are also examples in common law countries. The *Indian Contract Act 1872* was based on the English common law as it stood at the time. Its first 75 sections deal with general principles, with the remainder devoted to 'special' contracts such as those concerning guarantees or bailments. In the United States, there are two main codes, though their legal status differs. The Uniform Commercial Code is a set of rules on sales, leases, financial instruments and other common types of commercial transaction. It has been given effect, albeit with some variations, by legislation in all 50 States, the District of Columbia and most US territories. For other types of contract, reference is commonly made to the American Law Institute's *Restatement of the Law of Contracts*, the second edition of which was released in 1979. This legal treatise, drafted by expert scholars and practitioners, sets out the law in a series of 'black letter' propositions, backed by comments, examples and notes. Although not legally binding, it is highly influential and routinely cited both to and by American courts.

In Australia, there have been examples of partial codification. These include the colonial (and later State and Territory) statutes based on the *Sale of Goods Act 1893* (UK), which sought to capture many (though not all) of the common law rules concerning that type of transaction.[29] But there has been no attempt to adopt a more comprehensive code – or at least none with any real prospect of success. The Victorian Law Reform Commission did in 1992 put forward a radical plan to reduce Australian contract law to just 27 short articles. This was achieved by according a central role to the 'overriding' principle, captured in Article 27, that 'A person may not assert a right or deny an obligation to the extent that it would be unconscionable to do so.' The proposal, perhaps unsurprisingly, failed to attract any support from either the legal community or government.[30]

---

26   See eg Robertson 2012; Stewart 2012; Swain 2014c; Keyes & Wilson 2014; Eldridge 2018a.

27   See Svantesson 2008: 94–5; Attorney-General's Department 2012: 18–19.

28   See Swain 2012.

29   For the current versions, see *Sale of Goods Act 1923* (NSW); *Goods Act 1958* (Vic); *Sale of Goods Act 1896* (Qld); *Sale of Goods Act 1895* (WA); *Sale of Goods Act 1895* (SA); *Sale of Goods Act 1896* (Tas); *Sale of Goods Act 1954* (ACT); *Sale of Goods Act 1972* (NT).

30   See Victorian Law Reform Commission 1992. For later work by the Code's authors, see Ellinghaus et al 2005; Wright et al 2014.

2.13   Harmonisation

The 2012 discussion paper noted the potential value of reducing differences in contract law both between jurisdictions within Australia, and as between Australia and its major trading partners.[31] There are certainly differences in many of the State and Territory statutes that regulate specific types of transaction, such as building contracts. Some jurisdictions have legislated on issues such as the capacity of children, privity of contract or the consequences of frustration, where others have not: see **5.42**, **8.18–8.20**, **15.15–15.17**. But perhaps the more significant reform that might be considered is what the discussion paper termed the 'internationalisation' of Australian law. This might not just lessen barriers to trade and investment. It could 'make Australian law more attractive for parties from different countries when choosing a system of law to govern their contract'. That might in turn 'help promote Australia as a regional hub for finance and commercial arbitration bringing significant benefits to the Australian economy'.[32]

Two obvious models on which Australia might draw for inspiration were themselves the product of attempts to find common ground between common law and civil law regimes. The *United Nations Convention on the International Sale of Goods 1980* has already been given direct effect in Australia by State and Territory legislation, though few parties in practice seem to choose to apply it: see **1.13**. Then there is UNIDROIT's Principles of International Commercial Contracts, also mentioned in Chapter 1. Although the Principles 'only apply with obligatory force where the contract provides for them to do so, they are increasingly used by arbitral tribunals and courts striving to determine the issues in dispute before them in accordance with principles of international best practice'.[33] It remains possible that a future Australian government might see value in legislating to facilitate their adoption for international or even domestic transactions, at least on an optional basis.

Theoretical and critical analysis

2.14   Introduction

There are many different ways in which the rules and processes of contract law can be analysed. Some frames of reference are essentially descriptive in nature, seeking primarily to explain the nature or effect of the law as it stands. Others are more avowedly normative, in criticising aspects of the law and proposing why and how it should be reformed. Many are a mixture of the two. One increasingly common approach is to draw on the insights offered by *regulatory theory* to explore the forms and techniques of contract law.[34] As Collins (1999: 65–9) observes, the private law of contract offers an extreme example of 'responsive' or 'reflexive' law, in permitting parties to self-regulate their affairs;[35] although forms of 'command

---

31   See Attorney-General's Department 2012: 5–6.
32   Attorney-General's Department 2012: 6.
33   Attorney-General's Department 2012: 16. As to the arbitration of commercial disputes, see **3.09**.
34   For a recent example, see Brownsword et al 2017; and see generally Freiberg 2017.
35   See generally Ayres & Braithwaite 1992; Teubner 1993.

and control' regulation can also be found in the statutory regimes that have come to regulate both consumer and employment contracts.[36]

There is also work that has analysed contract law from certain critical perspectives. This includes *feminist* scholarship, which has sought to explore the ways in which various doctrines both reflect and entrench the subordination of women to men – including in what is or is not recognised as an enforceable agreement.[37] Exposing the assumptions implicit in rules that are presented as 'neutral' or 'value-free' was also a hallmark of the *critical legal studies* movement that flourished in the United States during the 1970s and 1980s, and which had its origins in earlier notions of legal realism.[38] While that movement has perhaps had its day, it is part of a broader tradition that seeks to expose the ideological underpinnings of classical contract law.[39] There has also been an ongoing debate between those who advocate a *formalist* approach to the making and application of rules, especially by judges, and supporters of more pragmatic or *contextualist* techniques.[40]

At the risk, however, of offending those interested in these and other perspectives, we have chosen below to highlight three broad strands of thinking strongly represented in modern writings on contract theory, at least in common law countries. These involve theories of contract that essentially present *moral or ethical* explanations for the rules concerning the enforceability of agreements; work that focuses on the *relational* aspects of contracting; and various forms of *economic* analysis.

2.15   Moral theories

Attempts to develop a moral theory of contracting have a long history.[41] In the last few decades, a few of these theories have been particularly prominent. All of them seek to present a normative view of contract which is prescriptive and evaluative, and at the same time seek to describe the law of contract as it actually exists in practice. Fried (2015) has argued that the binding force of contractual liability is derived from the fact that *promises* have moral force.[42] This analysis supports the classical law of contract because it places emphasis on values like party autonomy and freedom of contract. It arguably fits less well with aspects of contract doctrine which are derived from the law rather than the parties themselves. These aspects include the fact that intention is viewed objectively, the doctrine of consideration and the implication of terms.[43] A second approach, the *consent theory*, shares some common features with promissory theories but shifts the focus away from promising to 'a manifest intention to be legally bound'.[44] Party consent is said to bring about a transfer of rights to performance from the other party. Consent theory is open to many of the same objections as promissory theory

---

36   As, for example, with the prohibitions on misleading or unconscionable conduct discussed in Chapters 18 and 20, or the mandatory obligations imposed on suppliers or employers by the regimes considered in Chapter 9.

37   See eg Frug 1985; Mulcahy & Wheeler 2005; and see further **5.08**.

38   See eg Feinman 1983; Dalton 1985; Drahos & Parker 1990.

39   See eg Adams & Brownsword 1987.

40   Compare, for example, the approaches to contract law taken by Morgan 2013 and Mitchell 2013.

41   See eg Gordley 1991.

42   Promises have played a central role in contractual liability for centuries: see Swain 2013b.

43   Compare Fried 2015, which seeks to address these criticisms of an earlier version of his theory.

44   See Barnett 1986, 2012.

because it too struggles to explain aspects of contractual doctrine imposed by the law rather than the parties through their exercise of consent.

A third theory argues that contractual liability is a product of reasonable *reliance*. In the 1970s, it was suggested by writers like Gilmore (1974) that reliance had become so central to contractual liability that the boundary with the law of tort had broken down altogether. It turns out, however, that rumours of the death of contract have been somewhat exaggerated. One problem with reliance theories is that they need to provide a justification for why reliance is reasonable, and as a result they tend to be derivative of other theories. For example, reliance might be reasonable because it is the product of a promise.[45]

As noted in **1.07**, it is difficult for these theories to explain certain aspects of modern or indeed classical contract law. Dagan and Heller (2017) have recently identified another disadvantage. In seeking to promote general theories of contract, their proponents tend to exclude some transactions, thereby limiting the scope of contract law and party choice. Dagan and Heller favour a pluralistic model which recognises that different types of contracting are a result of different activities and different values that the parties wish, through the exercise of their choice, to promote.

2.16   Relational analysis

The classical model of contract assumes that contractual relationships consist of discrete one-off transactions. Many modern commercial transactions are of a quite different character. Building on the empirical insights of Macaulay (see **2.04**), a number of theorists, particularly in the United States, have developed an alternative model of contractual liability. The *relational contract* analysis, developed in particular by Macneil, sees contracting as a form of exchange which takes place within a relationship of cooperation. Macneil has refined his relational analysis over the decades,[46] but he has always emphasised that it reflects contracting practice in the real world. In what Macneil (2000) has come to call his 'essential contract theory', he has identified 10 common norms present in all contracts. Contracts can be seen as sitting on a spectrum from highly discrete transactions to ones that are highly relational.[47] Macneil's work is primarily directed at exposing the shortcomings of classical contract law,[48] but others have attempted to model what a 'relational' law of contract might look like.[49] It is true that classical contract doctrine is built around assumptions that do not fit well with a relational system of contracting. However, it can be argued that recent developments in doctrinal law have moved it more into alignment with relational and behavioural norms in the commercial world.[50] An obvious example here is the possible recognition of a duty of good faith and fair dealing, as noted in **2.08**.

---

45   An economic analysis may also support reliance theory: see eg Goetz & Scott 1990.
46   For a clear statement of the theory, see Macneil 1978. For a volume of his collected works with a useful commentary, see Campbell 2001.
47   The question of whether all contracts are relational is seen as an ambiguity in Macneil's work by those who otherwise adopt his analysis: see Campbell 2001: 54–8.
48   See Macneil 2003, emphasising the 'neutral' nature of his essential contract theory, which he regarded as merely one of countless possible relational theories of contracting.
49   See eg Austen-Baker 2009; Collins 2016.
50   See eg Goldwasser & Ciro 2002.

2.17   Economic perspectives

Recent decades have seen a great deal of analysis that seeks to use the 'dismal science' of economics as a framework for the description and criticism of contractual rules.[51] Economic analysis can clearly be useful in focusing attention on the incentives that particular rules or approaches may create, and hence on their potential costs and benefits.[52] But beyond that, the normative foundations of much work in this vein are highly contestable.[53] This is especially true of the *neoclassical economics* that dominated early writings of this type.[54] This prioritises the 'efficient' allocation of resources, including by (as far as possible) minimising transaction costs. It also assumes that individuals will generally act rationally to maximise their self-interest.[55]

There are many types of economic analysis today which rest on very different foundations. These include *new institutional economics*, which (among other things) views markets as being shaped by the complex interactions of individual, groups, organisations and governments, rather than existing in some kind of natural state.[56] In emphasising the importance of social norms, it can be linked to (and indeed helps inform) the relational contracting analyses noted above. *Behavioural economics* draws on psychological studies to explore the 'bounded rationality' (or indeed often plain irrationality) that, in fact, characterises human decision-making in relation to transactions.[57] Among other things, some behavioural economics research suggests an interest in distributive justice that is potentially at odds with the goals and assumptions of neoclassical economics.[58]

---

51   For an overview, see Katz 2014.
52   An example here is the 'contract theory' developed from the Nobel Prize-winning work of Oliver Hart and Bengt Holmström, which analyses how cooperation can most usefully be promoted under what must necessarily be incomplete contracts: see eg Aghion et al 2016.
53   See eg Trebilcock 1993.
54   See eg Kronman & Posner 1979.
55   For an Australian example of this type of law and economics analysis which nonetheless acknowledges its limitations, see Zhou 2011.
56   See generally Richter 2015.
57   See generally Sunstein 2000.
58   See Duke 2007.

3

RESOLVING CONTRACTUAL DISPUTES

3.01   Introduction

This chapter provides an overview of the methods by which disputes over the meaning, effect or performance of a contract can be resolved. It starts by considering ways in which the parties concerned may (lawfully) take matters into their own hands, before discussing negotiated settlements. In practice, most contractual disputes are resolved either by the parties reaching agreement on their own, or by one party simply conceding whatever point is being argued. But a few matters may need some external assistance or determination. We examine various forms of assisted dispute resolution, some of which the parties may have anticipated using when entering into their contract. Processes such as mediation, arbitration or expert determination are often considered cheaper, quicker or more effective alternatives to going to court. But where those processes are not used, or sometimes even when they are, a small percentage of matters will end up requiring judicial determination. Most of the *remedies* or formal orders that the courts can grant are explored in more detail later in the book. But we offer a broad summary of the main possibilities here, categorised according to their principal function or objective. Finally, we consider the difficult questions that can arise when a contract dispute involves parties, matters or adjudicators in different parts of Australia, or in different countries.

In discussing these various issues, we are principally concerned with the resolution of disputes that involve issues of general contract law, including the application of broadly applicable statutes such as the Australian Consumer Law (ACL). But we do, in passing, mention a number of mechanisms that have been adopted to deal with specific types of contractual disputes.

Self-help

3.02   Withholding performance

One of the simplest ways in which a party can seek to resolve a dispute over the meaning or effect of a contract is to withhold performance of some or all of their obligations. For example, a customer who is not satisfied with the quality of goods or services supplied may refuse to pay for them. A contractor who is concerned about not being paid for earlier work, or some other aspect of their treatment, may 'down tools' and refuse to continue. A purchaser of land who is worried about the non-fulfilment of an important condition for the sale, such as an environmental clearance or a rezoning application, may decline to tender some or all of the agreed price. In each of these cases, the party withholding performance may or may not be strictly entitled to take the stance they have. But their refusal puts the onus on the other party to object – and perhaps to take what may be expensive court action either to compel the relevant performance, or to seek compensation or restitution. While withholding performance can sometimes prove to be an expensive mistake if the other party successfully litigates, more often than not in practice it induces the other party either to accept the situation or negotiate a settlement.

The availability of these options depends of course on the order of performance agreed by the parties. More is said in Chapter 12 about some of the legal principles that help determine the point at which a party can *lawfully* withhold their own performance until the other does what they have promised. But at a more basic level, the practical ability to put pressure on the other party to perform or to rectify a situation, without having to litigate, often turns on the timing of any agreed payments.

3.03   Deposits and part payments

Most contracts involve the payment of money by at least one party. For contracts of a lengthy or possibly indefinite duration, regular payments may be expected or required; for example, of wages to an employee, or of premiums to an insurance company. But for more discrete transactions, payment schemes can be structured in very different ways. Consider, for example, a contract to perform building work. If the work has to be paid for only after completion, then the customer has a natural advantage. If they are not happy at any stage with the builder's performance, they can bar entry to the site, and/or refuse to pay for any work done. Conversely, if full payment must be made in advance, the advantage shifts to the builder. In practice, for work that must go on over any length of time, the agreed payment scheme will likely seek to balance the parties' interests. For example, the customer may have to pay a *deposit*, either when the contract is signed or at least before work commences. Such a payment, which is commonly measured as a percentage of the overall fee for the work, helps to act as a security to assure the customer's ongoing cooperation or commitment to the project. There may also be provision for *instalment payments*, to be made either at regular intervals or as particular stages of the work are completed. Finally, the *balance* of the price for the job may be payable only when the work has been completed to the customer's satisfaction. Similar schemes may be agreed for the purchase of land, or of goods that are not immediately available to be taken away, although it is more typical in those contexts to have just two payments: a deposit, then later the balance.

Given how common they are, it should be no surprise that a good deal of law has accumulated over the circumstances in which deposits and part payments can be demanded, retained or reclaimed. The relevant principles are examined in detail in Chapter 17.

3.04   Termination and rescission

As discussed in Chapter 16, a contract may expressly allow one party to *terminate* a contract in particular circumstances, either with or without cause (that is, a good reason). The common law permits one party to terminate a contract when the other party has in some significant way breached or repudiated their obligations. It may also, at least in limited situations, recognise an implied right for one party to terminate a contract with no fixed duration by giving the other reasonable notice. In each of these cases, termination is a remedy exercised by the terminating party, not ordered by a court. But the validity of a termination may still be challenged in court proceedings: see **16.03**.

The term *rescission* is sometimes used as a synonym for termination. But as explained in **16.02**, that word is better reserved for what is technically known as rescission ab initio (from the beginning). This involves a contract being cancelled or set aside on grounds such as misrepresentation, duress, undue influence or unconscionability. The High Court has stressed that rescission is 'always an act of the party': *Alati v Kruger* (1955) at 224. That would suggest it is correctly classified as a self-help remedy. Yet, as noted in **18.12**, that characterisation is challenged by the degree of control a court may exert over both the exercise of the remedy and the subsequent adjustment of the parties' rights. Some commentators have indeed argued that rescission should in some or possibly all cases be seen as a court-ordered remedy.[1]

Resolving disputes by agreement

3.05   Negotiated resolution

As the empirical studies mentioned in **2.04** reveal, many contractual disputes are resolved without going near a court – and often without even referring to any terms formally agreed between the parties, or the rights they may have under an applicable law. Those negotiations may be informal, though they can also be conducted through a lawyer or other representative. The latter is more likely if personal relations between the parties have broken down, or the matter involves a substantial amount of money. A negotiated settlement can also be reached even if court action has been commenced, or some other formal process has been initiated. Indeed, most court proceedings are settled either before any hearing, or during a break in a hearing that has already started.

Recent years have seen a great deal of research on the negotiating techniques and approaches that may be adopted by the parties or their agents, especially in extended or more structured negotiations. More is said about that in **4.02**.

3.06   Settlement agreements

Many disputes are resolved entirely informally, with the parties simply being satisfied that they have reached an outcome that they can both accept – or that one party feels compelled to accept, however unwillingly. A negotiated settlement may sometimes involve modifications to the original terms of the contract. For reasons explained in Chapter 13, however, it may be unclear whether such a variation is legally binding.

In a minority of cases, but particularly where lawyers are involved, the parties may choose to record their agreement in writing, often in a formal document known as a *deed* (see **5.47**). This is especially likely if one party wants to ensure that the other will not pursue certain claims in the future. There may also be a confidentiality clause, to preclude any disclosure of the terms of the settlement. Whether a settlement agreement is binding will depend on whether it satisfies the requirements for the formation of a valid contract set out in Chapter 5. In practice, an issue that sometimes arises in this context is whether a settlement is binding even before a formal document is drawn up to record its terms: see eg *Lucke v Cleary* (2011); *Pavlovic v Universal Music* (2015); and see further **6.06**. So long as the agreement is binding, however, it will preclude any attempt to litigate or re-litigate any matters that a party has undertaken not to pursue.

Assisted dispute resolution

3.07   Seeking assistance from third parties

Even where parties have not agreed in advance on a process for settling any disputes under their contract (see below), there are various ways of seeking assistance from third parties. For

---

1   See eg Heydon et al 2015: [25–095]–[25.110]; O'Sullivan 2000.

example, there are various types of *ombudsman* to assist consumers and/or small businesses to resolve complaints about their dealings with certain types of supplier. Notable examples include the Telecommunications Industry Ombudsman, the Australian Financial Complaints Authority, and the Australian Small Business and Family Enterprise Ombudsman.[2]

Parties who do take their disputes to court may also now be encouraged or even required to engage in some form of *alternative dispute resolution* (ADR). This may operate either within or outside the court or tribunal in question.[3] There are also examples of ADR processes designed as the primary way of resolving certain types of contractual dispute. For example, each State and Territory has legislation dealing with claims by contractors for progress payments in relation to building work. Such claims may be referred to an adjudicator for prompt determination, rather than requiring court proceedings.[4] Concerns have repeatedly been expressed, however, about the effectiveness of this legislation. A 2017 review conducted for the federal government recommended that the Commonwealth work with the States and Territories to create a nationally consistent scheme.[5] While little progress has yet been made towards that objective, some jurisdictions have made changes in response to recommendations in the review.[6]

3.08   Agreed dispute resolution processes

Parties may agree in advance to use a particular process to resolve either certain types of dispute that may arise under their contract, or indeed any type of dispute. This is especially common in certain transactions, such as building contracts or commercial leases. Alternatively, parties who are already in dispute may agree, whether formally or informally, to seek a particular form of assistance from an independent person or body. There are many different options, which may be used either singly or in combination. The more common forms of ADR include:

*   'facilitative' processes such as *mediation*, which involves a neutral person assisting the parties to identify, discuss and resolve issues;[7]

---

2   See *Telecommunications (Consumer Protection and Service Standards) Act 1999* (Cth) Pt 6; *Treasury Laws Amendment (Putting Consumers First – Establishment of the Australian Financial Complaints Authority) Act 2018* (Cth); *Australian Small Business and Family Enterprise Ombudsman Act 2015* (Cth). For details of the services these bodies provide, see www.tio.com.au, www.afca.org.au and www.asbfeo.gov.au.
3   See Sourdin 2016: ch 8; and see eg *Federal Court Rules 2011* (Cth) Pt 28.
4   See eg *Building and Construction Industry Security of Payment Act 1999* (NSW); though compare the somewhat different approach taken by the *Construction Contracts Act 2004* (WA). For discussion of the different models, see Coggins et al 2016: 50–70. As to the power of courts to review adjudications, see eg *Probuild Constructions v Shade Systems* (2018).
5   Murray 2017. The report favours the 'East Coast' model based on the New South Wales Act, although with modifications. Compare Coggins 2011, proposing a 'hybrid' scheme.
6   See eg *Building and Construction Industry Security of Payment Amendment Act 2018* (NSW).
7   An alternative possibility is *conciliation*, a term that is treated by some as a synonym for mediation, but by others as having different connotations: see Sourdin 2016: 190–3. One possible difference is that a conciliator exercising statutory functions – as, for example, with employment disputes resolved in the Fair Work Commission under the *Fair Work Act 2009* (Cth) – must seek to resolve the dispute in accordance with the provisions of the statute. A private mediator, by contrast, may simply be expected to facilitate a resolution on whatever terms the parties will accept.

- 'evaluative' processes such as *expert appraisal*, where a person with relevant expertise is asked to investigate a matter in dispute (such as the valuation of property) and provide advice on the facts and/or possible outcomes; and

- 'adjudicative processes' such as *expert determination*, where an expert is appointed to resolve a dispute over a particular issue; or *arbitration*, a more general and quasi-judicial process for hearing arguments from the parties and then determining their rights and obligations.[8]

Agreed dispute resolution processes are often 'tiered', so that parties may, for instance, have to negotiate, and/or seek the assistance of a mediator, before being able to proceed to arbitration.

The effect of an adjudicated *award* or determination is to define the parties' rights and liabilities under their contract and will be enforceable as such: see *TCL Air Conditioner v Judges of the Federal Court* (2013) at [75]–[79]. As a matter of common law (as opposed to the legislation considered in the next paragraph), there can be no 'appeal' unless the parties have agreed on such a mechanism. But even if the decision is described as final and binding, it will always be possible to ask a court to review it, to determine whether it was made in accordance with the parties' agreement: see eg *Shoalhaven City Council v Firedam Civil Engineering* (2011); *Mickovski v Financial Ombudsman Service Ltd* (2012); *Australian Vintage v Belvino Investments* (2015).[9]

3.09   The commercial arbitration legislation

Legislation in each Australian jurisdiction gives effect to agreements for the arbitration of commercial disputes, subject to a measure of judicial supervision. The legislation is based on UNCITRAL's Model Law on International Commercial Arbitration 1985, as amended in 2006.[10] At the federal level, Part III of the *International Arbitration Act 1974* (Cth) applies to arbitration agreements made in relation to international trade and commerce.[11] Part II also provides for the recognition and enforcement of arbitral awards made outside Australia, in accordance with another international instrument, the UNCITRAL *Convention on the Recognition and Enforcement of Foreign Arbitral Awards 1958* (the 'New York Convention').

In the mid-1980s (or 1990 in the case of Queensland), all States and Territories adopted uniform legislation to govern commercial arbitration. These regimes were subsequently updated by all jurisdictions to harmonise them with the Model Law, create more flexibility

---

8   One key difference between these processes is that an expert can base a decision on their own knowledge and opinion, whereas an arbitrator must pay due regard to the evidence and arguments advanced by the parties. Expert determination provisions may indeed make it clear that the expert is *not* acting as an arbitrator. Among other things, this may be intended to ensure that the procedure is not subject to the commercial arbitration legislation considered in the text below.

9   As to whether a determination may be set aside on the basis of apparent bias or partiality by the adjudicator, see *The Gull Lexington Group v Laguna Bay (Banongill) Agricultural* (2018).

10   Note that UNCITRAL has been preparing a new convention on the enforceability of settlement agreements reached through international commercial mediation: see https://uncitral.un.org/en/working_groups/2/arbitration/.

11   The constitutionality of these provisions was upheld in *TCL Air Conditioner v Judges of the Federal Court* (2013). As to whether the legislation can or should apply to cross-border consumer transactions, see Garnett 2017.

and limit the scope for judicial intervention.[12] Section 7 of the State and Territory statutes defines an arbitration agreement to mean any written agreement, whether contractual or not, to submit a dispute to arbitration. But s 1 of each Act makes it clear it is limited to 'domestic commercial' arbitration. The domestic requirement is satisfied by the parties having their place of business in Australia and the agreement not being covered by the 1974 federal Act. 'Commercial' is not defined. A note to s 1 indicates that the term 'should be given a wide interpretation'. But it has been held, for example, not to cover employment contracts: *Chief Executive Officer of ASADA v 34 Players* (2014).

The commercial arbitration legislation covers matters such as the appointment and powers of arbitrators, the conduct of proceedings, and the recognition and enforcement of awards made in the same or other jurisdictions. An award may only be challenged in court or denied recognition on limited grounds, which include the invalidity of the arbitration agreement, a failure to conduct the arbitration properly or a conflict with public policy (ss 34, 36).[13] The parties may, however, agree that an appeal can be made to a court on a question of law arising out of an award (s 34A).

Taking disputes to court

3.10 Court-ordered remedies

There are many different orders or *remedies* that a court may grant to resolve a contractual dispute. Most of these are explored in more detail later in the book, especially in Part VII. But in the paragraphs that follow we provide an overview of the main remedies, grouped into seven broad categories according to their main function or purpose: those of enforcement, compensation, adjustment, restitution, disgorgement, punishment and declaration.[14]

Besides classifying remedies according to their function, they may also be distinguished according to whether they are available as of right, or at the discretion of the court. The main common law remedies discussed below – those of debt and damages – fall into the former category. If a plaintiff establishes the necessary kind of breach of contract, and there is no applicable defence (such as that of illegality),[15] relief *must* be granted. By contrast, and as noted in **1.17** and **2.08**, it is a distinguishing feature of equitable remedies (those having their origins in the English Court of Chancery) that a plaintiff cannot automatically expect to obtain the order they are seeking. That does not mean, however, that judges can grant or refuse relief on a whim. The discretion must be exercised according to settled principles, such as those

---

12   See now *Commercial Arbitration Act 2010* (NSW); *Commercial Arbitration Act 2011* (Vic); *Commercial Arbitration Act 2013* (Qld); *Commercial Arbitration Act 2012* (WA); *Commercial Arbitration Act 2011* (SA); *Commercial Arbitration Act 2011* (Tas); *Commercial Arbitration Act 2017* (ACT); *Commercial Arbitration (National Uniform Legislation) Act 2011* (NT). For a detailed treatment, see Jones 2013.

13   As to this last exception, see eg *Gutnick v Indian Farmers* (2016).

14   Our list is similar but slightly different to the typology that appears in Witzleb et al 2015: 18, notably in adding adjustment of rights as a separate type of remedy.

15   As to illegality, see Chapter 21. Note that it is uncommon (unlike, say, in criminal law or tort law) to speak of 'defences' to an action for breach of contract, which is why there is no section in this book devoted to that topic. In practice, most of what might be considered defences are really arguments that there was no enforceable contract at the time of the breach; for example, because it had been rescinded or frustrated. See further Dyson et al 2017.

noted below in relation to the remedy of specific performance. It is also established that courts granting equitable remedies can attach conditions or make ancillary orders to achieve justice between the parties, in ways not typically possible with common law remedies.[16] Statutes too typically confer a discretion as to the availability of certain remedies. But the exercise of such a discretion is necessarily bounded by both the terms and overall objects (purposes) of the legislation.

3.11   Enforcement

Given that a contract is, by definition, a legally enforceable agreement, it might be thought that the standard remedy would be an order requiring a party in breach to comply with their obligations. But aside from compelling payments of money, that is not the case, as explained in Chapter 22. It is possible to seek an equitable order for *specific performance* of a contract. But there are many established reasons for a court exercising its discretion not to grant such relief. These include that damages (see below) would adequately compensate the plaintiff, a reluctance to supervise continuing obligations, and an unwillingness to require parties to work together when some kind of personal relationship is involved. In practice, and with the partial exception of contracts for the sale of land, specific performance is rarely granted.

It is slightly easier to get an *injunction*, especially of the 'prohibitory' kind. This can be used to restrain a party from breaching a negative stipulation – that is, a promise *not* to do something. But this too is an equitable remedy and courts will not grant it where the injunction would have the practical effect of forcing a party to perform a contract that would not be amenable to specific performance. Both injunctions and specific performance can also be declined, even where the circumstances might otherwise be suitable for such relief, on a range of other grounds. These include that the plaintiff is unable or unwilling to perform their own obligations, or has left it too long to seek relief.

In practice then, it is extremely hard to obtain enforcement of a contract – except where the obligation is to pay money that is already due. That is because the action for *debt* is available in such a case. Because this is a common law remedy, it is enough to show that money is owed to the plaintiff. The court does not have a general discretion to refuse such an order.

Statutory schemes may also offer remedies that can be used to compel the performance of statutory obligations. For instance, s 232(6) of the ACL allows a court to grant injunctions in response to an actual or threatened breach of various contraventions, including of the 'consumer guarantees' outlined in Chapter 9 of this book, or the prohibitions on misleading or unconscionable conduct considered in Chapters 18 and 20. Section 232(6) makes it clear that such orders may, among other things, require a person to transfer property or honour a promise.

3.12   Compensation

Along with debt, the action for *damages* is the principal remedy for breach of contract. Its purpose is to compensate a plaintiff for any loss they have suffered. That loss is almost always

---

16   There has been lively academic debate as to the nature of, and constraints on, 'discretionary remedialism': see eg Birks 2000; Evans 2001; Burns 2001.

assessed according to the position the plaintiff expected to be in if the contract had been performed ('expectation loss'), as opposed to the position they would have been in had the contract never been made ('reliance loss'). To be compensable, any loss must have been *caused* by the breach. It must also not be too *remote*, in the sense of being outside the reasonable contemplation of the parties at the time the contract was made. In addition, the doctrine of *mitigation* ensures that a plaintiff cannot recover damages for loss that they have taken steps to avoid, or that they could reasonably have avoided; for example, by finding someone else with whom to deal. Damages are generally oriented to economic or financial loss that can be expressed in monetary terms. It is rare that they can be recovered for *non-pecuniary loss* such as distress or disappointment. All of these matters are discussed further in Chapter 23.

Statutes regulating contracts or commercial behaviour may also permit orders for damages or compensation for loss suffered as a result of a breach of a statutory prohibition: see eg ACL ss 236–237. As discussed in **18.32**, however, it is often unclear on what basis such damages should be assessed.

Where a breach of contract also involves an equitable wrong, such as a breach of fiduciary duty (see **12.16**), *equitable compensation* may be available.[17] Statutes in each State and Territory also confer a power to award damages in addition to, or instead of, an order for specific performance or an injunction: see **23.23**.

3.13 Adjustment

Some remedies have the effect of adjusting the parties' contractual rights and obligations. At common law, the main example is *rectification* – an order to correct a contract, deed or other instrument to say what it was intended to say. This can be used to deal with instances of either a common (shared) or unilateral mistake as to the recorded terms of a transaction: see **18.43–18.44**. The capacity of a court to permit or order the partial rescission of a contract (see **18.12**) may also be an example.

Some statutory schemes likewise confer broad powers to vary a contract or declare particular terms to be void: see eg ACL ss 243(b), 250. The latter of those provisions relates to unfair terms and is discussed in **20.29**.

3.14 Restitution

As Chapter 24 explains, the idea of recognising certain remedies to be 'restitutionary' in nature is a relatively recent invention. But the common law had long provided for what were known as 'quasi-contractual' actions. For example, a party might bring an *action for money had and received* to recover money paid either under mistake or duress, or for an expected return which did not eventuate (a 'total failure of consideration'). The action for *quantum meruit* could also be used to obtain reasonable remuneration for services rendered, where the defendant had requested the services, freely accepted their benefit or (perhaps) been incontrovertibly benefited by their provision.[18]

---

17 As to this remedy and the basis on which it is assessed, see Heydon et al 2015: ch 23.
18 The action for *quantum meruit* can also be used in some cases to enforce a contractual obligation to pay a reasonable sum for work done: see **24.06**.

At one time, these actions were explained as resting on some form of 'implied contract' to repay the money or pay for the services. But this gradually came to be seen as a fiction, especially in cases where the parties had not otherwise entered into an agreement. The modern explanation, accepted by the High Court in *Pavey & Matthews v Paul* (1987), is that restitution is available in these and other situations in order to prevent the defendant from being *unjustly enriched* at the plaintiff's expense. More recent High Court decisions have muddied the waters by insisting (quite unnecessarily) on rediscovering an equitable basis for at least some of these actions: see **24.12**. Nevertheless, the rules that determine whether restitution will be awarded in certain common situations remain reasonably clear. This is the case, for instance, with claims to recover money paid, or remuneration for work done, under contracts that have since been terminated. The principles that apply in that context are discussed in Chapter 17.

Some statutes expressly confer a power to order restitution in order to remedy the effects of a contravention: see eg ACL s 243(d). The remedy of *rescission ab initio* can also be regarded as having a restitutionary function. As noted earlier, it can be used to cancel or annul a contract procured by (among other things) misrepresentation, duress or unconscionable conduct. It has the function of restoring the parties to the position they were in before the contract was made. Indeed, if that is not possible, the remedy will not generally be available: see **18.12–18.13**.

3.15 Disgorgement

As a matter of common law, it seems settled (at least in Australia) that a party in breach of their contractual obligations cannot be required to give up any profits they have made from their breach, to the extent those gains exceed any loss suffered by the other party: see **23.07**. But where a breach of contract also constitutes an equitable wrong, such as a breach of fiduciary duty or a breach of confidence, an *account of profits* may be awarded against the wrongdoer and anyone else knowingly involved in the breach: see eg *Warman International v Dwyer* (1995); *Optus Networks v Telstra* (2010); *Ancient Order of Foresters in Victoria v Lifeplan Australia* (2018). If property is obtained as a result of such a breach, another form of equitable relief is for a *constructive trust* to be imposed: see eg *Timber Engineering v Anderson* (1980). This requires the defendant wrongdoer (the trustee) to deal with the property on behalf of the plaintiff (the beneficiary).[19]

3.16 Punishment

There is no common law remedy that is directed to punishing a contract-breaker. *Exemplary* (or *punitive*) *damages* cannot be awarded for breach of contract: see **23.03**. But where a statute imposes obligations on a contracting party, it is not unusual today for a court to be able to impose monetary fines by way of *civil penalties* for certain types of contravention: see eg ACL s 224; *Fair Work Act 2009* (Cth) s 546. Despite their quasi-criminal nature, the ordinary rules of civil procedure still apply to the imposition of such penalties: see *Commonwealth v*

---

19   As to constructive trusts, see generally Dal Pont 2015a: ch 38.

Director, Fair Work Building Industry Inspectorate (2015). The High Court has also held that the power to impose a penalty may implicitly carry with it the capacity to direct that it be paid personally by the defendant: *Australian Building and Construction Commissioner v CFMEU* (2018).[20]

A person breaching their statutory obligations may also, in some cases, be required to advertise their culpability. For example, s 247 of the ACL expressly permits a court to make *adverse publicity orders* against those who have breached certain provisions, including the consumer guarantees.

3.17   Declaration

Most courts have the power to grant *declarations* as to the existence, scope or effect of a party's rights or obligations under a contract. This power exists in equity,[21] as well as under statutory provisions such as s 21(1) of the *Federal Court of Australia Act 1976* (Cth). But there must be a real dispute between the parties, and the court must be satisfied that granting a declaration will be of practical utility in resolving a controversy between them: see *Neeta (Epping) v Phillips* (1974).

A court may sometimes award *nominal damages* to a plaintiff who has established a breach of contract, but been unable to prove that they have suffered any loss as a result of that breach: see **23.01**. This too can be viewed as a form of declaratory relief.

3.18   Accessorial liability

At common law, the doctrine of privity of contract (see Chapter 8) means that direct liability for breaching a contract can only be borne by a party to that contract. So if a company breaches a contract, only the company itself can be sued, not its officers, employees or advisers. However, it is possible to sue a third party in tort for deliberately inducing a contracting party not to fulfil their obligations. For such liability to arise, the defendant must either know that the relevant contract exists or be recklessly indifferent to its existence. They do not need to know the precise term that is breached: *Daebo Shipping v The Ship Go Star* (2012) at [88]–[89]. Many statutory regimes also allow remedies to be pursued against a person knowingly involved in another person's contravention. These include the ACL, as discussed in **18.31**. Remedies are likewise available in equity, as noted in **3.15**, against third parties who knowingly participate in breaches of equitable duties.

3.19   Jurisdiction of Australian courts

Common law actions for breach of contract or for other remedies concerning a contract (including equitable relief or restitutionary claims) most naturally fall within the general civil jurisdiction of the State and Territory courts. Which particular court will be chosen within a given hierarchy may depend on the amounts at stake and the complexity of the matter. In South Australia, to take just one example, both the Supreme Court and the District Court are

---

20   Note that some statutes expressly forbid companies from indemnifying officers on whom such penalties are imposed: see eg ACL ss 229–230.
21   See Dal Pont 2015a: 1131–40.

empowered to hear such matters,[22] though the latter will more commonly be used for reasons of cost. A further option in South Australia is the Magistrates Court, though it can only generally deal with monetary or property claims involving up to $100,000 and is limited in the equitable relief it can grant.[23] The same court offers a special process for dealing with 'minor civil actions', including small claims involving up to $12,000. The procedure used is inquisitorial rather than adversarial, the normal rules of evidence do not apply, there are limits on legal representation, and the magistrate is expected to 'act according to equity, good conscience and the substantial merits of the case without regard to technicalities and legal forms'.[24] There are also specialist tribunals to deal with claims arising under particular statutory regimes. For instance, the South Australian Civil and Administrative Tribunal can deal with residential tenancy disputes,[25] while the South Australian Employment Tribunal has a broad jurisdiction over employment-related matters, including some that arise under the federal *Fair Work Act 2009*.[26]

The Federal Court and Federal Circuit Court generally have jurisdiction only where a federal statute expressly provides.[27] But in practice they commonly deal with actions for breach of contract and other common law claims. This is because once a statutory claim is validly before the court – for example for misleading or unconscionable conduct in breach of ss 18 or 21 of the ACL[28] – the court may deal with any other related claim or issue that arises as part of the same 'matter' or controversy between the parties: see eg *Fencott v Muller* (1983).

3.20 Limitation periods

Each State and Territory has general legislation dealing with the period within which certain actions must be brought. These *Limitation Acts* provide that actions for breach of contract must be brought within six years from the date on which the cause of action accrued, or three years in the Northern Territory. The same applies to 'quasi-contractual' (restitutionary) remedies.[29]

---

22   *Supreme Court Act 1935* (SA) s 17; *District Court Act 1991* (SA) s 8. New South Wales, Queensland and Western Australia also have a District Court, while the equivalent in Victoria is the County Court. Tasmania, the ACT and the Northern Territory do not have an intermediate court of this type.

23   *Magistrates Court Act 1991* (SA) s 8. Each of the States and Territories has an equivalent court, although in New South Wales and the Northern Territory it is called the Local Court.

24   *Magistrates Court Act 1991* (SA) s 38; and see also the definitions in s 3 of 'minor civil action' and 'small claim'.

25   *Residential Tenancies Act 1995* (SA) s 24. Both parties' consent is required if more than $40,000 is claimed. All States and Territories bar Tasmania now have a Civil and Administrative Tribunal, though their roles and functions vary.

26   *Fair Work Act 1994* (SA) Ch 2 Pt 1; *Fair Work Act 2009* (Cth) s 539. Unusually for tribunals of this kind, the jurisdiction conferred by s 10 of the 1994 Act extends to common law and equitable claims for damages, specific performance or injunctive relief relating to an employment contract. New South Wales, Queensland, Western Australia and Tasmania also have industrial tribunals, although again their functions (and names) vary.

27   See *Federal Court of Australia Act 1976* (Cth) s 19; *Judiciary Act 1903* (Cth) s 39B; *Federal Circuit Court of Australia Act 1999* (Cth) s 10.

28   The Federal Court or Federal Circuit Court will generally have such jurisdiction when the ACL applies as a federal law: see **1.15**.

29   *Limitation Act 1969* (NSW) s 14(1)(a); *Limitation of Actions Act 1958* (Vic) s 5(1)(a); *Limitation of Actions Act 1974* (Qld) s 10(1)(a); *Limitation Act 2005* (WA) s 13(1); *Limitation of Actions Act 1936* (SA) s 35(a); *Limitation Act 1974* (Tas) s 4(1)(a); *Limitation Act 1985* (ACT) s 11(1); *Limitation Act 1981* (NT) s 12(1)(a).

Where a deed is used, the limitation periods are longer. Some jurisdictions allow 12 years,[30] while in Victoria and South Australia, 15 years is used.[31] The date on which a cause of action accrues may vary according to the type of action.[32] But in actions for debt or damages for breach of contract, time will generally start to run from the date of the breach. Ignorance that a breach has occurred does not prevent time running. If that ignorance is a product of mistake or fraud, however, time does not generally start to run until the breach is discovered or could reasonably be discovered.[33] Where there is a failure to perform an ongoing obligation, a new cause of action will arise each day: see eg *Sheldon v McBeath* (1993). It appears to be open to parties to agree either to shorten or extend a limitation period for breach of contract: see eg *The New York Star* (1978).[34]

The *Limitation Acts* do not generally apply to equitable remedies. But where a 'corresponding' remedy at law is barred by statute, a court may apply that limitation period by analogy: see *Gerace v Auzhair Supplies* (2014). More generally, the grant of an equitable remedy may be refused under the doctrine of *laches*, where the plaintiff has been guilty of unreasonable delay in seeking relief: see eg **22.11**, discussing this principle in relation to actions for specific performance.

The equitable doctrine of *promissory estoppel*, discussed in Chapter 7, may also be invoked where one party leads another to believe that they will not invoke a statutory limitation period to bar an action. If the other party relies on that belief to their detriment, the first party may be estopped (precluded) from subsequently pleading the limitation period as a defence: see eg *Commonwealth v Verwayen* (1990). Alternatively, as some judges in *Verwayen* preferred to put it, the first party may be said to have waived their right to invoke the limitation period: see eg *Uren v Uren* (2018), and see further **13.18**.

Choice of law

3.21   Resolving conflicts of laws

It is not unusual, especially in a federation such as Australia, for questions to arise as to which laws govern a contract, or which court(s) may deal with any dispute that arises. Any or all of the parties, the subject matter of the contract or the place of performance may be located in different States or Territories, or indeed in different countries. The principles of *private international law* that are used to resolve conflicts between the laws of different jurisdictions are far too complex to cover in any detail in a book of this kind. But some basic principles are outlined in the paragraphs that follow.[35]

---

30   *Limitation Act 1969* (NSW) s 16; *Limitation of Actions Act 1974* (Qld) s 10(3); *Limitation Act 2005* (WA) s 18; *Limitation Act 1974* (Tas) s 4(3); *Limitation Act 1985* (ACT) s 13; *Limitation Act 1981* (NT) s 14.

31   *Limitation of Actions Act 1958* (Vic) s 5(3); *Limitation of Actions Act 1936* (SA) s 34.

32   See Handford 2017: [5.10.630]–[5.10.710].

33   *Limitation Act 1969* (NSW) ss 55–56; *Limitation of Actions Act 1958* (Vic) s 27; *Limitation of Actions Act 1974* (Qld) s 38; *Limitation Act 2005* (WA) s 38; *Limitation Act 1974* (Tas) s 32; *Limitation Act 1985* (ACT) ss 33–34; *Limitation Act 1981* (NT) ss 42–43. Compare *Limitation of Actions Act 1936* (SA) s 48, which confers a more general discretion on courts to extend limitation periods.

34   In Western Australia there is specific statutory provision to this effect: *Limitation Act 2005* (WA) s 45.

35   For a more detailed treatment, see Mortensen et al 2015, especially ch 17.

3.22 Taking jurisdiction

If an action is commenced in a court located in a particular place or *forum*, the first question is whether that court has any *jurisdiction* to deal with the dispute. As a matter of common law, a court can exercise personal jurisdiction in a contractual matter over anyone 'served' – that is, given a copy of a claim or application – within the physical boundaries of the forum, or who voluntarily submits to the court's jurisdiction: see eg *Laurie v Carroll* (1958). The practical difficulties created by that principle are significantly reduced by s 15 of the *Service and Execution of Process Act 1992* (Cth). This permits a process initiated in any State or Territory court to be served on a defendant anywhere in Australia. There is a similar rule for service in New Zealand, under s 9 of the *Trans-Tasman Proceedings Act 2010* (Cth). Beyond that, service depends on the rules of the forum court. Service outside Australia is generally possible if the defendant is domiciled or ordinarily resident in Australia, or has submitted to the jurisdiction of an Australian court, including through a term of the relevant contract. Service outside Australia is also permitted if a contract has various kinds of connection to Australia, including the contract being made or breached in the forum, the contract being governed by the law of the forum (see below), or one of the parties having a connection to Australia. But the court may grant leave to serve outside the jurisdiction even if none of these conditions are met.[36]

Once a court has jurisdiction, it may be asked to stay its own proceedings so the matter may be litigated elsewhere. If that is another Australian court, it is simply a matter of deciding whether that court is the 'appropriate' one: *Service and Execution of Process Act 1992* (Cth) s 20.[37] But different considerations arise where it is suggested that an overseas court should deal with the matter. If the parties have previously agreed to refer any disputes only to the courts of another jurisdiction, such a stay will likely be granted by an Australian court, in the absence of any compelling public policy considerations: *Oceanic Sun Line v Fay* (1988) at 224, 231, 259.[38] But if there is no such 'exclusive jurisdiction' clause, a defendant who wishes the matter to be heard by a foreign court must generally make a *forum non conveniens* argument. To succeed, it must be shown that the Australian forum is a 'clearly inappropriate' court to hear the matter: *Voth v Manildra Flour Mills* (1990); *Puttick v Tenon* (2008).

In some cases, a court may be asked to issue an *anti-suit injunction* restraining a court elsewhere from dealing with a matter. In the interests of 'comity' between courts, this will not lightly be granted: see *CSR v Cigna Insurance* (1997).

The position described above would change somewhat if, as recommended by a parliamentary committee,[39] Australia accedes to the *Convention on Choice of Court Agreements 2005*. Drafted by the Hague Conference on Private International Law, the Convention

---

36   See eg *Uniform Civil Procedure Rules 2005* (NSW) Pt 11, Sch 6.

37   An application may also be made under the 'cross-vesting' legislation in each Australian jurisdiction to transfer a proceeding to another Australian court 'in the interests of justice': see eg *Jurisdiction of Courts (Cross-vesting) Act 1987* (Vic) s 5.

38   Note that where a New Zealand court is nominated by an exclusive jurisdiction clause in a commercial contract, s 20 of the *Trans-Tasman Proceedings Act 2010* (Cth) generally requires Australian courts to defer to that choice. But this only applies where both litigants are parties to that contract: *Australian Gourmet Pastes v IAG New Zealand* (2017).

39   See Joint Standing Committee on Treaties 2016: 17–23; and see further Marshall & Keyes 2017; Douglas 2018.

generally requires contracting states to give effect to provisions in commercial contracts requiring the parties to submit exclusively to the courts of a nominated jurisdiction. It does not, however, apply to consumer transactions or employment contracts.

3.23   The proper law of the contract

If a matter is heard in the court of a particular forum, the procedural laws of the forum will generally apply. But the substantive law that governs the dispute may be another matter. The general rule in Australia is that a contractual dispute will be resolved by reference to the *proper law of the contract*. This is, in the first instance, a matter for the parties. If they have chosen to nominate the law of a particular place as governing their contract, even one to which the contract appears to lack a connection, that choice will generally be respected: *Vita Food v Unus Shipping* (1939). Even in the absence of an express term, it may be possible to imply an intention to choose a particular law: *Akai v People's Insurance* (1996) at 441–2. In the absence of any choice, however, the proper law of the contract will be determined on an objective basis. A court must decide which legal system has the closest and most real connection to the contract: *Bonython v Commonwealth* (1950).

As with exclusive jurisdiction agreements, it has been proposed that Australia legislate to strengthen party autonomy. The federal government has indicated an intention to enact an *International Civil Law Act* which, besides implementing the *Convention on Choice of Court Agreements*, would give effect to the Hague Principles on Choice of Law in International Commercial Contracts.[40]

3.24   Mandatory laws

Identification of the proper law of the contract is not the end of the matter. A forum court may still need to decide whether a statute that operates in the forum is to be regarded as having mandatory effect, notwithstanding the proper law of the contract being that of another place.

Some legislation provides explicit guidance in this regard. For example, s 11 of the *Carriage of Goods by Sea Act 1991* (Cth) provides that a sea carriage document, such as a bill of lading, is governed by the law in force at the place of shipment, wherever that might be. By contrast, s 67 of the ACL ensures that the 'consumer guarantees' discussed in Chapter 9 will apply whenever goods or services are supplied to an Australian consumer. It prevents a term in a contract for the supply of goods or services to a consumer from either: (a) displacing Australian law as the proper law of that contract; or (b) substituting the law of another country for the consumer guarantee provisions. The second of these rules was held in *Valve v ACCC* (2017) to apply even where the proper law of the contract would not have been the law of Australia. A similar though slightly less clearly worded provision appears in s 8(2) of the *Insurance Contracts Act 1984* (Cth). It was held in *Akai v People's Insurance* (1996) to mean that an insurance contract that had its closest connection to New South Wales was governed by the Act, even though the parties had clearly expressed an intention that the contract be subject to English law and that any disputes come before the English courts.

---

40   Australian Government 2016. For a critical analysis of the Hague Principles, see Marshall 2018. As to the laws most commonly chosen by parties to international contracts, see Cuniberti 2014.

Where a forum statute is silent, it is a matter of determining the intended scope of the legislation through a process of statutory interpretation. In *Old UGC v Industrial Relations Commission* (2006), it was held that a provision authorising the New South Wales Industrial Relations Commission to review the fairness of a contract relating to the performance of work was plainly intended to apply to any work performed within the State, even if the contract was otherwise governed by the law of another place. By contrast, in *Insight Vacations v Young* (2011), a provision in the *Civil Liability Act 2002* (NSW) dealing with the validity of exemption clauses in contracts for recreational services was found not to apply to services supplied wholly outside the State during an overseas holiday. This was despite the fact that the contract in question was otherwise governed by New South Wales law.

Even where it is determined that Australian legislation applies to a cross-border transaction, there may be practical difficulties in ensuring compliance. This is a particular challenge in relation to consumer transactions with overseas businesses.[41] One obvious answer lies in international cooperation. For example, the ACCC is part of the International Consumer Protection and Enforcement Network, which involves agencies from over 60 countries working together to combat fraud and other forms of malpractice in cross-border marketing.[42] Initiatives like this can help deal with some of the worst kinds of online scam. But many challenges remain, especially for consumers dealing with parties which have no office or resources within the reach of Australian regulators or their international partners.

---

41   See eg Malbon 2013.
42   See www.icpen.org/protecting-consumers-worldwide.

PART

II

MAKING A CONTRACT

4

PREPARING TO MAKE A CONTRACT

Preparing and settling the terms

4.01   The many ways to make a contract

As we noted at the start of Chapter 2, some contracts are the product of extensive *negotiation* – but in practice, most are not. Contracts can also differ dramatically in their level of *formality*. Many simple agreements are entered into with little more than a brief verbal exchange; for instance, when buying a coffee. At the other end of the spectrum, contracts may be expressed in printed or digitally stored terms that run to thousands of words.

But formality does not of itself signify negotiation. Some complex commercial deals are thrashed out between legal representatives whose goal is to capture what the parties have agreed in written terms. Such terms are often developed through a succession of drafts, proposals and counter-proposals. But it is much more common for carefully drafted terms to be prepared by one party and simply imposed on the other in a take-it-or-leave-it fashion. This is what typically happens when we open bank accounts, accept a mobile phone plan, or buy airline or event tickets online. Conversely, even informal contracts can be the product of intense negotiation, as when haggling to buy a product at a street market.

The principles that determine when the parties have reached agreement and actually formed a contract are dealt with in Chapter 5. In the remainder of this chapter, we briefly touch on five aspects of the process for preparing and settling the terms of different kinds of contracts. These are the approach to any *negotiation* that takes place; the use of *agents* to make a contract on behalf of someone else; the role of *standard form terms*; the various approaches that can be taken to *drafting* contracts; and the *types of provision* commonly included in a written agreement. We then go on to consider other pre-contractual issues such as obligations on parties to disclose information before making a contract; other types of regulation of pre-contractual conduct; and finally, what happens if one party does something in anticipation of a contract that never materialises.

4.02   Negotiation techniques

There are many ways in which to negotiate a contract. For most of us as individuals, a combination of our personalities and situational needs will influence whether we undertake any preparation, what strategies we consciously or instinctively adopt – and indeed whether we are prepared to negotiate at all. But for those who have to negotiate on a more regular basis, whether on their own behalf or for someone else, a great deal of guidance is now available. Particularly since the publication of Fisher and Ury's *Getting to Yes* in 1981,[1] a wave of academic studies and self-help books have explored the keys to successful negotiations, both to resolve disputes and for other purposes.[2]

---

1   Fisher & Ury 1981. This was one of the early products of the Harvard Negotiation Project, established at Harvard Law School in 1979 'to improve the theory and practice of conflict resolution and negotiation by working on real world conflict intervention, theory building, education and training, and writing and disseminating new ideas': see www.pon.harvard.edu/research_projects/harvard-negotiation-project/hnp/.

2   Even where the parties to a dispute do not already have a contract, the outcomes of a successful negotiation may well involve some form of settlement agreement, especially if the purpose is to end or avert litigation: see **3.05**. As to the legal issues that such agreements can raise, see eg **5.33**, **6.06–6.07**.

There is far too much in this literature to do it justice here.[3] But one consistent theme has been to distinguish between adversarial or 'positional' bargaining, and 'integrative' or interests-based bargaining. The former sees negotiation as a competitive process, in which the aim is to beat the other party and secure a better deal or a greater share. There is much emphasis on stating, modifying and, if necessary, abandoning a formal 'position'. The alternative is to focus on the parties' underlying interests or needs. The participants are encouraged to explore a range of options before settling on an outcome, and to maintain a focus on the issues involved rather than the people. This more cooperative approach is often said to be associated with a greater chance of *win-win* outcomes.[4] In practice, however, some contractual negotiations more naturally lend themselves to a positional approach, especially if the transaction involves a simple, one-off exchange between parties who do not expect to have to deal with one another in the future. There are also times where, for external or organisational reasons, negotiating parties are necessarily expected to state and defend certain positions.[5]

4.03   The use of agents

Organisations such as corporations and governments necessarily have to make contracts through the agency of individuals, who are generally (though not always) working directly for those organisations as employees. But there are also times when it is possible or even customary to engage the services of an external agent to help make a contract. Such agents can play a range of different roles.[6] Some are intermediaries who do little more than provide a 'matching' service for suppliers and potential clients. Many online booking services operate in that way. Others may play a more active role. Real estate agents, for example, can generally be expected not just to carry messages between potential buyers and sellers, but to advise one or both on whether they should make or accept a particular offer. Normally, however, they do not have the authority to make binding commitments on behalf of either party. They are not 'agents' in the strict legal sense of the term, as meaning someone empowered to act on behalf of another (their *principal*) in creating or affecting legal rights and duties: *Petersen v Moloney* (1951) at 94–5. The same is true of lawyers. Solicitors can certainly negotiate on behalf of their clients. But unless there is clear evidence to the contrary, they do not usually have the authority to make binding commitments on those clients' behalf: *Pavlovic v Universal Music* (2015).

Whether a particular agent *does* have the authority to enter into a contract on behalf of their principal depends on the circumstances. More is said about that in **8.04**. For now, it is sufficient to note that some agents can effectively act for both parties to a contract. At a traditional auction, for example, the auctioneer may be regarded as an agent for both the seller *and* the successful bidder: *Venuti v Toop Real Estate* (2004) at [19]–[20].[7] Similarly, while insurance

---

3   For a useful summary, see Sourdin 2016: ch 2, from which some of the following is taken. For a more detailed treatment, see eg Alexander et al 2015.

4   One particular type of cooperative approach to contracting, used particularly for construction projects, is known as *alliancing*: see eg Stephenson & Molck 2017.

5   See eg Provis 1996.

6   As to the different types of agency and agent, see Dal Pont 2013: ch 1.

7   It may be different with online auctions of the kind facilitated by eBay: see **5.21**.

agents are generally regarded as acting for insurers, and insurance *brokers* as representing those seeking insurance, in some situations these intermediaries may be agents of the other party as well.[8]

4.04   Standard form contracts

It has become extremely common for contracts to be entered into on standardised terms. Occasionally the form and substance of a particular contract are mandated by legislation, as for instance with some residential leases: see eg *Residential Tenancies Act 1995* (SA) s 49. But more commonly, contracts are privately drafted. Some standard forms are created by or for industry associations and made available for general use. Important examples in this category include agreements for the sale of land prepared by real estate institutes or law societies,[9] or the various building contracts prepared by Standards Australia Ltd.[10] Many organisations also have their own standard terms for doing business with customers and/or suppliers. Where two businesses are both intent on using their own terms for a single transaction, the resulting 'battle of the forms' may make it hard to determine whether a contract has been concluded, and if so on whose terms: see **5.23**.

A further source of standard terms are the 'precedent banks' maintained by law firms. These include standardised agreements, often with variable prompts and optional inclusions. They can be rolled out in their entirety, or customised to meet the needs of a particular client. Even where much of a contract is negotiated, the terms settled by the parties will often contain standardised inclusions drawn from these precedents.

There are obvious benefits to the use of standard forms. They can lower the cost of doing business by avoiding costly and protracted bargaining, as well as disseminating information more efficiently. Repeated use of the same terms can improve certainty and predictability. Standard forms can also (at least in theory) enable the incorporation and refinement of 'best practice' provisions. At the same time, however, many standard contracts are imposed on a take-it-or-leave-it basis.[11] Empirical studies and personal experience also suggest that most parties (including consumers *and* businesses) do not read the standard terms they are shown or given – although residential leases may be something of an exception.[12] Even where negotiation occurs, this is more likely to involve discussions over price or product specification, not the fine print.

Judges have long been aware of the risks presented by standard terms for consumers in particular.[13] As Chapter 9 will explain, this has led them to require businesses to ensure their

---

8   See Tarr et al 2009: 102–4.
9   See eg www.lawsociety.com.au/resources/areasoflaw/propertylaw/index.htm (New South Wales). A potential pitfall for such bodies is the need to comply strictly with statutory requirements as to the expression of certain terms: see eg *Advisory Services v Augustin* (2018); Houston & Vedelago 2018.
10   As to the use of these and other standard forms in the construction industry, see Sharkey et al 2014.
11   Agreements imposed in this way are sometimes called 'contracts of adhesion': see eg Rakoff 1983. See also Radin 2017, discussing the difference between what she terms 'massively distributed boilerplate' (contracts of adhesion) and 'high end boilerplate' (standard terms used for what may otherwise be 'bespoke' or customised contracts); and see further Radin 2013, discussing the implications of standard form contracts for both theories of contracting and the rule of law.
12   See eg Robertson 2005: 188–93; Bakos et al 2014.
13   For a particularly striking example, see *George Mitchell v Finney Lock Seeds* (1982) at 1043.

customers are given reasonable notice of the existence and content of such terms – and to highlight any unusual or especially onerous provisions that may be included. Courts have also been inclined to find ways to narrow the effect of standard clauses limiting or excluding a party's liability for what would otherwise be a breach of their obligations, as discussed in Chapter 11. But in both instances it is relatively easy for a party to frustrate these efforts. In the first case, this may be done by requiring a signed agreement (something that, as we will see, negates any need for special notice of unusual terms). In the second case, a party need only be more precise in drafting its exclusion or limitation clauses.

More recently, however, parliaments have intervened to provide increased protections for consumers. This has sometimes involved legislating to negate particular terms, as for instance with the controls on exemption clauses discussed in **11.09**. But more significantly now, Part 2-3 of the Australian Consumer Law (ACL) includes provisions that apply generally to unfair terms in standard form contracts. When these provisions first took effect in 2010 they were limited to contracts for the supply of goods, services or land to a consumer. But since November 2016, they have been broadened to cover standard form contracts with smaller businesses: see **20.22**. As a result of these reforms, many businesses have been obliged (or at least encouraged) to review their standard terms.[14]

4.05   Drafting styles

Subject to any statutory requirements, parties are free to draft written contracts in whatever way they choose. But in practice, most written terms are the work of lawyers – especially if the terms being used are in standard form. Where parties decide to 'do it themselves', they may be able to save some money. But the results are not always positive if a dispute subsequently arises.[15]

Drafting styles have always varied, even amongst legal professionals. But until recently, there was a general tendency to draft commercial contracts in terms intelligible only to other lawyers. Short sentences were unusual. Punctuation, especially in the form of commas, tended to be sparse. Legal jargon was common, as were antiquated terms such as 'howsoever', 'aforementioned' and 'hereinafter'. And drafters rarely used one word where two or three could be employed. Contracts, like other legal instruments, were sprinkled with doublets and triplets such as 'covenant and agree', 'let or hindrance', or 'right, title and interest'.

In the last few decades, thankfully, 'plain English' has become more common in legal drafting. Useful guides are now available to assist drafters in this regard.[16] These explain how to avoid legalese and keep language simple and direct. They emphasise the importance of breaking up long or convoluted sentences. They suggest greater use of headings and bulleted lists, as well as more 'white space' on a page to make it easier on the eye. It has also become common to draft some contracts in the first and second person. So rather than referring impersonally to 'the parties', or 'the purchaser', a contract may now speak of 'we' and 'you'. This is an especially useful technique for contracts that involve an ongoing relationship, such

---

14   See ACCC 2013a, 2016b.
15   For a notable example, see *Fletcher Challenge Energy v Electricity Corporation of New Zealand* (2002), discussed in **6.05**. See also the 'drafting disaster' described in *Alstom v Yokogawa* (2012) at [89]–[92].
16   See eg Asprey 2010; Butt 2013.

as an employment contract. There have even been examples of 'comic (strip) contracts' being prepared, using graphics and pictures to help convey complex legal concepts to workers or other parties who might find text alone less accessible.[17]

The uptake of plain language drafting has been uneven. But standard form contracts are noticeably easier to read than they used to be.[18] Sometimes, this has been prompted by legislative requirements. For example, s 35 of the *Insurance Contracts Act 1984* (Cth) prevents insurers from relying on various types of limitations or exceptions to insurance cover unless they have clearly been drawn to the attention of the insured.

What has not changed so much has been the amount of detail typically included in commercial contracts. Australian lawyers remain generally averse to drafting short agreements that set out general obligations. That style is more common with 'heads of agreement' or 'letters of intent'. But documents of that type, which are discussed further in Chapter 6, are often seen as preliminary to the preparation of more detailed contracts. It is not uncommon for complex transactions, such as joint ventures, to run to hundreds of pages. Even with simpler agreements, where the main obligations can be quickly described, the inclusion of 'boilerplate' (standardised) terms on some of the matters outlined below can add many pages to the length of a contract.

4.06   Common provisions in written contracts

It is impossible here to canvass all the different matters that might be dealt with in a contract. Something is said in the next chapter about the terms that are considered *essential* to contracts of a particular kind: see **5.36**, **5.38**. But there are some common inclusions in written contracts that are worth mentioning briefly.

A contract will generally start by identifying the parties to the agreement. Some contracts will then go on to 'recite' the nature, origins or purposes of the transaction. Recitals of this sort may, within certain limits, be used as an aid to interpreting the operative provisions of the contract: see *Franklins v Metcash* (2009) at [379]–[390]. The principal obligations of the parties will be detailed. There may also be ancillary obligations; for example, to 'warrant' (promise) that certain things have been done or that certain assumptions may be made, or to take out insurance against specified risks. Conversely, a provision may make it clear that *no* warranties have been given on a particular matter, or that no liability is to be incurred in particular circumstances. Clauses limiting or excluding liability are examined in Chapter 11. *Force majeure* clauses, which typically suspend performance in the event of some disruption outside the parties' control, are considered separately in Chapter 15. Where a contract is to operate for a particular duration, this will be specified, either by reference to a period of time or a certain contingency, such as the completion of a project. In addition, or alternatively, a contract may specify the circumstances in which it may be terminated. More is said about that in Chapter 16. Agreed terms may also seek to influence, expand or limit the remedies available for certain

---

17   See eg Keating & Andersen 2016.
18   The newer ones, that is. Compare the outdated standard form lease which, complete with handwritten deletions and typewritten inclusions, prompted the litigation in *Ecosse Property Holdings v Gee Dee Nominees* (2017).

types of breach.[19] A particularly important example is a provision for *agreed* (or *liquidated*) *damages*. Such clauses are discussed in Chapter 22, in the context of the rule against penalties.

Beyond those matters, it is common to find standardised or 'boilerplate' provisions on a further range of issues. Sometimes these are needed. But just as often, they seem to be included by lawyers out of habit. In some instances they may be ignored by the parties, or replicate the position that would apply anyway under the general law. Provisions in this category include:

- *entire agreement* clauses, stipulating that the written terms operate to the exclusion of any separate documents or verbal assurances (see **9.15**);
- stipulations that *variations* may only be agreed in writing (see **13.13**);
- requirements as to the giving of *notices* by one party to the other; for example, to address specified problems, or to terminate the contract;
- permission for one party to *assign* (transfer) their rights or obligations under the contract to another party (see Chapter 14);
- clauses purporting to make any invalid provision *severable* from the rest of the contract (see **5.40, 21.17, 21.28**);
- procedures for the *resolution of disputes* arising under the contract (see **3.08**); and
- *choice of law* provisions, indicating which jurisdiction's rules are to govern the contract, and/or whose courts are to have jurisdiction if any litigation is commenced (see **3.22–3.23**).

Obligations to disclose information

4.07   The general rule: silence is golden

As Gleeson CJ explained in *Lam v Ausintel* (1989) at 475:

> Where parties are dealing at arm's length in a commercial situation in which they have conflicting interests it will often be the case that one party will be aware of information which, if known to the other, would or might cause that other party to take a different negotiating stance. This does not in itself impose any obligation on the first party to bring the information to the attention of the other party, and failure to do so would not, without more, ordinarily be regarded as dishonesty or even sharp practice.

This principle is not limited to commercial negotiations. As a matter of general law, and subject to the exceptions noted below, a party contemplating or negotiating a contract is not obliged to disclose information, no matter how relevant or important. As explained in Chapter 18, a party's failure to reveal material information cannot usually be treated as a *misrepresentation* that would render a contract voidable: see eg *W Scott Fell v Lloyd* (1906). Nor, even if it is intentional, can it provide a basis for an action in the tort of *deceit*. However, it might be different if a defendant has taken active steps to prevent the plaintiff from discovering certain facts: see eg *Wood v Balfour* (2011).

---

19   For an overview of what can and cannot be done in this respect, see Carter & Tilbury 1998.

4.08   Common law exceptions

As that last qualification suggests, the rule permitting pre-contractual silence is by no means absolute.[20] For example, a *half-truth* can be a misrepresentation. This is where a statement is literally true, but in context implies something else that is false. A contract is also voidable for misrepresentation where a party *fails to correct* a statement that was originally true, but has since become false: see **18.10**. A contract may likewise be set aside where one party is aware that the other party is *mistaken* as to a fundamental term (such as the price or subject matter) of a contract and unconscionably fails to enlighten them: see eg *Taylor v Johnson* (1983), and see **18.39**.[21] In addition, silence at a key point in negotiations may be a ground for an action in *estoppel*, as noted later in this chapter: see **4.12**.

Then there are circumstances where the relationship between the parties is such as to compel disclosure of material information.[22] The most obvious example is where the relationship is of a *fiduciary* nature. This involves one party being obliged to act in the best interests of the other (see **12.16**), such as a solicitor in relation to their client. The two main obligations of a fiduciary are to avoid conflicts of interest and not to profit from their position. Technically, there is no positive duty to disclose.[23] But without full disclosure of the existence of a conflict or the possibility of a profit, the principal or beneficiary (the person to whom the fiduciary duty is owed) cannot give informed consent to what would otherwise be a breach of duty: see eg *Commonwealth Bank v Smith* (1991); *Oliver Hume v Investa Residential Group* (2017). Importantly, such a requirement may arise even when parties are in the process of establishing what will become a fiduciary relationship, but have not yet concluded a formal agreement: *United Dominions v Brian* (1985).[24] There may also be situations where a stronger party is effectively required to disclose certain information about the effect of a transaction in order to avoid any suggestion of exploiting a weaker party. Such an issue may, for example, arise under the doctrine of unconscionable bargains: see eg *Commercial Bank v Amadio* (1983), discussed in **20.04**.

Finally, there are certain special categories of contract that were historically viewed by the common law as involving a relationship of *utmost good faith*. Insurance contracts were the most significant example. As part of their duty of good faith, an insured party was expected to disclose any material facts both prior to and after the making of an insurance contract. As Lord Mansfield explained in *Carter v Boehm* (1766) at 1909:

> Insurance is a contract upon speculation. The special facts upon which the contingent chance is to be computed lie most commonly in the knowledge of the assured only; the underwriter trusts to his [sic] representation, and proceeds upon confidence that he does not keep back any circumstance in his knowledge to mislead the underwriter into a belief that the circumstance does not exist.

---

20   See Stewart & McClurg 2007, from which some of the following is taken.

21   But this does not apply where the mistake is as to the value or benefit of a contract: see Duggan et al 1994: 22–4, and note their use of economic analysis (at 155–7) to explain why this should be so.

22   See Finn 1989b.

23   As to the essentially negative nature of fiduciary obligations, see eg *Breen v Williams* (1996) at 113, 137–8.

24   It appears, however, that a fiduciary does not have a positive obligation to disclose any *past* misconduct: see eg *Blackmagic Design v Overliese* (2011).

A breach of this duty rendered the policy voidable at the option of the insurer: see eg *Khoury v Government Insurance Office* (1984). As explained below, however, this common law duty has now largely been overtaken by statutory regulation.

Contracts of guarantee, which are discussed in Chapter 11, are not generally treated as requiring utmost good faith. But a creditor is nonetheless expected to disclose to the guarantor any unusual aspect of the creditor's relationship with the debtor: see **11.13**.

4.09   Statutory obligations and prohibitions

The general obligation on parties to an insurance contract to use utmost good faith in dealing with one another now finds statutory form: see *Insurance Contracts Act 1984* (Cth) s 13, which is discussed in **12.17**. But the insured's duty of disclosure has been narrowed under this legislation. At common law, the insured was expected to reveal any information that a 'prudent insurer' might need to know in deciding whether and on what terms to accept the insurance: see *Mayne Nickless v Pegler* (1974) at 239. Section 21, by contrast, requires pre-contractual disclosure only of information that the insured knows, or that a reasonable person would realise, was relevant to the insurer. Disclosure is not required of matters that diminish the risk, that are of common knowledge, or that are known or ought to be known by the insurer in the ordinary course of its business. The insurer must also clearly inform the insured of the duty of disclosure (s 22). Under s 28, only a fraudulent failure to comply with the duty allows the insurer to avoid the contract. In all other cases, the insurer's liability in respect of a claim is merely reduced to an amount that would place it in the position it would have been in had the failure not occurred.[25] Section 21A also has special rules for certain common types of consumer insurance.[26] A duty of disclosure only arises for such contracts to the extent that the insurer asks specific questions relevant to its decision to insure. Once again, these need only be answered by reference to matters the insured would reasonably understand to be relevant. Importantly too, s 12 makes it clear that the general duty of good faith does not create any duty of disclosure on the part of an insured that goes beyond that laid down in s 21. Hence any *post-contractual* duty of disclosure can only be imposed by contract.

There are many other contexts now in which legislation requires parties to reveal information. In some instances, the disclosure must be to the public. For example, a combination of stock market rules and s 674 of the *Corporations Act 2001* (Cth) requires listed companies to disclose information that might affect the price of certain types of security.[27] But, more commonly, this type of obligation is imposed on parties to private transactions. There are many instances of consumers being protected in this way, including, for example, when buying a house or entering into a credit agreement.[28] But various types of disclosure are also

---

25   For the position in relation to life insurance contracts, see s 29.

26   These are motor vehicle insurance, home buildings insurance, home contents insurance, sickness and accident insurance, consumer credit insurance, and travel insurance: *Insurance Contracts Regulations 2017* (Cth) reg 6.

27   See eg *Forrest v ASIC* (2012), the facts of which are noted in **6.02**.

28   As to the purchase of real estate, see eg *Sale of Land Act 1962* (Vic) Pt II Div 2. For consumer credit contracts, see National Credit Code s 16; *National Consumer Credit Protection Regulations 2010* (Cth) regs 72–74.

frequently required now in relation to business transactions, such as retail leases or franchise agreements.[29]

A further statutory provision that has a potential bearing on almost any type of commercial or consumer transaction is s 18 of the ACL. This prohibits *misleading or deceptive conduct* in trade or commerce. Without trespassing too much on the discussion in Chapter 18, there can clearly be situations where the failure to reveal information is misleading: see eg *Henjo Investments v Collins Marrickville* (1988). This will most commonly be the finding when a court believes there was a 'reasonable expectation' of disclosure: see eg *Demagogue v Ramensky* (1992). But in practice, the courts have generally been reluctant to identify such an expectation: see eg *Clifford v Vegas Enterprises* (2011); *Traderight v Bank of Queensland* (2015). Their approach has closely mirrored that taken under the common law.[30] According to French CJ and Kiefel J, what is now s 18 'does not require a party to commercial negotiations to volunteer information which will be of assistance to the decision-making of the other party'. Nor does it impose 'an obligation to volunteer information in order to avoid the consequences of the careless disregard, for its own interests, of another party of equal bargaining power and competence': *Miller & Associates v BMW Australia Finance* (2010) at [21]–[22].

The prohibitions against unconscionable conduct in ss 20 and 21 of the ACL, discussed in Chapter 20, may also be relevant. Indeed one of the matters that a court may consider in determining whether a party has acted unconscionably is that they have unreasonably failed to disclose intended conduct that might affect the other party's interests, or risks from such conduct: ss 22(1)(i), (2)(i). In *Messer v Lotus Securities* (2018), a firm was found to have breached equivalent provisions in the *Australian Securities and Investments Commission Act 2001* (Cth) by inducing the plaintiff, who suffered from Alzheimer's disease, to purchase shares in a company. The shares were effectively worthless, given information about the company's finances known to the defendant but not disclosed to the plaintiff.[31]

Other regulation of pre-contractual conduct

4.10   The various forms of pre-contractual liability

Section 18 of the ACL does not just cover non-disclosure. Its prohibition on misleading or deceptive conduct covers anything done in relation to the formation of contracts (as well as their performance, termination, and so on). Its scope is bounded only by the requirement that the conduct occur in trade or commerce: see **18.20**. As such, it is routinely invoked to complain about pre-contractual conduct. The ACL also has other provisions that may be relevant to the parties' behaviour during this phase. These include the raft of provisions in Division 1 of Part 3-1 dealing with more specific forms of deceptive conduct (see **18.18**); the prohibitions on *unconscionable conduct* in ss 20–21 (see **20.11–20.20**); and s 50, which

---

29   As to retail leases, see eg *Retail and Commercial Leases Act 1995* (SA) s 12. In relation to franchises, see *Competition and Consumer (Industry Codes—Franchising) Regulation 2014* (Cth) Sch 1 cls 8–11, Annexures 1–2; *ACC v Ultra Tune* (2019).

30   See Gillies 2004; and see further **18.25**.

31   Compare the unsuccessful claim in *ACCC v Medibank Private* (2018).

proscribes physical force, undue harassment or coercion (see **19.08**). Other statutes have similar provisions in relation to specific types of commerce: see eg **18.19**, **20.11**.

At common law, liability for pre-contractual conduct may also arise in a number of ways. These include where:

- an assurance given by one of the parties becomes *incorporated* into a resulting contract, so that there is liability for breach of contract if the assurance is not met (see **9.11–9.16**);
- one party intentionally or recklessly deceives the other, exposing them to an award of damages for the tort of *deceit* (see **18.16**);
- a party is liable in the tort of *negligence* for careless conduct, for example in relation to the provision of information (see **18.17**); or
- a party's statements or conduct provide the basis for some form of *estoppel* (see eg **4.12**).

In addition, what happens during the period before a contract is concluded may provide a basis for a later argument that the contract has in some ways been *vitiated*. As noted in **5.48**, a contract may be void, or more commonly voidable, on a range of grounds discussed in Part VI of the book. These include mistake, misrepresentation, duress, undue influence and unconscionability.

4.11   A duty to negotiate in good faith?

In many of the legal systems that recognise a general duty of *good faith and fair dealing*, that obligation applies to the formation of a contract as well as its performance. For example, in UNIDROIT's Principles of International Commercial Contracts, Article 2.1.15 states that:

> (1)   A party is free to negotiate and is not liable for failure to reach an agreement.
>
> (2)   However, a party who negotiates or breaks off negotiations in bad faith is liable for the losses caused to the other party.
>
> (3)   It is bad faith, in particular, for a party to enter into or continue negotiations when intending not to reach an agreement with the other party.

Historically, both the English and Australian courts have refused to recognise such a duty. In *Walford v Miles* (1992) at 138, Lord Ackner was emphatic on this point. He considered that 'the concept of a duty to carry on negotiations in good faith is inherently repugnant to the adversarial position of the parties when involved in negotiations'. But as Carter and Furmston (1994: 5) have noted:

> in the application of doctrine, English and Australian courts have promoted good faith and achieved results which are, for the most part, consistent with the operation of a general concept of that kind. Rule formulation is today less emphatic than in the 19th century, and rule application is more pragmatic.[32]

This is apparent in the range of different ways that a party may be liable for acting unreasonably or without due regard to another party's interests in the course of negotiations.

---

32   See further Carter & Furmston 1995. As to whether parties can validly *agree* (as part of an enforceable preliminary agreement) to conduct further negotiations in good faith, see **6.09**.

Nevertheless, it remains significant that there is no *general* principle to help fill any gaps between the operation of the various principles or prohibitions noted above. Parties may sometimes expressly (but not always validly) agree to negotiate in good faith: see **6.09**. A duty to negotiate in good faith is also occasionally given statutory effect, as in cl 6(2) of the *Franchising Code of Conduct*, discussed in **12.18**. But this is very much the exception rather than the rule.[33]

Anticipated contracts that fail to materialise

4.12   Remedies for a disappointed party

Where parties are negotiating what they hope and intend to be a contract, it is not unusual for one or other to 'jump the gun' and start preparing for performance, or even commence performing their expected obligations. As Mason et al (2016: 404) note, one reason this can occur is because 'the contracting process often lags behind performance … Work is done while lawyers debate matters such as liability clauses, but the contract is never signed.'

Is there anything a party who has incurred expense or commenced performing can do if a contract fails to materialise? One possibility is to invoke s 18 of the ACL. Where a party's words or conduct suggest they are prepared to enter into a contract, but they ultimately decide not to go ahead, that will not of itself be misleading or deceptive: see eg *Leading Edge Events v Te Kanawa* (2007). It would be different, however, if they had never intended to make a contract, or if they had changed their mind but failed to reveal this while still purporting to negotiate: see eg *E K Nominees v Woolworths* (2006).

Another option for a party who has been encouraged to believe that a contract will be concluded, and who has relied on that to their detriment, is to argue that the other party is estopped (precluded) from denying a contract. As we will see in Chapter 7, this was the situation in the leading case on what is called promissory estoppel: *Waltons Stores v Maher* (1988). But for an estoppel argument to succeed, it must be shown that the party to be estopped has acted unconscionably. Once again, they must have done more than just indicate they were going to proceed, then walked away from the transaction: see eg *Austotel v Franklins Selfserve* (1989).

Finally, there is the possibility of a party seeking *restitution* for any benefits they have conferred on the other party in anticipation of the contract coming into existence. As Chapter 24 will explain, it is clear enough that restitution may be sought where benefits have been transferred in performance of what the parties believe to be a contract, but which turns out to be void; for instance, because it is uncertain or incomplete (see **5.36–5.40**). But the position is not quite so clear where a contract is simply never agreed.

Where a payment is made by one party to the other in anticipation of this being required under a contract, it can be recovered on the basis that there is a 'total failure of consideration'

---

33   But see *Paciocco v ANZ Bank* (2015) at [294], where Allsop CJ referred to a 'nascent doctrine of bargaining in good faith'. The basis for this observation was rather slender. It was that in identifying any breach of a statutory prohibition on unconscionable conduct, such as that in s 21 of the ACL, it is relevant to inquire whether the parties have acted in good faith: see **20.17**.

for the payment: see **24.04**, and see eg *Nu Line Construction v Fowler* (2014); *Diao v Cohen* (2016). It also seems to be accepted that if a party is allowed to complete work to be required under a contract that is never formally concluded, and that work is of benefit to the recipient, the performing party may bring a restitutionary claim for *quantum meruit* (reasonable remuneration): see eg *British Steel v Cleveland Bridge and Engineering* (1984).[34] On the other hand, no such claim can be made where a party incurs expense tendering or preparing for a contract that they know they may not be awarded: see *Brenner v First Artists' Management* (1993) at 259.

Another scenario is more difficult. It occurs where a party partially performs work that they expect to be contracted to undertake. On one view, such a party is simply taking a gamble and should bear the risk of any resulting loss.[35] But in *Sabemo v North Sydney Municipal Council* (1977) at 901, Sheppard J considered that it would matter *why* the contract had not gone ahead:

> If the transaction had gone off because the parties were unable to agree, then I think it would be correct ... to say that each party had taken a risk, in incurring the expenditure which it did, that the transaction might go off because of a bona fide failure to reach agreement on some point of substance in such a complex transaction. But I do not think it right to say that that risk should be so borne, when one party has taken upon itself to change its mind about the entirety of the proposal.

In this case, the defendant council had decided for its own reasons not to go ahead with a proposed land development. The plaintiff, which had spent a lot of money preparing various schemes for the council to consider, was held to be entitled to recover reasonable remuneration for that work. The decision is generally considered to be a controversial application of the principles of restitution discussed in Chapter 24. Were the facts to recur today, the case might instead be argued and decided on the basis of promissory estoppel. Nevertheless, it has been followed in at least some subsequent cases: see eg *Leading Edge Events v Te Kanawa* (2007).

---

34   But see **24.10**, noting the doubt cast on the basis for recovery in this type of case by the High Court's decision in *Lumbers v W Cook Builders* (2008).

35   See Mason et al 2016: 404–10.

5

FORMATION

Introduction

5.01   Requirements for a valid contract

The rough definition of a contract given in **1.02** states that a contract is an agreement between two or more parties, involving one or more promises that are given for something in return, and which the parties intend to be legally enforceable. Other than the concept of *parties*, which is discussed in Chapter 8, the other elements of the definition form the subject matter of this chapter. In practice, it will be fairly uncommon for a contract dispute to revolve around formation. It is much more likely to turn on how the contract should be interpreted, whether it has been breached, or the consequences of breach. Nevertheless, there are still some occasions where the existence of a contract is in doubt. The parties may, for example, have failed to *reach agreement*. In order to determine whether they have in fact agreed, it is necessary to inquire into the parties' intentions. People often agree to things without wanting to attach legal consequences. Social arrangements are one obvious example. Even business people may sometimes wish to enter into an agreement which is not legally enforceable. Having the requisite *intention to contract* is necessary to form a contract – but it is not sufficient. Unless a deed is used, as discussed in **5.47**, a valid contract also requires *consideration*. Consideration is the legal manifestation of the idea that contracts are founded on an exchange. The existence of consideration is usually uncontroversial, but it has caused problems in a few situations.

Two further points that may require attention are whether the terms of a contract are sufficiently *certain* to be understood, and whether they are *complete*, in the sense of dealing with all matters that are essential for whatever type of transaction is involved. There may also be other reasons why what appears to be a valid and enforceable contract is treated as invalid or cannot be the subject of an action for breach of contract. One example considered in this chapter involves the failure to ensure a contract is *recorded in writing* (a requirement that, as noted in Chapter 1, only applies to certain types of agreement). Another is that one of the parties lacks the necessary *capacity* to contract. But contracts may also be 'vitiated' by other factors, including that they have been obtained through misrepresentation, mistake, duress, undue influence or unconscionable conduct, or that their enforcement is prohibited by statute or would be contrary to public policy. These issues are largely left to later chapters.

In summary then, for a valid contract to be formed, the general requirements are that:

- the parties must intend to create legal relations;
- the parties must have reached agreement;
- each party must have provided consideration;
- any terms agreed by the parties must be certain and complete; and
- there must be no other factor vitiating the agreement.

It would be a mistake, however, to view these requirements as separate and distinct. To take just one example, the fact that proposed terms are uncertain or incomplete may indicate a lack of intention to create legal relations. Similarly, in cases like *Australian Woollen Mills v Commonwealth* (1954), which will be encountered a number of times in this chapter, the reasoning used to find that no contract was formed effectively cuts across some of the categories above, or at least can be explained on multiple bases. That is one reason why we have chosen to cover each of these elements in a single chapter, rather than splitting their treatment.

5.02   The objective approach to intention

The intentions of the parties are relevant in determining whether they have reached agreement (or *consensus ad idem* as it is sometimes said), whether that agreement is meant to have legal effect, what terms are to be part of the agreement, and what those terms mean.[1] In theory, intention can be ascertained using a subjective or objective test. A *subjective* inquiry focuses on what the parties believed they were intending. But the law of contract generally favours an *objective* test of intention. One justification for using an objective test is that a subjective test has the potential to undermine the security of transactions. A could argue that they did not subjectively intend to contract with B even though B thought, and a reasonable person would have thought, that was A's intention.

Objectivity requires looking at intention from the standpoint of a reasonable person and disregarding 'uncommunicated subjective motives or intentions': *Ermogenous v Greek Orthodox Community* (2002) at [25]. The words and conduct might be examined by a reasonable person in the place of the person to whom those words or conduct were addressed. Alternatively, behaviour could be assessed from the perspective of a wholly detached and reasonable observer.[2] The 'fly on the wall' or detached approach ignores any characteristics of the parties or the dealings between them. It means that a contract can be concluded even if a reasonable person in the position of one of the parties would not interpret the behaviour of the other as showing an intention to contract.

Detached objectivity has attracted some support in Australia. In *Taylor v Johnson* (1983) at 428 Mason ACJ, Murphy and Deane JJ stated that the law was not concerned 'with the real intentions of the parties, but with the outward manifestations of those intentions'. When, to an objective observer standing apart from the parties, it would appear that a contract was entered into on a particular set of terms, then a binding contract is formed on those terms.[3] Dawson J (at 444) pointed out that 'the necessity for certainty in commercial dealings requires such an approach'. These passages can be read as supporting a principle of detached objectivity. More recent authority, however, whilst accepting that the test is objective, is less inclined to utilise a detached reasonable person. The reasonable person is typically taken to be someone in the position of the parties, and the circumstances surrounding the transaction are regarded as relevant: see eg *Toll v Alphapharm* (2004) at [40]; *Electricity Generation v Woodside Energy* (2014) at [35].

An agreement which satisfies the objective test of intention can still be set aside. In *Taylor v Johnson*, the parties entered into a written contract for the sale of land; one party made a mistake as to the content of the contract and the other knew of the mistake. Applying an objective test of intention there was a contract, but because of the mistake, the majority thought that the contract was voidable in equity: see **18.39.** The impact of the objective approach will

---

1   As to these last two issues, see Chapters 9 and 10.
2   See Howarth 1984, who also identifies a third type of objectivity – that being the standpoint of a reasonable person in the place of the person speaking or acting.
3   Compare the approach taken in *Smith v Hughes* (1871) at 607. Despite insisting that a contract cannot be made without the parties being genuinely of one mind, Blackburn J noted that a party who reasonably appeared to be assenting to a proposed agreement 'would be equally bound as if he had intended to agree to the other's terms'. This effectively uses something like an estoppel to arrive at the same result as an objective analysis: see Paterson et al 2016: 73–4, 86–8.

depend then upon the ease by which it is possible to rescind contracts in equity. For example, in *Taylor v Johnson*, Dawson J took a narrower view of equitable mistake on the facts than his colleagues. The majority judges also left open the question of whether the objective approach should be applied in cases of oral contracts. It is difficult to argue that a written contract does not reflect what the parties intended. At the same time, it does not follow that written contracts are unique in this respect. The evidence is nearly as compelling if a contract is completed through an exchange of letters, even if the final agreement is not reduced into writing. In principle, there seems no reason why an objective test should not apply to *all* types of contract.

5.03   How far should objectivity be taken?

The objective test promotes a degree of certainty. The outcome will not depend on subjective intentions which may be more difficult to predict. But it is not perfect. In theory, a contract may be found to exist when *neither* party intends one. Some judges at least have suggested that this should not be allowed to happen. For example, in *Air Great Lakes v K S Easter Holdings* (1985) at 331, Mahoney J observed:

> The law would not, I think, impose the relationship of contract where, eg, A thought he was play-acting and B knew of that fact. A's actual subjective intention would be effective to prevent the contract arising. A fortiori, if both A and B had the intention that no contract should result, and each knew of it, then none would be imposed. And, I think, this notwithstanding that a reasonable bystander would take from what they said and did that there was an exchange of congruent promises and a mutual purpose to contract.

The opposite situation arises when the parties have an actual subjective intent to contract. It is quite difficult to see why a contract should not be formed, whatever an objective observer would say. One solution in this situation might be to regard the objective test as a default rule where actual *consensus ad idem* is absent.[4] Yet it is sometimes suggested that actual beliefs and intentions are entirely irrelevant: see eg *Equuscorp v Glengallan Investments* (2004) at 483. There are good reasons for this approach. Contract formation is about the outward manifestation of intention. Were it otherwise, parties could contract in silence.

Even so, there are recognised exceptions to the objective approach to contract formation. For example, it is permissible to have regard to the parties' actual or subjective intentions in determining whether a transaction is a *sham* (see **9.19)**, or in considering a plea of non est factum from a party unable to understand a document they have signed (see **18.42**).

Intention to create legal relations

5.04   Ascertaining the parties' intention

Not all agreements are contracts. A contract is an agreement that is intended by the parties to create legal relations. In *Australian Woollen Mills v Commonwealth* (1954) at 457, the High Court said that this requirement went to the 'very essence of contract'. Sometimes an intention to enter into a legal relationship will be expressly stated. Any such declaration will generally be

---

4   For this suggestion and a discussion of some of the issues around objectivity, see McLauchlan 2005a.

respected: *Forrest v ASIC* (2012) at [56]. But so too will a statement to the opposite effect. For example, in *Rose & Frank v JR Crompton & Brothers* (1925), a distribution arrangement was expressed not to be 'a formal or legal agreement'. It was not to be 'subject to the jurisdiction of either the British or American courts', but was simply 'a record of the intention of the parties to which they honourably pledge themselves'. When the parties fell into dispute and one (perhaps dishonourably) attempted to sue the other for breach of contract, the English Court of Appeal dismissed the claim. There was no reason why the parties' clear intention not to make a contract should not be respected.

5.05   The role of presumptions

When an agreement was silent on intention, the traditional approach was to rely on presumptions. A commercial agreement was presumed to be a contract: *Banque Brussels v Australian National Industries* (1989) at 521. By contrast, the law presumed that a contract was not intended when the agreement was between family members or made in a social setting: *Teen Ranch v Brown* (1995) at 310. In both situations, the presumption could be rebutted with contrary evidence. The use of presumptions emphasised the nature of the relationship at the expense of a more fundamental question: what did the parties intend?

In *Ermogenous v Greek Orthodox Community* (2002), however, the High Court questioned the value of such presumptions. The plaintiff had agreed to serve as an archbishop for a local community, under what was ultimately held to be an employment contract. In previous cases, ministers of religion had often been held to be in a 'spiritual' but not a contractual relationship with their churches. But the majority of the court expressed the view (at [25]) that it would be wrong to formulate rules as to 'the kinds of cases in which an intention to create contractual relations should, or should not, be found to exist'. The judges doubted (at [26]) the utility of using the language of presumptions in this context. Instead it was emphasised (at [25]) that it was necessary to make 'an objective assessment of the state of affairs between the parties'.

Subsequent authorities have been split as to the significance of what was said in *Ermogenous*. Some courts have endorsed the view that recourse should no longer be had at all to presumptions: see eg *Evans v Secretary, Department of Families* (2012) at [12]; *Ashton v Pratt* (2015) at [73]. Others, however, appear to have treated what the High Court said as simply a warning not to overstate the effect of any presumptions, rather than an instruction to abandon them. Hence, for example, mention can still be found of the presumption that 'family members do not intend to contract when they make arrangements amongst themselves', although this 'applies with diminishing force the more remote the familial connection': *Sion v NSW Trustee & Guardian* (2013) at [40]. It is particularly common still to find assertions that 'there is a presumption with commercial arrangements that parties intend to create legal relations': *Atco Controls v Newtronics* (2009) at [68]. The presumption is considered to be a strong one, which can 'only be rebutted with difficulty': *Helmos Enterprises v Jaylor* (2005) at [48]. In *Shahid v Australian College of Dermatologists* (2008) at [211], Jessup J expressed the principle as being that 'in a business context, and where the requirements of a contract are otherwise established, the person proposing that the parties did not intend to create legal relations bears the onus of so proving'. He emphasised the longstanding support for this proposition and could not accept that in *Ermogenous* – a case in which no mention at all was made of any of the relevant authorities – the High Court had intended to dispense with it. In practice, however, whichever approach is adopted should make little difference to the outcome in most cases.

5.06   Commercial dealings

There are some situations where even commercial parties wish to avoid their agreement having legal consequences. Besides the idea of being bound in honour only, a more common example occurs when an agreement is made 'subject to contract'. This phrase is often used in contracts for the sale of land. Subject to any statutory provision to the contrary, it allows either of the parties to withdraw from the deal prior to the exchange of contracts which concludes the sale. In *Masters v Cameron* (1954) at 363, the High Court explained that where a term like 'subject to contract' is used, then 'what has been agreed must be regarded as the intended basis for a future contract and not as constituting a contract'. The decision is analysed further in Chapter 6, in the context of the broader question of the status of 'preliminary' agreements. The cases examined in that chapter generally involve arguments that are not so much over whether the parties intended to create a contract, but *at what point* they intended to be bound. As will be seen, this has been a common source of dispute.

Assuming that there is no explicit indication as to whether a commercial arrangement is intended to be legally binding, the objective approach outlined above demands that the matter be assessed from the viewpoint of a reasonable person. This is exemplified by *Carlill v Carbolic Smoke Ball* (1893), one of the most famous of all English contract cases. In a newspaper advertisement, the defendant company offered to pay £100 – a considerable sum of money in those days – to anyone who used its smoke ball and still contracted influenza. When the plaintiff claimed this 'reward', the defendant unsuccessfully sought to deny that any contract had been formed. One of its arguments was that the advertisement was a 'mere puff' – an exaggerated promotional statement that was not to be taken seriously.[5] But the English Court of Appeal rejected this characterisation. Crucially, the advertisement had stated that £1000 had been deposited with a particular bank, 'shewing our sincerity in the matter'. This would clearly lead a reasonable person to believe both that a promise was intended and, if the stipulated condition was met, that it would be honoured. The contract found to exist was *unilateral* in nature (see **1.06**), with the plaintiff's use of the smoke ball and subsequent illness being the acts which simultaneously accepted the defendant's offer and provided the necessary consideration.

5.07   Problematic cases

One situation which has created difficulty in assessing intention to create legal relations has concerned 'letters of comfort'. These are statements reassuring a creditor that a debtor's obligations are likely to be met, if not by the debtor, then by the author of the letter (often a parent company of the debtor or some other associated entity). The letter is generally given to secure some form of loan, concession or arrangement for the debtor. Some courts have been prepared to regard such a statement as creating a binding contract: see eg *Banque Brussels v Australian National Industries* (1989); *Norman v FEA Plantation* (2011). But the language

---

5   The distinction between 'serious' statements and puffs is considered further in **18.07** and **18.23** in the context of liability for misrepresentation or misleading conduct.

used in these cases was fairly clear. More cautiously or vaguely worded letters have been found not to have any contractual effect in cases such as *Commonwealth Bank v TLI Management* (1990) and *Australian European Finance v Sheehan* (1993).[6]

The problems occasioned by letters of comfort are understandable. The issuer is often seeking to tread a delicate balance between inducing a positive response and avoiding the language of reciprocal obligation. It is also easy to see why courts have sometimes been reluctant to attribute contractual effect to promises of government subsidies or assistance, even when relied on by the businesses or individuals to which they are targeted: see eg *Australian Woollen Mills v Commonwealth* (1955); *Administration of Papua New Guinea v Leahy* (1961). The schemes concerned were regarded as being 'administrative' in nature and involving matters of 'policy' rather than commerce.

But other decisions are less easy to explain. For example, when a student enrols at a university they are typically required to promise that they will comply with the institution's policies. And in return the university appears to undertake that it will do the same, if not indeed provide the education or study opportunities featured in their advertising. Yet this type of 'consensual' arrangement has been found to be non-contractual, at least in the case of a government-subsidised research student: see eg *Mbuzi v Griffith University* (2016). A fee-paying student, by contrast, would have a much clearer case for establishing a contract: see eg *Clark v University of Lincolnshire and Humberside* (2000).[7]

5.08   Private arrangements

The law of contract has tended to stay outside the domestic sphere.[8] In *Balfour v Balfour* (1919), a husband's agreement to pay an allowance to a wife did not create an enforceable contract. An intention to create legal relations was lacking, as Atkin LJ explained (at 579):

> Agreements such as these are outside the realm of contracts altogether. The common law does not regulate the form of agreements between spouses. Their promises are not sealed with seals or sealing wax. The consideration that really obtains for them is that natural love and affection which counts for so little in these cold Courts ... In respect of these promises each house is a domain into which the King's writ does not seek to run ...

The same approach has traditionally been taken to arrangements between other family members as well as spouses: see eg *Jones v Padavatton* (1969). As a Full Court of the Federal Court has put it, courts are expected to be 'careful not to convert informal situations that frequently arise in circumstances that involve love, friendship and concomitant human

---

6   See also *Atco Controls v Newtronics* (2009), where the 'commitments' in question were, in any event, found not to be supported by any consideration.

7   As to the complications presented by the Higher Education Contribution Scheme (HECS), see Goldacre 2013: 188–9. As she notes (at 188–95), most commentators are in no doubt that the student–university relationship *should* be treated as contractual, though opinions differ on the nature and extent of any contract(s) involved. See further Rochford 2015.

8   For criticism of this tendency from a feminist perspective, see eg Graycar & Morgan 2002: 15–17. They present it as a classic example of 'how the dichotomy between the public and private has been constructed and supported by the legal system, to the detriment of women' (at 10). Compare Keyes & Burns 2002, whose criticism of the traditional distinction between family and commercial arrangements is grounded in relational contract and behavioural decision theories.

emotional feelings of duty or responsibility, into the stuff of daily commercial life': *Evans v Secretary, Department of Families* (2012) at [16].[9]

As noted above, it is unclear whether there remains a presumption to this effect. But even if there is not, it is still relevant to consider 'the relationship of the parties and the circumstances in which the arrangement was entered into': *Ashton v Pratt* (2015) at [73]. Hence, for example, it is more likely that there will be an intention to create legal relations between a husband and wife when they have separated: see eg *Merritt v Merritt* (1970).[10] Similarly, where there is significant detrimental reliance by the promisee, it will be more likely that the parties intended to enter into an enforceable contract. In *Riches v Hogben* (1986), for instance, a son incurred considerable expense in emigrating from England to Australia with his family to live with and care for his aged mother. He had done this on the faith of her promise that she would buy a house and transfer it into his name. Given the circumstances, the parties were taken to have intended this to be a legally binding arrangement.[11]

There is also no reason why a commercial agreement between family members should not have legal consequences. In *Roufos v Brewster* (1971), a Coober Pedy store owner struck a deal with the owners of a local motel. He would use his semi-trailer to take their truck to Adelaide for repair. In return, he could use their truck to bring back goods for his store. The fact that he was their son-in-law, and that his wife had helped make the arrangement, did not prevent this from being treated as a contract between two businesses.

5.09   Associations

Given that a purely social agreement is unlikely to give rise to an enforceable contract, it used to be thought that membership of a voluntary association failed to confer contractual rights by one member against the others: see eg *Cameron v Hogan* (1934). These days, however, a court is more likely to conclude that members of a voluntary association intend to enter into legal relations, especially where an association is large and fulfils important social functions, such as a political party: see eg *Baldwin v Everingham* (1993). To avoid any doubt, s 140(1) of the *Corporations Act 2001* (Cth) provides that a company's constitution and its replaceable rules have effect as a contract that requires their observance. The contract is taken to exist between the company and each of its members, between the company and its directors and company secretary, and between a member and each other member.

Establishing agreement

5.10   Ways of signifying agreement

There are many ways in which parties can reach agreement on a contract. In some instances, it may be understood that a document will be prepared to embody the terms of the agreement, to

---

9   See also *Magill v Magill* (2006) at [202].
10   The *Family Law Act 1975* (Cth), in any event, now provides for the legal enforcement of agreements for the distribution of property and the payment of maintenance between married and de facto partners.
11   The son's action for breach of this contract failed, because the agreement was not in writing as required by statute. But his alternative claim of proprietary estoppel succeeded: see **5.45**, **7.13**.

be signed by both parties, whether separately or at some kind of 'ceremony'. Only if that happens will a contract be concluded.[12] This approach is especially common with agreements concerning the sale or lease of land, though it can be and is adopted with many other types of transaction, especially where significant commitments are involved or the terms have been negotiated with the assistance of lawyers. But at least as a matter of common law, there is no necessity for this approach to be adopted.[13] An agreement may be finalised through a series of communications, which may be oral or written, or a mixture of the two. Sometimes the element of agreement will need to be inferred not from any communication as such, but simply the conduct of one or both parties.

There has been a persistent tendency to approach this issue by reference to a set of principles – the so-called 'rules' of offer and acceptance discussed below – that were developed by reference to contracts formed through structured communications. As we will explain, they are not readily suited to every situation. This is a point that modern courts have come to recognise. As Allsop J noted in *Branir v Ouston Nominees* (2001) at [369]:

> The essential question . . . is whether the parties' conduct, including what was said and not said and including the evident commercial aims and expectations of the parties, reveals an understanding or agreement or, as sometimes expressed, a manifestation of mutual assent, which bespeaks an intention to be legally bound to the essential elements of a contract.

5.11   The principles of offer and acceptance

The doctrine of offer and acceptance comprises a set of legal principles that can be used to determine not just whether parties have reached agreement, but the point at which this has occurred. Knowing exactly when and/or where a contract was made can sometimes matter a great deal. For example, in *Pharmaceutical Society v Boots Cash Chemists* (1952), the issue was whether a self-service pharmacy was complying with a regulatory requirement that sales of prescribed products be supervised. If, as the proprietors successfully argued, those sales were concluded at the cash register, the presence there of a registered pharmacist was sufficient. But it would have been different if, as discussed further below, the relevant contracts had been formed somewhere else in the store. Similarly, in *Brinkibon v Stahag Stahl* (1983), it mattered for jurisdictional purposes whether the relevant contract was concluded in England or – as was found to be the case – in Austria.

The offer and acceptance doctrine assumes that a contract is formed when one party, the *offeror*, makes an *offer* to contract upon certain terms, and that offer is accepted by another party, the *offeree*. An offer may be made to a particular person, to a group, or indeed the entire world.[14] A distinction is made between an offer, which upon acceptance will create a binding

---

12   As to what happens when counterpart documents are exchanged but turn out not to be identical, see *Sindel v Georgiou* (1984). Today, documents are often signed and exchanged electronically: see Whittaker 2016, discussing the legal principles concerning such 'remote signings'. More is said about the significance of signed agreements at **9.04**.

13   As to the statutory requirements for certain contracts to be recorded in writing and signed, see **5.44**.

14   See eg *Carlill v Carbolic Smoke Ball* (1893), rejecting the argument that an offer must be directed at a particular person.

contract, and other statements made in the course of negotiations. The latter include 'invitations to treat' and are not capable of acceptance. Likewise, a distinction is made between an acceptance, which creates a contract, and a 'counter-offer', which as the name suggests proposes new or different terms to be considered by the (original) offeror: see **5.17**.

5.12   Offers and invitations to treat

An *invitation to treat* refers to preliminary negotiations or expressions of interest which predate any offer. Whether a statement or conduct amounts to an offer which the other party can accept, thereby forming a contract, or is merely an invitation to treat, is ultimately a question of intention: did the person making the statement objectively intend to make an offer? In order to simplify the process, a series of *prima facie* 'rules' have been developed to help analyse the effect of advertisements, the display of goods, the conduct of auctions and requests for tenders. These rules can be displaced by evidence of contrary intention.

5.13   Advertisements and displays

An advertisement intended to lead to a bilateral contract is not usually treated as an offer, because further bargaining is expected. The contrary conclusion would make a trader liable to supply goods even where no stock was available. But different considerations apply when the advertisement is limited to a certain number of goods; for example, 'Sale – 10 laptops for sale at $400 each – first come, first served'. This scenario was considered in an American case, *Lefkowitz v Great Minneapolis Surplus Store* (1957). It was held (at 691) that if the advertisement 'is clear, definite and explicit, and leaves nothing open for negotiation, it constitutes an offer'. Advertisements intended to lead to a unilateral contract, like an advertisement of a reward, are also more likely to be treated as an offer: see eg *Gibbons v Proctor* (1891). The offer of a unilateral contract is only capable of being accepted by a person who performs the conditions required to claim the reward. It is not like a typical advertisement of a bilateral contract which may be capable of being accepted by anyone.

The general approach developed by the common law to advertisements is reflected in the *Electronic Transactions Acts* (see **2.10**) that apply in each Australian jurisdiction. A proposal to form a contract made through a generally accessible electronic communication, such as a website, is presumed to be an 'invitation to make offers'. But this can be displaced if the proposal clearly indicates an intention to be bound on acceptance.[15]

A display of goods in a self-service shop is also generally regarded as an invitation to treat, rather than an offer, but this is not an absolute rule. When the customer picks up an item from the shelf and takes it to the cash desk to pay, then they make an offer to the shopkeeper. The shopkeeper can then accept or reject the customer's offer. In *Pharmaceutical Society v Boots Cash Chemist* (1952) at 802, Lord Goddard gave the example of a customer in a bookshop. The

---

15   *Electronic Transactions Act 1999* (Cth) s 15B; *Electronic Transactions Act 2000* (NSW) s 14B; *Electronic Transactions (Victoria) Act 2000* (Vic) s 14B; *Electronic Transactions (Queensland) Act 2001* (Qld) s 26B; *Electronic Transactions Act 2011* (WA) s 18; *Electronic Transactions Act 2000* (SA) s 14B; *Electronic Transactions Act 2000* (Tas) s 12B; *Electronic Transactions Act 2001* (ACT) s 14B; *Electronic Transactions (Northern Territory) Act 2000* (NT) s 14B.

customer picks up a book and goes to pay but it turns out that the shopkeeper has promised the book to another customer. The customer makes the offer and the shopkeeper might refuse to accept it. If the display was regarded as an offer then the shopkeeper would be bound to sell the book when the customer picked it up off the shelf, even if the book was out of stock because it was already promised to someone else. Lord Goddard also argued that treating a display of goods as an offer would disadvantage a customer, because they would be bound to purchase an item by picking it up and thereby accepting a contract to purchase it. This justification is weaker. It would be perfectly possible to require a more unequivocal acceptance than removing an item from the shelf, such as taking it to the cash desk in order to pay. Nevertheless, the approach in *Boots Cash Chemist* is at least easy to apply.

By contrast, it would seem that the display of goods in a vending machine must be treated as an offer which is accepted when the customer inserts money. Similarly, taking a ticket at the entrance to an automatic car park would seem to constitute the acceptance of an offer: *Thornton v Shoe Lane Parking* (1971) at 169.

5.14   Auctions

When an auctioneer requests bids on a lot at an auction, it is generally seen as an invitation to treat: *Harris v Nickerson* (1873). The bidder makes the offer which is accepted by the fall of the auctioneer's hammer.[16] The contract is concluded between the bidder and the auctioneer, acting as an agent for the vendor. A typical auction involves a reserve price below which no bids will be accepted. Once the reserve is met, the auctioneer, like any other offeree, has a choice to reject or accept the offeror's bid. The law runs contrary to the general understanding of an 'auction without reserve', which is that the person who makes the highest bid will secure the auction lot. On ordinary offer and acceptance principles the auctioneer would be under no obligation to accept a bid, even if it were the highest. One way around this obstacle is to hold that the auctioneer is compelled in this situation to accept the highest bid: see eg *Warlow v Harrison* (1859). The bidder still makes the offer on the contract of sale but a collateral contract (which runs alongside the main contract) prevents the auctioneer from refusing to accept the highest bid. A collateral contract may also contain other terms relating to the way in which the auction is conducted: see eg *Futuretronics International v Gadzbis* (1992). An alternative solution for auctions without reserve suggested in *AGC (Advances) v McWhirter* (1977) was that the auctioneer is bound to accept the highest offer, but the vendor of the goods still remains free to withdraw the property from sale and decline to accept any bid. This runs counter to the usual idea that an accepted offer cannot be withdrawn.

5.15   Tenders

Where one party wishes to carry out a large project they may invite 'tenders' to do the work. A request of this sort will generally be an invitation to treat. The tenders that are submitted

---

16   This is confirmed by legislation: *Sale of Goods Act 1923* (NSW) s 60(2); *Goods Act 1958* (Vic) s 64; *Sale of Goods Act 1896* (Qld) s 59(1); *Sale of Goods Act 1895* (WA) s 57(2); *Sale of Goods Act 1895* (SA) s 57(1); *Sale of Goods Act 1896* (Tas) s 62; *Sale of Goods Act 1954* (ACT) s 60(3); *Sale of Goods Act 1972* (NT) s 60.

constitute offers: *Spencer v Harding* (1870). It is commonly stated that the lowest tender will be accepted. However, because the party making the bid or putting in the tender is the one making the offer, the requestor is generally free to accept or reject individual tenders as they see fit. The expense of putting together the bid falls on the tenderer. They do so knowing that their bid might be unsuccessful.

A tenderer is not usually entitled to have their bid considered. But in some situations the courts have been willing to imply a collateral contract, sometimes known in this context as a *process contract*. This ensures that those who invite tenders are under a duty to consider, but not necessarily accept, conforming bids: see eg *Blackpool & Fylde Aero Club v Blackpool BC* (1990). In *Hughes Aircraft v Airservices Australia* (1997) at 42, Finn J went further. He explained that a process contract might be implied to the effect that a party inviting tenders would conduct its tender evaluation fairly, and deal fairly with a tenderer in the performance of that contract. On the facts before him, the process had not been conducted fairly because a rival bid had been accepted after the date for submitting tenders had passed. In the wake of this decision, it has become common for organisations issuing requests for tender to include clauses that specifically seek to negate any possibility of a process contract.[17]

According to the terms of the tender, one bid may be more favourable than those from competitors because it is lower or higher than the rest. On ordinary principles, the party seeking bids is not bound to accept the most favourable bid. In *Harvela v Royal Trust of Canada* (1986), shares were to be sold to one of two parties who made the highest sealed bid. Only the plaintiff submitted a bid which conformed with the requirements of the tender, but the other bid was accepted. In the Privy Council, Lord Diplock reasoned that when a bid was invited there was a unilateral contract with the potential bidders to accept the highest bid for the shares. This unilateral contract became a bilateral contract between the Royal Trust and Harvela to sell the shares once Harvela had made the highest bid. The implication of a contract ensures that the tendering process meets the expectations of those who submit bids, but in *Harvela* it, in effect, compelled acceptance of the tender.

5.16 Termination of an offer

Once an offer is terminated it cannot be accepted. An offer will cease if it is expressly *revoked* by the offeror. The revocation must be communicated to the offeree. If the offer is accepted before the offeree learns of the revocation, a contract is formed: see eg *Byrne v Van Tienhoven* (1880); *Stevenson Jacques v McLean* (1880).[18] Notice of the withdrawal need not, however, come from the offeror. It is enough that they hear about it from a reliable source: *Dickinson v Dodds* (1876).

The offeree can also bring the offer to an end by rejecting it outright, or by making a counter-offer (see **5.17**). Once this has happened, the offeree cannot subsequently turn round and accept it: see eg *Fletcher v Minister for Environment* (1999). Offers may also be limited by time or other conditions and cannot be accepted after that period has elapsed or if those conditions are not met. If no time for acceptance is stated then the offer is treated as remaining

---

17   Compare Napier 2011, criticising this approach in the context of government tendering.
18   Note that, as these cases make clear, the postal acceptance rule (see **5.20**) does *not* apply to revocations.

open for a reasonable time: *Ballas v Theophilos* (1957). What is reasonable will depend on the nature of the contract. For example, it would not be reasonable for an offer of perishable goods to remain open for a long period.

In some cases, an offeror may promise to keep an offer open for a stipulated period of time, or to provide the offeree and nobody else with an opportunity to enter into a contract for a specified item. But estoppel aside, such a promise will only be binding if the offeree provides consideration: see eg *Goldsbrough Mort v Quinn* (1910). The effect of doing so is to create a binding *option*, though disagreement has persisted as to whether to regard such an arrangement as itself being a contract.[19]

The capacity to revoke an offer potentially creates a problem with unilateral contracts. As discussed further below, acceptance of a unilateral contract is generally understood to involve completion of a required act. It is only when the act is complete that the offer can be said to have been accepted. So, if A offers B $1,000 to walk from Melbourne to Sydney, A may in theory revoke the offer at any time before B reaches their destination. This outcome might cause hardship if B were just outside Sydney when A sought to withdraw. To counter this problem, in *Abbot v Lance* (1860) it was suggested that although the general rule was that an offer of a unilateral contract could be withdrawn before performance, part performance by the offeree amounted to sufficient consideration and the offer could not be revoked.

In *Mobil Oil v Wellcome International* (1998), however, the Full Court of the Federal Court rejected the idea of any such general rule. The Court suggested that when an offer of a unilateral contract was made, the offeror could be prevented from withdrawing it, but only if either there was an 'implied ancillary contract' not to revoke the offer or the principles of estoppel (discussed in Chapter 7) were brought into play. The latter would require the offeree to have acted to their detriment on the assumption that the offer would not be revoked. The factors to be considered would include whether the offeror knew that the offeree had commenced performance, whether the offeree understood that they ran the risk that the offeror might revoke the offer, whether the parties intended the offer to be revocable, and whether acts of performance by the offeree were detrimental or beneficial to them. In *Mobil*, the oil company had announced a new 'Circle of Excellence' program to a group of franchisees running service stations. If they met certain targets over a six year period, the company would 'find a way' to renew their franchises. The announcement was held not to have amounted to an offer, since its terms were vague and the audience could not reasonably have understood it to signal a definite commitment. But even if it had been, Mobil was free to revoke the offer. While the franchisees claimed to have spent time and money seeking to meet the targets, their actions had mostly been beneficial to their businesses rather than detrimental.

5.17 Acceptances and counter-offers

An *acceptance* is an unqualified assent to an offer. The motive for accepting is irrelevant. An acceptance must be unconditional, and correspond with the exact terms of the offer. The general principle is that the offer and acceptance must mirror each other. If the offeree seeks to vary the terms of the offer, they are considered to be making a *counter-offer*. This will

---

19   See Seddon & Bigwood 2017: 167–72.

obviously be the case if, for instance, the offeree proposes a different price to that originally offered: see eg *Hyde v Wrench* (1840). But even a communication that purports to be an acceptance can be treated as a counter-offer if it proposes new terms: see eg *Turner Kempson v Camm* (1922). Where a counter-offer is made, no contract will result unless that new offer is in turn accepted by the other party.

In some cases, however, what might appear to be a counter-offer may be treated simply as a request for information. In *Stevenson Jacques v McLean* (1880), the defendant offered to sell a quantity of iron for 40 shillings per ton. The plaintiff sent a telegram asking 'whether you would accept forty for delivery over two months or, if not, longest limit you would give'. A further telegram then purported to accept the original offer. A contract was held to have been made by the second telegram. The first telegram did no more than seek to clarify what the seller would be prepared to accept – it neither rejected the offer nor put a definite counter-offer.[20]

5.18 Methods of acceptance

Sometimes a method of acceptance is prescribed with a particular object in mind, like speed or reliability. Where this object can be achieved equally well or better by another method, then the acceptance is usually valid: *Manchester Diocesan Council v Commercial Investments* (1970). A contract can also be accepted by conduct. There is no need to use the words 'I accept'. Other types of conduct can amount to acceptance, notwithstanding the absence of specific assent. Acceptance can be implied from an objective consideration of all the relevant conduct and circumstances. As McHugh J explained in *Empirnall Holdings v Machon Paull* (1988) at 535: 'The ultimate issue is whether a reasonable bystander would regard the conduct of the offeree, including his [sic] silence, as signalling to the offeror that his offer has been accepted.' In that case, a property developer verbally engaged a firm of architects to act as a project manager. After starting work, the architects sent the developer a set of written terms. The developer refused to sign the proposed contract, but nonetheless made progress payments in accordance with the architect's terms. By taking the benefit of the work and not questioning the terms, the developer was held to have accepted them.

What an offeror cannot do, however, is to force a contract upon an offeree by insisting on treating silence as consent. In *Felthouse v Bindley* (1862), an uncle wrote to his nephew offering to buy a horse. The letter stated that: 'If I hear no more about him, I consider the horse mine.' The nephew intended to accept the offer, but did not communicate that, and the horse was sold by mistake to someone else. It was held that the uncle's offer had never been accepted. Arguably here, acceptance might have been found on the basis of the nephew's conduct, as he had instructed his auctioneer to set the horse aside for his uncle. Nevertheless, the case is valuable in emphasising the need for some act of consent. That view can also be seen to underpin ss 39–43 of the Australian Consumer Law (ACL), which prohibit various forms of 'inertia selling'. These involve a business supplying unsolicited goods or services and then asserting a right to payment.

---

20   See also *Brambles Holdings v Bathurst City Council* (2001), where a letter complaining about the proposed fees for certain work was described (at [156]–[157]) as 'merely part of the posturing that often accompanies negotiation' and containing 'nothing specific by way of offer or rejection'.

5.19 Acceptance and unilateral contracts

Unilateral contracts are exceptions to the rule, discussed below, that an acceptance must be communicated to the offeror. In this instance, meeting the conditions of acceptance laid down in the offer is generally enough. Hence in *Carlill v Carbolic Smoke Ball* (1893), discussed in **5.06**, the act of using the smoke ball was sufficient. No further acceptance needed to be communicated in order to recover the promised sum when Mrs Carlill became ill. It would be different, of course, if the offer itself specified the need for communication.

One issue that has sometimes arisen with unilateral contracts is whether the requested act needs to be performed with the *intention* of accepting the offer. It seems to be generally accepted that knowledge of the offer is essential. A person who returned a lost cat without knowing its owner had offered a reward could surely not say that they had accepted the owner's offer – though of course they might be paid anyway. If, on the other hand, a requested act is performed by someone who has knowledge of the offer, it will be presumed that they did so with an intention to accept: *The New York Star* (1978) at 271. But in some cases at least, the evidence may suggest the contrary. In *R v Clarke* (1927), the plaintiff claimed a substantial reward for information leading to the conviction of a murderer. His claim failed because he had admitted that in giving the necessary information, he had not been thinking of the reward, but had rather acted to clear his own name.[21]

5.20 Communication and the postal acceptance rule

The standard rule, at least for bilateral contracts, is that an acceptance cannot take effect unless and until it is communicated to the offeror. The offeror may waive the need for communication, but this requires clear evidence: *Latec Finance v Knight* (1969). The case of acceptance by letter is a longstanding exception. If the 'postal rule' applies then the contract is concluded when the acceptance is posted, rather than when it arrives: *Adams v Lindsell* (1818). The fact that the letter may arrive late, or never arrive at all, is irrelevant. The law could equally have required a letter to be received, but the postal rule was a pragmatic solution influenced by nineteenth century attitudes towards the postal system.[22] It effectively places the risk of non-delivery on the offeror. Questions remain, however, about when the postal rule can be applied.

In *Tallerman v Nathan's Merchandise* (1957) at 111, Dixon CJ and Fullagar J stated that the postal rule 'cannot be justified unless it is to be inferred that the offeror contemplated and intended that [the] offer might be accepted by the doing of that act'. There was no inference on the facts because, as was explained (at 112), the parties' solicitors were 'conducting a highly contentious correspondence, one would have thought that actual communication would be regarded as essential to the conclusion of the agreement on anything'. This version of the postal rule appears more restrictive than the English counterpart, which sees acceptance by posting rather than receiving the letter as valid if it was 'within the contemplation of the parties that according to the ordinary usage of mankind the post might be used as a means of

---

21 Compare *Williams v Carwardine* (1833), a decision distinguished in *Clarke* but which is hard to reconcile with the High Court's decision.
22 On the background to the rule, see Gardner 1992.

accepting the offer': *Henthorn v Fraser* (1892) at 33. In *Bressan v Squires* (1974) at 462, Bowen CJ suggested that no difference was intended.[23] The traditional threshold for applying the postal rule requires the post to be a reasonable method of acceptance. This might very well be the same situation in which it is most likely to be inferred that acceptance by post was contemplated and intended. But that doesn't mean that both versions will necessarily produce the same result. In any event, an offeror who wants to be absolutely sure that only receipt of the acceptance concludes the contract can oust the postal rule by the terms of the offer.

A letter may be overtaken by speedier means of communication. Suppose an offeree telephones the offeror before the offeror receives the acceptance letter and states, 'Ignore my letter. I do not wish to accept your offer'. If the contract is accepted by post it is difficult to see how such a statement would have any force, otherwise it would enable the offeree to speculate against the offeror. If they are able to find a more favourable deal elsewhere, then the offeree will be inclined to retract their acceptance. But it can be argued that the current default position favours the offeror to an even greater extent. The offeror controls the method of acceptance and is at perfect liberty to make clear that once the acceptance is posted, it cannot be withdrawn.[24]

5.21   Acceptance by other means

In *Bressan v Squires* at 462, Bowen CJ explained that 'courts in more recent times and in the light of modern means of communication have no disposition to extend the [postal rule] exception'. The general rule for instantaneous communication, such as the telephone, or virtually instantaneous methods of communication, such as a telex or fax machine, is that an acceptance must reach the offeror. Sending an acceptance is insufficient: *Entores v Miles Far East* (1955); *Reese Brothers Plastics v Hamon-Sobelco* (1988). The recipient will usually be an employee of the offeror and so for practical reasons effective communication is achieved when it is received at the offeror's office: see *Brinkibon v Stahag Stahl* (1983); *Leach Nominees v Walter Wright* (1986). Like the other default rules, however, the principle that the acceptance must be received can be displaced by contrary intention. Business practice and the allocation of risk are factors to be considered, as was emphasised in *Brinkibon*. Any fault on the part of the recipient may also be relevant in determining whether the contract is concluded. Sometimes it will be obvious when communicating instantaneously that the acceptance was not communicated. This is the case where a telephone line goes dead before acceptance can be communicated. On other occasions, it might not be so obvious that the acceptance has not got through. A voice on the telephone may become indistinct. In this situation, the offeror is at fault for not asking for the message to be repeated. The same idea applies when the offeree faxes an acceptance and the recipient has not refilled their fax machine with ink. The offeree believes that the acceptance has got through and has no way of knowing otherwise. The offeror is again at fault and it is as though the acceptance was communicated: *The Brimnes* (1975).

---

23   For a contrary view supporting a narrower rule, see *Nunin Holdings v Tullamarine Estates* (1994) at 83; but compare *Wardle v Agricultural and Rural Finance* (2012) at [135].

24   For a discussion of these issues, see Hudson 1966.

Contracts conducted over the internet have given rise to an entirely new set of problems. An interactive website typically requires a purchaser to click on a link. As a form of instantaneous communication, the default rule ought to be that the acceptance must be communicated to the offeror. Online auctions like those on eBay have some characteristics of traditional auctions, but they are also a form of instantaneous communication. It has been held that making the highest bid, when combined with an indication from the website that the bidder has won the item, amounts to acceptance of the seller's offer: *Smythe v Thomas* (2007).[25]

The postal rule has been extended to the telegram, but it is unlikely that it will apply to emails. So much was assumed by Logan J in *Olivaylle v Flottweg* (2009) at [25], although the point did not have to be decided. Yet email shares some features with the post.[26] There are several possible delays once an emailed acceptance is sent. There may be a short delay in sending the email after the writer presses send, particularly if the email contains a very large document. There may be a delay in the transmission process as a result of network congestion or mail server unavailability. A third delay occurs in the recipient retrieving the email.

Even if the rule for instantaneous communication applies to emails and therefore acceptance needs to be received, it still remains necessary to define receipt. The *Electronic Transactions Acts* do not purport to determine whether a contract is accepted when an email is dispatched or received, but they do provide a legal definition of dispatch and receipt in this context. Section 13(1) of the *Electronic Transactions Act 2000* (NSW) is mirrored in the other jurisdictions. The time of dispatch of an email, unless otherwise provided for by the parties, is defined as occurring when it leaves an information system under the control of the sender.[27] An email is received when it is capable of being retrieved from an email address designated by the recipient; or if a non-designated email address of the recipient is used, then the recipient must also know that it has been sent there (s 13A(1)).

A further provision that is potentially important in the context of contract formation is s 14D (also mirrored in other jurisdictions). This applies if a natural person 'makes an input error' in communicating with an automated message system and is not given an opportunity to correct it. Provided the error is notified as soon as possible, and no benefit has been received from the other party, the person (or a party for whom they were acting) may 'withdraw' the relevant communication – which could clearly include a purported acceptance.

5.22   Limits of offer and acceptance analysis

The requirement of a matching offer and acceptance puts the onus on the parties to be clear about the point at which the contract is entered into. It is open to the criticism that it is unduly mechanical and does not fit well with the reality of contracting. In his widely quoted judgment in *Integrated Computer Services v Digital Equipment* (1988) at 11,117–18, McHugh JA observed:

---

25   Note that in such a case there are in fact three contracts in all, since both the buyer and seller contract with the intermediary (eBay) and accept its terms for facilitating the sale.
26   For a detailed discussion of the problem of acceptance by email, see Mik 2009.
27   An information system is defined as a system for 'generating, sending, receiving, storing or otherwise processing electronic communications' (s 5).

It is often difficult to fit a commercial arrangement into the common lawyers' analysis of a contractual arrangement. Commercial discussions are often too unrefined to fit easily into the slots of 'offer', 'acceptance', 'consideration' and 'intention to create a legal relationship' which are the benchmarks of the contract of classical theory ... Moreover, in an ongoing relationship, it is not always easy to point to the precise moment when the legal criteria of a contract have been fulfilled ...

It has also been said that the doctrine comes unstuck 'outside the realms of commerce and conveyancing, to the everyday contractual situations which are a feature of life in modern urban communities': *MacRobertson Miller Airline Services v Commissioner of State Taxation* (1975) at 136.

Rather than seeking to identify an offer and acceptance, an alternative approach is to look at the conduct of the parties as a whole in order to determine whether a contract is concluded. Lord Denning used this method in *Gibson v Manchester City Council* (1978). On appeal to the House of Lords, it was held that the usual offer and acceptance rule could only be departed from in exceptional circumstances: *Gibson v Manchester City Council* (1979). Nevertheless, the more flexible approach has the merit of avoiding artificiality, and may more closely reflect the way that most contracting parties actually behave. In *Brambles Holdings v Bathurst City Council* (2001) at [74], the New South Wales Court of Appeal held that 'offer and acceptance is a useful tool in most circumstances'. But it also conceded that 'limited recognition' has been given to the idea that a contract can be formed without an offer and acceptance. As a result, it may not be necessary to identify a precise offer and acceptance in every case: *Mushroom Composters v IS & DE Robertson* (2015) at [60].

A note of caution was added in *Magill v Magill* (2006) at 617, however, when Heydon J said that just because the traditional offer and acceptance doctrine does not work well in all circumstances, that was not a good reason to abandon it entirely. The courts have also stressed that for a contract to be inferred, the parties' conduct must unequivocally support that conclusion. As Bond J observed in *King Tide v Arawak Holdings* (2017) at [21]: 'It is not enough that the conduct is merely consistent with the terms of the alleged binding agreement, the evidence must positively indicate that both parties considered themselves bound by that agreement.'

5.23   The battle of the forms

The application of the doctrine of offer and acceptance has proved especially troublesome in the so called 'battle of the forms' cases, as illustrated by the decision of the English Court of Appeal in *Butler Machine Tool v Ex-Cell-O* (1979). The plaintiff offered to supply a machine for a specific sum. The offer was expressed to be subject to a 'price escalation clause'. In reply to the offer, the buyer placed an order with a form setting out their own terms and conditions and omitting the price escalation clause. The reply also contained a tear-off strip to be signed by the seller and returned to the buyer stating that the seller accepted the order 'on the terms and conditions stated therein'. The seller signed and returned it along with a letter saying that they were 'entering' the contract 'in accordance with' their offer. A dispute arose over whether the contract was concluded on the buyer's or seller's terms.

Lawton and Bridge LLJ sought to determine whether an unequivocal offer was mirrored by an unequivocal acceptance. As noted earlier, where an apparent acceptance adds new terms, or varies those of the offer, it is treated as a counter-offer. On the facts, the buyer made a counter-offer. It was held, somewhat dubiously, that this counter-offer was accepted by the seller when they returned the tear-off strip. It was decided that the seller's accompanying letter was not a counter-offer because it did not refer to the price escalation clause. Arguably here, the 'mirror-image' analysis should have produced a stalemate where no contract was concluded. This would have put the onus on the parties to negotiate a solution between them, which might have been a better outcome. It is difficult to believe that the seller really intended to conclude an agreement without the price escalation clause, even if they had failed to refer to it in the accompanying letter. They found themselves bound by the buyer's terms because an employee had signed a tear-off strip. This approach favours the party who sends the last set of standard terms to the other. When the other party performs or accepts performance, they are then treated as dealing on those terms.

Lord Denning agreed that the return of the tear-off strip was decisive, but his reasoning was not consistent with the 'mirror-image' approach. He thought that there could be a contract, even if the terms on which the parties purported to deal varied. The court, he said (at 405), was able to reconcile the terms in order to give a 'harmonious result'; if not, 'then the conflicting terms may have to be scrapped and replaced by a reasonable implication'. Either situation would allow a court to rewrite the contract and would be a radical departure from the established approach.

In *Goodman v Cospak* (2004), Master Macready applied Lord Denning's solution to the facts before him. He explained (at [55]) that such an approach seeks 'to determine the ad idem of the parties from an objective rather than technical offer and acceptance perspective'. The dispute was about the terms that the parties had agreed upon. The contract could be construed to give a 'harmonious result', so there was no need to impose a 'reasonable implication'. It remains unclear when judges will depart from the traditional test of matching an acceptance to an offer. The application of Lord Denning's alternative approach has been restricted: see eg *Tekdata Interconnections v Amphenol* (2009). *Goodman v Cospak* may, therefore, be an exceptional authority. On the other hand, while not being quite as openly creative as Lord Denning, recent Australian courts dealing with battles of forms have tended to avoid offer and acceptance analysis. They have instead favoured a broad inquiry as to whether agreement on a set of terms can be objectively ascertained, based on a review of the totality of the parties' dealings: see eg *Eccles v Koolan Ire Ore* (2013); *Diploma Construction v Best Bar* (2015).

Conditional contracts

5.24 Conditions

The word *condition* has many different meanings in contract law. Besides being used loosely to refer to *any* term of a contract (as in 'the conditions of sale'), it can mean any of the following:

- an *essential term* (as opposed to an intermediate term or a warranty) – a term any breach of which will justify termination by the injured party (see **16.07**);
- a promise which, under the order of performance determined by the parties, one party is obliged to perform or make good before the other party can be called upon to perform certain of their obligations (see **12.07**); or

- an event or state of events which neither party has promised to bring about, but whose occurrence (or non-occurrence) will affect the creation or subsistence of a contract or of certain obligations in it.

The third of these categories includes unilateral contracts, under which the relevant promise only becomes binding if the requested act is performed, something that the promisee is *not* undertaking to ensure. Contingent conditions can also be found in 'aleatory' contracts such as insurance contracts or guarantees, where one party's principal obligations are triggered only by the occurrence of a fortuitous event. If an insurer agrees to insure against a particular risk, they are only obliged to indemnify the insured if the relevant event occurs, something that neither party is promising will happen. Similarly, a guarantor only becomes liable if the principal debtor defaults.

5.25   The effect of a contingent condition

As the examples just given demonstrate, a contingent condition may operate in one of two ways. The first possibility is that its fulfilment determines whether a contract comes into existence at all, as with a unilateral contract. In such a case, either party may as a general rule withdraw from the 'agreement' at any time before the condition is satisfied. The second possibility, illustrated by the aleatory contracts mentioned above, is that a contract has already come into existence. There the contingent condition dictates whether some or all of the obligations in that contract are to be performed. The precise effect of a condition of this latter variety varies according to its nature and intent. An insurance contract, for example, usually continues until the period of the risk has elapsed, with the insurer's obligation to indemnify being triggered as circumstances dictate. In other instances, the contingency may affect only some of the parties' principal obligations, leaving others untouched. In the most extreme case, it may be expressly or impliedly provided that the contract is to terminate automatically on the occurrence of a stipulated event.[28] In general, courts prefer to construe contingent conditions as conferring on one or both parties a right to terminate if they so choose: see eg *Suttor v Gundowda* (1950). But this is a principle of construction, not an absolute rule: see *MK & JA Roche v Metro Edgley* (2005).

In some instances, it may be difficult to determine whether a contingency operates as a condition precedent to the formation of a contract, or simply to the performance of some of its obligations. A specific example of this that has already been mentioned in **5.06**, and that will be discussed further in Chapter 6, involves an agreement being made subject to the preparation of a formal contract. But the same issue can arise with other types of condition. For example, the purchase of a house may be made 'subject to finance' – that is, subject to the buyer being able to borrow the money they need, often by way of a bank loan secured by a mortgage on the property they wish to acquire.[29] Or the purchase may be subject to the buyer being able to sell

---

28   A condition of this sort is sometimes called a *condition subsequent*, as distinct from a condition precedent. But compare *Perri v Coolangatta Investments* (1982) at 541, noting that it is more important to focus on the intended effect of a condition than the labels 'precedent' or 'subsequent'.

29   As to the effect of a requirement for such finance to be 'satisfactory' to the buyer, see *Meehan v Jones* (1982), rejecting an argument that this made the condition too uncertain. For a detailed consideration of subject to finance clauses, see Swanton 1984.

their own house. In each case, the question may arise whether one or other party is free to withdraw from the agreement prior to the condition being fulfilled.

Ultimately, this is a question of ascertaining the parties' intentions on the matter, on the basis of all relevant evidence, including the circumstances surrounding the agreement: see eg *Air Great Lakes v K S Easter Holdings* (1985). In *Whittle v Parnell Mogas* (2006), for example, an offer of a lease was made subject to certain work being done on the property and an environmental assessment being obtained. On the facts, the court was satisfied that the fulfilment of these conditions was necessary for a contract to be formed. But where the evidence is equivocal, the court will generally be inclined to treat a contingent condition as one precedent to performance rather than formation: see eg *Perri v Coolangatta Investments* (1982) at 552.[30] This allows the court to find that a contract does exist and, if it is appropriate, to imply into that contract an ancillary duty of cooperation. This duty does not require either party to fulfil the contingency. Rather, the parties are obliged to do whatever is reasonably necessary to allow the condition to be satisfied: see eg *Butts v O'Dwyer* (1952).[31] Hence, in the examples given above, the buyer would be under an implied obligation to make inquiries about finance or to put their property on the market. They might also be obliged to accept any reasonable offers they receive. Besides conferring on the other party a right to claim damages, breach of such a duty may preclude the party who has failed to cooperate from relying on the non-fulfilment of the condition: *Gange v Sullivan* (1966) at 441–2.

5.26   Fulfilling, waiving or relying on a contingent condition

Whatever the nature of a contingent condition, whether it involves a promissory term or not, it will generally be interpreted fairly strictly. Substantial but not exact fulfilment will usually be insufficient to trigger the relevant consequence: see eg *Tricontinental v HDFI* (1990). On the other hand, a party may be estopped from relying on the non-fulfilment of a condition where they have led the other to believe that the condition need not be satisfied: see eg *Update Constructions v Rozelle Child Care Centre* (1990). A party may also choose to 'waive' fulfilment of a condition precedent to performance and call upon the other to perform, so long as the condition has been stipulated solely for the benefit of the waiving party: *Gange v Sullivan* at 429–30, 443. But while accepting that this is so, the High Court made it clear in *Perri v Coolangatta Investments* that if such a condition has not been met within a reasonable time, nor waived, either party is still free to 'avoid' the contract.

Consideration

5.27   The need for consideration

Unless entered into using a deed (see **5.47**), a contract must be supported by *consideration* – or, as it is sometimes said, 'good' consideration or 'valuable' consideration. Consideration and

---

30   Or, as it is sometimes said, the contract will be treated as voidable rather than void: see eg *Gange v Sullivan* (1966) at 441.

31   Some contracts make this duty explicit: see eg *Margush v Maddeford* (2014).

motive are both reasons for contracting but they are quite different: *Thomas v Thomas* (1842) at 859. Motive is inherently subjective. Consideration is something that is defined by the law. It is a longstanding feature of the common law of contract. In essence, a promise can only be enforceable as part of a contract if something of value is provided in return. What is required is an element of *quid pro quo*, exchange or bargain, which are all ways of defining the key characteristic of consideration: *Australian Woollen Mills v Commonwealth* (1954) at 461. A gratuitous promise, no matter how seriously intended, is not legally enforceable unless expressed in a deed.

In the case of a bilateral contract, the consideration for one party's promise or set of promises is the promise or set of promises given in return by the promisee. Thus, even before either party has begun to perform, while the agreement remains wholly 'executory', the parties are bound merely through their exchange of promises. In the case of a unilateral contract, by contrast, there is only one promisor. The consideration for that party's promise(s) constitutes some act or forbearance requested by the promisor. The promisee in this situation is not obliged to do anything. But *if* what is requested is done, this brings the contract into existence, supplies consideration for the promise and thus renders the promise enforceable.

In what follows, we look first at the requirement for some form of exchange and then at the vexed question of what constitutes sufficient 'value'.

5.28   The element of exchange

For the requirement of consideration to be satisfied, there must be a causal connection between what each party is promising or doing. Thus, if A promises to do something for B and B, hearing this promise, responds by making a promise to do something for A, there is no contract, since the element of reciprocity is lacking. In order for these promises to represent a bargain, each must be given on the understanding that the other is to be made and honoured. Similarly, a promise cannot become contractually binding merely because the person to whom it was made incurs some cost or potential detriment in reliance on the promise being performed.

For example, in *Beaton v McDivitt* (1987), the defendants decided to subdivide a parcel of land. They agreed that the plaintiff would occupy one lot and work it rent-free, using a particular method of horticulture. They promised the plaintiff that they would transfer title to him once the land was re-zoned, something which never in fact happened. In the years that followed, the plaintiff not only farmed on the lot but built a house. After a falling out between the parties, the issue arose of whether the plaintiff had a contractual right to be on the property. At first instance, Young J held that it was enough that the defendants had made a promise and the plaintiff had relied upon it to his detriment. On appeal, both Kirby P and McHugh JA rejected this finding of reliance-based consideration as incompatible with the bargain theory of contract endorsed by the High Court in *Australian Woollen Mills v Commonwealth* (1954).[32] McHugh and Mahoney JJA were nonetheless willing (perhaps generously) to interpret the facts

---

32   The authorities relied upon by Young J in support of his reliance-based approach were treated as resting not on a contractual analysis, but on the equitable doctrine of proprietary estoppel: see **7.03**.

as involving a unilateral contract, on the basis that the defendants had requested the plaintiff to work the land in return for their promise to give him ownership.[33]

As *Beaton* illustrates, it can be difficult to distinguish between a conditional gift and a unilateral contract. If A makes a promise to be performed on condition that B does something, A's promise is only enforceable as part of a unilateral contract if B's act has been *requested* as the price for A undertaking a commitment. In practice, it is rarely obvious whether this is indeed the case and much will turn on the particular circumstances. This is illustrated by *Australian Woollen Mills*, where a government announcement that it would pay subsidies to companies purchasing Australian wool for domestic use was held by the High Court not to be contractually binding. An appeal to the Privy Council was dismissed: *Australian Woollen Mills v Commonwealth* (1955).

By contrast, an offer of a reward for information or for the return of a lost item will almost always be construed as being intended to create a bargain, unless the contrary is made clear: see eg *R v Clarke* (1927).

There is an intuitive appeal in the idea that a contract is based on exchange, but the continued existence of a doctrine of consideration is not entirely uncontroversial. The law might be simpler and more coherent if consideration were abolished in favour of a single rule that a contract must be seriously intended.[34] As matters stand, such a reform could only be accomplished by statute. What the common law has done, however, has been to find a way of protecting the position of those who act in reliance on a promise being fulfilled, even if they have not furnished the consideration necessary to make that promise contractually binding. This has been achieved through the concept of *equitable estoppel*, as discussed in Chapter 7.

5.29 Past consideration

The need for an exchange explains the rule that *past consideration* is not good consideration. Past consideration involves an act which predates a promise. For example, A paints B's fence on Monday, and on the following Wednesday B promises to pay A $100 for doing so. If B does not pay the $100, A cannot claim it in contract because it is past consideration: A did not paint B's fence in exchange for B's promise: see eg *Roscorla v Thomas* (1842).[35] However, if B's act or forbearance had originally been at A's request, it may be possible to imply an understanding that B was to be remunerated or rewarded on terms to be determined at a later date. In that event, a contract is taken to be formed at the time of the request, with A's promise simply representing the ascertainment of the remuneration or reward: see eg *Re Casey's Patents* (1892). Similarly, where B has been assured of some form of payment, though not in terms certain enough to create a contract, what B does in response may be good consideration for a later and more precise promise from A: see eg *Pao On v Lau Yiu Long* (1980).

---

33 Despite this finding the plaintiff's claim ultimately failed, since Mahoney JA held that the contract had been frustrated (see Chapter 15) when the land was not rezoned. He therefore agreed with Kirby P, albeit for a different reason, that there was no contract in force.
34 Compare Chen-Wishart 2013, 2016; and see further Paterson et al 2016: 111–14.
35 Compare *Bills of Exchange Act 1909* (Cth) s 32, which effectively creates an exception to this principle in the case of a bill of exchange.

5.30   The requirement of 'value'

It is difficult to arrive at a useful and accurate definition of what constitutes valuable consideration. The classic formulation is found in *Currie v Misa* (1875) at 162, where Lush J said:

> A valuable consideration, in the sense of the law, may consist either in some right, interest, profit or benefit accruing to the one party, or some forbearance, detriment, loss or responsibility, given, suffered, or undertaken by the other.

Ordinarily, what is provided by way of consideration for a promise from A to B will involve benefit and detriment on *both* sides; for example, a payment of money from B to A, or the performance of work by B that has some utility to A. But this need not be the case, as Lush J made clear. For instance, B may do something that in formal terms benefits someone other than A. This is the case with a contract of guarantee, where the consideration typically 'received' by the guarantor is the granting of credit to the principal debtor: see **11.11**. It is enough that consideration 'move' from the promisee;[36] it does not have to move *to* the promisor.

Despite the breadth of the *Currie v Misa* formula, it is not always completely clear what will suffice to constitute a benefit or detriment. Some older authorities in particular are hard to reconcile or explain. For example, in *White v Bluett* (1853), a father agreed not to sue his son on a debt that he owed. In return, the son agreed he would not annoy his father with complaints over the way the father distributed his property amongst his children. Chief Baron Pollock held that the son had not provided any consideration as he had 'no right to complain' to his father because it was up to the father to decide how he distributed his property. In contrast, in the American case of *Hamer v Sidway* (1891), an uncle promised to pay his nephew $5,000 if the nephew refrained from 'drinking liquor, using tobacco, swearing and playing cards or billiards for money' until the nephew was 21. It was held that there was a contract because the nephew had the legal right to engage in these activities. Giving up his legal rights was a detriment and therefore good consideration. It is doubtful, however, whether either of these decisions would now meet the threshold of an intention to enter into legal relations.

In practice, most of the modern problems with consideration do not centre on what constitutes a benefit or a detriment.[37] Rather, they turn on the scope and operation of rules that deem certain types of promise or act to be legally 'insufficient'. The most troublesome of these rules concern the performance of a pre-existing duty, an issue which is discussed below along with the concept of 'illusory' consideration. Before turning to those matters, however, it is necessary to say something about the difference between the sufficiency of consideration and its *adequacy*.

---

36   Where there are joint promisees, it is enough that one of them supplies consideration: *Coulls v Bagot's* (1967) (see **8.03**).

37   But see *Director of Public Prosecutions (Vic) v Le* (2007), where members of the High Court disagreed as to whether a wife's 'love and affection' could be good consideration for a promise by her husband to transfer property to her. However, this was in the context of a statutory requirement of 'sufficient consideration' – a term which the judges recognised could have different meanings in different legal contexts.

5.31   Adequacy of consideration

Although consideration requires an exchange, the value of that exchange is left to be determined by the parties. Hence while consideration must be legally sufficient, it need not be adequate: *Director of Public Prosecutions (Vic) v Le* (2007) at [115]. It is irrelevant for this purpose that a bargain may be unequal. For example, A and B can validly agree that A will sell B a car for $1, even if the actual value of the car is $100,000. When something with apparently little value is requested and given in exchange, it still amounts to good consideration.

The fact that consideration need not be adequate means that items of purely nominal value can be used as consideration. *Chappell v Nestlé* (1960) provides an extreme example of the operation of this rule. A chocolate manufacturer sold gramophone records for one shilling and sixpence, plus three wrappers of its sixpence bars of chocolate. It was held that the delivery of the wrappers formed part of the consideration, even though the wrappers were of little value and were in fact thrown away. In practice, it is not unusual for commercial agreements to stipulate a token amount or article as the price for what would otherwise be a gratuitous promise. Aside from a 'peppercorn rent' (a promise to pay a peppercorn for the right to occupy premises), a common example involves paying $1 or some other trivial sum to convert a revocable offer into a binding option (see **5.16**).

It might be argued that the acceptance of nominal consideration undermines the idea that consideration reflects a bargain or exchange. But there are good reasons why a court does not inquire into the adequacy of consideration: see *Woolworths v Kelly* (1991) at 193–4. People make bad bargains all the time. That should be their choice. If adequacy were to be put under scrutiny then there would be a risk that any bargain could be reopened. Even if it were possible to examine the adequacy of consideration it would be immensely difficult, outside the most obvious cases, to know where to draw the line. That said, a gross disparity in value may – depending on the context – suggest that a contract has been procured improperly or unfairly. As we will see, while the lack of a 'fair price' may not preclude the requirement of consideration being satisfied, it may become relevant in determining whether a contract can be set aside on grounds such as unconscionability: see **20.02–20.07**.

5.32   Performance of pre-existing duties

Where consideration is grounded in a promise to perform an existing duty, a problem arises. The other party is getting nothing more than they were already entitled to. A benefit or detriment is missing. Most commonly, the duty in question arises out of a pre-existing contract between the parties. As a general rule, the performance of an existing contractual obligation owed by A to B cannot be good consideration for any new agreement between those parties: *Wigan v Edwards* (1973) at 594. But not only are there a number of exceptions to this principle, it has been challenged in recent decades by the idea that consideration may be found in some 'practical benefit' obtained by B as a result of A fulfilling or recommitting to their original obligation: see eg *Musumeci v Winadell* (1994). Since this issue necessarily arises when the parties are attempting to vary or renegotiate their original agreement, it is given more detailed treatment in Chapter 13.[38]

---

[38]   As to whether the practical benefit principle can or should apply when parties are *forming* a contract, as opposed to varying it, see Giancaspro 2014a.

It has also been held that the performance of an existing 'moral 'duty is not sufficient consideration, in the absence of any more specific or tangible commitment: *Eastwood v Kenyon* (1840). Nor is there consideration in a promise to perform an existing legal duty of a 'public' character: *Collins v Godefroy* (1831). If the contract goes beyond that duty, however, the outcome is different. When a mine owner requested more police officers than the police thought necessary in order to control a group of striking workers, the police went beyond their legal duty and provided sufficient consideration for a contract with the mine owner to pay them: see *Glasbrook v Glamorgan County Council* (1925).

The reasoning in some of these authorities is rather artificial. In *Ward v Byham* (1956), a father promised to pay the mother of his child £1 per week 'providing you can prove that the child is well looked after and happy, and she is allowed to decide for herself whether or not she wishes to come and live with you'. Having looked after the child the mother was still able to enforce the contract to pay her, even though she was under an existing statutory legal duty to look after the child. The majority of the Court of Appeal, Morris and Parker LJJ, found additional consideration in the requirements of making the child 'happy' and 'able to choose' whether to live with the mother. Denning LJ went further and argued that the father received a benefit. The rise of the 'practical benefit' doctrine, as mentioned above, means that this analysis may have some appeal. There is scant Australian authority, but in *Popiw v Popiw* (1959) Hudson J cited Denning LJ's judgment with approval. A husband promised a wife that if she would return to live with him he would transfer half of the matrimonial home into her name. She returned, but only for four weeks when they quarrelled and she left again. It was said that the husband received 'something . . . far more advantageous to him than the right of cohabiting with his wife which he had no means of enforcing' and that the wife 'in returning was submitting to a detriment in placing herself in a position which she could not have been compelled to occupy'. Excluding existing legal duties from consideration can be justified on the basis that there are good public policy grounds not to allow someone to claim on a contract for something that they are already legally bound to do. At the same time, it runs up against the idea that when a contract appears to be intended, and there is some benefit attached, the courts tend to find other ways to enforce the contract.

5.33   Compromise agreements

Where there is a dispute as to the performance or requirements of an existing contract, the parties may reach a compromise and embody that in a new agreement. So long as that compromise has been struck in good faith, it will not matter that one of the parties is promising to fulfil an existing obligation. Giving up a seriously asserted claim may constitute good consideration, even if it transpires that the claim was unfounded: *Butler v Fairclough* (1917) at 96.

In *Wigan v Edwards* (1973), the plaintiffs contracted to buy a house owned and built by the defendant. They refused to complete the sale unless the defendant rectified what they claimed to be a number of defects. The defendant undertook to do that and also made a commitment to repair any major faults in construction discovered within five years of the purchase. No such promises had been made in the original contract. The plaintiffs completed the sale and later sued the defendant for failing to repair what they claimed to be a major fault in the concrete slab on which the house was built. The claim was dismissed by a majority of the High Court, on the basis that the fault identified did not fall within the promise of repair. But all members of the

Court agreed that there was consideration for the defendant's promise, even though on the face of it the plaintiffs' commitment in return to complete the sale involved doing no more than they were already bound to do. The trial judge had found that the purchasers genuinely (if wrongly) believed in their right to insist on the original defects being addressed. Moreover, the defendant's promise had been intended to induce them to complete. That was enough for the agreement to be one of compromise, even though it was not framed as such. It was not necessary for the plaintiffs to have threatened legal proceedings. It was enough that they had honestly made – and then agreed to withdraw – a claim that they were not bound to go through with the sale.[39]

5.34   Duties owed to third parties

The performance of an existing duty can also be sufficient consideration when that duty is owed to a third party. Suppose A enters into a contract with B, and A also wants to enter into a contract with C. A can furnish consideration for the agreement with C by promising C to perform the contract with B: see eg *Pao On v Lau Yiu Long* (1980). In *Shadwell v Shadwell* (1860), an uncle promised to pay his nephew £150 per annum on the nephew marrying his fiancée – something he was already obliged to do. It was held that there was detriment to the nephew in that 'he may have made a most material change in his position, and induced the object of his affection to do the same, and may have incurred pecuniary liabilities resulting in embarrassments'. The benefit to the uncle was that the marriage was 'an object of interest to a near relative'. Although consideration need not be adequate, it is difficult to explain here why the uncle receives a quantifiable benefit of any kind beyond the interest that the other party perform, which could be said of any gratuitous promise.

The third party exception also applies to the performance of non-contractual duties. In *Ailakis v Olivero* (2014), the defendants promised a large number of shares in a company to one of its directors if he rendered certain services that were important to the company. While admitting the agreement, and that the plaintiff had done what was requested, the defendants sought to escape liability by arguing that the plaintiff was doing no more than fulfil his duties as a director under the *Corporations Act 2001* (Cth). But even if that were true, those duties did not have a 'public' character. They were owed to the company, which was not a party to the contract. 'Happily', Martin CJ observed (at [2]), the law was 'not so out of step with basic commercial morality to sustain [the defendants'] propositions'.

5.35   Illusory consideration

A promise which is held not to constitute good consideration because it involves the perform-ance of a pre-existing duty may be described as an 'illusory consideration': see eg *Wigan v Edwards* (1973) at 594. The same may be said of past consideration. However, the term is more usually reserved for a promise which imposes no real obligation upon the promisor at all and thus cannot be valuable consideration. This may occur where the promisor is given an absolute discretion as to whether to perform the promise, as was found to be the case in *Placer Development v Commonwealth* (1969) (see **5.39**). A further example of illusory consideration

---

39   See also *Tallerman v Nathan's Merchandise* (1957).

is provided by *MacRobertson Miller Airline Services v Commissioner of State Taxation* (1975), where the conditions of carriage on an air ticket permitted the airline to cancel a flight or a booking without liability. The exemption clauses drafted by the airline to protect its interests were found to be so extensive that they precluded any suggestion that the airline was under an obligation to carry its passengers.

By contrast, in *Memery v Trilogy Funds Management* (2012), a loan facility agreement was held not to be an illusory contract. The lender's obligation to advance any monies was subject to a great many conditions, and it had a broad discretion to withdraw the facility. Nevertheless, the agreement obliged the lender to use its 'best endeavours' to advance the loan. This was considered to be sufficient consideration for the borrower's obligation to pay a loan application fee.

Certainty and completeness

5.36   The need for certainty and completeness

A contract which is incomplete or uncertain is void. An agreement will be treated as *uncertain* where it is too difficult for a court to determine if the parties have performed in accordance with the contract. A contract is *incomplete* when 'essential' matters are omitted: *Mushroom Composters v IS & DE Robertson* (2015) at [63]. Courts are reluctant to make a contract for the parties where key elements are missing. In determining what is essential, a court looks for evidence of what the parties see as important: *Australian Broadcasting Corporation v XIVth Commonwealth Games* (1988) at 458. It will also depend on the nature of the contract: *Vroon v Foster's Brewing* (1994) at [68]. The burden of challenging the contract lies on the party arguing that the agreement is incomplete or uncertain: *Whitlock v Brew* (1968) at 454.

There may be very good reasons why parties want to leave matters open. In some circumstances, commercial parties especially may want to preserve a degree of flexibility in their dealings: see eg *Prints for Pleasure v Oswald-Sealy* (1968) at 765. The courts have never insisted that everything must be absolutely settled. It is enough if, as was observed in *Scammell and Nephew v Ouston* (1941) at 255, the parties' 'meaning can be determined with a reasonable degree of certainty'.

There are limits, however, to the flexibility that can be permitted. For example, parties are not permitted to contract on the basis that certain matters are left for further agreement: see eg *Mushroom Composters*, where a contract for the supply of goods over a four year period was interpreted to leave the price for all but the first year to further negotiation between the parties. The invalidity of an 'agreement to agree' is considered further in Chapter 6, together with the related question of whether effect can be given to a requirement to negotiate in good faith over a change to existing obligations.

5.37   Meeting the requirements of certainty

Despite emphasising the need for certainty, judges are usually reluctant to find that a contract is void for uncertainty. The fact that a particular term in a contract is capable of more than one meaning does not necessarily make the contract uncertain. This is something that can be resolved through a process of construction by looking at the meaning that the parties intended. For example, in *Upper Hunter County District Council v Australian Chilling and Freezing* (1968), a contract for the supply of electricity contained a clause allowing the price to vary according to changes in 'the supplier's costs'. The High Court acknowledged that this phrase could be given more than one meaning, but was satisfied nonetheless that it could be interpreted. As Barwick CJ noted (at 437), 'the concept of a cost of doing something is certain in the sense that it provides a criterion by reference to which the rights of the parties may ultimately and logically be worked out, if not by the parties then by the courts'. Where the parties have previously performed an agreement on the basis that it is enforceable, it will be especially difficult to argue subsequently that it is uncertain: *Hillas & Co v Arcos* (1932).

However, while judges prefer to avoid finding an agreement uncertain, this outcome is not inevitable, as two High Court decisions involving contracts for the sale of land show. In *Whitlock v Brew* (1968), as part of the sale, the parties had purported to enter into a lease back agreement on 'such reasonable terms as commonly govern such a lease'. Because there was no evidence of any commonly agreed terms for this type of contract, it was too uncertain.[40] In *Hall v Busst* (1960), a contract included an option for repurchase at a specified price less a 'reasonable sum to cover depreciation of all buildings and other property on the land'. By a majority, the contract was held to be uncertain because there were a number of different ways to calculate depreciation, all of which might be considered reasonable.[41]

5.38   Incomplete contracts

The contract in *Whitlock v Brew* was not just uncertain, it was also incomplete because there was no provision for the length of the term or the amount of rent to be paid. Each of these matters is regarded as an *essential term* for any contract of lease, along with a clear identification of both the premises and the parties: *NZI Insurance v Baryzcka* (2003) at [31]. But with other types of contract, a far less demanding approach is taken. For example, when a contract for the sale of goods is silent on price, the law simply requires that a reasonable price must be paid.[42] The same is true if an employee is hired without any agreement as to their wages: see eg *Midya v Sagrani* (1999). Nor is the duration of an employment contract something that must be expressly agreed. If no period is set by the parties, a term will be implied that permits either party to end the employment by giving reasonable notice: *Byrne v Australian Airlines* (1995) at 429. It is hard to say why some contracts can be 'rescued' from incompleteness in this way and others cannot. It appears to be primarily a matter of historical accident.

---

40   Compare *Allcars v Tweedle* (1937), where the defendant agreed to hire a car from the plaintiff 'on terms of [the plaintiff's] usual hiring agreements or that of [the plaintiff's] nominee'. Although the plaintiff did not utilise a set of usual terms, evidence before the Court showed such terms *did* exist in the car hire market and therefore the contract could be enforced.

41   For further examples of uncertainty, see eg *Biotechnology Australia v Pace* (1988) (reference in employment contract to non-existent 'equity sharing scheme'); *National Australia Bank v Budget Stationery Supplies* (1997) (inconsistent and irreconcilable conditions of loan).

42   *Sale of Goods Act 1923* (NSW) s 13(2); *Goods Act 1958* (Vic) s 13(2); *Sale of Goods Act 1896* (Qld) s 11(2); *Sale of Goods Act 1895* (WA) s 8(2); *Sale of Goods Act 1895* (SA) s 8(2); *Sale of Goods Act 1896* (Tas) s 13(2); *Sale of Goods Act 1954* (ACT) s 13(2); *Sale of Goods Act 1972* (NT) s 13(2).

5.39   Discretion and uncertainty

A contract will not be regarded as too uncertain merely because one or other party is given a discretion as to the exercise of a power, or the satisfaction of a condition. In such a case, it is customary to interpret the contract as requiring the discretion to be exercised by reference to some established standard, such as honesty or reasonableness: see eg *Godecke v Kirwan* (1973); *Meehan v Jones* (1982). The basis for this approach is discussed in a later chapter: see **12.19**.

The law does, however, draw a distinction between a contract which allows discretion about whether or not to perform the contract and one which allows discretion as to the method of performance. The first type of contract can be regarded as illusory: see **5.35**. The second type of contract can be enforced: *Thorby v Goldberg* (1964); *Transfield v Arlo International* (1980). The distinction between the two contracts is not always clear. In *Placer Development v Commonwealth* (1969), the Commonwealth and Placer Developments entered into an agreement concerning importation of timber from Papua New Guinea which stated:

> If customs duty is paid upon the importation into Australia of the plywood veneers, logs and other products of [a company to be formed by Placer Development] and is not remitted the Commonwealth to pay [the company] a subsidy … of an amount or at a rate determined by the Commonwealth from time to time.

The majority held that there was no valid agreement. Kitto J stated (at 356) that, if the 'promisor is to have a discretion or option as to whether he will carry out that which purports to be the promise, the result is that there is no contract on which an action can be brought at all'. Yet, as Menzies and Windeyer JJ pointed out in dissent (at 363–4, 370), the contract gave no option to perform. Instead it left open how the contract should be performed in terms of the size of the subsidy to pay.

5.40   Mechanisms for resolving uncertainty and incompleteness

As the cases discussed above indicate, there are a number of methods open to a court wanting to resolve problems of incompleteness and uncertainty. Besides the ability to settle on a meaning for an apparently ambiguous provision, a court may also imply a term to fill what would otherwise be a major 'gap' in a contract. More is said about that in Chapter 9. On other occasions, the fact that there is an external body, such as an arbitrator, to settle matters may allow an otherwise incomplete or uncertain contract to be enforced. In *Booker Industries v Wilson Parking* (1982), for example, a lease gave the lessee an option of a new term, the rent for which was either to be agreed between the parties or determined by an arbitrator nominated by the President of the Queensland Law Society. The High Court held that the option was sufficiently certain to be enforced. Furthermore, if the option was exercised and no agreement could be reached on the new rent, a term should be implied requiring the parties to do whatever was reasonably necessary to procure the appointment of an arbitrator.[43]

---

43   See also *Godecke v Kirwan* (1973), discussed in **6.08**.

If these methods fail, it is sometimes possible to *sever* the uncertain or incomplete provision, leaving the rest of the contract enforceable. Severance is discussed in more detail later, in the context of illegality and public policy: see **21.17**, **21.28**. But the basic principle is that it will only be permitted where it is apparent that the parties could have contemplated the agreement being binding without the relevant provision: *Fitzgerald v Masters* (1956).

Capacity

5.41   The capacity to make a contract

Anyone recognised as having legal capacity can enter into a contract. For these purposes, an incorporated company is given the same standing in law as an individual: *Corporations Act 2001* (Cth) s 124(1).[44] The same is true of the Crown. At common law, the Crown could not be sued for breach of contract or other wrongs. But that immunity has been removed by legislation.[45] A person who has been declared bankrupt can also make a contract, though this is subject to the right of that person's trustee in bankruptcy to intervene and disclaim the contract: *Bankruptcy Act 1966* (Cth) s 126(1).

The law recognises, however, that certain classes of person are vulnerable to exploitation and restricts or excludes their capacity to contract to some extent. Minors, persons with mental incapacity and the intoxicated are all afforded varying degrees of protection.

5.42   Minors

The law relating to contracting by young persons is complex and, outside New South Wales, governed by a combination of statute and common law authority.[46] The basic principle is straightforward enough. A *minor*, defined as a person under 18,[47] is not generally bound by a contract entered into before coming of age. There are three main exceptions: contracts for necessaries, contracts over permanent interests, and contracts which are ratified when the minor becomes an adult.

When a minor purchases goods or services that are classified as *necessaries* then the contract is valid. Under sale of goods legislation, the minor is liable to pay a reasonable price.[48]

---

44   Where a person purports to enter into a *pre-incorporation contract* on behalf of a company that has not yet been registered, the contract may bind the company if it is registered and ratifies the contract. But this must happen within any time agreed by the parties or, if no time is agreed, within a reasonable time: *Corporations Act 2001* s 131; and see eg *Rafferty v Madgwicks* (2012).

45   *Judiciary Act 1903* (Cth) ss 56, 64; *Crown Proceedings Act 1988* (NSW); *Crown Proceedings Act 1958* (Vic); *Crown Proceedings Act 1980* (Qld); *Crown Suits Act 1947* (WA); *Crown Proceedings Act 1992* (SA); *Crown Proceedings Act 1993* (Tas); *Court Procedures Act 2004* (ACT) s 21; *Crown Proceedings Act 1993* (NT).

46   For a detailed account, see Seddon & Bigwood 2017: ch 17.

47   *Minors (Property and Contracts) Act 1970* (NSW) s 6(1); *Age of Majority Act 1977* (Vic); *Law Reform Act 1995* (Qld) s 17; *Age of Majority Act 1972* (WA); *Age of Majority (Reduction) Act 1971* (SA); *Age of Majority Act 1973* (Tas); *Age of Majority Act 1974* (ACT); *Age of Majority Act 1974* (NT).

48   *Goods Act 1958* (Vic) s 7; *Sale of Goods Act 1896* (Qld) s 5; *Sale of Goods Act 1895* (WA) s 2; *Sale of Goods Act 1895* (SA) s 2; *Sale of Goods Act 1896* (Tas) s 7; *Sale of Goods Act 1954* (ACT) s 7; *Sale of Goods Act 1972* (NT) s 7.

The statutory definition of 'necessaries' goes beyond food and drink and typically includes 'goods suitable to the condition in life' of the minor. The authorities on what this covers, however, are usually too old to provide very useful guidance. The onus of proving that the goods or services are necessaries, and that the contract with the minor is therefore valid, is on the seller or supplier. If the minor is already adequately supplied, then the contract does not qualify: *Bojczuk v Gregorcewicz* (1961).

Special rules apply at common law if the minor purchases something permanent, such as land or shares: see eg *Davies v Beynon-Harris* (1931). These contracts are potentially binding unless they are repudiated during the minority or within a reasonably time of the minor coming of age. As a consequence of the Torrens system, once the land is registered the sale cannot be repudiated if the purchaser was unaware that the vendor was a minor: *Percy v Youngman* (1941).

Contracts falling outside the previous two categories will generally not be treated as binding on the minor, unless they choose to ratify the contract after attaining majority. In some jurisdictions, any such ratification must be in writing.[49] In Victoria, by contrast, contracts of this type generally cannot be ratified, though a new commitment can validly be given for good consideration, other than to pay a debt contracted during minority.[50]

The current law in most jurisdictions is unsatisfactory and uncertain. A seller will not know, for example, whether a laptop or a mobile telephone falls within the legal definition of necessaries. Nor is the law internally consistent. There is no obvious reason, other than a historical one, that some contracts should be binding, or some should be voidable and the onus placed on the minor to repudiate the contract, whereas the majority are unenforceable unless ratified on reaching adulthood.

The *Minors (Property and Contracts) Act 1970* (NSW) is an improvement in some respects. It is certainly more coherent. Youth by itself does not render a contract unenforceable. Contracts which benefit a minor (s 19) or involve dispositions of property for consideration (s 20) are, in the wording of the statute, 'presumptively binding'. This means that the law treats the minor as if they were an adult (s 6(3)). In consequence, any challenge to the contract must be through one of the standard vitiating factors such as duress or unconscionability: see **19.02–19.08, 20.02–20.07.** Youth will only be relevant where there is such a lack of understanding that the presumption does not apply (s 18). Contracts falling outside the presumption can still be affirmed by the minor on reaching their majority, in which case they become presumptively binding (s 30). Where an adult guarantees the performance of a minor's obligations, the guarantee can be enforced to the same extent as if the minor had been of age when making the contract (s 47).[51]

---

49   *Minors' Contracts (Miscellaneous Provisions) Act 1979* (SA) s 4; *Mercantile Law Act 1962* (ACT) s 15. This is also the position in Western Australia and the Northern Territory, owing to the continuing operation of the *Statute of Frauds (Amendment) Act 1828* (Imp) ('*Lord Tenterden's Act*').

50   *Supreme Court Act 1986* (Vic) ss 50–51. Section 49 also declares certain types of contract to be void. These include loan contracts, which cannot be ratified on turning 18.

51   South Australia and Tasmania have similar provisions: *Minors' Contracts (Miscellaneous Provisions) Act 1979* (SA) s 5; *Minors Contracts Act 1988* (Tas) s 4. The common law position is more complex: see eg *Land & Homes v Roe* (1936).

5.43 Mental incapacity and intoxication

Mental incapacity, including intoxication, only renders a contract unenforceable if the incapacity is sufficiently serious that it robs the individual of understanding at the time the contract was entered into, and the other party knew or ought to have known of this: *Gibbons v Wright* (1954). Mental incapacity renders a contract voidable rather than void (see **5.48**). This means that the contract is valid unless and until it is rescinded. The burden of proving insufficient mental incapacity is on the party seeking to avoid the contract. Mental incapacity may also be relevant as part of other doctrines, notably non est factum (see **18.42**) and unconscionability (see **20.02–20.07**).[52]

Formalities

5.44 Contracts in writing and the *Statute of Frauds*

There is no general rule that contracts have to be in writing. Hence, oral contracts are usually valid. There are still advantages, however, of reducing a contract to writing. In particular, writing is valuable evidence of what has been agreed. To the extent it still applies, the *parol evidence rule* prevents evidence which is extrinsic to a written agreement being used to vary or add to the written words in the contract: see **9.13**, **10.05–10.06**.

Writing *is* compulsory, on the other hand, for certain types of contract. Some of the more significant requirements in this area are derived from the *Statute of Frauds 1677* (Imp), which was enacted to minimise the risk of promises being invented by fraudulent witnesses.[53] It stipulated that in order for various types of agreement to be enforceable against a party, they must be recorded in a document signed by that party. Parts of this law remain in force in Australia, though in most cases local statutes have either supplanted the original requirements or, in some instances, abolished them.

The two most important categories that remain concern *guarantees* and contracts for the *sale of land*. In a contract of guarantee, one party (the guarantor) agrees to guarantee the liabilities of a third party to another (the guarantee). The guarantor and guarantee are both at risk. The guarantor may derive very little, if any, benefit from the contract. The guarantee runs a significant risk that the guarantor may not keep their word if the third party defaults. Accordingly, some jurisdictions still require that guarantees be recorded in writing.[54] What constitutes a guarantee, and how it is differentiated from an *indemnity*, is discussed in Chapter 11.

As for land sales, they tend to be high value transactions where the requirement of writing can be justified because of the risk of dishonesty. A sale of land usually involves three stages: an oral agreement, a written agreement, and finally a conveyance which passes title to the property. In all jurisdictions, a contract to sell land must be evidenced in writing. So too must

---

52 See eg *Hanna v Raoul* (2018), where an incapacity argument failed because the respondent had a general understanding of the contract he had signed. The contract was nonetheless set aside as being unconscionable.

53 See Rabal 1947; Simpson 1975b: 599–620.

54 *Instruments Act 1958* (Vic) s 126; *Property Law Act 1974* (Qld) s 56; *Law Reform (Statute of Frauds) Act 1962* (WA) s 2; *Law of Property Act 2000* (NT) s 58.

any other type of contract for the disposition of an interest in land, such as a lease or a mortgage.[55]

Besides these two categories, some States retain requirements of writing for other types of contract originally covered by the *Statute of Frauds*. These include the sale of goods of more than a specified amount,[56] as well as contracts not to be performed within a year.[57]

5.45 The *Statute of Frauds* requirements

The provisions derived from the *Statute of Frauds* do not necessarily require an affected contract to be fully set out in writing. It is enough that *either* the relevant agreement, *or* some 'note or memorandum' of that agreement, be in writing. The relevant document must also be signed by the 'party to be charged' (that is, the person against whom the contract is being enforced) or their agent. But it is not necessary that the party seeking to enforce the contract has signed anything: *Heppingstone v Stewart* (1910).

Over the years, there have been many disputes over the satisfaction of these requirements. A large body of case law has built up concerning issues such as what constitutes an 'interest' in land or a 'signature', how detailed a note or memorandum of an oral agreement must be, and the circumstances in which different documents can be read together to constitute such a note. A book of this type lacks the space even to summarise these authorities, especially given their limited relevance today beyond land transactions.[58] It suffices here to make four brief points about the operation of this legislation.

Firstly, the requirement of writing has created problems where affected contracts are modified. The courts have come to draw a distinction in this context between an oral agreement to *vary* an existing contract, which is unenforceable, and an oral agreement to *terminate* it, which may be given effect: see **13.13**. Secondly, in each jurisdiction the statutory requirements of writing and signature can be met by electronic equivalents, in accordance with the *Electronic Transactions Acts*.[59] Exceptions that used to exist for certain land transactions in New South Wales and South Australia have been removed in recent years, as part of the adoption of a national system of e-conveyancing.[60]

---

55   *Conveyancing Act 1919* (NSW) s 54A; *Instruments Act 1958* (Vic) s 126; *Property Law Act 1974* (Qld) s 59; *Law Reform (Statute of Frauds) Act 1962* (WA) s 2; *Law of Property Act 1936* (SA) s 26(1); *Conveyancing and Law of Property Act 1884* (Tas) s 36; *Civil Law (Property) Act 2006* (ACT) s 204; *Law of Property Act 2000* (NT) s 62.

56   *Sale of Goods Act 1895* (WA) s 4; *Sale of Goods Act 1896* (Tas) s 9.

57   *Mercantile Law Act 1935* (Tas) s 6. Note that a provision such as this does not apply to contracts which are *capable* of being performed within a year, no matter how long the parties in fact contemplate they might operate: *Clarke v Tyler* (1949).

58   For detailed discussion, see eg Seddon & Bigwood 2017: ch 16.

59   See eg *Electronic Transactions (Victoria) Act 2000* (Vic) ss 8–9; and see also *Instruments Act 1958* (Vic) s 126(2), specifically confirming the operation of these provisions. As to the problems that may occur when multiple people have access to a person's electronic signature, see *Williams Group v Crocker* (2016), discussed in Skilbeck 2017.

60   The system allows certain types of land transaction, including sales and mortgages, to be completed and registered through an electronic lodgment network, the first of which is operated by PEXA (Property Exchange Australia). As to the rules governing this system, see *Electronic Conveyancing (Adoption of National Law) Act 2012* (NSW) and its equivalents in other jurisdictions.

Thirdly, the effect of non-compliance is that the contract in question is *unenforceable*, at least against a party that has not signed the contract or a document recording its terms. No action for breach of contract may be brought against that party. Nor, it seems, may the contract be pleaded by way of defence to an action brought by that party on some other basis: *Perpetual Executors & Trustees v Russell* (1931). But the contract is not void: *Maddison v Alderson* (1883) at 474. While a party may not be able to sue for breach of contract, they may still be able to bring a restitutionary claim. This may be used to reclaim or seek payment for any benefits conferred in the course of performing the contract, at least where the contract is discharged by performance or for breach: see *Horton v Jones* (1934) at 367.[61]

Fourth, even if a contract is apparently unenforceable for lack of writing, various equitable doctrines may allow the effect of the relevant statute to be evaded. The most notable is the doctrine of *part performance*, developed to mitigate the harshness of the *Statute of Frauds*. Its effect is to offer equitable relief in the form of an order for specific performance. As such, it has almost exclusively applied to contracts involving land, the type of contract most often amenable to specific enforcement: see **22.03**. But there is no reason in principle why it could not apply in other contexts, provided the contract in question is capable of attracting an order for specific performance: *JC Williamson v Lukey* (1931) at 297. The doctrine requires the party seeking relief to show part performance of the contract, making it inequitable for the other party to plead the statute. But the acts alleged to constitute part performance 'must be unequivocally and of their own nature referable to some such agreement as that alleged': *Maddison v Alderson* (1883) at 479. The strictness of that requirement, which was reaffirmed by the High Court in *Pipikos v Trayans* (2018), has sometimes made the doctrine difficult to invoke: see eg *McBride v Sandland* (1918).[62] For that reason, it has become common for plaintiffs to seek relief under other equitable doctrines. For example, a claim to property may succeed on the basis of a *constructive trust*: see eg *Ogilvie v Ryan* (1976). More commonly, an undocumented promise to grant an interest in land may be enforced through the doctrines of either *promissory or proprietary estoppel*. In *Waltons Stores v Maher* (1988) at 408, 433, Mason CJ, Wilson and Brennan JJ were clear that because the plaintiffs' claim rested in equity rather than contract, any lack of writing could not be a bar. Similarly, it was on the basis of proprietary estoppel that the claim in *Riches v Hogben* (1986) succeeded: see **5.08**.[63]

5.46   Other statutes

Besides the provisions discussed above, a wide variety of other statutes require particular types of agreement to be recorded in writing, or to contain certain standard terms. For the most part, these agreements are consumer transactions, with the obligation being placed on the business party to ensure compliance. Without going into detail (given the wide variation between the

---

61   For a further example of a restitutionary claim for benefits conferred under an unenforceable contract, see *Pavey & Matthews v Paul* (1987), discussed at **24.08**.

62   Compare *Regent v Millett* (1976), where the acts concerned were found to be sufficient to meet the requirement. For a detailed treatment of the doctrine, see Dal Pont 2015a: ch 12.

63   As to what must be established to make out such a claim, when the promise is contained in a contract that is unenforceable for lack of writing, see the different views expressed in *Tipperary Developments v WA* (2009) at [21]–[24], [130]–[146].

provisions involved), they include consumer credit agreements and home building contracts.[64] However, contracts made by corporations are no longer required to be made under the company's seal, as was once the case. They may instead be entered into in the ordinary way by a person acting under the express or implied authority of the company: *Corporations Act 2001* (Cth) s 126(1).

5.47 Deeds

Whether it is required or not, writing provides valuable evidence of a contract. It does not eliminate the need for consideration. But *deeds* are different: they can be a substitute for consideration. A deed is a special form of written contract. Historically, this method of contract was characterised by great formality. A deed was required to be 'signed, sealed and delivered'. To varying degrees, these requirements have been relaxed; although a valid deed must still be witnessed.[65]

Deeds are particularly useful in situations in which the law is reluctant to find consideration. Some examples of this are discussed later in the book in the context of contractual variations: see **13.04**. Deeds are also commonly used by lawyers to embody agreements settling disputes, as noted in **3.06**. But they do have one limitation. Because of the principle that 'equity will not assist a volunteer', it may not be possible to secure an order for specific performance to enforce a gratuitous promise embodied in a deed: see **22.02**.

Where a deed is not properly executed, it may still take effect as an ordinary contract. This may be the case even where a purported deed has not been signed by one of the parties, provided there is evidence that the party in question has accepted the obligations set out in it: *Nurisvan Investment v Anyoption Holdings* (2017).

Vitiating factors

5.48 Formed contracts and vitiating factors

The grounds under which a contract might be set aside are known collectively as *vitiating factors*. Besides uncertainty, incompleteness and incapacity, which have already been considered, they are discussed in detail in subsequent chapters. Contract law makes a distinction here between void and voidable contracts. If a contract is *void*, or as it is more technically correct to say, void ab initio (from the beginning), then it never existed. The consequences are serious for third parties because property can never pass under a void contract. However, very few contracts are void. Some contracts that are illegal or contrary to public policy may be void, though generally only where a statute specifically says so: see **21.06**. Common law mistake is another example: see **18.36–18.41**.

---

64 See eg National Credit Code s 14; *Home Building Act 1989* (NSW) ss 7(1), 7AAA(2).
65 *Conveyancing Act 1919* (NSW) s 63; *Property Law Act 1958* (Vic) ss 73, 73A; *Property Law Act 1974* (Qld) ss 45, 47; *Property Law Act 1969* (WA) s 9; *Law of Property Act 1936* (SA) s 41; *Conveyancing and Law of Property Act 1884* (Tas) s 63; *Civil Law (Property) Act 2006* (ACT) s 219; *Law of Property Act 2000* (NT) ss 47, 49.

A *voidable* contract is different. It exists until it is rescinded (or 'avoided'). This means that prior to rescission property can pass under the contract. Indeed, the fact that this has happened may in some cases preclude the contract being rescinded: see **18.13**. Rescission is an equitable remedy. It puts the parties back in the position that they would have been in had they never contracted. Rescission may be granted where a contract is the product of misrepresentation, equitable mistake, duress, undue influence or unconscionability, as discussed in Chapters 18–20. At the same time, damages may also be payable, for example in the case of misrepresentation. Whether or not rescission is ordered is a matter for the court's discretion: see eg **18.12**.

6

PRELIMINARY AGREEMENTS

Introduction

6.01   The prevalence of preliminary agreements

It was noted in Chapter 5 that disputes over the formation of a contract are not as common as disagreements over the meaning, performance or termination of what is acknowledged by both parties to be a binding agreement. But when formation disputes do arise, it is surprising how often some kind of *preliminary agreement* is involved. Cases of this kind typically involve an attempt to set out the basis or framework for a transaction (or series of transactions) that is under discussion, before the parties have finalised all the details.

There are many reasons why parties may wish to do this. It may simply be to assist further negotiations, by recording what the parties have agreed on to date. It may be intended to demonstrate the parties' mutual trust and their commitment to dealing with one another. The parties may have had only limited time to reach agreement: as, for example, where a deal is struck to settle a dispute just before it is due to go before a court, or at the conclusion of a mediation process. A preliminary agreement may also have the function of providing a framework or template for further transactions that are anticipated to occur. Or its primary purpose may be to have something to show to a third party, such as a financier or a government agency, which wants or needs an indication that the parties have reached agreement.

It may be clear enough in such instances that the parties intend at some point to enter into a contract, or perhaps a series of contracts. The question is whether they have *yet* reached that point, when they stop to record what they have agreed.

6.02   The legal issues involved

The resolution of disputes over the status of a preliminary agreement generally involves the application of the principles considered in the previous chapter. In particular, a court will usually need to consider whether the agreement is intended by the parties to be legally binding; and, if it is, whether the terms are sufficiently certain and complete.[1]

There are two main reasons why the case law on preliminary agreements is discussed separately in this chapter. One is simply to draw attention to how common it is for preliminary agreements to end up being the subject of litigation – and to highlight how the pitfalls that often attend them can be avoided.[2] The other is that certain issues frequently encountered with preliminary agreements have come to generate principles and precedents that merit separate study. Two such issues are considered later in this chapter: the effect of making an agreement conditional on some further process of formalisation; and agreements to conduct further negotiations.

At this point in the book, we are concerned principally with whether a preliminary agreement may be considered legally binding as a contract – or, to put it another way, whether a party who walks away from such an agreement may be sued for breach of contract. There are also other ways for such a party to be held liable, besides the agreement being found to be a

---

1   See generally Tarrant 2006.
2   See Knowler & Stewart 2004, from which some of what follows in this chapter is taken.

contract. They may, for example, be *estopped* from denying that the agreement is binding, under the principles outlined in Chapter 7. Such an estoppel might arise if one party induced the other party to believe that a contract existed and that party has relied on that belief to their detriment: see eg *Skilled Group v CSR* (2012).[3] Conversely, one party might claim that they had been led to believe that there was *no* binding agreement and that the other party was estopped from denying that: see eg *McKenry v White* (2003). There may also be cases where conduct of either type may be found to have infringed the statutory prohibitions on misleading and deceptive conduct considered in Chapter 18.[4]

A question of intention

6.03 The form of the agreement

Preliminary agreements may, in some cases, be set out in a document titled 'heads of agreement' or a 'memorandum of understanding'. There appears to be a degree of confusion about these terms, especially in the business community. Some people automatically equate them with a lack of intention to contract, while others appear to assume exactly the opposite. There is in fact no hard and fast rule as to how terms such as 'heads of agreement' should be understood: they have no settled legal meaning. Rather, a court will look at each document in its particular context to determine what the parties must have intended. The same applies where one party sends the other a 'letter of intent'. Depending on the circumstances, this may signal or confirm an acceptance of terms offered by the other party (and hence the creation of a contract). Or it may simply indicate a desire to go ahead with a contract, which still requires some formal expression of assent.[5]

As Gleeson CJ noted in *Geebung Investments v Varga Group Investments* (1995) at 14,552:

> The fact that parties to negotiations have agreed upon the major matter under discussion, confidently believing that the remaining matters to be decided will be sorted out later between them or their lawyers, without any difficulty, can sometimes create a misleading appearance of consensus. Such parties may well believe that they have a 'deal' or a 'bargain', and speak and act accordingly, whilst at the same time knowing and intending that further and more detailed agreement is necessary. For that reason, conduct such as shaking hands, or using the language of agreement, can be ambiguous.

---

3   Cases such as *Waltons Stores v Maher* (1988) (see **7.06**) can also be regarded as examples of this. See further Silink 2011, discussing the differing views that have been taken as to the requirements to establish an estoppel in this situation.

4   Compare *Forrest v Australian Securities and Investments Commission* (2012), rejecting a claim that the defendants had misled investors into believing that they had entered into binding agreements with certain Chinese companies, when in fact the agreements were incomplete. The High Court ruled that the relevant communications would not have been understood by an ordinary reader to suggest that the agreements were necessarily enforceable in an Australian court.

5   See eg *Coogee Esplanade Surf Motel v Commonwealth* (1983), where the four judges who heard the case at trial and on appeal split 2:2 as to whether a contract had been made. The majority view on appeal was that the letter did not evidence a contract.

6.04   Ascertaining the parties' intention

In determining whether a preliminary agreement is intended to be immediately binding as a contract, a court will use the objective approach outlined in **5.02**. The parties' intention 'must be objectively ascertained from the terms of the document when read in the light of the surrounding circumstances': *GR Securities v Baulkham Hills Private Hospital* (1986) at 634–5. It is permissible for this purpose to have regard to the parties' subsequent conduct: *Australian Broadcasting Corporation v XIVth Commonwealth Games* (1988) at 547–8. In particular, if the parties have carried on negotiations, this may well show an intention not to be bound until further matters are resolved or a formal agreement is drawn up: *Sagacious Procurement v Symbion Health* (2008) at [101]–[105].

In some instances, the very nature of the transaction may suggest that no contract is intended until there is some kind of formal 'ceremony' to mark its creation. That will often involve the exchange of signed documents, as noted in **5.10**. There is no reason in principle why parties cannot intend a preliminary agreement to be binding before that happens. But if there is any doubt, it will tend to be resolved in accord with what is considered to be standard practice for the type of dealing in question. This is certainly true of contracts for the sale of land, as noted below in discussing the High Court's decision in *Masters v Cameron* (1954). But it also applies in relation to major commercial leases, as Giles JA noted in *Long v Piper* (2001) at [52]–[55]. In that case, the court held that no lease agreement had been concluded for a hotel, even though the parties had agreed on the terms and the tenant had actually taken possession. The 'commercial circumstances' here included the fact that both parties had retained solicitors, who were 'engaged in the normal conveyancing steps towards execution and registration of a formal lease' (at [51]). Since this process had not been completed, the tenant was free not to go ahead.

6.05   Completeness of terms

A further indication that no binding contract has been intended is that the parties have not yet resolved key terms. This is true even if the agreement is not legally incomplete, in the sense discussed in **5.38**. For example, in *Factory 5 v Victoria* (2012), a signed agreement indicated that a company would be appointed to sell merchandise for the 2006 Commonwealth Games in Melbourne, subject (among other things) to the parties 'reaching agreement on a legally binding Long Form Concessionaire Agreement'. The preliminary agreement was held not to be a contract, primarily because of the important matters that had not at that point been resolved during the negotiations to date.

In that case, the evidence showed that negotiations were still in progress. But where parties have apparently reached some form of (perhaps provisional) conclusion, it may be more difficult to determine the status of what they have agreed. A particularly striking example is provided by the New Zealand Court of Appeal's decision in *Fletcher Challenge Energy v Electricity Corp of New Zealand* (2002). The deal being negotiated here was for a long-term supply of gas by the plaintiff to the defendant's power station, for a total price expected to exceed NZ$1 billion. Negotiations had proceeded unsuccessfully for over a year, before a breakthrough came as a result of telephone conversations between the two companies' chief executives. Over the next two days, senior officials from the companies met to thrash out a deal, with their respective lawyers excluded from the process. The outcome was a four-page heads of agreement. This appeared to settle all essential terms and allowed the parties to go ahead with a related transaction. But the document was later ruled by a majority of the Court (at 450) to be no more than 'an important staging post on the way to final agreement'. Since no final sale and purchase agreement was ever concluded, this allowed the defendant to walk away from the deal. An important reason for reaching this conclusion was that two clauses in the heads of agreement had been marked 'not agreed'. Yet, as Thomas J pointed out (at 463) in his dissenting judgment, the majority did not regard the absence of consensus on these matters as rendering the agreement either incomplete or uncertain. Had the parties simply deleted the clauses in question, as their lawyers would likely have done had they been in the room, the result may have been different.[6]

6.06 *Masters v Cameron*

As should be clear from the discussion so far, many of the cases on preliminary agreements involve situations in which the parties contemplate a further process of formalisation. One conceptual framework often used to help analyse the various possibilities was set out by the High Court in *Masters v Cameron* (1954) at 360:

> Where parties who have been in negotiation reach agreement upon terms of a contractual nature and also agree that the matter of their negotiation shall be dealt with by a formal contract, the case may belong to any of three cases. It may be one in which the parties have reached finality in arranging all the terms of their bargain and intend to be immediately bound to the performance of those terms, but at the same time propose to have the terms restated in a form which will be fuller or more precise but not different in effect. Or, secondly, it may be a case in which the parties have completely agreed upon all the terms of their bargain and intend no departure from or addition to that which their agreed terms express or imply, but nevertheless have made performance of one or more of the terms conditional upon the execution of a formal document. Or, thirdly, the case may be one in which the intention of the parties is not to make a concluded bargain at all, unless and until they execute a formal contract.

The *first category* identified here covers situations where the agreement is intended to take immediate effect as a contract, whether or not a formal document is ever drafted and signed. In *Stirnemann v Kaza Investments* (2011), for example, the parties had been negotiating a contract for the sale of land. Over the course of two days, there was an exchange of faxes that appeared to resolve all the essential matters. The last of these indicated that the purchaser would 'arrange for further necessary paperwork to be prepared by a lawyer'. It was held that these communications evidenced an immediate intention to be bound. There was no suggestion that any of the agreed terms were to be renegotiated or varied.

The *second category* also involves a binding contract being formed right away. The difference is that until formal terms are drawn up and signed, no further performance may be required. But if one party seeks to resile from the agreement, an order for specific performance may be granted requiring them to execute the necessary document: see eg

---

6   See further McLauchlan 2002, criticising the majority's decision on this and other grounds.

Niesmann v Collingridge (1921). On a conventional view of both this and the first category, the final version of the contract is not meant to contain new terms. But an exception is made where the person preparing it has been authorised to flesh out the original agreement by dealing with incidental matters in a reasonable way: see eg *Godecke v Kirwan* (1973), where this was expressly envisaged by the parties (see **6.08**).

In the *third category*, there is no contract unless and until the agreement is formalised, meaning that either party is free to walk away from the deal prior to that point. This is what was found to be the case in *Masters v Cameron*. A contract for the sale of land was expressed by the vendor to be 'subject to the preparation of a formal contract of sale which shall be acceptable to my solicitors'. Language of this kind, including the pithier phrase 'subject to contract', has long been understood by conveyancers to mean that a contract will only arise when the formal terms are executed.[7] In *Stirnemann*, discussed above, it was the *absence* of such words that helped persuade the court that the arrangement negotiated by fax was to be immediately binding.

In recent decades, it has become customary for courts to suggest that there is a *fourth category*. This is said to cover the situation where parties intend to be bound immediately by the terms they have agreed, but expect to make a subsequent contract in lieu of the first one which will, by consent, contain additional terms: see eg *Baulkham Hills Private Hospital v G R Securities* (1986) at 628; *Anaconda Nickel v Tarmoola* (2000); *Lucke v Cleary* (2011). What is said to differentiate this category from either the first or the second is that the parties contemplate the possibility of the formalised agreement differing in substance and not merely detail from the preliminary agreement. The idea has prompted a lively academic debate as to the need for a fourth category – or indeed whether there should just be two, covering those cases in which there either is a binding contract or is not.[8] In any event, as Beazley P noted in *Pavlovic v Universal Music* (2015) at [69], 'the *Masters v Cameron* classifications are no longer, if ever they were, applied as strict categories'. The key question will always be: what was it that the parties reasonably appear to have intended?

6.07 Express declarations of intent

The obvious way to avoid any uncertainty as to whether there is an immediate intention to contract is to address the matter expressly. If it is explicitly stated that an arrangement is not to be treated as contractually binding, either at all or until some further step is taken, this will generally be respected by the courts: see **5.04**. Likewise, parties can make it clear that a preliminary agreement *is* intended to constitute a contract. For example, in *LMI v Baulderstone Hornibrook* (2001), the enforceability of an agreement was upheld on the basis of this express provision: 'If any of the Bids are successful the parties intend to enter into a more formal Facility Management Agreement, but, in the meantime intend this Heads of Agreement to be

---

7   Historically, the use of such provisions to defer the creation of a contract for the sale of land has been more common in some States than in others: see eg Moore et al 2016: [8.275], comparing New South Wales with South Australia in this respect. Note also that the common law position described here may be affected by statutory regulation: ibid, [8.275]–[8.335]. This commonly allows a purchaser of land for residential purposes a 'cooling off' period of several days, during which they can withdraw even from a binding contract: see eg *Conveyancing Act 1919* (NSW) ss 66R–66X.

8   See eg McLauchlan 2005b; Tolhurst et al 2011.

legally binding.'[9] It is still possible that a preliminary agreement that contains such a declaration may be found to be too uncertain or incomplete: see eg *Coal Cliff Collieries v Sijehama* (1991), discussed below at **6.09**. But at least the parties' intention will be clear.[10]

The question may be posed then: why not *always* include a declaration of intent in any preliminary agreement, to avoid any doubt? Sometimes, the failure to do just that will be a mistake. But on other occasions, there may be good commercial reasons for not taking that course. These might include a belief that if the issue of legal enforceability is pressed too hard, or even raised at all, it may effectively destroy the prospects of reaching final agreement. Sometimes in business it is necessary to strike while the iron is hot and not sit around worrying about the legal niceties. And sometimes a deal is so finely balanced, or a relationship so fragile, that it is better to 'fudge' the question of whether a binding contract has been concluded. This is especially true in the context of negotiations to resolve a dispute. The parties or their representatives may feel that it is enough to have thrashed out the main points of settlement and that merely discussing its legal status may be a risky move. The price to be paid, however, is uncertainty as to whether one party can renege before a formal agreement is drawn up. The frequency with which this issue comes before the courts certainly attests to the scale of that risk.[11]

Agreements to negotiate

6.08   Agreements to agree

As noted in **5.36**, parties cannot validly leave matters in a contract for further agreement. If the matter in question is peripheral to the main subject of the transaction, it may be possible to sever the offending provision and enforce the rest of the contract: see eg *David Jones v Lunn* (1969). Partial enforcement may also be feasible in the case of a framework agreement where the parties have fully agreed on the terms for some transactions, but not others: see eg *Mushroom Composters v IS & DE Robertson* (2015). But otherwise the contract will be void for uncertainty.[12] So, for example, in *May & Butcher Ltd v The King* (1934), a contract for the purchase of tents at a price 'to be agreed' was held not to be enforceable. Had the parties said nothing at all about price, a term might have been implied that a reasonable sum be paid: see **5.38**. But that could not happen here because, the House of Lords held, it would have been inconsistent with the parties' explicit intention to defer agreement on the matter.

---

9   See also *Anaconda Nickel v Tarmoola* (2000) (description of heads of agreement as 'an agreement in itself' taken to indicate an intention that it be enforceable); *Malago v AW Ellis Engineering* (2012) (clause referred to 'the binding nature of these Heads of Agreement').

10   Compare *Nurisvan Investment v Anyoption Holdings* (2017), concerning what was described as a legally binding heads of agreement relating to the sale of shares in a company. Although this was found to be a contract, it was no more than an agreement to negotiate in good faith to finalise the terms of the sale. As such, it was not a contract for the sale of the shares that could be enforced by an order for specific performance.

11   See eg the case law surveyed in Spencer 2015; and see also *Lucke v Cleary* (2011); *Grave v Blazevic Holdings* (2012); *Pavlovic v Universal Music* (2015); *Queensland Phosphate v Korda* (2017).

12   Compare McLauchlan 1998, challenging the strictness of this view, while accepting that the deferral of agreement over certain matters may indicate an intention not to be bound.

It is different, as also pointed out in Chapter 5, if the parties have provided a mechanism for resolving the terms of their agreement. This may involve nominating an arbitrator to break any deadlock between the parties: see eg *Booker Industries v Wilson Parking* (1982). Or the parties may agree that non-essential matters can be settled by one of them. In *Godecke v Kirwan* (1973), a purchaser agreed to sign a formal contract drawn up by the vendor's solicitors, containing the terms already agreed and 'such other covenants and conditions as they may reasonably require'. The imposition of a requirement to act reasonably is sufficient in such a case to avoid any argument that the contract is illusory: see **5.35**.

6.09   Agreements to negotiate in good faith

If an agreement to leave certain matters to further negotiation is too uncertain to be enforced, does it matter that the parties agree to do so in good faith? In *Walford v Miles* (1992), the House of Lords thought not, treating such a commitment as just an illusory agreement to agree.

In Australia, however, a different view has been taken since the decision of the New South Wales Court of Appeal in *Coal Cliff Collieries v Sijehama* (1991). The heads of agreement for a mining venture contained a commitment that the parties would 'forthwith proceed in good faith to consult together upon the formulation of a more comprehensive and detailed joint venture agreement'. The document made clear that 'the actions of the parties in so consulting and in negotiating on fresh or additional terms shall not in the meantime in any way prejudice the full and binding effect of what is now agreed'. When three years of negotiations failed to result in agreement, one of the parties withdrew. The other party's action for breach of contract failed, on the basis that the agreement was too uncertain to be enforced. The venture was a complex one and would ordinarily call for a lengthy and very detailed contract. As Kirby P noted (at 27), 'a court would be extremely ill-equipped to fill the remaining blank spaces . . . How mining executives, attending to the interests of their corporation and its shareholders might act in negotiating such a complex transaction is quite unknowable.'[13]

Nevertheless, a majority of the Court accepted as a matter of principle that a promise to negotiate in good faith may be enforceable. Kirby P argued that to universally reject terms of this sort was to disregard the intentions of the parties and interfere with their freedom of contract. Handley JA dissented on the basis that it was impossible for a court to determine the content of an obligation to negotiate in good faith and whether it was breached. The difference between the two positions may not be very great in practice. Kirby P conceded it would be difficult to breach an obligation of good faith because such contracts will necessarily contemplate that negotiations might come to nothing.

Still, in the wake of this decision, there have been a number of cases in which courts have been willing to treat promises of this kind as enforceable. In *United Group Rail Services v Rail Corporation* (2009), the commitment was to undertake 'genuine and good faith negotiations'

---

13   For a further example of such a view, see *Baldwin v Icon Energy* (2016), where a memorandum of understanding requiring the use of reasonable endeavours to negotiate a gas supply agreement was held to be unenforceable. Compare Paterson 1996: 129–130, challenging this sort of reasoning and arguing that whether a commitment to negotiate in good faith should be considered enforceable should not necessarily depend on the complexity of the matters involved or the court's ability to 'complete' the agreement.

to resolve any disputes arising under a contract for the design and building of rolling stock for a rail operator. In contrast to the open-ended nature of the negotiations called for in *Coal Cliff Collieries*, it was far easier to determine what was involved here. As Allsop P put it (at [71]), the clause would simply require an 'honest and genuine' approach, rooted in a commitment or 'fidelity' to the bargain that the parties had made.[14]

The possibilities here are demonstrated by *Masters Home Improvement v North East Solution* (2017). It was agreed that the plaintiff would develop a home improvement store for Woolworths and then lease it to a related company. The agreement could be terminated if the parties, acting reasonably and in good faith, were unable to resolve any disagreement that arose in relation to certain costs. Woolworths purported to terminate on this basis, but were found at trial to have breached its commitment to negotiate in good faith. Among other things, it had failed to communicate properly with the plaintiff, including by disclosing relevant information. An award of over $10 million in damages was made in favour of the plaintiff. The decision was overturned on appeal, because of errors in the trial judge's factual findings. But it was accepted that the relevant provision imposed an enforceable obligation.[15]

Perhaps the strongest argument for allowing agreements to negotiate in good faith to stand is that they reflect what the parties intend. After all, these cases generally concern legally advised commercial parties. Such an approach fits with the way that the courts generally strive to uphold agreements between commercial parties where possible, rather than striking them down as uncertain: see **5.37**.

---

14   As will be discussed in **12.22**, this same approach has been applied by Allsop P and some other judges to the question of recognising and applying what is suggested to be an implied obligation to perform contracts in good faith.

15   See also *Reading Properties v Mackie Group* (2012), where a 'negotiation agreement' for a land development required the parties to negotiate in good faith. It was also provided that if either party withdrew from the negotiations in certain circumstances, one party would pay the other $1 million. The agreement was assumed without argument to be enforceable, with the litigation focusing on the proper interpretation of the payment clause.

7

PROTECTING RELIANCE: THE DOCTRINE OF ESTOPPEL

7.01   Introduction

This chapter explains the concept of *estoppel* and how it can be used to affect the scope and enforcement of contractual obligations. As we will see, both from what follows and from later parts of the book, estoppel may be used in many different ways. For instance, a person may plead an estoppel in order to:

- enforce a promise made for their benefit under a contract to which they are not a party (see **8.17**);
- hold another party to a contract to an assurance that is not formally a term of the contract (see **9.15**, **18.04**);
- enforce a promise by one party to modify the obligations under a contract, despite the absence of any consideration for that variation (see **13.16**); or
- prevent another party from terminating a contract in the face of an indication that they would not do that: see eg *Legione v Hateley* (1983), discussed in **7.07**.

The reason for dealing with estoppel at this point in the book, however, concerns two other uses, which are perhaps more striking. One is to enforce a gratuitous promise that could not be the subject of a contract, because of the absence of any consideration from the promisee. The other is to hold a person to an assurance that they will agree to a contract, despite the contract never actually being formed. In these instances, estoppel is effectively acting as an alternative to the law of contract.

In most, if not all, of the situations just mentioned, the type of estoppel being invoked will be *equitable* in nature. But this is not true of all forms of estoppel. Hence, before saying more about the two forms of equitable estoppel that are typically recognised today, it makes sense first to explain the nature of estoppel and its various categories.

Nature and types of estoppel

7.02   What is estoppel?

An estoppel arises where A successfully claims that B should be *estopped* (prevented) from putting a particular argument in legal proceedings. To 'raise' (establish) the estoppel, A must show that: (1) B has created or helped to create a particular belief or assumption by A about a relevant matter; (2) A has acted in reliance on that assumption; and (3) it would now be unjust for B to be permitted to question or act inconsistently with the assumption.

There has long been a distinction between common law and equitable forms of estoppel. *Common law estoppel* is said to operate only upon assumptions or representations that relate to matters of *existing fact*: see eg *Low v Bouverie* (1891). As such, a common law estoppel is merely a rule of evidence which precludes a party's denial of certain facts. Its role is limited to the establishment of the facts upon which the parties' legal rights are to be decided. It creates no substantive rights as such. *Equitable estoppel,* by contrast, can relate to assumptions or promises as to what will happen in the future. It can be used to determine the parties' respective rights and obligations.[1]

---

1   On the distinction between the 'substantive' equitable estoppels and the 'procedural' common law estoppels, see Swadling 2016: 18–21.

Estoppel may be deployed defensively, to prevent a party from asserting a legal right or invoking a defence that would otherwise be available. It can also, at least in its equitable forms, operate positively to enable a party to assert rights against the estopped party that the first party would not otherwise have had.

7.03   Categories of estoppel

There are three main categories of *common law estoppel*:

* *estoppel by deed*, which precludes certain challenges to an assertion or allegation of fact that the estopped party has made in a deed;
* *estoppel by judgment* (or *by record*), which in its various forms (including cause of action estoppel, issue estoppel and *Anshun* estoppel) seeks to prevent the litigation of matters that either have already or could have been resolved in earlier proceedings;[2] and
* *estoppel by conduct* (or *in pais*), which can be used to prevent a party from acting inconsistently with an assumption which they have either induced the other party to accept (*estoppel by representation*), or which the two parties have jointly adopted as the basis for their dealings (*estoppel by convention*).[3]

Historically, there were considered to be two distinct species of *equitable estoppel*. The older of these, *proprietary estoppel*, allowed a person who had been led to believe that they would be granted an interest in land to seek an order that it be conveyed to them, where they had either been encouraged or allowed to build on or otherwise improve that land.[4] The more general doctrine of *promissory estoppel*, concerning promises as to the creation or enforcement of rights that might or might not concern property, emerged in the late nineteenth century but was not refined until more recently, as explained below.[5]

In *Waltons Stores v Maher* (1988), a majority of the High Court effectively brought together promissory and proprietary estoppel to create a single, broader doctrine of equitable estoppel. The 'common thread' between the two species was said by Mason CJ and Wilson J (at 404) to be the idea that where A has acted to their detriment on an assumption induced by B, equity may come to A's aid on the ground that it would be unconscionable for B to ignore the assumption. Brennan J observed (at 420) that:

---

2   See *Tomlinson v Ramsey Food Processing* (2015) at [22], noting among other things the relationship between the first of these forms and the common law principle of *res judicata*.

3   For a detailed discussion of the common law forms of estoppel by conduct, see Handley 2016: chs 2–5, 8. For an example of estoppel by convention, see *Mineralogy v Sino Iron* (2017).

4   Where the plaintiff was actively induced to improve the land, they could plead *estoppel by encouragement*: see eg *Dillwyn v Llewelyn* (1862). *Estoppel by acquiescence* was adopted for cases in which the owner of land passively (but knowingly) stood by and allowed the plaintiff to incur expense, in the belief the land would be theirs: see eg *Ramsden v Dyson* (1866).

5   Although, it has been argued that an earlier line of equity cases provides authority for the view that representations as to future conduct (that is, promises) could give rise to an estoppel. The basis of these cases was said to be that to resile from the representation would be to commit a fraud on the representee: see Lunney 1994: 569.

> If cases of equitable estoppel are in truth but particular instances of the operation of the general principles of equity, there is little purpose in dividing those cases into the categories of promissory and proprietary estoppel which are not necessarily exhaustive of the cases in which equity will intervene ...

Nonetheless, he added (ibid), the 'familiar categories' of promissory estoppel and proprietary estoppel retained some value in identifying 'the characteristics of the circumstances which have been held to give rise to an equity in the party raising the estoppel'.

Consistently with the notion of a unified doctrine of equitable estoppel, both species share the same general requirements. Both operate as a cause of action and may apply even in the absence of any pre-existing legal relationship. As noted below, however, some small points of difference may remain. Recent High Court decisions have continued to maintain a formal distinction between the two categories, while emphasising their close connection: see eg *Sidhu v Van Dyke* (2014) at [1]; *Crown Melbourne v Cosmopolitan Hotel* (2016) at [139], [217].

In *Waltons Stores*, Deane J advocated (at 451) a more ambitious unification of equitable estoppel with common law estoppel to create a general doctrine of estoppel by conduct.[6] The suggestion has generated spirited academic debate.[7] But it is yet to be taken up by the courts.

Using equitable estoppel to enforce express or implied promises or assurances

7.04   The development of promissory estoppel

As discussed above, the common law doctrines of estoppel by conduct are confined to representations of existing fact. This is a result of the House of Lords decision in *Jorden v Money* (1854), which sought to ensure that the enforcement of a promise or representation as to future conduct remained the sole province of contract law, with its attendant requirement of consideration. *Jorden v Money* originally confined both common law and equitable estoppel in this way.[8] However, in time, two exceptions came to be recognised in equity. The first was the doctrine of proprietary estoppel, which as noted above operated in respect of induced assumptions concerning interests in land.[9] There was no difficulty in proprietary estoppel operating to found a cause of action and a pre-existing legal relationship was not required. The second exception to *Jorden v Money* had its origins in the principle expounded by Lord Cairns in *Hughes v Metropolitan Railway* (1877) at 448, that:

---

6   See further *Foran v Wight* (1989) at 435; *Commonwealth v Verwayen* (1990) at 413, 440.

7   See eg Bant & Bryan 2015; Hudson 2017.

8   There had previously been a well-established equitable jurisdiction to 'make representations good': see Dawson 1982; Finn 1985.

9   There has been support in England for the view that proprietary estoppel can extend to promises relating to interests in forms of property other than land: see eg *Western Fish Products v Penwith District Council* (1981).

> If parties who have entered into definite and distinct terms involving certain legal results ... afterwards by their own act or with their own consent enter upon a course of negotiation which has the effect of leading one of the parties to suppose that the strict rights arising under the contract will not be enforced, or will be kept in suspense, or held in abeyance, the person who otherwise might have enforced those rights will not be allowed to enforce them where it would be inequitable having regard to the dealings which have thus taken place between the parties.

This was seized upon by Denning J in *Central London Property Trust v High Trees House* (1947) as the basis for the modern doctrine of promissory estoppel. He saw (at 134) this type of estoppel as operating where:

> A promise was made which was intended to create legal relations and which, to the knowledge of the person making the promise, was going to be acted on by the person making the promise, and which was in fact so acted on.

The case involved a lease of a block of flats in London entered into in September 1937. With the outbreak of the Second World War in 1939, only a few of the flats were let and the defendant lessee struggled to pay the rent. In early 1940, the plaintiff lessor agreed to accept a reduced ground rent, although the period for which that reduction was to apply was not specified. On 21 September 1945, with the war over and the flats now fully let, the receiver of the plaintiff company wrote to the defendant demanding that full rent be paid for the future and claiming arrears of rent for past periods. 'Friendly proceedings' were subsequently instituted to test the legal position as to the rent payable. The claim was for the difference between the full rent and the reduced rent for the last two quarters of 1945. Denning J concluded that the promise of reduced rent had been understood by the parties to apply only while the conditions operating at the time of the promise prevailed. Since the block had been fully let from early 1945, the reduction ceased to apply from that date. The receiver's claim therefore succeeded. However, Denning J noted that the doctrine of promissory estoppel would have prevented the plaintiff from claiming the full rent for the periods prior to early 1945.

In an attempt to pre-empt objections that it was being used as an alternative to the law of contract, and hence undermining it, the English doctrine of promissory estoppel was confined to operating defensively and in situations involving pre-existing legal relationships. Unlike proprietary estoppel, promissory estoppel could not be used to found a cause of action. It must be a 'shield not a sword': *Combe v Combe* (1951) at 224.[10] This 'confined' doctrine of promissory estoppel was accepted by the Australian High Court in *Legione v Hateley* (1983). It was not long, though, before it was released from its shackles and consolidated with proprietary estoppel in the landmark case of *Waltons Stores v Maher* (1988). In developing a far broader doctrine of estoppel, Australian law has clearly diverged significantly from its English roots. As such, the English estoppel authorities are no longer directly relevant to the Australian context.

---

10 As McKendrick (2017: 106) has commented, it has never been convincingly explained why, in English law, detrimental reliance upon a promise relating to an interest in property can found a cause of action but detrimental reliance upon any other promise does not.

7.05   The elements of equitable estoppel

In *Waltons Stores*, Brennan J formulated the elements of equitable estoppel as follows (at 428–9):

(1)   the plaintiff assumed that a particular legal relationship then existed between the plaintiff and the defendant or expected that a particular legal relationship would exist between them and, in the latter case, that the defendant would not be free to withdraw from the expected legal relationship;

(2)   the defendant has induced the plaintiff to adopt this assumption or expectation;

(3)   the plaintiff acts or abstains from acting in reliance on the assumption or expectation;

(4)   the defendant knew or intended him [sic] to do so;

(5)   the plaintiff's action or inaction will occasion detriment if the assumption or expectation is not fulfilled; and

(6)   the defendant has failed to act to avoid that detriment whether by fulfilling the assumption or expectation or otherwise.

Although neither definitive nor exhaustive,[11] this much quoted formulation provides a convenient starting point and structure for discussion.

7.06   Assumption or expectation

Equitable estoppel, as already explained, operates in respect of assumptions as to future conduct, whereas common law estoppel is confined to matters of present fact. The distinction is illustrated by the facts of *Waltons Stores* itself. Waltons had been negotiating for a lease of land owned by Mr and Mrs Maher. The proposed lease agreement involved the Mahers demolishing an existing building and constructing a new one for the purposes of a store Waltons planned to operate. A draft lease having been produced, Waltons' solicitors indicated on 7 November 1983 that they had received verbal instructions that certain proposed amendments were acceptable to their client, but would inform the Mahers' solicitors the next day if this were not the case. Having received no communication, the Mahers' solicitors forwarded Waltons' solicitors a signed amended lease for execution on 11 November. Given the urgency of the construction work, the Mahers began demolishing the existing building. On 21 November, Waltons began to have second thoughts about proceeding with the lease and instructed its solicitors to 'go slow'. Despite knowing (from 10 December) that demolition work had commenced, it simply retained the copy of the lease and remained silent. It was not until 19 January 1984 that Waltons indicated that it did not intend to proceed with the lease. By that stage, the Mahers had completed 40 per cent of the building work contemplated by the agreement.

The High Court held that, despite the absence of a formal exchange of contract, Waltons was estopped from denying the existence of a binding contract. Gaudron and Deane JJ found an assumption of existing fact (that the exchange had taken place). By contrast, Mason CJ and

---

11   As to the importance of not 'mechanically' applying the six requirements, see eg *Doueihi v Construction Technologies* (2016) at [166].

Wilson J, along with Brennan J, decided the case on the basis of an equitable estoppel built on the Mahers' assumption that the lease *would* be executed (an assumption as to future conduct).[12]

There is some doubt as to whether the assumption must relate to an *existing or expected legal relationship*, as Brennan J's formulation above might suggest. On that basis, estoppel would not be available in the simple situation of a gratuitous promise by A to pay B a sum of money. In the proprietary estoppel cases, by contrast, the absence of an expectation of a legal relationship had never been considered an impediment. In *Austotel v Franklins Selfserve* (1989) at 610, Priestley JA accommodated these cases within the much broader formulation of the creation or encouragement of 'an assumption that a contract will come into existence or *a promise be performed* or *an interest granted* to the plaintiff by the defendant' (emphasis added).[13]

It has been insisted in some New South Wales Court of Appeal decisions that this broader formulation is true only of proprietary estoppel. Promissory estoppel, it has been claimed, operates as 'a restraint on the enforcement of rights, and thus, unlike a proprietary estoppel, it must be negative in substance': *Saleh v Romanous* (2010) at [74]; and see also *DHJPM v Blackthorn Resources* (2011) at [47]. As a differently constituted bench of that court acknowledged in *Ashton v Pratt* (2015) at [138], there have been many judicial observations that are inconsistent with such a limitation, not least in *Waltons*. Although the Court did not see the need to resolve the controversy, the better view is that both proprietary *and* promissory estoppel can operate positively to create rights, even where the parties had not envisaged creating a contract or other legal relationship.[14]

7.07 Inducement

Brennan J's formulation in *Waltons Stores* requires that the plaintiff was *induced* to adopt the assumption or expectation by the defendant, but makes no reference to any *representation* on the part of the defendant. A 'clear and unequivocal' representation was a requirement of the earlier case law on promissory estoppel.[15] In *Legione v Hateley* (1983), the plaintiffs had been served with a notice requiring payment of the balance of the purchase price due under a contract for the sale of land within 14 days. Their solicitors informed an employee of the vendors' solicitors that the plaintiffs had now arranged finance and would be in a position to settle the transaction, albeit on a date after expiry of the period. The employee responded: 'I think that'll be all right but I'll have to get instructions'. A majority of the High Court held that this was too equivocal to amount to a representation that the vendors would extend the time for settlement to the relevant date. However, the requirement of a clear and unequivocal representation did not mean that an *express* representation was required or that the representation had to be clear *in its entirety*. As Mason and Deane JJ explained (at 438–9):

---

12   Deane J concluded that there were assumptions of both existing fact *and* future conduct.
13   See also *Doueihi v Construction Technologies* (2016).
14   See Robertson 2013.
15   See *Low v Bouverie* (1891); *Woodhouse AC Israel Cocoa v Nigerian Produce Marketing* (1972).

> Such a clear representation may properly be seen as implied by the words used or to be
> adduced from either failure to speak where there was a duty to speak or from conduct . . .
> It will suffice if so much of the representation as is necessary to found the propounded
> estoppel satisfies the requirement. Thus, a representation that a particular right will not be
> asserted for at least x days is not rendered equivocal merely because the words used are
> equivocal as to whether the relevant period is x days, x plus one day or x plus two days.

In *Waltons Stores*, for example, no express representation had been made that the lease would
be executed, but a promise to do so could be implied from Waltons' inaction and silence.

The question has arisen whether a representation that is too vague, ambiguous or imprecise to give rise to a contract can nonetheless found an estoppel. In *Woodhouse Israel Cocoa v
Nigerian Produce Marketing* (1972) at 757, Lord Hailsham stressed the importance of the
requirement that the representation be clear and unequivocal and the need for coherence with
the law of contract. He shared Lord Denning's incredulity at the idea that a 'letter which is not
sufficient to *vary* a contract is, nevertheless, sufficient to work an *estoppel* – which will have the
same effect as a *variation*': see *Woodhouse Israel Cocoa* at 757. A number of Australian
courts have nonetheless held that a degree of uncertainty and vagueness fatal to the formation
of a valid contract can still found an estoppel: see eg *Flinn v Flinn* (1999); *Tadrous v
Tadrous* (2012).

The High Court recently considered the issue in *Crown Melbourne v Cosmopolitan Hotel*
(2016). At the heart of the case was a statement made by a landlord in the course of
negotiations for a five year lease of restaurant premises. The landlord's employee had told
the tenant that, despite the absence of any option for renewal in the lease currently under
negotiation, the tenant would be 'looked after at renewal time'. When the landlord later refused
to renew the lease, the tenant sought to recover its refurbishment costs through claims either
for breach of a collateral contract (see **9.16**) or in estoppel. The estoppel claim failed because
the tenant's assumption (that the lease would be renewed *on the same terms as the original
lease*) did not correspond with the objective meaning of the landlord's statement, as found at
first instance. That had been that the lease would be renewed for a further period of five years
on terms at the landlord's own discretion. Hence, it could not be said that the landlord had
induced the assumption. Nonetheless, the decision contains some important (though conflicting) observations on the question of the requisite degree of clarity and certainty of the
representation.

Dealing with the case as one based on promissory estoppel, French CJ, Kiefel and Bell JJ
considered the statement that the tenants would be 'looked after at renewal time' to be
incapable of conveying to a reasonable person that the tenants would be offered a further
lease. Keane J echoed (at [143]) Lord Hailsham's comments on the need for coherence
between promissory estoppel and the law of contract. Characterising promissory estoppel as
operating 'in relation to contracts', he stressed the importance of commercial certainty in this
context. In contrast, concerns about coherence with the law of contract and commercial
certainty did not arise in proprietary estoppel, which he described (at [145]) as 'concerned
with the recognition of interests in property by way of relief against unconscionable conduct'.
He was therefore happy to countenance a lower standard of certainty and clarity than that
required by the law of contract, though only in proprietary estoppel cases. Nonetheless, even if
the case were characterised as one of proprietary (as opposed to promissory) estoppel, he too

considered the statement to be incapable of bearing the meaning that an interest in land would be granted.

Nettle J, in contrast, had no difficulty with the idea of a representation that was too ambiguous or equivocal to form a binding contract nonetheless founding a promissory estoppel. In his view, this was just one, albeit important, factor to be considered in determining the broader question of whether and to what extent the assumption or expectation can fairly and reasonably be attributed to the representation.[16] He explained that the foundational question – is it unconscionable for the defendant to depart from an assumption or expectation created in the mind of the plaintiff? – is always highly context-dependent. As such, the requisite degree of certainty necessarily varies according to the relationship in question and the particular circumstances of the case. It follows that far less in the way of certainty and clarity may be required, for example, in the context of dealings between family members than in those between experienced commercial parties.[17]

7.08   Reliance

The requirement that the party seeking to plead equitable estoppel must have acted or abstained from acting *in reliance* on the relevant assumption or expectation involves establishing a causal connection between their conduct and the assumption or expectation. The burden of proof on this issue was considered by the High Court in *Sidhu v Van Dyke* (2014). The case involved assurances, in the course of a sexual relationship, that Mr Sidhu would (subject to certain conditions) transfer to Ms Van Dyke the cottage in which she then resided. At first instance, Ward J found Van Dyke's evidence 'equivocal' on the question of whether she would have acted differently if the promise had not been made. Her claim, accordingly, failed. The New South Wales Court of Appeal allowed her appeal on the basis that where inducement can be inferred from the promisee's conduct, the burden shifts to the promisor to show that the promisee did not rely on the promise.

On a further appeal, the High Court rejected any such presumption of reliance. According to French CJ, Kiefel, Bell and Keane JJ (at [58]), reliance was too fundamental to the doctrine of estoppel to be 'imputed on the basis of evidence which falls short of proof of the fact'. It was this element that answered concerns that equitable estoppel not be allowed to outflank *Jorden v Money*. The judges reiterated that it was the *promisor's responsibility for the promisee's reliance*, rather than the breach of the promise itself, that made it unconscionable to resile from the promise. Statements in earlier decisions about the drawing of a 'prima facie inference of reliance', where the natural consequence of the assumption is the action or inaction alleged by the relying party,[18] were to be read as involving no more than an inference of fact. However, the assumption or expectation need not be the *sole* reason for the relying party's action or inaction. It is sufficient if it is a 'contributing cause': *Sidhu* at [71]–[73]. Unusually, after

---

16   This relates to the point made in *Commonwealth Bank v Carotino* (2011) at [145] that 'it must be reasonable for the [relying party] to adopt the assumption in question on the strength of the representation made'.

17   But compare *Doueihi v Construction Technologies* (2016) at [173]–[178], rejecting the suggestion that a clear distinction should be drawn between the operation of equitable estoppel in 'arms-length/ commercial cases' and 'domestic/family cases'.

18   See eg *Newbon v City Mutual Life* (1935) at 735.

reviewing the whole of the evidence in the case, the High Court departed from the view of the facts taken at first instance and concluded that Van Dyke had made out a compelling case of detrimental reliance.[19]

Reliance on the assumption or expectation is not necessarily sufficient in itself. There have been statements that the relevant action (or inaction) of the relying party must also be reasonable: see eg *Standard Chartered Bank v Bank of China* (1991) at 180; *Commonwealth Bank v Carotino* (2011) at [145]. In *Sidhu,* Van Dyke had allegedly relied upon the expectation in three ways: carrying out works on the cottage and the land on which it was situated, refraining from looking for full time employment, and refraining from seeking a property settlement in divorce proceedings with her former husband. At first instance, Ward J accepted that Van Dyke had, in fact, relied on the expectation in the third way (but not the first two). However, the transfer of the cottage was necessarily dependent upon the ultimate subdivision of the land, which involved circumstances beyond Sidhu's control. These included the obtaining of planning approval, finance and the consent of Sidhu's wife or the arising of circumstances making such consent unnecessary. In these circumstances, Ward J did not find it 'objectively reasonable' for Van Dyke to refrain from seeking a property settlement. On appeal, the New South Wales Court of Appeal disagreed with this conclusion and this aspect of the decision was not challenged before the High Court.

Courts are generally reluctant to accept that it is reasonable for a negotiating party to rely on the expectation that a contract *will* be concluded. This is evident even in 'subject to contract' cases (se **6.06**), in which the terms of the contract have been fully settled: see eg *Attorney-General of Hong Kong v Humphreys Estate* (1987); although *Waltons Stores* is a notable exception to this. The reluctance is even greater where the full terms of the anticipated contract are yet to be worked out: see eg *Austotel v Franklins Selfserve* (1989); *DHJPM v Blackthorn Resources* (2011). While they are not precluded from establishing an estoppel, it can be an uphill struggle for a well-resourced, experienced commercial party – which can be expected to look after its own interests – to persuade the court that its reliance was reasonable in this type of situation, or that it would be unconscionable for the other party to exercise its right not to go ahead and reach agreement. It may be different, however, where the parties are negotiating for an arrangement that was never likely to be formalised: see eg *Doueihi v Construction Technologies* (2016).

7.09 Detriment

In *Thompson v Palmer* (1933) at 547, Dixon J explained the requirement of detriment in terms of the relying party taking up 'a position of material disadvantage' as a result of adopting the relevant assumption or expectation. Detriment is based on the notion of reliance loss: that is, the idea that the plaintiff has been made worse off in some way as a result of relying on the assumption. It is *not* the expectation loss that flows from the non-performance of the promise: see *Delaforce v Simpson-Cook* (2010) at [41]–[42].[20]

Detriment is a broad notion. Some of the most common examples in the case law are financial expenditure, the expenditure of other resources (including time and effort), and the

---

19   The issue of detriment is dealt with below.
20   On the difference between reliance loss and expectation loss, see **23.06**.

foregoing of other opportunities. In *Commonwealth v Verwayen* (1990), the Commonwealth represented that it would not plead certain defences available to it in a personal injuries action commenced by Mr Verwayen. A majority of a seven-judge High Court held that the Commonwealth was precluded from pleading the defences in question. Gaudron and Toohey JJ found for Verwayen on the basis of the doctrine of waiver (see **13.18**); Deane and Dawson JJ on the basis of estoppel. Significantly, all judges who based their decision on estoppel[21] recognised that the exacerbation of illness, anxiety and stress and inconvenience that Verwayen claimed to have suffered by continuing with the action in reliance on the Commonwealth's representation was capable of amounting to detriment.

Detriment need not involve a disadvantage capable of quantification in the same way as an award of damages: *Ashton v Pratt* (2015) at [147]. But it must be 'significant' (*Verwayen* (at 444)), 'substantial' (*Donis v Donis* (2007) at [20]; *Ashton v Pratt* (2015) at [147]) or 'material' (*Newbon v City Mutual Life* (1935) at 734; *Australian Financial Services v Hills Industries* (2014) at [150]). It cannot be equated with the doctrine of consideration. As Handley JA explained in *Hawker Pacific v Helicopter Charter* (1991) at 307–8:

> While a single peppercorn may constitute valuable consideration which can support a simple contract it seems to me that the loss of such an item would not constitute a 'material detriment', 'material disadvantage', or a 'significant disadvantage' for the purposes of the law of estoppel. It may seem strange that there should be such a distinction. However in the first case the consideration has been accepted as the price of a bargain which the law strives to uphold. Promissory estoppels and estoppels by representation lack this element of mutuality, and the relevant detriment has not been accepted by the party estopped as the price for binding himself to the representation or promise.

In England, detriment has been dispensed with in the context of promissory estoppel, it being sufficient that the promisee 'acted upon the promise': *WJ Alan v El Nasr Export & Import* (1972) at 213. The Australian courts, in contrast, have reaffirmed the importance of the detriment requirement within estoppel: see eg *Je Maintiendrai v Quaglia* (1980).

The question of detriment is 'part of a broad inquiry as to whether departure from a promise would be unconscionable in all the circumstances': *Donis* at [20]. Such an approach obviously necessitates consideration of the particular circumstances of the relying party. In *Je Maintiendrai*, a majority of the Full Court of the South Australian Supreme Court found that the relying party (the tenant) would suffer detriment if the landlord were allowed to resile from its promise to accept reduced rent for an indefinite period. The effect was that 18 months of rent arrears would become payable as a lump sum.[22] In reaching the conclusion that this amounted to a detriment, King CJ and White J considered it material that the tenant, the proprietor of a small hairdressing business who had requested the rent reduction because of financial difficulties, was a person who would find it easier to make small periodic payments than to find a lump sum.

---

21   Mason CJ, Deane, Dawson, Brennan and McHugh JJ.
22   That is, it was not in dispute that the landlord was entitled to revert to the strict legal position of full rent in relation to future payments, upon giving due notice.

7.10   Knowledge or intention?

Brennan J's formulation in *Waltons Stores v Maher* (1988) at 428–9 requires the defendant to *actually know of or intend* the plaintiff's reliance on the assumption or expectation. Brennan J added (at 423) that the requisite knowledge is easily inferred where the assumption or expectation has been induced by a promise, but that this inference would be more difficult where an already formed assumption has merely been encouraged or acquiesced in. There is no mention of any requirement of knowledge or intention in Mason CJ's and Wilson J's joint judgment in the case. For them, the question (at 445) was simply whether the other party had 'played such a part in the adoption of the assumption that it would be unfair or unjust if he [sic] were left free to ignore it'. In *Verwayen*, Deane J suggested (at 445) that it was sufficient if the representor 'clearly ought to have known that the other party would be induced by [their] conduct to adopt, and act on the basis of, the assumption'. Although the High Court is yet to resolve the issue and it is not clear whether there is any freestanding requirement of knowledge of any sort, Deane J's view has been preferred in a number of decisions: see eg *New Zealand Pelt Export v Trade Indemnity New Zealand* (2004) at [99]; *Leading Synthetics v Adroit Insurance* (2011) at [69].

7.11   Failure to avoid detriment

It follows from the final element of Brennan J's formulation that a defendant may, for example, validly give notice that the assumption should no longer be maintained, provided the plaintiff has not already been irretrievably prejudiced by relying on the assumption: see *Vella v Wah Lai Investment* (2004) at [169]. In such a case, the estoppel will cease to operate on the expiry of a period of reasonable notice. Another way of putting this is that estoppel may be merely suspensive, where the other party has been given a reasonable opportunity to resume their original position: see eg *Tool Metal Manufacturing v Tungsten Electric* (1955).

7.12   The role of unconscionability

In *Waltons Stores*, the basis for equity's intervention in estoppel was said to be the defendant's unconscionable conduct. On one view, unconscionability is a separate ingredient of the doctrine: see eg *Silovi v Barbaro* (1988) at 472; *Forbes v Australian Yachting Federation* (1996) at 287. But on another, it is merely a conclusion that is drawn about the defendant's conduct when the other elements of the doctrine have been established: see eg *Anaconda Nickel v Edensor Nominees* (2004) at [40]. It remains unclear which is correct, although the first view seems more accurately to capture what judges do. It suggests the need for a discretionary assessment of the justice of the situation, to determine whether equitable intervention is warranted.

7.13   Fashioning a remedy

The potential remedies in estoppel can be divided into two main categories: reliance-based remedies and expectation-based remedies. Reliance-based relief aims to repair the loss or detriment resulting from reliance on the assumption. The object of expectation-based remedies is to fulfil the expectation created by the promise; the relying party is to be put in the position they would have been in had the promise been fulfilled.[23] Whether the remedy granted pursuant to an estoppel should protect the expectation or reliance interest is a vexed issue that is linked to fundamental questions about the very nature of estoppel.[24]

When, prior to *Waltons Stores*, promissory estoppel operated purely defensively and in the context of pre-existing legal relationships, the remedial effect was simply to preclude the other party from enforcing its strict legal rights against the relying party. So, for example, in *Je Maintiendrai*, the landlord was prevented from recovering the alleged arrears of rent. In contrast, in proprietary estoppel cases, the courts enjoyed discretion as to how to satisfy the 'equity' raised by the estoppel. It was said that 'the Court must look at the circumstances of each case to decide in what way the equity can be satisfied': *Plimmer v Wellington* (1884) at 714. In *Crabb v Arun District Council* (1976) at 198, it was claimed that the remedy should be the 'minimum equity to do justice'. This might suggest limiting any relief to the extent of the plaintiff's reliance. But in practice, the courts have tended to grant expectation-based relief, such as an order that the relevant land be transferred.[25]

In *Waltons Stores*, the High Court sought to address objections that, if estoppel were allowed to operate as a cause of action, it would effectively outflank the law of contract with its requirement of consideration. Brennan J, for example, observed (at 425 and 421) that the object of estoppel is not 'to make a promise binding' or to fulfil expectations, but to 'avoid the detriment which the promisee would suffer if the promisor fails to fulfil the promise'. The difficulty was that the remedy actually awarded in the case – damages for the loss of the expected value of the lease, in lieu of specific performance – *looked* unambiguously expectation-based, although the reason for taking this approach was not explained.

The subsequent High Court decision in *Commonwealth v Verwayen* (1990) was seen as endorsing a reliance-based approach. While only Deane and Dawson JJ found for the plaintiff on the basis of estoppel, an overall majority of judges in the case (Mason CJ, Brennan, Dawson, Toohey and McHugh JJ) appeared to interpret the 'minimum equity' principle as entailing reliance-based relief. Nonetheless, they accepted that there would be situations where avoidance of the detriment would require the assumption to be made good, or, in other words, expectation-based relief. Only Deane J considered that expectation-based relief was the primary remedy, suggesting that:

> there is a prima facie entitlement to expectation based relief. A lesser form of relief should only be awarded where relief framed on the basis of the assumed state of affairs would be inequitably harsh.

In the subsequent proprietary estoppel case of *Giumelli v Giumelli* (1999), the Full Court of the Supreme Court of Western Australia had given effect to the estoppel through an expectation-based remedy – a constructive trust (see **3.15**) in favour of the plaintiff. On appeal to the High Court it was argued that *Verwayen* precluded, as a matter of principle, the grant of relief extending beyond the reversal of detriment. That contention was firmly rejected. Gleeson CJ, and McHugh, Gummow and Callinan JJ referred with approval to a number of points made in

---

23 This is the normal measure of contractual damages: see **23.06**.
24 See eg the reliance-based approach advocated in Finn 1985; Robertson 1996, 1997, 1998; Spence 1999. In support of an expectation-based approach, see eg Mescher 1990; Birks 1996; Cooke 1997.
25 See Robertson 1996: 809–17.

cases such as *Riches v Hogben* (1985) at 301 and *Verwayen* at 454, with a view to assuaging concerns about the outflanking of contract law and the doctrine of consideration. They stressed that in estoppel, unlike contract, there is no legally binding promise; if there is such a promise, the plaintiff must resort to contract law to enforce it. It is not the existence of an unperformed promise that invites the intervention of equity, but the conduct of the plaintiff in acting upon the expectation to which it gives rise. Furthermore, relief in equitable estoppel is discretionary in nature. They also appeared to adopt (at [50]) Deane J's approach of a prima facie entitlement to expectation-based relief, albeit obliquely. Ultimately, they considered the particular form of expectation-based relief awarded by the court below – the constructive trust – to be inappropriate in the circumstances, because of the potential for prejudice to third-party interests. They therefore substituted another form of expectation-based relief – damages representing the value of the promised land.

In *Sidhu v Van Dyke* (2014), another proprietary estoppel case, the High Court confirmed that the effect of *Giumelli* was the adoption of a prima facie entitlement to expectation-based relief approach.[26] French CJ, Kiefel, Bell and Keane JJ explained (at [77]) that 'this category of equitable estoppel serves to vindicate the expectations of the representee against a party who seeks unconscionably to resile from an expectation he or she has created'. They added (at [84]) that had Mrs Van Dyke made only a 'relatively small, readily quantifiable monetary outlay' in reliance on the assumption, it would have been appropriate to depart from this prima facie position. However, this was not such a case. On the contrary, the detriment here involved 'life-changing decisions with irreversible consequences of a profoundly personal nature ... beyond the measure of money'.[27] As such, expectation-based relief was entirely appropriate. This took the form of an order for equitable compensation reflecting the value of the promised property. An order that Mr Sidhu transfer the property to Mrs Van Dyke (another form of expectation-based relief) was considered inappropriate due to the adverse effect it would have had on the interests of Mrs Sidhu as co-owner of the property.[28]

There have been suggestions that while an expectation approach might be appropriate for proprietary estoppel, promissory estoppel 'is concerned with what needs to be done in order to avoid detriment': *Harrison v Harrison* (2013) at [138]; and see also *ACN 074 971 109 v National Mutual Life* (2008) at [161]. If so, the 'minimum equity' approach might still apply in that context. *Sidhu*, however, suggests that the prima facie entitlement to fulfilment of the expectation should apply equally to cases involving promissory estoppel. French CJ, Kiefel, Bell and Keane JJ commenced their judgment (at [1]) by emphasising that the various types of equitable estoppel are all 'intended to serve the same fundamental purpose'.[29] They went on (at [85]) to outline a principle that seems as applicable to promissory estoppel as its proprietary counterpart:

---

26   This had been the view taken by a number of lower courts: see eg *Donis v Donis* (2007); *McKay v McKay* (2008); *Delaforce v Simpson-Cook* (2010).

27   Quoting Nettle JA's judgment in *Donis v Donis* (2007) at [34].

28   Compare *Priestley v Priestley* (2017), where a constructive trust over the property in question was imposed in favour of the claimant.

29   Quoting Mason CJ in *Verwayen* at 409.

> While it is true to say that 'the court, as a court of conscience, goes no further than is necessary to prevent unconscionable conduct', where the unconscionable conduct consists of resiling from a promise or assurance which has induced conduct to the other party's detriment, the relief which is necessary in this sense is usually that which reflects the value of the promise.[30]

It is hard to see this emphasis on the 'value of the promise' as anything other than an expectation-based measure, to be departed from only in cases where it would be 'wholly inequitable and unjust to insist upon a disproportionate making good of the relevant assumption': ibid, quoting *Verwayen* at 413. Such cases will, of their nature be 'unusual': *Priestley v Priestley* (2017) at [164].

---

30   This accords with the approach in *Delaforce v Simpson-Cook* (2010) at [3], [56], [59]. See also *Sullivan v Sullivan* (2006) at [23].

8

THE PARTIES TO A CONTRACT

Who are the parties to a contract?

8.01   Identifying the parties

The *parties* to a contract are the persons or organisations who agree to be bound by its terms. By giving that consent, they become entitled to enforce the contract, but must also fulfil any obligations the contract imposes.[1] Whether or not a particular person is a party is a matter to be determined objectively, by reference to the circumstances surrounding the contract, its purpose and (where relevant) events after the contract was made: *Lederberger v Mediterranean Olives* (2012) at [19], [31].

8.02   Multi-party contracts

As noted in **1.03**, most contracts involve two parties, but contracts may also be entered into between multiple parties. For example, an unincorporated association, such as a club, has no legal personality of its own. It may be constituted by each member entering into a contract with every other member to abide by the rules of the association: see eg *Baldwin v Everingham* (1993).[2] A single event may sometimes work in the same way. In *Clarke v Dunraven* (1897), the competitors in a yacht race were held to be bound by the rules of the race because they had entered into contracts with each other.[3] Multi-party contracts are also used in a commercial setting. A syndicated loan agreement, for instance, allows a borrower to enter into a loan agreement with a number of lenders (the syndicate), using one contract rather than a series of separate contracts.

In each of the situations just mentioned, the number of parties may vary over time, as members join or leave an association, or competitors sign up for an event, or the membership of a syndicate changes. It is also possible, even under a two-party contract, for one of the parties to be replaced by someone else. This requires a process known as *novation*. The requirements for that are considered separately in Chapter 14, along with various circumstances in which a party can transfer or *assign* their rights under a contract to someone else.

Despite the fact that there can be more than two parties to a contract, the term *third party* is commonly used to mean a person or organisation who is *not* party to a contract, but who is affected by it or (more particularly) stands to benefit from its performance. In keeping with convention, we will also use the term in that sense over the rest of this chapter.

8.03   Joint parties

One type of multi-party contract involves two or more persons acting in a joint capacity. For instance, where an agreement is made to sell property jointly owned by a couple, both owners

---

1   In the case of a unilateral contract (see **1.06**, **5.19**), only one of the parties (the promisor) will incur any obligations, since by definition the promisee will already have completed their performance.
2   This is assuming, however, that the necessary intention to create legal relations can be identified. Difficulties have sometimes arisen in determining whether groups have the legal status of an unincorporated association or are something more informal: see **5.09**.
3   See also *Raguz v Sullivan* (2000), applying a similar analysis to athletes nominating for Olympic selection.

would usually be named in the contract as vendors. Sometimes, however, disputes can arise about whether a particular person is a joint party. In *Coulls v Bagot's Executor and Trustee* (1967), a company was granted the right to quarry Mr Coulls' land, in return for the payment of royalties to both Mr Coulls and as his wife 'as joint tenants'. Mrs Coulls signed the contract along with her husband, although the agreement was stated to be made between the company and him alone. After Mr Coulls' death, the question arose of whether the company was obliged to pay royalties to Mrs Coulls, or just to the deceased's estate. On the facts, the High Court disagreed about whether Mrs Coulls was a joint promisee, and therefore a party, with her husband. The majority (McTiernan, Taylor and Owen JJ) held that she was not. Barwick CJ and Windeyer J took the opposite view. As explained in **8.06**, the finding that she was not a party to the contract meant she had no claim on the royalties.

Where X and Y jointly promise to pay Z $1000, both X and Y are liable to pay that amount. Their liability cannot be divided. Once Z is paid, neither are liable. No more than $1000 can be claimed. X and Y may alternatively make separate contracts to pay Z $1000. In this case, liability is cumulative and Z may bring a claim against both for $1000. A third situation combines elements of both. X and Y may be joint promisors and at the same time make separate contracts as well. The law treats this situation like a joint promise.

Similar principles apply with promisees. Sometimes, as was argued in *Coulls,* there may be more than one promisee. X may agree to pay Y and Z $1000 jointly. X's liability is limited to the $1000 that is owing. If X makes separate promises to Y and Z, however, X will be liable to each for $1000.

X may breach a contract with Y and Z in such a way as to create a right to terminate the contract, under the principles discussed in Chapter 16. If so, then either of the joint promisees can elect to exercise that right, even if the other wishes to keep the contract alive: *Legal Services Commissioner v Sheehy* (2018). But it is different if X repudiates the contract before the time for performance has arrived. Such an 'anticipatory breach' (see **16.05**) can only be used as a basis for termination if both Y and Z agree: *Lion White Lead v Rogers* (1918) at 551.[4]

8.04   Agency

In many situations, a contract that appears to be made with one person is in fact made with someone else, because of the concept of *agency*. For example, when you walk into a shop and buy something, the chances are that you are not contracting with the person (if any) who serves you. In most cases, that person will be acting as the *agent* for another, usually (though not always) their employer. It is that other person or organisation, known in this context as the *principal*, with whom you are actually contracting.[5]

In order to enter into a contract that is binding on their principal, an agent is required to have *authority* from the principal. 'Actual authority' is the product of express or implied assent on the part of the principal. Authority may also be 'apparent' or 'ostensible'. Where C says or does something to induce B to believe that another person, A, has authority to act on C's behalf, then A is treated as C's agent even if A lacks the required authority. Any contract

---

4   For a more detailed treatment of the rules concerning joint and several rights and liabilities under a contract, see Davis 2016.

5   For a detailed treatment of the law of agency, see Dal Pont 2013.

entered into by A will bind C. As Diplock LJ explained, the inducement 'operates as an estoppel, preventing the principal from asserting that he [sic] is not bound by the contract': *Freeman & Lockyer v Buckhurst Park* (1964) at 503. Whether or not C could bring a claim under the contract is more difficult. A's apparent authority merely stops C from denying the contract: it does not give C the right to sue. But another doctrine may provide a solution. If C *ratifies* the act of A, in a situation where A has previously acted without authority, C will have a claim against B: see eg *Bolton Partners v Lambert* (1888).

Ordinarily, A will disclose to B that they are contracting on C's behalf. C is bound by all contracts of an authorised agent when their identity is disclosed to A. C may be disclosed by name, or be an unnamed disclosed principal. In the situation where C is disclosed, it is quite clear that A is acting as C's agent. The way that C is generally bound by, and able to enforce, a contract when they are *not* disclosed is more difficult to reconcile with the doctrine of privity that is discussed below. In this situation, as between A and B, C seems to fit the role of a third party. Various attempts have been made to explain this anomaly, but ultimately it may be best rationalised on the grounds of commercial convenience: see *Siu Yin Kwan v Eastern Insurance* (1994) at 207.

In some cases, it may be unclear whether a person is entering into a contract as an agent on behalf of a principal, on their own behalf, or indeed in both capacities. This last was found to be the case in *Harris v Burrell* (2010). The plaintiff company agreed to loan money to Hardel Pty Ltd and certain associated entities, of which the defendant, Harris, was the sole director. The two-page contract prepared to document this agreement was expressed to be made between the two companies, but with provision for signature by their respective directors, each of whom were named. The contract also contained a clause whereby the 'director of the borrowing entities acknowledges personal liability for all debt remaining after the loan repayment'. It was held that a reasonable person would have understood the document to mean that Harris was signing the contract in two capacities, as a director of Hardel *and* in his personal capacity. On that basis, he was a party to the contract and could be held personally liable for the loan repayment.

8.05 Privity of contract

As long ago as *Gandy v Gandy* (1885) at 69, Bowen LJ explained that:

> At law the rule in general is, no doubt, that a contract between two parties that one should do something for the benefit of a stranger, cannot be enforced by the stranger, except in certain exceptional cases.

For a long time, this statement was thought to represent the law in Australia. However, the current status of what is known as the *privity* rule is more ambiguous. As traditionally understood, contracts only took effect between parties. There are two elements to the rule. The first is uncontroversial. It states that non-parties cannot be *burdened* by a contract to which they are not 'privy' (party). When A enters into a contract with B that requires C to pay B $5000, C is not usually bound by that contract. There is one significant exception to this principle, however, which allows the passing of the burden of a freehold covenant in property law: see **8.21**.

The second manifestation of the rule – that a non-party cannot enforce a contract made for their *benefit* – has been much more widely debated, not least because many legal systems have adopted a different and more flexible approach. In England, the strict application of the privity doctrine to deny claims by third parties was confirmed by the House of Lords in *Dunlop Pneumatic Tyre v Selfridge* (1915). In the United States, by contrast, a distinction has come to be drawn between third parties who are *intended* beneficiaries of a contractual promise and those who merely stand to benefit *incidentally* from the performance of a contract. The former can, with some qualifications, take action if the promise made in their favour is not fulfilled: see *Restatement (Second) of Contracts*, Chapter 14 and especially Article 302.

In Australia, as we will see, the English approach held sway for most of the twentieth century. But in recent times, that position has been challenged, both at common law and through statutory reforms. And in both countries, various ways have been found to circumvent the privity doctrine. One of the problems with the doctrine is that it undermines the idea of freedom of contract. If the parties wish to benefit a third party, many would argue that there is no obvious justification why they should not be allowed to do so.[6]

Conferring a benefit on a third party

8.06   The orthodox position

When A enters into a contract with B to pay C a sum of money, the privity rule has traditionally (at least in England and Australia) been taken to mean that C has no remedy if A fails to perform. Hence, in *Coulls v Bagot's* (1967), the majority finding that Mrs Coulls was not a party to the contract meant that she was not entitled to receive any of the royalties that she had been promised.

The rule also applies where the promised benefit is in the form of a defence by way of a contractual exemption or limitation clause. For example, suppose A contracts to transport valuable goods owned by B. There is a clause in the contract excluding liability or limiting compensation to a set amount if the goods are damaged during transportation. The benefit of the exemption or limitation is expressly extended not just to A, but to any employees, subcontractors or agents used by A to help transport the goods. A subcontracts some part of the transportation or the handling of the goods to C. The goods are damaged while in C's care and B brings an action against C in the tort of negligence. As the High Court held in *Wilson v Darling Island* (1956), the privity rule means that C is unable to rely on the clause excluding liability or limiting a claim for damages by B, since C is not a party to the contract between A and B.

8.07   Privity and consideration

The rule preventing a third party from bringing a claim is sometimes expressed in two different ways. The so-called 'parties only' rule means that only a party to a contract can bring a claim. Alternatively, it is sometimes said that the reason that a non-party cannot bring a claim is that they have not provided any consideration for the contract. The first formula was traditionally applicable to contracts entered into using sealed deeds. The second formula was applied to informal contracts enforced through the action of assumpsit, where consideration was a key

6   This is not, however, a universally held view: see **8.22**.

component.[7] In most modern cases, the claim of a third party will fail for both of these reasons. The fact that there are separate requirements does not usually matter in practice. The non-party will generally not have provided any consideration.

There are instances, however, where the difference in formulas is more critical. Suppose A makes a promise to B and C as joint promisees to pay $100 to C in exchange for consideration provided by B. It might be argued that although C is a party they still cannot bring a claim because they have not provided any consideration. Both rules must be satisfied and therefore the claim fails. It appears, however, that where there are joint promisees, consideration provided by one of the two might be enough. In *Coulls v Bagot's* (1967), Barwick CJ and Windeyer J thought that the husband's consideration was sufficient to allow his wife to enforce the contract as a joint promisee. Taylor and Owen JJ expressed agreement with this view, although as noted earlier they rejected the wife's claim on the separate basis that she was not a joint promisee.

8.08 *Trident v McNiece*

Trident General Insurance v McNiece Bros (1988) is the leading modern authority on the privity doctrine. The decision merits detailed examination because the seven High Court judgments contain a detailed account of the current common law within Australia. Trident General Insurance agreed to indemnify a company against liability for personal injury on its building sites. The insured was described under the policy as 'Blue Circle Southern Cement Ltd, all its subsidiary, associated and related companies, all contractors and sub-contractors and/or suppliers'. Following the issue of the policy in 1978, McNiece were engaged as the principal contractor. In 1979, an employee of a subcontractor was injured through the fault of McNiece, who were found liable to pay compensation. McNiece sought to enforce the indemnity. Today, a Commonwealth statute applies and McNiece would recover: *Insurance Contracts Act 1984* (Cth) s 48. Because the contract was entered into prior to the legislation, however, the parties were thrown back on the common law. It was held, by a majority of the Court, that McNiece could recover the amount of its loss from Trident, though they arrived at this conclusion in different ways.

Some members of the High Court were attracted to the idea of a new common law exception. Mason CJ and Wilson J accepted (at 119) that there were problems with the privity rule. It caused uncertainty, they said, not so much because of the rule itself, but in the techniques that the courts have developed for avoiding it. At the same time, they recognised that the privity rule had some virtues. They were most convinced (at 122) by the 'important' argument that '[t]he recognition of an unqualified entitlement in a third party to sue on the contract would severely circumscribe the freedom of action of the parties, particularly the promisee'. The situation that Mason CJ and Wilson J highlighted arises if A and B are unable to modify the contract between them without gaining C's consent or giving C a right of action. As we will see, the difficulties thrown up by this scenario are recognised in various statutes reforming the privity rule, under which the parties are prevented from rescinding or modifying the main contract without C's consent, once C accepts the benefit of obligation: see **8.18–8.20**.

---

7   For a discussion of the history of the privity doctrine, see Ibbetson & Swain 2008.

Balancing the interests of the parties in this manner would not be possible if the rule were simply abolished at common law.

Nevertheless, Mason CJ and Wilson J were still prepared to reconsider the privity rule. Seemingly influenced by the fact that the statutory provision mentioned above had been introduced to confer rights on a third party insured, they were prepared to create a common law exception here – but only in the end for insurance contracts. They pointed out (at 123) that:

> the injustice which would flow from [the privity rule] arises not only from its failure to give effect to the expressed intentions of the person who takes out the insurance but also from the common intention of the parties and the circumstances that others, aware of the policy will order their affair accordingly.

A very similar justification for making an exception in the case of insurance contracts was put forward by Toohey J.

As Brennan J noted (at 127), the obvious problem with treating insurance contracts differently is that it then becomes necessary to find a way to distinguish such contracts from any other sort of transaction. When any contract is expressed to be for the benefit of a third person, it can just as easily be said that if it is not enforced the parties' intentions are frustrated. The fact that legislation was enacted on insurance can be used to support the argument that there was a common law privity rule which still operated in that context. Both Brennan and Dawson JJ saw privity as a settled rule which ought not to be overturned.

Two other members of the High Court, Deane and Gaudron JJ, were prepared to retain the rule but circumvent it with another legal device. This is a familiar technique. It has the advantage of preserving the integrity of the rule without the difficulty of carving out some special exception. Deane J found the insurance company presumptively liable to indemnify on the basis that Blue Circle held its promise to do this on trust for McNiece, though this would have required further proceedings. As noted in **8.14**, where the trust idea is discussed further, such reasoning is problematic. In many situations it may be quite difficult to find the relevant intention to create a trust without resorting to artificiality.

Gaudron J's judgment is a puzzle. She developed a rationale based on the principle of 'unjust enrichment', even though this ground was not relied on in argument before the High Court. She considered (at 176) that the plaintiff had a claim in unjust enrichment, because:

> a promisor who has accepted agreed consideration for a promise to benefit a third party is unjustly enriched at the expense of the third party to the extent that the promise is unfulfilled and the non-fulfilment does not attract proportional consequences.

In some general sense, the insurance company was indeed unjustly enriched, in that it had received premiums on certain terms which it had not then been prepared to meet. But this sense of the word is not relevant. As unjust enrichment scholars have always insisted, it is the legal sense of unjust enrichment which matters: see **24.11**. This requires any unjust enrichment to be at the plaintiff's expense. It is difficult here to see how the insurance company was enriched at McNiece's expense. If the enrichment was at anyone's expense it was at the expense of the contracting party, Blue Circle, who paid the insurance premiums. In *Benson v Rational Entertainment* (2018), the New South Wales Court of Appeal made clear its view that the principle stated by Gaudron J is not recognised under Australian law.

8.09 The current status of the privity rule

Extracting a ratio from the High Court's decision in *Trident* is no easy task. The result was that the plaintiff recovered under an insurance contract to which it was not a party. A clear majority preserved the existing privity rule in an unaltered form. There was no enthusiasm in the judgments of Brennan, Dawson, Deane and Gaudron JJ for carving out a common law exception to cover a contract of insurance for the benefit of a third party. The three judges who went down that route – Mason CJ, Wilson and Toohey JJ – were in a minority. Nevertheless, in the wake of the decision it has generally been accepted that such an exception now exists: see eg *Woodside Petroleum v H & RE & W* (1999).[8] Some have also been prepared to reason by analogy to create further exceptions. For example, in *Gate Gourmet Australia v Gate Gourmet Holding* (2004) it was suggested that a letter of guarantee issued by a holding company could be enforced by its subsidiary, even if that company was not a party to the contract in question.

It is possible that if the right case had come before the High Court soon after *Trident*, some judges at least might have been willing to develop a broader exception. Conceivably, this might have looked something like the option formulated (but not ultimately adopted) by Mason CJ and Wilson JJ (at 123):

> A simple departure from the traditional rules would lead to third party enforceability of such a contract, subject to the preservation of a contracting party's right to rescind or vary, in the absence of reliance by the third party to his [sic] detriment, and to the availability in an action by the third party of defences against a contracting party.

But any chance of that happening now seems remote, given the generally more cautious and technical approach taken by recent judges on the court (see **1.11**). As matters stand, therefore, it seems reasonable to suppose that any general reforms to the privity doctrine will need to come from parliament – something that, as we will see, has already happened in three Australian jurisdictions. Before getting to those provisions, however, it is first important to understand various ways in which the privity doctrine can be sidestepped, even under the common law.

8.10 Enforcement by the promisee: actions for damages

Even if a third party cannot enforce a contractual promise made for their benefit, the party to whom that promise was made may seek to enforce it on their behalf. One problem with doing this is the principle, discussed in **23.03**, that only those who suffer loss can recover damages for breach of contract. At least as a general rule, it is not possible to recover the loss suffered by a third party beneficiary even if the promisee is willing to bring a claim. The way in which the promisee's loss is characterised is crucial. In *Trident v McNiece* (1988) at 118–19, Mason CJ and

---

8   See also *Hannover Life v Sayseng* (2005), extending the exception to require an insurer to act in good faith towards a superannuation fund member, when making decisions affecting the availability of TPD (total and permanent disability) benefits offered by the fund. This was despite the fact that the fund member was not an insured as such – the insurance being taken out by the fund to allow it to provide the promised benefits. The *Insurance Contracts Act 1984* (Cth) has since been amended to create an enforceable duty of good faith for third party beneficiaries: see **12.17**.

Wilson J approved a passage in the judgment of Windeyer J in *Coulls v Bagot's* (1967) at 501–2. In it, he describes a situation where A enters into a contract with B in which B promises to pay C $500. A might not be able to recover $500 but might still recover substantial damages if B fails to pay. Sometimes it will be possible to characterise the loss as A's. Windeyer J gave the example of an instance where A was relying on the payment to reduce or discharge A's indebtedness to C, or where C was to use the $500 in a joint venture with A. In these situations, it can be said that A suffers a loss. But any damages recovered will be for A, not C, the third party.[9]

Some English cases have sought to challenge this orthodoxy. In *Jackson v Horizon Holidays* (1975), a father brought an action on behalf of himself and his wife and children after the luxurious holiday they were expecting proved to be anything but. When calculating the damages for mental distress,[10] Lord Denning held that the Court need not confine itself to the father's own distress but also consider that of his wife and children. Not long afterwards, the rule that it is normally possible only to recover for one's own losses was reaffirmed by the House of Lords, although Lord Wilberforce accepted that family holidays might be an exception: *Woodar Investment v Wimpey* (1980) at 283. The Australian status of the exception is unclear. Mason CJ and Wilson J in *Trident v McNiece* (1988) at 119 described *Jackson v Horizon Holidays* as having 'uncertain status'.

Another attempt to stretch the definition of loss was revived by Lord Diplock in *The Albazero* (1977) at 847 where he stated that:

> In a commercial contract concerning goods where it is in the contemplation of the parties that the proprietary interests in the goods may be transferred from one owner to another after the contract has been entered into and before the breach which causes the loss or damage to the goods, an original party to the contract, if such be the intention of them both, is to be treated in law as having entered into the contract for the benefit of all persons who have or may acquire an interest in the goods before they are lost or damaged, and is entitled to recover by way of damages for breach of contract the actual loss sustained by those for whose benefit the contract is entered into.

The difficulty identified arises from the rules about the passage of property. A is the original owner of the goods and enters into a contract with B to transport the goods. The property in the goods passes to C at the time of the contract. Before the goods reach C they are damaged. A does not have property in the goods, but has the contract with B. C has the property in the goods, but has no contract with B. Lord Diplock held that A can recover damages even though the property in the goods has passed to C. This is a narrow exception: it only concerns commercial parties, the contract must concern goods, and the third party must have acquired an interest in the goods before the breach and loss. In *The Albazero* itself, C, as a consignee on a bill of lading, had their own contract claim and therefore the principle did not apply. This is not strictly an exception to the privity rule. It is another situation in which the law is prepared to characterise the loss as A's.

Some English cases have suggested that a similar principle will apply in a new context, where A enters into a contract with B, a builder, and following construction the building is then

---

9   It is different, however, where a trust of the promise can be identified: see **8.14**.
10   On the wider problem of recovering damages for distress in contract law, see **23.13**.

conveyed to C. In some situations the property will have passed but the new owner will have no right of action in contract against the builder: see eg *Linden Gardens Trust v Lenesta Sludge Disposals* (1994). It has been doubted whether these authorities would even apply in Australia to give A a right of action: *Nicholson v Hilldove* (2014) at [77]. At the same time, in *Trident* Brennan J conceded (at 139) that:

> A development of the rules relating to damages rather than the acceptance of a third party's right to sue offers the prospect of an orderly development of the law if such a development be needed to avoid injustice.

8.11   Enforcement by the promisee: specific performance

Ordinarily then, A cannot recover any more than nominal damages from B for failing to confer an agreed benefit on C. But sometimes that very fact can be used to generate a different remedy. In *Beswick v Beswick* (1968), Peter Beswick, a coal merchant, retired and transferred the business to his nephew, John Beswick. In return, John agreed to pay Peter £6 10s a week. In the event of Peter's death, John agreed to pay Peter's widow, Ruth Beswick, an annuity of £5 a week. Peter died, and after paying one instalment John stopped paying Ruth. In the Court of Appeal, Lord Denning had suggested that 'nothing could be more unjust' than if the widow was unable to enforce the contract. Unlike the majority in the Court of Appeal, the House of Lords held that Ruth could not bring a claim for the money in her own capacity, since she was not a party to the contract. Fortuitously, however, and unlike her counterpart in *Coulls v Bagot's* (1967), Ruth was the administratrix of Peter's estate. In this capacity, she stood in his shoes and could bring an action as a party to the contract. The estate could show no loss from John's failure to perform. But the very fact that damages would not be an adequate remedy persuaded the House of Lords to grant Ruth (as administratrix) an order for specific performance, requiring John to pay the agreed annuity.[11]

Despite the unusual nature of the facts in *Beswick*, there is no reason why the same reasoning cannot be used in other situations to permit promisees to obtain orders for specific performance, where they are willing to assist third parties. So much was indeed recognised by a number of judges in both *Coulls* (at 478, 503) and *Trident* (at 119–20, 138, 158).[12]

A further example of enforcement by the promisee, although not involving specific performance, is provided by *Broken Hill v Hapag-Lloyd* (1980). There, a carrier of goods obtained a stay of proceedings to prevent the owner from breaching a promise not to sue a subcontractor which had damaged the goods. This was despite the fact that, as confirmed in *Wilson v Darling Island* (1956), the subcontractor itself could not have relied upon the exemption by way of a defence, not having been a party to the relevant contract.

8.12   Avoiding privity through agency arrangements

There is nothing new about attempts to draft contracts so as to avoid the consequences of the privity rule, especially in the type of situation just mentioned where work is subcontracted.

---

11   As to the relevance of adequacy of damages to an award of specific performance, see **22.03**.
12   See eg *Swift v McLeary* (2014).

One early example, *Elder Dempster v Paterson, Zochinos* (1924), rests on somewhat uncertain principles, and was long ago distinguished in Australia: *Wilson v Darling Island* (1956) at 68–71. By the 1950s, commercial parties were beginning to develop more secure ways of drafting contracts in order to defeat the privity rule and allow their intentions to be met. The so-called 'Himalaya clause'[13] is designed to allow a third party to rely on an exemption or limitation in a contract to which they are not a party. This is vital in the context of carriage of goods. The contract is made between A, the owner of the goods, and B, the carrier. During the course of the voyage, the goods may pass through the hands of third parties, especially stevedores, who load and unload goods from ships. The head contract, known as a bill of lading where shipping is involved, acknowledges that the carrier has received the goods and sets out the conditions of carriage. Bills of lading can also be used to transfer title in the goods from the owner A to the current holder of the bill. In addition, holders of the bill are, by virtue of legislation, given a right of action on the contract of carriage, as if they were the original party.[14]

The 'Himalaya clause' utilises the law of agency. In *Scruttons v Midland Silicones* (1962), Lord Reid accepted that under certain circumstances the law deems that a carrier is acting as agent for a third party stevedore. In order for that argument to succeed he suggested (at 474) that:

(1) the bill of lading under which the goods are shipped must make clear that the stevedore is intended to be protected by the provisions which limit liability;

(2) the bill of lading must make clear that the carrier is contracting as agent for the stevedore in relation to the defence or limitation;

(3) the carrier was authorised by the stevedore to act as their agent or there is later ratification;

(4) any difficulties about consideration from the stevedore can be overcome.

On the facts, the majority held that the carrier was not an agent for the stevedore. As Lord Reid put it (at 474), 'there is certainly nothing to indicate that the carrier was contracting as agent for the stevedore in addition to contracting on his own behalf'.

The conditions laid down by Lord Reid led parties to redraft their contracts. His requirements were satisfied in a subsequent authority, *The Eurymedon* (1975). A holder of a bill of lading brought a claim in negligence against a stevedore who damaged cargo during unloading. The relevant clauses included a number of exceptions. No servant or agent (including an independent contractor) of the carrier was to be liable for any act or default in the course of their employment. Every limitation available to the carrier was to be available to such persons. And, crucially, the carrier was to be regarded as the agent or trustee of such persons, so as to make them to that extent parties to the contract. A majority of the Privy Council held that the stevedore could rely on the clause. There was little difficulty in finding a relationship of agency because the stevedore habitually acted for the carrier and indeed they were part of the same group of companies. Finding a solution to Lord Reid's final requirement was potentially trickier. The stevedores were still required to show that they had provided consideration to be able to rely on the clause. Lord Wilberforce said (at 167–8) that:

---

13   The name is taken from that of the ship in *Adler v Dickson* (1955).
14   See eg *Carrington Slipways v Patrick Operations* (1991) at 751.

> The bill of lading brought into an existence a bargain initially unilateral but capable of becoming mutual between the shipper and the [stevedores] made through the carrier as agent. This became a full contract when the [stevedores] performed services by discharging the goods.

By performing an existing duty owed to the carrier, in unloading the goods, the stevedores provided consideration for a contract with the holder of the bill of lading. This reflects the general principle that performing a duty owed to a third party amounts to good consideration: see **5.34**.

8.13   Himalaya clauses in Australia

The High Court had an opportunity to consider the application of *The Eurymedon* in *The New York Star* (1978). A majority of the High Court agreed that a stevedore could take advantage of a limitation provision in a contract between the shipper and the carrier in an action by the holder of a bill of lading. Mason and Jacob JJ followed Lord Wilberforce's reasoning in *The Eurymedon*. Barwick CJ rejected this analysis. He did not share the view that there was a unilateral contract that became mutual. Rather, he thought (at 244) that:

> [W]e have here an arrangement, a compact with agreed conditions to attend performance of certain acts, which are not promised to be done ... The performance of the contemplated act both supplies the occasion for those conditions to operate and the consideration which makes the arrangement contractual.

The parties to the arrangement were the shipper (and through them the holder of the bill of lading) and on the other side the stevedore, through the agency of the carrier. This reasoning is problematic because it creates an 'arrangement' without legal force which on performance generates legal consequences. Lord Wilberforce's reasoning is not easy to understand either. A unilateral contract usually requires an offer to be made which is accepted through performance as stipulated in the offer. On the facts, it is quite difficult to see that either of those conditions were present, as was noted by Stephen J (at 257). The High Court thought that the limitation failed to protect the stevedore as a matter of construction. The decision was reversed on the construction issue by the Privy Council: *The New York Star* (1980).

Some remarks of Lord Wilberforce in the Privy Council (at 144) get to the core issue: 'their Lordships would not encourage a search for fine distinctions which would diminish the general applicability, in light of established commercial practice, of the principle'. In part, this is an expression of the view that when commercial parties organise their contractual relationships in this way then the law should not hinder their intentions. It also reflects a particular view of commercial practice within a given market.[15] Support for this rationale can also be found in some observations of Lord Goff in the *The Mahkutai* (1996) at 664. He said that 'there can be no doubt of the commercial need of some such principle', although in the end he stopped short of recognising what he termed a 'fully-fledged exception' to the privity of contract rule.

---

15   This view of commercial practice was not one shared by all of the High Court in *The New York Star*: see Stephen J at 258–60 and Murphy J at 284–5.

In Australia, the same technique has been used outside the context of carriage of goods by sea. In *Toll v Alphapharm* (2004), a drugs distribution company (Alphapharm), through a subsidiary (Thomson), entered into a contract with a carrier (Finemores). The subsidiary purported to enter into the contract on behalf of, among others, 'persons having an interest in the goods'. During transit, the drugs were stored at below the minimum temperature required. Finemores was sued in negligence and for breach of duty as a bailee by Alphapharm and relied on an exemption clause in the contract with the subsidiary. The High Court held that the exemption clause was binding. Thomson was authorised to act as an agent for Alphapharm. It was said (at 193) that such a result, 'may be more obvious than a conclusion that a carrier at the time of shipment was authorised to act on behalf of an unknown stevedore in a foreign country'. It seems to be generally accepted in Australia that when applying Lord Reid's conditions, set down in *Scruttons v Midland Silicones*, the courts will not look for fine distinctions. As Hutley JA observed in *Life Savers v Frigmobile* (1983) at 438:

> The form of contract here used, patterned on provisions in favour of stevedores and other subcontractors in bills of lading, strains doctrines of privity of contract and consideration but these difficulties have been overcome. There would appear to me to be no reason why the same form is not applicable to all forms of transportation of goods, and, if used, should be given the same effect in all cases.

Using drafting to circumvent the privity rules has enjoyed some notable successes in the courts. Well drafted contracts should not end up in litigation, although this approach is still at the mercy of judicial construction. Beyond the fact that these contracts concern commercial parties seeking to make profits, the practice of those in the industry may play a part in the process of interpretation. A further problem arises when a clause runs into conflict with other legal rules. The regime for carriage of goods by sea is governed by what are known as the Hague/Visby rules.[16] It was held in *The Starsin* (2004) that when a clause was drafted in such a way that it conflicted with these or other legal rules, then those rules prevailed. In his dissent, Lord Steyn expressed (at 749) some disquiet that this outcome failed to give weight to the commercial expectations of the parties and was an example of creating a 'fine distinction'. Lord Bingham, who delivered the leading speech for the majority, thought (at 744) that were that view to be correct then it 'would be to elevate form over substance and to invest what is essentially a legal device with a wholly disproportionate legal significance'.

8.14   Inferring a trust of a third-party promise

Suppose B promises A that B will confer a benefit on C. As just noted, this means that A can sue B for breach of contract if B fails to perform. The right to sue someone is regarded as a form of property, known as a 'chose in action'. That, in turn, raises the possibility of that property being held on trust for C.

A *trust* is an arrangement whereby one person (the *trustee*) is under an obligation to deal with certain property in the interests of another (the *beneficiary*). Trusts may sometimes be

---

16   See *International Convention for the Unification of Certain Rules of Law relating to Bills of Lading 1924*. The version given effect in Australia by the *Carriage of Goods by Sea Act 1991* (Cth) Pt 2 reflects changes made by a 1968 Protocol.

created automatically or imposed in response to wrongdoing. But the type of trust relevant here is an *express trust*, one that is intentionally created.[17] It can be argued that by making a contract that contains a promise in favour of C, the parties implicitly intended that A (the trustee) should hold the benefit of the right to sue B on trust for C (the beneficiary).

Recognising the existence of a trust has two major advantages for C. Firstly, if A does sue for breach of contract as a trustee, any damages recovered will be measured by reference to C's loss, not A's, and then held on trust for C: see *Lloyd's v Harper* (1880). Secondly, if A refuses to sue, C can sue B directly, provided A is joined in the proceedings as a co-defendant: see *Wilson v Darling Island* (1956) at 67.

The trust of a promise as a solution appealed to Deane J in *Trident v McNiece* (1988). But the idea has a long antecedence and was approved by the House of Lords in *Les Affréteurs Réunis v Leopold Walford* (1919) nearly a century ago. A broker negotiated a charterparty under which the ship owner promised the charterer that they would pay the broker a commission. It was held that the charterer was a trustee of this promise for the broker and therefore could enforce it against the owner. On the facts before him, Lord Birkenhead LC was influenced by longstanding commercial practice in this market. Otherwise, however, the difficulty is that the law requires an intention on the part of the promisee to irrevocably benefit the third party by way of trust. The courts have traditionally been reluctant to find the requisite intention to create a trust, especially where commercial parties are involved. In *Wilson v Darling Island* (1956) at 67, Fullagar J challenged this view, commenting that it was 'difficult to understand the reluctance which courts have sometimes shown to infer a trust' in cases where there was an intention to benefit a third party. This view was later echoed by a number of the judges in *Trident* (at 120, 146, 156).[18] In that case, Mason CJ and Wilson J suggested (at 121) that:

> The apparent uncertainty should be resolved by stating that the courts will recognise the existence of a trust when it appears from the language of the parties, construed in its context, including the matrix of circumstances, that the parties so intended.

It was useful to highlight the sorts of factors which will be relevant in deciding whether a trust of a promise is to be imposed. But, to some extent, these remarks merely restate the problem in another form. These elements are somewhat vague. There is no indication as to how the various factors are to be weighed against one another. The fact is that if a court wishes to infer a trust in order to create a remedy for a third party, it can readily do so: see eg *Kowalski v Mitsubishi Motors Superannuation Fund* (2018). But if it is not so inclined it can readily cite the absence of any clear intention to create a trust: see eg *Winterton Constructions v Hambros* (1991). If privity of contract is really a problem, there are surely better ways to solve it.[19]

8.15 The law of tort and third parties

The law of trusts is not the only area of private law which has had an impact on the position of third parties. The law of tort has also played a part in circumventing the privity restriction in

---

17   See Dal Pont 2015a: 504–6.
18   See also *Bahr v Nicolay* (1988) at 618–19.
19   See Stewart 1999.

contract. This is seen most clearly in cases of a disappointed beneficiary. In these cases, the negligence of a solicitor means that a beneficiary of a will did not receive the bequest that was intended by the testator. The contract in these cases is between the testator, or their estate should they die, and the solicitor. Neither the testator nor estate suffers any loss, which is suffered instead by the third party beneficiary. A majority of the House of Lords in *White v Jones* (1995) nevertheless found that a duty of care was owed, and when the solicitor was negligent the disappointed beneficiary had a claim. One of the reasons that Lord Keith dissented was because English law does not allow a contract for the benefit of a third party. He was not prepared to allow that rule to be circumvented by allowing a claim in tort. Lord Goff, for the majority, also discussed this issue. Whilst he did not think that it was an appropriate occasion to revisit the question of privity and consideration, he was of the view that in the circumstances there was no 'unacceptable' circumvention of contract law. He described it (at 259) as 'extraordinary' that if the solicitor did not owe a duty then the only person with a claim suffered no loss, and the only person who suffered a loss had no claim. On the grounds of 'practical justice' Lord Goff thought that he was justified in finding that a duty of care was owed. In so doing he stressed the fact that if there was no liability there was an exceptional gap in the law. He sought to limit the duty to testamentary dispositions under a will. Lord Browne-Wilkinson and Lord Nolan reached the same result but their emphasis was slightly different. They suggested that liability was grounded in the way in which the solicitor had assumed responsibility for the beneficiaries. This reasoning potentially has broader application. Lord Mustill dissented. He argued that there was no duty of care because the requirement of an undertaking by the solicitors towards the beneficiary was lacking.

Not long afterwards, the High Court faced a similar situation in *Hill v Van Erp* (1997). A solicitor prepared a will for a client which was to include a testamentary disposition to a friend of the client. When the will was being executed, the solicitor asked the husband of the intended beneficiary to attest it. As a result of statute the involvement of the husband made the disposition null and void. After the death of the client the intended beneficiary brought a claim against the solicitor in negligence. Once more, the court was divided, but a majority favoured finding a duty of care between the solicitor and the intended beneficiary. In finding that the plaintiff could recover, Gummow J sought to distinguish the situation before him from the typical third-party beneficiary in contract. It was not a situation, he contended, where a solicitor agreed to confer a benefit on a third party. Instead the solicitor had agreed to carry out work for the testator. Rather than a contractual situation, this was one which Gummow J argued (at 233) was 'equivalent to contract'. A number of members of the High Court explicitly limited such claims to testamentary dispositions. It was said that *inter vivos* (among the living) transactions were to be treated differently. One of the key reasons given for dissenting by McHugh J was that he thought that it was extremely difficult to distinguish the transaction at issue from those entered into by other professionals such as accountants.

White v Jones was extensively referred to in *Hill v Van Erp*. The law of negligent claims for pure economic loss in England and Australia has diverged since then.[20] As a result, it is difficult to predict whether, contrary to some of the remarks that were made in both decisions, the principles articulated may have broader application. Determining whether a duty will be found

---

in novel cases of pure economic loss is a matter of applying a multi-factoral analysis. There is no complete list of factors that will be used to determine a duty of care and how they will be weighted. But in *Perre v Apand* (1999) at 220 McHugh J listed five factors that he thought would always be relevant in cases of pure economic loss: 'reasonable foreseeability of loss, indeterminacy of liability, autonomy of the individual, vulnerability to risk and the defendant's knowledge of the risk and its magnitude'.

8.16   Collateral contracts and third parties

The classic illustration of a 'three party' collateral contract is found in *Shanklin Pier v Detel Products* (1951).[21] The plaintiff owned a pier. The defendant was a manufacturer of paint. They told the plaintiff that the paint would last for at least seven years before the pier needed to be repainted. In reliance on that statement, the plaintiff instructed some contractors to buy the defendant's paint. The contractor entered into a contract to buy paint from the defendant but the paint only lasted three months. There were found to be three contracts. The main contract was between the contractor and the manufacturer. The contractor also had a contract with the plaintiff. The difficulty was in allowing the plaintiff to bring a claim against the manufacturer when the paint proved not to be durable. A third and 'collateral' contract was said to exist between the plaintiff and defendant. This contract was collateral to the 'main' contract for the sale of the paint. Consideration for the collateral contract was provided by the benefit that the manufacturer received when the pier owner instructed the contractor to buy their paint.

There is a degree of artificiality in this process. If the owner of the pier had wanted to enter into a contract with the paint manufacturer they could easily have done so. Many of the relevant authorities in this area date from the 1950s. A collateral contract was more common then, when a car was bought on a hire purchase arrangement. The main contract was between the car dealer and the hire purchase company, while a collateral contract was said to exist between the customer and the dealer: *CJ Grais & Sons v F Jones* (1962). This particular situation is now governed by statute.[22] The more recent attitude of the English courts can perhaps be best summarised by the words of Jackson J in *Fuji Seal v Catalytic Combustion* (2005) at [158]: 'It is not appropriate for this court to supplement the contractual arrangements which experienced and well-advised commercial parties choose to make'. There is little recent authority, but there is nothing to suggest that Australian judges would not concur with these sentiments.

8.17   Estoppel and third parties

Estoppel plays a significant role in Australia, as Chapter 7 has demonstrated. One possible application concerns the situation where A and B enter into a contract for the benefit of C. If C is induced to believe that they will benefit from the contract, and in reliance on that inducement suffers a detriment, they may be able to raise an estoppel against the parties to the contract. In the right circumstances it may also be possible for A to raise an estoppel against B, if B fails to confer a promised benefit on C. In practice, however, demonstrating a detriment on A's part may be rather more difficult. Estoppel was not raised in the course of argument in

---

21   Collateral contracts can also be identified between just two parties: see **9.16**.
22   See *National Consumer Credit Protection Act 2009* (Cth) Sch 1 (National Credit Code).

Trident v McNiece (1988), but neither Brennan nor Deane JJ, who both mentioned estoppel, ruled out its application.

8.18   Statutory reform of the privity rule

Statute has had a major impact on the doctrine of privity. Commonwealth legislation has provided exceptions in contracts of a particular sort. Section 48 of the *Insurance Contracts Act 1984* (Cth) (see **8.08**) is just one important example, although some very common types of insurance, including marine and third-party motor accident insurance, are excluded from its operation (s 9). The various types of 'negotiable instruments', such as cheques and bills of exchange, are also a special category of contract governed by legislation: see **14.09**.

More generally, the legislatures in Western Australia, Queensland and the Northern Territory have all enacted statutes which make significant inroads into the privity doctrine. Although found in legislation regulating property interests and transactions, the relevant provisions are not subject matter specific but have general application. Despite their importance as litigation centres, similar legislation has yet to be enacted in Victoria or New South Wales.

8.19   Third-party claims in Western Australia

The oldest and narrowest of the three statutory regimes is found in Western Australia. Section 11(2) of the *Property Law Act 1969* (WA) states that 'where a contract expressly in its terms purports to confer a benefit directly on a person who is not named as a party to the contract, the contract is ... enforceable by that person in his [sic] own name'. Consideration is not expressly mentioned, but to require consideration on the part of the beneficiary would largely defeat the object of the legislation: *Westralian Farmers v Southern Meat Packers* (1981) at 245–6.

The reference to 'expressly' in the statute has been interpreted to mean that the beneficiary must be intended, rather than someone who happens to benefit.[23] The term purporting to confer a benefit must generally be express. Implied terms purporting to confer a benefit are more difficult. In *Jones v Bartlett* (2000), the adult son of tenants of a house was injured when he walked into a glass door. The landlord would have been liable to the tenants on the basis of a contractual duty of care, as implied into the lease as a result of the *Residential Tenancies Act 1987* (WA). The son argued that by virtue of s 11 of the *Property Law Act 1969* he might also bring a claim on the contract. His claim failed. There was nothing in the lease which purported to confer a benefit upon him which made it unnecessary for the High Court to decide whether implied terms fell within the legislation. But later Western Australian authority suggests that s 11 'confers only limited recognition of third party rights' and that 'a right is not acquired by implication. It is necessary that the contractual provision relied on expressly in its terms purport to confer a benefit directly on the claimant': *Westina v BGC Contracting* (2009) at [46].

Other aspects of the legislation have also been narrowly construed. It only applies to written and not oral contracts: see *Westpac v Bell Group* (2012). On the other hand, it is not necessary the third party must be identified by name at the time the contract is entered into. It is sufficient that they can be identified as part of a particular class: *Westina* at [43].

---

23   For an example of a third party being able to satisfy this test, see *Jaddcal v Minson* (2011).

Section 11(2)(a) provides that any defence that was available against the promisee is available against the third party. Section 11(2)(b) requires that the beneficiary join the promisee in any action against the promisor, a provision unique to Western Australia. Unless the contract provides otherwise, it may be cancelled or modified by the parties, though only until the third party beneficiary 'adopts' the contract, whether expressly or by conduct (s 11(3)).

8.20   Queensland and the Northern Territory

The legislation in Queensland and Northern Territory is almost identical. There is also considerable overlap with the earlier legislation in Western Australia. In some ways, the latter statutes are more liberal. Section 55(1) of the *Property Law Act 1974* (Qld) states that:

> A promisor who, for a valuable consideration moving from the promisee, promises to do or refrain from doing an act or acts for the benefit of a beneficiary shall, upon acceptance by the beneficiary, be subject to a duty enforceable by the beneficiary to perform the promise.

This is mirrored by s 56(1) of the *Law of Property Act 2000* (NT).

Provided that the beneficiary was in existence at the time of the contract's formation, they need not be identified by name. Nor, in Queensland, need a contract be wholly in writing in order to fall within the legislation, although it is different in the Northern Territory (Qld s 55(6); NT s 56(6)). In common with the Western Australia legislation, incidental beneficiaries are excluded. This follows from the definition of a promise as one 'which is or appears to be intended to be legally binding' and 'which creates or appears to be intended to create a duty enforceable by the beneficiary' (ibid). In *Northern Sandblasting v Harris* (1997), the High Court interpreted this provision narrowly. It held that, in Queensland, only an express term which confers a benefit is covered by the legislation. A statutory implied term could not generate a claim.

Upon accepting the benefit, the beneficiary may then sue in their own name and recover damages, as well as gain specific performance and injunctions (Qld s 55(3)(a); NT s 56(3)(a)). Acceptance, like adoption, is a key concept. Prior to acceptance of the benefit, the promisor and promisee are able to change the terms of the contract and may even decide to no longer confer a benefit (Qld s 55(2); NT s 56(2)). Once the benefit is accepted, any change requires the consent of the beneficiary as well as the promisor and promisee (Qld s 55(3)(d); NT s 56(3)(d)). Acceptance, whether by words or conduct, must be communicated to the promisor and must be given within any time specified or, where there is no such time, within a reasonable time (Qld s 55(6); NT s 56(6)). The legislation allows the beneficiary to take the benefit of a contract to which they are not a party, but does not allow burdens to be imposed upon them: *Rural View Developments v Fastfort* (2009). It is, however, possible to impose conditions by which the beneficiary is bound when they accept (Qld s 55(3)(b); NT s 56(3)(b)).

As in Western Australia, any defence that was available against the promisee is available against the third party (Qld s 55(4); NT s 56(4)). Even where the defence is personal against the promisee – for example, where the promisor contracts under duress – it has parasitic effects on a beneficiary who may be blameless. There will be situations in which the legislation cannot be relied upon – for example, where the beneficiary does not communicate their acceptance – in which case, the common law applies as usual (Qld s 55(7); NT s 56(7)).

Imposing a burden on a third party

8.21 The general rule and restrictions on property use

The general rule is that burdens cannot be imposed on a third party to a contract. One obvious exception, however, is found in property law. A freehold covenant is a device by which the owner of one piece of land typically imposes a restriction on the freedom of the owner of another piece of land to do as they please with that property. Typically a covenant places restrictions on the right to build on the neighbouring land. There is no difficulty between the original covenantor and covenantee. Such an arrangement is only problematic when the covenantor conveys the land to a third person who is not a party. A covenant is not likely to be very useful if it lapses when the covenantor conveys the land. At the same time, to allow a burden to be imposed on the new owner runs counter to the doctrine of privity of contract. In *Austerberry v Oldham* (1885), the English Court of Appeal held that the burden of the covenant did not pass in law. Several ways around the problem have long existed. A chain of covenants can be used. The original covenantor remains liable on the covenant, but when the land is transferred the new owner agrees to enter into an indemnity which covers any damages to the original covenantee or their successor in title. The relative ease with which the chain can be broken and the risk that the original covenantor will die or disappear are significant disadvantages of this method.

This is also a situation in which equity generates an exception to the privity doctrine. In *Tulk v Moxhay* (1848), Lord Cottenham argued that a covenant should be enforced against a party with notice of its existence. The rule in *Tulk v Moxhay* only applies to negative covenants; namely, those which prevent the covenantor doing something such as building. There are other limits as well. The covenant must accommodate the dominant tenement. This means that there must be some land to which the covenant attaches. The servient land, which is subject to the restriction, must be reasonably close to the dominant land. The covenant must be for the benefit of the dominant land and be intended to run with the land after it is conveyed.

It has sometimes been suggested that the concept of 'privity of estates' might have wider application. In *Lord Strathcona Steamship v Dominion Coal* (1926), the Privy Council appeared to apply a similar principle outside of the context of real property. It was held that a time charterer of a ship had an interest in the vessel which could be enforced against a purchaser with notice of the charterparty. As a result, the new owner could be restrained by an injunction from refusing to perform the charterparty. *Lord Strathcona* has been distinguished in Australia. In *Shell Oil v McIlwraith McEacharn* (1945) at 150, Jordan CJ said that the decision turned on the peculiar value of a ship to a charterer, and it was limited to the situation where an injunction was sought. Later authorities have doubted the Privy Council's decision.[24] Australian courts are no longer bound by the Privy Council, and *Lord Strathcona* may not be an authority from which a general principle can be extracted.

---

24   In England, see *Port Line v Ben Line* (1958). In Australia, see *Howie v NSW Lawn Tennis Ground* (1956).

Reform of the privity doctrine

8.22   Is reform warranted?

In the end, the majority of the High Court in *Trident v McNiece* (1988) decided against a major qualification of the doctrine of privity of contract that would have made it easier for third-party beneficiaries to enforce promises made in their favour. The case for reform of the common law rule is a matter of particular relevance in States like New South Wales, which are yet to introduce a statute that might mitigate some of the impact of the privity rule. Arguments can be made for preserving privity, beyond its historical pedigree.[25] It may be difficult to reconcile an abolition of the privity doctrine with the idea that contract law is grounded in the idea of a bargain. A third party who is able to bring a claim gives nothing to the promisor in exchange. They receive something by way of a benefit that they have not bargained for. The consideration is provided by the promisee rather than the third party. The idea that there is a bargain, albeit one between the promisor and the promisee, fails to explain how it is that the third party, who is not party to that bargain, can enforce a contract. The same argument can be supported by reference to a promissory theory of contract,[26] if it is accepted that what matters is that the promise is made to the beneficiary. If A makes a promise to B to benefit C, the promisee is B rather than C. These objections flow from the fact that a contract is a voluntary obligation only undertaken to a particular person. Some of these objections fall away, however, once it is noted that the presence of a bargain may be less important than it once was. For example, recent applications of the doctrine of consideration may weaken the force of the idea that a contract is founded on a bargain: see **5.28**, **13.07–13.08**. Many contract scholars would also reject a promissory theory of contract: see **2.15**.

The Law Commission (1996), in a report which preceded the statutory reform in England in the form of the *Contracts (Rights of Third Parties) Act 1999*, put forward a number of justifications for reform which are just as relevant in Australia. It was said that the privity rule thwarts the intention of the contracting parties. This argument has some superficial attraction. The same sentiments can be found in some of the judgments in *Trident*, but it suffers from a flaw. It assumes that contract law is just about the fulfilment of the parties' intentions. Intention is an important element in contract law. A contract is an agreement which is intended to have legal force. At the same time, intention is not enough. To intend to contract, or in this situation for the parties to intend to benefit a third party, is a necessary condition of liability, but not a sufficient one. A second justification put forward by the Law Commission is that a third party may rely on a contract made for their benefit. This was certainly true of the plaintiff in *Trident*. The Australian statutes recognise that a third party who has adopted or accepted the benefit, is in a different position to one who has not. Only the former has a right of action. The claims of the contractual parties to modify the contract are also less strong in this case. Estoppel might cover situations in which a third party has acted in reliance on the expectation that they will receive a benefit.

All in all, the arguments about the value of the privity doctrine are not all one way. As things stand, however, it is difficult to disagree with the Law Commission, when it observed (1996: 41) that '[t]he existence of the rule, together with the exceptions to it, has given rise to a complex body of law and to the use of elaborate and often artificial stratagems'.

---

25   See eg Kincaid 1989, 1997; Smith 1997.
26   See eg Fried 2015.

PART III

CONTRACTUAL OBLIGATIONS

9

TERMS AND OBLIGATIONS

Introduction

9.01 The different types of contractual term

A *term* of a contract is a provision or identifiable component that sets out what the parties are to do or how their agreement is to operate.

There are many different ways in which contractual terms can be categorised. One of the most important distinctions is between express and implied terms. An *express term* is generally understood as one that has explicitly been identified by the parties, whether verbally or in writing, or the existence of which can otherwise be inferred from their conduct. In this chapter, we explore two common issues that can arise with such terms. The first is whether and how a set of written terms prepared by one party can be said to be incorporated or included in a contract. The second concerns the status of statements or assurances made before the parties have reached agreement.

An *implied term* is a provision on which the parties have not actually agreed, but which is nonetheless taken to be part of their contract. There are at least four different types of implied term, those which are implied: (1) in fact, or on an ad hoc basis; (2) by custom and practice; (3) by law (that is, the common law); or (4) by statute.[1] More is said about each of these categories later in the chapter. For now, it is sufficient to note that the first two rest on the notion of presumed agreement. They involve identifying a provision that the parties are taken to have wanted to be part of their agreement, even though they have not said as much. The third and fourth, by contrast, involve a term being imposed on the parties by the operation of a legal rule. But it is important not to exaggerate these distinctions. Terms implied by law, like those implied in fact or by custom and practice, can only take effect if they are consistent with what the parties have expressly agreed. The same is true for at least some terms implied by statute. So the process for implying terms is necessarily linked to the ascertainment of any express terms.[2]

A further way of classifying terms relates to the consequences of their being breached and more specifically whether the 'innocent' (non-breaching) party may terminate the contract. As Chapter 16 will explain, contractual terms may be divided for this purpose into three classes. An *essential term* is sufficiently important that any breach of it will justify termination. An *intermediate term* is one that, if breached in a serious or 'fundamental' way, will create a right to terminate, but not if breached with less serious consequences. And a *non-essential term* is one that can never, on its own, lead to termination if breached. Essential and non-essential terms may also be referred to as *conditions* and *warranties* respectively. But those labels can have other, very different meanings – as indeed will become apparent later in this chapter, when we discuss the difference between a representation and a warranty. For that reason, in this book we generally prefer the language of essential and non-essential terms.

---

1   Two further categories are sometimes suggested: see eg Carter et al 2015: 209. These are the implication of terms by a course of dealing (see **9.08**), and implication by construction (see **9.23**). But the first of these are better regarded as express terms: see eg *La Rosa v Nudrill* (2013) at [43]. The same is true more generally for 'inferred' terms: see **9.22**. Compare Seddon & Bigwood 2017: 476–7, distinguishing between what they call universal, generic and specific implied terms.

2   See further **9.23**, discussing the difficulty of distinguishing between the processes of implication and interpretation.

9.02   Contractual and non-contractual obligations

The terms of a contract are in various ways concerned with creating, defining or limiting the parties' mutual rights and obligations. They may, for example, impose a duty to do something, or provide an excuse for not doing something. They may set a start or end date for the contract, or stipulate circumstances in which the contract may automatically cease to operate, or be terminated by one of the parties. They may also provide for how disputes are to be resolved, or for the remedial consequences of a certain type of breach.

A breach of the obligations directly created by a contract may lead to an award of one of the remedies outlined in Chapter 3 and explored in more detail in Part VII. This will typically involve a claim for debt or damages, or less commonly other orders such as specific performance or an injunction.[3] It is important, however, to bear in mind that the parties to a contract may also incur obligations that have other legal sources. For example, if a lawyer undertakes to provide a client with advice, they will be under a duty to take reasonable care as to the quality or accuracy of that advice. That duty will typically arise under an implied term of their contract with the client, but its breach will also give rise to an action in the tort of negligence: see eg *Astley v Austrust* (1999). The parties to a contract may also have equitable obligations that are enforceable through remedies (such as an account of profits) that are not otherwise available for breach of contract: see **3.15**, **12.16**.

There are also many instances in which legislation imposes duties on contracting parties. Sometimes these go beyond what the common law of contract would otherwise require; for example, in relation to the disclosure of information (see **4.09**) or the form of a contract (see **4.04**, **5.44–5.46**). But they may also impose obligations which either replicate or extend the effect of terms previously implied by the common law. Sometimes, as discussed in the final section of this chapter, statutes of this kind simply imply terms of their own, which are then enforceable through the common law remedies for breach of contract. But it is becoming increasingly common for legislative regimes to avoid this technique and instead impose duties directly. These can then be enforced through an array of statutory remedies that are typically much broader than the common law would provide. We look in particular at the most general and practically significant example of this approach: the *consumer guarantees* created by the Australian Consumer Law (ACL) in relation to the supply of goods or services to a consumer.

Incorporation of written terms

9.03   Types of incorporation

A business or other organisation will frequently wish to enter into a contract on the basis of a set of written terms that they (or someone representing them) have drawn up. These may have been put together for a specific transaction. But more commonly today they are standardised terms, intended to be used for a class of transactions: see **4.04**. If *both* parties are intent on using their own terms, the resulting 'battle of the forms' may create doubt as to whether any contract has been formed: see **5.23**. More commonly, however, it is clear that the parties have

---

3   A distinction is sometimes drawn in this respect between the 'primary' obligations originally created by a contract and the 'secondary' or remedial obligations imposed in the event of a breach: see **17.01**.

entered into a contract. The issue is more specifically whether the written terms (and in particular often an exclusion or limitation clause) put forward by one of them can be taken to have been *incorporated* into that contract.

The general rule here is that for terms to be validly incorporated, the other party must have indicated their assent to those terms. This most commonly happens in one of three ways: through *signed* acceptance; through a failure to object after being given *reasonable notice*; or through agreement inferred from a *prior course of dealing*.

9.04   Signature

A person is generally bound by any document that they sign, whether or not they have read or understood it. The strictness of this rule is illustrated by *L'Estrange v Graucob* (1943). The plaintiff purchased an automatic cigarette machine from the defendant. She signed an order form containing a clause excluding liability for all express and implied warranties (promises) as to the quality or working of the machine. The machine was faulty, and the plaintiff brought a claim for breach of contract on an implied warranty. The English Court of Appeal held that the plaintiff was bound by the exclusion clause, which was incorporated into the contract by the signature even though it was in 'regrettably small print' and had not been read by the plaintiff.

This approach was affirmed by the High Court in *Toll v Alphapharm* (2004) at [57]:

> The general rule … [is that] a person who signs a document which is known by that person to contain contractual terms, and to affect legal relations, is bound by those terms, and it is immaterial that the person has not read the document.

The case involved a contract for Toll to transport a batch of flu vaccine, which was damaged in transit. It was held that Toll could rely on an exclusion clause in a 'credit application' signed but not read by a representative of the client. As the Court noted (at [45]), the act of signing a document will generally suggest that the person concerned 'either has read and approved the contents of the document or is willing to take the chance of being bound by those contents … whatever they might be'.[4]

As the Court also observed (at [54], [57]), however, there have always been exceptions to what is often called the rule in *L'Estrange v Graucob*. It does not apply where there is some 'vitiating element' such as misrepresentation, mistake or duress. Nor, as the extract above from *Toll* makes clear, does it operate if the document signed was not one which would reasonably have been understood to have contractual effect.

Both possibilities are illustrated by *Curtis v Chemical Cleaning and Dyeing* (1951). The plaintiff, who wanted a wedding dress cleaned, was asked to sign a document headed 'Receipt'. When she asked why, a store assistant told her it was because the defendant would not accept liability for certain risks, such as damage to beads or sequins. The document in fact purported to exclude liability for 'any damage howsoever arising'. The dress was returned with a stain and the plaintiff sued for damages. It was held that the defendant could not rely on the exclusion clause because its employee had misrepresented the effect of the document in which it was contained. Denning LJ also expressed the view that even in the absence of this

---

4   See further Peden & Carter 2005a.

misrepresentation, the plaintiff's signature may not have resulted in the incorporation of the terms in the document, given that she might reasonably have understood it to be no more than a receipt to be presented when reclaiming the dress.

9.05   Is an electronic acceptance a signature?

It is common today for terms to be made available electronically; for example, on a website or on a screen that pops up on a mobile device. The terms might relate to the use of an app or program, or the acquisition of goods or services, or simply access to certain information. Consumers or customers are routinely asked to agree to such terms by clicking or tapping a box marked 'I agree', or words to that effect. The question is whether this should be taken to be a 'signature', for the purpose of the general rule discussed above. If it is, then in the absence of misrepresentation, the terms will automatically be part of any contract with the business or organisation responsible for the terms. If not, then it would usually be necessary to show, in accordance with the principles outlined below, that reasonable notice had been given.

Despite the prevalence of electronic terms, the point has very rarely arisen for decision. In *eBay v Creative Festival Entertainment* (2006) at [49], Rares J described the online purchase of tickets to the Big Day Out music festival in these words (with emphasis added):

> By clicking on the relevant buttons and, by the computer bringing up all terms needed to purchase a ticket, on behalf of Ticketmaster as agent for [the festival promoter], the whole transaction was in writing, *signed* and agreed by the parties.

Despite using the language of 'signature', however, the judge went on to find that online purchasers could not be said to have accepted additional terms contained on tickets subsequently sent to them. This was despite the fact that the existence of such terms was highlighted in a policy on the website which purchasers had agreed to accept. The reasoning on this point strongly suggests that reasonable notice was lacking. Indeed, Rares J referred (at [52]) to the need for specific attention to be drawn to any 'unusual or significant terms'. Yet, as noted in **9.07**, this requirement does *not* apply to terms in signed documents. The judge may well have taken a different view if the relevant terms had been immediately accessible by a link from the webpages visited by purchasers. Nevertheless, the decision cannot be taken to support the proposition that clicking 'I agree' has exactly the same effect as a traditional signature. As a matter of principle, the routine process of clicking or tapping through a series of screens arguably does not have sufficient formality to be equated to inscribing one's name.[5] However, it *might* be different if, for instance, a consumer were required to insert their name and type words of assent.

Before leaving this point, it should be noted that the *Electronic Transactions Acts* (see **2.10**) in each Australian jurisdiction do have a provision allowing an electronic communication to be treated as satisfying a legal requirement for a signature, providing certain conditions are met.[6] But it is far from clear that the rule in *L'Estrange v Graucob* can be called a 'requirement' as such. Nor is it self-evident that a mere click or tap can be said to be a reliable

---

5   See Macdonald 2011.
6   See eg *Electronic Transactions Act 2000* (NSW) s 9; and see further **5.45**.

method of identifying a person, which is one of the conditions imposed by the provision. On the face of it, therefore, the point remains one to be resolved as a matter of common law.

9.06   Reasonable notice

Besides the electronic examples just given, there are many ways in which a party may seek to communicate its preferred terms. They may be printed on tickets, receipts or invoices, or included in a catalogue or brochure advertising the party's products. Or they may simply be displayed on a sign.

A series of English decisions starting in the nineteenth century and often called the 'ticket cases' established the principle that, even in the absence of a signature, a customer can be taken to have accepted any terms shown or given to them merely by going ahead with a transaction without objection. But for this to be the case, either the customer must be aware of the terms,[7] or (more commonly) the party putting forward the terms must have taken reasonable steps to bring them to the customer's attention: see eg *Parker v South Eastern Railway Co* (1877) at 423.

What constitutes reasonable notice very much depends on the circumstances,[8] but three broad propositions emerge from the case law. The first is similar to a point already made above about signed documents. This is that merely giving a document to a customer is not sufficient, unless the customer would reasonably be expected to know that the document was likely to contain contractual terms. In *Causer v Browne* (1952), another case involving a dress being taken for dry cleaning, an exclusion clause printed on a docket was found not to be part of the contract. In the Court's opinion, the plaintiff would reasonably have understood the docket to have been no more than a 'voucher' to be presented when collecting the dress. It is interesting to speculate, however, whether the decision might be different today, when there is arguably greater awareness in the community about the use of 'fine print' to disclaim or limit liability.

The second proposition is that, to be effective, any notice must be given *before* the relevant contract is formed. In *Oceanic Sun Line v Fay* (1988), for example, passengers booking and paying for a cruise were given documents that could be exchanged for tickets when boarding the cruise ship. A term on the tickets purported to deal with the jurisdiction of courts to resolve any disputes, but was found by the High Court not to be part of the contract. By the time the passengers received the tickets, it was too late to give them notice of the term, as the relevant contracts had already been made. A similar conclusion was reached in *eBay*, not just for tickets purchased online, but also for those bought 'over the counter' at Ticketmaster outlets. When the tickets were handed over, customers had already paid their cash or had their cards debited. The same reasoning was used in *Olley v Marlborough Court* (1949) to deny any effect to a notice in a hotel bedroom, visible to a guest only after they had checked in. *Thornton v Shoe Lane Parking* (1971) provides a further example. Tickets issued by a machine at the entrance to a car park referred to terms displayed inside the premises. In practice, a driver could only discover these after they had accepted the ticket and gone through the barrier, by which time a contract had been formed.

---

7   For an example of actual notice of incorporated terms, see *Ange v First East Auction Holdings* (2011).
8   Compare Freilich & Webb 2009, arguing for different approaches to be taken in consumer and commercial transactions.

9.07   Onerous or unusual terms

A third principle that emerges from the cases on the incorporation of written terms is that some terms require more notice than others. In *J Spurling v Bradshaw* (1956) at 466, Denning LJ expressed the view that:

> the more unreasonable a clause is, the greater the notice which must be given of it. Some clauses which I have seen would need to be printed in red ink on the face of the document with a red hand pointing to it before the notice could be held to be sufficient.

The idea that 'onerous' or 'unusual' terms require additional warning or explanation has become firmly accepted: see eg *Oceanic Sun Line* at 229; *Baltic Shipping v Dillon* (1991) at 8–9, 24–5. In *Interfoto Picture Library v Stiletto Visual Programmes* (1989), a business which borrowed a set of photographic transparencies was charged an unusually high 'holding fee' for not returning them within 14 days. The fee was stipulated in a set of conditions printed on a delivery note that came with the transparencies. The English Court of Appeal accepted that the borrower would have recognised this as a contractual document. But the library had not done enough to draw the attention of its client to what was variously described (at 436, 445) as an 'exorbitant' or 'extortionate' fee.

In *Toll v Alphapharm* (2004), however, the High Court rejected the suggestion that the principle should apply to terms in signed documents. Quite apart from the difficulty of determining the criteria for designating terms as onerous or unusual, the Court warned (at [54]) that 'to introduce the concept of sufficient notice into the field of signed contracts' would carry the 'danger of subverting fundamental principle based on sound legal policy'.

9.08   Prior course of dealing

Besides signature or implied consent through reasonable notice, a third means of incorporating written terms is through a regular and consistent course of dealing, from which an acceptance of the terms in question may be inferred. In *Balmain New Ferry v Robertson* (1906), the plaintiff, who had missed his ferry, sought to evade a charge that was imposed on anyone leaving the wharf. The ferry company had posted a sign explaining that this charge applied to anyone who entered and then sought to exit its wharf, regardless of whether they had travelled on a ferry. The High Court held that the plaintiff had impliedly agreed to the charge – but not because of the sign. As Griffith CJ pointed out (at 386), if the plaintiff had been a stranger visiting the wharf for the first time, the company might have sought to establish, in line with the ticket cases, that it had taken reasonable steps to give him notice of the conditions of admittance to the wharf. But here there was no need to show that the plaintiff had seen the sign, or should have done so. It was sufficient that, having taken the defendant's ferries many times, he must have been aware of their practice of charging an exit fee to everyone leaving their wharves.

The basis for finding consent in this type of situation was spelled out by the House of Lords in *Henry Kendall & Sons v William Lillico & Sons* (1969). A regular practice had evolved for ordering animal feed from a supplier, Grimsdale. An oral contract would be made, following which Grimsdale would send the purchaser, SAPPA, a contract note. SAPPA was aware that the note had conditions on the back, which were held to have contractual effect. As Lord Pearce explained (at 113):

> The question ... is not what SAPPA themselves thought or knew about the matter but what they should be taken as representing to Grimsdale about it or leading Grimsdale to believe. The only reasonable inference from the regular course of dealing over so long a period is that SAPPA were evincing an acceptance of, and a readiness to be bound by, the printed conditions of whose existence they were well aware although they had not troubled to read them.

In *DJ Hill v Walter H Wright* (1971), the defendant had repeatedly contracted to carry goods for the plaintiff. On each occasion when the goods were delivered, a representative of the plaintiff was asked to sign a form accepting conditions of carriage printed on the back. A Full Court of the Victorian Supreme Court held that these conditions were not incorporated into what were otherwise oral contracts. It was said (at 753) that the parties had never treated the forms as 'contractual documents'. The Court's reasoning on this point appeared to suggest that this was because they had only ever been presented after an oral contract had already been formed. But that cannot be correct, because there have been many cases (including *Henry Kendall*) in which a post-contractual document has been incorporated through a course of dealing. On the first few occasions, the supply of the document would be too late to affect a contract already formed. But eventually, the acceptance of the document without dispute might lead the other party to believe that the terms had been accepted – depending on the circumstances.

The simpler and more obvious explanation for the result in *DJ Hill* should have been the Court's finding that the plaintiff had no reason to believe that the forms were anything other than delivery documents. In *La Rosa v Nudrill* (2013), another case involving the carriage of machinery, the Western Australian Court of Appeal held that terms contained in an invoice supplied when seeking payment were not incorporated into the contract of carriage, despite similar documents having been used on previous occasions. There was nothing to suggest *in this case* that the invoices had ever been accepted or treated by the customer as contractual documents. But, as Buss JA in particular made clear (at [71]), it is not essential for there to be incorporation through a prior course of dealing that the relevant terms be communicated prior to or at the time of making the relevant contract.

9.09   Incorporation by reference

It is common for parties to be given or shown documents that make reference to terms set out elsewhere, often in standard form. As a matter of principle, it is clearly possible for such terms to be incorporated into a contract, so long as there is evidence that both parties have agreed to that. The most straightforward situation is where the terms in question are attached to, or presented with, a signed document. For the reasons discussed earlier, a party's signature will be sufficient to indicate their assent to terms being incorporated, provided there has been no misrepresentation as to their content or effect: see eg *Toll v Alphapharm* (2004). Even if the external terms are not in fact attached, it is sufficient that they have previously been made available to the other party: see eg *Ange v First East Auction Holdings* (2011). But where the terms are not immediately available, the matter is more complicated. In some instances, the parties' dealings may be such as to infer a clear acceptance by one party of the other's standard terms, even though they may never have been provided: see eg *Maxitherm Boilers v Pacific Dunlop* (1997). Otherwise, however, it becomes a matter of reasonable notice – and in accordance with the principles outlined above, specific attention may have to be called to any unusual terms: see *Oceanic Sun Line* at 228–9; and see eg *Pritchard v Trius Constructions*

(2011). In the context of online transactions, a hyperlink that takes the reader to the relevant terms *may* be sufficient. But it is different where the relevant terms can only be accessed after the contract has been made: see eg *eBay v Creative Festival Entertainment* (2006).

Even if external documents are successfully incorporated, there may still be questions of whether particular provisions in them have contractual effect. Where a standard set of terms is inconsistent with other provisions that the parties have drawn up and agreed, it is usually the specific terms that will be given precedence: see eg *Giliberto v Kenny* (1983); *Walker v Citigroup Global Markets* (2006). Some incorporated documents may also contain vague language that sets out values or objectives to guide the parties' dealings with one another. Whether these should be construed as binding commitments or merely 'aspirational' statements will be determined objectively, according to how a reasonable person would view them. This has repeatedly become an issue with policy documents provided by employers to their employees: see eg *Goldman Sachs v Nikolich* (2007); *Romero v Farstad Shipping* (2014); *Gramotnev v Queensland University of Technology* (2015). To overcome any uncertainty in this respect, some policies are expressly declared not to have contractual effect, at least as against the employer: see eg *Yousif v Commonwealth Bank* (2010).[9]

One question that arises with the incorporation of external documents is whether the relevant terms can be varied after the contract has been formed. In the first instance, this is a matter for interpretation. If a set of terms or policies are taken to be incorporated only as they stand as at a particular date (generally the date of formation), then they cannot be varied without mutual consent: see eg *Bostik v Gorgevski* (1992). A party who wants a power of unilateral variation can stipulate this expressly; for example, by specifying that terms are incorporated 'as varied from time to time'. But it is generally implied that a power to introduce such changes may only be exercised in a reasonable or rational way, not arbitrarily or capriciously: see eg *Akmeemana v Murray* (2009); and see further **12.19**, **13.14.** Terms allowing for unilateral variation may also in certain circumstances be challenged as unfair: see **13.14**.

9.10 Rectifying mistakes

As discussed in **18.43–18.44**, a court may make an order for the *rectification* of a written contract, or of a document forming part of a contract, to ensure that it reflects the agreement the parties actually intended to make. But this process can only be used to correct a mistake as to the *content* of a document, not its meaning or effect.

Treating pre-contractual statements as express terms

9.11 Determining the status of pre-contractual statements

Much can be said, done, and suggested in the period before a contract is made. The question here is whether it is possible to identify a particular statement by one of the parties and give it contractual effect. The statement may have been made verbally, or in writing; for example, in

---

9 See further Stewart et al 2016: 282–5.

an advertisement, or a quote for a product or work to be supplied, or an email or other message passing between the parties. The party to whom the statement was directed may want to argue that they were led to believe that the statement was true, and sue for breach of contract if it turns out not to be.

For a pre-contractual statement to be a term, two hurdles need to be overcome. The first is to show that the statement was a *warranty*. In this particular context, the word 'warranty' means a promise that something is true,[10] as opposed to a *mere representation*. The latter involves simply stating that something is true, but not going so far as to guarantee its truth. If a contract is induced by a false statement, it may be possible to rescind the contract for *misrepresentation*. If the statement is made in trade or commerce, there may also be liability for breaching a statutory prohibition on misleading and deceptive conduct, such as s 18 of the ACL. Both of these possibilities are discussed in Chapter 18. But the falsity of a statement will not lead to an action for breach of contract, unless the statement can be categorised as a warranty.

Secondly, even if a warranty can be identified, it must be established that it was intended to have contractual effect. This will present particular difficulties where the parties have agreed to written terms that do not include the statement, or indeed contradict it.[11] In what follows, we examine each of these issues in turn.

9.12   Warranty or representation?

Whether a statement should be regarded as a warranty or a mere representation depends on the objective intentions of the parties. In *Oscar Chess v Williams* (1957) at 375, Denning LJ explained the process:

> The question whether a warranty was intended depends on the conduct of the parties, on their words and behaviour, rather than on their thoughts. If an intelligent bystander would reasonably infer that a warranty was intended, that will suffice.

There are no hard and fast rules when it comes to working out what the parties intend. There are, however, factors that may be relevant.

The wording used is an obvious starting point. Promissory words are required, as opposed to an expression of opinion, before a statement can be regarded as a contract term: see eg *JJ Savage & Sons v Blakney* (1970). The greater the importance attached to the statement, the more likely it is that it was intended to be a term of the contract. In *Couchman v Hill* (1947), a heifer (a young cow) was put up for sale at an auction, but no warranty was given as to its condition. The plaintiff asked the defendant whether the heifer was in calf, and said that he was not interested in purchasing it if it was. He was told that the heifer was not in calf. This was untrue and the heifer died as a result of a miscarriage. The plaintiff attached a great deal of importance to the representation that the heifer was not in calf, which made it a term. Timing may also matter. A statement made just before a contract is formed, in response to a question

---

10   Compare the narrower use of 'warranty' to mean a non-essential term: see **16.06**.
11   Note, however, that express warranties relating to goods or services may in some cases be given effect under s 59 of the ACL, as one of the 'consumer guarantees' outlined later in this chapter: see **9.36**.

about an important matter, is more likely to be a warranty: see eg *Van den Esschert v Chappell* (1960), concerning an assurance by the vendor of a house that it had no white ants.

The relative knowledge and expertise of the parties is also a relevant consideration. In *Smythe v Thomas* (2007), the seller of an aeroplane on eBay stated that it was capable of being flown from Albury to South Australia, and would possess a current airworthiness certificate. These were statements about matters within the seller's knowledge alone, and which were important to the buyer. As a result, they were warranties. The same principle was applied in *Dick Bentley v Harold Smith* (1965), when a prestige car dealer wrongly (though innocently) claimed that a second-hand Bentley had done far fewer miles than it really had. These cases can be contrasted with *Oscar Chess*, where a private seller incorrectly claimed that his vehicle had been made in 1948 (as its registration book suggested), when in fact it was a 1939 model. This was held *not* to be a warranty. The dealer who purchased the car was in just as good a position here as the seller to know its true age.

9.13   The parol evidence rule

Many contracts, even if negotiated orally, are reduced into writing. In these cases pre-contractual statements which are not included in the final document necessarily have limited relevance. This is reflected in the *parol evidence rule*. In its classic form, the rule prevents any recourse to verbal statements, or other 'extrinsic' materials, 'to add to or subtract from, or in any manner to vary or qualify [a] written contract': *Goss v Nugent* (1833) at 64–5. The rule has traditionally had two distinct functions. One of these, to identify the evidence that a court can consider in *interpreting* written agreements, is considered in the next chapter: see **10.05**. But here we are concerned with its impact on attempts to add or change terms in such agreements.

The parol evidence rule rests on the importance traditionally attached to writing. In *Equuscorp v Glengallan Investments* (2004), the High Court held that a group of investors were bound by written loan agreements that they had signed. They could not rely on certain terms said to be part of earlier oral agreements with the lender, because any such agreements had clearly been superseded by the written versions. As the Court explained (at [33]):

> Having executed the document, and not having been induced to do so by fraud, mistake, or misrepresentation, the [borrowers] cannot now be heard to say that they are not bound by the agreement recorded in it.

The Court went on to note that this approach can be justified by the objective approach to determining contractual intention. Moreover, resolving disputes as to oral agreements 'is commonly difficult, time-consuming, expensive and problematic' (at [35]).

At its height, the parol evidence rule was applied very strictly. If there was a document that *appeared* to be a complete record of the parties' contract, then no evidence could be relied upon to suggest otherwise. For example, in *LG Thorne v Thomas Borthwick* (1956), it was apparent that the parties to a sale of neatsfoot oil had orally agreed that it was to be a sale by sample. But because nothing was said about this in the document drawn up to record the agreement, the Full Court of the New South Wales Supreme Court refused to give effect to that intention. The Court acknowledged a qualification to the parol evidence rule previously noted by Isaacs J in *Hoyt's v Spencer* (1919) at 143. This is that the rule will by definition only apply if the parties actually intended the written terms to be 'the complete record of their bargain'. But according to a majority of the Court, so long as the written terms purported to be complete, that was the end of the inquiry.

9.14 The modern version of the rule: a presumption of integration

These days, however, the parol evidence rule may be expressed in a less rigid way. In *State Rail Authority v Heath Outdoor* (1986) at 191–2, McHugh JA rejected the idea that a document that appears on its face to be a complete record of an agreement must be *conclusively* presumed to have that status. Evidence will always be admissible to determine whether the parties intended their whole agreement to be 'integrated' or 'merged' into the document, or instead to make a contract with a mixture of oral and written terms. This is a view that has repeatedly been reaffirmed in later cases: see eg *Branir v Ouston Nominees* (2001) at [280]–[281]; *Masterton Homes v Palm Assets* (2009) at [90]. The 'rule' is best now regarded as expressing no more than a presumption, the strength of which will vary according to the nature, form and content of the document: see *Nemeth v Bayswater Road* (1988) at 414.[12]

On the facts in *State Rail Authority*, an oral assurance that a discretionary power set out in the written terms of a contract would seldom be exercised was found by the New South Wales Court of Appeal not to be intended to have any contractual force.[13] By contrast, in *Nicolazzo v Harb* (2009), an oral agreement as to the terms on which certain loans would be made *was* held to be enforceable, despite a written agreement being drawn up to document the loans. The difference from the facts in *Equuscorp*, as Dodds-Streeton JA pointed out (at [79]), was that the written terms here were set out in 'a patently incomplete and defective document which disregards fundamental drafting conventions and leaves uncertain the most basic matters, including the identity of the parties'. In other words, there was convincing evidence here that the real contract was to be found at least partially in what had been verbally agreed.

9.15 Entire agreement clauses

Transactions between a commercial party and a consumer commonly include an *entire agreement clause* (or a *merger clause* or *integration clause*, as it is sometimes known).[14] This type of provision expressly states that the written document constitutes the entire agreement of the parties. It may also contain a formal acknowledgment that there has been no reliance on any additional promises or representations given by one or other party. An entire agreement clause undoubtedly strengthens the presumption of integration, making it difficult to argue that the

---

12   For an older expression of the rule as a presumption, see eg *Gordon v McGregor* (1908) at 323; and see further Stewart 1987: 120–5. But compare *Branir* at [293], cautioning against using the language of presumptions in this context.

13   McHugh JA did take the view that the assurance could be enforced in equity through the doctrine of promissory estoppel, but the majority of the Court disagreed: see **18.04**.

14   For detailed discussion, see Peden & Carter 2006; Mitchell 2006.

contract was not wholly in writing. But, consistently with the modern view of the parol evidence rule, the task is not impossible.[15] For example, in *Keays v JP Morgan* (2012), a job description agreed before an employee was hired was treated as part of his employment contract, even though a later letter of offer made no mention of it and contained an entire agreement clause.

Whatever effect they have in identifying express terms, entire agreement clauses do not usually preclude the implication of additional terms under the principles discussed later in the chapter: see eg *Hart v McDonald* (1910); *Vakras v Cripps* (2015). Nor can they preclude one party from seeking to use the doctrine of promissory estoppel to give effect to a pre-contractual assurance: see eg *Saleh v Romanous* (2010), discussed in **18.04**. Likewise, an entire agreement clause cannot be used to bar a claim for rectification of a document to include a term omitted by mistake: see *Russell v RCR Tomlinson* (2016) at [132].

9.16 Collateral contracts

A *collateral contract* can be inferred where A makes a promise to B, in return for which B agrees to enter into a separate (or 'main') contract. Sometimes, as discussed in **8.16**, that main contract is with a third party, C. For example, in *DH MBI v Manning Motel* (2014), the plaintiff was induced to lease a motel from one company by a related company's promise to 'purchase' a certain number of rooms in the hotel each month. The plaintiff successfully argued that the promise was enforceable as part of a collateral contract, the consideration for which was the plaintiff's commitment to the lease.

More commonly, however, there are only two parties involved. It is in this context that a promisee may seek to set up a collateral contract as a way of avoiding the effect of the parol evidence rule. In *Shepperd v Ryde* (1952), for example, the plaintiff bought a house that was part of a land development project by a local council. The plaintiff had been attracted by the fact that the house was opposite two parks. Having communicated that to a council representative, he was shown plans confirming that these areas would be reserved for that purpose. When the council subsequently decided to subdivide the parks and build houses on them, the plaintiff successfully sought an injunction to restrain it from doing so. The High Court was satisfied that the plaintiff had an arguable case that the council was in breach of a collateral warranty, that it would maintain the public areas in the project in accordance with the plan, in return for which the plaintiff agreed to purchase the house.

In *Shepperd*, the contract of sale said nothing about the land surrounding the lot purchased by the plaintiff, or other aspects of the land development. Indeed, Dixon, McTiernan, Fullagar and Kitto JJ stressed (at 13) that any promise about such matters was not one that would have been expected to appear in the main contract. Had it been otherwise, it would have been harder to establish a collateral contract. The High Court has also taken the view that such a contract must be consistent with the main contract. In *Hoyt's v Spencer* (1919), a written lease stated that the lessor could terminate the lease by giving the lessee four weeks written notice. It was argued that there was a collateral contract that restricted the situations in which the lessor would give notice. Because this was inconsistent with the terms of the lease, it effectively altered the terms, rather than adding to the lease, ensuring that it was not enforceable. The

---

15   But compare Jackman 2015, arguing for much stricter application of such clauses.

reluctance in this case to countenance any conflict between main and collateral contracts has been criticised by commentators,[16] but endorsed in subsequent decisions: see eg *Maybury v Atlantic Union Oil* (1953); *Gates v City Mutual Life* (1986).[17]

A more fundamental objection to an argument for a collateral contract is that no promise has effectively been given. In *Crown Melbourne v Cosmopolitan Hotel* (2016) (see **7.07**), a majority of the High Court refused to find a collateral contract in the statement by a landlord during negotiations for a lease, that the tenant would be 'looked after at renewal time'. It was pointed out (at [28]) that these words 'did not have the quality of a contractual promise of any kind', especially given the lack of any agreement on the terms of a new lease.

Limits on express terms

9.17   Unlawful or unenforceable terms

There are a number of circumstances in which a term expressly agreed by contracting parties, as part of an otherwise valid contract, cannot be enforced if a dispute over its performance or effect goes to court. One possibility, which has already been discussed in Chapter 5, is that a term may be too *vague or uncertain* to be given effect. Another is that legislation may specifically prohibit the inclusion of a particular term in a contract. A number of instances of this are discussed in Chapter 21, along with the possibility that a term may be regarded as unenforceable by the courts because it is *contrary to public policy*. A common example of a term being unenforceable on policy grounds is one that involves an unreasonable *restraint of trade*. A further example of a term being contrary to public policy is considered separately in Chapter 22. This is where a clause is considered to impose an extravagant or unconscionable *penalty* for non-performance or non-fulfilment of a particular stipulation.

Where a particular term is found to be uncertain, unlawful or against public policy, the remainder of the contract may still be enforceable, provided the invalid term can be *severed*: see **5.40**, **21.17**, **21.28**.

9.18   Unfair terms

Under the classical law of contract (see **2.05**), the fact that a particular term might be capable of operating unfairly made no formal difference to its enforceability. Various doctrines were developed to address unfair conduct in the *process* of making contracts, as explained in Chapters 18–20. Issues of fairness could also sometimes creep into the application of particular doctrines. This can be seen in judicial attitudes to the imposition of standard form terms on consumers, whether in relation to the amount of notice needed for their incorporation (see **9.06–9.07**), or their interpretation (see **10.17**, **11.02**). Some courts may also be influenced by considerations of fairness or balance in determining whether or how to fill gaps by the

---

16   See eg Seddon 1978.
17   It appears that the existence of an entire agreement clause in the main contract will not of itself preclude a collateral contract, unless the clause specifically rules that out: *McMahon v National Foods Milk* (2009) at [38]–[39]. But compare the stricter view adopted by the UK Supreme Court in *MWB Business Exchange Centres v Rock Advertising* (2018) at [14].

development of implied terms: see **9.26**. Nonetheless, *substantive fairness* has not been an explicit concern of the common law: see **20.01**.

Increasingly, however, parliaments have gone where judges may have feared to tread. There are now many statutes which confer a discretion on courts to invalidate, or sometimes even rewrite, terms which are substantively unfair. The broadest of these regimes can be found in Part 2-3 of the ACL. This applies to standard form contracts for the supply of goods, services or land to a consumer, or involving a small business. This and other unfair contract regimes are discussed in Chapter 20.

9.19   Shams and pretences

A court will occasionally conclude that what objectively appears to be a contract is in fact a *sham*. In its traditional sense, the term is used to mean a 'disguise' or a 'facade' that is deliberately constructed in order to conceal a 'real' transaction: *Scott v Federal Commissioner of Taxation* (1966) at 279. As Lockhart J put it in *Sharrment v Official Trustee in Bankruptcy* (1988) at 454:

> A 'sham' is . . . something that is intended to be mistaken for something else or that is not really what it purports to be. It is a spurious imitation, a counterfeit, a disguise or a false front. It is not genuine or true, but something made in imitation of something else or made to appear to be something which it is not. It is something which is false or deceptive.[18]

Where the existence of a sham is alleged, the parol evidence rule does not prevent a court from looking past the terms of a written instrument in order to determine the parties' actual intention: *Raftland v Federal Commissioner of Taxation* (2008) at [33], [147].

Historically, most sham transaction cases have been associated with tax avoidance or minimisation, and typically result in a whole agreement being disregarded: see eg *Millar v Federal Commissioner of Taxation* (2016).[19] But it appears that an individual term may also be ignored or treated as ineffective, even though the transaction of which it is part is otherwise intended to have legal effect. This is apparent in decisions involving the characterisation of contracts for the occupation of land, or for the performance of work. Residential leases and employment contracts are subject to statutes that seek to protect tenants or employees. To avoid those regimes, a landlord or hirer may prepare agreements that appear to have the features of a licence to occupy premises, or a commercial contract for services. For example, the contract may state that other people may be licensed to share the relevant property with the occupant, or that the worker can delegate or subcontract the relevant labour rather than having to perform it personally. In cases such as *AG Securities v Vaughan* (1990) and *Autoclenz v Belcher* (2011), the UK courts have been willing to disregard such provisions as being a 'pretence', where the evidence (including the parties' conduct after making the relevant contract) suggested that there was never any genuine intention that they be given effect in practice.

It is unclear whether the broader doctrine of *pretence* suggested by these cases is part of Australian law, although the UK decisions have been cited with apparent support in cases such

---

18   As to the scope of the sham doctrine in Australia, see Stewart 2013.
19   Interestingly, the majority in this case largely based their finding on the intention of the adviser who designed the transaction, rather than the parties for whom he was acting.

as *Raftland* at [47] and *Fair Work Ombudsman v Quest South Perth* (2015) at [144]–[145].[20] Assuming it exists, however, there are still a number of important questions to be resolved. For example, there is some doubt as to whether the intention that a particular term have a pretended rather than actual effect must really be that of both parties, or just the 'stronger' party who imposed the term.[21]

Terms implied in fact

9.20   The tests for implication in fact

A term is *implied in fact* when a court is satisfied that the parties to a particular contract would have intended that term to be part of their agreement, had they considered the matter when making the contract.[22] Such a term is sometimes called a *tacit term*, to distinguish it from a standardised or default term 'imposed' by law: see eg *Byrne v Australian Airlines* (1995) at 447. It is a term specific to a single transaction.

Historically, the English courts identified two separate bases or rationales for implying a term on an ad hoc basis. One, articulated by Bowen LJ in *The Moorcock* (1889) at 68, is to give 'business efficacy' to a contract – that is, to fill a gap in the terms expressly agreed by the parties and make the contract work in a 'business-like' way. In that case, the contract was for the plaintiff's boat to be moored at the defendant's wharf on the river Thames in London. At low tide, the boat was damaged when it settled on a ridge of hard ground. The defendant was held liable for this damage, on the basis of an implied warranty that the river bed would be safe for use. It may well be that this was really a case of a term being implied by law, on the basis that the wharf owner was better placed to know the wharf's condition.[23] But the concept of business efficacy has become an important basis not just for implying a term in fact, but for denying any implication into a contract that would be workable without the suggested term.

The second basis involves a test based on obviousness. As Mackinnon LJ put it in *Shirlaw v Southern Foundries* (1939) at 227, a term can be implied if it is 'so obvious that it goes without saying'. He imagined an 'officious bystander' suggesting a provision on a particular matter, and the parties responding 'Oh, of course!'

In *BP Refinery v Hastings Shire Council* (1977) at 283, the Privy Council took the view that a term can only be implied in fact if it satisfies five potentially overlapping requirements:

---

20   In cases on the status of workers, it is established that any 'label' put on a relationship by the parties themselves may be disregarded: see *Hollis v Vabu* (2001) at [58]. There have also been Australian decisions in which importance has been attached to the substance or practical reality of an arrangement, as opposed to the formal terms agreed by the parties: see eg *ACE Insurance v Trifunovski* (2013); Bomball 2015; Stewart et al 2016: 209–13. But these decisions have not tended to go so far as the UK Supreme Court in designating particular terms as a sham or pretence. The language of 'sham' is more often used in the employment context to describe a contract that purports to be with one party, but is really with another: see eg *Fair Work Ombudsman v Ramsey Food Processing* (2011).
21   See Bright et al 2013; Davies 2013; Bomball 2019.
22   As to the hypothetical nature of the intention being assessed, see Paterson 1998.
23   See Collins 2014: 8–10.

(1) it must be reasonable and equitable; (2) it must be necessary to give business efficacy to the contract so that no terms will be implied if the contract is effective without it; (3) it must be so obvious that 'it goes without saying'; (4) it must be capable of clear expression; (5) it must not contradict any express term of the contract.

This test has repeatedly been endorsed by the High Court: see eg *Secured Income Real Estate v St Martins Investments* (1979) at 605–6; *Commonwealth Bank v Barker* (2014) at [21]. It can, however, be criticised for requiring *both* the business efficacy and obviousness tests to be satisfied, when arguably they should be regarded as alternatives.[24]

In *Byrne v Australian Airlines* (1995), the High Court did not question the *BP Refinery* requirements. But it did (at 422, 442) add an important qualification, first suggested by Deane J in *Hawkins v Clayton* (1988) at 573. This is that a different and simpler test applies to a contract not wholly set out in writing. In such a case, a term can be implied if it is 'necessary for the reasonable or effective operation of a contract of that nature in the circumstances of the case'.

9.21   Establishing necessity

It is certainly possible to find instances of terms being implied in fact. For example, in *Gwam Investments v Outback Health Screenings* (2010), the plaintiff needed a mobile unit to conduct drug and alcohol testing of mining industry employees. It engaged the defendant to design and construct such a unit, to be mounted on a particular truck. The combined weight of the truck and the unit delivered exceeded the weight limit for public roads. It was held that the defendant had breached an implied term that the unit be fit for the purpose of lawful use on such roads. *Regreen Asset Holdings v Castricum Brothers* (2015) involved a contract to purchase equipment for rendering meat from slaughtered animals. The equipment was contained on land being sold separately. The plaintiff company agreed to buy the equipment, while its sole director and shareholder, Mr Tahiri, was to acquire the land. When Tahiri pulled out of the latter contract, it was held that the defendant (the vendor under both contracts) was also entitled not to proceed with the sale of the equipment. A term was implied into the equipment contract that its completion was subject to the settlement of the land contract. The evidence showed that, although the purchasers were different, the transactions were very much intended to be linked.

In general, however, it is very hard to establish that a term is necessary to make a contract work – or, even where it might be, that the suggested term is the one that the parties would necessarily have agreed. This is illustrated by three High Court decisions.[25] In *Codelfa Construction v State Rail Authority* (1982), a construction company undertook to build an underground railway. For reasons outside its control, it was unable to complete the work according to the original schedule. The delay caused it to incur additional costs, which it sought to

---

24   That is indeed the position now taken in the UK: see *Marks and Spencer v BNP Paribas* (2015) at [21], where Lord Neuberger also questioned whether the first requirement in *BP Refinery* really added anything. If a suggested term satisfied the other requirements, it was 'hard to think that it would not be reasonable and equitable'. Compare Robertson 2016, proposing a different set of rationales for implication in fact.

25   For more recent decisions in which courts have refused to imply terms in fact, see eg *Ozyjiwsky v Ettridge* (2014); *Grocon Constructors v APN DF2* (2015); *Bull v Australian Quarter Horse Association* (2015).

recover from the Rail Authority. But the Court refused to imply a term entitling the company to compensation. As Mason J pointed out (at 355–6), if the parties had considered what to do if a delay of the relevant sort occurred, it was not obvious what they would have decided. There would have been a negotiation, which 'might have yielded any one of a number of alternative provisions, each being regarded as a reasonable solution'. The company did, however, succeed on a different basis, that being that the original construction contract had been frustrated: see **15.05**.

In *Byrne*, the issue was whether a term should be implied requiring an employer not to dismiss an employee in breach of an industrial award, which prohibited 'harsh, unjust or unreasonable' termination of employment. The suggested term would have allowed the plaintiff employees to claim damages for breach of contract if they were unfairly dismissed, a remedy not otherwise available under the legislation governing the award. The High Court held that there was no need to imply such a term to make the contract operate effectively. McHugh and Gummow JJ also stressed (at 442–3) that the suggested term would 'operate in a partisan fashion', favouring the employees' interests at the expense of their employer. Likewise, in *Breen v Williams* (1996), the Court refused to imply a term entitling patients to inspect or obtain medical records held by their doctors. Once again, the contracts for advice and treatment were considered entirely workable without such a term.

9.22   Inferred terms

As Dawson and Toohey JJ noted in *Breen* at 91, the line between inference and implication will not always be easy to draw. But it is established that *inferred terms* are those which 'can properly be inferred from all the circumstances as having been included in the contract as a matter of *actual* intention of the parties': *Hawkins v Clayton* (1988) at 570 (emphasis added). The existence of any such terms is to be considered before any question of implication arises: *Byrne* at 422, 442.

In practice, the kind of contracts in which terms are likely to be inferred are those not fully set out in writing. The concept has little application to 'detailed written agreements': *Grocon Constructors v APN DF2* (2015) at [191]. In *Uren v Uren* (2018), two brothers had for many years operated a cattle farm, under an undocumented partnership. One, a farmer, contributed all his capital to the partnership and worked on it full-time. The other put less money in and worked as a broker, using the losses from the farming business to help minimise his tax. It was held that a term should be inferred, as part of the partnership agreement, that the farmer be remunerated for his labour and also paid interest on the capital he had contributed.

9.23   The dividing line between implication and interpretation

In *Codelfa* at 345, Mason J described the process of implying a term in fact as an 'exercise in interpretation', in the sense that it raised issues 'as to the meaning and effect of the contract'. But it was not, he thought, 'an orthodox exercise in the interpretation of the language of a contract, that is, assigning a meaning to a particular provision'. This can be contrasted with the more radical view adopted by Lord Hoffman in *Attorney-General of Belize v Belize Telecom* (2009) at [16]–[27], in giving judgment for the Privy Council. He suggested that the implication of a term in fact is *always* an exercise in the construction of the contract in question.[26] An implication of this sort, he said (at [18]), does not result in any 'addition' to the parties' instrument. Rather, it 'spells out what the instrument means'. To accept this, however, would mean overturning the established tests for implication in fact set out above.[27] In *Marks and Spencer v BNP Paribas* (2015) at [25] and [76], a majority of the UK Supreme Court subsequently expressed their disagreement with Lord Hoffman's conflation of what they regarded as two separate processes.[28]

Even if the orthodox view of the difference between implication and interpretation is accepted, however, this does not mean the dividing line is always easy to draw. For example, the general duty of cooperation, mentioned below and discussed in more detail in **12.15**, has variously been expressed as a term implied in law or as a principle of construction. As Carter (2013: 95–7) points out, there are also many cases in which terms are effectively 'implied by construction', as a direct inference from what the parties have expressly agreed. One example is the engagement of a theatrical performer. Even if the contract does not say as much, the producer will be under an implied obligation to give the performer an opportunity to use their talents and enhance their public reputation: see eg *White v Australian and New Zealand Theatres* (1943).[29] Another involves the grant of an exclusive licence to distribute products. It will be implied that the licensor must not grant others a similar right in relation to the same territory: see eg *JC Williamson v Lukey* (1931). Carter goes on (at 97–8) to identify construction as the basis for a further range of default rules that are typically described as implied terms, but which he suggests are too general to be explained as terms implied in law. These include implications that performance happen within a reasonable period when no time is set by the parties themselves (see **12.05**), or that an apparently indefinite contract may be terminated by either party giving reasonable notice (see **16.20**). The characterisation of those particular terms may or may not be correct. But the fact that there is room for debate underscores the failure of the courts to articulate either the conceptual underpinnings or the precise scope of the concept of implication. As we will see, this becomes especially important in considering the basis for implying new terms in law.

Terms implied by custom and practice

9.24   Establishing custom and practice

Historically, many commercial transactions were conducted informally, against the background of established customs and practices in a particular industry, market or region. These are far less important today, given the greater prevalence of documented terms. But in principle, it is still possible to imply a term on the basis of a *custom* or *usage* so well known in the relevant trade that the parties must be presumed to have intended it to be part of their contract.

---

26   As to the distinction (if any) between the processes of 'interpretation' and 'construction', see **10.01**.
27   See Carter & Courtney 2015.
28   Compare *Commonwealth Bank v Barker* (2014) at [22], where French CJ, Bell and Keane JJ were content to note the 'debate' over Lord Hoffman's approach, without indicating a view one way or the other.
29   As to the broader question of when an employer is obliged to provide work for an employee to perform, and not merely pay them wages, see Stewart et al 2016: 437–40.

In *Con-Stan v Norwich Winterthur* (1986) at 236–8, the High Court summarised the case law on this point in four propositions. Firstly, the existence of the relevant custom or usage is a question of fact. Secondly, and crucially, there must be evidence that it 'is so well known and acquiesced in that everyone making a contract in that situation can reasonably be presumed to have imported that term into the contract' (at 236). Thirdly, the term must be consistent with the express terms of the contract.[30] Fourthly, however, if the other requirements are satisfied, a party may be bound even if they had no actual knowledge of the custom or usage.

In practice, it is hard to establish that a custom is sufficiently notorious to provide the basis for an implied term. In *Con-Stan*, an insurer sued to recover premiums due under insurance policies arranged by a broker on behalf of the defendant. The defendant had paid the money to the broker, which had gone into liquidation, and failed to pass it on. The defendant sought to argue that it was customary for brokers to be liable for unpaid premiums, but was unsuccessful. The fact that a broker normally made such payments, and that an insurer's first demand would be to the broker rather than its client, did not establish a custom that the insurer would *only* look to the broker for payment, not the insured. Similarly, in *Byrne v Australian Airlines* (1995) (see **9.21**), there was simply no evidence that award provisions were customarily treated as part of the employment contracts they regulated.[31]

Terms implied by law

9.25   Implied terms as default rules

It has occasionally been said that the various types of implied term sit along some kind of 'continuous spectrum': see eg *Liverpool City Council v Irwin* (1977) at 254. They can all, in different ways, be seen as having the function of filling gaps left by the parties.[32] Yet, in principle at least, Australian courts have come to insist on a clear distinction between terms implied in fact or by custom and practice, and terms *implied by law*: see eg *Castlemaine Tooheys v Carlton and United Breweries* (1987) at 486–90; *Con-Stan* at 237; *Byrne* at 447–52. Terms implied by law are effectively default rules developed by the judiciary, on the basis that they are appropriate for a particular type of contract. They are taken to be part of such a contract unless it can be shown that the parties have agreed something different: *Heimann v Commonwealth* (1938) at 695–6; *Castlemaine Tooheys* at 492. They can sometimes make the difference between an incomplete agreement and a valid contract, filling a gap that might otherwise exist even on an essential matter such as price or duration: see **5.38**.

There are at least two possible examples of a term that is capable of being implied into *all* types of contract.[33] One is the duty of cooperation discussed in **12.15** – assuming it does indeed operate as a term. The other is a general duty to perform contracts in good faith, an

---

30   Compare *Summers v Commonwealth* (1918).

31   For a further example of a claim failing for lack of evidence as to the relevant custom or usage, see *Elkerton v Milecki* (2018).

32   As to the various possible rationales for such a role, see Paterson et al 2016: 360–5, summarising some of the literature on this topic.

33   The logical possibility of a term being implied in law 'in all classes of contract' was noted in *Commonwealth Bank v Barker* (2014) at [21]. But see Carter et al 2015: 211–15, strenuously objecting to the very concept.

obligation some Australian judges at least have been prepared to identify: see **12.19–12.23**. But more usually, a term is recognised as being a legal incident of a *particular class* of contract. Almost all common types of contract have attracted some form of standard implication. Here, for instance, is a list compiled by Williams (1945: 403) and cited in *Byrne* at 448:

> Examples of such terms 'implied' into contracts by rules of law are the implied conditions of reasonable fitness and merchantable quality on a contract of sale of goods, the rule that payment and delivery of goods are concurrent conditions, the implied warranty of seaworthiness [for ships], the implied condition on the letting of a furnished house that it is reasonably fit for habitation, the implied promise by one who agrees to build a house that the house will be reasonably fit for habitation, the implied promise by a servant not to disclose secret processes, not to hand over to a rival written work completed for the master, and not, while still in his [sic] master's employment, to solicit the master's customers to transfer their custom to himself, the implied promise by an employer (in some cases) to furnish work, the implied duty of care in the carriage of passengers and in looking after bailed goods, and the implied promise by a banker not to disclose the state of his customer's account.

A number of these established terms are now enshrined in legislation, along with many others. As discussed later in the chapter, they are given effect either as terms implied by statute or, as with the ACL's consumer guarantees, as statutory obligations. But there are some types of contract for which the common law implied terms retain their importance. For any type of professional services, for example, there is an implied duty to render these with appropriate care and skill: see eg *Astley v Austrust* (1999). Implied terms also play an especially significant role in relation to employment contracts. Statutes such as the *Fair Work Act 2009* (Cth) have a great deal to say about the obligations of employers. But most of the core duties owed by employees still derive from the common law, in default of any express provision. Besides the examples given by Williams (using the old language of 'masters' and 'servants'), these include the basic obligation to obey any lawful and reasonable instructions from the employer: see *R v Darling Island Stevedoring & Lighterage* (1938) at 621–2.

9.26   Recognising new terms: necessity or policy?

One of the striking features of the various terms just mentioned is that they were recognised as legal incidents of particular relationships well before it became common to speak of implied terms, let alone distinguish between terms implied in law and fact. In most cases, they evolved out of established trade customs or usages, or were imposed in consequence of one party having a certain status (for example, as a servant or agent). The concept of a term implied by law really only became an established part of English (and in turn Australian) law after *Lister v Romford Ice* (1957), a case dealing with an employee's implied duty to take care not to injure anyone in the course of their work. By that stage, there were many legal rules about the performance of contracts that could be, and duly were, rationalised as implied terms.[34]

In principle, the categories of contract into which terms may be implied by law 'are not closed': see *Castlemaine Tooheys* at 487. The possibility of identifying a new term is illustrated

---

34   See Peden 2013.

by *Liverpool City Council v Irwin* (1977). The House of Lords held that the landlord of a high-rise apartment block was under an obligation to keep the common areas of the building, including the stairwells and lifts, in a state that was reasonably fit for the tenants' use.

In recent years, however, the High Court has come to insist that a term should only be implied by law where it is strictly necessary to ensure that the rights created by a contract are not rendered 'worthless' or 'seriously undermined': see *Byrne v Australian Airlines* (1995) at 450; *Breen v Williams* (1996) at 124. The difficulty this poses for the recognition of new terms was illustrated in *Commonwealth Bank v Barker* (2014). The Court refused to recognise an implied obligation not to do anything that might unreasonably damage or destroy the 'mutual trust and confidence' in an employment relationship. This was despite this term having become an established feature of English law after the House of Lords' decision in *Malik v Bank of Credit and Commerce International* (1998). French CJ, Bell and Keane JJ stressed (at [29]) that implied terms must be 'justified functionally by reference to the effective performance of the class of contract to which they apply'. The suggested term here was simply not necessary to make the contract effective. They also noted (at [40]) that recognising the term would involve 'complex policy considerations' that were better left to parliament.[35]

The reasoning in *Barker* suggests that it may be difficult in the future to persuade an Australian court to recognise *any* new implied term. This may be especially important in the context of the unresolved debate over the implication of a general duty of good faith and fair dealing, to which we return in Chapter 12. It is perhaps unlikely that any established terms would be called into question. But there might be room for debate as to whether some of them would meet the High Court's current standard.

The approach taken by the High Court can be contrasted with the willingness of the UK courts to treat the implication of a new term as a matter that calls for a policy decision: see eg *Malik* at 45–6.[36] In *University of Western Australia v Gray* (2009) at [136]–[142], the Full Court of the Federal Court had warned about the danger of taking too narrow a view of the concept of necessity. Implication in law, the Court pointed out, is not concerned with giving 'business efficacy' to a contract. Rather, it should be informed by 'more general considerations'. These may include 'the inherent nature of the contract and of the relationship thereby established', issues of 'justice and policy', and even 'social consequences'. But there was little evidence of such reasoning in *Barker*.

As things stand then, the narrow and functional view of necessity adopted by the High Court makes it hard to see any difference between the test for implying a new term in law and the business efficacy criterion for ad hoc implication. Indeed, it is notable just how often judges (including on the High Court) respond to what would plainly seem to be attempts to imply a term in law by relying on the *BP Refinery* criteria set out in **9.20**: see eg *TCL Air Conditioner v Judges of the Federal Court* (2013) at [74]; *Brennan v Kangaroo Island Council* (2013). The recent emphasis on a narrow view of necessity may be symptomatic of what Collins (2014: 306) has called the tendency of courts to go through periods of 'collective amnesia', in which they confuse or conflate implication in fact and law.

---

35   For critical analysis of these and other aspects of the decision in *Barker*, see Golding 2015, 2016; Gray 2015; Carter et al 2015.
36   See further Peden 2001.

Statutory obligations for the supply of goods and services

9.27   Terms implied by statute

Statutes sometimes imply terms into a particular type of contract. One of the leading examples involves contracts for the sale of goods. For instance, the *Sale of Goods Act 1923* (NSW) implies conditions or warranties as to:

- the seller's title, or right to sell the goods (s 17(1));
- the buyer's right to enjoy 'quiet possession' of the goods (s 17(2));
- the freedom of the goods from any charges or encumbrances in favour a third party, other than those disclosed to the buyer (s 17(3));
- the correspondence of the goods with any description given to the buyer (s 18);
- the goods being reasonably fit for any purpose required by the buyer, if made known to the seller (s 19(1));
- the goods being of 'merchantable quality' (s 19(2)); and
- the correspondence of the goods with any sample given or shown to the buyer (s 20).

Similar terms are implied by legislation in the other States and Territories.[37]

Whether parties can exclude such terms depends on each statute. The implied terms in the sales of goods legislation can be modified or omitted.[38] Hence, they can be described as *default* rules. But some terms implied by statute are *mandatory*. This is typically the case in consumer protection statutes. To give just one example, s 12EB(1) of the *Australian Securities and Investments Commission Act 2001* (Cth) makes it clear that it is not permissible to exclude the terms implied by s 12ED into contracts for the supply of financial services to consumers.

9.28   A different approach: the consumer guarantees

As noted at the beginning of this chapter, it is becoming increasingly common for legislation to regulate contractual dealings by the imposition of rules that are enforceable through statutory remedies, rather than having the status of contractual terms. This is true, for instance, of the minimum standards on leave, working hours and dismissal created for employees by the National Employment Standards in Part 2-2 of the *Fair Work Act 2009* (Cth).[39] But perhaps the most significant example is provided by the consumer guarantees in Division 1 of Part 3-2 of

---

37   *Goods Act 1958* (Vic) ss 17–20; *Sale of Goods Act 1896* (Qld) ss 15–18; *Sale of Goods Act 1895* (WA) ss 12–15; *Sale of Goods Act 1895* (SA) ss 12–15; *Sale of Goods Act 1896* (Tas) ss 17–20; *Sale of Goods Act 1954* (ACT) ss 17–20; *Sale of Goods Act 1972* (NT) ss 17–20. As to the significance of these terms being described as either conditions or warranties, see **16.07**.

38   See eg *Sale of Goods Act 1923* (NSW) s 57.

39   See Stewart et al 2016: ch 12. Compare *Minimum Conditions of Employment Act 1993* (WA) s 5(1)(c), which specifically provides that the minimum standards established by the Act are implied into the terms of certain employment contracts. The Act only applies to employees not covered by the federal *Fair Work Act*.

the ACL. In 2011, these replaced ss 69–74 of the *Trade Practices Act 1974* (Cth), which used to imply certain terms into contracts for the supply of goods or services to a consumer by a corporation.[40]

The consumer guarantees were intended to remedy three key defects with the previous system of implied terms: a lack of clarity in the legislation; a lack of awareness of the law on the part of consumers and suppliers; and difficulties experienced by consumers seeking to enforce their rights.[41] It is doubtful whether those objectives have been achieved.[42] Nevertheless, there are key differences from the previous regime. Besides the fact that the remedies afforded to consumers are statutory rather than contractual, the consumer guarantees operate independently of any contract. As such, their application is not restricted to suppliers; some also apply to manufacturers. In addition, recipients of gifts of goods are entitled to the same remedies as if they had acquired the goods themselves: ACL s 266.

The consumer guarantee provisions are based on New Zealand's *Consumer Guarantees Act 1993*. The case law on that Act is therefore relevant in interpreting the ACL provisions. So too are decisions on the former provisions of the *Trade Practices Act*, to the extent that similar language has been retained.

As s 131C of the *Competition and Consumer Act 2010* (Cth) makes clear, the State and Territory sale of goods legislation continues to apply alongside the provisions of the ACL. In practice, however, the main significance of that legislation is to regulate sales made to someone other than a consumer.

9.29   The scope of the consumer guarantees

The consumer guarantees generally apply to the supply of *goods* or *services*, as defined in s 2 of the ACL. These terms are defined broadly, so as to include the likes of gas, electricity and software. But work performed under a 'contract of service' (that is, an employment contract) does not count as services. Section 131A of the *Competition and Consumer Act 2010* (Cth) also precludes the guarantees from applying to the supply of financial services or products. Contracts for the supply of such services and products are regulated instead by implied terms as to due care and skill or fitness for purpose: see *Australian Securities and Investments Commission Act 2001* (Cth) s 12ED.

The guarantees in the ACL also require supply to a 'consumer'. For these purposes, the term is defined in s 3 by reference to both the *price* and *kind* of goods or services acquired.[43] A person acquires goods or services as a consumer if either of two general conditions is satisfied. The first is that the price of the goods or services does not exceed $40,000, or any higher figure prescribed by regulation.[44] In such a case, it does not matter

---

40   For a detailed treatment of the consumer guarantees, see Clarke & Erbacher 2018: chs 11–14.

41   Explanatory Memorandum to the Trade Practices Amendment (Australian Consumer Law) Bill (No 2) 2010 (Cth), [25.22]. In the footnotes below, this source is abbreviated as EM 2010.

42   See Paterson 2011. For a recent evaluation of the existing regime see CAANZ 2017: 13–31.

43   The definition also applies to the provisions concerning unsolicited consumer agreements (Pt 3-2 Div 2), layby-sales agreements (Pt 3-2 Div 3), itemised bills (Pt 3-2 Div 4), and linked credit contracts (Pt 5-5 Div 1).

44   At the time of writing, no such figure had been prescribed. Note also the provisions of ss 3(4)–(9) as to how price is to be ascertained in various situations.

who is buying or acquiring the goods or services – even the largest of businesses can qualify as a consumer. Secondly, where the price is higher, the goods or services must be 'of a kind ordinarily acquired for personal, domestic or household use or consumption'.[45] But under s 3(2), goods are not taken to be supplied to a consumer if they are acquired for the purposes of resupply. The provision also excludes the commercial acquisition of goods to be used up or transformed in the course of production or manufacture, or of repairing or treating other goods or fixtures on land. However, biscuits purchased by a manufacturer for its staff to eat while working would not, for example, fall within this 'non-consumer use' exception: *Laws v GWS Machinery* (2007). In general, a person acquiring goods or services is presumed to do so as a consumer. The onus of establishing otherwise rests on the other party (s 3(10)).

The rationale of the definition, which was retained from the *Trade Practices Act*, was supposedly to bring 'small business consumers' within the scope of protection. However, in affording large corporations identical protection to small business consumers and 'pure' consumers, the definition is over-inclusive. Indeed, in the case of a supply of goods or services by a small business to a large corporation, the latter will able to invoke the consumer guarantees *against* the former. In focusing on the *ordinary* use or consumption of goods or services of the kind in question, as opposed to the *subjective or actual* use for which they are acquired,[46] the definition can also be criticised for under-protecting genuine consumers. The courts have taken a broad approach in ascertaining the relevant purpose, interpreting 'ordinarily' as 'commonly' or 'regularly', as opposed to 'predominantly': see eg *Bunnings Group v Laminex* (2006), where a high-cost product used almost exclusively in commercial or industrial applications, but which was still suitable for domestic applications, was held to fall within the definition. Nevertheless, the approach remains problematic. A large corporation purchasing a commercial knitting machine costing $39,999 for use in its business is protected, while a private individual buying an identical machine for personal use at a cost of $40,001 may not be. The Legislative and Governance Forum on Consumer Affairs (CAF) has recently accepted a recommendation by Consumer Affairs Australia and New Zealand (CAANZ) to increase the $40,000 threshold to $100,000, to account for the decline in the real value of the threshold since it was originally set at that figure in 1986.[47] Regrettably, though, the opportunity seems to have been lost for a fundamental rethinking of the definition of 'consumer', with a view to eliminating the incoherence and complexity created by the multiple, differing meanings given to the term in the ACL.[48]

---

[45] This is not required in the case of a vehicle or trailer acquired for use principally in the transport of goods on public roads: s 3(1)(c). A person acquiring such goods will always be treated as a consumer, regardless of the price paid.

[46] As is the case in the definition of 'consumer contract' in s 23(3) for the purposes of the unfair contract terms provisions: see **20.24**.

[47] See CAANZ 2017: 72–4; CAF 2018. See also the Consultation Regulatory Impact Statement issued on this proposal, together with some other proposals coming out of CAANZ's review of the ACL that are discussed below: CAANZ 2018 ch 1.

[48] See eg the different definition of 'consumer goods' in s 2, and the definition of 'consumer contract' in s 23(3). For criticisms of this 'confused and confusing approach' of multiple definitions, see Carter 2010: 227–8; and see further Griggs et al 2011; O'Sullivan 2016.

9.30   Guarantees for goods

Nine guarantees apply where goods are supplied to consumers.[49] These cover:

* title or ownership (s 51);
* undisturbed possession (s 52);
* undisclosed securities (s 53);
* acceptable quality (s 54);
* fitness for any disclosed purpose (s 55);
* supply of goods by description (s 56);
* supply of goods by sample or demonstration model (s 57);
* repairs and spare parts (s 58); and
* express warranties (s 59).

Each of these guarantees applies to suppliers, other than s 58, which covers only manufacturers (s 259). Section 271 has the effect that manufacturers are also subject to the guarantees in ss 54, 56 and 59.[50] The guarantees in ss 54–59 only apply where the supply is made 'in trade or commerce', so that they do not cover 'private' sales.[51] Nor do those guarantees cover goods sold at auction. The rationale for this exclusion is that, in the context of a traditional auction, the consumer has the opportunity to identify any defects in the goods through inspection. A 'sale by auction' is defined in s 2 as a sale 'that is conducted by an agent of the person (whether the agent acts in person or by electronic means)'. Online auctions conducted by the likes of eBay, where the website operator does not act as agent for the seller, fall outside this definition and therefore attract the full consumer guarantees regime, provided they are conducted in trade or commerce. But where a website *does* act as the seller's agent, a buyer is denied the benefit of the guarantees in ss 54–59, even though they may not have had the opportunity to inspect the goods. Although the ACL review recommended that the consumer guarantees apply to *all* online auctions,[52] CAF (2018) has agreed to maintain the current exemption for goods sold via auctions, pending completion of a review of recent consumer law reforms in New Zealand.

9.31   Ownership and possession

The guarantees in ss 51–53 roughly correspond with the implied terms as to title, quiet possession, and freedom from charges or encumbrances in s 17 of the *Sale of Goods Act 1923* (NSW) and its equivalents in other jurisdictions. To ensure that consumers are not disadvantaged by potential third party claims, s 51 guarantees that the supplier has the right to dispose of the property in the goods at the time when that property is to pass to the consumer. The guarantee does not apply, however, where it was intended that the seller would transfer only limited title to the goods, or in a supply by way of hire or lease. Under s 52, there is a guarantee that the consumer's possession of the goods will be undisturbed. But again

---

49   For the definition of 'supply', which is not limited to sale but also covers leased or hired goods, see s 2. See also the definition of 'supplier'.
50   The term 'manufacturer' is defined in s 7.
51   For a detailed discussion of the meaning of 'trade and commerce', see **18.20.**
52   See CAANZ 2017: 69–70; CAANZ 2018: ch 4.

this does not apply to a supply of limited title, or where the existence of a security, charge or other encumbrance was disclosed to the consumer prior to the agreement. Section 53(1) guarantees freedom from any security, charge or encumbrance that was not disclosed to the consumer in writing prior to the agreement or created with their consent.[53] Section 53(3) also guarantees that all securities, charges and encumbrances known to the supplier but unknown to the consumer are disclosed prior to the agreement. Once more, these guarantees do not apply to supplies by way of hire or lease (s 53(4)).

9.32   Acceptable quality

The ACL has abandoned the archaic terminology of 'merchantable quality' formerly used in the *Trade Practices Act* and still found in sale of goods legislation. That term, which can mean different things in different contexts,[54] was said to have failed to provide consumers with 'clear and meaningful guidance on the essence of the law'.[55] Instead, s 54 speaks of goods having to be of 'acceptable quality'. According to s 54(2):

> Goods are of ***acceptable quality*** if they are as:
>
> (a)   fit for all the purposes for which goods of that kind are commonly supplied; and
> (b)   acceptable in appearance and finish; and
> (c)   free from defects; and
> (d)   safe; and
> (e)   durable
>
> as a reasonable consumer fully acquainted with the state and condition of the goods (including any hidden defects) would regard as acceptable ...

The relevant time for this determination is the time of supply. However, all relevant information known at the time of trial can be taken into account: *Medtel v Courtney* (2003). The phrase 'including any hidden defects' ensures that goods will not be of acceptable quality merely because they have not yet failed. It is enough that they carry an 'inherent risk': see *Medtel*; *APS Satellite v Ipstar* (2016); *Vautin v BY Winddown* (2018). Since the focus, as far as fitness for purpose is concerned, is on all the *common* purposes for which goods of the type are supplied, the actual purpose for which the goods were acquired is irrelevant under s 54.

In applying s 54(2), the 'reasonable consumer' is taken to have regard to factors which include the nature of the goods, their price (if relevant), any statements made about the goods on their packaging and labelling, and any representations by the supplier or manufacturer about the goods (s 54(3)). Thus, while second-hand goods are covered by the guarantee of acceptable quality, their age, price and condition must all be taken into account.[56]

The s 54 guarantee does not require goods to be 'indestructible'.[57] Hence, a consumer cannot obtain the benefit of the guarantee where they have damaged the goods by abnormal

---

53   This does not apply in the case of a fixed charge: s 53(2).
54   See *Rasell v Cavalier Marketing* (1991) at 400.
55   EM 2010, [25.25]
56   EM 2010, [7.31].
57   EM 2010, [7.35].

use (s 54(6)). The same is true where the consumer examined the goods prior to agreeing to their supply, and should reasonably have discovered that the goods were not of acceptable quality (s 54(7)). If a particular fault was drawn to the consumer's attention before the agreement for their supply, the goods are deemed to be of acceptable quality (s 54(4)). But this does not preclude the consumer from relying on the guarantee in respect of other faults. The guarantee can also be excluded, in the case of goods that are displayed, by an accompanying 'transparent' written notice drawing attention to any faults (s 54(5)).

9.33   Fitness of goods for purpose

Under s 55, there is a guarantee that the goods are reasonably fit for any purpose disclosed by the consumer, and also for any purpose for which the supplier represents them as being reasonably fit. The consumer's purpose must be made known either to the supplier, the person who conducted the negotiations or made arrangements in respect of the consumer's acquisition of the goods, or the manufacturer. This may be done either expressly or impliedly. It has been held that the mere acquisition of medication for human consumption does not impliedly communicate to a dispensing pharmacist 'some generalised purpose of safety or absence of adverse side-effects': *Merck Sharp & Dohme v Peterson* (2011).

The s 55 guarantee ordinarily requires a higher degree of quality than the 'general standard' of acceptable quality provided by s 54.[58] For example, under s 54, a lawnmower might be expected to be capable of mowing the lawn of an ordinary suburban house once a week for several years without significant problems. But a higher standard will be required under s 55 if the consumer indicates that it will be used to mow a 4 hectare block of land every week.

The fitness for purpose guarantee is excluded if it is apparent from the circumstances that the consumer did not rely on the skill or judgment of the supplier or that it was unreasonable for them to do so (s 55(3)). Clearly this would be the case if, after being informed by the supplier that the goods were not suitable for the consumer's disclosed purpose, the consumer decided to go ahead with the supply. It has been said that it would not be reasonable for a consumer to rely on the supplier's skill or judgment where the purpose was disclosed only to a checkout operator at a discount department store.

9.34   Conformity to description or sample

Where goods are supplied by description, there is a guarantee under s 56 that they will correspond with that description. This covers differences in colour, size and kind.[59] The fact that the goods had been exposed for sale or hire and selected by the consumer does not absolve the supplier or manufacturer.

Section 57(1)(c) also requires that goods correspond with any sample or demonstration model shown to the consumer, in terms of their 'quality, state or condition'. It was recognised that this right would be meaningless in practice unless consumers were actually given the opportunity to compare the goods with which they have been supplied with a sample they

---

58   EM 2010, [7.40], [7.43].
59   EM 2010, [7.44].

had originally been shown. Hence, a reasonable opportunity to make that comparison is also guaranteed under s 57(1)(d).[60] Finally, if the sample or demonstration model contained defects that would not be apparent on a reasonable examination and would cause the goods to be not of acceptable quality, there is a guarantee that the goods supplied to the consumer will be free from such defects (s 57(1)(e)). The ACCC et al. (2016a: 16) have suggested, consistently with the decision in *Rasell v Cavalier Marketing* (1991), that the guarantee of correspondence with a sample or demonstration model will apply even if the discrepancy is unavoidable.

9.35   Spare parts and repair

Section 58 provides a guarantee that the manufacturer will take reasonable action to ensure that any relevant repair facilities and spare parts are available for a reasonable period after the goods are supplied. The nature of the goods is important here.[61] While it may be reasonable to expect tyres for a new car to be available for many years, it may not be reasonable to expect spare parts for an inexpensive children's toy to be available at all. The guarantee is excluded where the manufacturer has taken reasonable steps to ensure that the consumer was advised in writing, at or prior to the agreement for the supply, that repair facilities and spare parts would not be available after a specified period (s 58(2)).

9.36   Express warranties for goods

Section 59 provides for two guarantees, applicable to suppliers and manufacturers respectively, of compliance with any express warranty given in relation to the goods. Each applies only to the party who has given the warranty. 'Express warranty' is broadly defined in s 2 as an 'undertaking, assertion or representation' made in connection with the supply or promotion of the goods, which has the natural tendency to induce persons to acquire the goods and relates to:

- the quality, state, condition, performance or characteristics of the goods;
- services and parts that may be required for the goods; or
- the future availability of identical goods, or of goods forming part of a set of which the goods in question form part.

In *Norman Enterprises v Deng* (2013), an express warranty, in the form of a 'money back guarantee', was held to have been provided in respect of a 'hair restoration product'. The guarantee stated that the manufacturer had such confidence in the product's ability to create 'thicker, fuller and healthier hair' that any purchaser dissatisfied with their results after 12 months of use would receive a refund. When, after 12 months of use, the consumer had patently not achieved the desired results, the manufacturer was held liable under s 59.

---

60   It was considered too onerous to expect suppliers to retain demonstration models for the purposes of subsequent comparison: see EM 2010, [7.48]. This aspect of the guarantee is therefore restricted to supplies by reference to a sample.
61   See EM 2010, [7.52].

9.37 Guarantees for services

Consumers are provided with three guarantees when acquiring services. These relate to the exercise of due care and skill (s 60), fitness for a particular purpose or desired result (s 61), and a reasonable time for supply (s 62). These guarantees apply to suppliers, but only when the services are supplied in trade and commerce. They do not apply to the transportation or storage of goods for business purposes (s 63(1)(a)),[62] or to the services supplied under a contract of insurance (s 63(1)(b)).

9.38 Due care and skill

Section 60 provides a guarantee that services will be rendered with 'due care and skill'. This has two aspects.[63] Firstly, the provider of the services must actually possess an acceptable level of skill in the relevant area. Thus a consumer, on discovering a provider's lack of skill, should be entitled to terminate the contract forthwith and without waiting to see how performance turns out. Secondly, the provider must exercise due care in actually providing the services. So, for example, in *Mayne Nickless v Crawford* (1992) a defendant who installed a burglar alarm in such a way that it could be easily bypassed was held not to have performed to the necessary standard. The same was true in *Read v Nerey Nominees* (1979) of repairs to a car that had been extensively damaged in an accident. The mechanic in question was found to have either failed to correctly diagnose a fault in the car's safety system or been responsible for incorrect wiring.

9.39 Fitness of services for purpose

Section 61 contains two separate guarantees. Section 61(1) provides a guarantee that both the services and any product resulting from them will be reasonably fit for any purpose the consumer makes known to the supplier. In *TLK Transport v Thornthwaite* (2014), the applicant had informed a motor vehicle repairer that the truck that it had brought in for repair was used in its transport business. In performing the repairs inadequately and defectively, the repairer had failed to ensure that the truck was reasonably fit for that stated purpose, as well as breaching the guarantee of due care and skill.[64] There is also a guarantee under s 61(2) that, where the consumer makes known the result they wish to achieve,[65] the services and any product resulting from them will be of such a nature, and quality, state or condition, that they might reasonably be expected to achieve that result. Neither of the s 61 guarantees apply to a supply of services of a professional nature by a qualified architect or engineer (s 61(4)). Nor do they apply where the circumstances show that the consumer did not rely on the supplier's skill or judgment or that it was unreasonable to do so (s 61(3)).

---

62   But see s 63(2), added by the *Treasury Laws Amendment (Australian Consumer Law Review) Act 2018* (Cth) Sch 9. This makes it clear that the exception does not apply 'if the consignee of the goods is not carrying on or engaged in a business, trade, profession or occupation in relation to the goods'. For the background to this amendment, see CAANZ 2017: 28–9.

63   EM 2010, [7.59].

64   For a case where the purpose had not been adequately made known to the supplier, either expressly or by implication, see *Ueda v Ecruising* (2014).

65   Either to the supplier or a person who conducted the negotiations or made the arrangements in relation to the supply.

9.40   Time of supply

Section 62 provides a guarantee that a supplier of services will supply the services within a reasonable time. This does not apply if the timeframe has been fixed by the contract or is to be determined in a manner agreed by consumer and supplier. What is 'a reasonable time' is inevitably highly context-dependent and will vary according to the nature of the services provided.[66] In *TLK Transport*, it was concluded that a period of six days was reasonable to ascertain the problem with the truck, itemise the parts needed and issue the invoice, taking into account the fact that the mechanic's business was a small one which had other customers. However, given the amount of time that had already been lost, the delay in commencing the work and the applicant's known need to recover the vehicle, the period of 15 days it took to complete the repair after all the parts had been received from Japan was found not to be reasonable.

9.41   Excluding and limiting the consumer guarantees

Section 64 makes it clear that none of the consumer guarantees can be excluded by contract. But under s 64A, it is possible to agree to *limit* liability for failure to comply with the guarantees in ss 54–57 and 59 to the provision of a replacement or repair, or the cost of such replacement or repair. It is also possible, as far as the guarantees in ss 61–63 are concerned, to restrict liability to an obligation to resupply the services or to the cost of resupply. Such limitations are only possible, however, in respect of supplies of goods and services of a kind not ordinarily acquired for personal, domestic or household use or consumption. They are also inapplicable if the consumer can establish that reliance on such a limitation of liability would not be fair or reasonable.

Section 139A of the *Competition and Consumer Act 2010* (Cth) also permits a contract for the supply of 'recreational services' (including sporting or leisure activities) to exclude, modify or limit liability under the consumer guarantees for death, illness or injury. But this cannot be done for reckless conduct by the supplier of the relevant services.

More generally, s 275 of the ACL has the effect that State or Territory laws that limit or exclude liability for breaches of a contract to supply services may also be relied upon to defeat any equivalent liability under the consumer guarantees.[67]

9.42   Remedies against suppliers

One of the significant consequences of a regime based on consumer guarantees, as opposed to implied terms, is that the remedial consequences of non-compliance are governed by statute rather than the law of contract. Under the remedial regime in Part 5-4, redress is possible against suppliers for breaches of the guarantees in ss 51–57, 59(2) or 60–62.[68] The remedial regime is built around a fundamental distinction between major and non-major failures.[69]

---

66   EM 2010, [7.64].
67   See Dietrich 2012, discussing the extent to which this preserves the operation of certain provisions in the *Civil Liability Acts* in each State and Territory.
68   There is, however, no right of redress against a supplier (the s 60 guarantee aside) where the non-compliance occurs solely because of acts, omissions or subsequent events not attributable to the supplier: s 267(1)(c).
69   For a detailed review of the remedial regime, see Paterson 2016.

A *major failure* is defined in ss 260 (for supply of goods) and 268 (for supply of services). A failure is major if:

- the goods or services would not have been acquired by a reasonable consumer fully acquainted with the nature and extent of the failure;
- the goods depart in one or more significant respects from any description, sample or demonstration model;
- the goods or services are substantially unfit for a purpose for which that kind is commonly supplied, or a disclosed purpose, and they cannot easily and within a reasonable time be made fit for that purpose;
- the services (and any product resulting from them) are not of such a nature, or quality, state or condition, that they can reasonably be expected to achieve a desired result made known to the supplier, and they cannot easily and within a reasonable period of time be remedied to achieve that result;
- the goods are not of acceptable quality because they are unsafe; or
- the supply of services creates an unsafe situation.

In the case of a major failure relating to goods, or of a *non-major failure* that cannot be remedied, the consumer can either notify the supplier that they are rejecting the goods, or retain them and claim compensation for the reduction in their value below the price paid or payable for them (s 259(3)). If the goods are rejected, the supplier must give a full refund or replace the goods, at the consumer's option (s 263(4)). For services, the equivalent right is for the consumer to terminate the contract for their supply or, again, claim compensation (s 267(3)). Where a contract is terminated, the consumer is entitled to a refund for any services not already consumed (s 269(3)). If a contract for services is terminated, any goods supplied in connection with the services must ordinarily be returned (s 270).[70]

Where the failure is non-major and can be remedied, the consumer has no right to reject goods or terminate a contract for supply of services. Instead, the supplier must first be given a reasonable period to remedy the defect (ss 259(2)(a), 267(2)(a)). In the case of goods, the supplier may do so by repair, replacement or refund, at its choice (s 261).[71] If the supplier fails to remedy the failure within a reasonable time, the consumer may then have the failure remedied by a third party and recoup the costs from the supplier. Alternatively, they may reject the goods or terminate the contract for the supply of services, with the same rights of refund or replacement as those set out above (ss 259(2)(b), 267(2)(b)).

In the case of both major and non-major failures, the consumer is also entitled to recover from the supplier damages in respect of any reasonably foreseeable consequential loss (ss 259(4), 267(4)).[72]

---

70   If the consumer insists on retaining such goods, this may be taken as indicating an intention not to terminate the contract for services, notwithstanding any statements to the contrary: *Coliban Heights v Citisolar* (2018).

71   Or, where the failure relates to title, by curing any defect in title.

72   As to the application of State and Territory laws that seek to limit such damages, see Dietrich 2012.

Uncertainty in respect of the 'major failure' test emerged as a serious problem in the ACL review. This is significant, as what often matters most to consumers is the ability to *choose* their remedy (such as the options of refund or replacement given in the case of a major failure), rather than having to submit to the supplier's choice (which may often be repair). Once a failure has been identified, it is imperative that the consumer should be able to determine with certainty whether it is major. Two situations, in particular, have been the focus of attention: a failure to meet the guarantees within a short period of time after the purchase, and multiple failures in relation to the same goods.[73] As CAANZ (2018: 2–3) stressed:

> consumers in these situations can still spend a disproportionate amount of time and resources determining whether a major failure has occurred and negotiating with the trader to obtain a remedy which may not be their preference or may leave them unsatisfied.

CAF (2018) has agreed to clarify the existing provisions of the ACL so as to put it beyond doubt that multiple non-major failures can amount to a major failure. It has also directed CAANZ to undertake further work on options relating to failures within a short time after purchase.

9.43   Remedies against manufacturers

Remedies can also be pursued directly against manufacturers of goods, but only in respect of non-compliance with the guarantees in ss 54 (acceptable quality), 56 (correspondence with description), 58 (spare parts and repairs) and 59(1) (express warranties).[74] In the case of s 54, redress cannot be obtained where the only reason for non-compliance is certain acts, omissions and subsequent events not attributable to the manufacturer (s 271(2)). The remedy against the manufacturer is damages, rather than replacement and repair, unless they have provided an express warranty to that effect (s 271(6)). In this context, damages represent the reduction in value of the goods calculated in accordance with s 272(1)(a). Damages for reasonably foreseeable consequential loss are also available against the manufacturer (s 272(1)(b)).

9.44   False or misleading representations

Finally, suppliers and manufacturers must take care not to make false or misleading representations concerning the existence, exclusion or effect of any condition, warranty, guarantee, right or remedy (s 29(1)(m)). This includes representations in relation to the consumer guarantees discussed above and any rights or remedies a consumer may have in relation to them. Nor must they make such representations concerning a requirement to pay for a contractual right that is equivalent to any condition, warranty, guarantee, right or remedy a

---

73   On the question of whether a number of non-major failures cumulatively amount to a major failure, contrast *Prestige Auto Traders v Bonnefin* (2017) with *Australia Rong Hua Fu v Ateco Automotive* (2015).

74   Where the consumer seeks redress against the supplier, the supplier is able to seek an indemnity from the manufacturer in a narrow range of circumstances: see s 274.

person already has, including under the consumer guarantee provisions (s 29(1)(n)).[75] In *ACCC v MSY Technology* (2017), fines of $750,000 were imposed for misrepresentations about consumers' rights to remedies for faulty products. An even larger penalty of $3 million was imposed in *Valve v ACCC* (2017) for misleading Australian users of Steam, an online game distribution network, as to the applicability of the consumer guarantees.

---

75   See also *Competition and Consumer Regulations 2010* (Cth) reg 90, requiring that any warranty against defects contain a mandatory statement about the non-excludable consumer guarantees provided under the ACL. Regulation 90 was amended by the *Competition and Consumer Amendment (Australian Consumer Law Review) Regulations 2018* (Cth) to clarify this mandatory text in respect of services and services bundled with goods.

10

INTERPRETING CONTRACTS

10.01   Introduction

Many disputes turn on the 'true' meaning or effect of contractual terms. Sometimes the parties are genuinely at odds about what they have agreed. But just as often, a competing view is put forward as a means to an end; for example, to excuse what would otherwise be a breach, or to escape from what has become an undesirable commitment by establishing a basis for the contract to be terminated. Either way, an adjudicator must resolve the dispute by *interpreting* the relevant contract.

In this chapter, we explain some general points about the way courts, tribunals or arbitrators go about this process, and the evidence to which they may have regard.[1] We look in particular at what (for wholly unnecessary reasons) has become one of the most contentious issues in modern Australian contract law. This is the extent to which reference may be made to the background or context surrounding the agreement in question, and not just the text of any written terms. We then go on to look more briefly at some of the various maxims or principles that are commonly invoked in tackling questions of interpretation.

A final note by way of introduction concerns terminology. The word *construction* can be used as a synonym for interpretation. But it is also sometimes suggested that the two terms are different. On one view, construction is the process of ascertaining legal effect, whereas interpretation simply involves working out what particular words mean. One historical explanation for that distinction is that matters of interpretation were questions of *fact* which could be left to a jury, whereas construction was treated as an issue of *law* for the judge.[2] With juries long since having disappeared in Australia from the process for resolving contractual disputes, however, there is little reason today to maintain that separation. In *Collector of Customs v Agfa-Gevaert* (1996) at 396, the High Court described the suggested distinction between construction and interpretation as 'artificial, if not illusory'. In this book, we use the two terms interchangeably, though we generally prefer to speak of interpretation, purely because it is the less technical word.

How courts ascertain meaning

10.02   The objective approach

However it is called, it is important to understand that the process involved in determining the meaning of a contractual term is not purely linguistic in nature. The search is not for meaning in some abstract sense, but for what the parties concerned *intended* their contract to mean. As Carter (2013: 45–52) points out, the 'intention' being assessed here is usually not the parties' *actual* (or subjective) intention. Rather, it is the intention *expressed* in the terms on which they have agreed or, if no such intention can be identified, in whatever intention can be *inferred* from relevant and admissible evidence. This reflects the objective approach to contractual intention noted in **5.02** and reiterated by the High Court in *Toll v Alphapharm* (2004) at [40]:

---

1   For more detailed treatments, see Lewison & Hughes 2012; Carter 2013.
2   See Lewison & Hughes 2012: 133–4.

It is not the subjective beliefs or understandings of the parties about their rights and liabilities that govern their contractual relations. What matters is what each party by words and conduct would have led a reasonable person in the position of the other party to believe. References to the common intention of the parties to a contract are to be understood as referring to what a reasonable person would understand by the language in which the parties have expressed their agreement.[3]

Spiers Earthworks v Landtec Projects (2012) offers a simple and straightforward example. A contract for the performance of earthworks, drainage and road works on a parcel of land specified that the price was inclusive of goods and service tax (GST). The contractor complained that its attention was not drawn to this provision and that the price was meant to exclude GST. Indeed, it had issued some invoices with GST added and had them approved by the superintendent of the works. But the Western Australian Court of Appeal held that the contractor was bound by the contract it had signed. Neither its subjective understanding, nor the apparent acceptance of its view by a representative of the other party, could displace the objective meaning of the contract, which was entirely clear. It might have been different if the contractor had sought to have the contract rectified (see **18.43–18.44**), on the basis that it did not reflect the parties' agreement. But no such claim was made.[4]

10.03   The challenge of interpretation

There is more disagreement than there should be about certain aspects of the law on contractual interpretation, as will become evident when we discuss the use of 'factual matrix' or 'surrounding circumstances' evidence. But even where judges agree on the principles to be applied, they can still arrive at very different conclusions.

Schwartz v Hadid (2013) provides a striking example. A deed of agreement stated that Dr Schwartz 'agreed at his discretion to buy one or more properties' at a certain location, as part of a joint venture with Mr Hadid. Three properties were under consideration. Schwartz bought one, but made no attempt to secure the other two. Hadid sued for breach of contract, claiming that Schwartz should have attempted either to buy or take an option on all three properties. Schwartz denied that he was under any such obligation. At trial, Hadid succeeded. The judge held that the provision quoted should not be given a literal interpretation. On the basis of the parties' prior communications, it should be taken to mean that the only 'discretion' for Schwartz in relation to the second and third properties was that he could either purchase them or secure an option to purchase them.

This finding was overturned by a majority of the New South Wales Court of Appeal. Macfarlan JA considered that the disputed provision gave Schwartz a discretion as to whether to buy *any* of the properties. Even if it was permissible to have regard to the details of the parties' prior negotiations, the language used was clear. Meagher JA agreed that there was no breach, but on a different basis. He considered that the provision was ambiguous. In accordance with the principles discussed at **10.06**, this justified taking account of the negotiations. But the interpretation he preferred was that Schwartz had a discretion as to whether to buy

---

3   For an attack on this approach, see eg McLauchlan 2012.
4   Compare *Alstom v Yokogawa* (2012), where such a claim succeeded in similar circumstances.

one, two or three of the properties. As he had bought one, there was no breach. Basten JA dissented. He agreed with Meagher JA that the provision was ambiguous, but differed as to the conclusion to be drawn from the evidence as to the parties' negotiations. In his view, Schwartz was obliged to buy one property, and either buy or option the other two. But rather than interpret the disputed provision as simply meaning that, as the trial judge had done, he would have regarded the contract as being partly written and partly oral. So the four judges to consider this contract effectively came up with four different ways to make sense of what the parties had agreed!

10.04   Interpretation as a balancing exercise

Catterwell (2019) describes interpretation as a sequential process through which objective intention is inferred from the choice of words in a contract. It involves four steps. These are:

(1)   identifying a discrete question as to what the parties have agreed;

(2)   articulating competing constructions or possible answers;

(3)   advancing arguments in favour of those alternatives, based on the admissible evidence; and

(4)   weighing and balancing considerations to reach a conclusion as to what the parties probably intended.

That does indeed seem to capture what is involved not only when an adjudicator resolves a dispute as to interpretation,[5] but when lawyers examine a contract to determine how it might be construed. Understanding the process, and in particular how competing considerations tend to be identified and then weighed, certainly makes it easier to give advice on possible outcomes. Unfortunately, as Allsop P put it in *OneSteel Manufacturing v BlueScope Steel* (2013) at [61]:

> construction is not a process necessarily concluded by logical reasoning or a priori analysis. It involves the weighing of different considerations partly logical and partly intuitive (though rational) leading to a choice.

As cases such as *Schwartz v Hadid* show, predicting how that choice will be made by a particular judge can sometimes be very difficult.

Admissible evidence in interpretation disputes

10.05   The parol evidence rule and its effect on interpretation

The *parol evidence rule* is concerned with the use of *extrinsic evidence* in any dispute over the scope or effect of a written contract or other instrument. Such evidence relates to anything said,

---

5   See eg *Wood v Capita Insurance Services* (2017) at [11]–[12].

done or written that is not part of the instrument itself.[6] In its traditional form, as discussed in **9.13**, the rule provides that extrinsic evidence may not be admitted to qualify, vary, add to or detract from the terms of the instrument. Our concern here is not with the effect of the rule on the *identification* of the terms that form part of a contract, but how it constrains the process of *interpreting* those terms. The rule suggests that courts should, at least as a general rule, determine the meaning of documents from the bare words alone. In particular, they should not have regard to anything said or done by the parties in the process of negotiating their contract. For example, in *Hope v RCA Photophone* (1937), the plaintiff agreed to lease 'electrical-sound reproduction equipment' of a kind described in a schedule to the lease agreement. The defendant argued that the equipment supplied must be new. But the High Court held that no such intention was apparent on the face of the agreement and refused to allow the defendant to adduce evidence to show that the parties had discussed the supply of new equipment.

The rationale for excluding evidence of *prior negotiations*, as Lord Wilberforce noted in *Prenn v Simonds* (1971) at 1384, does not rest on either technicality or convenience. It is simply that such evidence tends to be 'unhelpful'.[7] In *Codelfa Construction v State Rail Authority* (1982) at 352 Mason J explained:

> Obviously the prior negotiations will tend to establish objective background facts which were known to both parties and the subject matter of the contract. To the extent to which they have this tendency they are admissible. But in so far as they consist of statements and actions of the parties which are reflective of their actual intentions and expectations they are not receivable. The point is that such statements and actions reveal the terms of the contract which the parties intended or hoped to make. They are superseded by, and merged in, the contract itself.[8]

10.06 Exceptions to the rule

There has long been controversy as to the scope and effect of the parol evidence rule.[9] That has only intensified as the courts have become progressively more willing to consider evidence as to the context or background of the relevant contract, as discussed below. But even in its traditional form, various exceptions to the rule have been recognised.

In *Codelfa*, for example, Mason J was prepared (at 352–3) to accept 'one situation in which evidence of the actual intention of the parties should be allowed to prevail over their presumed intention'. If the parties had deleted or refused to include a particular provision in their contract, evidence as to that decision could properly be given to negate an inference that might otherwise be drawn from the rest of their agreement. That qualification has been relied on in a number of cases: see eg *Mrocki v Mountview Prestige Homes* (2012); *Ecosse Property Holdings v Gee Dee Nominees* (2017).

---

6   It may also cover evidence of anything said or done after the making of the contract: see Carter 2013: 247, 270. As to the permissible uses of such evidence, see **10.13**.
7   For a contrary view, see McLauchlan 2009.
8   As to the further precondition set by Mason J for considering 'objective background facts', see **10.09**.
9   See eg Carter 2013: chs 8–9.

More generally, extrinsic evidence can be given to help resolve an *ambiguity* in a written contract, as to the parties or subject matter. In *Giliberto v Kenny* (1983), one part of a contract for the sale of a house named the plaintiff as the purchaser, while another referred to her now-deceased husband as the buyer. It was held that since the contract was patently ambiguous, it was permissible to look at evidence of the making of the contract to clarify that it had been signed by the plaintiff both on her own behalf and as an agent for her husband. In *White v ANZ Theatres* (1943), two artists undertook to supply their 'sole professional services' to a theatre company, 'as required and directed' for a set period. The company claimed that the two had been employed purely as performers. But it was held that in identifying the 'professional services' in question, it was permissible to consider evidence that the purpose of the contract was to engage the artists to devise and produce a particular revue.

A court may also be persuaded that particular words used in a contract are intended to be given a specialised meaning, according to the *custom* in a particular trade or location: see eg *RW Cameron v L Slutzkin* (1923). This may be done even where the words in question might otherwise have a plain and ordinary meaning: see eg *Appleby v Pursell* (1973), concerning an agreement to 'push and stack' timber. But as with the implication of terms on this basis (see **9.24**), it must be established that the relevant meaning or usage is 'so notorious, uniform and certain' that anyone making a contract in the relevant trade or location would have intended it to operate: *Homestake v Metana Minerals* (1991) at 447.

A further purpose for which extrinsic evidence can be received is to establish whether the parties have validly concluded a contract. For example, it may be used to show that the parties have agreed that an apparently binding contract is not to take effect unless and until a particular condition is satisfied: see eg *Pym v Campbell* (1856). Conversely, evidence as to the parties' common intention may be given that an agreement *is* to take legal effect, despite the non-fulfilment of a stated condition: see *Air Great Lakes v K S Easter Holdings* (1985).

10.07   The rise of 'commercial construction'

In interpreting written terms, judges have traditionally sought to determine the plain, natural or ordinary meaning of the words chosen by the parties: see eg *Southern Cross Assurance v Australian Provincial Assurance* (1935) at 636; *Manufacturers' Mutual Insurance v Queensland Government Railways* (1968) at 321. That objective has never been abandoned. Nevertheless, the modern tendency has been to adopt a more contextual approach, especially in relation to commercial transactions.[10] According to Peden and Carter (2005b: 179) the concept of *commercial construction* includes the following elements or principles:[11]

- taking the 'surrounding circumstances' or 'factual matrix' into account, as the external context of a contract, in all cases;
- taking internal context – construction of the contract as a whole – into account in a practical manner, so as to give the agreement a reasonable business operation;

---

10   There are similarities in this respect to the modern approach to statutory interpretation: see eg Dharmananda & Firios 2015.

11   See further Carter 2013: 16–17.

- assertion of a common sense approach under which lack of clarity may be ignored for the purpose of giving effect to a commercially sensible construction;

- generally, the adoption of a uniform approach to the construction of all contracts, so that the applicable principles do not depend on the nature of the contract (or document) at issue;

- adoption of a construction which will prevent the contract failing for uncertainty or lack of subject matter;

- a concern to reject particular construction approaches, such as 'strict' or 'literal' construction in favour of a general approach based on the view which a reasonable commercial person would take as to the intended meaning or application of a contract; and

- a preference for rationalising conclusions by reference to the meaning and effect of the express terms of the contract, without the need to imply any further term.

In general terms, this approach has been firmly embraced by the High Court. The following observation by French CJ, Hayne, Crennan and Kiefel JJ in *Electricity Generation v Woodside Energy* (2014) at [35] is typical of the support for 'businesslike' outcomes:

> The meaning of the terms of a commercial contract is to be determined by what a reasonable businessperson would have understood those terms to mean ... [U]nless a contrary intention is indicated, a court is entitled to approach the task of giving a commercial contract a businesslike interpretation on the assumption 'that the parties ... intended to produce a commercial result'. A commercial contract is to be construed so as to avoid it 'making commercial nonsense or working commercial inconvenience'.[12]

Unfortunately, however, the Court has struggled to be clear or consistent on one key aspect of the principle of commercial construction – the extent to which evidence of the circumstances surrounding the making of a written contract can be used to interpret its terms.[13]

10.08 The relevance of surrounding circumstances

As Lord Wilberforce noted in *Prenn v Simonds* (1971) at 1383–4, even the most formal agreements should not be 'isolated from the matrix of facts in which they were set and interpreted purely on internal linguistic considerations'. The same judge considered in *Reardon Smith Line v Yngvar Hansen-Tangen* (1976) at 995–6 that:

> In a commercial contract it is certainly right that the court should know the commercial purpose of the contract and this in turn presupposes knowledge of the genesis of the transaction, the background, the context, the market in which the parties are operating.

Although still drawing the line at admitting evidence of the parties' negotiations or subjective intention,[14] the English courts have repeatedly stressed the relevance of what they have called the *factual matrix* in construing written contracts. Any doubts on this score were removed by

---

12   For similar statements, see eg *Pacific Carriers v BNP Paribas* (2004) at [22]; *Ecosse Property Holdings v Gee Dee Nominees* (2017) at [17].

13   As to whether the parties themselves can dictate whether such evidence may or may not be used in interpreting their contract, see Mitchell 2006; Byrne 2013.

14   See eg *Chartbrook v Persimmon Homes* (2009).

the House of Lords' decision in *Investors Compensation Scheme v West Bromwich Building Society* (1998). In restating the principles of contractual interpretation, Lord Hoffmann spoke (at 912–3) of the need to take account of 'absolutely anything which would have affected the way in which the language of the document would have been understood by a reasonable man [sic]', provided it was 'reasonably available to the parties'. Later decisions have perhaps retreated somewhat from certain aspects of Lord Hoffmann's restatement.[15] Nevertheless, the influence of the contextual approach it embodied is still very much apparent. This, for example, is how Lord Neuberger put it in *Arnold v Britton* (2015) at [15]:

> When interpreting a written contract, the court is concerned to identify the intention of the parties by reference to 'what a reasonable person having all the background knowledge which would have been available to the parties would have understood them to be using the language in the contract to mean' … And it does so by focussing on the meaning of the relevant words … That meaning has to be assessed in the light of (i) the natural and ordinary meaning of the clause, (ii) any other relevant provisions of the [contract], (iii) the overall purpose of the clause and the [contract], (iv) the facts and circumstances known or assumed by the parties at the time that the document was executed, and (v) commercial common sense, but (vi) disregarding subjective evidence of any party's intentions.

10.09   *Codelfa* and the 'true rule'

As discussed in the previous chapter, *Codelfa Construction v State Rail Authority* (1982) involved a construction project on which work was delayed, for reasons outside the parties' control. In their judgments, both Mason and Brennan JJ referred with approval to Lord Wilberforce's comments in *Prenn* and *Reardon* about the relevance of the factual matrix. The High Court took account of the circumstances surrounding the making of the construction contract, both in rejecting the contractor's argument for an implied term entitling it to extra payments (see **9.21**) and in considering whether the contract had been frustrated (see **15.05**).

However, in the course of reviewing the approach to be adopted in considering evidence of this type, Mason J insisted (at 352) on a requirement that has come to bedevil the development of Australian law in this area:

> The true rule is that evidence of surrounding circumstances is admissible to assist in the interpretation of the contract if the language is ambiguous or susceptible of more than one meaning. But it is not admissible to contradict the language of the contract when it has a plain meaning.

His Honour accepted that the parties' presumed intention was to be ascertained by reference to the 'objective framework of facts within which the contract came into existence'. But this would *only* be the case when a court was deciding 'which of two or more possible meanings is to be given to a contractual provision'. On the face of it then, the judgment was proposing what

---

15   See McLauchlan 2016. But compare *Wood v Capita Insurance Services* (2017) at [13]–[14], rejecting the idea that there has been a change of approach.

has subsequently come to be called an 'ambiguity gateway' for the reception of factual matrix evidence.[16] If that is correct, a court must first look at the words chosen by the parties. If they have a clear meaning on their face, the inquiry ends. It is only if multiple interpretations *appear* from the text to be possible that the court may consider the background to the contract to help resolve that uncertainty.

10.10   *Royal Botanic* and the High Court's puzzle

By the early 2000s, it appeared that the High Court had opted to follow the English courts in treating the factual matrix as relevant in *every* case. For example, in *Maggbury v Hafele* (2001) at [11], Gleeson CJ, Gummow and Hayne JJ quoted Lord Hoffmann's judgment in *Investors Compensation Scheme* with approval. Yet, just months later those same judges, now joined by Gaudron and McHugh JJ, appeared to backtrack. In *Royal Botanic Gardens v South Sydney Council* (2002) at [39], they offered this mysterious comment:

> It is unnecessary to determine whether [the House of Lords has taken] a broader view of the admissible 'background' than was taken in *Codelfa* or, if so, whether those views should be preferred to those of this Court. Until that determination is made by this Court, other Australian courts, if they discern any inconsistency with *Codelfa*, should continue to follow *Codelfa*.

This perhaps suggested that it might be possible to reconcile Mason J's 'true rule' with the much broader recourse to factual matrix evidence endorsed by the House of Lords. But there was no attempt to explain how that could be so.

   Royal Botanic involved a 50 year lease of land to allow the construction and operation of the Domain Parking Station in Sydney. Although formally concluded in 1976, after lengthy negotiations, the lease was taken to have started in 1958. Clause 4(b) allowed the lessor to fix an annual rent and provided that in doing so it 'may have regard to' certain costs and expenses. Although originally set at a low figure, the rent was eventually raised to something more appropriate for such commercially valuable property. The lessee eventually challenged the rent determinations. Its argument was that clause 4(b) should be interpreted to mean that the lessor could *only* have regard to the matters listed in the clause in setting the rent. The lessor, by contrast, argued that the provision meant exactly what it appeared to say: that it 'may' have regard to the factors listed, but was also free to consider others. By majority, the High Court ruled in favour of the lessee, by reference to evidence that suggested that the transaction had never been intended to have a commercial character. The majority judges were willing to treat what was really no more than a difficulty of interpretation as an 'ambiguity', so as to justify recourse to the factual matrix. They also seemed to have little reluctance in considering detailed evidence of the parties' prior negotiations to establish the necessary context.[17]

---

16   For support for such an approach, see eg Spigelman 2011; Prince 2015. Compare Mason 2009: 3, where the judge himself, writing extra-judicially, admitted that his judgment had been 'imperfectly' expressed and that he 'should not have been thinking in terms of gateway'.

17   For a critical analysis of the Court's approach, see Carter & Stewart 2002: 186–90. See further Catterwell 2012, highlighting the difficulty of distinguishing permissible and impermissible uses of evidence as to prior negotiations.

10.11 A 'gateway' requirement for surrounding circumstances evidence?

In the wake of *Royal Botanic*, the High Court continued to express views about the relevance of the factual background that seemed to flatly contradict the idea of a gateway requirement. To take just one example, in *Toll v Alphapharm* (2004) at [40], the Court stated (with emphasis added):

> The meaning of the terms of a contractual document is to be determined by what a reasonable person would have understood them to mean. That, *normally*, requires consideration not only of the text, but also of the surrounding circumstances known to the parties, and the purpose and object of the transaction.

There was no suggestion here of any need to find ambiguity first. Statements such as this led intermediate courts of appeal to believe that the High Court had effectively abandoned the 'true rule': see eg *Lion Nathan v Coopers Brewery* (2006); *Franklins v Metcash Trading* (2009). Yet, in *Western Export Services v Jireh International* (2011), the High Court once again muddied the waters. In refusing leave to appeal from what was treated as a correct decision on interpretation by the New South Wales Court of Appeal, Gummow, Heydon and Bell JJ excoriated the lower courts for ignoring what was said in *Royal Botanic*. Statements such as those in *Toll* were said to be entirely consistent with the gateway requirement adopted in *Codelfa*. Yet bafflingly, and infuriatingly, the judges once again refused to say how this could be so.

Following *Jireh*, the previous pattern resumed. In *Electricity Generation v Woodside Energy* (2014) at [35] French CJ, Hayne, Crennan and Kiefel JJ once again emphasised that ascertaining the meaning of a commercial contract 'will require consideration of the language used by the parties, the surrounding circumstances known to them and the commercial purpose or objects to be secured by the contract'.[18] This led the New South Wales Court of Appeal in *Mainteck Services v Stein Heurtey* (2014) to reaffirm its previous view that there cannot be an ambiguity gateway. As Leeming JA explained (at [77]), it is only *after* the context of a statement is considered that its possible legal meanings can be ascertained:

> [T]o say that a legal text is 'clear' reflects the outcome of [the] process of interpretation. It means that there is nothing in the context which detracts from the ordinary literal meaning. It cannot mean that context can be put to one side ...

He did not regard this as inconsistent with the assertion in *Codelfa* that surrounding circumstances evidence cannot be used to contradict language that has a plain meaning. As he observed (at [80]):

> Mason J was indicating that there are very real limits to the extent to which grammatical meaning can be displaced by contextual considerations. However, in order to determine whether more than one meaning is available, it may be necessary first to turn to the context.[19]

---

18   See also *Ecosse Property Holdings v Gee Dee Nominees* (2017) at [16]. It is clear that the 'circumstances' in question must be reasonably known to *both* parties: see eg *QBE Insurance v Vasic* (2010). The relevant circumstances may also include 'matters of law, including relevant legislation': *Westfield Management v AMP Capital Property* (2012) at [36].

19   For a reaffirmation of this view, see *Cherry v Steele-Park* (2017).

Other intermediate courts of appeal have taken a similar view.[20] But some have felt constrained to maintain the gateway requirement.[21]

For its part, the High Court has continued to refuse even to acknowledge the problem it has created, let alone attempt to resolve it. In *Mount Bruce Mining v Wright Prospecting* (2015) at [47]–[50], French CJ, Nettle and Gordon JJ insisted that the process of interpreting a commercial contract 'will require' reference to its context and purpose – but also that this is only 'sometimes' necessary. How both propositions can be true was left unexplained. They also declined to comment on the existence of any gateway requirement – or, as they put it (at [49]), 'whether events, circumstances and things external to the contract may be resorted to, in order to identify the existence of a constructional choice'. For their part, Kiefel and Keane JJ hinted (at [110]–[113]) that Mason J in *Codelfa* might not necessarily have intended to suggest such a requirement. They also pointedly observed that, as a decision on a special leave application, *Jireh* is not a binding precedent. Bell and Gageler JJ made a similar point (at [119]), but offered no further comment on the controversy. Disappointingly, no reference was made (whether positive or otherwise) to the cogent analysis in *Mainteck*.

So, more than 35 years on from *Codelfa*, the High Court has still not clarified whether contractual terms must *always* be interpreted by reference to the circumstances in which they were made, or whether reference to context is permissible *only* in the case of language that can be seen on its face to have multiple possible meanings.[22] In practice, it is easy enough for a judge who wants to refer to surrounding circumstances evidence to do so, simply by declaring the existence of ambiguity. Indeed, in *Mainteck*, *Mount Bruce Mining* and many other recent cases on this point, ambiguity was readily identified. As McHugh JA once observed, 'few, if any, English words are unambiguous or not susceptible of more than one meaning': *Manufacturers' Mutual Insurance v Withers* (1988) at 75,343. But there should be no need to have to circumvent a gateway requirement that may or may not exist. It is to the High Court's lasting discredit that so fundamental a point of contract law has been left not just unresolved, but in such a state of utter confusion.

10.12 Absurdity and unlikelihood

In *Australian Broadcasting Commission v Australasian Performing Right Association* (1973) at 109 Gibbs J warned that:

> If the words used are unambiguous the court must give effect to them, notwithstanding that the result may appear capricious or unreasonable, and notwithstanding that it may be guessed or suspected that the parties intended something different. The court has no power to remake or amend a contract for the purpose of avoiding a result which is considered to be inconvenient or unjust.

---

20   See eg *Stratton Finance v Webb* (2014); *Huntingdale Village v Corrs Chambers Westgarth* (2018).
21   See eg *Technomin v Xstrata Nickel* (2014); *Apple and Pear Australia v Pink Lady America* (2016). See also *McCourt v Cranston* (2012) at [20]–[26], highlighting the practical difficulties the High Court has caused for lower courts.
22   There is now a vast literature on this issue. Besides the sources already cited, see eg Wong & Michael 2012; Martin 2013; Acreman 2016.

This passage has often been cited, even by judges otherwise committed to the principle of commercial construction. As Macfarlan JA put it in *Jireh v Western Export Services* (2011) at [55]:

> So far as they are able, courts must of course give commercial agreements a commercial and business-like interpretation. However, their ability to do so is constrained by the language used by the parties ... In the case of absurdity, a court is able to conclude that the parties must have made a mistake in the language that they used and to correct that mistake. A court is not justified in disregarding unambiguous language simply because the contract would have a more commercial and businesslike operation if an interpretation different to that dictated by the language were adopted.

As this passage recognises, there are cases where, to quote Lord Hoffmann in *Investors Compensation Scheme* at 115, 'something must have gone wrong with the language' of a contract. In order to correct an obvious drafting error, judges may be willing to add, delete or change the words the parties have used. For instance, in *Fitzgerald v Masters* (1956), a contract for the sale of an interest in a farm purported to incorporate certain standard conditions 'so far as they are inconsistent' with the other terms of the contract. To make sense of the provision, the word 'inconsistent' was taken to mean 'consistent', or 'not inconsistent'.

The challenge, however, is to draw the line between rescuing parties from 'absurdity' and allowing an unambiguous but commercially unlikely interpretation to stand.[23] It is interesting in this regard to contrast two decisions of the Full Court of the Supreme Court of South Australia. *Dockside Holdings v Rakio* (2001) involved a lease with rents that automatically increased in certain years, while in others were subject to review by an independent valuer in the absence of agreement. The valuer's determination was to be based on 'the annual rent payable at the time of the review varied in accordance with any variation in the market rental for the Demised Premises since the commencement date or the last review of rental (as applicable)'. The first review was due to occur in the fifth year. If given its plain meaning, the formula would mean taking the Year 4 rent and increasing it by the percentage variation in market rents over the first four years of the lease, not just the most recent year. The automatic increases had already taken the Year 4 rent above the market figure. That rent would now jump up again by a substantial figure – and the Year 5 rent would become the base for further increases, compounding the gap between the calculated rent and the market. The Court took the view that so 'ridiculous' an outcome could not possibly have been intended.[24] The provision was interpreted as if it said something entirely different: that the rent would be set at a market rate in the event of any dispute.

In *Quirke v FCL Interstate Transport* (2005), FCL asked Mr Quirke, a director of a company for which FCL had agreed to transport a consignment of oranges, to sign a personal guarantee. This was for any amounts owing by the company in respect of 'all such goods as may be sold' to it. Since FCL was providing transportation services, not selling goods, the guarantee made no sense. The Court refused to allow evidence as to the background to the transaction to be used to show that the guarantee was intended to cover amounts owing for services. Since the contract was unambiguous, Doyle CJ explained (at [48]), the Court had no power to correct it,

---

23   See eg the difference of opinions in *Ecosse Property Holdings v Gee Dee Nominees* (2017), and in particular the dissenting comments (at [98]) of Nettle J.

24   See also *Westpac v Tanzone* (2000), involving a similar problem and conclusion.

no matter how fair and reasonable that might seem. No reference was made, however, to the many cases – including those discussed above – where courts have been prepared to do exactly that, if sufficiently swayed by the incongruity of a literal approach. As these two cases show, it is hard to draw a consistent line between absurdity and unlikelihood.

10.13   Post-contractual conduct

It is not at all unusual for one or other party to seek to rely on evidence of conduct and statements after the making of the relevant contract, to help determine its meaning. The law on this point was at one stage unclear, thanks to a series of conflicting decisions or observations by the High Court and the Privy Council. But in *Agricultural and Rural Finance v Gardiner* (2008) at [35], Gummow, Hayne and Kiefel JJ endorsed the general principle that 'it is not legitimate to use as an aid in the construction of [a] contract anything which the parties said or did after it was made'.[25] This stance may mean ignoring what might well happen to be the most persuasive or helpful evidence as to the parties' intentions in choosing the words in question.[26] Nevertheless, in *Franklins v Metcash Trading* (2009), the New South Wales Court of Appeal took the view that the decision in *Gardiner* had settled the law.

As Campbell JA noted in *Franklins* at [324], however, the bar on *subsequent conduct* evidence is not an absolute one:

> If, for example, a contracting party admitted, after the contract had been made, the truth of some fact that was a relevant part of the context in which the contract had been made, I see no reason why that admission could not be used as part of the means of proof of that background fact.

It has also been accepted that evidence of later conduct may be adduced to help determine whether the parties intended to make a contract at all, or to identify the parties: see eg *Australian Broadcasting Corporation v XIVth Commonwealth Games* (1988); *Nurisvan Investment v Anyoption Holdings* (2017). Likewise, post-contractual evidence or statements may be relevant in identifying the terms of a contract that is partly oral and partly in writing: see eg *Lym International v Marcolongo* (2011). Conversations and events that are not admissible for the purpose of interpretation may be relevant to a claim in estoppel: see eg *Stevens v Standard Chartered Bank Australia Ltd* (1988). They may also be relied upon to help characterise a contract for regulatory purposes, such as in determining whether an agreement for the performance of work is an employment arrangement.[27]

10.14   Admissible evidence: the position summarised

The uncertain status of the parol evidence rule, and the confusion created by the High Court over the permissible uses of surrounding circumstances evidence, make it hard to state the

---

25   Quoting Lord Reid in *James Miller & Partners v Whitworth Street Estates* (1970) at 603.

26   See McLauchlan 2009: 42–6. Compare the approach taken by the Supreme Court of New Zealand in *Gibbons Holdings v Wholesale Distributors* (2008). See also article 4.3(c) of the UNIDROIT Principles of International Commercial Contracts, which treats 'the conduct of the parties subsequent to the conclusion of the contract' as necessarily relevant in interpreting a contract. Article 4.3(a) takes the same approach to 'preliminary negotiations'.

27   See Bomball 2015.

current law with any certainty. However, we can say that when an adjudicator is interpreting a written contract, the following type of extrinsic evidence (that is, evidence of matters beyond the text itself) *can* be considered:

- contextual matters known or reasonably available to both parties that help establish the origins, purpose and nature of the transaction – these matters being relevant either in all cases (the better view) *or*, if the 'true rule' still holds, if it is apparent from the face of the contract that there is ambiguity or at least a 'constructional choice';
- details of the negotiations conducted by the parties, to the extent they establish a definite decision to delete or exclude a particular provision, or to resolve an ambiguity over the parties or subject-matter of the contract; and
- a custom or usage in a particular trade or industry, to help establish that certain words have a specialised meaning.

By contrast, it is *not* permissible to refer to:

- evidence which seeks to establish the subjective intentions of one or both parties; or
- anything said or done after the contract was made.

Principles of interpretation

10.15 The canons of construction

In earlier centuries, as explained in **1.10**, the operation of the English legal system was dominated by the need to bring any law suit within a recognised 'form of action'. This was also a time in which a range of formal rules were developed for the interpretation of documents. As Carter (2013: 141) explains:

> Although those rules originated in deeds, they were long ago adopted as canons of construction applicable to all instruments. The canons survive today. Indeed, they are frequently still rendered, as 'maxims', in their original Latin formulations.

Importantly, however, these canons or maxims are today no more than aids to interpretation. As Kirby J noted in *McCann v Switzerland Insurance* (2000) at [74], they are 'subordinate to the [court's] primary duty, which is to uphold the contract between the parties'.

10.16 Considering the whole of the contract

A number of the canons of construction are concerned with the interrelationship of different parts of a contract. One of the most powerful relates to the need to have regard to everything in the contract. In *Metropolitan Gas Co v Federated Gas Employees' Industrial Union* (1925) at 455, for example, Isaacs and Rich JJ said:

> It is a received canon of interpretation that every passage in a document must be read, not as if it were entirely divorced from its context, but as part of the whole instrument ... In construing an instrument 'every part of it should be brought into action, in order to collect from the whole one uniform and consistent sense, if that may be done; or, in other words, the construction must be made upon the entire instrument, and not merely upon

disjointed parts of it; the whole context must be considered, in endeavouring to collect the intention of the parties, although the immediate object of inquiry be the meaning of an isolated clause' . . .

A corollary of this principle is sometimes said to be that courts should find ways of giving effect to every provision in a contract, to avoid 'surplusage'. In *Chapmans v Australian Stock Exchange* (1996) at 411, Lockhart and Hill JJ explained:

> A court will strain against interpreting a contract so that a particular clause in it is nugatory or ineffective, particularly if a meaning can be given to it consonant with other provisions in a contract. Likewise where there are general provisions in a contract and specific provisions, both will be given effect, the specific provisions being applicable to the circumstances which fall within them.

There are limits to this principle, however, especially where standard form commercial contracts are concerned: see *Big River Timbers v Stewart* (1999) at [16]. The drafting techniques involved in such contracts mean that there is often a risk of redundant provisions being included either by mistake or from an abundance of caution.

10.17 Resolving ambiguities

One of the most enduring canons of construction has come to be known as the *contra proferentem* principle. This requires any ambiguities in a written provision to be resolved against the interests of the *proferens*, the person who is 'putting the provision forward'.[28] Ironically, however, the principle itself is ambiguous. It has never been entirely clear whether the *proferens* is taken to be the party who prepared the document in question, or the one for whose benefit the relevant provision has been included: see eg *J Fenwick v Federal Steam Navigation* (1943) at 5. Indeed, there have been a number of different formulations of the principle, each involving a different sense of the term *proferens*: see *North v Marina* (2003) at [57]–[72].

In practice today, the maxim seems to have three main operations. The first is as a general principle of interpretation. An ambiguous provision in a standard form contract will be construed against the party who has been responsible for drafting it, such as an insurer or an employer: see eg *Halford v Price* (1960); *Carr v Blade Repairs* (2010).[29] The second is specific to clauses that seek to exclude or limit a party's liability for what would otherwise be a breach of contract, or some other wrong. Here the principle has the effect that such a clause is 'construed strictly against . . . the party for whose benefit it is inserted': *Thomas National Transport v May & Baker* (1966) at 376. That aspect of the maxim is discussed further in **11.05**. Thirdly, as discussed in **11.15**, there is a principle that guarantees should be construed 'strictly' in favour of the guarantor. It appears that this too can be regarded as an example of the *contra proferentem* principle: see eg *Andar Transport v Brambles* (2004) at [19].[30]

---

28 The original maxim is most commonly given as '*verba cartarum fortius accipiuntur contra proferentem*' (the words of documents are to be taken strongly against the one who puts them forward).

29 But compare *Wilkie v Gordian Runoff* (2005) at [17], where the principle was treated as inapplicable to a contract between insurers.

30 But compare *Gardiner v Agricultural and Rural Finance* (2007) at [16], disputing this interpretation of what was said in *Andar*.

Importantly, however, the maxim is not to be read as favouring *any* available interpretation that is contrary to the interests of the *proferens*. It is only applicable where a contract is genuinely ambiguous, so that a court is 'choosing amongst meanings that are fairly open by reason of the application of other rules of construction': *Rava v Logan Wines* (2007) at [56]. It has indeed been described as a principle 'of last resort': *McCann v Switzerland Insurance* (2000) at [74].

10.18   Other maxims

There are many more canons of construction, beyond those already mentioned.[31] It is impossible to do justice to these in a book of this nature, but a few of the more commonly applied ones include:

- *expressio unius est exclusio alterius* (if one option or alternative is expressed, that suggests an intention to exclude others) – see eg *SCN v Smith* (2006) at [7];
- where a list of specific items concludes with a general or 'other' category, the general words may be confined or 'read down' to cover only things *eiusdem generis* (of the same kind) as those previously listed – see eg *Goldsbrough Mort v Tolson* (1909);
- a party should not normally be permitted to take advantage of their own wrongdoing to obtain a benefit under the contract – see eg *Hope Island Resort Holdings v Jefferson Properties* (2005) at [47]–[49];
- the presumption of legality suggests that a contract should if possible be construed to have a lawful operation – see eg *Langley v Foster* (1906); and
- a contract should if possible be interpreted so that it has a valid operation, as opposed, for example, to being void for uncertainty – see eg *Hillas & Co v Arcos* (1932) at 367; *Meehan v Jones* (1982) at 589.

---

31   See Lewison & Hughes 2012: ch 7.

11

LIMITING OR EXTENDING LIABILITY

11.01   Introduction

This chapter examines the rules relating to three contractual mechanisms used either to limit or extend liability. We first consider *exemption (or exclusion) clauses*. Their function, as the label suggests, is to provide one party with an exemption – either complete or partial – from a liability for breach of contract, or for some other wrong. We then outline how a *guarantee* may be used to require one person to take responsibility for another person's failure to perform their obligations. Finally, we look at *indemnities*, which in their various forms may be used either to extend *or* limit liabilities.

The nature and use of exemption clauses

11.02   The use of exemption clauses

Contractual provisions may seek to exclude or limit liability for breach of contract, and/or for some other form of wrongdoing (such as a tort or a breach of a statutory duty). Most exemption clauses are an incidental (albeit often an important) feature of a contract concerning the supply of goods or services, or some form of property. But occasionally the only purpose of a contract is to exclude or limit liability that might otherwise arise, as where a disclaimer must be accepted as a condition of gaining access to information, or an otherwise free event.

The systematic imposition by powerful businesses of sweeping exemption clauses in standard form contracts with weaker parties (typically consumers) resulted in a degree of judicial hostility towards such provisions in the twentieth century. In *George Mitchell v Finney Lock Seeds* (1982), Lord Denning reflected on 'ticket cases' such as *Thompson v London, Midland and Scottish Railway* (1930). There, a railway company was held to have validly excluded its liability for injury to passengers, whether fatal or otherwise, and howsoever caused. As Lord Denning explained (at 1043), exemption clauses of this type:

> were printed in small print on the back of tickets and order forms and invoices. They were contained in catalogues or timetables. They were held to be binding on any person who took them without objection. No one ever did object. He [sic] never read them or knew what was in them. No matter how unreasonable they were, he was bound. All this was done in the name of 'freedom of contract'. But the freedom was all on the side of the big concern which had the use of the printing press. No freedom for the little man who took the ticket or order form or invoice. The big concern said, 'Take it or leave it.' The little man had no option but to take it. The big concern could and did exempt itself from liability in its own interest without regard to the little man. It got away with it time after time. When the courts said to the big concern, 'You must put it in clear words,' the big concern had no hesitation in doing so. It knew well that the little man would never read the exemption clauses or understand them.

Despite this potential for abuse, exemption clauses are far from entirely negative. Where the contract is a product of genuine negotiation between parties who can be expected to read and understand its terms or are legally advised, such clauses are generally unobjectionable and, indeed, may have positive function. Exemption clauses play a vital role in the management and allocation of risks.[1] There is nothing objectionable in A negotiating with B to provide a service to B at a reduced cost in exchange for exclusion of its (A's) liability, particularly where B can most appropriately insure against the risk in question. The certainty created by a contract which clearly spells out what each party will and will not be liable for has the benefit of reducing potential litigation costs. It should also be borne in mind that some contracts could not be entered into in the absence of an exemption clause. The size and indeterminacy of the potential consequential losses of the other party may, for example, render it impossible for a party to contract at all (or at least not at a viable price) without the protection of such a clause.

An interesting counterpoint to a case like *Thompson* where, to modern eyes, the exemption clause seemed so repugnant, is *Photo Production v Securicor Transport* (1980). The case involved a fire at the plaintiff's factory, caused by the negligence of a security guard engaged by the defendant to help provide night patrol services. The defendant successfully invoked a provision in its contract with the plaintiff that excluded any liability for the acts and defaults of its employees. The House of Lords made it clear that the clause was perfectly reasonable in the circumstances.[2] This was so even though the damage caused was the very type of risk it was the purpose of the contract to protect against. Their Lordships emphasised the relatively modest contract price, the fact that these were commercial parties of roughly equal bargaining power capable of looking after their own interests and deciding how the risks should be borne, and that the risk had been allocated to the party (the plaintiff) who could most appropriately (and economically) insure against it.

11.03   The nature and types of exemption clauses

Exemption clauses come in a variety of shapes and forms. Exclusions may be total or partial. The label *limitation clause* is sometimes used to distinguish partial exclusions of liability (such as 'any liability arising out of the relationship established by this contract shall be limited to $500') from an *exclusion clause* that involves a total exemption. As will be seen below, the English courts have advocated treating these two types of clauses differently. However, the term 'exemption clause' is used here to refer to both partial and total exclusions of liability, unless the context suggests otherwise. Some exemption clauses are expressed as operating as a defence to liability that would otherwise arise: for example, 'the seller excludes all liability for loss and damage howsoever caused'. Others are expressed as excluding or limiting a party's obligations; for instance, 'any warranty, condition or other undertaking as to goods' correspondence with sample is hereby excluded'. But similar effects can be achieved by subjecting the enforcement of a party's rights to time limits or procedural steps; for example, 'The buyer must notify the seller of any defect in the goods within 2 days. Any claim arising therefrom must be made within 6 months.' Similarly, an exemption clause can be expressed in the form of an indemnity, such as 'The buyer will indemnify the seller in respect of any liability of the seller to the buyer resulting from any breach of the seller's obligations under this contract.'

---

1   See von Mehren 1982.
2   Strictly speaking, the issue of reasonableness did not arise, the events in question having occurred before the *Unfair Contract Terms Act 1977* (UK) took effect. The actual decision turned on the construction of the exemption clause: see **11.06**.

Questions of form aside, there has been significant debate about the essential nature of exemption clauses. On one view, they are terms which simply define the extent of the obligations assumed by the parties.[3] If this view is correct, there is no more reason for the law to regulate exemption clauses than any other term of a contract. On another view, they are a distinct type of term whose role is to provide a party with a *defence* to liability, but which does not in itself affect the other party's rights. In other words, exemption clauses deny the other party enforcement of their rights. The flaw in this second analysis is that it fails to identify the source of these rights, which must clearly be extra-contractual, given the difficulty in suggesting that parties to a contract can create rights which, at the same time, they intend to be unenforceable.[4] Both views of exemption clauses are represented in the case law,[5] but the defensive view has generally prevailed.[6]

Interpreting and applying exemption clauses

11.04 Judicial control of exemption clauses

Faced with what they saw as the routine abuse of exemption clauses by businesses, for much of the twentieth century some judges at least were determined to keep them in check. This could be seen in rulings on whether such terms were incorporated into a contract, as discussed in Chapter 9. But judicial hostility to exemption clauses was also evident in the many rules developed to limit their scope, under the guise of determining 'the true construction of the contract'. This concept was memorably (if somewhat impractically) described by Lord Denning in *George Mitchell* at 1043 as a 'secret weapon' used by judges to stab the 'idol' of freedom of contract in the back. As he acknowledged, it in fact involved constructions that were anything but 'true'. Time and time again courts departed from the natural meaning of words used in clauses to reach strained and unnatural interpretations that would constrain their operation.

11.05 Rules of interpretation

This interpretative approach consisted of a number of rules. Firstly, an exemption clause was to be construed strictly and against the party for whose benefit it was inserted: see eg *Thomas National Transport v May & Baker* (1966). This was an example of the *contra proferentem* principle discussed in **10.17**. A classic example of this approach is *Wallis v Pratt* (1911). The House of Lords refused to read the clause, 'sellers give no *warranty* as to growth, description or any other matters' (emphasis added), as extending to a *condition* that the goods sold would correspond with their description.[7] While it was open to the sellers to exclude such a condition, clearer language was needed to do so. Strictly speaking, only *ambiguous* words are meant to be construed *contra proferentem*. However, as Carter (2018: 295) has noted, courts

---

3   See Coote 1964.
4   See Coote 1964: 1–7.
5   Contrast, eg, the different approaches of Lord Wilberforce and Lord Diplock in *Photo Production v Securicor Transport* (1980) at 842–3 and 851 respectively.
6   See Macdonald 2009.
7   As to the use of the terms 'warranty' and 'condition' in this context, see **16.06–16.09**. The condition in question was implied into the contract by s 13 of the *Sale of Goods Act 1893* (UK).

often created ambiguities through the use of strict and literal interpretations: see eg *Ernest Beck v K Szymanowski* (1924).

In the 1950s, the English courts began developing a doctrine of 'fundamental breach'. This originated in the so-called 'deviation rule' that applied in relation to contracts for the carriage of goods by sea and was later extended to agreements for other forms of transport. The effect was to deny the carrier the benefit of any exemption clause in the contract where the agreed, usual, or customary route had been departed from without lawful excuse. The rule was explained in the following terms in *Joseph Thorley v Orchis Steamship* (1907) at 669:

> A deviation is such a serious matter, and changes the character of the contemplated voyage so essentially, that a shipowner who has been guilty of a deviation cannot be considered as having performed his [sic] part of the bill of lading contract, but something fundamentally different, and therefore he cannot claim the benefit of stipulations in his favour contained in the bill of lading.

An example of an Australian deviation case is *Thomas National Transport*, where the driver of the vehicle carrying the plaintiff's goods stored the goods in his garage overnight because the carrier's depot was closed. A fire broke out in the garage, resulting in damage to the goods. A majority of the High Court found that this deviation amounted to a breach of an implied term that the goods would be stored in the depot at the end of each collection round. It followed that a clause excluding the carrier's responsibility for any loss of or damage to the goods 'either in transit or in storage for any reason whatsoever' could not be relied upon by the carriers after that deviation.

Closely related to the deviation cases were those such as *Council of the City of Sydney v West* (1965), where the party seeking to rely on an exemption clause had acted 'outside the four corners of the contract'.[8] The plaintiff had parked his car in the defendant's car park. He received a ticket which included a term excluding the defendant's 'responsibility for the loss or damage to any vehicle ... however such loss, damage or injury may be caused'. It also stated that the ticket had to be presented to an attendant to obtain release of the vehicle. The evidence suggested that the plaintiff's car was stolen from the car park with the assistance of a duplicate ticket. The thief had obtained this by fraudulently claiming to have lost his ticket for a car with a different registration number and giving a false name and address. He then drove the plaintiff's car to the barrier at the car park exit and tendered the duplicate ticket. The attendant failed to check that the registration number on the ticket matched the car and allowed the thief to drive away. In these circumstances, a majority of the High Court held that the defendant was not exonerated by the exemption clause. Barwick CJ and Taylor J explained that, on its true construction, the clause's operation was restricted to loss or damage resulting from the carrying out of obligations under the contract. Loss or damage resulting from acts that were not authorised or permitted by the contract (in other words acts outside the 'four corners of the contract') was beyond the purview of the clause. The attendant's act of allowing the car to exit the car park without the appropriate ticket was an unauthorised delivery of possession of the car to the thief, rather than merely an act of negligence in relation to an act authorised by the contract.

---

8   See also *Gibaud v Great Eastern Railway* (1921).

In its decision in the same case, the New South Wales Supreme Court had largely adopted the English doctrine of fundamental breach, which had been formulated by Denning LJ in *Karsales (Harrow) v Wallis* (1956) at 940 as a substantive rule of law. According to Denning LJ:

> Exempting clauses … no matter how widely they are expressed, only avail the party when he [sic] is carrying out his contract in its essential respects … they do not avail him when he is guilty of a breach which goes to the root of the contract.

On this view, some types of breach and contractual term were so fundamental that no clause, however broadly and clearly drafted, could exclude them. However, in its decision in *Council of the City of Sydney,* the High Court declined to adopt any substantive 'rule of law' doctrine of fundamental breach, with Windeyer J noting (at 500) its 'many difficulties'.[9] Instead, the case was decided purely on the basis of the construction of the contract. In subsequent cases, Australian courts were willing in appropriate cases to construe exemption clauses as covering fundamental breaches: see eg *Metrotex v Freight Investments* (1969); *H and E Van der Sterren v Cibernetics* (1970).

11.06   The modern approach

The advent of statutory controls on exemption clauses in consumer contracts, discussed in more detail below, has left courts free to give these clauses their natural meaning when used in purely commercial transactions. In the UK, the catalyst for this new approach was the introduction of the *Unfair Contract Terms Act 1977.* This expressly permitted the courts to strike down exemption clauses for being 'unreasonable'.[10] In *Photo Production v Securicor Transport* (1980), the House of Lords endorsed the *contra proferentem* principle, but rejected any substantive rule of law preventing parties from excluding liability for fundamental breach. It was stressed that the courts' new statutory power had rendered resort to strained constructions and 'judicial distortion of the English language' unnecessary.

This approach was followed (after a fashion) by the Australian High Court in *Darlington Futures v Delco* (1986). The case involved a broker which had engaged in unauthorised transactions, thus acting outside the 'four corners of the contract' with its client. The question was whether the losses sustained as a result of these transactions were covered by either or both of two exemption clauses. The first (clause 6) provided that 'the [Broker] will not be responsible for any loss arising in any way out of any trading activity undertaken on behalf of the Client whether pursuant to this Agreement or not'. The second (clause 7(c)) limited the broker's liability to $100 for any claims 'arising out of or in connection with the relationship established by this agreement or any conduct under it or any orders or instructions given to the [Broker] by the Client'. The Court concluded that on its proper interpretation, clause 6 only contemplated losses caused by trading activity undertaken with the client's authority, whether pursuant to the agreement or not. However, it considered that the words 'in connection with' in clause 7(c) were intended to cover a claim in respect of an unauthorised transaction. The Court stated (at 510) that:

---

9   On these difficulties, see Coote 1967.
10   The Act also imposed an outright prohibition on excluding certain types of liability, such as for negligently caused death or personal injury.

> [T]he interpretation of an exclusion clause is to be determined by construing the clause according to its natural and ordinary meaning, read in the light of the contract as a whole, thereby giving due weight to the context in which the clause appears including the nature and object of the contract, and where appropriate, construing the clause contra proferentem in case of ambiguity.

It also took the opportunity to disapprove English decisions such as *Ailsa Craig Fishing v Malvern Fishing* (1983) and *George Mitchell v Finney Lock Seeds* (1983) which had advocated the less rigorous application of the *contra proferentem* rule to limitation as opposed to exclusion clauses.

The only difficulty created by the decision in *Darlington* is that the Court insisted that its previous decisions, in cases such as *Council of the City of Sydney*, were entirely consistent with the principle of giving an exemption clause its natural and ordinary meaning. That may be doubted. Nevertheless, the endorsement of the need to avoid strained or unnatural constructions has plainly induced courts to be more willing to give exemption clauses their intended effect: see eg *Nissho Iwai v Malaysian International Shipping* (1989); *Victorian Alps Wine v All Saints Estate* (2012); *Electricity Generation v Woodside Energy* (2013); *Thistle v Bretz* (2018).

11.07   Excluding liability for negligence

One other set of 'rules' for interpreting exemption clauses that may still apply concerns the question of whether a provision is broad enough to cover liability for negligence, whether in tort or for breach of a contractual duty of care. In *Canada Steamship Lines v R* (1952) at 208, Lord Morton, speaking for the Privy Council formulated a set of principles that may be summarised as follows:

(1)   Effect must be given to any clause using language which expressly excludes liability for 'negligence' or a synonym for negligence.

(2)   Where more general words are used, the court must decide whether they are broad enough, on their ordinary meaning, to cover liability for negligence. In accordance with the *contra proferentem* principle, any ambiguity must be resolved against the party for whose benefit the clause was inserted.

(3)   Words which are wide enough to cover liability for negligence must not be read as doing so if they could have been intended to cover some other form of liability.

The effect is that liability for negligence can only be excluded if the clause expressly mentions negligence or a synonym for negligence, or uses general words which could not have been intended to cover a more strict form of liability. The operation of these principles is illustrated by *White v John Warwick* (1953). The plaintiff had hired a bicycle from the defendant, who provided him with a replacement bicycle while they repaired the first one. The seat of the spare bicycle was loose and the plaintiff suffered injuries as a result. A clause in the contract provided that 'nothing in this agreement shall render the owners liable for any personal injuries to the rider of the machines'. The clause was potentially broad enough to cover both the defendant's strict liability for breach of an implied warranty of fitness for purpose, and liability in the tort of negligence. However, the English Court of Appeal construed it as limited to contractual liability. 'Clear words' were required before it would be read as extending to tortious liability as well.

By contrast, where the *only* possible basis for liability is negligence, it is hard to argue that the general words were *not* intended to apply to negligence liability.[11] This was certainly a factor in the High Court's decision in *Davis v Pearce Parking Station* (1954). A clause in a parking contract provided that the car was 'garaged at owner's risk' and that the defendant was 'not responsible for loss or damage of any description'. Since the defendant's only responsibility was to take reasonable care of the plaintiff's vehicle, these words were considered broad enough to exclude liability for the defendant's negligence. The very small amount of the fee charged for parking in the defendant's car park relative to the value of the plaintiff's car and hence the potential loss was also material. In these circumstances, the clause would have been reasonably understood as putting the onus on the plaintiff to insure.

11.08   The status of the *Canada Steamship* rules

The principle that exclusions of liability for negligence require clear expression has been accepted by the Australian courts on numerous occasions: see eg *Commissioner for Railways v Quinn* (1946); *Davis v Commissioner for Main Roads* (1968). The rationale for having specific rules for negligence liability is said to be the inherent improbability 'that one party to a contract should intend to absolve the other from liability from the consequence of his [sic] own negligence': *Gillespie Brothers v Ray Bowles Transport* (1973) at 419. However, the status of the *Canada Steamship* principles has been called into question by *Darlington*. As negligence liability was not in issue in the case, those principles were not discussed. Nonetheless, they seem incompatible with the High Court's general emphasis on 'ordinary and natural meaning'. In particular, the third limb operates to frustrate the intention of parties who might wish to exclude both tortious and other forms of liability with general words. However, some have suggested that these principles *can* be reconciled with the approach in *Darlington Futures*.[12]

The Australian courts have been divided on the issue. This is apparent from a number of cases involving indemnity clauses, which had long been governed by the same rules of construction as exemption clauses. Courts of appeal in Victoria, New South Wales and South Australia have each treated the *Canada Steamship* principles as being inconsistent with *Darlington*: see *Schenker v Maplas Equipment and Services* (1990); *Glebe Island Terminals v Continental Seagram* (1993); *Valkonen v Jennings Construction* (1995). In *Valkonen*, the first and second limbs were described (at 12) as 'acceptable working rules', but the third was said to impose 'an artificial and inflexible rule of interpretation that is as likely as not to frustrate the intention of the parties'. However, other courts have taken a different view: see eg *Graham v Royal National Agricultural and Industrial Association* (1989); *Allied Westralian Finance v Wenpac* (1995).

The High Court was given an opportunity to clarify the law in *Andar Transport v Brambles* (2004). But the Court side-stepped the question, making no reference to the *Canada*

---

11   See eg *Alderslade v Hendon Laundry* (1945); although compare the rather strained construction adopted in *Hollier v Rambler Motors* (1972).

12   See eg Carter 1995; Carter & Yates 2004.

Steamship rules. Instead, it held that indemnities are governed not by the principles laid down in *Darlington*, but by the rules of strict construction applicable to guarantees (see **11.15**). In *BI (Contracting) v AW Baulderstone Holdings* (2007), a case discussed in more detail in **11.25**, the New South Wales Court of Appeal took the view that the third *Canada Steamship* principle was incompatible with the strict rule of construction adopted in *Andar*. If that conclusion is correct, then a fortiori that principle is incompatible with the *Darlington* approach based on 'natural and ordinary meaning'. The abandonment of the *Canada Steamship* rules is certainly evident in recent cases: see eg *MWH Australia v Wynton Stone Australia* (2010); *Stewart v White* (2011). But the matter ultimately awaits authoritative determination by the High Court.

Statutory controls on exemption clauses

11.09   Specific restrictions

Many statutes either preclude parties from contracting out of some of the obligations they impose, or at least require any exemptions to be reasonable. As noted in **9.41**, the ACL has examples of both approaches. Under s 64, any term of a contract is treated as void to the extent that it purports to exclude, restrict or modify the consumer guarantees in ss 51–62 of the ACL. Section 64A does make an exception to that blanket rule, by permitting certain limitations (though not exclusions) of liability for breaching some of the guarantees. But a supplier cannot rely on such a limitation if the consumer establishes that it would not be 'fair and reasonable' to do so. The factors to be taken into account in determining the reasonableness of a limitation include the relative bargaining power of the parties, any inducement offered to the consumer, the availability of the relevant goods or services without such a limitation, whether the consumer knew or should reasonably have known about the relevant term, and (in the case of goods) whether they have been customised to the needs of the consumer.

There is a surprising paucity of case law, either under s 64A or its predecessor, s 68A of the *Trade Practices Act 1974* (Cth), on the fairness and reasonableness of such limitations.[13] One rare example is *Indico Holdings v TNT Australia* (1990). Here, the plaintiff had arranged for one of its products to be advertised on television. It subsequently entered into an agreement with the defendant for the provision of telemarketing and fulfilment services for the product. This would involve the defendant providing a dedicated telephone line, the number for which was included in the television advertising. The defendant's staff were to take calls from potential customers, take orders, arrange payment and despatch the orders. Although the market at which the advertising was directed was predominantly callers within the Sydney telephone district, the phone line the defendant initially provided could only take calls from outside Sydney. This was admitted to be a breach of the implied term that the services would be rendered with due care and skill under s 74(1) of the 1974 Act. However, the defendant relied on a clause in its standard terms and conditions limiting its liability to an obligation to supply the services again or to pay for the cost of such resupply, at its option. Giles J in the New South Wales Supreme Court held that the limitation was not fair and reasonable under s 68A(2). He stressed that all the circumstances of the case had to be taken into account. Of particular

---

13   See Finlay 1997.

relevance here was the nature of the services, which were such that their resupply (or the payment of the cost of resupply) would be of no real value to the plaintiff, unless it embarked upon a new and extremely costly advertising campaign.

Section 139A of the *Competition and Consumer Act 2010* (Cth) also allows some contractual exclusions, restrictions or modifications of the consumer guarantees in respect of the supply of 'recreational services'. In essence, these are services involving sporting or other leisure activities which entail a significant degree of physical exertion or risk. It is possible to limit liability for death, illness or injury caused in the course of using such services, though not where significant injury is caused by the reckless conduct of the supplier.

In a similar vein, s 52 of the *Insurance Contracts Act 1984* prevents contracts from excluding, restricting or modifying the operation of the Act, except to the extent that the statute expressly authorises a particular provision. Likewise, s 191 of the National Credit Code declares that a contractual provision that seeks to avoid or modify the effect of the Code is void.[14]

State and Territory laws may also contain prohibitions of this kind. In New South Wales, for instance, examples can be found in s 219 of the *Residential Tenancies Act 2010*, s 7 of the *Retail Leases Act 1994* and s 7E of the *Home Building Act 1989*.

The absence in a statute of an express prohibition on 'contracting out' does not mean that parties are necessarily free to exclude or limit liability for breaching the legislation. Depending on how the relevant legislation is interpreted, it may still be possible to conclude that such a provision is contrary to public policy: see **21.14**. There can be no doubt, for instance, that an employer cannot validly ask employees to exempt it from liability for breaching the National Employment Standards or other obligations imposed under the *Fair Work Act 2009* (Cth), even though that Act does not generally address the issue of contracting out.[15]

11.10   More general controls

Exemption clauses are also potentially subject to challenge under the unfair terms legislation discussed in Chapter 20, in particular those set out in Part 2-3 of the ACL. It is clearly possible for such a provision to satisfy the criteria, in s 24 of the ACL, of creating a significant imbalance in the parties' rights and obligations, not being reasonably necessary to protect a legitimate interest, and causing detriment if relied upon. Indeed, the very first of the examples listed in s 25 of a term that *may* be unfair is 'a term that permits, or has the effect of permitting, one party (but not another party) to avoid or limit performance of the contract'. *ACCC v JJ Richards* (2017), discussed in **20.31**, provides an example. Clause 6 of the standard terms of a waste services supplier provided that it would 'use all reasonable endeavours to perform the collection at the times agreed but accepts no liability where such performance is prevented or hindered *in any way*' (emphasis added). The Federal Court declared the term unfair. It was significant that it purported to exclude the supplier's liability even where the customer was in no way responsible for the prevention or hindrance or where the supplier was better placed to manage or mitigate the risk of that prevention or hindrance occurring. Similarly, an exclusion in the form of an indemnity clause was declared unfair in proceedings brought against an internet

---

14   The Code is found in Schedule 1 to the *National Consumer Credit Protection Act 2009* (Cth).
15   For a rare exception, see s 326, dealing with unreasonable deductions from wages; and see further Stewart et al 2016: 295.

service provider, ByteCard.[16] Here the clause required the consumer to indemnify ByteCard in any circumstance, even where there was no breach on the consumer's part and where the liability, loss or damage was caused by the provider's own breach of contract.

Guarantees

11.11   The nature of guarantees

A contract of guarantee involves a tripartite relationship between:

- a principal *debtor* (or obligor);
- a *creditor* (or obligee); and
- a *guarantor* (sometimes referred to as a *surety*).

The terms 'debtor' and 'creditor' are commonly used in this context because such contracts are typically (although not always) used to guarantee obligations to pay money: see *Sunbird Plaza v Maloney* (1988) at 254–5.[17]

Under a contract of guarantee, the guarantor promises to be responsible, in addition to the principal debtor, for the due performance of obligations owed by the principal debtor to the creditor. So, for example, if A wishes to borrow money from B Bank, B Bank may only be prepared to provide the loan if A's mother, C, guarantees A's obligations to B Bank under the proposed loan contract. If C enters into the desired contract of guarantee, she will be liable in the event that A defaults on the loan repayments. The beneficiary of the contract of guarantee is the creditor (here, B Bank). The effect of the contract of guarantee between B Bank and C is to extend the liability under the contract of loan beyond the immediate parties of that contract (A and B Bank).

The difference between a contract of guarantee and one type of contractual indemnity discussed at **11.22** below (referred to as a 'guarantor indemnity') is that the guarantor's liability is *secondary*. It is consequential upon the primary liability of the principal debtor and contingent upon that party's default. The indemnifier's liability under a 'guarantor indemnity', in contrast, is *primary* and independent: *Re Taylor* (1995). As Davey LJ explained in *Guild v Conrad* (1894) at 896:

> [T]here is a plain distinction between a promise to pay the creditor if the principal debtor makes default in payment, and a promise to keep a person who has entered, or is about to enter, into a contract of liability indemnified against that liability, independently of the question whether a third person makes default or not.

In *Sunbird Plaza v Maloney* (1988) at 254, Mason J explained that what is meant by the 'primary liability' of the principal debtor is *ultimate liability*. As will be seen, a guarantor who is called upon by the creditor to answer for the principal debtor's default is, after making such payment, generally entitled to recover amounts paid from the principal debtor. A consequence of the secondary nature of a guarantor's liability is that it is co-extensive with that of the

---

16   See ACCC 2013b; and see further **20.30**.
17   For a general treatment of the law relating to guarantees, see Phillips & O'Donovan 2014.

principal debtor: see eg *McDonald v Dennys Lascelles* (1933). If the principal debtor's under-lying obligation turns out to be void or unenforceable, or ceases to exist, the guarantor will not generally be liable.

A guarantee is usually (although not always) entered into in the form of a separate, but collateral contract. All the normal prerequisites for an enforceable contract, including the requirement of consideration, apply. A guarantee is generally entered into prior to, or simul-taneously with, the transaction between the creditor and principal debtor. In such a case, the consideration which moves from the creditor is the creditor's agreement to enter into the other transaction with the principal debtor. The rule that consideration must not be past (see **5.29**) poses problems in cases where the contemplated guarantee relates to a pre-existing liability of the principal debtor: see *Ahern v Power* (1935). In this situation, a deed will be required. Contracts of guarantee are subject to some special rules, such as the formality requirements and rules on disclosure of information discussed below.

11.12   The use of guarantees

Guarantees are used in a wide range of commercial and consumer situations. They perform a valuable function in facilitating access to credit in situations where it would not otherwise be available, or only at greater cost. As is apparent from the wealth of case law in this area, guarantees are onerous obligations with potentially grave consequences. As such, they should only be entered into with open eyes. Once a guarantee has been given, the guarantor often has little or no effective control over whether they will ultimately incur liability under it. Guarantees are commonly used in situations involving a close personal relationship between the guarantor and the principal debtor. For that reason, the problem of so called 'sexually transmitted debt' has been a particular source of concern.[18] The typical, but not invariable, example of a guarantee entered into in the context of a close relationship is that of a wife (or de facto wife) providing a guarantee, often secured by a mortgage over the family home, in respect of her husband's business borrowings. But there is also a high incidence of parents providing guarantees to support the borrowing of adult children.

Empirical studies have shown that, in the context of close personal relationships, guaran-tees are commonly entered into for emotional rather than financial reasons.[19] The decision to provide the guarantee is often motivated by fears that a refusal will damage their relationship. Such guarantors commonly feel that they have no choice, particularly where they are finan-cially dependent upon the principal debtor. Lack of understanding of the transaction and its potentially grave consequences is another common and worrying feature of guarantees given in this context. So too is the fact that such guarantees are sometimes agreed to in complete ignorance of the financial situation of the principal debtor or the relevant business. These concerns are amplified where the guarantee is an 'all-moneys' guarantee. This is an open-ended guarantee covering all *future* amounts advanced by the creditor to the principal debtor, whether under an existing credit contract or future credit contracts.[20] In 1991, the Martin

---

18   See eg Fehlberg 1997. The labels 'emotionally transmitted debt' and 'relationship transmitted debt' have also been used in this context.
19   See eg Lovric & Millbank 2003.
20   An example of such a clause is provided by the facts of *Garcia v National Australia Bank* (1998): see **20.09**.

Committee made a number of proposals designed to assist the guarantor's understanding of the transaction to which they are agreeing. It also recommended an outright ban on all-moneys guarantees.[21] Despite subsequent support,[22] the latter recommendation was never put into effect.

11.13   Formality requirements and information disclosure

A number of formality and information disclosure requirements apply to guarantees. This reflects the potentially grave consequences of entering into such transactions. In Victoria, Queensland, Western Australia, Tasmania and the Northern Territory, all contracts of guarantee must be in writing or evidenced in writing.[23]

The provisions of the National Credit Code (NCC) and the Code of Banking Practice (CBP) may also be relevant.[24] The NCC applies to a contract of guarantee entered into by a natural person or strata corporation in respect of a 'credit contract' regulated by the Code (s 8). 'Credit contract' is defined in s 5 so as to exclude credit for business purposes, with the result that the typical guarantee to support business borrowing discussed above would not be covered by the NCC. The CBP applies to guarantees entered into by an individual with a bank which has adopted the CBP in respect of credit granted to an individual or a small business. The CBP applies in addition to any applicable provisions of the NCC.

Where the NCC applies, the guarantee must be in writing and signed by the guarantor (s 55 (1)). The guarantee must contain a prescribed warning immediately above the place for the guarantor's signature.[25] Besides urging the guarantor to read the guarantee and the credit contract, the warning includes the following information:

- You should obtain independent legal advice.
- You should also consider obtaining independent financial advice.
- You should make your own inquiries about the creditworthiness, financial position and honesty of the debtor.
- Understand that, by signing this guarantee, you may become personally responsible instead of, or as well as, the debtor to pay the amounts which the debtor owes and the reasonable expenses of the credit provider in enforcing the guarantee.
- If the debtor does not pay you must pay. This could mean you lose everything you own including your home.
- You may be able to withdraw from this guarantee or limit your liability. Ask your legal adviser about this before you sign this guarantee.

---

21   House of Representatives Standing Committee on Finance and Public Administration 1991: [20.179].

22   See Trade Practices Commission 1992a, 1992b.

23   *Instruments Act 1958* (Vic) s 126(1); *Property Law Act 1974* (Qld) s 56; *Law Reform (Statute of Frauds) Act 1962* (WA) s 2; *Mercantile Law Act 1935* (Tas) s 6; *Law of Property Act 2000* (NT) s 58.

24   The CBP is produced by the Australian Banking Association: see www.ausbanking.org.au/code/banking-code-of-practice/. At the time of writing, a new version of the Code had just been approved. Banks that have adopted the Code must comply with it by 1 July 2019. All references below are to this new version. For background on the role of the Code, as well as the review that led to the new version being adopted, see Royal Commission into Misconduct in the Banking Industry 2018: 165–70.

25   Form 8, as required by s 55(3) of the NCC and reg 81 of the *National Consumer Credit Protection Regulations 2010* (Cth).

- You are not bound by a change to the credit contract, or by a new credit contract, that increases your liabilities under the guarantee unless you have agreed in writing and have been given written particulars of the change or a copy of the new credit contract document.

Before signing the guarantee, the guarantor must be given a copy of the credit contract and a document, 'Things You Should Know about Guarantees', explaining their rights and obligations (s 56).[26] Non-compliance with any of these requirements renders the guarantee unenforceable.[27] Clauses 96–106 of the CBP also impose a number of disclosure requirements on banks in relation to guarantees. These include the provision of a warning notice in substantially the same terms as that required by s 55(3) of the NCC.

Significantly, a contract of guarantee is not a contract *uberrimae fidei* (of utmost good faith),[28] so there is no general duty at common law for the creditor to disclose all matters that are relevant to the guarantor's decision to enter into the contract. A duty of disclosure has, however, been said to exist in respect of unusual matters: *Commercial Bank v Amadio* (1983) at 454–8, 485; *Westpac v Robinson* (1993). This extends to anything which has taken place between the creditor and principal debtor 'that might not naturally be expected': *Hamilton v Watson* (1845) at 119. This test is a difficult one to satisfy. In *Cooper v National Provincial Bank* (1946), for example, the creditor bank failed to disclose to the guarantor the facts that the principal debtor's husband had authority to draw cheques on the relevant account, that the husband was an undischarged bankrupt and that nearly a dozen cheques drawn on the account had been dishonoured. None of these matters was considered sufficiently unusual to give rise to a duty of disclosure.[29] However, for guarantees covered by the CBP, clause 97 requires the bank to disclose any notice of demand it has made on the borrower within the previous two years and whether any existing loan of the borrower will be cancelled if the guarantee is not provided. The guarantor must also be provided, among other things, with a copy of any related credit report from a credit reporting agency and any financial accounts or statements of financial position given to the bank by the principal debtor for the purposes of the loan facility (clause 99). In addition, the bank has an *ongoing* duty to disclose some matters relating to the deterioration of the borrower's financial position in so far as they are relevant to the guaranteed loan (clause 101).

11.14 Protections in relation to future credit and 'all-moneys' guarantees

To address concerns about exposure to open-ended liability, s 60(4) of the NCC allows a guarantor of liabilities under a continuing credit contract to subsequently limit its liabilities, by notice to the creditor, to credit already provided under that credit contract.[30] Where an

---

26   See *National Consumer Credit Protection Regulations 2010* (Cth) reg 82, Form 9.
27   See also the requirements of s 57 in respect of the provision of copies of documents *after* signature.
28   As to such contracts, see **12.17**.
29   See also *Goodwin v National Bank of Australasia* (1968); *Behan v Obelon* (1985).
30   A 'continuing credit contract' is defined in s 204 as 'a credit contract under which multiple advances of credit are contemplated and the amount of available credit ordinarily increases as the amount of credit is reduced'. An example is a credit card account.

all-moneys guarantee extends to liabilities under *future* credit contracts, it will be unenforceable in respect of those future liabilities unless the guarantor was provided with a copy of any future contract and subsequently accepted the extension of the guarantee in writing (s 59(2)). Similar rules apply where the terms of the underlying credit contract are changed to increase the debtor's liability in certain ways, for example by increasing the amount of credit granted to the debtor (s 61(1)). The CBP prohibits unlimited guarantees (clause 94) and, subject to certain exceptions, allows the guarantor to limit their liabilities under the guarantee by giving written notice (clause 95).

11.15   Interpretation of guarantees

Special rules of construction (interpretation) have been applied to guarantees. In *Ankar v National Westminster Finance)* (1987) at 561, the High Court expressed the view that:

> the liability of the surety is *strictissimi juris* [given the strictest interpretation of the law] and that ambiguous contractual provisions should be construed in favour of the surety.

The rationale for this approach is said to be that guarantees are potentially onerous obligations, typically given (historically at least) by the principal debtor's relatives or friends without reward. But, as Kirby P observed in *Corumo Holdings v C Itoh* (1991) at 377, this approach ignores the modern reality that guarantees are also commonly entered into by commercial parties for reward or compensation. Although the strict rule of construction described above has been restricted to *uncompensated* guarantors in the United States,[31] any such distinction was rejected by the High Court in *Ankar*. Nonetheless, the strict rule of construction must not be taken too far: see *Mineralogy v BGP Geoexplorer* (2018) at [56]. As Santow J emphasised in *Burke v State Bank of NSW* (1995) at 72:

> [W]here ambiguity is absent, such guidelines must yield to clear language expressing a contrary intention, though subject to being interpreted by reference to their context and to the commercial purpose served. Where ambiguity is present, or where the language is not wholly clear, any doubt in the case of guarantees, should be resolved, where the language permits, in favour of the guarantor and . . . so as to avoid absurdities or results which could not sensibly have been contemplated.

11.16   Enforcing a guarantee

Once default on the part of the principal debtor has occurred, the creditor can sue the guarantor. In general, unless the contract of guarantee provides otherwise, there is no requirement for the creditor to first take proceedings against the principal debtor: *Moschi v Lep Air Services* (1973) at 356–7. Where, however, the NCC applies, s 90 provides that a judgment can only be enforced against the guarantor in the following circumstances:

---

31   See *Chapman v Hoage* (1936). In fact, the provisions of a guarantee are construed strictly against (rather than in favour of) a compensated guarantor in the United States.

(a) the creditor has obtained a judgment against the principal debtor for payment of the guaranteed liability and the judgment remains unsatisfied for 30 days after the creditor has made a written demand for payment of the judgment debt; or

(b) the court has relieved the creditor from the obligation to obtain a judgment against the principal debtor on the ground that recovery from them is unlikely; or

(c) the creditor has made reasonable attempts to locate the principal debtor but without success; or

(d) the principal debtor is insolvent.

The CBP contains a similar provision (clause 114), which also prevents the enforcement of a judgment against the guarantor unless the bank has first enforced any mortgage or other security provided by the borrower in respect of the guaranteed liability. However, this is specifically expressed not to apply where the principal debtor is a small business.

11.17 The rights of the guarantor after payment

On making payment to the creditor, the guarantor can seek indemnity (that is, reimbursement) from the principal debtor. This right of indemnity can arise either by express agreement between the principal debtor and the guarantor, or by implication: *McColls Wholesale v State Bank of New South Wales* (1984). There is generally no difficulty in implying such a term into a contract of guarantee which was entered into by the guarantor at the express or implied request of the principal debtor: see eg *Israel v Foreshore Properties* (1980). But courts are unlikely to do so outside of this situation: see eg *Conaghan v Cahill* (1932). In practical terms, this right of indemnity is often of little value, as the whole reason why the creditor is enforcing the guarantee is generally the principal debtor's inability to make payment.

However, once the creditor has been paid in full,[32] the guarantor also acquires important rights under the doctrine of *subrogation*: *Sunbird Plaza v Maloney* (1988) at 254. The guarantor is said to be 'subrogated' to the rights of the creditor as against the principal debtor, which means that they can stand in the shoes of the creditor and enforce every remedy, right, security or means of payment that was available to the creditor against the principal debtor: *Craythorne v Swinburne* (1807). Significantly, this allows the guarantor to enforce their right to indemnity against the principal debtor by calling for an assignment of any securities – for example a mortgage granted by the principal debtor over their property – held by the creditor in relation to the transaction with the principal debtor. Although the guarantor's right to call for such securities does not arise until the creditor has been paid in full, the right of subrogation has implications from the moment the guarantee is entered into for the way in which the creditor deals with any securities granted, as discussed below. The right of subrogation can be excluded by express provision in the contract of guarantee, or by conduct rendering enforcement of that right inequitable: *Equity Trustees Executors & Agency v New Zealand Loan and Mercantile Agency* (1940) at 205; *Bofinger v Kingsway Group* (2009) at [52]. However, in a

---

32 Where there is more than one guarantor, it is not necessary that the guarantor claiming the right of subrogation discussed in the text below has discharged the entire obligation themselves. It is enough that they have made a payment which reduced the debt in part: *Equity Trustees Executors & Agency v New Zealand Loan and Mercantile Agency* (1940).

guarantee covered by the NCC, a term purporting to limit the guarantor's right to indemnity against the principal debtor, or to postpone or limit the guarantor's right to enforce that indemnity, is void (s 60(5)).

11.18 Escaping liability under a guarantee

A guarantor may avoid liability under a contract of guarantee on the basis of any of the vitiating factors such as mistake, misrepresentation, fraud, duress, undue influence and unconscionable conduct discussed elsewhere in this book. The unconscionable bargains doctrine and the special equity for married women discussed in Chapter 20 have proved particularly important in this context.

There are also a number of more specific bases on which a guarantor may escape liability. For example, where the creditor's conduct has the effect of altering the guarantor's rights without their consent, the guarantor's obligations are discharged, unless the alteration is insubstantial and the guarantor is not prejudiced: *Ankar v National Westminster Finance* (1987) at 559. For example, in *Australian Joint Stock Bank v Bailey* (1897), the name of one co-guarantor was struck out of a joint and several guarantee without the consent of all co-guarantors. This meant that all the co-guarantors were discharged. Similarly, in *Egbert v National Crown Bank* (1918), guarantors were discharged where, without their consent, the creditor and principal debtor agreed to increase the rate of interest payable under the principal contract. The same occurred in *Deane v City Bank of Sydney* (1904), where the creditor agreed with the principal debtor to extend the time for the latter's performance beyond that provided in the original contract.[33]

The guarantor will also be discharged, either wholly or in part, where the benefit of securities taken by the creditor for the guaranteed debt has been lost or diminished by the acts or neglect of the creditor: *Williams v Frayne* (1937) at 738; *Buckeridge v Mercantile Credits* (1981) at 675. For example, in *Re Kwan* (1987) the creditor had obtained a security, in the form of a bill of sale over property owned by the principal debtor (a company), as well as a guarantee from its directors. The creditor failed to register the bill of sale within the period required by statute, with the result that it was ineffective. As the assets over which the bill of sale had been given would have been sufficient to discharge the principal debtor's entire debt (had the bill of sale been effective), the guarantor was discharged. However, the creditor is under no duty to actually *exercise* their rights over the security: *McMahon v Young* (1876); *Omlaw v Delahunty* (1995).[34]

Finally, where the guarantee is governed by the NCC, the guarantor may be relieved on the grounds that it is an 'unjust transaction' under s 76. On reopening an unjust transaction, the court has wide remedial powers under s 77, including the power to set a guarantee aside.

---

33   Compare *Mineralogy v BGP Geoexplorer* (2018), where the guarantee expressly contemplated that the principal contract might be varied, without affecting the guarantee.

34   Although, clause 113 of the CBP prevents a bank enforcing a mortgage or other security given by the guarantor unless it has *first* enforced any mortgage or other security given by the principal debtor in respect of the guaranteed liability.

Indemnities

11.19   Insurance

A contractual *indemnity* has been described as a promise to 'save and keep harmless against loss': *Victorian WorkCover Authority v Esso Australia* (2001) at 529. Contractual indemnities are used in a wide range of situations and, as will be seen, the term covers a wide variety of contractual arrangements.[35]

The notion of an indemnity is central to the law of *insurance*, which distinguishes between 'indemnity insurance' and 'non-indemnity insurance'. Indemnity insurance – for example, property insurance or professional indemnity insurance – involves a promise by the insurer to indemnify the insured for *loss suffered*. It is the suffering of loss rather than the happening of an event which entitles the insured to payment under the policy. In contrast, in 'non-indemnity' insurance – for example, life insurance or personal accident and illness insurance – the liability of the insurer arises on the happening of the event insured, it generally being unnecessary for the insured to prove any loss. Indemnity insurance is probably the most obvious example of a contractual indemnity. Insurance is a form of risk management. Contracts of insurance allow the insured to transfer the risk of a certain event happening – for example, damage to the insured's property, or the insured becoming legally liable to a third party – to the insurer, at a price (or *premium*) calculated by the insurer.

Detailed discussion of the law of insurance is outside the scope of this book.[36] Insurance is governed by a complex mix of federal, State and Territory legislation. The most generally applicable of these statutes, the *Insurance Contracts Act 1984* (Cth), is mentioned at various points throughout this book.[37] This includes a discussion in the next chapter of one of the fundamental features of contracts of insurance – the duty of utmost good faith (see **12.17**).

11.20   Types of indemnity

Outside of the insurance situation, the label 'contractual indemnity' covers a wide range of contractual arrangements. Carter (2009) identifies four main types of contractual indemnity:[38]

(1)   A must indemnify B against any breach of this contract by A (a *party–party indemnity*);

(2)   A must indemnify B against any loss arising from B's contract with C (a *guarantor indemnity*);

(3)   A must indemnify B against any claim by a third party against B in connection with specified matters or transactions (a *third-party claims indemnity*); and

(4)   A must indemnify B against any breach of this agreement by B (a *reverse indemnity*).

We consider each of these categories briefly below.

---

35   For a general treatment of indemnities, see Courtney 2014.
36   For detailed coverage, see Enright & Merkin 2015.
37   Other federal statutes include the *Insurance Act 1973* (Cth), *Life Insurance Act 1995* (Cth), *Marine Insurance Act 1909* (Cth) and *Private Health Insurance Act 2007* (Cth). State and Territory legislation typically covers matters such as workers' compensation and compulsory third party motor vehicle insurance: see eg *Workers Compensation Act 1987* (NSW); *Workplace Injury Management and Workers Compensation Act 1998* (NSW); *Motor Vehicles (Third Party Insurance) Act 1942* (NSW).
38   See also the categorisation in Courtney 2011: 1–2.

11.21   Party–party indemnities

At first glance, this type of indemnity is puzzling as, in the absence of an exemption clause, A is *in any event* required at common law to compensate B for any loss occasioned by their breach of contract. Upon closer examination, however, it becomes apparent that one of the main purposes of such indemnities is the circumvention of some of the common law limitations on damages, such as the rules on remoteness of loss (see **23.16–23.17**) and the duty to mitigate (see **23.18**). Indeed, the term 'indemnity' has sometimes been used as a synonym for *complete* recovery of loss, in contradistinction to damages: see *Victoria Laundry v Newman Industries* (1949) at 539. The extent to which rules such as remoteness and the duty to mitigate apply to claims on indemnities is, in fact, far from settled. However, Courtney (2011: 11) describes the lack of reference to these principles in the indemnity case law as 'striking' and notes that the general approach has been to assume that they do not apply where the loss is within the scope of the indemnity: see eg *Mediterranean Freight Services v BP Oil International* (1994) at 522; *Zaccardi v Caunt* (2008) at [33].

11.22   Guarantor indemnities

As discussed in **11.11**, an indemnity of this type closely resembles a contractual guarantee.[39] It is a contractual arrangement whereby A promises C to guarantee the performance of B's obligations under a contract between B and C. This type of indemnity is commonly used in banking and finance. In fact, guarantees and indemnities of this type are often used in tandem in banking and finance transactions. From the creditor's perspective, this type of indemnity has advantages over a guarantee. Firstly, the indemnifier's liability, unlike that of a guarantor, is *primary* and independent: *Sunbird Plaza v Maloney* (1988) at 254. Hence, the indemnity will be unaffected if the principal debtor's underlying obligation is void or unenforceable, or ceases to exist (because, for example, the principal debtor has been discharged). Secondly, indemnities are not subject to the State and Territory formality requirements applicable to guarantees (see **11.13**). However, both the NCC and the CBP define a 'guarantee' as including an indemnity, so all the provisions discussed above in relation to guarantees will apply. Finally, it should be noted that an indemnity does not carry with it the rights of indemnity and subrogation discussed in relation to guarantees at **11.17**

11.23   Third-party claims indemnities

This is the most common type of contractual indemnity. The object is to ensure that any loss suffered by the indemnified party as a result of claims by third parties in respect of matters within the scope of the indemnity will be covered by the indemnifier. Such third-party indemnities are sometimes more narrowly drafted to cover only liability to (as opposed to claims by) third parties.

Third-party indemnities are used across the spectrum of commercial activity. Publishers, for example, routinely require authors to indemnify them in respect of any claims brought by third parties for loss, injury or damage resulting from publication of the author's work. Such

---

39   As to the distinction between the two, see D'Angelo 2011.

indemnities typically cover claims in respect of matters such as infringement of copyright and other intellectual property rights, breach of confidence and defamation. In the context of the construction industry, the Australian Standard General Conditions of Contract AS2124–1992 include the following indemnity clause:[40]

17.1 Indemnity by Contractor

The Contractor shall indemnify the Principal against – . . .

> (b) claims by any person against the Principal in respect of personal injury or death or loss of or damage to any property, or any other loss or damage,

> arising out of or as a consequence of the carrying out by the Contractor of the work under the Contract, but the Contractor's liability to indemnify the Principal shall be reduced proportionally to the extent that the act or omission of the Principal or employees or agents of the Principal may have contributed to the loss, damage, death or injury.

11.24   Reverse indemnities

Where A agrees to 'indemnify B against any breach of this agreement by B', the effect is simply to exclude B's liability for its *own* breach of contract. But reverse indemnity clauses are often drafted more broadly to cover not only breaches of contract by B, but also any *claim* by A against B on the contract. Such a clause not only exempts B from liability for its own breach of the agreement, but requires A to indemnify B for any costs B incurs in defending a claim brought on the contract by A. The ultimate effect of an indemnity in these terms is to bar any claim by A. Such a claim would have to be dismissed to prevent circuity of action: see *Carr v Stephens* (1829); *Eastern Extension Australasia & China Telegraph v Federal Commissioner of Taxation* (1923) at 441.

11.25   The interpretation of indemnities[41]

Earlier in the chapter, mention was made of the 'rules' set out in *Canada Steamship Lines v R* (1952) for determining whether an exemption clause covers liability for negligence: see **11.07**. It was clear from Lord Morton's opinion that these principles applied to both the exclusion clause *and* the reverse indemnity clause with which the case was concerned. Subsequent English decisions took the view that these rules of construction were not restricted to reverse indemnities and that, if anything:

> A heavier burden lay on the proferens seeking to establish that the other party to an agreement had agreed to indemnify him [sic] against liability for his [sic] negligence and that of his servants than when he is merely seeking to establish exemption from liability for his negligence.[42]

---

40   This standard form construction contract is widely used in Australia, including by many government departments.

41   There are also a number of rules and principles peculiar to the interpretation of contracts of indemnity insurance that are not covered here: see Enright & Merkin 2015: ch 10.

42   *Smith v South Wales Switchgear* (1978) at 168.

A recent English Court of Appeal decision has confirmed that, in so far as they survive, the *Canada Steamship* principles are now more relevant to indemnity clauses than to exemption clauses, at least in commercial cases: see *Persimmon Homes v Ove Arup* (2017) at [55]–[56].

Working on the assumption that this analogy between exemption clauses and indemnity clauses was valid, Australian courts initially considered that the approach taken in *Darlington Futures v Delco* (1986) (see **11.06**) was as applicable to indemnity clauses as to exemption clauses.[43] But, as explained earlier, the High Court in *Andar Transport v Brambles* (2004) preferred to analogise indemnities to *guarantees*. Consequently, indemnities are now governed by the strict rules of construction set out in *Ankar v National Westminster Finance* (1987), rather than the emphasis in *Darlington* on identifying the 'natural and ordinary meaning' of a provision. However, the absence of any reference in *Andar* to the *Canada Steamship* principles has left doubts as to their continued applicability to indemnities. In *BI (Contracting) v AW Baulderstone Holdings* (2007), the indemnifier argued that the strict rules of construction now applicable to guarantees mandated the application of the third *Canada Steamship* principle. The New South Wales Court of Appeal rejected this argument and noted (at [94]) the incompatibility it saw between this principle and the strict approach set out in *Ankar*:

> The third principle, upon which [the indemnifier] relies, is very specific. It requires the reading of a clause on a particular basis in that it requires the court to look for ambiguity as a first approach, rather than construing the clauses strictly and, if there still be ambiguity, in favour of the surety as against the proferens in accordance with the approach stated in *Ankar* and *Andar*.

It observed, too, that the principle had never been expressly endorsed by the High Court in previous decisions. Against that background, had the High Court in *Andar* considered application of that principle mandatory, express reference to it would have been expected.

---

43   See eg *Schenker v Maplas Equipment* (1990); *Glebe Island Terminals v Continental Seagram* (1993); *Valkonen v Jennings Construction* (1995); *Pendal Nominees v Lednez Industries* (1996).

12

PERFORMANCE OF CONTRACTUAL OBLIGATIONS

12.01   Introduction

This chapter is concerned with various issues or questions that commonly arise in relation to the performance of contractual obligations. In particular, we consider:

- What *standard* of performance is expected, and how much choice does the promisor (the party under an obligation to perform) typically have over their *method* of performance?

- At what *time*, or over what period, must performance occur?

- Who must perform first? And where a promisee's own performance only falls due if the promisor fulfils certain obligations, what happens if the promisor renders partial but not complete performance?

- To what extent, in performing obligations or exercising powers under a contract, must a promisor *cooperate* with the promisee or have regard to the promisee's interests?

This final question, as we will see, takes us into what is arguably the single greatest controversy in modern Australian contract law – the extent to which parties are subject to a duty of *good faith and fair dealing* in the performance of their otherwise agreed obligations.

12.02   Breach of contract and its consequences

There are various ways in which a promisor may fail to comply with a contractual obligation. They may not do something they have promised to do, or conversely may do something they have promised not to do. They may fulfil a promise, but not to the standard required; for example, by delivering goods that are not of acceptable quality, or performing work that does not meet certain specifications. They may complete the necessary performance, but not by the time required under the contract. Or they may have given a promise (or 'warranty') as to the truth or accuracy of certain information, which turns out to be incorrect.[1] In each of these cases, subject to any defence for which the terms allow, there will be a *breach of contract*.

The burden of establishing that a breach has occurred is generally on the promisee: see eg *Hart v McDonald* (1910). But exemption clauses or *force majeure* clauses (see **15.04**) may sometimes effectively reverse that burden, by requiring a promisor to establish a particular excuse for non-performance. There is also a special rule applicable at common law to contracts of *bailment* – that is, arrangements to look after someone else's goods; for example, while storing or transporting them. If the goods are not returned, or are returned in a damaged state, the burden of proof is on the bailee (the person looking after the goods) to show that the loss or damage was not due to any lack of reasonable care: see eg *Hobbs v Petersham Transport* (1971).

Where a breach of contract occurs, various legal consequences may follow, either singly or in combination:

- The promisee may be entitled to *withhold performance* of some or all of their own obligations, as discussed in **12.07** and the paragraphs that follow.

- The breach may trigger certain consequences under the contract, such as an obligation on the promisor to pay money or return property. But this is subject to the *rule against penalties* discussed in **22.19–22.24**.

---

1   As to the potential difficulty in distinguishing between warranties and 'mere representations', see **9.12**.

- The promisee will be entitled to obtain *damages*, irrespective of whether they have suffered any loss: see **23.01**. Depending on the circumstances, the promisee may also seek either *enforcement* of the promisor's obligations, or *restitution* of any benefits they have previously conferred on the promisor, using the remedies discussed in Chapters 22 and 24.
- The promisee may be entitled to seek to *terminate* the contract in response to the breach. Such a right may be conferred by an express term in the contract, either immediately or subject to certain processes being followed: see **16.18**. But even in the absence of such a provision, a right to terminate may arise at common law for any breach of an *essential term*, for a *fundamental breach* of an intermediate term, or for a *repudiation*. Each of those concepts is explained in Chapter 16.

Standards and methods of performance

12.03   The different types of obligation

Contractual obligations can vary dramatically in terms of what they require of a promisor. Ultimately, everything turns on the terms of the contract and how they are interpreted in the event of any dispute. But a number of general points can be made.[2]

The first is that most contractual obligations are taken to be *strict* in nature. If a promisor fails to perform, they will generally be liable for breach of contract even if they have done their reasonable best to comply with their obligations. For example, if goods sold are not of acceptable quality, it is irrelevant that the seller is not responsible for the defect: see eg *Grant v Australian Knitting Mills* (1936). Similarly, if a party fails to pay money or complete work, it will not matter that they did not intend to breach their obligations, or that circumstances may have conspired to hinder their performance. That said, it is rare today for obligations to be *absolute* in nature, in the sense that a promisor can have no excuse whatsoever for non-performance. For one thing, the dependency of most obligations (see **12.07**) means that promisors are often excused from performance if the promisee is unable or unwilling to perform their side of the bargain. For another, the doctrine of *frustration* discussed in Chapter 15 means that a promisor may (at least in some cases) be discharged from their obligations if their performance is hindered or rendered impossible by circumstances outside their control and for which the contract makes no provision.

There are in any event certain obligations that call for a lesser standard of performance, where the promisor is not undertaking that something will be done, or that some definite outcome will be achieved, but merely that they will exercise due care, skill or diligence in the performance of a task. This is true of many contracts for professional services. For example, when a lawyer is engaged to assist with a commercial transaction, their obligation is generally to take reasonable care in giving advice, not to obtain a successful outcome for their client: see eg *Winnote v Page* (2006) at [77]. The same is true of a doctor treating a patient, or a financial advisor recommending certain investments. That said, contracts of this type are rarely limited entirely to obligations of care and skill. A professional who contracts to give advice or provide

---

2   For more detailed discussion of some of the points covered below, see Carter 2019: ch 2.

assistance is also likely to be under other obligations that *are* strict in nature, such as to provide reports by agreed dates or safeguard any confidential information they are given.[3]

Another example of a less strict obligation is one that expressly calls for 'reasonable endeavours' or 'best efforts' to be used in striving for a particular result. Such provisions are commonly found in distribution agreements, intellectual property licences and mining ventures. As French CJ, Hayne, Crennan and Kiefel JJ pointed out in *Electricity Generation v Woodside Energy* (2014) at [41], the nature and extent of such an obligation 'is necessarily conditioned by what is reasonable in the circumstances, which can include circumstances that may affect [the promisor's] business'.[4]

12.04   Methods of performance

The means by which a contractual obligation may be discharged are sometimes specified in great detail; for instance, when employees are required to comply with detailed policies and procedures in the way they go about their work.[5] Some contracts may prescribe different options for performance. In that event, it is usually (though not invariably) the promisor who is considered to have the choice as to which method to use: see eg *Timmerman v Nervina Industries* (1983). Beyond that, a promisor may have a discretion as to their method of performance, within the limits of what would be considered reasonable. For example, in the absence of any specification to the contrary, an obligation to pay money may usually be discharged not just by paying cash, or arranging a bank transfer, but by presenting a cheque: see eg *George v Cluning* (1979).[6] Payment in another country's currency may also suffice, if the payment is to be made in that country. But the amount in question must still be calculated by reference to the 'money of account' – the currency in which the amount is expressed.[7] Transactions in this country are presumed to involve Australian currency unless the parties indicate otherwise.[8] Whether it would be acceptable to tender payment in some form of cryptocurrency, such as Bitcoin, is less clear.

It is also well understood that where the promisor is a corporation or government agency, any performance on its part will necessarily be undertaken by employees or other agents acting on its behalf. But can a party delegate or subcontract performance to a different organisation? The answer is generally yes. Indeed, this is common with certain types of contract, as explained in **14.06**. But such *vicarious performance* will not be possible where the nature of the contract suggests a personal commitment by the promisor: see eg *Australis Media Holdings v Telstra* (1998) at 118–19. This will most obviously be true in the case of employment contracts, or agreements with artists or performers.

---

3   As to the strict nature of confidentiality obligations, see Dal Pont 2015b: 267–8.

4   For a critical analysis of the decision in this case, see Carter et al 2014b.

5   Such policies and procedures, however, do not always have direct contractual force: see **9.09**.

6   As to permissible methods of payment of wages to employees, see eg *Fair Work Act 2009* (Cth) ss 323–326.

7   See eg *Bonython v Commonwealth* (1948), decided at a time when matters were complicated by the Australian currency having diverged from that of the UK, but still being pound sterling.

8   See *Currency Act 1965* (Cth) s 9.

Time of performance

12.05   When performance is required

Contracts often expressly specify either a precise time for performance or, more commonly, a deadline by which certain obligations must be performed. But in the absence of any express time stipulation, the common law will generally imply that performance must take place within a reasonable time: *Canning v Temby* (1905) at 424; and see eg *Woolcock Engineering v SWF Hoists & Industrial Equipment* (2000). As mentioned in **9.40**, s 62 of the Australian Consumer Law (ACL) likewise stipulates that services must be supplied to a consumer within a reasonable time, where the relevant agreement is silent on the matter.

Late performance will ordinarily constitute a breach of contract and entitle the promisee to claim damages. It may also be possible for the promisee to terminate the contract, in the circumstances discussed in **16.15–16.17**. But if the only reason for the performance being late is that the promisee has wrongfully prevented or hindered it, the promisor is the one who is entitled to pursue those remedies, depending on the terms of the relevant contract: see eg *Spiers Earthworks v Landtec Projects* (2012). On the other hand, if performance is delayed for reasons outside both parties' control, it may sometimes be possible to conclude that the contract has been frustrated: see **15.08**.

12.06   Duration of contracts

Contracts which involve a discrete exchange, such as a sale of a single item, batch of goods or parcel of land, last only for as long as it takes for the major obligations to be performed. The same is often true of construction contracts, even though in the case of major infrastructure projects the timeframe required may stretch into years or even decades. But other contracts are intended to involve ongoing obligations in which the relevant type of performance will be repeatedly rendered or available. Most employment contracts fall into this category, as do leases, insurance policies, distribution agreements, and contracts for mobile phones, internet services or bank accounts. In some instances, the parties may not agree on a duration at all and simply assume that the contract may operate indefinitely. In such a case, it is common for the contract to provide for a party to be able to end the contract whenever they choose, on giving a specified period of notice to the other party. If no such provision has been agreed in an otherwise indefinite contract, the law may imply a power to terminate on reasonable notice: see **16.20**.

Although employment contracts in particular are often indefinite in nature, some are agreed to operate for a fixed term – and that is perhaps the more common arrangement for some of the other types of ongoing agreement mentioned above. Where a contract for a fixed term expires, the parties may agree to renew the agreement for a further period, in which case a new contract is created. A new contract can also be inferred when the parties continue to deal with one another after a previous agreement has expired, even though nothing has been formally agreed. But in that case the new contract may not have a fixed period. Under the rules discussed in Chapter 16, it can still be terminated at any time by mutual consent, or if one of the parties commits a breach or repudiation that is sufficient at common law to permit unilateral termination. Alternatively, it may be possible for one party to exercise an implied right to give reasonable notice of termination: see eg *Brambles v Wail* (2002).[9] In some cases, legislation may explicitly deal with this type of situation. In South Australia, for example, a residential tenancy that expires without either party giving a notice of termination is automatically converted to 'a periodic tenancy with a tenancy period equivalent to the interval between rental payment times'.[10]

Order and completeness of performance

12.07 Dependent and independent obligations

If a contract is unilateral in nature (see **1.06**), there can be no doubt about the order of performance. Unless and until the condition stipulated by the offeror is met, there can be no contract. But once an offeree performs the requested act(s), a contract is formed and the offeror becomes obliged to fulfil their promise. With bilateral contracts, however, the position is more complex. Who has to perform first, and whether a promisor can withhold performance until the promisee has fulfilled their side of the bargain, hinge on the relationship between the respective obligations.

In *Kingston v Preston* (1773) at 690–1, Lord Mansfield identified three types of what he called 'covenants' (promises). They might be (1) 'mutual and independent', (2) 'conditions and dependant', or (3) 'mutual conditions to be performed at the same time'.

The first category covers obligations that are *independent* of one another, in the sense that neither party can use the other's non-performance as an excuse for failing to do what they have promised. Originally, many contractual obligations were treated as independent of one another; for example, a tenant's obligation to pay rent and a landlord's obligation to keep premises in good repair. But by Lord Mansfield's time the courts were stressing that the matter was one of interpretation, or what he called (at 691) 'the evident sense and meaning of the parties'. The modern approach, as Leeming JA explained in *Hillam v Iacullo* (2015) at [107], 'favours a construction whereby most obligations are construed to be dependent', so that 'clear words are required to discern a relation of independency'. In practice then, it is relatively rare for contractual obligations today to be treated as independent. That said, there is no reason why parties cannot make such an intention clear; for instance, by specifying that goods must be paid for irrespective of whether they have yet been supplied.

In the more normal situation of obligations being dependent, that still leaves two distinct possibilities. Lord Mansfield's second category covers situations where the performance of one party's obligation is *conditional* on the other performing first. This is typically the case with employment contracts. Under what has come to be known as the 'no work no pay' principle, an employee cannot generally claim any wages unless they have performed work

---

9   It is not uncommon for employment arrangements to be inadvertently converted from fixed term to indefinite engagements terminable only by reasonable notice: see eg *Quinn v Jack Chia* (1992). But compare *Heldberg v Rand Transport* (2018), where an intention was inferred that the new contract be terminable in accordance with a notice provision previously included in the expired contract.

10   *Residential Tenancies Act 1995* (SA) s 79A(1). Compare *Retail and Commercial Leases Act 1995* (SA) ss 20D–20G, 20J, concerning the expiry or extension of commercial leases. As to the expiry of leases and the creation of periodic tenancies, see generally Moore et al 2016: 668–71, 735–6.

as directed. This holds true, at least as a matter of common law, even where the employer has wrongfully prevented any work from being performed. While the employee may seek damages for breach of contract, they cannot bring a claim in debt, because they have not earned the wages in question: see *Automatic Fire Sprinklers v Watson* (1946).[11] The question of conditional performance is discussed further below by reference to the concept of entire obligations.

The other type of dependency is the subject of Lord Mansfield's third category. Here, the expectation is that performance will be *concurrent*. This is not to be taken literally. Parties with concurrent obligations may, and commonly will, perform them at different times. The point is rather that neither can sit back and simply wait for the other party to perform. Each party must, when the time comes, be ready, willing and able to perform their respective obligations. If one party fails to do what they have promised, the other cannot sue for breach of contract unless they themselves were at the relevant time in a position to provide the agreed counter-performance. In contracts for the sale of goods, for example, the default rule is that payment and delivery are treated as concurrent conditions. Unless the parties agree otherwise, the seller must be ready and willing to give possession of the goods, while the buyer must be able to pay the agreed price.[12] The same applies to contracts for the sale of land. '[T]he vendor's obligation to deliver a good title and the purchaser's obligation to pay the purchase money are concurrent and mutually dependent obligations': *Foran v Wight* (1989) at 396.[13]

12.08   Entire contracts

An *entire contract* is one where, as a matter of interpretation, a party is required to perform *all* their obligations before any right to the contract price (or any part of it) arises. In other words, complete performance is a condition precedent to recovery. This is most obviously true of a contract to do 'an entire work for a specific sum': see *Phillips v Ellinson Brothers* (1941) at 233–4. In *Cutter v Powell* (1795), a sailor was employed on a voyage from Kingston, Jamaica, to Liverpool, England, for a lump sum of 30 guineas. His contract was construed as being entire. Hence, after he died part-way through the voyage, his estate was held to have no entitlement to any part of that sum. Significantly, the entire contracts doctrine operated here despite the absence of any breach of contract on the sailor's part.

Although payment by way of lump sum is a characteristic of entire contracts, it has been stressed that it is not 'in the least decisive of the character of the contract': *William Thomas & Sons v Harrowing Steamship* (1915) at 63; and see also *Hoenig v Isaacs* (1952). The crucial question is whether the true agreement between the parties was that the promisor's ability to recover payment was to be conditional upon complete performance of its obligations.

---

11   See further Stewart et al 2016: 435–46.
12   *Sale of Goods Act 1923* (NSW) s 31; *Goods Act 1958* (Vic) s 35; *Sale of Goods Act 1896* (Qld) s 30; *Sale of Goods Act 1895* (WA) s 28; *Sale of Goods Act 1895* (SA) s 28; *Sale of Goods Act 1896* (Tas) s 33; *Sale of Goods Act 1954* (ACT) s 32; *Sale of Goods Act 1972* (NT) s 31.
13   It was recognised in *Foran*, however, that a defaulting party may sometimes be estopped from asserting a lack of readiness and willingness to perform by the other party: see **16.22**.

12.09   Divisible contracts

In contrast to an entire contract, the defining characteristic of a severable or *divisible* contract is the parties' intention that the promisor will earn the contract price in stages. Separate parts of the contract price can, in other words, be attributed to performance of separate parts of the promisor's obligations. As a result, a party will be able to recover the contract price attributable to that part of its obligations it has performed, notwithstanding its failure to provide *complete* performance. A classic example of a severable contract is an agreement providing for delivery of goods in instalments, with the buyer paying for each instalment upon delivery: see eg *Mersey Steel and Iron v Naylor Benzon* (1884). Another is a construction contract that provides for a series of progress payments as various stages of the work are completed: see eg *Stocznia Gdanska v Latvian Shipping* (1998). But just as the existence of a lump sum is not conclusive of an entire contract, so the existence of a series of instalments or progress payments is not conclusive of a severable one: see eg *Gilbert-Ash v Modern Engineering* (1974) at 717.

As Carter (2018: 641–2) points out, the terminology of entire *contracts* can be misleading, as one aspect of a party's obligations may be entire, while another is severable. Moreover, even where a contract is clearly severable, it may be divided into a series of obligations that are themselves entire. For example, in *Steele v Tardiani* (1946), the plaintiffs, who were Italian wartime internees, contracted to cut an unascertained quantity of timber for the defendant. The timber was to be cut to particular dimensions and the plaintiffs were to be paid per ton of timber cut. In the event, the plaintiffs cut 1500 tons of timber, but not all of it to contractual specifications. The contract was found to be severable, in that each ton of timber had to be cut in compliance with the specifications. Nevertheless, as Dixon J put it (at 401), 'each divisible application of the contract' was itself entire. It is more accurate, therefore, to speak of *obligations* being entire, rather than contracts.

12.10   Statutory provisions

In some instances, an otherwise entire contract, or a set of entire obligations, may be rendered severable by statute. What is known as the *apportionment legislation* provides for severability in respect of 'all rents, annuities, dividends and other periodical payments in the nature of income', although this is subject to express contractual provision to the contrary.[14]

In the employment context, the common law position may also be modified by virtue of the numerous awards or registered enterprise agreements that set minimum wages for workers in various industries, occupations or workplaces. These may, for example, have the effect that pay accrues for each hour worked: see eg *Re Waterside Workers Award* (1957). Historically, industrial instruments have not always been clear on this point. But the Fair Work Commission has indicated a willingness to include standard provisions on the matter in most 'modern awards' operating under the *Fair Work Act 2009* (Cth): see *4 Yearly Review of Modern*

---

14   See *Conveyancing Act 1919* (NSW), ss 144(1), 144(5); *Supreme Court Act 1986* (Vic), ss 54, 53(4); *Property Law Act 1974* (Qld), ss 232, 233(2); *Property Law Act 1969* (WA), ss 131, 134(2); *Law of Property Act 1936* (SA), ss 64, 68; *Apportionment Act 1871* (Tas), ss 2, 7; *Civil Law (Property) Act 2006* (ACT), ss 250, 253(2); *Law of Property Act 2000* (NT), ss 212(1), 213(2).

Awards – Payment of Wages (2017) at [19]–[22]. These are likely to provide for either daily or hourly accrual of wages.

12.11 Can partial performance suffice?

The general assumption at common law is that the performance required under a contract must be exactly as specified. As Lord Atkin put it in *Arcos v EA Ronaasen & Son* (1933) at 479, '[a] ton does not mean about a ton, or a yard about a yard'. Still less, he suggested, would this be true of a contract using more 'minute measurements'. This is by no means an absolute rule. Under what is known as the *de minimis* principle,[15] truly insignificant or trivial discrepancies may be ignored: see eg *Condon Investments v Lesdor Properties* (2012) at [61]. For example, the fact that a consultant's report contains a few typos or the occasional factual error would not be a basis for the client who commissioned it refusing to pay for the work. Sometimes too, what might appear on its face to be an exact requirement may be interpreted as requiring only approximate satisfaction. In *Luna Park v Tramways Advertising* (1938), for instance, a require-ment to display advertisements for 'at least eight hours per day' was considered on its proper construction to be satisfied by display for *substantially* eight hours a day. Generally speaking, however, a failure to meet whatever specifications, targets or deadlines are set for performance will constitute a breach of contract.

Despite this, the courts have been prepared in some instances to recognise that incomplete or defective performance by a promisor may be good enough to warrant some form of reward. The possibility of a *quantum meruit* claim for reasonable recompense is considered further below. But first it is necessary to consider the doctrine of *substantial performance*.

12.12 The doctrine of substantial performance

Under this doctrine, a promisor who has rendered substantial performance may be allowed to recover the contract price set for their work, subject to a set-off or counterclaim by the promisee for damages in relation to the cost of having the work completed or rectified: see eg *Hoenig v Isaacs* (1952). In this situation, there is still a breach of contract – hence, the promisee's right to claim damages. But the promisor is nonetheless taken to have done enough to earn the agreed counter-performance. If that constitutes a payment, they may sue in debt to recover it.

Application of the doctrine poses no conceptual difficulty in the context of contracts where complete performance is not a condition precedent to payment. But the position in relation to entire obligations is more problematic, even though courts have often assumed that the doctrine can operate in such a case: see eg *Phillips v Ellinson Brothers* (1941) at 246; *Steele v Tardiani* (1946) at 401.[16] The fairness and logic of allowing a promisor to recover for incom-plete performance in circumstances where payment was intended to be conditional on *complete* performance is surely questionable. In *Hoenig v Isaacs*, the English Court of Appeal

---

15 The full expression is *de minimis non curat lex* (the law does not concern itself with trifles).

16 But compare *Condon Investments v Lesdor Properties* (2012), where an obligation to execute a strata plan for land under development by the parties was conditional on the completion of building works. It was held that for this particular purpose, substantial completion would *not* suffice.

attempted to reconcile its earlier decision in *H Dakin v Lee* (1916), allowing recovery on the grounds of substantial performance, with the entire contracts doctrine of *Cutter v Powell*. Rather than viewing the doctrine of substantial performance in *Dakin* as an exception to the entire contracts doctrine, Somervell LJ stressed (at 179) that *Dakin* reinforced his view that the court in *Cutter v Powell* had not construed *all* of the sailor's obligations as entire:

> [The court] clearly decided that his continuing as mate during the whole voyage was a condition precedent to payment. It did not decide that if he had completed the main purpose of the contract, namely, serving as mate for the whole voyage, the defendant could have repudiated his liability by establishing that in the course of the voyage the sailor had, possibly through inadvertence, failed on some occasion in his duty as mate whereby some damage had been caused.

In other words, while there would have been no scope for the doctrine of substantial performance with respect to the *continuation* of performance, there could have been in respect of the *manner* in which that continuing performance proceeded.

12.13   When is performance substantial?

Determining when incomplete or defective performance is sufficiently 'substantial' is not straightforward. In *Hoenig v Isaacs* (1952), the defendant contracted to decorate and furnish the plaintiff's apartment for a total of £750. The Court found that this was not an entire contract and that, despite defects costing nearly £56 to rectify, the defendant had substantially performed his obligations under the contract. Accordingly, the defendant recovered the contract price minus a deduction reflecting the cost of remedying the defects.

In *Bolton v Mahadeva* (1972), by contrast, the plaintiff had contracted to install a heating and hot water system for the defendant for the price of £560. The installation was defective in a number of ways and the defendant refused to pay. The principal matters complained of were a defective flue resulting in fumes, making a number of rooms uncomfortable and inconvenient to use, and the installation of insufficient radiators and insulation, rendering the system incapable of generating adequate heat. In deciding whether there was substantial performance, Cairns LJ took into account both the nature of the defects and the proportion between the cost of rectifying them (£174.50) and the contract price. He also rejected (at 1013) the proposition that the contractor was only entitled to payment if the defects were so trifling as to be *de minimis*. In concluding that this was not a case of substantial performance, both Cairns LJ and Sachs LJ emphasised that the system as installed was generally ineffective for its primary purpose.

12.14   *Quantum meruit* claims

A *quantum meruit* claim seeks to recover reasonable recompense for work done. As a general rule, such an action cannot be used to obtain payment for partial performance of an entire obligation. This was indeed the claim that failed in *Cutter v Powell* (1795). The Court took the view that to allow the deceased sailor's estate to recover the value of the services he had provided up to his death would conflict with the contract he had made.

Importantly, however, there are cases where a *quantum meruit* claim can succeed. For example, a court may be prepared to infer that the promisee has *waived compliance* with the requirement of complete performance, or indeed that the parties have agreed to vary the original contract. That is what happened in *Steele v Tardiani* (1946). The defendant had stood by while the plaintiffs did the work and subsequently sold the timber they had cut, even the bundles not cut to the original specifications. For those bundles, the plaintiffs were entitled to receive a fair price measured by market rates.

A further argument that may be made – and indeed another possible explanation for the successful claim in *Steele v Tardiani* – is that the promisee has *freely accepted* the benefit of the promisor's performance. The limited circumstances in which such a plea will be accepted are considered further in Chapter 17. So too is the capacity of a promisor who has been *wrongfully prevented* from completing their performance to bring an action in *quantum meruit*, as an alternative to suing for damages for breach of contract: see **17.08–17.09**.

Cooperation, good faith and fair dealing

12.15   The duty of cooperation

The parties to any contract are obliged to cooperate with one another to ensure that the contract is performed. This duty has at times been expressed either as a principle of interpretation or as a term implied by law. The latter suggestion is perhaps more logical, since it is possible to envisage cooperation being implicitly required even in the most informal of agreements. In *Commonwealth Bank v Barker* (2014) at [25] and [37], however, French CJ, Bell and Keane JJ seemed willing to accept that the duty can operate in both of those ways.

Whatever its conceptual basis, the duty has both positive and negative elements. From a negative perspective, the parties are obliged not to do anything which would hinder or prevent the fulfilment of the purpose of an express term of the contract: *Shepherd v Felt and Textiles* (1931) at 378. More positively, each party is expected to do whatever is necessary to 'enable the other party to have the benefit of the contract': *Butt v McDonald* (1896) at 71; *Secured Income Real Estate v St Martins Investments* (1979) at 607. More particularly, as Lord Blackburn explained in *Mackay v Dick* (1881) at 263:

> where in a … contract it appears that both parties have agreed that something shall be done, which cannot effectually be done unless both concur in doing it, … each agrees to do all that is necessary to be done on his [sic] part for the carrying out of that thing.

At an obvious level, this can include allowing contractors or employees to access workplaces, or accepting payments or deliveries. But it can also, as explained in **5.25**, oblige parties to take reasonable steps to allow the satisfaction of a condition on which the operation of the contract hinges.

As the High Court stressed in *Barker*, however, for the duty to be engaged, there must be an express promise of a particular 'benefit'.[17] The plaintiff had been made redundant by the Commonwealth Bank. His contract provided that he would be entitled to a severance payment if his job became surplus to requirements and the bank was unable to place him in an alternative position. He argued that the bank had breached its duty of cooperation by failing to take steps to

17   See also *Australis Media Holdings v Telstra* (1998); *WIN v Nine Network* (2016).

redeploy him. But this argument was rejected. The bank's lack of action could only have breached the duty of cooperation if it had failed to help the plaintiff secure a benefit that was actually being promised under the contract. The only benefit to which he was positively entitled was a payment. The contract here did not confer any *right* to be redeployed.[18]

In a similar vein, other courts have resisted any suggestion that the duty requires parties to behave nicely or even reasonably towards one another: *Council of the City of Sydney v Goldspar* (2006) at [162]; *Beerens v Bluescope Distribution* (2012) at [54]. Nor does it require a party to abandon self-interest: see eg *Famestock v Body Corporate* (2013). It is also clear that, like all implied terms, the duty must operate in a way that is consistent with the express terms of the contract: see *Campbell v Backoffice Investments* (2009) at [168].

12.16   Fiduciary duties

In some instances, parties may be required to go beyond cooperation. For example, a party who owes a *fiduciary duty* must generally act in someone else's best interests and avoid any situation in which there might be a conflict between that person's interest and their own.[19] Any breach of such a duty may attract equitable remedies, such as an account of profits, that are not available for breach of an ordinary contract: see **3.15**.

Fiduciary relationships may be, but do not have to be, contractual in nature. Ordinarily, a contracting party is entitled to pursue their own self-interest, at least within the bounds of the obligations they have accepted. But some contracts are different.[20] As Mason J noted in *Hospital Products v United States Surgical* (1984) at 96, the categories of what might be considered fiduciary relationships are not closed. But accepted relationships which attract this higher level of obligation include trustee and beneficiary, agent and principal, solicitor and client, employee and employer, and director and company. Each of those relationships involves 'vertical' duties, where the first party is expected to subordinate their own interest to that of the second party. But some fiduciary duties can also operate 'horizontally' or reciprocally, as in the case of a partnership. In that instance, each of the partners is expected to put the *joint* interests of the partnership ahead of their own.

In *Hospital Products* at 96–7, Mason J explained what it is about a relationship that will mark it out as having a fiduciary character:

> The critical feature of these relationships is that the fiduciary undertakes or agrees to act for or on behalf of or in the interests of another person in the exercise of a power or discretion which will affect the interests of that other person in a legal or practical sense. The relationship between the parties is therefore one which gives the fiduciary a special opportunity to exercise the power or discretion to the detriment of that other person who is accordingly vulnerable to abuse by the fiduciary of his [sic] position.

The courts have sometimes struggled to find a dividing line between such relationships and what might be regarded as ordinary commercial dealings. Some joint ventures, for example,

---

18   As to the rejection of the plaintiff's alternative argument, based on an implied duty of mutual trust and confidence, see **9.26**.

19   See generally Dal Pont 2015a: ch 4.

20   See Finn 1989a.

are taken to have a fiduciary dimension, where others do not. Much will turn on whether the venture is akin to a partnership: see eg *United Dominions v Brian* (1985) at 10–11.[21] *Hospital Products* itself concerned an agreement for an Australian company to have exclusive distribution rights for a US firm's products. The High Court split 3:2 in ruling that there was no fiduciary relationship, with Mason and Deane JJ dissenting.

More recently, however, the courts have perhaps been a little firmer about resisting the incursion of fiduciary duties into commercial relationships.[22] *John Alexander's Clubs v White City Tennis Club* (2010) involved a series of agreements between multiple parties, concerning the sale and use of land on which a tennis club operated. The most recent of these granted John Alexander's Clubs (JACS) an option to purchase the land. The High Court could find nothing in this contract to suggest a fiduciary relationship between JACS and the club. It commented (at [83]) that the club's only vulnerability 'was that which any contracting party has to breach by another'. Nor, it added (at [90]), was there any 'entrustment or custodianship to be abused'. It also adopted (at [91]) the following statement by Mason J in *Hospital Products* at 97:

> The fiduciary relationship, if it is to exist at all, must accommodate itself to the terms of the contract so that it is consistent with, and conforms to, them. The fiduciary relationship cannot be superimposed upon the contract in such a way as to alter the operation which the contract was intended to have according to its true construction.

The Court added (at [92]) that '[w]here a term to like effect as the suggested fiduciary obligation cannot be implied, it will be very difficult to superimpose the suggested fiduciary obligation'.

12.17   Contracts of utmost good faith

Some agreements, although not involving fiduciary relations, were treated by the common law as contracts 'of utmost good faith' (*uberrimae fidei*). Historically, these included certain kinds of family settlement: see eg *Gordon v Gordon* (1817). But by far the most significant example was a contract of insurance. As noted in **4.08**, the requirement of good faith applicable to such arrangements included a duty on the part of the insured to disclose any material facts. The more general duty has now been put on a statutory footing by the *Insurance Contracts Act 1984* (Cth).[23] For all contracts of insurance covered by the Act,[24] s 13(1) implies 'a provision requiring each party to it to act towards the other party, in respect of any matter arising under or in relation to it, with the utmost good faith'. Following a 2013 amendment, it is now clear that this duty applies not just in relation to the parties to the contract, but any third party to whom the benefit of the insurance cover extends (s 13(3)).[25] Section 14 also provides that a party may

---

21   See further Knowler & Rickett 2011.

22   See eg *Streetscape Projects v City of Sydney* (2013); *Adventure Golf Systems v Belgravia Health & Leisure Group* (2017). But compare Finn 2014: 135–44, criticising the *Streetscape* decision.

23   See generally Enright & Merkin 2015: ch 6.

24   Contracts not covered by the Act are listed in s 9. These include contracts of reinsurance, private health insurance, contracts of insurance with friendly societies, marine insurance, workers' compensation insurance, and compulsory third party motor vehicle insurance.

25   But this extension only applies after the contract is made (s 13(4)). As to this and other aspects of the changes to the duty of good faith made by the *Insurance Contracts Amendment Act 2013* (Cth), see McGivern 2013.

not rely on a provision of an insurance contract, if to do so would involve failing to act with the utmost good faith.

The Act does not define 'utmost good faith'. But in *CGU Insurance v AMP Financial Planning* (2007), the High Court rejected the view that the duty is breached only by dishonest conduct. Rather, as Gleeson and Crennan JJ explained (at [15]), good faith encompasses a duty to act 'consistently with commercial standards of decency and fairness' and with regard to the interests of the other party. That said, it does not require the insurer to 'surrender any commercial advantage which they may seek to take advantage of': *Allianz Australia Insurance v Vitale* (2014) at [125]. Non-compliance with the duty may lead to a party being liable for breach of contract. ASIC may also take action against an insurer that breaches its duty in handling or settling claims (s 14A). In the event of a breach by the insured, the insurer has the right to cancel the policy (s 60(1)).

12.18 Statutory obligations

Aside from the *Insurance Contracts Act 1984*, few other Australian statutes impose a broadly framed duty of good faith. But examples can be found in some of the industry codes given statutory effect under s 51AE of the *Competition and Consumer Act 2010* (Cth). These include the Franchising Code of Conduct in Schedule 1 of the *Competition and Consumer (Industry Codes—Franchising) Regulation 2014* (Cth).[26] Clause 6 of the Code requires each party to a franchising agreement to act towards any other party with good faith, in any matter arising under either the agreement or the Code itself. The duty, which cannot be limited or excluded, expressly extends to negotiations and other pre-contractual dealings: see eg *ACCC v Ultra Tune* (2019). Good faith is expressed to operate 'within the meaning of the unwritten law from time to time' – that is, the common law. But to avoid any doubt, it is expressly stated that a court may consider whether a party 'acted honestly and not arbitrarily', or 'cooperated to achieve the purposes of the agreement'. It is also provided, however, that the obligation to act in good faith does not prevent a party from acting in their 'legitimate commercial interests'. As we will see, all this is consistent with the common law conception of good faith: see **12.22**.

Beyond those more general instances, specific statutory obligations are often couched in terms of a need to act in good faith. They may also make the presence or absence of good faith a relevant factor in determining whether some other standard of behaviour has been breached. Important examples of this can be found in ss 22(1)(l) and (2)(l) of the ACL. These permit a court to have regard to the extent to which each party has acted in good faith in deciding whether a party has engaged in unconscionable conduct, in breach of the prohibition in s 21: see **20.17**.[27]

---

26 For a further example, see eg cl 28 of the Food and Grocery Code of Conduct in Schedule 1 to the *Competition and Consumer (Industry Codes—Food and Grocery) Regulation 2015*. This covers commercial dealings between retailers, wholesalers and suppliers in a grocery supply chain. Unlike the Franchising Code of Conduct, however, this is a voluntary rather than mandatory code.

27 The same applies for the purpose of the similar prohibition in s 12CB of the *Australian Securities and Investments Commission Act 2001* (Cth): see ss 12CC(1)(l), (2)(l). Examples can also be found in other types of legislation dealing with unconscionable conduct: see eg *Retail Leases Act* 2003 (Vic) s 77(2)(k).

12.19   A general duty of good faith?

There is nothing to stop the parties to a contract from expressly demanding the exercise of good faith in the performance of a particular obligation. A common example of this, as discussed in **6.09**, is to require negotiations to be conducted in good faith. Occasionally, a contract may go further. In *Macquarie International Health Clinic v Sydney South West Area Health Service* (2010), for example, a series of agreements made in conjunction with a land development project obliged the parties to act in good faith not just in performing any duties or exercising any powers under the contracts, but 'in their respective dealings with each other'.

The question, however, is whether such a duty might be imposed as part of the general law of contract, even in the absence of agreement. This is an issue on which countries have taken very different paths. In the UK, the courts have long accepted that where one party is accorded an apparently unfettered discretion under the express terms of a contract, the exercise of that discretion may be limited by an implied requirement of reasonableness. The discretion must be exercised 'rationally' by reference to the purposes for which the power was granted, rather than capriciously or arbitrarily.[28] In recent cases, the UK Supreme Court has been prepared to use the language of 'good faith' to describe this requirement: see eg *British Telecommunications v Telefónica O2* (2014) at [37]; *Braganza v BP Shipping* (2015). But there has been no great interest in identifying a more general duty to act in good faith.[29] This is despite the fact that the concept is hardly unfamiliar. Besides the concept of utmost good faith in insurance law, many rules of English law incorporate requirements of this type, for example in dealing with property.[30]

By contrast, US law has readily embraced the idea of a general duty of good faith. Section 205 of the *Restatement (Second) of the Law of Contracts* provides: 'Every contract imposes upon each party a duty of good faith and fair dealing in its performance and enforcement.' Section 1-203 of the Uniform Commercial Code is to similar effect. In Canada, the concept took longer to take root. But, in *Bhasin v Hrynew* (2014) at [33], the Canadian Supreme Court identified 'good faith contractual performance [as] a general organizing principle of the common law'. More specifically, it recognised (at [73]) what it termed 'a general duty of honesty in contractual performance'. Good faith is also a standard obligation in the codes of civil law countries, often expressed in very general terms.[31] The same is true of UNIDROIT's Principles of International Commercial Contracts. Article 1.7 imposes an overriding duty to 'act in accordance with good faith and fair dealing in international trade'.

In Australia, the position is completely unsettled. Like their UK counterparts, courts in this country have been willing to accept that discretionary powers may be subject to an implied requirement that they be exercised 'honestly and conformably with the purposes of the contract': *Silverbrook Research v Lindley* (2010) at [6]; and see also *Mineralogy v Sino Iron* (2017) at [419].[32] But, for the last three decades, there has been an ongoing debate among both judges and commentators as to whether to go further and embrace at least a US-style duty to

---

28   The sense of 'reasonableness' adopted in this context has clear parallels to the standard used in administrative law to review official decisions: see Daintith 2005.

29   For a rare exception, see *Yam Seng v International Trade* (2013).

30   See Lücke 1987.

31   See eg *German Civil Code* arts 157, 242; *Contract Law of the People's Republic of China* arts 6, 60, 125.

32   See generally Paterson 2009a.

perform contracts in good faith. Despite having many opportunities to settle on a consistent approach, judges in the lower courts have persisted in taking differing views, to the point where it almost seems that the doctrine of precedent has completely broken down. For its part, as will be seen, the High Court has ignored its one clear opportunity to clarify the law.[33]

12.20   A duty implied in law?

The starting point for the current debate in Australia was provided by *Renard Constructions v Minister for Public Works* (1992). The case concerned a construction project. In the event of any default by the contractor, the contract permitted a notice to be served requiring the contractor to 'show cause to the satisfaction of the principal' why certain powers (including termination of the contract) should not be exercised. The New South Wales Court of Appeal held that the principal was required to act reasonably in determining whether there was cause for action against the contractor. On the facts, the principal had not done so, having acted on misleading, incomplete and prejudicial information. Handley and Meagher JJA decided the case on conventional grounds, invoking (albeit in different ways) principles concerning the need for this type of discretion to be exercised reasonably.[34] Priestley JA was prepared to do likewise. But, in a groundbreaking judgment, he went further, reviewing case law from both Australia and other jurisdictions (notably the US) on the idea of good faith in performance. His conclusion (at 268) was a radical one:

> [P]eople generally, including judges and other lawyers, from all strands of the community, have grown used to the courts applying standards of fairness to contract which are wholly consistent with the existence in all contracts of a duty upon the parties of good faith and fair dealing in its performance. In my view this is in these days the expected standard, and anything less is contrary to prevailing community expectations.

This duty, he considered, should be implied into contracts both by law *and* in fact.

There was initial resistance to this suggestion from some judges. In *Service Station Association v Berg Bennett* (1993) at 94, for example, Gummow J insisted that controls on the exercise of powers and discretions are grounded in construction, not implied terms.[35] This view has been strongly supported by Peden, who has argued that good faith is a principle that already informs the interpretation of contractual terms. Indeed, it is the very 'essence of contract'. That being the case, she suggests, there is no need to imply any term to support its operation.[36]

Nevertheless, in the wake of *Renard*, the idea of implying a duty of good faith as a matter of law became widely accepted: see eg *Hughes Aircraft Systems v Airservices Australia* (1997) at 192; *Alcatel Australia v Scarcella* (1998) at 368–9. The decision in *Burger King v Hungry Jack's* (2001) provided a particularly striking example of the duty at work. Burger King, the US fast

---

33   There is a vast literature on this subject. For a survey of some of the earlier contributions, see Munro 2009. For more recent contributions, besides those mentioned below, see eg Allsop 2011; Corcoran 2012; Paterson 2014; Gray 2015.

34   For an earlier example of such an implication, concerning an architect's power to issue instructions as to building work, see *Carr v JA Berriman* (1953).

35   See also *Pacific Brands Sport & Leisure v Underworks* (2005) at [64].

36   See Peden 2003; and see further Carter & Peden 2003; Carter 2018: ch 2.

food giant, had purported to terminate its agreement with its Australian franchisee, Hungry Jack's, because the latter had failed to develop new outlets as required under the agreement. But this failure had only occurred because Burger King had effectively put a 'freeze' on such developments. The US company's motive was apparently to clear the way for direct development of the Australian market. It was held to have acted unreasonably and in bad faith and accordingly could not validly rely on the franchisee's breaches as a basis for termination.

It was significant, however, that in some of these later cases the courts had started to speak of implying such a duty into 'commercial contracts', rather than all contracts: see eg *Burger King* at [159]. In *Vodafone v Mobile Innovations* (2004) at [204]–[206] the New South Wales Court of Appeal once again accepted that the basis of the duty lay in a term implied by law, expressly rejecting Peden's view. But in giving the leading judgment, Giles JA expressed doubts (at [191]) as to the 'width and indeterminacy' of commercial contracts as a potential class of contract.

Vodafone also confirmed the orthodox view that no duty will be implied where to do so would be inconsistent with the express terms of a contract.[37] It was held that there could be no scope for implying a duty of good faith in the face of provisions that in some instances gave one party absolute discretion, but in others explicitly required powers to be exercised reasonably or in good faith. It was also noted that the contract contained a 'whole of agreement' clause that purported to exclude any implied terms.[38] On the other hand, Giles JA was careful to reserve the possibility that the use of any absolute discretion might still be challenged on the basis that it had been exercised arbitrarily, capriciously or for an extraneous purpose. Whether that more specific basis for judicial intervention could ever be excluded by express words in a contract remains an open question. As Finn J observed in *GEC Marconi Systems v BHP Information Technology* (2003) at [920], it is 'difficult to envisage an express provision authorising dishonesty'.

12.21 A duty implied in fact?

By the mid-2000s, the balance of authority was plainly in favour of recognising a general duty of good faith, even if not all courts agreed with the idea. But in *Esso v Southern Pacific* (2005), the Victorian Court of Appeal seized on the comments in *Vodafone* to reject the case for implying the term by law into *any* type of contract. At most, the Court suggested, it might be appropriate to imply a term *in fact* – and then only to protect one of the parties from what Buchanan JA termed (at [25]) 'exploitive conduct which subverts the original purpose for which the contract was made'. According to Warren CJ (at [4]):

> Ultimately, the interests of certainty in contractual activity should be interfered with only when the relationship between the parties is unbalanced and one party is at a substantial disadvantage, or is particularly vulnerable in the prevailing context. Where commercial leviathans are contractually engaged, it is difficult to see that a duty of good faith will arise, leaving aside duties that might arise in a fiduciary relationship.

---

37 See also *Central Exchange v Anaconda Nickel* (2002); and see generally **9.01**.
38 Compare *Vakras v Cripps* (2015) at [422], where an entire agreement clause that made no mention of implied terms was not sufficient in itself to exclude any implied duty.

In subsequent cases, these comments have been invoked to justify implying a duty of good faith to protect franchisees against exploitation by franchisors: see eg *Meridian Retail v Australian Unity Retail Network* (2006) at [210]–[212]; *Video Ezy v Sedema* (2014); *Marmax Investments v RPR Maintenance* (2015) at [122]. The problem, however, is that terms are only meant to be implied in fact when they are *necessary* to the effective operation of a contract: see **9.20–9.21**. It is hard to see why a duty of good faith is genuinely needed to give business efficacy to a franchise agreement. It would make far more sense to imply it in law as a default term. Indeed, that is how the term was actually described in *Video Ezy* and *Marmax*.

A more convincing example of a necessary (but limited) implication of good faith is provided by *Specialist Diagnostic Services v Healthscope* (2012). A hospital leased part of its premises to a pathology laboratory, with a covenant not to allow any other business to provide similar services on site. The hospital subsequently altered its building to facilitate the delivery of pathology specimens to and from another company. The covenant was ultimately held to impose an unreasonable restraint on trade, under the principles discussed in Chapter 21. But the Court expressed the view that, if it had been valid, the hospital would have been in breach of an implied obligation of good faith not to undertake such alterations. This was justified because, as the Court put it (at [89]), '[t]he tenant was necessarily vulnerable to such conduct'.

Returning to the general debate, the judgments in *Esso* seemed for a time to have marked a turning point. They had plainly struck a chord with judges wary of the implications of a universally applicable duty of good faith and fair dealing: see eg *Tote Tasmania v Garrott* (2008) at [16]; *Specialist Diagnostic Services* at [86]. In *CGU Workers Compensation v Garcia* (2007) at [132], the New South Wales Court of Appeal stressed that its earlier decisions 'do not establish that such an implied term is to be inserted into every contract or even into every aspect of a particular contract'.

But once again, any chance of consensus quickly vanished. In *United Group Rail Services v Rail Corporation* (2009) at [61], a differently constituted Court of Appeal led by Allsop P made no mention of *Garcia* in reaffirming the proposition that 'good faith, in some degree or to some extent, is part of the law of performance of contracts'.[39] In *Paciocco v ANZ Bank* (2015) at [287], the same judge, now the Chief Justice of the Federal Court, reaffirmed that view with the concurrence of other members of the Full Court. The Victorian Court of Appeal, however, has continued to insist that a duty should only be implied where it is truly necessary: see eg *Vakras v Cripps* (2015) at [423].

12.22   What *is* good faith?

For some, the doubts about the concept of good faith have centred on the difficulty in defining it. As Warren CJ noted in *Esso* (at [3]):

---

39   See also *Adventure World Travel v Newsom* (2014) at [26]. But not all New South Wales judges agree: see eg *Starlink International v Coles Supermarkets* (2011) at [18]–[33]; *Caswell v Sony/ATV Music Publishing* (2014) at [46]–[47].

The difficulty is that the standard is nebulous. Therefore, the current reticence attending the application and recognition of a duty of good faith probably lies as much with the vagueness and imprecision inherent in defining commercial morality. The modern law of contract has developed on the premise of achieving certainty in commerce. If good faith is not readily capable of definition then that certainty is undermined.

In fact, however, most judges have tended to agree on what good faith means. Reference has frequently been made to the suggestion by Mason (2000: 69) that it involves 'no less than three related notions':

(1) an obligation on the parties to co-operate in achieving the contractual objects (loyalty to the promise itself);
(2) compliance with honest standards of conduct; and
(3) compliance with standards of conduct which are reasonable having regard to the interests of the parties.

In *Overlook v Foxtel* (2002) at [67], Barrett J agreed with this approach and added:

Viewed in this way, the implied obligation of good faith underwrites the spirit of the contract and supports the integrity of its character. A party is precluded from cynical resort to the black letter. But no party is fixed with the duty to subordinate self-interest entirely which is the lot of the fiduciary ... The duty is not a duty to prefer the interests of the other contracting party. It is, rather, a duty to recognise and to have due regard to the legitimate interests of both the parties in the enjoyment of the fruits of the contract as delineated by its terms.

Both Mason's formulation, and the caution that parties are not expected to forego the pursuit of their own interests, have repeatedly been endorsed: see eg *Macquarie International Health Clinic v Sydney South West Area Health Service* (2010) at [146]–[147]; *Masters Home Improvement v North East Solution* (2017) at [99]. In *Paciocco* (at [289], [294]), Allsop CJ expressed the duty in these terms:

[T]he notion is rooted in the bargain and requires behaviour to support it, not undermine it, and not to take advantage of oversight, slips and the like in it. To do so is akin to theft
Trickery and sharp practice impede commerce by decreasing trust and increasing risk. Good faith and fair dealing promote commerce by supporting the central conception and basal foundation of commerce: a requisite degree of trust. Business people understand these things.[40]

The aspect that has tended to generate most controversy has been the requirement of reasonableness.[41] In *Virk v YUM! Restaurants* (2017) at [164], however, a Full Court of the Federal Court provided a helpful explanation of what it involves in this context:

Reasonableness is not to be approached in a case such as this as akin to a tortious duty to exercise due care and skill or to produce a reasonable outcome. Rather it goes to the

---

40   On this last point, see Duke 2007, using insights from behavioural economics literature to support the view that fair dealing is indeed an appropriate and accepted standard for commercial dealings.
41   See eg Peden 2005.

> quality of the conduct ... to discern whether it was capricious, dishonest, unconscionable, arbitrary or the product of a motive which was antithetical to the object of the contractual power.

The case concerned the power of the Pizza Hut franchisor to set the prices for pizzas sold by its franchisees. It was conceded that the exercise of the discretion was subject to an implied duty of good faith and reasonableness. But the defendant was held not to have breached this duty when cutting prices below what the franchisees believed was a figure that would enable them to operate profitably. The Court stressed that the franchise contracts did not contain any promise that each business would be profitable. Indeed, they contemplated losses being made. On the facts, there was nothing to suggest the franchisor had acted irrationally or capriciously. Whether it had taken sufficient care in making its decision, or had in some broad sense been unreasonable towards the franchisees, was irrelevant.

12.23   The prospects for a general duty of good faith

Unless and until the High Court produces a definitive ruling on this subject, it seems likely that uncertainty and disagreement will persist. The Court did have the opportunity to deal with the issue in *Royal Botanic v South Sydney* (2002), a case turning on the interpretation of the rent-fixing power in a lease: see **10.10**. But, although the point had been fully argued, the Court felt able to decide the case without addressing it. Kirby J did, however, observe (at [88]) that the idea of any general duty of good faith 'appears to conflict with fundamental notions of caveat emptor that are inherent (statute and equitable intervention apart) in common law conceptions of economic freedom'. More recently, the matter was touched upon in *Commonwealth Bank v Barker* (2014). Four members of the Court noted (at [42], [104]–[107]) that no argument had been put to it about the existence of a general contractual obligation to act in good faith. They declined to comment on how they would have reacted if it had been raised, although Kiefel J, now the Chief Justice of the Court, was far from dismissive in her judgment.

In the wake of *Barker*, attempts to establish a general duty to perform employment contracts in good faith have consistently met with failure: see eg *New South Wales v Shaw* (2015); *Gramotnev v Queensland University of Technology* (2015). But some judges have left open the possibility that a duty of good faith might be implied as a matter of fact where an employee is especially vulnerable to the exercise of managerial power: see eg *Whelan v Cigarette & Gift Warehouse* (2017) at [224]–[226], although this was *not* considered to be true of the executive involved in that case.

If a further case on good faith comes before it, the High Court would have at least four options. It could take the view that there is no need to recognise any principle of good faith and fair dealing at all. It could view the principle as being part of Australian law, but based on interpretation rather than an implied term (the Peden view). It could acknowledge the possibility of a term being implied in fact, but only where 'necessary', as per *Esso*. Or it could recognise that a term requiring good faith and fair dealing should be implied by law into all contracts, all commercial contracts, or at least some classes of contract.[42]

---

42   Compare Dixon 2005, suggesting that the duty should only be implied in 'relational' contracts (see **2.16**).

At present, it is perhaps easiest to imagine the High Court opting for something like the view expressed by the Full Court of the Supreme Court of Tasmania in *Tote Tasmania v Garrott* (2008) at [16]–[17]. This is that good faith may be necessary for any contractual power that is either 'concerned with co-operation between the parties to produce a result which benefits all the parties to the contract', or that is exercisable if the party concerned 'considers that a certain state of affairs or condition exists'. But it is not appropriate in the case of a 'quite unqualified power'.[43] This type of approach concentrates on moderating the exercise of certain types of a discretionary power. It does not create a freestanding duty to behave in a particular way, of the type proposed (albeit on the different basis of 'mutual trust and confidence') and rejected in *Barker*: see **9.26**. Significantly, the notion of constraining discretionary powers is capable of being embraced either with or without reference to the concept of good faith.

---

43   See further *Bartlett v ANZ Bank* (2016), discussed at **16.25**; and note also the views expressed by Edelman J, since appointed to the High Court, in *Mineralogy v Sino Iron* (2015) at [1003]–[1019].

PART **IV**

ADJUSTING A
CONTRACT

13

VARYING TERMS

How contracts can be varied

13.01 The need for contract variation

A great many commercial contracts do not involve a simultaneous one-off transaction. Parties are contracting against the backdrop of a long-term relationship. As noted in **2.16**, contract scholars such as Stewart Macaulay, Ian Macneil and others have highlighted the importance of the process of relational contracting.[1] One practical consequence of parties dealing in this manner is that the precise details of that contractual relationship are not necessarily set down in the contract. Instead, the relationship is framed by strong implicit understandings between the parties. Even where the precise details are set down in the contract itself, the circumstances may have changed since the parties entered into the contract. This is more likely when the contract involves a long-term continuing relationship. It may even be difficult to perform the contract for the original contract price. Circumstances in a particular market may change. Some markets, such as those involving the sale of commodities or charterparties, are particularly volatile. There will also be events that are unforeseen at the time of the contract. Both, or more commonly one, of the parties may wish to vary the original agreement. Although this may seem like a perfectly natural response to a change in circumstances, traditionally contract law does not always make the process of contractual modification easy.[2]

In this chapter we examine the rules that apply when the terms of a contract are varied. Chapter 14 looks separately at changes to the *parties* to a contract and the transfer of contractual rights. Chapter 15 is concerned with the effect of post-contractual changes that make performance impossible or radically alter the nature or context of an agreement. In particular, it explains the circumstances in which a contract may be *frustrated* – that is, automatically terminated – by such events.

13.02 Methods of variation

There is nothing to prevent parties from providing in the terms of a contract for the possibility of later changes. If so, variations may be made in accordance with whatever process is laid down. It is not unusual for parties with superior bargaining power to reserve the right to make unilateral changes to specified terms, or (in the most extreme cases) to any term at all. But as we will see later in the chapter, the exercise of such discretionary powers may be subject to certain controls: see **13.14**.

Assuming, however, that the parties wish to make a change for which their original agreement does not provide, it will be necessary for them to reach agreement on a variation. The starting point here is that when an original contract is modified by a subsequent agreement, the law treats the modified contract as a new contract: *Commissioner of Taxation v Sara Lee Household & Body Care* (2000) at 533. As a result, the requirements of contract modification are the same as those relating to the formation of the original contract, as explained by Finn J in *GEC Marconi v BHP Information Technology* (2003) at 63. One benefit in this approach is that it confirms the general need not only for both parties to agree, but for both

---

1   See eg Macaulay 1963; Macneil 1978.
2   See Carter 1998.

parties' obligations to be adjusted. At the same time, there is something odd about treating parties who are in a pre-existing relationship in the same way as those who are yet to contract. The surrounding circumstances are quite different. It need not be like this. Civilian legal systems adopt a much more liberal approach to contract variation. Their approach is reflected in Article 3.1.2. of the UNIDROIT Principles of International Commercial Contracts, which simply requires the agreement of the parties for any modification.[3]

Aspects of contract doctrine may hinder the process of variation. It is always possible to vary a contract using a deed. But in the absence of a deed, consideration for the variation is required. Once the doctrine of consideration is applied to variation, problems start to arise. There are some longstanding rules relating to consideration which appear to restrict the ability of parties to modify their contract. In the last few decades, the courts have sought to ensure that the law better reflects the pragmatic reality of the modern contractual relationship, but this has not always been without discord. Nor are the arguments for facilitating contractual variation all in one direction.

13.03   Variation or replacement?

Before going on to look at the ways in which the rules on consideration impact on contractual modifications, one other preliminary point needs to be noted. This is the distinction between merely varying the terms of a contract, and replacing the original agreement with a new contract. In many instances, it makes no difference whether a change has one effect or the other. But sometimes it *does* matter; as, for instance, in relation to the issue of statutory formalities: see **13.13**.

Whether a variation replaces the original contract, or simply modifies it, is ultimately a matter of ascertaining the parties' intention: *Commissioner of Taxation v Sara Lee Household & Body Care* (2000) at [22]–[23]; *Balanced Securities v Dumayne* (2017) at [78]. In the absence of more explicit guidance, the courts will take their lead from the nature and extent of the changes made. For example, in cases involving employees being transferred or promoted to new positions, the tendency has been to infer that the original contract has been replaced. This may have significant (and sometimes costly) consequences if, as in *Quinn v Jack Chia* (1992), the effect is that certain terms agreed for the old job are held to have no application to the new one. By contrast, in *Concut v Worrell* (2000), the High Court considered that when a manager was offered a formal contract to replace the verbal agreement under which he had initially been engaged, this resulted in a variation of his original employment contract, rather than the substitution of a new one.

The requirement for fresh consideration

13.04   The problem of 'one-sided' variations

If a variation involves an additional undertaking from both parties, the requirement for consideration is satisfied. Likewise, a variation will be supported by consideration if each party agrees to accept something less. But if only one party agrees to take on a new obligation, or to

---

3   See Giancaspro 2014b: 27–8.

grant the other a concession, there will, on the face of it, be no consideration for that promise, even if the promisee reaffirms their original commitments.

As Chapter 5 explained, there is no universal rule preventing the performance of an existing legal duty from amounting to good consideration. If the promise to perform an existing legal duty is made to someone who is not a party to the contract, then it amounts to good consideration: see **5.34**. Equally, there is nothing to prevent the parties from entering into a compromise agreement to settle a genuine dispute, even if one of them is promising to do no more than fulfil their original promises: see **5.33**.

When the parties wish to vary their contract, they are also at liberty to agree to terminate their existing contract and enter into a new contract. So long as both parties still have obligations to perform, the agreement to release one another from those obligations will be sufficient to discharge the old contract (see **16.27**), leaving the parties free to substitute another. Yet there may be good reasons why, rather than entering into a new contract, the parties prefer to modify the existing contract. But difficulties arise when the consideration for a modification purports to rest on one party promising to perform, or performing, what the contract already requires. These restrictions are grounded in old English authority.

13.05 Performance of an existing contractual duty: a history

In *Stilk v Myrick* (1809), two sailors deserted a ship part way through a voyage. The ship's master agreed to share the wages of those who had left between the remaining crew. When one of the sailors sought to collect his payment, the master refused to pay. Lord Ellenborough rejected an action on the sailor's contract. The two reports of the case gave different accounts of his reasoning. In the report by Espinasse, the claim is said to have failed on the grounds that it was contrary to public policy. In Campbell's report on the other hand, Lord Ellenborough is said to have declared (at 319) that the contract was 'void for want of consideration'. Campbell's version has proved more durable. There are a number of reasons for this. Campbell was perceived as a more reliable reporter. The fact that he rose to the high judicial office of Lord Chancellor no doubt added to his credibility. The result in *Stilk* is not too difficult to explain. Sailors' contracts of service at the time were regulated by statute. There was a fear that sailors would demand higher wages when the ship was in danger or when it was short of crew. It is hardly surprising that in the early nineteenth century judges would be more likely to side with a ship owner than a crew member. In *Harris v Watson* (1791), nearly 20 years earlier, Lord Kenyon had rejected a similar claim by a sailor 'upon a principle of policy'. In Campbell's report of *Stilk* (at 319), Lord Ellenborough accepted the outcome in the earlier decision but doubted the reasoning. He preferred instead to rationalise it as a rule of consideration.

It is not without some irony that, in the 1850s, Lord Campbell himself questioned whether Lord Ellenborough had been too ready to disregard public policy in *Stilk*: see *Harris v Carter* (1854). In *Hartley v Ponsonby* (1857), Lord Campbell also held that where a ship's crew was so diminished that it had become dangerous to sail, then a contract for additional wages was enforceable. His justification was significant. He stated (at 878) that there was 'a voluntary agreement upon sufficient consideration'. These cases involving sailors are hardly typical of contract modification. They were decided against the backdrop of maritime custom and statutory regulation. In *Hartley*, the sailors had agreed to do more than under their original contracts, thus providing consideration for a promise of higher wages. Finding that additional element was not too difficult on the facts. A further factor that was taken into account was whether the contract was freely entered into. On the facts, there was a 'free bargain', or as Coleridge J put it (at 878), in terminology with a more contemporary resonance, there was no 'duress'.

Despite the quite specific factual matrix of these decisions, they have come to stand for a series of broader propositions. Firstly, where the promise or performance of the modification consisted of what was already agreed under the contract, then consideration was absent. Secondly, where more was promised than was agreed under the contract, then there was sufficient consideration for a modification. Thirdly, even in the second situation, the variation must not have been brought about by one party exercising duress against the other. There matters rested until the 1990s, when the first proposition began to be judicially undermined by shifting the focus of what amounts to good consideration.

13.06   A tension between the needs of contracting parties and legal doctrine

Beneath the debate lies a deeper tension alluded to in *Hartley v Ponsonby*. On the one side is the argument that parties, especially commercial parties, should be able to vary their contract to take account of new circumstances if that is their intention. It can be said that to do otherwise is to refuse to respect their autonomy. In many of these situations, the modification may even be in the interests of both parties. In *Stilk v Myrick*, the ship's master benefited from getting the ship safely to port even though it was short-handed. The sailors also benefited from the promise of an increase in wages. There was no evidence in the reports that the sailors had abused their position, so it could not be said that they were guilty of duress or extortion. More generally, contract modification by its nature is always likely to run into the fear that one party may exploit their bargaining position in order to attain a more favourable arrangement. Suppose, for example, that A has a contract with B to undertake work for B at the price of $20,000. A informs B that the work will cost $30,000 and asks B to agree to modify the contract. It may be that A has put in a bid under a tender that is too small to make a profit. It may also be that B needs the work completed quickly and cannot find an alternative to A at short notice. The question then becomes whether the behaviour of A is so exploitative that the contract ought not to stand. The older cases prevented exploitation by adopting a blanket rule that agreeing to do what is required under the contract does not amount to good consideration for a contractual modification. This rule was fairly certain: the only doubt concerned whether there was an agreement to do more under the contract, in which case there was good consideration. The rule also restricted the ability of parties to contract even in the absence of exploitation. More recent decisions in England and Australia have attempted to strike a different balance between freedom of contract and avoiding exploit-ation, by appealing to the idea that a *practical benefit* may constitute good consideration. There is, as yet, no entirely satisfactory determination of these issues.

13.07   Contractual modification and the concept of practical benefit

The modern restatement of the law in this area is found in a decision of the English Court of Appeal in *Williams v Roffey Brothers* (1991). The defendants were the main contractors in the construction of an apartment block. They entered into a subcontract with the plaintiff, under which the plaintiff was to carry out carpentry work for a price of £20,000. The plaintiff found himself in financial difficulty because the agreed price was too low for him to operate satisfactorily and make a profit. The main contract contained a time penalty clause and the defendants became worried that this would be activated. They therefore entered into an oral agreement to pay the plaintiff an additional sum of £10,300 at the rate of £575 for each apartment on which the carpentry work had been completed. Seven weeks later, when the plaintiff had substantially completed eight more apartments, the defendants had only made one further payment of £1,500. The plaintiff ceased work and brought a claim for the additional sum promised. At the trial the judge held that the plaintiff was entitled to the additional sum. The defendants appealed.

On the basis of *Stilk v Myrick*, it might be thought that the plaintiff's claim here would fail. He had only promised to do what he was already contractually bound to do, albeit that he would achieve a larger sum for his trouble. In fact, the Court of Appeal allowed the claim. The key passage occurs (at 15–16) in the judgment of Glidewell LJ. Because it is the basis of later Australian decisions it is worth reproducing in full:

> (i) If A has entered into a contract with B to do work for, or to supply goods or services, to B in return for payment by B; and (ii) at some stage before A has completely performed his [sic] obligations under the contract B has some reason to doubt whether A will, or will be able to, complete his side of the bargain; and (iii) B thereupon promises A an additional payment in return for A's promise to perform his contractual obligations on time; and (iv) as a result of giving his promise, B obtains in practice a benefit, or obviates a disbenefit; and (v) B's promise is not given as a result of economic duress or fraud on the part of A; then (vi) the benefit to B is capable of being consideration for B's promise, so that the promise will be legally binding.

Glidewell LJ argued that he was not overruling *Stilk*. Rather, he said (at 16), his propositions were designed to 'refine, and limit the application of that principle, but they leave the principle unscathed eg where B secures no benefit by his promise'.

There are a number of issues raised by the outcome and the reasoning in *Williams*.[4] It was said that the plaintiff had not met the threshold for duress. Had he done so, then any threat not to perform a contract would amount to duress and therefore prevent contract modification. At the same time, it is difficult to feel much sympathy for the plaintiff. He had negotiated a price that was too low and had failed to properly supervise his workers. These factors had led him into financial difficulty in the first place. He was, in effect, seeking to be rescued from a bad bargain. The idea that economic duress can police these sorts of situations with any degree of consistency is highly questionable. The doctrine of economic duress is still fairly new when applied to contract modification and its contours are yet to be fully worked out: see **13.11–13.12**. It may not be a good way of separating ordinary commercial pressure from the sort of pressure that the law will not countenance.

Contrary to Glidewell LJ's protestations, it is also not easy to reconcile his reasoning with the outcome in *Stilk*. The advantages which the Court of Appeal identified as amounting to

---

4   For extended analysis, see eg Carter et al 1995; Chen-Wishart 1995.

'practical benefits' are difficult to distinguish from the benefits that the defendants were due to receive by the plaintiff's performance of the contract. The benefits were said to lie in the plaintiff's continued performance, the avoidance of the trouble and expense of finding another subcontractor and the avoidance of a penalty being imposed on the defendants for breaching its own obligations under the main contract. Yet, these all flowed from the plaintiff fulfilling his contractual obligations. It is difficult to see what additional benefits to those agreed under the original contract were present. Even if it can be accepted that the benefits were sufficiently 'practical' to make them distinct there are other problems. It is difficult to see why the avoidance of trouble and expense in finding a replacement would not be present in almost any case where there is a threat to breach a contract. The key factor then becomes the penalty clause in the main contract. This is a standard arrangement in building contracts, despite the restrictions on the enforcement of such provisions considered in Chapter 22. Just as in *Stilk*, it makes the context of the industry in which the contract was made critical to the outcome. The penalty clause aside, the benefits that the ship's master received in *Stilk* were just as practical.

At its heart, the decision in *Williams* amounts to little more than a recognition of the fact that when commercial parties both intend to enter into a contractual modification then they should not be prevented from doing so. This outcome is consistent with the idea that the law supports nominal consideration. The line between nominal consideration, such as a pepper-corn, which is valid, and the consideration in a typical case of modification is likely to be wafer thin. Arguably then, as suggested earlier in the chapter, it might be better simply to abandon the requirement of consideration in this context.[5]

13.08   Practical benefit in Australia

The decision in *Williams v Roffey Bros* has been widely cited and adopted around the common law world.[6] In Australia, it was approved and arguably extended in *Musumeci v Winadell* (1994). The plaintiffs were tenants of a greengrocers shop owned by the defendant. The plaintiffs found themselves in financial difficulty when the defendant rented a nearby property to a larger greengrocer. The plaintiffs asked for a one-third reduction in rent. The defendant agreed. Despite the agreement the defendant then sought to terminate the lease and gain possession, following the failure of the plaintiffs to pay the full amount of rent. The situation here was unlike the one in *Williams*, in that the defendant was agreeing to take a lower sum rather than pay a higher one. Santow J thought it made no difference. He suggested (at 741) that Glidewell LJ's third condition be amended to include the words, 'or other concession (such as reducing A's original obligation)'. On the facts, he said (at 748), there was a practical benefit to the defendant:

> [T]he lessor had greater assurance of the lessees staying in occupation and maintaining viability and capacity to perform by reason of their reduction in their rent, notwithstanding the introduction of a major, much larger competing tenant.

Santow J also sought to identify the essence of a 'practical benefit'. He thought that this could be found in whether the concession was worth more to the party making it than any likely

---

5   See Giancaspro 2014b. But compare Roberts 2017.
6   See Giancaspro 2013: 26–7.

damages that would be gained from bringing a claim for breach of contract. This does not necessarily narrow the application of the doctrine. In many cases, the party who wants to modify, like the greengrocers in *Musumeci* or the joiner in *Williams*, will be in a perilous financial position and will not therefore be in a position to pay damages to cover the cost of their expected performance under the unmodified contract. In any event, rather than scrupulously applying Glidewell LJ's six point test, or the amended version from *Musumeci*, the Australian courts have tended to emphasis just the fourth point: 'as a result of giving his promise, B obtains in practice a benefit, or obviates a disbenefit'.[7]

The precise status of *Williams v Roffey Brothers* in Australia is difficult to determine with absolute certainty. The High Court is yet to address the issue of practical benefit, outside of a passing reference by Gummow and Hayne JJ in *Department of Public Prosecutions (Vic) v Le* (2007) at [43]. The need for an extended doctrine of consideration in Australia may be less urgent because promissory estoppel (see **13.16**) plays a more prominent role than in England. Nevertheless, there has been support for Santow J's approach in other decisions: see eg *Mitchell v Pacific Dawn* (2003) at [36]–[39]; *Tinyow v Lee* (2006); *W & K Holdings v Mayo* (2013). The impact of this approach will depend on how willing the courts are to find a 'practical benefit' in any given situation: see eg *Schwartz v Hadid* (2013), in which there was found to be no practical benefit on the facts. When the decision is set against an Australian law of contract, which, for some decades, has shown a pragmatic streak, it would be surprising if this sort of approach does not eventually receive the explicit approval of the High Court.

However, a second and very specific sort of contractual modification has given rise to difficulties. Once again, it generates an outcome that may fail to accommodate what the parties intend. The source of the problem is once more a venerable English authority.

13.09 Part-payment of debts: the rule in *Foakes v Beer*

A situation not unconnected from the one just discussed arises when A owes B $1000, and B agrees to accept $500 in full payment of the debt. Once again, the question is whether there is consideration to support the modification of the parties' obligations. Traditionally, the answer to this question was negative. Here, A is not even fulfilling an existing obligation; instead, they are seeking agreement to reduce their obligation to B. These are not quite the same set of facts as those facing Santow J in *Musumeci v Winadell* (1994). The plaintiffs there agreed to rent the premises for a lower sum. The agreement was to pay less for the same lease for the remainder of the lease. They were not arguing that a one-off lower payment settled all their liabilities under the lease. The case in which it is argued that part-payment of a debt amounts to settlement of the whole is distinct. A creditor in this situation may be in a stronger position than someone who promises to pay more for the same. This sort of claim is for a fixed sum. If A owes B $1000, then that is what B must pay. There is no question of remoteness or mitigation which might be unfavourable to the claimant. Yet, there are some parallels too. There may be very good reasons to accept a lower sum in satisfaction of a debt. It may be perfectly rational to accept a lower sum now rather than wait for full payment later on. If the creditor waits until a later date they may find that the debtor is unable to pay anything. In

---

7   See Giancaspro 2013: 29–30, noting that this has also been true of courts in other jurisdictions.

addition, a creditor faces the trouble and expense of recovery, not to mention the risk that there may be other creditors under insolvency rules.

As so often happens, the facts of the leading authority, *Foakes v Beer* (1884), are not entirely typical. After a judgment against him, Foakes found the he owed Beer £2090 19s by way of judgment debt. Foakes agreed to pay an initial £500 and the rest of the debt in instalments until the whole of the £2090 19s 'have been fully paid and satisfied'. Beer agreed. The debt was paid but not the interest that Beer was due on that debt. The interest came to the considerable sum (for the 1880s) of £302. Foakes argued that as a result of the agreement he was not bound to pay the interest. The House of Lords disagreed. Lords Selbourne, Watson and Fitzgerald all appeared to reject Foakes' argument on the basis that there was no benefit to Beer in the agreement. Foakes was merely agreeing to what he was already bound to do. A second strand of the reasoning was more specific. It rested on a much earlier authority – *Pinnel's Case* (1602). As Ames (1899: 522–3) pointed out, this was a poor authority for the conclusion. *Pinnel's Case* was not concerned with consideration. It was a decision about the rules of 'accord and satisfaction' in the action of debt.[8] The House of Lords simply transposed a version of the same rule into the doctrine of consideration. Lord Blackburn agreed with his colleagues, but he put (at 622) a good case for reaching a different outcome on the basis that there could be a benefit in such an agreement:

> All men of business, whether merchants or tradesmen, do every day recognise and act on the ground that prompt payment of a part of their demand may be more beneficial to them than it would be to insist on their rights and enforce payment of the whole. Even where the debtor is solvent, and sure to pay at last, this is often so. Where the credit of the debtor is doubtful it must be more so.

The rule in *Foakes v Beer*, that an agreement to accept a lower sum in satisfaction of a larger sum was invalid, was never an absolute rule. It only applies if the transaction concerned is one for repayment of a fixed sum of money or for an agreed sum for goods or services. It does not apply to 'unliquidated' sums – that is, an amount that has to be fixed by a process of assessment, such as compensation. This reflects the origin of the rule in the action of debt. In addition, there are several major inroads into the application of a seemingly restrictive rule. The most obvious is where the debtor agrees to do something they were not bound to do under the contract in return for the creditor accepting a lower sum in settlement: see *Martech International v Energy World* (2006) at [141]. So, for example, a debtor who agrees to pay a lower sum a day before the debt was originally due, or who hands over a token item in addition to the money, provides consideration. The consideration is found in the fact that the debtor is providing something extra, even if it is very trivial. Equally, where the debtor disputes the claim in good faith and pays something, even if it is less than the amount claimed, then they provide good consideration: *Cooper v Parker* (1885). This reflects the view that the debtor is providing the creditor with something to which they may not otherwise be entitled, should they successfully defend the claim. Where several creditors jointly agree to forgo part of each of their debts and accept a lower sum, the rule likewise does not apply: *ET Fisher v English, Scottish & Australian Bank* (1940). This arrangement is known as a composition agreement.

---

8   An *accord and satisfaction* is an agreement (the 'accord') to release someone from an obligation, in return for some form of consideration (the 'satisfaction'). Until the satisfaction is provided, the obligation remains binding: *McDermott v Black* (1940) at 183–4.

Where a third party agrees to pay the lower sum, rather than the debtor, there is good consideration for that contract as well: *Hirachand Punamchand v Temple* (1911); *Sheahan v Carrier Air Conditioning* (1997) at 431.

It could quite easily be said that, in the example given by Lord Blackburn, the creditor enjoys a 'practical benefit', and therefore, by analogy with *Musumeci*, the debtor ought to be able to enforce the agreement. Some English courts have rejected this argument. In *Re Selectmove* (1995) at 481, Peter Gibson LJ said that 'if the principle of *Williams v Roffey* is to be extended to an obligation to make payment, it would in effect leave the principle in *Foakes v Beer*, without any application'. Given that *Foakes v Beer* was a decision of the House of Lords, and therefore binding upon them, it was understandable that the Court of Appeal in this case felt unable to reach a different result. It does, however, mean that the outcome probably owes more to the doctrine of precedent than any real conviction.[9] More recent authority, in the form of *MWB Business Exchange Centres v Rock Advertising* (2016), suggests that the Court of Appeal may now be more willing to find a solution to the *Foakes v Beer* conundrum through the doctrine of consideration. On appeal, the Supreme Court in *MWB Business Exchange Centres v Rock Advertising* (2018) declined the opportunity to reassess *Foakes v Beer,* though Lord Sumption said (at [18]) that he thought the rule was 'probably ripe for re-examination'.

13.10   The rule in *Foakes v Beer* in Australia

The Australian courts are not shackled by English precedent in the same way. If *Pinnel's Case* (1602) is taken out of the equation, *Foakes v Beer* (1884) becomes less compelling. This is because the courts have departed from the other strand of the House of Lords' reasoning. A promise to do something that one is already bound to do *can* amount to consideration if there is a practical benefit. In *Musumeci v Winadell* (1994), Santow J was rather equivocal about whether the principle he was expounding applied where there was an agreement to take a smaller sum in settlement of a larger debt. He observed (at 739) that the rule that there is no consideration 'has not been over-ruled' and yet noted that 'the underlying rationale for the rule is the same'. His view (at 740) was that 'there has been a continuing trend to side-step the artificial results of a strict doctrine of consideration'. This could easily be interpreted as a call to abandon the rule in *Foakes v Beer*. There are some advantages in abandoning the rule. It would no longer be necessary to rely on exceptions. Because the benefit received may be so trivial the exception hardly differs factually from the rule. It would also align these cases rather better with the approach in *Musumeci*. On a practical level, an agreement to reduce the rent to be paid over the course of a lease does not look notably different from an agreement to accept a lower sum in satisfaction of a larger debt.

Policing variations

13.11   Economic duress

One of the arguments that is sometimes made for restricting the scope of consideration in variation cases is that the process of varying a contract can be the result of undue pressure by

---

9   See also *Corbern v Whatmusic Holdings* (2003); and see further Thampapillai 2015.

one of the parties. As a result, it might be said that the other party is not acting entirely of their own free will. They may agree to a variation because they feel that they have no choice. The doctrine of *economic duress* is concerned with the threat of economic harm to induce the conferral or promise of a benefit. It is used to police contract variations, but it is not confined to contract variation. As Chapter 19 will explain, it applies to the process of contract formation as well. If successfully pleaded, it may result in a contract – or, in this case, the new contract created by a variation – being rescinded. As variation of contracts has become easier because of the relaxation of the rules of consideration, so the role played by the doctrine of economic duress has been strengthened. Commercial parties who enter into contracts do so expecting to make a profit. Ordinary commercial pressure is a legitimate part of ordinary business dealings. Economic duress is designed to distinguish between legitimate commercial pressure and situations in which the law regards the modification as coerced. The narrow rules of consideration avoided these difficult questions by ensuring that, in certain situations, contracts were not enforceable, irrespective of the way in which that variation was obtained. As a rule, this was something of a blunt instrument because it meant in cases like *Stilk v Myrick* (1809), where both parties benefited from the variation and there appeared to be no undue pressure, there was no consideration and the contract could not be enforced. Whilst the traditional approach is very rigid, the doctrine of economic duress can sometimes be troublesome to apply and can generate uncertainty.

13.12   Examples of economic duress

A good illustration of a situation in which economic duress might prevent a contractual variation from being enforced can be found in the English case, *Atlas Express v Kafco* (1989). The defendant was a small importer of basketware. The plaintiff was a carrier who agreed to deliver those goods to a major retailer. A price was agreed at a rate per carton. The plaintiff sought to vary the agreement and set a minimum charge per load. Initially the defendant refused to change. The plaintiff retaliated by refusing to carry the defendant's goods unless it agreed to the variation. Believing that it would be impossible to arrange alternative carriage and fearing that it would be in breach of contract with the retailer, the defendant agreed to the new terms. When the plaintiff sought to enforce the new version of the contract, the defendant argued that there was no consideration for the variation and that, in any event, it was entered into under economic duress. Tucker J accepted both arguments. On the question of duress, he stressed the difficulty of finding an alternative carrier at short notice and the extent to which the defendant's business depended on the one retailer. In these circumstances, he took the view that the variation of the contract was agreed to under coercion.[10]

The English courts have struggled to come up with a single approach to determining the presence of economic duress. The Australian courts have more clearly focused on two questions. Firstly, was the pressure illegitimate? Secondly, was the illegitimate pressure a reason for entering into the variation? Establishing that the pressure was illegitimate may not always be very

---

10   For a further example, see *North Ocean Shipping v Hyundai Construction* (1979), although in this instance a variation obtained by duress could not be set aside because the plaintiff had waited too long to seek relief: see **19.07**. Here, the variation *was* supported by fresh consideration, since a promise of extra payment by the plaintiff was met by an increase in a letter of credit opened by the defendant in the plaintiff's favour.

easy. The most straightforward instance occurs where the pressure is unlawful. Such pressure is always illegitimate. On the basis of the existing case law and statute, it is not too difficult to work out if the conduct falls within this category. For example, an actual or threatened breach of contract is necessarily treated as unlawful for these purposes: *Electricity Generation v Woodside Energy* (2013) at [26]. As a result, an Australian court might very well reach the same result as Tucker J did in *Atlas Express*. Illegitimate pressure may, however, be broader than this case suggests: see eg *Crescendo Management v Westpac* (1988) at 46. Once the definition goes beyond these core cases, the application of the doctrine inevitably becomes more uncertain. It has been suggested that even when a victim of pressure was left with little choice, this did not necessarily mean that there was illegitimate pressure: *Bank of New Zealand v Equiticorp Finance* (1992). The courts are unlikely to find economic duress lightly. This may be why it is sometimes suggested that illegitimate pressure should be confined 'to conduct which is unlawful or wrongful, by reference to some external standard': *Electricity Generation* at [176]. These issues go to the nature and scope of the legal concept of duress: see **19.04–19.05**.

Having established that illegitimate pressure was exerted, it is unnecessary to prove that the pressure was the sole, or even the main reason, for entering into the contractual variation. It is sufficient to show that the duress was *a* reason: *Crescendo Management* at 46. It may be one of many reasons. The onus then shifts to the other party to demonstrate that the illegitimate pressure was not a factor in the other party entering into variation.

There is a degree of uncertainty in the process of distinguishing between illegitimate pressure and legitimate commercial pressure for the purposes of economic duress. This is perhaps inevitable. Santow J addressed the question of exploitation in *Musumeci v Winadell* (1994). In the context of setting out the type of conduct by a promisee that would prevent them from relying on the practical benefit principle, he went further than the English Court of Appeal, which had confined itself to economic duress and fraud. He suggested that there may be other reasons why a variation may be unenforceable. He was also prepared to include undue influence and unconscionable conduct. Given that the doctrine of unconscionability plays a much more significant role in Australia than in England, as explained in **20.02–20.07**, the fact that it was included is unsurprising. To those grounds he added 'unfair pressure'. Santow J conceded that the term encompassed economic duress, but was nonetheless broader. He stated (at 744) that 'undue pressure' was a 'more precise and apposite' description than requiring 'good faith'. There are few clues about how unfair pressure is to be actually determined, although it seems the proportionality of the pressure is a factor. The inclusion of 'unfair pressure' simply adds another layer of uncertainty.

13.13   Formalities

It is not unusual for the terms of a contract – especially when in standard form – to require any variations to be agreed in writing. It appears, however, that such provisions cannot actually prevent an oral variation from taking effect. If parties are free to change the substantive terms of a contract, then they must logically be able to agree to dispense with a previous requirement of writing at the same time. On the face of it then, if a variation 'satisfies the necessary elements of contract' it may take effect, regardless of any previous specification as to form: *Musumeci v Winadell* (1994) at 750; and see *GEC Marconi v BHP Information Technology* (2003). In *MWB Business Exchange Centres v Rock Advertising* (2018), the United Kingdom Supreme Court took a different view, holding that a variation will be ineffective if it fails to comply with any formalities that the parties have previously agreed to require. But this has not yet prompted a reconsideration of the settled position in Australia: see *Cenric Group v TWT Property Group* (2018).

The more significant issue concerns those contracts which, as noted in **5.44–5.46**, are required by legislation to be evidenced in writing. Where a contract of this sort is modified by an oral agreement for which written evidence is lacking, the effect of the modification depends upon how it is classified. If the parties intended simply to vary the terms of the contract, the variation will be ineffective, leaving the original terms in force: *Phillips v Ellinson Brothers* (1941). But if the intent was to replace the original contract with a new, oral agreement, the parties may be left without any binding obligations at all. This is because the oral agreement can be effective to discharge the original contract, yet be unenforceable because of the relevant statute: see eg *Morris v Baron* (1918). However, if it is clear that the parties intended to substitute a new contract only if the new contract were valid, the proper conclusion would be that the original contract remained on foot: *Tallerman v Nathan's Merchandise* (1957) at 123. A third possibility is that an oral modification represents a mere 'forbearance'. This will often be the case where the parties agree to a different manner or time of performance, without affecting the nature of the obligations involved. Such a forbearance may not be enforceable as such, other than through the law of estoppel (for which, as we will see, detrimental reliance is required). But nor need it be evidenced in writing: *Dowling v Rae* (1927).

13.14   Limits on unilateral variation

As noted at the beginning of the chapter, some contracts expressly permit one party to vary some or all their terms unilaterally. There is no common law rule that prohibits this. But in theory, a discretionary power to alter terms that is so broad that it can be used to remove any obligation at all might render the contract 'illusory': see **5.35**. For that reason, among others, it is generally implied that a power to introduce changes may only be exercised in a reasonable or rational way, not arbitrarily or capriciously: see eg *Akmeemana v Murray* (2009); and see further **12.19**

There are also important statutory limits on contract terms which may impact on the ability to vary a contract. Part 2-3 of the Australian Consumer Law (ACL) governs unfair terms in standard form consumer and small business contracts, as discussed in Chapter 20. It is clear that some types of unilateral variation permitted under a contract may fall within the definition of an unfair term in s 24(1): see eg *ACCC v JJ Richards* (2017).[11]

Estoppel and waiver

13.15   Facilitating informal modifications

Despite – or perhaps because of – the inflexibility of the requirement that a contractual variation satisfy the same requirements as for the formation of the original contract, the common law has developed various other ways in which agreed modifications can be given

---

11   See further Paterson & Smith 2016.

effect. These can be used for formal but ineffective variations, where consideration is found to be lacking. But, as Lücke (1991) points out, they can also be used for the kind of informal concessions or adjustments that are so frequently granted or made in commercial dealings, especially where the parties have an ongoing relationship.

The main arguments that can be deployed for this purpose involve the doctrine of *promissory estoppel* and the more nebulous concept of *waiver*, which are discussed below. But as Lücke notes, there are also many cases that invoke the concept of *forbearance*.[12] This idea has been invoked in a number of different contexts, including (as noted in **13.13**) to permit minor modifications to be given effect without falling foul of a statutory requirement of writing. Some of the older authorities reviewed by Lücke would probably now be decided on the basis of estoppel. But there are at least a few cases in which the parties' conduct, despite not apparently involving any agreement as such, has been held to result in a change to their obligations. For example, in *Electronic Industries v David Jones* (1954), the defendant retailer requested the postponement of some demonstrations of television equipment that the plaintiff had agreed to give. The plaintiff indicated its willingness to do that and proposed an alternative date. During the inconclusive discussions that followed, the original date passed without anything happening. The defendant then sought to resile from the agreement and was found liable for breach of contract. The High Court held that although there had been no agreed variation, the parties' forbearance during the negotiations meant that there was no longer a fixed date for performance. Instead, emphasising the parties' implied duty of cooperation (see **12.15**), the Court found that the plaintiff was entitled to call upon the defendant to schedule the demonstrations within a reasonable time.

13.16   Promissory estoppel

In Australia, it is accepted that promissory estoppel can be used to generate a cause of action on an agreement as well as proving a defence to a claim by the other party for breach of contract: see **7.13**. Variation cases fall into the latter category. There is no reason why estoppel might not provide an alternative solution in cases of modifications that are unsupported by consideration. This can be illustrated by reference to a South Australian Supreme Court decision, *Je Maintiendrai v Quaglia* (1980). The facts were not very dissimilar from *Musumeci v Winadell* (1994). A landlord agreed to accept a lower rent from a tenant for an indefinite period. Eighteen months passed and the landlord sought back-dated payment of the full rent. It was held on the facts that the landlord was estopped from claiming the difference between the contractually agreed rent and the lower rent.

From the point of view of the party seeking to raise the estoppel, there are two major disadvantages compared with a contractual variation supported by consideration. Firstly, estoppel does not necessarily act as a permanent bar on returning to the position agreed in the contract. It may do so, but only where to resile from the representation would be unconscionable. In *Je Maintiendrai*, the landlord promised a reduction for an indefinite period, which made it unconscionable to later demand the full rent. The issue of a permanent reduction was not discussed. Reliance was placed on Denning J's judgment in *Central London*

---

12   See also Stoljar 2018.

Property Trust v High Trees (1947), in which he made clear that while estoppel might serve to suspend an obligation, it did not necessarily extinguish it. Secondly, detriment, one of the elements required to establish an estoppel, may prove extremely difficult to establish in cases of variation. A variation may benefit both parties but it will almost always benefit the party seeking to rely on the estoppel. It is difficult to regard paying a lower rent as a detriment to that party. That hurdle was supposedly overcome in *Je Maintiendrai* when the majority held that to require a lump sum to become payable rather than periodic payments was detrimental. Even King CJ for the majority conceded (at 107) that the 'evidence as to detriment is sparse'. In addition, White J suggested (at 115) that by remaining in the shop the tenants did not make other changes open to them, even taking a risk that they might be subject to a claim for breach of contract, and that amounted to a detriment. The problem of establishing a detriment may be even more acute in a case like *Williams v Roffey* (1991), which is presumably why no estoppel argument was pursued in that case.

13.17 Using promissory estoppel as a way around *Foakes v Beer*

On the assumption that a practical benefit can be identified for the landlord, then following *Musumeci v Winadell* (1994), there would be no longer be any need to resort to estoppel in a case like *Je Maintiendrai Pty Ltd* (1980). Whether estoppel is to have much of a role in the context of contractual variation is likely to depend on the status of *Foakes v Beer* (1884) in Australia. In *Collier v P & MJ Wright* (2007), the English Court of Appeal, whilst accepting the continued applicability of *Foakes v Beer*, were prepared to accept that estoppel could be deployed in these circumstances. Arden LJ suggested that when a promise by the creditor to accept part payment of the debt is made, and the debtor relies on the promise, that in itself makes it inequitable to resile from the promise. This approach seems to strip the element of unconscionability of much of its content. The element of detriment, although raised in argument, was not squarely addressed in Arden LJ's judgment. By stretching the scope of estoppel in this way, it was possible to ameliorate the impact of the rule in *Foakes v Beer*. But the idea that it will always be inequitable to resile from a promise to accept part payment has recently been questioned. In *MWB Business Exchange Centres v Rock Advertising* (2016), Kitchin LJ re-emphasised the requirements of detriment that are central to traditional notions of estoppel: see **7.09**. This will make it harder to argue for an estoppel in this context, since it will often be difficult to show detriment where the other party agrees to accept part payment in satisfaction.

13.18 Waiver

The term 'waiver' is generally understood to cover a situation where a person voluntarily and intentionally abandons a legal right by acting in a way that is inconsistent with that right: *Commonwealth v Verwayen* (1990) at 406. But that simple statement masks a range of possibilities.[13] One type of waiver is simply a matter of *election* between alternative rights –

---

13   See eg Stoljar 2013, identifying no less than 11 different categories of waiver.

as, for example, where a party 'waives' a right to terminate by doing something to affirm the contract: see **16.23**. Some old cases that speak of waiver would also be regarded today as instances of promissory estoppel. It has indeed been suggested that, in the wake of comments made by members of the High Court in *Agricultural and Rural Finance v Gardiner* (2008) at [98], [162], there is no longer an 'independent' doctrine of waiver, at least in relation to contractual rights. On this view, a party can only waive such rights if: (a) they do so as part of a variation supported by consideration; (b) the other party relies to their detriment on an indication that the rights will not be exercised, such as to estop the first party; or (c) there is a 'true' election between inconsistent rights.[14]

The better view, however, is that there remain at least limited instances in which a party can be considered to have waived their rights under a contract without any variation, estoppel or election: see *Badat v DTZ Australia* (2008) at [52], [148]. One example is where a party waives the right to invoke a condition that has been inserted solely for their benefit, a concept acknowledged by the High Court in cases such as *Gange v Sullivan* (1966) and *Perri v Coolangatta Investments* (1982): see **5.26**. But there are also cases where a party merely forebears the exercise of their rights under the contract. A waiver of this sort can be retracted. It is 'temporary in the sense that, unlike variation, it does not alter the terms and conditions of the contract but only prevents the enforcement of the relevant contractual right': *Badat* at [54]. So where A contracts to deliver goods to B on Tuesday, B may waive their right to receive the goods on Tuesday in favour of Friday. B's waiver doesn't give A a cause of action, but it does allow A a defence if B brings a claim for breach of contract for late delivery.

Rectification

13.19   The limited scope of rectification

Rectification is a remedy that can be sought when a written contract fails to represent the real agreement of the parties. The allegation is that the contract was incorrectly recorded in the written document. More is said about rectification in Chapter 18, in the context of the law on mistake. For now, it suffices to note that is an equitable remedy, and its exercise is governed by discretion. It is nevertheless extremely difficult to persuade a court to amend a written contract. Convincing proof that the written contract fails to accord with the intention of the parties is required. This is a high threshold to meet. It is not enough that the parties were operating under a mistake when they entered into the contract. The role of rectification is different. It is granted when the common intentions of the parties at the time of the agreement are not reflected in the written document: *Pukallus v Cameron* (1982). Rectification can also be used when one party mistakenly believes that the document reflects the common intention of both parties and the other knows that it does not. It is regarded as unconscionable, knowing of the error, to enforce the written contract without rectification, because it is inconsistent with the common intentions of the parties at the time of the contract: see *Franklins v Metcash Trading* (2009) at [444].

---

14   See eg Bevan 2009. But compare Stoljar 2013: 488, 492–3, emphasising the limited scope of the arguments before the Court in *Gardiner*.

Statutory powers of variation

13.20   Key examples of statutory variation powers

Statutory provisions may sometimes empower one party to vary a contract without the consent of the other. This is a capacity commonly granted to government agencies; for instance, in the context of employment conditions for their staff: see eg *Litchfield v Chief Executive, Department of Manufacturing* (2014).

It is not just the parties, however, who may vary a contract. In certain circumstances, courts are given statutory powers to vary contracts. Some of these powers are quite specific in scope. Section 72 of the National Credit Code, enacted through the *National Consumer Credit Protection Act 2009* (Cth), gives consumers with a credit contract the right to seek to vary the terms of the repayment of a loan in cases of financial hardship.[15] There are slightly broader powers contained in Part 2-3 of the ACL: see **20.29**. Where a term in a standard form contract with a consumer or small business is deemed unfair, it is void. If the contract can still continue, it operates with the unfair term omitted (s 23(2)). The same legislation allows a court to vary a contract in response to misleading or deceptive conduct, or conduct by one of the parties that is unconscionable (s 243): see **18.33**, **20.20**. In New South Wales, s 7 of the *Contracts Review Act 1980* (NSW) gives a court power to grant relief, including variation, when a contract or term of a contract is unjust, provided that it was not entered into in the 'course of business': see **20.32**. A further example can be found in Part 3 of the *Independent Contractors Act 2006 (Cth)*, which, as the name suggests, applies to contracts for the performance of work by independent contractors – that is, persons or organisations who perform work as part of their own business, rather than as employees. The statute empowers the federal courts to vary or set aside contracts that are found to be 'harsh' or 'unfair'. Variations have, for instance, been ordered to require a client to provide reasonable notice of termination of the contractor's services: see *Fabsert v ABB Warehousing* (2008).

---

15   See Ali et al 2016.

14

TRANSFERRING RIGHTS AND OBLIGATIONS

14.01   Introduction

This chapter briefly explains the processes for transferring contractual rights and obligations from the original parties to someone else.[1] The first two parts of the chapter are concerned with *voluntary* transfers. An important distinction is drawn here between the 'assignment' (as a transfer is typically termed in this context) of rights, and of obligations.

As will be explained, it is generally possible for one person (the *assignor*) to transfer to another (the *assignee*) the right to demand performance of a contractual obligation, even without the consent of the original promisor who is to provide that performance. So if A makes a contract with B, B may seek to transfer the right to receive the benefit of some or all of A's promises to C. Provided the assignment is effective, under the rules discussed below, C will be able to take legal action against A in the event of non-performance, even though C is not a party to the contract.

With contractual obligations, however, the position is different. The duty to perform a contract cannot generally be assigned without the consent of the promisee – the original party to whom that duty is owed. If C is to assume obligations formerly owed by A to B, this will generally require the creation of a new contract between B and C. This process, to which all three parties must consent, is known as a *novation*.

The chapter concludes by looking briefly at some of the rules that provide for the *involuntary* transfer of contractual rights and obligations, such as when a party dies or is declared bankrupt. It also notes the special rules that apply to the transfer of certain types of promise to pay money, under what are called *negotiable instruments*.

Assignment of contractual rights

14.02   The use of assignments

There are many circumstances in which a person or organisation may wish or be asked to transfer one or more of their rights to receive performance under a contract. One typical situation is where some or all of a business is being sold. The purchaser is likely to want to acquire not just the physical assets of the business and any accumulated goodwill, but the benefit of various contracts the vendor may have. These may be with key suppliers or employees, the lessor of any premises in which the business is conducted, the licensor of any trademarks or other intellectual property used in the business, and so on. In each of those cases, however, a simple assignment will probably not be possible. This is because the contracts just mentioned will tend to involve *ongoing* arrangements. The purchaser cannot in practice hope to acquire any rights under those contracts without promising to assume the vendor's obligations in return. As already mentioned, this will require a process of novation, not assignment.[2]

---

1   For a more complete account of this very technical and complex subject, see Tolhurst 2006. See also *Pacific Brands v Underworks* (2006) at [32], summarising many of the propositions set out below.

2   Hence, for example, employees cannot as a matter of common law be transferred from one employer to another without their consent: *Nokes v Doncaster Amalgamated Collieries* (1940) at 1020, 1026; *Minister for Employment v Gribbles Radiology* (2005) at [48].

In practice, therefore, assignments of contractual rights tend to involve situations where the assignor has already performed their obligations and is expecting, but has not yet received, the agreed counter-performance. The most common and straightforward situation involves a monetary debt for goods or services already supplied. The assignor may wish to assign that debt to someone else, to clear a debt of their own. Or they may do so because the assignee is more likely to be able to collect that debt. This is how some debt collection agencies work. Rather than merely charging a fee to collect money on behalf of a creditor, they may purchase – that is, take an assignment of – a number of debts owed to a business, in return for something less than the full value of those debts. Businesses will agree to such an arrangement to save themselves the time and trouble of chasing up their debtors, while agencies will rely on their specialist expertise to recoup more than what they have paid for the debts.[3]

14.03   How contractual rights can be assigned

As explained in **8.14**, the right to sue for breach of contract is treated as a form of property known as a 'chose in action'. It is that property that can be assigned in one of two ways.

The first is that each State and Territory has *statutory provisions* that permit the assignment of debts and other choses in action.[4] The legislation requires the assignment to be in writing and signed by the assignor. Written notice must be also given to the promisor/debtor. Most of the relevant provisions are limited to 'absolute' assignments, which means that all of the relevant right must be transferred and there must be no condition attached to the transfer.[5] If the statutory requirements are met, however, the assignee does not have to provide any consideration for the assignment to take effect: *Norman v Federal Commissioner of Taxation* (1963) at 28. Nor does the assignee even need to be aware of the transfer: *Grey v Australian Motorists & General Insurance* (1976).

The second, an alternative way, is that an assignment which does not satisfy the statutory requirements may take effect *in equity.*[6] For this to happen, the assignor will ordinarily need to be joined in any proceedings brought to enforce the right in question, either as a co-plaintiff or a co-defendant. The promisor/debtor need not be given notice of the assignment for it to take effect in equity: *Thomas v National Australia Bank* (1999). But if the relevant money is paid or performance is rendered to the assignor before the promisor/debtor is notified of the transfer, their obligation will be discharged: *Squires v SA Steel & Sheet* (1987). An assignment can take effect in equity even without consideration being provided to the assignor, provided the assignment is of a debt or right that already exists, as opposed to one that may be created in the future: *Shepherd v Federal Commissioner of Taxation* (1965).

---

3   The States and Territories typically have laws that require either debt collectors or the agencies for which they work to be licensed: see eg *Commercial Agents and Private Inquiry Agents Act 2004* (NSW).

4   *Conveyancing Act 1919* (NSW) s 12; *Property Law Act 1958* (Vic) s 134; *Property Law Act 1974* (Qld) s 199; *Property Law Act 1969* (WA) s 20; *Law of Property Act 1936* (SA) s 15; *Conveyancing and Law of Property Act 1884* (Tas) s 86; *Civil Law (Property) Act 2006* (ACT) s 205; *Law of Property Act 2000* (NT) s 182.

5   But compare *Property Law Act 1969* (WA) s 20(3), which allows the absolute assignment of part of a debt or chose in action.

6   See Dal Pont 2015a: ch 3; Heydon et al 2015: chs 6–7.

14.04   Rights that cannot be assigned

There are some contractual rights that cannot be assigned. This will be the case, for example, where the contract itself forbids any assignment, whether expressly or impliedly: *Linden Gardens Trust v Lenesta Sludge Disposals* (1994) at 106.[7] Nor can the benefit of contractual performance involving 'personal skill and confidence' be transferred, unless the contract itself contemplates assignment: *Devefi v Mateffy Pearl Nagy* (1993) at 235. This category covers arrangements where the identity of the original promisee is important to the promisor; for instance, because of some personal skill which the promisee possesses or some element of trust and confidence between the parties: see eg *Bruce v Tyley* (1916). There may also be cases where a contractual right cannot validly be assigned without the transfer of other rights to which it is inseparably linked: see eg *Pacific Brands v Underworks* (2006).

In addition, certain types of assignment are considered to be contrary to public policy. For example, it is not generally permitted to assign a 'bare' right to claim damages for a wrong which has already occurred: see eg *May v Lane* (1894).[8] But this principle does not apply where the assignee is considered to have a genuine commercial or proprietary interest in the proceedings: *Equuscorp v Haxton* (2012) at [50]–[51], [79]. In practice, it would be unusual today for such an interest not to be recognised: see eg *Dover v Lewkovitz* (2013), reviewing the case law in this area.[9]

14.05   Effect of an assignment

The effect of an assignment is to put the assignee in the same position as the assignor would have been had the transfer not occurred: *Pacific Brands v Underworks* (2006) at [55].[10] This means, for example, that the promisor/debtor can rely on any defence that would have been available against the assignor. If sued by the assignee, they can also set off (or have deducted) a claim for damages arising from a previous breach by the assignor: see eg *Mitchell v Purnell Motors* (1960).

Assignment of obligations and novation

14.06   Transferring responsibility for performance

It is not at all unusual for a contracting party to arrange for someone else to carry out the obligations they have undertaken. They may, for example, choose to subcontract some or all of the tasks involved to other firms or individuals. This is a very common feature of building projects, where the head builder or contractor will typically engage specialists to do the electrical work, carpentry, plumbing and so on. It is only where a contract expressly or impliedly requires the original promisor to carry out performance personally, perhaps because

---

7   As to the precise effect of such a prohibition, see the discussion in Tolhurst & Carter 2014.
8   This is an aspect of the law concerning 'maintenance' and 'champerty': see **21.12**.
9   See further Anderson 2016.
10 As to how damages are to be assessed in relation to breaches occurring *before* the transfer, see the discussion in Tolhurst 2008.

of some particular skill they possess, that subcontracting will be forbidden: see eg *Davies v Collins* (1945).

If a subcontractor fails to perform, it is the contractor who remains liable under the original contract. The contractor may in turn seek to sue the subcontractor to recover damages, measured by the cost of that liability. But the subcontractor cannot be directly liable to the original promisee, since they are not privy to that contract.

While delegation or subcontracting may be possible, a promisor cannot unilaterally assign to someone else an obligation they have undertaken: *Tolhurst v Associated Portland Cement* (1902) at 668. Even if the benefit of a contractual right has been validly assigned, that will not of itself fix the assignee with the burden of the obligations originally undertaken by the assignor: see eg *Konstas v Southern Cross Pumps & Irrigation* (1996). If a contractual obligation is to be transferred, as a matter of common law this must usually be through the process of novation.

14.07   Novation

The term 'novation' has two distinct meanings: *ALH Group v Chief Commissioner of State Revenue* (2012) at [27]. It can refer to the replacement of a contract by a new contract between the same parties. But, more commonly, it connotes a tripartite arrangement. This involves the parties to a contract agreeing that one of them will be replaced by someone else, with the consent of both the original parties *and* the new party. Technically, the process does not involve an 'assignment' as such. Rather, the parties are agreeing to terminate the original contract and replace it with a new one: *Olsson v Dyson* (1969) at 388. This may be found to be the parties' intention even if they have not expressly used the language of novation: see eg *ALH Group*; *Fu Tian Fortune v Park Cho* (2018). But consent to novation will not lightly be inferred. For example, if a business assigns its customer contracts to a related company, there must be clear evidence that the customers have consented. The fact that some customers may have noticed a change in the name of the company invoicing them will not be sufficient: see eg *ACCC v Harrison* (2016).

It is not unusual for a contract to contain a term expressly allowing one party to substitute another party in its place, without the need for any further agreement. In *Leveraged Equities v Goodridge* (2011), it was held that there is no reason why consent cannot be given to a novation in advance, so long as it is clear that the substituted party is to assume the original party's rights and obligations. It may be different if the term contemplates the imposition of new but unspecified obligations, although this was held not to be the case in *Leveraged Equities*.

Involuntary assignments

14.08   Death, bankruptcy and other situations

Where a contracting party dies, the principles of succession law provide that any rights and obligations arising under the contract are transferred to the deceased's legal personal representative as part of their estate.[11] The death of a party may sometimes have the effect of

---

11   See Seddon & Bigwood 2017: 409–10; and see eg *Beswick v Beswick* (1968), discussed in **8.11**.

automatically terminating the contract, on the basis that their identity is integral to the contract: see **15.07**. Even in that case, however, the person administering the estate may still be able to enforce rights accrued prior to the original party's death.

Similarly, where a person is declared bankrupt, s 58 of the *Bankruptcy Act 1966* (Cth) ensures that their contractual rights and obligations are vested in their trustee in bankruptcy. This is subject to the power of the trustee under s 133 to disclaim the contract or, where it is not 'unprofitable', to seek a court's permission to do so.[12]

There may also be other situations where legislation provides for the transfer of contractual rights and obligations from one party to another, without the need to secure the consent of all concerned. This is a common feature, for example, of statutes providing for the restructuring, replacement or privatisation of government agencies.[13]

Negotiable instruments

14.09   'Negotiating' promises to pay money

The law has long made special provision for the transfer of certain types of financial instrument, such as bills of exchange, cheques and promissory notes. These permit promises to pay money to be passed on or 'negotiated' to a third party, without the necessity for complying with the requirements of an ordinary assignment of contractual rights.[14]

---

12   See Symes & Duns 2015: 106–9.

13   To take just one of many possible examples, see *Electricity Corporations (Restructuring and Disposal) Act 1999* (SA).

14   See eg *Bills of Exchange Act 1909* (Cth); *Cheques Act 1986* (Cth); and see further Tyree 2017: 159–60.

15

IMPOSSIBILITY AND CHANGE OF CIRCUMSTANCES

Introduction

15.01   The impact of post-contractual changes

The conditions under which a contract is to be performed may change between the time that the parties enter into a contract and the time that performance falls due. As noted in **13.01,** this is especially true if the contract is anticipated to run for a lengthy period. Goods or buildings may be damaged or destroyed. Supplies that one party was relying upon to enable their performance may be delayed. One of the parties may become ill or even die. A change in the law may impact on the performance of the contract or its intended benefits. Fluctuations in market prices or the value of a currency may affect the expected profitability of a contract. In all of these situations and more, one party may argue that they should be released from their obligations because it has become impossible, or at least onerous, for them to perform.

There would be little security in transactions if contracts were too easily discharged when circumstances changed. Trade would quickly become impossible.[1] Furthermore, many changes of the type just mentioned are foreseeable. It may be reasonable to expect that the risk of their happening can or should be addressed by express contractual terms. In the absence of such terms, it may be inferred that one or other party is to bear the risk of the relevant change. Nevertheless, a contract can sometimes be disrupted by an event outside the parties' control that is so extreme or unusual that they cannot reasonably be expected to have provided for it. There may also be situations where, even though the change is one that might have been anticipated, it was not feasible for the party most affected by it to negotiate any protection or to insure against the relevant risk.[2]

15.02   Absolute obligations and the doctrine of frustration

The traditional rule in contract law was harsh: a change in circumstances was considered irrelevant to the performance of a contract. As explained in *Paradine v Jane* (1647), if the parties wanted to provide for a change of circumstances then they must do so in the contract itself. Even if the contract had become impossible to perform, the parties were not absolved from obligations which were considered to be 'absolute' in nature. Any failure to perform would be a breach of contract, giving rise to the remedies discussed in Part VII. Gradually, however, it came to be accepted that in some very limited situations, changes in circumstances should be treated as sufficient to *frustrate* a contract.

The doctrine of frustration developed in the nineteenth century in cases where the subject matter of the contract had been destroyed. In *Taylor v Caldwell* (1863), the defendant contracted to let the plaintiff have use of his music hall on four days for giving concerts. Before the first concert could take place, the music hall was destroyed in a fire. Blackburn J rejected the plaintiff's claim for breach of contract. He held that the parties had contracted on the basis that

---

1   The same difficulties arise where it is pleaded that a common mistake as to events or circumstances *prior* to the making of a contract should invalidate it. There, too, the law makes it difficult to vitiate a contract: see **18.41**.

2   For an economic perspective on the allocation of post-contractual risks, see eg Posner & Rosenfield 1977; Triantis 1992.

the subject matter of the contract, the music hall, which was essential to the performance of the contract, would continue to exist. When performance becomes impossible from the 'perishing of the thing without the fault of the contractor', he said (at 834), then all future obligations are discharged. The more common situation of the destruction of goods which are the subject of a contract for sale is now covered by statute. Where there is an agreement for the sale of specific goods, which subsequently perish before the risk under the contract passes to the buyer, legislation in each State and Territory provides that the contract is 'avoided'.[3]

Taylor v Caldwell came to stand for a broader doctrine that went beyond the destruction of the subject matter of the contract and allowed contracts to be frustrated in a range of other situations. Today, it is sufficient that matters are 'radically different' from those the parties contemplated when they entered into their agreement: *Davis Contractors v Fareham UDC* (1956) at 729. The authorities are not always easy to reconcile, partly because different justifications for frustration have been offered at different times. These have included explaining the doctrine as resting on an implied term, or on a 'failure of consideration'.[4] However, the modern understanding is that a finding of frustration hinges on the 'true construction' of the contract in question: see **15.05**.

15.03   The consequences of frustration

Frustration has the effect of automatically terminating a contract. It is typically raised as a defence by a party who is subject to a claim for breach of contract. Under the common law, the precise impact of frustration depends on when the frustrating event has occurred. Obligations that are due to be performed post-frustration are extinguished. By contrast, obligations that have accrued before the frustrating event may still be enforced. It is only in very limited circumstances that money paid under a frustrated contract can be recovered under the law of restitution. However, statutory rules in some States have amended the common law, broadening the circumstances in which restitutionary claims can be brought for money paid, or work done, prior to frustration. More is said about this later in the chapter.

15.04   The role of contract planning

Despite the broadening of the modern doctrine to encompass cases that go beyond the outright impossibility of performance, it remains difficult to show that a contract is frustrated. It is insufficient that a change of circumstances makes performance more difficult or onerous. A frustrating event is still something exceptional. The courts have consistently sought to keep the doctrine within narrow limits. The fear is that to do otherwise would be to make it too easy to escape from the consequences of a breach of contract. For the reasons already mentioned, the law takes the view that parties, especially to commercial contracts, can generally be expected to make provision for events outside their control, at least when those events are reasonably foreseeable.

---

3   *Sale of Goods Act 1923* (NSW) s 12; *Goods Act 1958* (Vic) s 12; *Sale of Goods Act 1896* (Qld) s 10; *Sale of Goods Act 1895* (WA) s 7; *Sale of Goods Act 1895* (SA) s 7; *Sale of Goods Act 1896* (Tas) s 12; *Sale of Goods Act 1954* (ACT) s 12; *Sale of Goods Act 1972* (NT) s 12.
4   See Carter 2018: 767–71.

One way of doing this is to build in a degree of flexibility in order to accommodate the possibility of changing circumstances. Besides allowing for either consensual or unilateral variations to the terms themselves (see **13.02**), a contract may, for example, allow for payments to be varied according to changes in costs or market conditions: see eg *Upper Hunter County District Council v Australian Chilling & Freezing* (1968), discussed in **5.37**. 'Rise and fall' clauses of this type are a particularly common inclusion in building contracts.

Another way of providing for more dramatic changes is to include a *force majeure clause* in the contract. This kind of provision will typically cover events such as war, industrial action, a natural disaster (sometimes referred to as an 'act of god'), or a terrorist act. More uncommon situations might be added as well.[5] For the clause to apply, it is enough if the events that occur fall within the wording of the clause and are not brought about by the party seeking to rely on it. The change in circumstances need not be sufficient to frustrate the contract. The usual effect of a force majeure clause is to suspend certain obligations, and/or shield one or both parties from liability for what would otherwise be non-performance. More complex clauses might require the parties to renegotiate certain terms, use the services of an arbitrator, or settle on a new contract price. The great advantage of a force majeure clause is that the parties know where they stand at the time they enter into a contract and can plan accordingly.[6]

There will still, however, be situations in which even large commercial parties fail to make provision for a particular eventuality. In the absence of a relevant express provision, the contract is either frustrated or breached. In determining which of those is the case, a court will still pay close attention to the terms of the contract. As we will see, even the failure to provide for an event can be highly relevant in determining whether a contract is frustrated.

Defining frustration

15.05   *Codelfa* and the construction theory

Building on earlier English authority, the definitive modern statement of the doctrine of frustration in Australia can be found in *Codelfa Construction v State Rail Authority* (1982). Codelfa, a construction company, contracted with the State Rail Authority of New South Wales to build an underground railway. The work was to be completed in a fixed period. It was understood that work would be carried out six days a week and without any restrictions on Sunday working. It was also assumed, incorrectly as it turned out, that Codelfa would enjoy the Authority's statutory immunity from injunctions to restrain any nuisance caused to nearby residents. When the work generated noise and vibrations, an injunction was issued to restrain Codelfa from working between 10pm and 6am. Codelfa also undertook not to work on a Sunday, which significantly increased its costs.

As noted in **9.21**, the High Court refused to imply a term that if the company had its activities restrained by an injunction then they were to be indemnified for the additional costs. However, a majority of the Court went on to find that the contract was frustrated. This allowed

---

5   For a detailed examination of these kinds of terms, see McKendrick, 2007; and see also Robertson 2009.

6   As to other types of term that may be used to deal with post-contractual changes, including 'hardship' clauses and 'stabilisation' provisions, see Robertson 2011: 75–9.

Codelfa to recover the additional costs by way of an action for *quantum meruit*: see **15.14**. The leading judgment, delivered by Mason J, drew on the earlier English authority, *Davis Contractors v Fareham UDC* (1956). In the House of Lords, Lord Reid had said (at 720–1) that whether or not a contract is frustrated depended 'on the true construction of the terms which are in the contract read in the light of the nature of the contract and of the relevant surrounding circumstances when the contract was made'. Lord Radcliffe observed (at 729) that frustration would only arise where 'the circumstances in which performance is called for would render it a thing radically different from that which was undertaken by the contract'. He added (at 727) that 'frustration is not to be lightly invoked'.

When parties enter into a contract they make certain assumptions which will necessarily be met if the contract is to be performed. For example, they might both assume that war will not break out and delay or even stop performance of the contract. On the other hand, they may make provision for these eventualities. If they do, then risk is allocated under the contract and it is not frustrated. What has become known as the 'construction theory' of frustration involves the court asking whether, on its true construction, the contract applies in the situation that has actually arisen during the performance of the contract. As Mason J explained in *Codelfa* (at 337):

> a contract will be frustrated when the parties enter into it on the common assumption that some particular thing or state of affairs essential to its performance will continue to exist or be available, neither party undertaking responsibility in that regard and that common assumption proves to be mistaken.

The parties' assumptions are gleaned from the contract. The surrounding circumstances may also be relevant in situations where the plain meaning is not evident from the contract alone. On the facts, Mason J thought that the contract was frustrated because the granting of an injunction made the situation fundamentally different from the one contemplated by the contract on its true construction. Aickin and Wilson JJ likewise treated the contract as frustrated.

15.06 *Codelfa* criticised

Brennan J dissented in *Codelfa* on the basis that the granting of an injunction was not a frustrating event. He stressed the limited scope of frustration. His more restricted application of the doctrine fitted better with the earlier High Court decision in *Scanlan's New Neon v Tooheys* (1943). The defendant hired neon advertising signs from the plaintiff which were installed and illuminated. The Second World War broke out before the hire period had expired. As a result of 'black-out' legislation, the use of illuminated advertisements was prohibited. The defendant stopped paying the hire charge and argued that the contract was frustrated. Latham CJ considered the various theories of frustration, including the construction theory. He concluded (at 194) that:

> it is clear without further evidence that the parties expected that the signs would be used as illuminated signs. But that they made an express provision that rent was to be paid whether the signs were used or not. The court, therefore, would not be justified in holding that the basis of the contract was that no rent should be paid if the signs were not used.

The High Court's judgment in *Scanlan's New Neon* is quite different in tone from the majority in *Codelfa*. The Court in *Scanlan's New Neon* stressed that, for a substantial period of the contract, it had been possible to illuminate the signs and even the unilluminated signs had some value. Williams J noted (at 231) there was a 'fair business risk' that the signs might not be able to be illuminated. He found it 'impossible to believe that the plaintiff would have agreed to take the risk that all its contracts should be terminated in the event of the illumination of the signs being prohibited or restricted'. Once the surrounding circumstances were considered, the Court thought it unlikely, even aside from the express provision, that on the construction test the contract would be frustrated.

It is difficult to see how, on the true construction of the contract, the High Court in *Codelfa* were able to conclude that the contract was frustrated. Both parties were large organisations with legal advisors. It was Codelfa's business to enter into building contracts of this sort. Provision was made in the contract for 'noise, pollution or nuisance', including restrictions on working hours. Mason J concluded that the provision was insufficiently 'wide ranging' to prevent the contract from being frustrated. But it looked very little different in intent to the express provision in *Scanlan's New Neon*, which an earlier High Court thought precluded a finding of frustration. These decisions demonstrate how difficult it can be to predict whether the doctrine of frustration will apply. It is helpful, nonetheless, to identify certain common situations in which the courts have treated a contract as frustrated.

Examples of frustration

15.07   Contracts which are impossible to perform

Frustration covers more than just impossibility. In *Codelfa*, although it was still possible to carry out the building work, the contract was frustrated because the disruption meant that performance was not in the manner contemplated by the contract. Nevertheless, the typical case of frustration remains the situation where a contract has become impossible to perform. Impossibility may occur, as in *Taylor v Caldwell* (see **15.02**), because the subject matter of the contract no longer exists. There are also other kinds of impossibility. For example, the death of a party will frustrate a contract where, as in the case of an employee, personal performance by that party was required: see eg *Cutter v Powell* (1795). In *Cornish v Kanematsu* (1913), the parties entered into a contract for the sale of onions with 'shipment per P&O steamer sailing from Japan about 8th Sept and coming direct to Sydney'. The onions were not shipped because no P&O steamer sailed at the time stated in the contract. The purchaser refused to accept the onions shipped otherwise than in accordance with this term of the contract. It was held that the vendor gave no warranty that the P&O steamer would leave at the time specified in the contract. Although both parties expected the ship to sail on that date, it was not possible for the ship to do so without fault on either side. The contract was therefore frustrated.

The courts have always been careful to distinguish between the situation in which performance becomes impossible and those where it merely becomes more expensive. As a result of a blockade of the Suez Canal in 1956, ships travelling between Europe and Asia were forced to take the much longer and therefore more expensive route around Africa. In *Tsakiroglou v Noblee* (1962), the House of Lords took the view that on its true construction a contract was not frustrated because it could still be performed by shipping the cargo around the Cape of Good Hope. The alternative route was just more expensive. It was conceded that the outcome would have been different if the contract had specified the Suez Canal as the required route.

15.08   Temporary impossibility

A situation that makes performance temporarily impossible is also capable of frustrating a contract. The longer the temporary impossibility, set against the contract duration, the more likely it will be that the contract will be frustrated. In *Ringstad v Gollin* (1924), a contract was entered into for the sale of calcium carbide with delivery to begin on the completion of an earlier contract in early 1917. Wartime restrictions on the import of the chemical were imposed between 1917 and 1919. The High Court held that the contract was not frustrated. It was stressed that the parties did not contract on the basis of a fixed and definitive final delivery date. Nor, as Isaacs J explained (at 315–16), were the goods 'articles of fleeting demand, or passing fashion, nor are they shown to be of abandoned or greatly diminished application in commerce or industry'. The arrival of the chemical in 1919 did not make the contract performed significantly different from the one agreed upon. In other situations, however, a change in the law that directly prohibits the performance of a contract or declares it void may be treated as frustrating the contract: see eg *Maine v Lyons* (1913); *RS Howard & Sons v Brunton* (1916). This may occur, for example, where it becomes illegal to trade with an 'enemy' government or business: see eg *Re Continental C & R Rubber* (1919).

Where a contract requires work to be performed by a particular person, even a temporary incapacity on their part may, if it is sufficiently serious, have the effect of frustrating a contract: see eg *Chapman v Taylor* (2004). This principle has been applied to cases where an employee is expected to be absent from work for a lengthy period because of injury or imprisonment: see eg *Simmons v Hay* (1964); *FC Shepherd v Jerrom* (1986). But, in many instances, the possibility of frustration is raised by an employer solely to deny the employee access to statutory benefits or claims which hinge on them having been 'dismissed'. In *Finch v Sayers* (1976), it was suggested that courts should be reluctant to conclude that an employment contract is frustrated where it can be terminated by giving notice or has a short fixed term.

15.09   Frustration of common purpose

The notion of frustration of common purpose can be illustrated by two decisions that arose out of the cancellation of the coronation of Edward VII. Both cases were heard by the same panel of the Court of Appeal around the same time and produced different outcomes. In *Krell v Henry* (1903), the plaintiff hired a room in London's Pall Mall for two days during which the coronation procession for the new monarch was planned to take place. The plaintiff's motivation for hiring the room was to view the procession, but this was not expressly stated in the contract. The contract was held to be frustrated when the events were postponed due to illness of the King. Performance was not impossible. The plaintiff could have used the room on the day in question. It was held that the contract was entered into on a premise that could not be fulfilled – namely, that the coronation would take place. A different outcome, however, was reached in *Herne Bay Steam Boat v Hutton* (1903). A boat was hired 'for the purpose of viewing the naval review and for a day's cruise round the fleet'. The naval review, forming part of the celebrations planned for Edward VII's coronation, was cancelled when he fell ill. This time the contract was held not to be frustrated. It was explained (at 689) that the naval review 'was not the foundation of the contract'. It was still possible to cruise around the fleet even though the King was not in attendance.

When the purpose of a contract cannot be fulfilled, it appears then that in some circumstances it will be frustrated. But these cases should probably be regarded as exceptional. If it were it too easy to argue frustration of purpose then it would be too easy to escape from a bad bargain. In *oOh! Media v Diamond Wheels* (2011) it was observed (at [92]) that whilst *Krell v Henry* may have been rightly decided, 'there was substantial evidence of surrounding circumstances that the parties entered into an agreement on the basis of a common assumption'. On the facts before the Victorian Court of Appeal (see **15.12**), such substantial evidence was lacking.

Brisbane City Council v Group Projects (1979) is a High Court case in which a contract was held to be frustrated for failure of purpose. Group Projects, a property developer, entered into a contract with Brisbane City Council. Under the contract, the Council was to apply to the Minister to have some land re-zoned for residential development. In return, the developer agreed to contribute towards the cost of new footpaths, sewage systems, water mains, electricity cables, the construction of a bridge and landscaping. Before the re-zoning could take place, the land vested in the Crown. Group Projects found itself left with the onerous obligations under the contract over land in which it no longer had an interest. It argued that the contract was frustrated. Despite the change of circumstances, the developer might still have provided the new amenities. It was held that the contract was frustrated because the parties were now in 'a fundamentally different situation from that contemplated when the contract was entered into' (at 162). The amenities were required for a residential development. Once the land vested in the Crown it was to be used for a school. It was also stressed (at 163) that the Council was in an unusual position: 'If the contract be declared to be frustrated the Council will not be deprived of some commercial advantage which it sought to attain when it entered into the contract.' Because of its very unusual facts it is unsafe to draw any wider conclusions. As Stephen J pointed out (at 163), earlier decisions 'provide little more than single instances of solutions'.

Limits on frustration

15.10   Self-induced frustration

Suppose that there is a contract between A and B and B fails to perform. A then brings an action for breach. If, on its true construction, the contract does not apply in the new set of circumstances, the situation falls within the definition of frustration. But this is not necessarily the end of the matter. B may be unable to argue that the contract is frustrated if the frustration was self-induced. This outcome can be justified because B should not gain advantage from their own wrong. The burden of proving that frustration is self-induced is on the party seeking to defeat the accusation that the contract is frustrated: *Joseph Constantine SS Line v Imperial Smelting* (1942); although compare *Allied Mills v Gwydir Valley Oilseeds* (1978) at 30.

The rule that self-induced frustration does not discharge a contract is easier to state than to apply. In *Scanlan's New Neon* (1943) at 186, Latham CJ suggested that it reflected the idea of 'a state of facts brought about by the act of a party'. His observation provides little by way of concrete guidance of what amounts to self-inducement. In *Joseph Constantine SS Line*, the question of whether fault was required for the frustration to be self-induced was raised but not definitely settled. Some sort of blameworthiness may be needed: a conscious act or omission may not be enough. This may explain why in *Codelfa* (1982) the frustration was not self-induced. Codelfa were acting on the advice of the State Rail Authority that they would be the subject of a statutory immunity. Codelfa's legal advisors expressed no recorded reservations on the issue. Mason J suggested (at 359) that the fact that Codelfa was owned by an Italian company might explain why they were willing to rely on what they were told by the State Rail Authority. Yet, equally, it could be argued that a major commercial party that acted in this way was at least partly culpable and that any frustration was self-induced.

The self-induced rule has sometimes been applied in ways that may seem quite harsh at first sight. In *Maritime National Fish v Ocean Trawlers* (1935), the defendants chartered a trawler from the plaintiff with the intention of operating an otter trawl. Both parties knew that an otter trawl required a licence. The defendants applied for five licences but were only given three which they used for other ships. Their argument that the charterparty was frustrated was rejected. The Privy Council held that it was the act and election of the defendants in using the licences for other vessels that ensured the frustration was self-induced. The dilemma facing the defendants in *The Super Servant Two* (1990) was even starker. They owned two ships, the Super Servant One and the Super Servant Two. The Super Servant Two was allocated to the plaintiff, but sank before the contract could be performed. Because it was required on another voyage, the Super Servant One could not be redeployed to the plaintiff's contract. The Court of Appeal held that the fact the defendants chose to perform the other contract meant that the frustration in relation to the plaintiff's contract was self-induced. Even then, when a defendant has no practical choice, it appears frustration may still be self-induced.

15.11   Contractual provision for a potentially frustrating event

The contract itself may operate as a major limitation on frustration which goes beyond the simple application of a force majeure or hardship clause. If the terms of the contract address the situation that has arisen, then, on its true construction, the contract is not frustrated: see eg *Ange v First East Auction Holdings* (2011). That said, there have been occasions when greater emphasis is put upon the surrounding circumstances than the contract itself. In *Codelfa* (1982), it was held that a clause about restricted working hours and undue noise, pollution or nuisance did not prevent the contract from being frustrated. Mason J took the view (at 362) that the provision was 'quite consistent with the contemplated method of work being an essential element of the contract'. On the facts, as noted earlier, the opposite conclusion could have been reached just as easily.

Where the parties have expressly provided for some events and not others, it may lead the court to make conclusions about where the risk should fall. In *Meriton Apartments v McLaurin and Tait* (1976), a buyer of land refused to go ahead with the transaction when a 'green ban' was imposed which prevented development of the land. The contract was silent on the subject of 'green bans'. Because other risks were allocated under the contract, silence in the contract was taken to suggest that the risk lay with the buyer. As a result the contract was not frustrated.

15.12   Foreseeable events

The fact that a potentially frustrating event is not provided for in the contract may not be enough to ensure that the contract is frustrated. If the event was one that was foreseen or reasonably foreseeable by the parties the contract is not frustrated. Foreseeability is relevant to the question of whether the contract on its true construction applies to the new circumstances. On a more fundamental level, it shows how frustration remains bound up with questions of the allocation of risk. Where the event was foreseen or reasonably foreseeable, then the risk ought to lie where it falls. It can be safely assumed that the parties might have made provision for the events and when they fail to do so they should not be allowed to fall back on frustration. In *Davis Contractors* (1956), the possibility of a shortage of labour and materials was reasonably foreseeable and, as such, provision might have been made for the eventuality in the contract. The construction contract in that case, performance of which had been affected by the shortage, was held not to have been frustrated.

A similar conclusion was reached in *oOh! Media* (2011). The appellant was licenced by a predecessor in title of the respondents to use the site for outside advertisement hoardings. Before the term of the licence was complete a building was constructed which obscured the sign. The appellant purported to terminate the licence. The respondents brought a claim for the loss of the benefit of the licence agreement. The appellant argued that the contract was frustrated. As Nettle JA made clear, the fundamental issue for the court to determine was the common assumptions of the parties at the time that they entered into the contract. Where an event is foreseen then it is difficult to conclude that the parties had entered into a contract on the fundamental assumption that the event could not occur. It was different where the events were foreseeable, but not actually foreseen. A high degree of foreseeability was required before the contract would not be frustrated. Within Melbourne, urban development that would partially or completely obstruct the sign was held (at [74]) to be foreseeable as 'a real possibility'. The fact that the appellant might easily have included a reduced visibility clause in the licence agreement did not help its cause in arguing that the contract was frustrated.

15.13   Frustration and contracts concerning land

Contracts relating to land are quite different from normal contracts. They create both proprietary and personal obligations. Frustration applies differently as well. Land is rarely destroyed. Where land is sold, the risk of destruction of the land passes on conclusion of the contract.[7] Frustration is only likely to have any relevance if the land is destroyed between the making of the contract and the time fixed for completion. This would cover cases where land collapses into the sea or the land is subject to a compulsory acquisition by a government body: see eg *McRoss Developments v Caltex Petroleum* (2004).

A much more common situation concerns an executed lease. In *National Carriers v Panalpina* (1981), despite some earlier contrary authority, the House of Lords held that the doctrine of frustration is capable of applying to leases. It will still be rare, however, for a lease to be frustrated. Some leases run for long periods, such as 99 years, and it is difficult to conceive of such a lease being frustrated because parties must anticipate major changes during a term of that length. Many of these changes will be reasonably foreseeable. Different considerations may apply where a lease is only for a short period. The lease of ten years' duration in *National Carriers Ltd* fell between these two extremes. Access to the property was blocked for

---

7   This rule is derived from the old case of *Paine v Meller* (1801). In New South Wales, the position is slightly different as a result of s 66K of the *Conveyancing Act 1919* (NSW).

a period of about 20 months. Given the period in which access to the premises was unavailable and the likely continuation of the lease, it was held that the contract was not frustrated. This was despite the fact, as Lord Wilberforce put it (at 697), that the lessees' business would have been 'severely dislocated'.

It is difficult to be entirely sure whether frustration applies to leases in Australia. At the trial in *Halloran v Firth* (1926), it was suggested that frustration did not apply to a lease. The majority of the High Court agreed with the trial decision. Isaacs J accepted the result and thought that the contract was not frustrated. He nevertheless suggested (at 269) that leases were capable of being frustrated. Later authorities fail to speak with one voice. In *Scanlan's New Neon* (1943) at 228, Williams J suggested that frustration applies to leases, provided that the lessee has not taken possession.[8] This version of the rule would exclude the possibility of frustration on facts similar to those in *National Carriers*. State decisions can be found supporting the application of frustration to leases and others saying that it does not apply.[9] In *Progressive Mailing House v Tabali* (1985) at 41 and 52, Brennan and Deane JJ expressly left the question open. Mason J hinted (at 29) that he would be prepared to apply frustration to a lease. There seems no reason in principle why the English approach should not apply to leases in Australia. If so, this would mean that whilst the doctrine of frustration applies to leases, it will be difficult to argue successfully.

The effects of frustration

15.14   The common law rules

Once a contract is frustrated, it is automatically terminated, without either party having a say in the matter or needing to give notice. The effect is to release the parties from their future obligations: *Scanlan's New Neon* (1943) at 203. The impact of frustration on obligations that arise prior to a frustrating event is less straightforward. New South Wales, Victoria and South Australia are governed by statutory regimes. The common law continues to apply in other Australian jurisdictions, or where the statutes are excluded by the parties themselves, or because of the type of contract involved.

Prior to the contract becoming frustrated, obligations may already have fallen due. These obligations must be performed. The traditional rule was that payments that fell due still had to be paid and money paid could not be recovered. This outcome follows on from the fact that obligations are only discharged at the point at which the contract becomes frustrated. In *Re Continental C & R Rubber* (1919), a contract was entered into for the construction and installation of machinery. Construction of the machinery began. The contract provided that payments were to be made at the rate of 90 per cent 'on the value of the machinery in progress' as certified by an engineer. Payments totalling £6,000 were made and certificates were issued. The recipient of the machinery, a foreign owned company, fell within wartime restrictions

---

8   The same judge expressed a contrary view a year later in *Minister of State for the Army v Dalziel* (1944) at 302.

9   For cases affirming that leases can be frustrated, see eg *Shiell v Symons* (1951); *Robertson v Wilson* (1958); *Tim Barr v Narui Gold Coast* (2010). For decisions taking the opposite view, see eg *Thearle v Keeley* (1958); *Lobb v Vasey Housing Auxiliary* (1963).

relating to trading with the enemy. As a result, the contract was frustrated prior to the delivery of the machinery. When the company was wound up, the controller standing in the place of the company sought to recover the payments. It was held that the money already paid could not be recovered. This outcome was justified on the basis of the terms of the contract itself, the fact that there was no 'failure of consideration', and as a matter of principle.

In *Chandler v Webster* (1904), referred to in argument in *Re Continental C & R Rubber*, the English Court of Appeal had held that a payment made under a contract could only be recovered on the basis of total failure of consideration if the contract could be rescinded ab initio. A frustrated contract is not rescinded ab initio, but rather discharged at the point it is frustrated. In *Fibrosa Spolka Akcyjna v Fairbairn Lawson Combe Barbour* (1943), however, the House of Lords rejected the view that it was necessary to rescind a contract ab initio. This meant that money paid prior to a frustrating event could be recovered, at least in some circumstances. The House of Lords made clear that when used in the quasi-contractual (or what we would now call restitutionary or unjust enrichment) sense, the concept of failure of consideration refers to a lack of performance: see **24.04–24.05**. The fact that there was consideration for a contract to be formed and that it had not been rescinded ab initio would not of itself preclude a claim to recover a payment made under the contract. In *Fibrosa*, the defendant agreed to manufacture some machinery for the plaintiff who was based in Poland. The plaintiff paid part of the purchase price but no machinery was delivered because of the outbreak of the Second World War. The outbreak of war frustrated the contract. It was held that the plaintiff could recover the payment because there was a total failure of consideration, in the sense that nothing had been received in return for it. In so far as there was any conflict between the approach in *Fibrosa* and *Re Continental C & R Rubber*, Mason CJ would later suggest that *Fibrosa* ought to be followed in Australia: *Baltic Shipping v Dillon* (1993) at 355.

Money is not the only benefit that might fall due or be received prior to the frustrating event. But the common law has adopted a different attitude toward the receipt of money and non-monetary benefits. In *Appleby v Myers* (1867), the plaintiff agreed to manufacture and install machinery in the defendant's factory and to service the machinery for a further two years. The price was calculated by item but payment was to take place on completion of the whole installation. After part of the machinery was installed, an accidental fire destroyed the factory. The contract was frustrated but it was held that the plaintiffs were unable to recover for the value of the machinery that was already installed. The contract between the parties was 'entire', because the contract stated entire payment was only due on completion of the work: see **12.08**. This meant that the right to payment had not accrued before the frustrating event. In *Appleby v Myers*, the recipient did not retain any benefit because the machinery was destroyed. The result would have been the same, however, had the machinery remained intact. If, rather than being a lump sum contract, payments had been by instalment, the recipient of the benefit would have been required to pay the instalments which fell due prior to frustration. By contrast, when benefits are conferred *after* a frustrating event, because, for example, the parties fail to realise that the contract is frustrated, the value of the benefit conferred can more readily be recovered: see eg *Codelfa* (1982).

The common law in this area is unsatisfactory. Money paid prior to a frustrating event can only be recovered when the failure of consideration is total. As a result, where some performance, however trivial, is received in return for the payment, then it remains impossible to recover payments made. It is worse in situations where a non-monetary benefit is received.

Significant benefits may be rendered by way of part performance without any compensation becoming payable if the contract is entire. This may leave the recipient with a valuable product without requiring any payment from them. Dissatisfaction with the common law rules has led legislatures in New South Wales, Victoria and South Australia to make statutory provision for the consequences of frustration.[10]

15.15   New South Wales

In New South Wales, frustrated contracts are governed by the *Frustrated Contracts Act 1978* (NSW). A frustrated contract includes for this purpose a contract for goods that perish before sale (s 5(1)). But certain kinds of charterparty, other contracts for the carriage of goods by sea, and contracts of insurance are not covered by the Act. The parties are also free to exclude the legislation (s 6(1)). The legislation diverges from the common law in several important ways. At common law, unperformed obligations falling due prior to the frustrating event remain to be performed whether that obligation is to pay money or to confer some other benefit. In New South Wales, unperformed obligations are now discharged except as necessary to support a claim for breach of contract (s 7).

Where money is paid prior to frustration, the recipient is required to pay an equal sum in return, provided the money was paid in return for performance (s 12). This is easier to satisfy than the common law requirement of a total failure of consideration. The rules governing other types of performance prior to frustration are more complex. Where one party fully performs their obligations under the contract prior to frustration, s 10 provides that they are entitled to an amount equal to the 'value of the agreed return for the performance'. But a situation like *Appleby v Myers* (1867), where there is partial performance of an entire obligation prior to frustration, is covered by a completely new scheme. Section 11 lays down a formula for calculating what can be recovered. The recipient is required to pay the party who performs the 'attributable value' of that performance. This is equated with the contract price, subject to a deduction representing the extent to which the performance falls short of the contractually agreed performance. Where the cost of performance exceeds the 'attributable value' then, in addition to the attributable value, the performing party is entitled to receive half of those costs from the recipient.

When a contract is frustrated, some expenditure may be wasted, without the other party receiving money or any other benefit. At common law, wasted expenditure cannot be recovered. Section 13(1) makes provision for the recovery of wasted expenditure when a party suffers a detriment 'by reasonably paying money or doing or suffering any other act or thing for the purpose or giving performance under the contract'. This section could be utilised in a factual situation one step removed from *Appleby v Myers*. Suppose that the manufacturers of the machines had begun construction away from the defendant's factory and, before the machinery could be delivered, the factory was destroyed in the fire. This counts as wasted expenditure because no benefit has been received by the customer. Under the statute, on these facts, the manufacturers would be able to recover one-half of the amounts expended as 'fair compensation'. Where a valuable product is produced, the manufacturer is still required to pay

---

10   For a detailed analysis of these provisions, see Stewart & Carter 1992.

half the value of the end product or the improvement to the other party (s 13(2)). This solution involves sharing the loss between both parties. The manufacturer receives fair compensation but has to pay back half the value of any end product.

In certain circumstances, a court may exclude the provisions in ss 10–13. This may be done where the terms of the contract or the events that occur are such that to apply these sections would be 'manifestly inadequate or inappropriate' and would either cause 'manifest injustice' or would be 'excessively difficult or expensive' to apply. In that case, a court may substitute such adjustments 'in money or otherwise as it considers proper' (s 15(1)). This provision is potentially far reaching. It allows the courts to ignore the detailed statutory provisions about apportionment of loss. The question of what is 'proper' is inherently vague and gives neither the parties nor the judiciary much guidance.

15.16 South Australia

Like its New South Wales counterpart, the *Frustrated Contracts Act 1988* (SA) does not apply to certain types of contract, or where the parties exclude it (s 4). It does, however, include contracts for goods that perish before sale (s 3(1)). The guiding principle behind the legislation is explained in s 7(1), which states that when a contract is frustrated 'there will be an adjustment between the parties so that no party is unfairly advantaged or disadvantaged'. With the exception of obligations which on the construction of the contract are designed to continue, any unperformed obligations are discharged on frustration (s 6(1)). There is no distinction between money and non-monetary benefits. The Act simply requires a calculation of the aggregated contractual benefits received by each party prior to frustration and then a deduction for the aggregated value of each party's contractual performance. The figure left over is then notionally divided between the parties in equal shares, followed by a further adjustment to ensure an equalisation of the contractual return of each party (s 7(2)). A court is given a residual discretion to be exercised on an 'equitable basis' (s 7(4)). If anything, this provision is even vaguer than the New South Wales equivalent, which at least identifies situations in which the discretion can be exercised.[11]

15.17 Victoria

Frustration in Victoria is governed by Part 3-2 of the *Australian Consumer Law and Fair Trading Act 2012* (Vic).[12] In common with the other legislation, it excludes a charterparty, other contracts relating to the carriage of goods by sea and insurance (s 35(3)), and the parties themselves may agree on provisions that effectively override the legislation (s 41). Contracts for goods that perish before sale are, however, included (s 35(1)(c)).

Section 36(1) provides that any money paid prior to frustration is recoverable. The obligation to pay any money due but not yet paid is discharged (s 36(2)). This provision is subject to s 37, which allows the recipient to retain money paid or recover money payable up to the level of any expenses that they have incurred.

---

11   For a detailed analysis of the legislation and its shortcomings, see Stewart 1992.
12   These provisions were originally enacted as the *Frustrated Contracts Act 1959* (Vic).

When one of the parties receives a valuable benefit other than money, prior to frustration, a court may award the other party a 'just' sum not exceeding the value of the benefit received (s 38(2)). This provision mirrors s 1(3) of the *Law Reform (Frustrated Contracts) Act 1943* (UK), which has proved very difficult to interpret. In *BP Exploration v Hunt* (1979), Robert Goff J laid down some general principles. The starting point was to value the benefit received. The benefit might consist of an end product, though in some situations this might have no market value. Robert Goff J gave the example of redecoration in execrable taste. Here the benefit was valued according to the service provided. He thought that the same measure should be used where there was no end product, because the contract merely involved the provision of a service such as transporting goods. A third situation is like the one in *Appleby v Myers* (1867). Here, an end product is produced but it is destroyed. According to Robert Goff J, there is no benefit because any benefit was reduced to zero by the destruction. As such, these facts apparently fall outside the legislation. If this interpretation were to be adopted in Victoria, the common law would effectively continue to apply in a case of this sort.

Having valued the benefit, this sum acts as a ceiling on the claim when calculating a 'just sum'. In determining this sum, the court may have regard to expenses incurred by the recipient of the benefit and 'the circumstances giving rise to the frustration' (s 38(3)). Relevant factors are identified in the statute but a court retains a considerable degree of discretion in determining a just sum. No provision is made in the legislation for obligations, other than the payment of money, which are not fulfilled by the time the contract is frustrated. This means that the common law applies and the obligations must be performed.

Is the doctrine of frustration unsatisfactory?

15.18   Criticisms of the law on frustration

One former Chief Judge of the Commercial Division of the Supreme Court of New South Wales, Andrew Rogers QC, has expressed the view that (Rogers 1995: 245):

> The operation of the doctrine of frustration is one of the least successful efforts of lawyers to meet the needs of commerce. Unforeseen occurrences are surely a common event. Yet the response of the law of contract is both uncertain and inadequate.

Rogers makes some very valid points. Determining whether a contract is frustrated is not a very precise exercise. A leading case such as *Codelfa* (1982) could just as easily have gone the other way. Nor is the way the law apportions loss after frustration entirely satisfactory. Legislation has improved matters but even allowing for the absence of statutes in some States, the legislation itself is far from perfect.

The old law required contracts to be performed and put the onus on parties to make provisions for the unexpected. This was at least certain. In the absence of a contrary provision, the contract must be performed and the loss lay where it fell. The problem with that solution is that there are some events that cannot be predicted. The modern law deals with risk allocation in a more subtle way. The construction theory requires a court to assess the contract and surrounding circumstances in order to determine whether the contract covers the new factual situation. This produces an outcome that is less 'all or nothing' than the old law. It means that, sometimes, the loss no longer need lie where it falls.

Concerns about the operation of frustration should not be exaggerated. It is quite rare for a contract to be frustrated. The clearest cases of frustration, reflected in many of the authorities, are brought about by events like wars or through acts of destruction outside the control of the parties. Such events happen, but they are hardly commonplace. There are nevertheless those who would like to see the law of frustration reformed. Some believe that the modern law is too flexible and others argue that it is not flexible enough.

As for the statutory rules on apportionment, they are a long way from satisfactory. Much of the legislation is difficult to apply and uncertain in scope. The New South Wales and South Australian Acts are particularly open to criticism in this regard. It is striking that the statutes have received virtually no judicial attention,[13] suggesting that they are routinely being excluded or ignored. Their inadequacies should come as no real surprise. Loss apportionment is not something that the courts do in the ordinary course of enforcing contracts. It does not fit well within the dominant individualistic model of contract law that still holds sway in Australia. Some of the resistance to loss apportionment may be reflected in the way in which judges are generally reluctant to treat a contract as frustrated. The rules about self-induced frustration are only the most blatant example. In a broad sense, loss apportionment may protect those who are in a weaker bargaining position, but in reality even this assumption may be flawed when the statutory schemes can be excluded.

15.19   Alternatives to the current law

Some writers have suggested that no separate doctrine of frustration is required. Kull (1991) has argued that where the parties have failed to allocate risk then there is no justification for a court to fill the gap. He favours what he terms a 'principle of inertia' under which the loss lies where it falls. As Kull concedes, this is ultimately a moral and political choice between requiring parties to make proper provision and allowing courts to intervene when they do not. This approach would return the law to its traditional state. It would remove any role for the courts in apportioning losses between the parties.

A very different suggestion would be to follow the lead of many civil law systems and attach greater importance to the *adaptation* of contracts affected by supervening circumstances, rather than their termination. As Robertson (2011) notes, this is already a feature of provisions typically included in long-term contracts associated with international trade and investment. By way of illustration, he cites (at 76) Article 6.2 of the UNIDROIT Principles of International Commercial Contracts. This deals with the 'hardship' caused by post-contractual events that fundamentally alter the 'equilibrium' of a contract and disadvantage a party who could not reasonably have been expected to address or assume that risk. That party is entitled to ask for the contract to be renegotiated, something that must be done in good faith, in

---

13   For a limited exception, see *Lobb v Vasey Housing Auxiliary* (1963).

accordance with the duty noted in **12.19**. If the parties cannot agree, a court or arbitrator may be asked either to terminate the contract or to adapt it in such a way as to restore its equilibrium.[14]

---

14   For an example of a US court assuming such a power, see *Aluminium Co of America v Essex Group* (1990). The case concerned a long-term contract with a price indexing formula. When unexpectedly high increases in energy costs caused the price to skyrocket and made the contract unprofitable, the Court rewrote the formula to produce results more in line with the parties' original expectations.

PART V

ENDING A CONTRACT

16

TERMINATION OF CONTRACTS

How and why contracts can end

16.01   Discharge and termination

The vast majority of contracts are performed. When a contract is fully performed in accordance with its terms, the parties are *discharged* from their obligations. Parties are also discharged from their obligations when a contract has an agreed duration and reaches its *expiry date*: see **12.05–12.06**.[1]

A contract can be discharged in a number of other ways. For example, *frustration* discharges the parties from any contractual obligations falling due for performance after the frustrating event. At common law, obligations which have not been performed as of the date of frustration remain binding, although these may now also be discharged in some States as a result of statutory regulation: see **15.14–15.17**. As explained in Chapter 15, it is very uncommon for a contract to be frustrated. The threshold for proving frustration is high and the parties have often made express provision for a change of circumstances.

After performance or expiry, the next most important kind of discharge occurs through *termination*.[2] Termination may occur in a number of ways. The parties may agree that in certain circumstances the contract may be terminated. Termination clauses are very common in commercial contracts. Even without such a clause there is nothing to stop the parties subsequently entering into a contract to terminate their earlier agreement. Termination can also occur without agreement. A series of common law rules mean that non-performance of the contract by one party may, in some circumstances, allow the other party to terminate the contract. Whether a contract can be terminated at the time that performance becomes due depends on the nature of the breach. A contract may also be repudiated *before* performance is due, allowing the other party to terminate. Both of these situations are discussed later in the chapter.

Australian law does not allow an innocent party to *suspend* their performance in response to the other's breach, unless the contract includes a special provision allowing suspension.[3] A force majeure clause is a good example: see **15.04**. In contrast to the common law, Article 71 of the Vienna Convention allows the innocent party to an international contract of sale to suspend their performance when it 'becomes apparent that the other party will not perform a substantial part of his [sic] obligations'.

16.02   Termination and rescission

Many judges and lawyers insist on using *rescission* as a synonym for termination. They will speak, for instance, of 'rescinding' a contract in response to certain breaches. But this risks serious confusion, because rescission is more commonly understood to mean rescission ab initio (from the beginning). Where a contract is rescinded in that sense, it is as if the contract never existed. The parties are put back in the position that they were in before contracting.

---

1   Some obligations, however, may be intended to continue operating even after others have been discharged: see the examples given in **17.01–17.02**.
2   For discussion of the distinction between discharge and termination, see eg Carter 2012.
3   As to the operation of this principle in relation to employment contracts, see eg *Coal & Allied Mining Services v MacPherson* (2010) at [63]–[71]; Stewart et al 2016: [17.62].

A contract may be rescinded ab initio in a number of situations. These include where a contract is entered into after a misrepresentation (see **18.05**), or as the result of undue pressure (see **19.01**, **19.07**). Rescission ab initio occurs where something is wrong in the way that a contract has been formed. The consequences of termination, by contrast, are quite different. An express clause may set down what happens on termination, but this almost never involves undoing any previous performance.[4] Similarly, when a contract is terminated at common law for non-performance a series of rules determine what happens to the parties' obligations. Unlike rescission ab initio, when a contract is terminated it is not as though there never was a contract. Some obligations can survive termination: see **17.01–17.02**. It is better, therefore, to speaking of *rescinding* a contract for misrepresentation or one of the other vitiating factors, and of *terminating* a contract for breach.[5]

16.03   Termination as a self-help remedy

Courts are not initially involved in the process of terminating for non-performance. As a self-help remedy (see **3.04**), the innocent party can bring the contract to an end quickly without the cost and inconvenience of going to court. If a deposit has been received, this can be retained to cover any expenses or other loss. The onus is then placed on the contract-breaker to challenge the termination. Sometimes, it will not be worth the cost of litigating.

It may be different, however, if the terminating party has incurred expenses, or has suffered a loss for which they want compensation. In that situation, an action may be initiated to recover damages, and/or to seek restitution for any benefits conferred on the contract breaker. Restitution is a limited remedy, because it can only be used in limited circumstances: see **24.05**, **24.09**. A claim for damages in this situation may include not only any loss directly caused by the breach that has created the right to terminate, but *loss of bargain damages*. These cover the loss of benefits that were expected from the remainder of the contract: see **23.04**. However, suing may open the way for the defendant to challenge the termination. Indeed, the defendant may counter-claim that the plaintiff's wrongful termination was itself a repudiation that entitled the defendant to terminate the contract and claim damages: see **16.13**. It is not at all unusual then for a court to have to rule between parties who are each claiming to have (lawfully) terminated the contract and to be entitled to redress. By definition, both parties cannot be right in this situation. Usually, the outcome will be a ruling in one party's favour. But occasionally, as in *DTR Nominees v Mona Homes* (1978), a court may determine that neither party had a right to terminate: see **16.28**.

16.04   Why terminate?

There are often good practical reasons why an innocent party may wish to terminate the contract when they are able to do so. A customer or employer may, for instance, be unhappy with the

---

4   The main exception here involves the non-fulfilment of certain types of contingent condition, which courts tend to speak of as making the contracts in question 'voidable'. see **5.25**. But, even here, it can be argued that 'termination' is the better usage. This is apparent from the fact that, unless the parties have expressly provided otherwise, the consequences of a contract being 'cancelled' for non-fulfilment of a contingent condition are the same as if the contract had been terminated for breach: see eg *Westralian Farmers v Commonwealth Agricultural Service Engineers* (1936); and see further **17.03**.

5   But compare the express provision considered in *Carbone v Metricon* (2018).

performance they are receiving from a supplier or employee and want to engage someone else instead. Conversely, an employee or contractor may be unhappy with their treatment and prefer to find work somewhere else. Continuing to perform may be risky in some circumstances; for instance, where there is a serious breach and the party in breach is in financial difficulties. It will usually be better to bring the contract to an early end, and avoid the expense of performance, rather than risk becoming an unsecured creditor in a claim for damages.

There may be other situations, however, in which a decision to terminate has nothing to do with any real dissatisfaction with the other party. It may be motivated by a desire to escape what may have become a disadvantageous transaction – or to take advantage of a better deal that is now on offer. Such scenarios are especially likely where markets are volatile and prices can shift. Suppose that A agrees to purchase some goods for $100,000 from B to be delivered on 1 October. The price of the goods in the market on the date for delivery is now $50,000. Assuming that there is a breach by B of the relevant sort, terminating the contract and going out into the market and purchasing the goods for a lower price would make sense. In some cases, this may mean that even when a breach which appears quite small occurs, provided it is one that supports termination, the party in breach will lose the benefit of a bargain which is quite disproportionate to the small harm caused by their breach.

A party may even decide that it makes sense to end a contract where there is no lawful power to terminate. In theory, and occasionally in practice, the other party may be able to resist such a move and keep the contract alive: see **16.26**. But, given the reluctance of courts to order parties to perform their obligations, as discussed in Chapter 22, the more common outcome is that the other party will be forced to accept the termination. The wrongfully terminating party may head off any damages claim by offering to pay compensation, in effect 'purchasing' their release. A common and highly visible example of this practice occurs in professional sports, with the sacking of managers or head coaches. The latter have rarely done anything to trigger the termination of what are usually fixed-term contracts for their services. But clubs generally go ahead anyway, under pressure from supporters, players or the media. Proceedings may be threatened or commenced, but in practice a pay out will usually be negotiated and it is very rare for such cases to end in court.[6]

Termination for non-performance: common law rights

16.05   Types of breach: anticipatory and actual breach

Non-performance may occur at different times in relation to the date fixed for performance of the contract. A breach that is identified before the time specified in the contract for performance or completion of performance has arrived is known as an *anticipatory breach*, even though technically the breach has not yet occurred. An anticipatory breach is brought about

---

6   It is sometimes different with departing players: see eg *Bulldogs Rugby League Club v Williams* (2008), where an injunction was granted to prevent Sonny Bill Williams from leaving the Bulldogs to play rugby in France. But even here a settlement quickly eventuated. As to the availability of an injunction in such a case, see **22.14–22.15**.

when one of the parties repudiates the contract (see **16.11**) by indicating that they do not intend to fulfil their obligations under the contract, or acts in such a way that it will not be possible to perform the contract. In the face of an anticipatory breach it is unnecessary for the innocent party to wait until the time for performance falls due before they can elect to terminate. Termination and the claim for damages can usually be brought forward: see *Hochster v De La Tour* (1853). In that case, the plaintiff was engaged to accompany the defendant on a tour to Europe and act as his courier. The defendant changed his mind a few weeks before the tour was to begin. It was held that the plaintiff, who subsequently found other work, could immediately sue for damages, rather than having to remain at the defendant's disposal.

This general rule may, however, have some limits. In *Mackenzie v Rees* (1941) at 15–16, Dixon J suggested that when the innocent party has fully performed their own obligations under the contract they are unable to terminate and claim damages until an actual breach has occurred. This restriction is of uncertain scope, but may be limited to the situation in which the repudiating party owes an obligation to the innocent party to pay them money: see *Progressive Mailing House v Tabali* (1985) at 44–6.

A breach occurring at the time performance is required by the contract is termed an *actual breach*. Whether an actual breach gives rise to a right to terminate depends on the classification of the term that is breached – in particular, whether it is an essential, non-essential or intermediate term.

16.06   Types of term: essential, non-essential and intermediate terms

Until comparatively recently the English – and, by extension, the Australian – law of contract only recognised two kinds of term: *conditions* and *warranties*. Both of these words have multiple legal meanings: see **5.24**, **9.11**. In this context, a warranty – or, as it can more usefully be called, a *non-essential term* – was understood to be a term which, when breached, gave a right to claim damages, but no right to terminate. By contrast, any breach of a condition (or *essential term*),[7] no matter how minor, conferred a right on the other party to terminate the contract.

Eventually, however, the dichotomy of conditions (breach of which could lead to termination), and warranties (breach of which merely gave rise to a claim for damages) came to be seen as too inflexible. In *Hong Kong Fir Shipping v Kawasaki* (1962), the facts of which are discussed below at **16.10**, the English Court of Appeal invented a new category of term – the *intermediate* or *innominate term*. All terms which are not conditions or warranties are now considered to fall into this category. Whether a breach of this sort of term allows termination in

---

7   On one view, there is a distinction between a condition and an essential term: see eg *VIP Home Services v Swan* (2011) at [45], [48]. But the High Court now appears to treat them as synonyms: see eg *Gumland Property Holdings v Duffy Brothers* (2008) at [58]. For practical purposes, it is easier to follow that course, provided it is borne in mind that the word 'condition' can also have very different meanings. Indeed, that is why we generally prefer 'essential term' – even though this too can mean something slightly different in the context of determining whether an agreement is sufficiently 'complete' to be enforceable as a contract. There, it refers to the type of matter on which the parties must have reached agreement for a particular class of transaction: see **5.38**.

addition to damages depends on the extent and consequences of the breach. If the breach is a serious or *fundamental* one that deprives the terminating party of substantially what was expected from performance of the contract, the contract can be terminated.

The Australian courts were slow to recognise this third category, although there had long been a hint of its existence in judgments that appeared to distinguish between conditions that called for either 'strict' or 'substantial' compliance: see eg *Tramways Advertising v Luna Park* (1938) at 641–2, discussed below at **16.08**. But the concept of an intermediate term was endorsed by the High Court in *Koompahtoo Local Aboriginal Land Council v Sanpine* (2007): see **16.10**.

16.07 Classifying a term as essential

Some terms are classified by statute. As a result of legislation, various implied terms in contracts for the sale of goods (see **9.27**) are designated as either conditions or warranties.[8] Other terms are classified in a particular way because of earlier court rulings. This means that some terms are always treated as essential. For example, in *The Mihalis Angelos* (1971), a clause in a voyage charter requiring the ship to be ready to load at a particular time was treated as a condition because this was how earlier authorities had classified it. Terms of this kind appear in commercial contracts all the time. Commercial parties often contract on standard terms and particularly value consistency in interpretation which enables them to plan their activities – a point that the House of Lords stressed in *Bunge v Tradax* (1981), in considering whether a time stipulation was essential (see **16.16**). It is why it is necessary to consider the particular characteristics of a contract when determining the nature of the clause: *Ankar v National Westminster Finance* (1987).

More typically, the parties themselves will designate a term as 'essential'. Labelling a term a 'condition' does not necessarily mean that it will have that effect, given the different meanings of that word. In *L Schuler v Wickman Machine Tool Sales* (1974), Lord Reid accepted that when the parties used the word 'condition', it was a strong indication that the term was to be interpreted as a condition. But he added that the fact that a particular construction leads to a very unreasonable result must also be a relevant consideration in the other direction. The more unreasonable the result, the more unlikely it is that the parties intend it, and if a condition is really intended then they need to make that intention abundantly clear.

In general, however, parties are perfectly at liberty to make performance of a particular term essential to the contract. When they do so, any breach is enough to allow the contract to be terminated, even if, from an objective perspective, the breach may be a trivial one: see eg *Gumland Property Holdings v Duffy Brothers* (2008), upholding the designation of an obligation to pay rent on time as an essential term. Indeed, terms are frequently designated as essential in commercial contracts.

---

8   *Sale of Goods Act 1923* (NSW) ss 17–20; *Goods Act 1958* (Vic) ss 17–20; *Sale of Goods Act 1896* (Qld) ss 15–18; *Sale of Goods Act 1895* (WA) ss 12–15; *Sale of Goods Act 1895* (SA) ss 12–15; *Sale of Goods Act 1896* (Tas) ss 17–20; *Sale of Goods Act 1954* (ACT) ss 17–20; *Sale of Goods Act 1972* (NT) ss 17–20. Note, however, that in New South Wales the concept of an intermediate term is also now recognised: *Sale of Goods Act 1923* (NSW) s 4(5).

16.08   Inferring that a term is essential

A term need not actually be described as essential in order to be treated as having that character. Other terms can, as a matter of fact, be essential. Jordan CJ's judgment in *Tramways Advertising v Luna Park* (1938) at 641–2 has been subsequently adopted as the correct approach when identifying an essential term:

> The test of essentiality is whether it appears from the general nature of the contract considered as a whole, or from some particular term or terms, that the promise is of such importance to the promisee that he [sic] would not have entered into the contract unless he had been assured of a strict or a substantial performance of the promise, as the case may be, and that this ought to have been apparent to the promisor.[9]

On appeal to the High Court in *Luna Park v Tramways Advertising* (1938), there was a clear division. The majority, who found that the relevant clause was essential, adopted the more traditional approach and focused on the grammatical construction of the clause. Dixon J dissented. He explained (at 409) that his own choice 'may be the result of giving greater weight to context and subject matter than to the exact grammatical construction'. Dixon J's approach is favoured by modern courts. The test of whether a term is essential involves a broader inquiry. It requires an understanding of the term within the whole context of the transaction.

The process of identifying an essential term is usefully illustrated by *Associated Newspapers v Bancks* (1951). The defendant was a cartoonist employed by the plaintiff's newspaper. The defendant agreed to produce a weekly full-page drawing of a popular cartoon, 'Us Fellers'. In return, the plaintiff undertook that each weekly full-page drawing would be presented on the front page of the comic section of the *Sunday Sun and Guardian*. Until February 1951, the plaintiff honoured the agreement. Then, on three Sundays in succession, owing to a shortage of newsprint, the defendant's cartoon was printed in the colour magazine on the third page and not on the front page of the comic. The defendant argued that the plaintiff had repeatedly, and in the face of his protests, broken its undertaking, and that he was therefore entitled to treat the contract as at an end. After applying Jordan CJ's test, the High Court concluded that the plaintiff had breached an essential term which went to the root of the contract and therefore entitled the defendant to terminate the contract. The High Court stressed that the defendant was not like an ordinary employee. Continuity of publication and the appearance of the cartoon on the front of the comic were of vital importance to him, such that he would never have agreed to the contract without these terms.

Whether a term is essential is a matter of intention. The focus is on the importance of the term from an objective point of view. So, for example, in *Gough v South Sky Investments* (2012), the name of a development on the Gold Coast was changed as part of a rebranding. It was found that there was nothing to suggest that maintaining the original name should be regarded as an essential term of an agreement to purchase units in a tower block there. It has indeed been suggested that judges should not be too ready to classify a term as essential,

---

9   For approval of this passage, see eg *Associated Newspapers v Bancks* (1951) at 337; *Koompahtoo Local Aboriginal Land Council v Sanpine* (2007) at [47]–[48].

because the preference should be to encourage performance rather than allowing a contract to be terminated: *Ankar v National Westminster Finance* (1987) at 556–7.

16.09   Non-essential terms

A warranty, or non-essential term,[10] forms the second category of contract term. When such a term is breached, the innocent party has no right to terminate. The contract continues. The innocent party is restricted to recovering damages for the breach. Some terms are classified as a warranty by statute, as with the sale of goods legislation mentioned in **16.07**. The parties may also deliberately designate a term as a warranty in order to ensure that if it is breached then the contract cannot be terminated. But the emergence of the category of intermediate terms means that, outside of these examples, this classification is far less important than it once was.

16.10   Intermediate terms

A warranty and a condition were traditionally identified by looking at the nature of the term. This meant assessing the intentions of the parties at the time that they entered into the contract. But the actual consequences of breach could only be determined at the time of the breach, rather than when the contract was formed. The twofold classification was very rigid. It meant that a very serious breach would not allow a contract to be terminated if the term breached was a warranty. Equally, a very minor breach would allow a contract to be terminated if the term was a condition. This all or nothing approach was inflexible. It was particularly problematic when a term could be breached in different ways – some trivial, others more serious.

In *Hong Kong Fir Shipping v Kawasaki* (1962). The case involved a requirement in a time charterparty (an agreement to charter or hire a ship for a set period) for the vessel to be seaworthy. Such a clause could be breached in minor ways or in ways that were very serious. Upjohn LJ gave examples of trivial breaches of seaworthiness, including a wooden ship with one missing nail. It was, he said (at 62), 'contrary to common sense' to think that the parties intended to treat the contract as at an end for such trivial breaches. But whilst the term was not classified as a condition, its non-performance could still be grounds to terminate the contract if the consequences of the breach were sufficiently serious. The Court achieved this result by treating the term as intermediate in nature – something between a condition and warranty. The threshold for termination is a high one, with such a term. According to Diplock LJ (at 73), the breach must deprive the innocent party 'of substantially the whole benefit which he [sic] should obtain from the contract'.

In *Koompahtoo Local Aboriginal Land Council v Sanpine* (2007), the majority of the High Court endorsed *Hong Kong Fir*. The Land Council and Sanpine entered into a joint venture for the commercial development of land. Liabilities in excess of $2 million were incurred on the security of mortgages of the land. Because the project was controversial in the Koompahtoo community, it could not attract financial backers, and the project never reached the stage of rezoning the land. The mortgagee took possession. The administrator tried to get

---

10   Note that 'non-essential term' is sometimes used simply to mean a term that is not essential, but which may still be an intermediate term: see eg *Koompahtoo Local Aboriginal Land Council v Sanpine* (2007) at [49]. But we prefer to be clearer by using it as a synonym for warranty.

information from Sanpine about the financial records of the joint venture, but Sanpine had failed to keep proper books of accounts. The administrator, acting on behalf of Koompahtoo, then terminated the joint venture. Sanpine argued that the termination was invalid. A clause in the contract imposed an obligation on Sanpine to ensure that proper account books were kept. According to Gleeson CJ, Gummow, Heydon and Crennan JJ (at [69]), it was 'difficult to resist a conclusion that such an obligation was essential. The ability to make an assessment of the affairs of the joint venture, at all times from the commencement of the agreement was vital'. However, they did not decide the case on that basis, instead holding that it was an intermediate term and the breach that occurred was sufficiently serious to allow Koompahtoo to terminate the contract.

The majority confirmed (at [47]) that the correct approach in determining whether a term is essential is to consider the common intention of the parties. The addition of a category of intermediate term was said (at [51]) to allow for 'greater flexibility'. As they went on to explain (at [52]):

> First the interests of justice are promoted by limiting rights to rescind to instances of serious and substantial breaches of contract. Secondly a just outcome is facilitated in cases where the breach is of a term which is inessential.

Kirby J dissented. He did not favour a third category. He thought that two categories were sufficient. A contract could be terminated for breach of an essential term. A second, additional, category of non-essential term would allow for termination where a breach caused substantial loss of benefit. This analysis is tidier, although it would mean that the parties could not deliberately classify a term as a warranty so as to ensure that non-performance could not allow termination – however serious the breach. Kirby J was critical of using common intention to identify a condition which he described (at [101]) as a 'fiction'. It was better, he considered (ibid), to 'inquire into the objective significance of a breach of the term'. Undoubtedly, there is often a degree of artificiality about the process of contractual interpretation: see **10.02–10.04**. It is also correct to suggest that, at least where the parties have not expressly designated a term as essential, the objective significance of a breach of the term is likely to be critical, as is evident from *Associated Newspapers v Bancks* (1951).

The breaches in *Koompahtoo* were held to justify terminating the contract. The majority stressed that they were frequent, and the consequences serious. They were enough to deprive the Land Council of 'a substantial part of the benefit for which it contracted' (at [71]). In contrast, the ship in *Hong Kong Fir* was unseaworthy for part of the charterparty, but (perhaps surprisingly) this was not considered enough to deprive the charterers of 'substantially the whole benefit'. The onus of proving that the breach is one that can justify termination is on the party seeking to terminate. A key factor in determining whether the breach qualifies as 'fundamental' will, as in *Koompahtoo*, be the extent to which the innocent party is deprived of benefits that would have been gained by performance. A range of other factors may also be relevant, including the length of any delay, the value of performance received or tendered by the innocent party, and whether damages would be adequate compensation.[11]

---

11 For a detailed discussion of these and other factors which have been seen as relevant to whether the breach is sufficiently serious, see Carter 2019: [6–56]-[6–83].

16.11 Repudiation by renunciation

The term *repudiation* is used in a number of different senses by contract lawyers. Sometimes it is used to describe any breach of contract which gives the innocent party a right to terminate the contract. Used in this way, repudiation would, for example, cover the breach of an essential term. More narrowly (and indeed more traditionally), it refers to a range of behaviour in which one party indicates, whether through words or conduct, that they will not or cannot perform the contract to an extent that is sufficiently serious for the contract to be terminated for non-performance. Repudiation in this sense usually occurs before the time that performance of the contract falls due, in the form of an anticipatory rather than an actual breach. But there is nothing to stop a repudiation occurring at the time that the contract is due to be performed. This sense of repudiation is better captured by the idea of *renunciation*. The majority in *Koompahtoo* (at [44]) defined this as being 'conduct of a party which evinces an intention no longer to be bound by the contract or to fulfil it only in a manner substantially inconsistent with the party's obligations'.

In practice, the requirement (discussed below) that a repudiation reach a certain level of seriousness means that the doctrine significantly overlaps with the two grounds of termination previously discussed. Many breaches of essential terms and (more especially) fundamental breaches of intermediate terms will also constitute repudiation. Indeed, courts frequently conflate the concepts of repudiation and fundamental breach.

There are two situations, however, where termination for repudiation does not overlap with the other grounds. One is that of anticipatory breach. A number of different justifications for allowing repudiation to bring a contract to an end by such a breach have been put forward.[12] All of these may rest on the notion that a contract generates an expectation that the other will perform. By renunciating, one party makes clear that those expectations will not be fulfilled. If the innocent party was unable to bring the contract to an end, despite a repudiation, they would be wasting resources in continuing to perform: *Hochster v De La Tour* (1853) at 690.

The other situation is where there is a cumulative series of breaches, none of which on their own would justify termination, but which taken together can be regarded as evidence of a party's unwillingness or inability to comply with their obligations. For example, in *Progressive Mailing House v Tabali* (1985), the High Court held that a series of breaches by a tenant fell into this category, even though none of the terms breached was essential.

16.12 Types of renunciation and the requirement of seriousness

In the simplest instance, a renunciation will involve a clear statement that a party no longer intends to perform the contract. Sometimes though, renunciation can be inferred from conduct. In *Carr v JA Berriman* (1953), a building owner contracted to engage a builder. Part of the contract involved the fabrication of steel, which was particularly profitable to the builder because of their contract with the manufacturer. The building owner informed the builder that he had placed the fabrication order with a third party. The owner also failed to clear the site

---

12 See Carter 2019: [7-17]–[7-23]; and see further Carter et al 2018.

ready for building work to begin. In combination, this behaviour was such (as explained at 351) that:

> A reasonable man [sic] could hardly draw any other inference than that the building owner does not intend to take the contract seriously, that he is prepared to carry out his part of the contract only if and when it suits him.

Whether conduct is sufficient to amount to renunciation is assessed objectively, from the perspective of a reasonable person in the place of the innocent party. In *Woodar Investment v Wimpey Construction* (1980) at 287–8, Lord Keith explained:

> The matter is to be considered objectively. The claim being for wrongful repudiation of the contract it was necessary that the plaintiff's language should amount to a declaration of intention not to carry out the contract, or that it should be such that the defendant was justified in inferring from it such intention.

It has been said that renunciation should not 'be lightly found or inferred': *Shevill v Builders Licensing Board* (1982) at 633. Where there is a total renunciation, because a party states that they will not perform the contract at all, there are few difficulties. The innocent party is entitled to elect to terminate the contract. Such a refusal is, by definition, serious. But where the renunciation is less than total – for example, because the party indicates that they will deviate from the agreed mode of performance – then the situation is more complex. One of the parties is, in effect, saying that they will not perform one of more of the terms of the contract – not that they will not perform the contract as a whole. Whether a renunciation of this sort allows termination will depend on the type of term that the party is purporting to renounce, or the nature of the breach. It is sometimes said that the repudiation must go to the 'root of the contract' or be 'fundamental': *Foran v Wight* (1989) at 395, 416, 441.

A renunciation of an essential term, for example, would entitle the innocent party to terminate, provided that the other conditions for termination were met. But, in the case of an intermediate term, whether a renunciation is sufficient to allow a contract to be terminated must depend on the seriousness and likely consequences of the breach. If the breach has not yet occurred, a court will have to speculate. For example, in *Federal Commerce and Navigation v Molena Alpha* (1979), a threat by a shipowner to breach an intermediate term in a charterparty was held to be an anticipatory breach, allowing the charterers to terminate. Had the breach actually occurred, the Court was satisfied that the charterer would have been unable to carry out various contracts of carriage, thereby exposing them to considerable liability that could not be adequately compensated by damages.

16.13   Repudiation based on a misapprehension

Suppose that a party mistakenly makes a statement that they will not perform contractual obligations because of incorrect advice from their lawyer, or because they are otherwise convinced they are entitled to withhold performance. The general rule is that refusal to perform amounts to a repudiation and, if sufficiently serious, then the other party can terminate. Nevertheless, if a party, in good faith, believes that their non-performance is justified it is sometimes said that there is no repudiation. These cases are exceptional, however, and concern repudiations which pre-date the time due for performance.

In *Woodar*, the plaintiff agreed to sell land to the defendant. Completion was to occur after gaining planning permission. The defendant purchaser resiled from the deal, invoking in good faith, but mistakenly as it turned out, a purported contractual right to withdraw. In fact, the defendant had no such right. The majority held that the defendant had not repudiated. They were instead purporting to rely on an escape clause. The required intention to repudiate was missing. It was perhaps significant on the facts that the purchaser said throughout that they would perform, should their interpretation of the contact be wrong. In *DTR Nominees v Mona Homes* (1978) at 432, this sort of scenario was explained:

> No doubt there are cases in which a party, by insisting on an incorrect interpretation of a contract, evinces an intention that he [sic] will not perform the contract according to its terms. But there are other cases in which a party, though asserting a wrong view of a contract because he believes it to be correct, is willing to perform the contract according to its tenor. He may be willing to recognize his heresy once the true doctrine is enunciated or he may be willing to accept an authoritative exposition of the correct interpretation. In either event an intention to repudiate the contract could not be attributed to him.

It is far more likely that an inference of repudiation will be drawn where a party acts on an obviously untenable interpretation: see eg *Sopov v Kane Constructions* (2007).

16.14   Repudiation by an inability to perform

If one party indicates to the other that they are unable to perform, this has the same effect as an express refusal to perform: it amounts to a repudiation: *Bell v Scott* (1922) at 395–6. Similarly, if a party does something which has the effect of disabling themselves from performing the contract, this may be a repudiation. Disposing of a unique thing which is the subject matter of the contract is the clearest example: see eg *Schaefer v Schuhmann* (1972).

It has also been held that a party may terminate if they can establish that the other party is in fact unable to perform, regardless of any admission or action on their part. For example, in *Rawson v Hobbs* (1961), legislation in Western Australia required ministerial approval for the transfer of grazing land. Before the sale was complete, the purchasers were informed that the sale would not be approved. A majority of the High Court found that, although an express right of cancellation in the contract did not apply, the vendor did not have an ability to gain approval within the time for completion of the contract. The purchaser was therefore justified in terminating the contract.

In cases of renunciation, it does not matter whether or not the renouncing party could have performed. But where repudiation is based on an inability to perform that is said to exist in fact, it must be shown that the relevant party was wholly and finally disabled from performing. In *Universal Cargo Carriers v Citati* (1957), charterers were under an obligation to completely load a ship by a specified date. Before that time had expired, the ship owner terminated the contract on the grounds that the loading would not be possible within the time remaining. Loading of the ship was not an essential term. This meant that the owner could only have been justified in terminating if the delay had become so serious by then that it had frustrated the purpose of the charter. The case was remitted to an arbitrator to make findings on that matter.

In this case, Devlin J expressed the view (at 449) that repudiation cannot be based on an *inferred* (as opposed to actual) inability to perform, no matter how reasonable the basis for the belief.[13] On this approach, the doctrine of anticipatory breach cannot be invoked where a party appears to be unable to perform when the time comes, unless they admit this or have done something to disable themselves from performing. The innocent party in this situation must wait until an admission comes, or the time for performance arises.[14]

16.15   Termination for delay in performance

There will be some contracts, as in the case just discussed, where the time of performance is important. By reason of a delay in performance, one party may want to terminate the contract. This depends in the first instance on whether the parties have included a *time stipulation* in their contract.[15] This is simply a stipulation that performance must be rendered by a certain time, or within a specified period. Even in the absence of an express term to that effect, an obligation to perform within a reasonable time may sometimes be implied: see **12.05**.

A delay in performance by one party, unless excused by some other term, will confer a right on the other party to sue for damages for any loss caused by the delay. But whether it also allows that party to terminate the contract depends on the general rules set out above, together with some particular principles that, as explained below, have their roots in equitable doctrine.

In summary, a delay in performance will confer a right to terminate where: (a) there has been a breach of an essential time stipulation; (b) there has been non-compliance with a valid notice to perform (see below); or (c) the delay in performance is sufficiently serious to amount either to a repudiation or (possibly) a fundamental breach.

As with other types of term, whether a time stipulation is essential depends on the express or implied intentions of the parties. Including a statement that '*time is of the essence*', as is common in contracts for the sale of land, is perhaps the most obvious way of achieving that: see eg *Legione v Hateley* (1983) at 445.

16.16   Time stipulations at common law and in equity

Historically, the common law and equity treated time stipulations differently. The common law required strict compliance, whether time was of the essence or not. In the absence of a contrary intention, *any* breach of a time stipulation allowed the contract to be terminated. But the impact of that approach could be mitigated by a court exercising equitable jurisdiction. If, for example, a purchaser of land failed to tender the purchase price at the agreed time, then the court might (provided certain conditions were met) still order specific performance against the vendor. At the same time, however, the courts of equity developed a procedure whereby time could in effect be made of the essence, by serving on the defaulting party a notice to complete. If performance was not then rendered within a reasonable time, termination would be permitted.[16]

---

13   See also *Elders v Incitec Pivot* (2006).
14   But see Carter 1984.
15   See generally Lindgren 1982.
16   Technically, the notice does not actually make time of the essence, though it is often described as having that effect. Rather, non-compliance with the notice, if valid (see **16.17**), is treated as evidence of repudiation: *Ciavarella v Balmer* (1983) at 446.

When the administration of law and equity in England was fused in the nineteenth century, legislation was passed to confirm that the equitable approach should be taken to prevail. That statutory rule still exists today. For example, s 13 of the *Conveyancing Act 1919* (NSW) provides that:

> Stipulations in contracts, as to time or otherwise, which would not before the commencement of this Act have been deemed to be or to have become of the essence of such contracts in a court of equity, shall receive in all courts the same construction and effect as they would have heretofore received in such court.

Similar provisions are enacted in all States and Territories.[17] The statutes make clear that the equitable rules prevail. Unfortunately, however, there is disagreement about their precise application. According to the orthodox position, as stated by Kitto J in *Holland v Wiltshire* (1954) at 418–19, the legislation has limited relevance. It only applies if the party seeking to avoid the effect of a 'time of the essence' clause is also claiming equitable relief, by way of specific performance or injunction. For example, they may have paid late and, on the refusal of the seller to perform, be seeking specific performance. On this view, many situations are excluded because equitable relief will not always, or indeed often, be appropriate. For example, the remedy of specific performance is relevant to contracts for the sale of land, because land is treated as unique, but will not be granted for most other contracts: see **22.03**. In such instances, it is suggested, the statute cannot be used to justify construing a contract to allow completion within a reasonable time, as opposed to time being of the essence: *Louinder v Leis* (1982) at 524–5.

A more unorthodox interpretation of the equivalent English legislation was adopted by the House of Lords in *United Scientific Holdings v Burnley Borough Council* (1978). It held that a timetable in a rent review clause in a commercial leasing agreement did not make time of the essence. The surprising aspect of this reasoning was that it was justified on the basis of the statute, even though no equitable relief was sought. But orthodoxy was reasserted by the same court a few years later in *Bunge v Tradax* (1981). A clause requiring a buyer to nominate a port of loading within 15 days was held to be a condition which, when breached, entitled the seller to terminate the contract. Lord Roskill doubted whether the statute could be used as a general means of mitigating the impact of a time stipulation. Whether a time stipulation would allow termination if breached should be determined by the parties' intention. Further, it was held that in a 'mercantile' (or major commercial) contract, it would be assumed, even where it was not expressly stated, that time was intended to be of the essence. Australian courts have consistently adopted the orthodox and more limited interpretation: see eg *Michael Realty v Carr* (1977) at 561, 574; *Louinder v Leis* (1982) at 532.

16.17   Termination for delay where time is not of the essence

If a time stipulation is not essential, then Lord Wilberforce in *Bunge v Tradax* (at 715) doubted whether the intermediate term analysis was useful. He argued that a time stipulation is either

---

17   *Property Law Act 1958* (Vic) s 41; *Property Law Act 1974* (Qld) s 62; *Property Law Act 1969* (WA) s 21; *Law of Property Act 1936* (SA) s 16; *Supreme Court Civil Procedure Act 1932* (Tas) s 11(7); *Civil Law (Property) Act 2006* (ACT) s 501; *Law of Property Act 2000* (NT) s 65.

performed or it is not, because there is only one form of breach – namely, to be late in performing. But this analysis ignores the variable nature and consequences of lateness. To be a minute late may be a breach, but the consequences of performing a week late may be more serious. Arguably then, it should be possible to terminate for breach of a non-essential time stipulation where the delay is so serious as to substantially deprive the other party of the benefit of the contract, consistent with the discussion in **16.10**. In any event, such a delay is capable of being treated as repudiation. For example, in *Laurinda v Capalaba Park Shopping Centre* (1989) a lessor's failure for nine months to comply with its obligation to register a lease was held to have that quality, allowing the lessee to terminate.

Even when a time stipulation is not essential, nor the breach serious, the contract might still be terminated by issuing a notice against the party in breach, using the procedure originated by the courts of equity. In *Louinder v Leis* (1982), the High Court discussed the operation of a valid notice. A contract for the sale of land lacked a fixed date for completion and did not state that time was of the essence. Instead, the contract required that, within 28 days from the time that the vendor delivered their statement of title, the purchaser should tender a transfer to the vendor for execution. No transfer was tendered. The vendor issued a notice requiring completion of the contract within 21 days. When the notice was not complied with, the contract was terminated. The High Court held that whilst a notice requiring tender was permissible, a notice requiring completion was not. Because no time for completion was specified in the contract, completion in a reasonable time could be implied. No unreasonable delay had occurred which would have justified the issuing of a notice. A notice could only be issued after a breach of an express or implied time stipulation – though once a breach had occurred, the notice could be served right away. Mason J at 527 sought to justify the doctrine of notice:

> This solution is not unfair to the party who is guilty of a mere breach of contract. He [sic] is entitled to a notice which fixes a reasonable time in all the circumstances and those circumstances will include the fact that he has not been guilty of a serious breach of contract or of unreasonable or gross delay.

As Mason J made clear, the notice period must be reasonable. In *Laurinda*, a notice issued to the lessor to complete the registration of the lease within 14 days was held to be invalid on that basis, since registration would normally take longer than that. Furthermore, the notice did not clearly state that the time fixed for performance would be of the essence or, at the very least, that the lessee would regard a failure to complete in accordance with the notice as grounds to terminate the contract. But the invalidity of the notice did not prevent the lessee from terminating on the separate ground of repudiation.

Express rights to terminate

16.18 Termination clauses

The parties are at liberty to include a term within the contract that allows the contract to be terminated on breach, for certain types of breach, or on a certain event occurring or failing to occur, whether that amounts to a breach or not. A party may also be authorised to terminate whenever they choose – a provision sometimes called a *termination for convenience* clause. A termination clause may also deal with the consequences of termination. A contract may be terminated at common law – for example, because of a fundamental breach – yet still be subject to a process for termination laid down in the contract. A clause in the contract may also provide for certain remedies to be granted on termination. An express termination clause has the obvious advantage that it provides certainty. The parties are clearly informed about the consequences that will flow from a failure to perform. A well drafted clause may also provide a strong incentive to exact performance. An express right to terminate is common in commercial contracts and contracts involving the sale of land.

An express termination clause is easy enough to justify between two large commercial parties who are legally advised. In other situations, it might be objected that this type of clause may potentially allow exploitation of a weaker party. A clause can be inserted and used to escape from a bad bargain, particularly when a market has shifted. There is some limited statutory regulation of express termination clauses, as discussed in Chapter 20. Under s 23 of the Australian Consumer Law (ACL), an unfair term in a standard form consumer or small business contract will be treated as void. Section 25(1) of that legislation lists the type of terms that the law regards as unfair and includes '(b) a term that permits, or has the effect of permitting, one party (but not another party) to terminate the contract'. The existence of such clauses has indeed been highlighted in some of the examples to date of a contract being found or conceded to be unfair: see **20.30–20.31**.

Express termination clauses are subject to the usual rules of contractual interpretation.[18] In the face of ambiguity, there is a tendency for courts to read clauses of this sort narrowly in order to favour performance, rather than allowing a trivial breach to be a ground for a contract to be terminated. As Weinberg J observed in *Wallace-Smith v Thiess Infraco* (2005) at [131], 'in general such provisions are construed strictly, limiting the right to terminate where breaches are relatively innocuous'. This is an illustration of the *contra proferentem* principle: see **10.17**, **11.05**. There are other potential limits on the operation of express termination clauses. When a clause is so broadly drafted that the slightest breach might allow termination, a requirement of reasonableness and good faith has sometimes been implied into a commercial contract in order to restrict its operation: see eg *Burger King v Hungry Jack's* (2001) at 572–3, discussed in **12.20**.

Termination clauses generally require notice to be given as a prerequisite for terminating the contract. Notice will often come with conditions attached. Older authorities suggested that any conditions must be exactly complied with: see eg *Nund v McWaters* (1982). More recently, courts have been less inclined to worry too much about technical default in relation to the notice requirements, especially in a commercial contract: see eg *Pan Foods v ANZ Banking Group* (2000). Nevertheless, it is still best to be careful in adhering to termination procedures, because a failure to do so may amount to a repudiation of the contract: see eg *Commonwealth v Amann Aviation* (1991), discussed at **23.09.**

Unless the parties agree otherwise, an express contractual right to terminate is considered to run concurrently with a more general legal right to terminate; for example, because there is a breach of a term classified as essential: see eg *Holland v Wiltshire* (1954). In other words, the fact that the parties have expressly stipulated circumstances in which their contract may be terminated will not be taken to supersede or exclude any right

---

18   See generally Carter 1990.

at common law to terminate for breach of an essential term, a fundamental breach of an intermediate term, or a repudiation.

Whilst a contract may be terminated at common law for breach, or through a termination clause, the consequences are not identical. Unless the contract provides otherwise, the default position is that when a termination clause is invoked, there is no automatic right to claim 'loss of bargain' damages, as there would be at common law (see **23.04**). In *Shevill v Builders Licensing Board* (1982), a lessor terminated a lease under a termination clause and claimed damages for rent covering the full term of the lease. The High Court held that, because the failure to pay rent on time was not a breach of an essential term, termination was not justified at common law, and therefore loss of bargain damages could not be recovered. Had the lessor wanted to recover for rent for the entire term, then the termination clause needed to make that provision. Had they done so, there was no reason why the parties' intentions should not be respected: *Gumland v Duffy Brothers* (2008) at 259. It would also have been different had the lessee's breach (or breaches) amounted to a repudiation of their obligations: see eg *Progressive Mailing House v Tabali* (1985). That would have created a common law right to terminate and made loss of bargain damages available.

16.19   Statutory rights to terminate

Some statutes that regulate a particular type of contract confer a right on one or other party to terminate a contract. For example, s 60 of the *Insurance Contracts Act 1984* (Cth) permits an insurer to cancel an insurance contract where, for instance, the insured has acted in bad faith, failed to comply with their duty of disclosure or breached any provision in their policy. Any cancellation has to be notified in writing (s 59). Similarly, ss 178A–179 of the National Credit Code in Schedule 1 to the *National Consumer Credit Protection Act 2009* (Cth) permit the lessee to terminate a consumer lease in various circumstances. Sections 82–88 of the ACL likewise authorise and regulate the termination of an agreement for the supply of unsolicited goods or services to a consumer.

In other instances, a court or tribunal may be empowered to terminate a contract in remedying a statutory breach. For example, in making orders for the redress of loss or damage suffered as a result of a breach of the ACL, s 243(a)(ii) makes it clear that a court may declare a contract to be void as from a certain date (as opposed to ab initio). A statutory power to vary a contract to prevent it operating unfairly may also sometimes be used to create or modify a right to terminate: see **13.20**.

Implied rights to terminate without cause

16.20   Termination without cause

Although a contract can be terminated for actual or anticipatory breach, providing that the conditions discussed earlier are met, the common law makes no general provision for termination where there is no breach or cause. It is usually left to the parties to determine whether to make any express provision. It is common, for instance, for employment contracts to contain provisions permitting either the employer or the employee to end the relationship at any stage, without needing to have or state a particular reason.

Ordinarily, the absence of such a provision in a contract would not create any difficulty. But it may be different if the parties have not agreed on any duration for their arrangement and the agreement is not one that, like a sale, involves a single exchange. In such a case, in order to fill what would otherwise be a problematic gap, the law may imply a right to terminate the contract without cause.

In the case of an agreement to provide personal labour, the reason for doing this should be obvious. Without such a right, an indefinite contract of employment would be one of slavery. By default, therefore, a term is implied as a matter of law that such a contract may be terminated by either party giving reasonable notice: *Byrne v Australian Airlines* (1995) at 429. What constitutes a reasonable period for this purpose, at least when given by an employer, tends to increase with the duration of the employment and the degree of responsibility exercised by the employee.[19]

Although there is far less authority on the point, courts have also been willing to imply a term permitting the termination of other types of ongoing commercial arrangement. In *Crawford Fitting v Sydney Valve & Fitting* (1988), it was explained that whether such a term will be implied must depend on the subject matter of the agreement, the circumstances in which it was made, and the terms already included or omitted from the contract.[20] The contract here was a valuable commercial distribution agreement for the sale of technical products which required ongoing customer support and which had been operating for nearly 15 years. In this situation, six months was regarded as a reasonable period of notice on the basis that it would allow the parties to bring the contract to an end in a 'businesslike' manner.

In *Energy World v Maurice Hayes & Associates* (2007), by contrast, one month's notice was sufficient in relation to a contract for consultancy services of 'limited scope'. In *IOOF Building Society v Foxeden* (2009), however, 12 months' notice was considered to be appropriate in relation to a contract to operate a branch of a building society. The significant factors here were the substantial upfront expenses that the plaintiff had incurred in taking over the branch, and the fact that the agreement had only been in operation for just over two years, giving the plaintiff little time to have seen a return on its investment.

Exercising a right to terminate

16.21   Finding a basis for termination

Unless it contains an express provision to that effect, no contract is terminated automatically as a result of a serious breach or repudiation. The innocent party must *elect* (choose) to terminate, as discussed below. At the time of election, there needs to be a valid ground to terminate, but it need not be correctly identified. Even if the innocent party only becomes aware of those valid grounds after the purported termination, they may still use those grounds to (retrospectively) justify the termination: see eg *Concut v Worrell* (2000). Similarly, a party who incorrectly

---

19   See Stewart et al 2016: 718–20, 724–5; and see further Irving 2015.
20   Compare *Sante Wines v Paxton Wines* (2018), where the implication of a term requiring reasonable notice would have been inconsistent with an express term permitting written 'notification' of termination with immediate effect.

purports to exercise an express right of termination may, if challenged, rely upon a right to terminate that has arisen under the common law: see eg *Rawson v Hobbs* (1961). In *Downer EDI v Gillies* (2012) at [131], Allsop P summarised the effect of the leading High Court decision in *Shepherd v Felt and Textiles* (1931) when he spoke of the:

> well-known feature of the common law ... that a contracting party who gives a reason for a contractual position being taken (such as termination) does not by the giving of that reason (which may be wrong) deprive itself of a justification which existed, whether known of or not at the time.

Shepherd was dealing with the situation where termination could not be justified on the grounds originally given for terminating by the innocent party. It may be that the innocent party relies on a perfectly valid ground to terminate and then wishes to rely on a different ground for termination which is more favourable to them. This issue is especially likely to arise in the context of employment contracts. In *Melbourne Stadiums v Sautner* (2015), the employer, having purported to terminate an employee's contract under a clause requiring it to give six months' salary in lieu of notice, discovered misconduct on the part of the defendant and a few days later attempted to terminate the contract under a second clause which gave it the power to summarily dismiss the employee. A majority of the Full Court of the Federal Court took the view (at [112]) that the *Shepherd* principle does not allow a contract that has been lawfully terminated to be 'resuscitated and then re-terminated upon some ground not known at the time of the termination'. The suggested solution in such cases was to include in a termination clause a requirement that, should it later emerge that the contract could have been terminated for misconduct, any salary paid in lieu of notice must be repaid. On the facts of the case, however, it was found that the original attempt to terminate had not been effective. Under the terms of the contract, termination would only occur if the requisite payment was actually made. Since that had not yet happened, it was still open to the employer to change its mind and terminate summarily instead.

16.22   Election to terminate

A contract does not come to an end just because it has been seriously breached or repudiated, whatever the practical effect on the parties' relationship: *Visscher v Giudice* (2009) at [53]. As a general rule, the innocent party has a choice. They can either elect to terminate the contract or keep it alive by *affirming* it. Where there is an express right to terminate, then termination must take place in accordance with the contract. Typically, in this situation it will be necessary to give notice or even allow the other party an opportunity to remedy the breach. A contract may sometimes allow for automatic termination on the occurrence of a specified event; for example, a force majeure clause (see **15.04**) may terminate a contract when a particular event which is outside the control of the parties occurs. But where termination can be brought about by one of the parties, the courts are less inclined to conclude that the parties intended the contract to terminate automatically: *Gange v Sullivan* (1966) at 429, 441–2.

Aside from cases where the process of termination is governed by a contract or statute, election occurs according to the rules of the common law. These include the principle that an election, once made, is final. A contract cannot subsequently be revived after an election to terminate, unless the parties enter into a new contract: *Ogle v Comboyuro Investments* (1976) at 451. By contrast, as discussed further below, a contract that has been affirmed *can* subsequently be terminated, provided a new ground for termination has arisen or can be relied upon.

A valid election to terminate consists of words or conduct that unequivocally indicate an intention to take that step: see *Tropical Traders v Goonan* (1964). It is enough for the election to come to the other party's attention; it need not be communicated by the party purporting to elect: *Majik Markets v S & M Motor Repairs* (1987) at 54. Conduct by the party seeking to elect which is inconsistent with an intention on their part to perform is generally sufficiently unequivocal. A simple failure to perform, if sufficiently unequivocal, can sometimes amount to an election to terminate the contract: see eg *Vitol SA v Norelf* (1996).

Where a contract expressly confers a right to terminate, it does not matter that the terminating party may previously have breached or repudiated the contract: *Allphones Retail v Hoy Mobile* (2009). But otherwise, the general rule is that a party can only terminate if they themselves are ready, willing and able to perform their obligations under the contract: *DTR Nominees v Mona Homes* (1978) at 433.[21] A breach of an essential term or a fundamental breach will disqualify a party from exercising a common law right to terminate – though not, it would seem, more minor breaches: see *Almond Investors v Kualitree Nursery* (2011).[22]

This requirement can sometimes cause practical difficulties. In *Foran v Wight* (1989), shortly before the date fixed for completion of a contract for the sale of land, the vendors told the purchasers that they would be unable to complete in time. The purchasers failed to treat the repudiation as an anticipatory breach. They waited until the date for completion had passed and then sought to terminate. The vendors alleged that the purchasers did not have funds to complete on that day, and because they were not ready and willing to perform they were unable to terminate. Although the purchasers had failed to terminate for the anticipatory breach, they were not 'substantially incapable' of raising the purchase price. At that point in time, they were ready and willing to perform. The purchasers then failed to seek finance because of the representation by the vendors. According to Brennan, Deane and Dawson JJ, this meant that the vendors were estopped from arguing that the purchasers were not ready and willing to perform at the moment of actual breach.

16.23   Election to affirm

In order to affirm, the innocent party needs to know that it has a choice to either continue with the contract or to terminate it. Clearly, therefore, a party cannot be held to have affirmed by continuing to perform their own obligations if they were unaware at the time

---

21   As to whether this should be true even in a case of anticipatory breach, see the differing views noted in *Upside Property Group v Tekin* (2017) at [14]–[15]. It was held in that case that even if a purchaser could terminate a contract for sale in response to the vendor's repudiation, the fact that the purchaser lacked the finance to complete the sale precluded it from claiming damages.

22   For critical analysis of the case law on this issue, see O'Brien 2014. In *Highmist v Tricare* (2005) at [61], Keane JA suggested that it makes little commercial sense to say that where both parties are resolved not to perform the contract, the contract continues 'in existence in some legal limbo' because neither party is ready, willing and able to perform.

that the other party had breached or repudiated the contract. But how precise or accurate their knowledge must be for this purpose is unclear.[23] A party may be aware of facts that give them the right to terminate, but not that the right exists. It is possible that a distinction may be drawn here between an express right of termination and one arising under the common law: see eg *Peyman v Lanjani* (1985).[24] In the case of the former, the High Court's decision in *Sargent v ASL Developments* (1974) establishes that knowledge of the facts will be sufficient. Mason J considered (at 658) that the same would be true in relation to a common law right of termination. But Stephen J (with whom McTiernan ACJ agreed) left the point open (at 644–5). In *Khoury v Government Insurance Office* (1984) at 634, Mason, Brennan, Deane and Dawson JJ reiterated that where rights arise under the terms of a contract, knowledge of the facts will be sufficient for there to be an affirmation, but did not resolve the difference in opinion in *Sargent* about rights arising under the common law.

Although the innocent party need not make an immediate choice to terminate or affirm, if they fail to do so in a reasonable time then they run the risk that they will be taken to have affirmed the contract. Giving the other party more time to perform need not, however, amount to affirmation. In *Tropical Traders v Goonan* (1964), in a contract for the sale of land to be paid for by instalments, time was made of the essence. The purchaser sought an extension to pay the final instalment, which was granted by the vendor 'without prejudice to and in no way varying the [vendor's] right to the strict enforcement of the contract'. The purchaser failed to pay the vendor by the agreed extension date, so the vendor was entitled to terminate. Time remained of the essence. Nor was there an affirmation in the face of this breach, because the vendor's rights were expressly preserved and merely meant that the time for electing either way would be delayed. The fact that the vendor had previously accepted late payments, thereby affirming the contract on each occasion, did not prevent a new right to terminate arising and being exercised when the final instalment was late.

When a contract is affirmed, it continues despite the breach. As a result, the party in breach may themselves gain a right to terminate if the party affirming commits a breach. In *Bowes v Chaleyer* (1923), a contract of sale provided that goods were to be delivered in two stages: 'Half as soon as possible. Half two months later.' After the first consignment had arrived, the buyer purported to repudiate the contract, but the seller affirmed. When the goods were delivered, the mode of delivery put the seller in breach of a condition and the buyer was held to be entitled to terminate.

If an affirming party does not perform their side of the contract, they may nevertheless be absolved of the need to perform their obligations where the other party intimates that the performance would be futile. For example, in *Peter Turnbull v Mundus Trading* (1954), a seller clearly intimated to a buyer that it was useless to perform a condition in the contract and that the buyer need not do so. This is seen as a kind of waiver or estoppel: see *Foran v Wight* (1989) at 396, 434.

---

23   See Bigwood 2011.
24   According to *Coastal Estates v Melevende* (1965), this is the position in relation to a right to rescind a contract for misrepresentation: see **18.13**.

16.24   Relief against forfeiture

The right to terminate is not entirely without limits. In recent decades, the subject of relief for unfair termination has become bound up in the wider debate about the place of equity in Australian contract law. One established basis for equitable intervention is provided by the doctrine of promissory estoppel. As the High Court confirmed in *Legione v Hateley* (1983), a party may be estopped from unconscionably exercising a right to terminate where they have led the defaulting party to believe that they will not terminate and the defaulting party has relied on that belief to their detriment: see **7.07**. Beyond that, there is no general jurisdiction to protect a party in breach by relieving against the loss of benefit of the contract they will suffer by the termination. Nevertheless, equity has traditionally granted *relief against forfeiture* where termination would result in the loss of a real or personal proprietary or possessory right. Rather than removing a property right, relief against forfeiture may allow a party in breach extra time to perform. Relief against forfeiture is particularly important for breaches of leasehold covenants. It may be used to restrict a landlord's right to forfeit a lease for breach of covenant by a tenant, in return for the tenant rectifying the breach. By contrast, the courts are usually more reluctant to grant relief against forfeiture to commercial parties: see *The Scaptrade* (1983).

A series of High Court decisions have considered the application of relief against forfeiture in contracts for the sale of land. When a person enters into a valid agreement to purchase land, they are considered to obtain an equitable interest in that land that is commensurate with their ability to obtain an order for specific performance of the agreement. In *Legione v Hateley*, a majority held that, in principle, a court might grant relief against forfeiture of the purchaser's beneficial interest in the land, even where he had failed to comply with a time of the essence condition. It was stressed that relief was exceptional. Mason and Deane JJ gave a useful list of factors (at 449) that a court will consider in granting relief:

> In the ultimate analysis the result in a given case will depend upon the resolution of subsidiary questions which inevitably arise. The more important of these are: (1) Did the conduct of the vendor contribute to the purchaser's breach? (2) Was the purchaser's breach (a) trivial or slight, and (b) inadvertent and not wilful? (3) What damage or other adverse consequences did the vendor suffer by reason of the purchaser's breach? (4) What is the magnitude of the purchaser's loss and the vendor's gain if the forfeiture is to stand? (5) Is specific performance with or without compensation an adequate safeguard for the vendor?

By contemplating an order for specific performance, the decision conflicted with longstanding Privy Council authority that no relief against forfeiture by way of specific performance could be granted when there was a breach of a time of the essence condition. Mason and Deane JJ explained (at 447) that 'if there be fraud, mistake, accident, surprise or some other element which would make it unconscionable or inequitable to insist on forfeiture of the purchaser's interest', then it was proper to order specific performance.[25] Since the point had not been fully argued at trial, the matter was remitted for further consideration, though the case appears to have settled before any further hearing.

---

25   As to the meaning of the terms fraud, mistake, accident or surprise in this context, see **20.02**.

Relief against forfeiture was actually granted in *Stern v McArthur* (1988). A contract for the sale of land provided for payment of the price by instalments over a number of years. The purchasers, a husband and wife, went into possession and built a house on the land. In 1977, they separated and the husband defaulted on the payment of instalments without the wife's knowledge. She then made up the arrears. On her failure to pay the balance, the vendors terminated the contract. Before the action was commenced the balance was tendered and refused. A majority granted relief on the grounds that the vendors had acted unconscionably. It was stressed that, had the vendors been allowed to terminate, they would get a windfall through the increase in value of the property. In his dissent, Mason CJ signalled that he favoured a more cautious approach. He warned (at 505) that relief against forfeiture did 'not authorise a court to reshape contractual relations into a form that a court thinks more reasonable or fair where subsequent events have rendered one side's situation more favourable'.

More recent High Court authority has clarified the position. *Tanwar Enterprises v Cauchi* (2003) again involved the sale of land. A deposit was paid and the date for completion was extended. For the new date, time was of the essence. Funds for the purchase were coming from overseas and arrived a day after the agreed completion date. The vendor knew that the purchaser wished to complete, but sought to terminate the contract anyway. The purchaser sought specific performance, among other grounds on the basis of relief against forfeiture. Gleeson CJ, McHugh, Gummow, Hayne and Heydon JJ identified the 'special heads' of fraud, accident, mistake or surprise which justified equity's intervention and then continued (at [58]):

> No doubt the decided cases in which the operation of these 'special heads' is considered do not disclose exhaustively the circumstances which merit this equitable intervention. But, at least where accident and mistake are not involved, it will be necessary to point to the conduct of the vendor as having in some significant respect caused or contributed to the breach of the essential time stipulation.

At the same time, they stressed (at [59]) that there was no justification for treating relief as 'exceptional'. Kirby J, having exhaustively examined the basis for relief, disagreed. It was proper, he said (at [106]), to consider whether the party seeking relief was 'disadvantaged' or 'vulnerable', or whether it is a commercial contract. Callinan J also insisted (at [145]) that relief would only be granted in exceptional circumstances. The High Court was in agreement, however, that no relief against forfeiture should be granted on the facts.[26]

16.25   A broader restriction on unfair termination?

Some of the language used in the relief against forfeiture cases, and others, hints at a broader doctrine of relief against unconscionable termination.[27] For example in *Stern v McArthur* (1988) at 526, Deane and Dawson JJ said:

---

26   For a further example of relief being refused, see *Auburn Shopping Village v Nelmeer Hoteliers* (2018).
27   Indeed, it has been suggested that the principle endorsed in *Tanwar* is not concerned with relief against forfeiture at all, but should be seen as a new head of equitable relief: see Heydon et al 2015: [18–340]; *Barrak v Jaswil Properties* (2016) at [69]. But how widely it might extend, beyond contracts for the sale of land, is not clear.

> The circumstances must be such as to make it plain that it is necessary to intervene to avoid injustice or, what is the same thing, to relieve against unconscionable – or, more accurately, unconscientious – conduct.

Similar statements were made by Mason and Deane JJ in *Legione v Hateley* (1983) at 444 and by Mason CJ in *Foran v Wight* (1989) at 394. Expressed in these terms there is no reason in theory why intervention should be limited to those cases which fall within the traditional scope of relief against forfeiture. The language used might allow relief where there was no threat to a property right by termination, and no basis for any claim in estoppel. However, whether or not relief against unconscionable termination extends beyond those cases remains unclear.[28]

The same is true in relation to the duty of good faith and fair dealing that, at least according to some judges, should routinely be implied into all contracts, or at least certain types of contract. Without repeating the discussion in Chapter 12, there have been cases in which a duty of this kind has been invoked to require that a contractual power to terminate be exercised reasonably and in good faith: see eg *Burger King v Hungry Jack's* (2001); *Adventure World Travel v Newsom* (2014) at [26], [44]. Furthermore, even in the absence of a duty of good faith, courts may interpret a power to terminate on specified grounds as requiring an honest and reasonable assessment of whether those grounds exist: see eg *Renard Constructions v Minister of Public Works* (1992). By contrast, the unqualified discretion conferred by a termination for convenience provision is less likely to attract any implied requirement of good faith: see eg *Trans Petroleum v White Gum Petroleum* (2012) at [155].[29]

A decision which neatly illustrates these propositions is that of the New South Wales Court of Appeal in *Bartlett v ANZ Bank* (2016). The contract here provided that an employee could be summarily dismissed if, in the bank's opinion, he had engaged in serious misconduct. The Court rejected the bank's argument that, so long as it actually held the necessary opinion, it did not need to prove the employee's guilt. The relevant term was construed to mean that the bank's opinion was only relevant to the assessment of the seriousness of any proven misconduct. Furthermore, even if the bank's opinion was sufficient, it was obliged to act reasonably in forming that opinion. The deficiencies in its investigation meant that it had failed to do this. The dismissal was therefore wrongful. But, in assessing damages for the bank's breach of contract, the Court took account of the fact that if the employee had not been summarily dismissed, the bank would have exercised a separate power to give four months' notice of termination 'for any reason'. That power was found *not* to be subject to any duty to act reasonably.

On the other hand, whatever the uncertainties about the doctrine of relief against forfeiture or a duty of good faith, they do not affect the operation of the type of statutory prohibition on unconscionable conduct found in s 21 of the ACL (see **20.15–20.16**). A provision of this kind may be invoked to challenge instances of unfair termination, whether or not any property rights are involved, though only if the conduct concerned is clearly unreasonable: see eg *Garry Rogers Motors v Subaru* (1999); *Allphones Retail v Hoy Mobile* (2009).

---

28   Compare the more cautious view expressed in *Tenth Vandy v Natwest Markets* (2012) at [133]–[134].
29   This is not to deny that there have been suggestions to the contrary: see Dixon 2017 for a discussion of the case law on this and other issues concerning termination for convenience clauses.

16.26   Unfair affirmation

The general rule is that the innocent party can always choose to affirm should they so wish, even when to do so would cause hardship to the party in breach. The case law has emphasised this element of choice: see eg *Peter Turnbull v Mundus Trading* (1954) at 250. In many instances, however, an affirmation that the other party is unwilling to accept will be an empty gesture. If the party in breach is unwilling to perform, there may be little that the innocent party can do to obtain any benefit from the contract. For example, if a vendor of goods persistently refuses to deliver, there is little point in the purchaser keeping the contract alive. They will not usually be able to obtain any order for specific performance (see **22.03**), and unless the purchaser accepts delivery, they cannot claim the price. Similarly, if an employer wrongfully dismisses an employee, the latter may affirm the contract and try to turn up to work. But, unless the employer relents, or their contract is an unusual one, they will be unable to earn any wages: see **12.07**. Nor, again, can they compel the employer to allow them to work: see **22.07**. Furthermore, if the employee tries to sue for damages, the principle of mitigation of loss (see **23.18**) means that they may be denied any claim for income that they could have obtained from another employer.

Occasionally, however, an innocent party may be able to keep a contract alive in the face of a repudiation, perform their side of the contract without any cooperation from the other party, and earn a sum of money which they can claim through an action for debt. Since their action is not one for damages, then the principle of mitigation of loss should have no application.

This is what happened in *White & Carter v McGregor* (1962). The defendant agreed to renew a contract under which the plaintiff agreed to display advertisements for the defendant's business on plates attached to litter bins. Later the same day, the defendant wrote to the plaintiff stating that they no longer wished to renew the contract. The plaintiff refused to accept the cancellation, proceeded to display the advertisements, and in due course brought an action to recover the contract price. The House of Lords held by majority that the plaintiff was not under any obligation to accept the defendant's breach, even though it was unfortunate that the defendant had been left with 'an unwanted contract causing an apparent waste of time and money' (at 445). Had the plaintiffs terminated they could only have recovered damages for breach of contract. Given they had not yet begun to perform, these were likely to be small. By continuing the contract, however, they could claim the much higher contract price by way of an action in debt. Importantly too, they did not need the defendant's cooperation, since they already had all the material they needed for the advertisements.

One member of the majority, Lord Reid, expressed a tentative qualification. He suggested (at 431) that 'it may well be that, if it can be shown that a person has no legitimate interest, financial or otherwise, in performing the contract rather than claiming damages, he ought not to be allowed to saddle the other party with an additional burden with no benefit at all'. To say that there are problems with this observation would be an understatement. Lord Reid did not put forward any legal basis for such a restriction. Nor did he explain what would or would not count as a 'legitimate interest' – or what that interest was in the case before him, given that he agreed that the plaintiff could recover.

Nevertheless, despite the absence of any support for such a limitation in the other majority judgments, it has subsequently been applied in later English cases. For example, in *The*

Alaskan Trader (1984), a ship that was chartered by the defendant for two years required extensive repairs part way through the charter. The defendant stated that it had no further use for the ship, but the plaintiff nevertheless spent large sums repairing the ship and, when it was repaired, kept the ship and its crew ready to receive instructions from the defendant for the remaining eight months of the charter. The defendant had paid the plaintiff for the hire period in advance. The plaintiff refused to return the hire. It was held that the plaintiff had acted wholly unreasonably in refusing to accept the breach and that on (unspecified) 'equitable grounds' it was not entitled to retain the hire payments. In the absence of the defendant's liability for the hire charges, the plaintiff was limited to damages, which in a case like this could be readily assessed.

It does not appear that the issue has arisen for decision in Australia. If and when it does, it will be interesting to see whether the orthodox position articulated by the other members of the majority in *White & Carter* will be applied, or whether Lord Reid's qualification is accepted. It is possible that the limitation on unreasonable claims might be justified by reference to an overriding duty of good faith – if such a duty exists.[30]

Termination by agreement

16.27   Mutual consent to termination

The parties to a contract may agree at any time to bring it to an end. This agreement is itself regarded as a contract. As such, the usual requirements for contract formation, outlined in Chapter 5, need to be met. Where both parties have yet to perform any or all of the original contract then finding consideration, which is required for a binding contract without a deed, is not too difficult. Each party is agreeing to give up some, or all, of the other party's performance. Where one of the parties has completely performed their obligations under the contract, however, then the reciprocity required by consideration is missing. Only one party is agreeing to give up a right to performance. The only option in this situation may be to use a deed, or for the party whose obligations are being discharged to agree to pay or do something extra in return, even something nominal.

In some instances, the parties intend to continue to deal with one another, but on new terms. A subsequent agreement in this situation will not always expressly state if it is terminating or simply varying the existing contract. The distinction between the two has been described as 'a matter of degree': *Tallerman v Nathan's Merchandise* (1957) at 113. Ultimately, it is a matter of ascertaining the parties' intentions: see **13.03**. One situation where termination is likely to be inferred, however, is where the later agreement deals with the whole of the subject matter of the earlier agreement, but in a way that is inconsistent with it: see eg *Hillam v Iacullo* (2015); *Balanced Securities v Dumayne* (2017). Where a contract is replaced in this way, this is sometimes referred to as a novation, though as noted in **14.07** the more common use of that term involves a substitution of one of the parties, not just the terms.

---

30   See Dahdal 2015.

16.28   Abandonment

A contract can be *abandoned* even without a subsequent agreement. Care, however, has to be taken with this concept. If one party simply walks away from a contract and refuses to perform it, this is a repudiation, in accordance with the principles described earlier in the chapter. The innocent party in this situation may accept the repudiation as terminating the contract and sue for damages, but it is still the innocent party's election that brings the contract to an end.[31] Abandonment, by contrast, means that *both* parties are treating the contract as being at an end, without either party being able to justify the termination as a response to wrongdoing on the part of the other.

In *DTR Nominees v Mona Homes* (1978), the parties disagreed on the correct interpretation of a contract for the sale of land. Both purported to terminate the contract, but neither were entitled to do so. The High Court held that the parties had conducted themselves in such a way that they had abandoned the contract.[32] The facts made it fairly easy to reach this conclusion because both parties had believed – albeit incorrectly – that they were entitled to terminate for breach and repudiation respectively. Abandonment requires some kind of consensus to abandon. This will be easier to find when a contract is executory. Where there is part performance by the parties it will be more difficult to argue the contract has been abandoned even where many years pass without performance by either party. In *Fitzgerald v Masters* (1956) at 432 it was said that:

> There can be no doubt that, where what has been called an 'inordinate' length of time has been allowed to elapse, during which neither party has attempted to perform, or called upon the other to perform, a contract made between them, it may be inferred that the contract has been abandoned . . . What is really inferred in such a case is that the contract has been discharged by agreement, each party being entitled to assume from a long-continued ignoring of the contract on both sides that . . . 'the matter is off altogether'.

The contract in this case concerned a sale of land to be paid in instalments. More than half the purchase price was paid. The purchaser had an equitable interest in the property which was registered. The High Court held that it was impossible in these circumstances to suppose that the purchaser intended to allow the vendor to keep the money and the land. Ultimately, abandonment is determined by looking at the intention of the parties. In common with intention in contract formation, an intention to abandon is judged objectively from the conduct of the parties, rather than inquiring into their subjective intentions: see *CMG Investments v Chelliah* (2003) at [18]; *Técnicas Reunidas SA v Andrew* (2018) at [52].

---

31   But see Stewart et al 2016: 740–1, noting a different view taken in certain cases dealing with 'abandonment' by employees.

32   For other recent examples, see *Protector Glass Industries v Southern Cross Autoglass* (2015); *JR Consulting & Drafting v Cummings* (2016).

17

CONSEQUENCES OF TERMINATION

Effect of termination

17.01   Primary and secondary obligations

Termination is effective from the moment of election – that is, the point at which the terminating party elects to terminate a contract rather than affirm it (see **16.22**). The exact consequences of that termination will depend on the nature of the contractual obligations in question. In *Photo Production v Securicor Transport* (1980) at 848–9, Lord Diplock examined the effect of termination for breach or repudiation in some detail.[1] He explained that when a contract is terminated both parties are discharged from their future *primary obligations*. Primary obligations are at the core of a contract. The term describes those obligations placed on the parties to perform as agreed under the contract. These can arise before and after the contract is terminated. Future primary obligations are those which fall due to be performed after termination. If a contract is terminated on 1 June, any obligation to perform that arises on 2 June will be a future primary obligation.

A terminating party, even though innocent of the breach of contract that led to the termination, needs to be careful. As explained in the next section, any primary obligations which have fallen due before the termination, and are therefore not future obligations, may still be enforceable, including by the party in breach.[2] In addition, damages remain payable for any breaches of contract that predate the termination. Future primary obligations are different. When the contract is terminated, the general rule is that the party in breach, as well as the innocent party, is released from those obligations. In the case of the innocent party, they are no longer required to perform post-termination obligations. The contract-breaker is in a different position. There is no clean slate. Their unperformed future primary obligations are replaced by a *secondary* (remedial) obligation to pay compensation by way of 'loss of bargain' damages: see **23.04**. The right of the innocent party to claim performance is therefore turned into a right to claim damages.

The principle that future primary obligations are discharged on termination does admit some exceptions. In particular, if the parties clearly intend a primary obligation to continue in effect after termination, it may do so. An obvious example here is a post-employment restraint. An employee may promise that, after their employment comes to an end, they will not work for or establish a competing business. Under the doctrine of restraint of trade, considered in **21.23–21.30**, many promises of this type are treated as contrary to public policy. But subject to one exception mentioned below, there is no doubt that a reasonable restraint may be enforced even if contained in an employment contract that has otherwise come to an end.

17.02   Ancillary obligations

Primary obligations are obligations to perform, while secondary obligations require the payment of compensation in the event of a breach. A third group of obligations are known as ancillary obligations. These will not occur in every contract. Whilst the obligation to perform does not

---

1   In the earlier Australian case of *McDonald v Dennys Lascelles* (1933) at 476–7, Dixon J used different terminology, but offered a similar (and very widely cited) analysis.

2   This is subject, however, to the availability of certain restitutionary remedies, as discussed later in the chapter.

usually survive termination, *ancillary obligations* are different. They are often, by their very nature, designed to survive termination. For example, a clause in a contract may provide for arbitration in the event of a dispute arising over a breach. A provision of this type is considered to remain binding even after the termination of the contract: *Heyman v Darwins* (1942). Similarly, when, on its true construction, a limitation or exclusion clause covers a particular breach, the fact that the breach may have led to the contract being terminated will not preclude the party in breach from relying on such a clause: see *Photo Production v Securicor Transport* (1980), as discussed in **11.06**. A commercial contract may also often contain an agreed (or 'liquidated') damages clause. Its purpose is to fix the sum to be recovered in the event of a breach. Provided the clause is not classified as a penalty (see **22.19–22.24**), it too may survive termination.

Both exclusion and limitation clauses may, by their nature, be relied on by a party in breach. A different rule seems to apply to restraint of trade clauses. Despite the fact that provisions of this kind may be intended to survive termination in the same way as an exclusion or limitation clause, they cannot generally be enforced by a party whose breach or repudiation led to a termination: see **21.29**.

17.03   Termination other than for breach

The principles outlined above and discussed further in the sections that follow have generally been developed in cases dealing with termination for breach or repudiation. There are situations where a contract can be terminated other than for breach. The contract may contain terms which allow termination by the parties. A good example is provided by a termination for convenience clause. A clause such as this allows a party to terminate without incurring liability to the other party in damages: see **16.18**. The precise consequences of the clause will depend on the parties' intentions. In the absence of any contrary indication, the same rules that apply when a contract is terminated for breach will operate by default: see *Larratt v Bankers and Traders Insurance* (1941) at 225–6. This means that it will be inferred that any termination operates to discharge only future obligations, leaving accrued rights enforceable. As we have seen, this is the position where a contract is frustrated, at least as a matter of common law: see **15.14**. It applies where a contract comes to an end because of the occurrence or non-fulfilment of some type of contingency: see eg *Westralian Farmers v Commonwealth Agricultural Service Engineers* (1936) at 369, 379. The same is true where a contract is abandoned (see **16.28**), unless the parties clearly intend otherwise: *Cedar Meats v Five Star Lamb* (2014).

Recognition and enforcement of accrued rights

17.04   Accrued rights after termination

As pointed out in **16.02**, termination is not like rescission, in that some rights survive termination. Rights that have accrued under a terminated contract remain enforceable, unless the contract provides otherwise.[3] The most important accrued right is a right to damages. The

---

3   This is true even of rights accrued between the point at which one party repudiates and the other elects to terminate: see eg *Kyren v Wunda Projects* (2012).

party who terminates may recover damages for breaches arising prior to termination. They may themselves also be guilty of a breach, in which case they too may have to pay damages. The fact that they have terminated does not absolve them of their own breaches.

Unperformed primary obligations, as already noted, are generally discharged by termination. Once the contract is at an end, there is no longer any requirement to perform unless the contract provides otherwise. The most common example of a situation in which a contract provides otherwise is the right to payment of a fixed sum under the contract which has unconditionally accrued prior to termination. For instance, in *Elkhoury v Farrow Mortgage Services* (1993), when a contract was repudiated by a creditor, the principal plus interest on a loan was still payable by the debtor. This sum is usually claimed as a debt. It is unconditional because payment is required, irrespective of complete performance by the other party. In these cases, termination does not discharge the primary obligation.

An accrued right to payment which arises before termination but is payable at a future point, after the contract has been terminated, may also remain enforceable. In *Westralian Farmers v Commonwealth Agricultural Service Engineers* (1936), the plaintiff agreed with an American manufacturer to import tractors into Australia. The defendant agreed to purchase agreed quantities of the tractors at a fixed price and pay the plaintiff a percentage of the price by way of commission. The fixed price was to be paid to the manufacturer, and the commission was to be paid to the plaintiff on the arrival of the tractors. It was held that a commission for the sale of tractors could be recovered, because the commission had been earned prior to the termination, despite the fact the termination occurred prior to the arrival of the tractors with the defendant. Payment of the commission was merely contingent on the later arrival of the tractors.

17.05   Part payments

Whether money due under the contract is an accrued right which survives termination is determined by the intentions of the parties. There are plenty of examples of accrued rights. A hire purchase contract usually requires an initial payment and then the purchaser is required to make periodic payments for the use of the goods. Even if the goods are repossessed for non-payment the hirer remains bound to pay for hire of the goods during the period prior to termination: *Brooks v Bernstein* (1909).

In the case of such an agreement, the hirer had received the benefit of the goods for a period of time. The hire price was earned. Contracts which require progress payments, which are common in the construction industry, can be explained in the same way. A progress payment is an instalment of the total price paid as the work is carried out. In *Stocznia Gdanska v Latvian Shipping* (1998), it was held that such a payment was earned by the shipbuilder's performance in designing and building part of the ship. They were entitled to payment, despite the termination, and despite the fact that the ship was never delivered.[4]

---

4   But see Carter & Tolhurst 2009: 202, seeking to explain this decision on the basis of the particular term in the contract that permitted the builder to claim the relevant payments once notice was given of keel laying. The authors criticise the House of Lords' earlier decision to allow such recovery in *Hyundai Heavy Industries v Papadopoulos* (1980), although the reasoning in the two cases seems hard to distinguish.

Other types of liquidated sums are not generally recoverable. They have not been earned. For example, when a contract to perform a service for a fixed price is terminated before it is complete, the innocent party will be limited to an action in damages or a claim in restitution. They will not be able to recover the contract price in debt. Provided that affirmation is not unfair (see **16.26**), a better option might be to elect to affirm in the face of breach and complete performance.

McDonald v Dennys Lascelles (1933) concerned a sale of land. The purchasers paid an initial deposit and subsequently paid instalments for a number of years. They then defaulted. The vendor terminated the contract. It was held that the vendor was not entitled to retain the instalments. Dixon J explained (at 477):

> When a contract stipulates for payment of part of the purchase money in advance, the purchaser relying only on the vendor's promise to give him [sic] a conveyance, the vendor is entitled to enforce payment before the time has arrived for conveying the land; yet his title to retain the money has been considered not to be absolute but conditional upon the subsequent completion of the contract.

The right to payment of instalments in a contract for the sale of land is not an accrued right. Payment is conditional upon completion. Once the contract is terminated, the condition cannot be met. If instalments have already been paid, they can usually be recovered by the purchaser, using an action for money had and received: see **17.07**.

Dixon J also discussed what would happen if a contract expressly provided that instalments could be retained on termination. Whilst this would make the payment an accrued right, he suggested (at 478) that it may be subject to a claim by the payer for *relief against forfeiture*. In accordance with the equitable principles outlined in **16.24**, the payer would need to show that it would unconscionable for the payee to retain the payment. The mere fact that the payee would be enriched by retaining the payment would not be sufficient.

17.06   Deposits

A *deposit* is treated differently to a payment by instalment. It has a dual character. It is a payment of part of the purchase price. But it has also been described as a payment 'in earnest' – that is, a payment designed to secure performance by the payer: see eg *Ashdown v Kirk* (1999) at 8. In contracts for the sale of land, it is customary to pay anywhere up to 10 per cent of the sale price by way of a deposit. It is generally accepted that a deposit will be forfeited by the purchaser if they do not complete the sale. As Bryson JA explained in *Luu v Sovereign Developments* (2006) at [24]:

> Where parties make an agreement for a sale which is to be completed at some time in the future it is unremarkable and only to be expected that the vendor will require the purchaser to pay some part of the purchase money straight away so as to show that the purchaser is in earnest in committing himself to pay the rest, on the understanding that the purchaser will not get his earnest money back if he does not complete the sale.

Deposits can create accrued rights, as illustrated by *Bot v Ristevski* (1981). Under a contract for the sale of a house and land, part of the deposit was payable on the signing of the sale note, the balance of the deposit within seven days thereafter, and the residue of the purchase money at a later date. After payment of the initial part of the deposit, and before the balance of the deposit was paid, the purchasers repudiated the contract and the vendors terminated. It was held that the vendors could recover the balance of the unpaid deposit. Payment of a deposit is different from the payment of an instalment because it is not conditional on completion of the sale.

A deposit of up to 10 per cent will generally be enforceable without much difficulty. But there are limits. For historical reasons, the rule against penalties does not apply to genuine deposits: see *Andrews v ANZ Banking Group* (2012) at [43].[5] It does not matter that the amount of a deposit does not represent a genuine pre-estimate of the payee's loss if the transaction fails to go ahead. Deposits have a different purpose to agreed damages clauses: see *NLS v Hughes* (1966) at 589. Nevertheless, a deposit must still be reasonable: see *Workers Trust Bank v Dojap* (1993) at 579. How much – or how much more than 10 per cent – will be considered reasonable depends on the circumstances of each case. For example, in *Freedom v AHR Constructions* (1987), payments totalling more than one-third of the purchase price of an apartment were treated as instalments rather than a deposit, at least to the extent they exceeded 10 per cent. But in *Coates v Sarich* (1964), a deposit of 27 per cent was considered reasonable, in the context of a purchase price that was to be paid off over many years.

Furthermore, what is called a deposit may sometimes be structured in a way that it *does* constitute a penalty. In *Luu v Sovereign Developments* (2006), a much-amended contract for the sale of land provided for a sum of less than one per cent of the purchase price to be paid on the making of the contract. But a further condition made the 'balance' of what was described as a 10 per cent deposit payable by the purchaser in the event of default. The New South Wales Court of Appeal held that this condition was a penalty. As Bryson JA put it (at [24]), it did not 'truly have the character of earnest money paid on or in relation to entering into the contract'. The fact that the parties could simply have provided for a 10 per cent deposit in the first place was irrelevant.

In New South Wales and Victoria, there are statutory powers for a court to order the return of a deposit in a contract for the sale of land where a court refuses to grant specific performance.[6] The application of the power is a matter for the court's discretion. But it has been held that the key question is whether it is 'unjust and inequitable' to retain the deposit: *Lucas and Tait (Investments) v Victoria Securities* (1973) at 272; and see eg *PC Developments v Revell* (1991).

Finally, it should be noted that where it is the *vendor* who defaults, the usual understanding is that any deposit paid by the purchaser must be returned. This will be the case even if the deposit has been described as 'non-refundable': *CCP Australian Airships v Primus Telecommunications* (2004). The right to recover a deposit in such a case is achieved by bringing a restitutionary claim, to which we now turn.

Restitutionary claims

17.07   Claims for the return of money

The precise theoretical basis of restitution remains contested. Some have argued that it is based on the idea of unjust enrichment. This is not the prevailing view in Australia, where the courts

---

have said that such claims are justified on the grounds that retention of the money is unconscionable. This debate is discussed in more detail in **24.12**. Nevertheless, it is not in dispute that a claim may be brought to recover money paid prior to a contract being terminated, under an action for money had and received. But such a claim can only succeed if the payer can show a *total failure of consideration*. 'Consideration' in this context simply means counter-performance. This is quite different to the standard meaning of the term, as described in **5.27–5.35**. Even if sufficient consideration was supplied to form a valid contract, a payer may still be able to show a total failure of consideration for a payment made under that contract. It is enough that the payer has not received what they bargained to get in return for that payment. This applies even if it was the payer's own breach or repudiation that led to the termination of the contract.

Everything depends then on the purpose of the payment. For example, a reasonable deposit cannot normally be recovered because it has been paid to secure a right to purchase land or goods, or to obtain services. Even if the contract is not fully performed, the payment will still have achieved its purpose, since the contract has been made. The only exception, as mentioned above, will be where the vendor defaults. In that case, the purchaser may recover the deposit on the basis of a total failure of consideration: see eg *Foran v Wight* (1989); *CCP Australian Airships v Primus Telecommunications* (2004).

By contrast, an advance payment of part of the price for land *can* usually be recovered by a defaulting purchaser, provided it is an instalment rather than a deposit: *McDonald v Dennys Lascelles* (1933) at 478. Until the land is transferred, the failure of consideration is usually total. But this need not be the case with every type of sale. For example, when the purchaser of a business paid instalments and took possession and enjoyed the goodwill of the business, without formal assignment of a lease, prior to termination, there was no total failure of consideration: *Shaw v Ball* (1962). A restitutionary remedy was therefore denied.

In *Baltic Shipping v Dillon* (1993), the plaintiff was a passenger on the defendant's cruise ship. Nine days through a 14 day voyage, the ship sank off New Zealand. The plaintiff had prepaid the cost of the cruise. The defendant refunded the cost of the cruise for the period after the sinking. The plaintiff sought to recover for the entire cost of the cruise. The High Court held that she was unable to do so. She had enjoyed nine days of the cruise, and as a result there was no total failure of consideration. During this period she had received transport, food and entertainment before the ship sank. Deane and Dawson JJ made the point (at 378) that these benefits were not merely incidental, like food and an inflight movie during an aeroplane journey – they were what she had paid for as part of the overall experience.[7]

Enjoyment of goods, even ones which are defective, will bring about the same result. The purchase price cannot be recovered because there is no total failure of consideration. But it is different if the plaintiff has not received good title to the goods; for example, because the property is stolen. In *Rowland v Divall* (1923), the Court of Appeal held that, when a plaintiff

---

7   Compare *Ferme v Kimberley Discovery Cruises* (2015), where passengers who had paid in advance for a cruise that was cancelled because of a cyclone were entitled to recover their money, even though they had been transported to the location where the cruise would start. It was held that the 'substantial' or 'primary' benefit which they had contracted to receive was the cruise, not the transfers that preceded it. Nor did it matter that the cruise operator made alternative travel arrangements after the cancellation, since this was not part of the original 'consideration' for the payment.

was sold a stolen car, he had 'not received any part of that which he had contracted to receive' because of the absence of a good title. He could therefore recover his purchase money, despite having used the car and sold it on.

17.08   Claims for work done

In contrast to money claims, it is far harder to seek restitution reflecting the value of the benefit of work performed under a terminated contract. If full or substantial performance of a particular service has been rendered, the performer may be able to claim the agreed payment.[8] But where work has only been partially performed, so that no right to payment has accrued, the traditional rule is that the performer cannot bring a claim in *quantum meruit* to recover reasonable remuneration, unless there has been *free acceptance* of the benefit of the work.

In the classic case of *Sumpter v Hedges* (1898), the plaintiff had entered into a contract with the defendant to build two houses and stables for the defendant. Much of the work was completed, but before the job could be finished the plaintiff became insolvent and was unable to continue. He sought to recover for the work done by way of *quantum meruit*, but the claim failed. It was held that the owner had not freely accepted the benefit of the work, despite having subsequently completed the construction. The owner was not considered to have had a *practicable* choice as to whether to accept or reject the builder's works. He could hardly leave unfinished (and potentially dangerous) buildings on his land. A separate claim, however, succeeded for the value of materials which the builder had left on the site and which the owner had used in completing the buildings.[9] In this instance the owner *did* have a choice.

The failure of the main claim in *Sumpter* has been justified on the basis that the contract was entire (see **12.08**) and the builder was only entitled to be paid once the work was complete. As a result, there was no total failure of consideration, because payment was conditional on completion of the work.[10] But arguments for allowing recovery on a *quantum meruit* for partial performance can also be made. After all, the defendant certainly received a benefit in this case, even if it was not the precise one that he contracted for.[11]

17.09   Work done by a party terminating for breach

The general rule that a restitutionary action does not lie for work partially performed under a terminated contract does not apply to a party terminating a contract in response to a breach or repudiation. It will rarely be necessary or desirable for such a party to seek restitution in this situation. They can recover any pre-termination losses by way of damages for breach of contract: see **23.24**. Nevertheless, it has long been held that where the completion of work has been wrongly prevented by the defendant, an action for *quantum meruit* can be brought to recover reasonable remuneration, even if the work has been of no benefit to the defendant: see eg *Planché v Colburn* (1831).

---

8   As to substantial performance, see **12.12–12.13**.
9   Technically, the successful claim for the materials involved an action for *quantum valebat*, not *quantum meruit*. The former is used to recover the reasonable value of goods, as opposed to services.
10   See McFarlane & Stevens 2002.
11   For a range of arguments supporting recovery, see Burrows 2011: 356–61.

In this situation, the rule against double recovery means that the innocent party has a choice. They cannot recover in both contract and restitution, but must either seek damages for the loss suffered by performing work without payment or sue in *quantum meruit* for a sum measured by the prevailing market rate for their services. In practice, the choice will probably hinge on how good or bad the contract price is, since that will necessarily affect the calculation of damages: see **23.24**. The kind of case where restitution is more attractive is illustrated by the famous American case of *Boomer v Muir* (1933). A building contract was terminated. The innocent party, the building contractor, would have been due only the $20,000 that remained to be paid under the contract. Instead, he was held to be able to recover over $250,000, representing the value of the work done. This outcome allows an innocent party to recover more than the contract price and effectively escape from a bad bargain.

English judges have been reluctant to allow *quantum meruit* to be used in this manner: see eg *Taylor v Motability Finance* (2004). Australian judges have taken a different view. In *Renard Construction v Ministry for Public Works* (1992), the New South Wales Court of Appeal allowed a builder to recover a sum exceeding the one to which it was entitled under the contract, using *quantum meruit*. Meagher JA explained (at 277) that:

> There is nothing anomalous in the notion that two different remedies, proceeding on entirely different principles, might yield different results. Nor is there anything anomalous in the fact that either remedy may yield a higher monetary figure than the other. Nor is there anything anomalous in the prospect that a figure arrived at on a quantum meruit might exceed, or even far exceed, the profit which would have been made if the contract had been fully performed.[12]

The Court of Appeal in Victoria came to a similar conclusion in *Sopov v Kane Constructions* (2009), whilst at the same time noting that using *quantum meruit* in this way has been heavily criticised by commentators.[13] Despite acknowledging the power of their arguments, the Court felt constrained by authority to reaffirm the position taken in *Renard* and other cases. That stance has since been reiterated in *Mann v Paterson Constructions* (2018).

---

12   For further discussion, see **24.07**.
13   The issue continues to attract debate: see eg Morris 2015; Raghavan 2016.

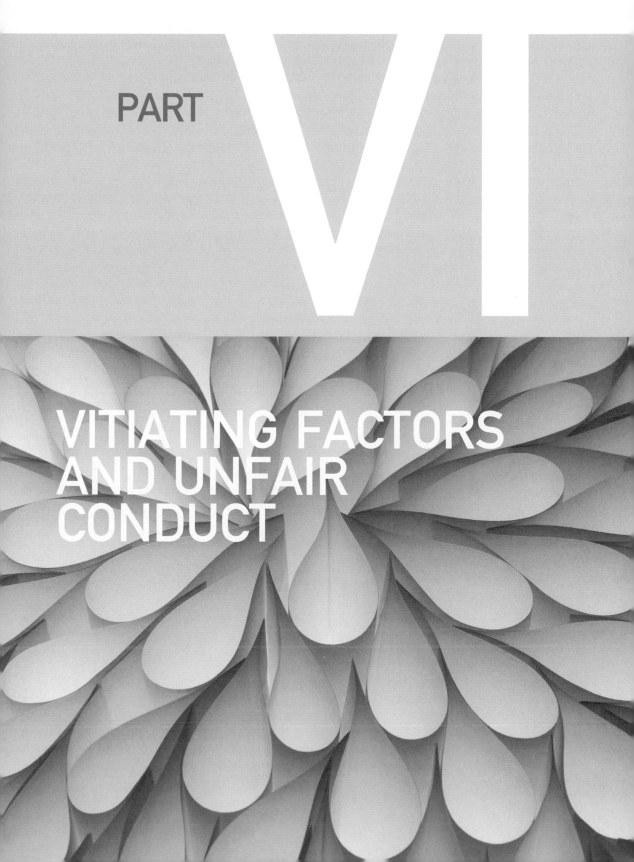

PART

VI

VITIATING FACTORS
AND UNFAIR
CONDUCT

18

MISINFORMATION

18.01   Introduction

In an ideal world, a contract will be formed between two parties fully informed of the circumstances surrounding the transaction. The reality of many contract transactions is rather different. Often there is a significant asymmetry in the knowledge of the parties, particularly where one of them is a consumer.[1] In this chapter, we are concerned with any situation in which a party enters into a contract under some sort of misapprehension as to a matter relevant to the transaction. It may concern the nature, subject, terms or benefits of the contract, or something incidental. In each case, the question is whether, after discovering the truth, there is anything the misinformed party can do to escape the contract or seek some other form of relief.

18.02   The different remedies for misinformation

One possible argument is that either one or both of the parties have been labouring under a *mistake*. The common law has never been particularly generous towards those who make a mistake, especially when it is self-induced. Mistake is only rarely a basis for finding a contract to be void. Equity, however, is more sympathetic. Where it is unconscionable to take advantage of another party's mistake, the contract may be rescinded or set aside. The equitable doctrine of *rectification* also allows a court to rewrite a written contract so that it more accurately reflects the intentions of the parties, where the transaction is mistakenly recorded.

More typically, a misapprehension has been created by the other party. The purpose of the misinformation may be to induce the contract on a favourable set of terms. At common law, a statement as to a current or future state of affairs which is made before a contact is entered into may be treated as a *warranty* – that is, a promise that is a term of the contract. If the statement turns out to be untrue, then a breach of contract occurs. It may also be possible to use the doctrine of *estoppel* to hold one party to a promise or representation they have made.

If the misinformation is the product of a *misrepresentation* which is fraudulent or careless, the torts of *deceit* or *negligence* may have been committed and damages may be recovered. In some jurisdictions, legislation has been passed to expand these liabilities. Where a misrepresentation is neither fraudulent nor negligent, damages cannot generally be recovered. However, at common law, the contract can still be rescinded for misrepresentation, even when innocent.

A further alternative is likely to be more attractive when there is a contract between a commercial party and a consumer, or two commercial parties. If the misinformation constitutes *misleading or deceptive conduct* and takes place 'in trade or commerce', s 18 of the Australian Consumer Law (ACL) will be contravened. There is no need to prove fault, nor indeed that the conduct has occurred before a contract has been made. A wide range of remedies are available for breach of this prohibition, which are not confined to damages or rescission. Section 18 is complemented by more specific prohibitions in the ACL, concerning misleading conduct in relation to various types of commercial transaction.

In this chapter, we consider each of these possibilities, though it is important to understand that the main focus should always be on the ACL. So long as the 'trade or commerce'

---

1   There is a large literature in the field of behavioural economics about asymmetrical information in contracting. For a seminal contribution, see Akerlof 1970.

requirement is satisfied, which it generally can be, the statutory regime will generally offer much greater scope for relief than all the other options with which we deal.

Pre-contractual statements as warranties

18.03   Misinformation as breach of contract

Most of the remedies discussed in this chapter do not arise as a result of a breach of contract. There will be occasions, however, when a statement has become incorporated into a contract as a term. When this happens and the statement turns out to be false, then a breach of contract occurs. The legal issues that determine whether a pre-contractual statement by one of the parties can be given effect as a term of the contract have already been considered in **9.11–9.16**. In summary, if A tells B something prior to them making a contract, and what A says turns out to be wrong, B can sue A for breach of contract if:

- A's statement would reasonably be understood to be warranting (promising) that something was true, not merely representing that to be the case; and
- the statement can be regarded as part of either the main contract entered into by the parties or a collateral contract, notwithstanding any difficulties created by the parol evidence rule, or by an entire agreement clause.

Where these requirements are satisfied, B can seek damages for any loss they have suffered as a result of the falsity of the statement. In accordance with the usual measure of damages for breach of contract (see **23.06**), their claim will typically reflect the monetary difference between the position they are in as a result of the breach, and the position they would have been in had the statement been true.

If a statement is incorporated into the contract as a non-essential term (see **16.06**, **16.09**), the plaintiff will be limited to an action for damages. The contract cannot be terminated. It may still, however, be possible to rescind the contract for misrepresentation, despite the fact that the statement is also a term of that contract.[2]

Estoppel

18.04   Estoppel as a remedy for misinformation

There are various ways in which estoppel may be invoked to obtain a remedy for misinformation. For instance, if A misleads B into thinking that A either has agreed or is about to agree to enter into a contract with B, A may be estopped from denying the existence of the contract: see eg *Waltons Stores v Maher* (1988), as discussed in **7.04–7.06**.

Estoppel may also be used where there is a pre-contractual assurance that certain rights under the contract will only be exercised in a particular way. If that assurance was given to secure those

---

2   In some States and Territories, there is a general provision to this effect: *Misrepresentation Act 1972* (SA) s 6(1)(a); *Civil Law (Wrongs) Act 2002* (ACT) s 173. In others, rescission is possible in more limited circumstances: see eg *Sale of Goods Act 1923* (NSW) s 4(2A)(a) (contracts for the sale of goods); *Australian Consumer Law and Fair Trading Act 2012* (Vic) s 24(2) (contracts for the supply of goods).

rights in the first place, then it may be unconscionable to insist on their strict legal interpretation. For example, in *Saleh v Romanous* (2010), a purchaser of land was verbally assured that the vendor's brother, who owned an adjoining property, would participate in a development venture. If this did not happen, the sale would not proceed and the purchaser could recover their deposit. When this assurance was not made good, it was held that the vendor was estopped from enforcing the written contract of sale, which said nothing about these conditions.

But estoppel can only be invoked where it would be reasonable to rely on the representation. In *State Rail Authority of NSW v Heath Outdoor* (1986), a written contract for the exhibition of advertisements by the Authority contained a clause permitting it to terminate the contract at any time by giving one month's notice. When the advertiser tried to have this clause removed, a representative of the Authority made it clear that he had no power to do this, but suggested that the clause was seldom invoked. A majority of the Court of Appeal found that this 'assurance' provided no basis for an estoppel, but rather reinforced the fact that the termination power existed and might be used. Kirby P expressed concern (at 177) about the potential for estoppel to be invoked in this kind of commercial context:

> Too great a willingness by the courts to discern, in pre-contract negotiations, a basis for estoppel will have the effect of introducing a serious element of uncertainty into our law of contract. It may also encourage expensive litigation in which the terms of the writing are put to one side and the courts busily engaged (as we have been) in a minute examination of the wilderness of pre-contract conversations.

Rescission for misrepresentation

18.05   The remedy of rescission

Rescission is a drastic remedy which allows the contract to be undone, so that both parties are restored to the position they were in before contracting. The consequences of rescission are different from termination for breach. It was explained in **17.01** that, where a contract is terminated, any unperformed future obligations are discharged, although obligations arising prior to termination may still be enforced. When a contract is rescinded, by contrast, all of the obligations are wiped away. This includes those that arose prior to rescission. It is as if the contract never happened. Rescission is also used to remedy certain types of mistake, as discussed later in the chapter, and also duress, undue influence and unconscionability. The latter doctrines are considered separately in Chapters 19 and 20.

At common law, contracts could always be rescinded where there was fraud. The modern definition of fraud, as set down in *Derry v Peek* (1889), is difficult to satisfy: see **18.16**. Fortunately, equity allows a contract to be rescinded even where the misrepresentation is non-fraudulent.[3] There is no requirement that a loss is suffered by entering into the contract. This outcome means that one party making an entirely innocent misrepresentation is disadvantaged over another innocent party who relies on the misrepresentation. Both parties may be

---

3   As to the distinction between the common law and equitable remedies of rescission, and also the differences that apply in equity where fraud is or is not present, see *Nadinic v Drinkwater* (2017) at [22]–[49].

under a genuine misapprehension. The act of making a statement which turns out to be false is nevertheless enough to favour the other party. Because the impact of rescission is so serious, there are a number of conditions to its use. The most important of these, as discussed below, is that it must be possible to substantially restore the parties to the position that they were in prior to the contract.

18.06   The definition of an actionable misrepresentation

A misrepresentation will only provide a basis for rescinding a contract if it involves one party (the representor) making a false statement to the other party (the representee), which induces them to enter into a contract. That statement must be of existing or past *fact* – although the courts have been quite prepared to stretch that category to include situations in which the representor conveys more than just factual information. This has allowed greater scope for rescission. This technique can be illustrated with reference to statements of intention or opinion. First, however, it is necessary to say something about puffs.

18.07   Puffs

Some exaggerated statements made before a contract is concluded have no legal conse-quences. These are known as 'mere puffs'. Statements of this sort are a form of sales talk. This kind of hyperbole is typical in advertising. It can be expected not to be taken too seriously. One characteristic of a mere puff is that it tends to be vague. Hence, in *Dimmock v Hallett* (1866), the description of land as 'fertile and improvable' was a mere puff. But the line between statements of fact and puffery can be a hard one to draw. In *Mitchell v Valherie* (2005), the advertisement for the sale of a house stated that there was 'nothing to spend – perfect presentation' and the property was in 'immaculate style'. Once the purchase was complete, it turned out that the property suffered from structural problems which had to be remedied at a considerable cost. All three judges of the Full Court of the Supreme Court of South Australia were satisfied that 'immaculate style' was mere puffery. But they disagreed on 'nothing to spend'. Sulan J, who dissented, thought this was an actionable misrepresentation. He stressed that the purchasers were not investors, but consumers on modest incomes without legal advice who would take the words to mean that no expenditure was needed on the property in the short term. White J disagreed. He noted (at [81]) that the words were being used here 'in a context in which some hyperbole is commonplace. Exaggerated descriptions of houses are a common, even expected, feature of real estate advertising'. Layton J offered a third view. She thought that the words 'nothing to spend' *were* a representation of fact – but only as to a purchaser being able to move in with no need to spend money on its appearance. She did not believe that the phrase conveyed anything about the structural integrity of the house, or indeed any other aspect that might require expenditure.

18.08   Statements of intention or opinion

A person who makes a statement that something will happen in the future does not misrepre-sent a fact merely because they fail to carry out their intentions. Statements of this sort are only actionable if they are promissory in nature and included as a term of the contract. To allow statements of intention to be grounds to rescind a contract would convert a non-contractual statement into one which had some of the characteristics of a contractual one.

Statements of future intention of the non-actionable sort have been distinguished, however, from ones in which a person misrepresents their present intention. This is treated as a statement of current fact – the fact of the representor's state of mind. In *Edgington v Fitzmaurice* (1885), the directors of a company invited the public to subscribe for debentures on the basis that the money raised would be used to expand the business. It was held that the directors were guilty of misrepresenting their actual intention, because it was not their intention to expand the business. The misstatement of their current intention was a misrepresentation of fact.

Opinions are treated in much the same way. A true statement of opinion or belief does not give grounds to rescind a contract. In *Bisset v Wilkinson* (1927), the vendor of a farm in New Zealand, which had never been used for sheep farming, represented to a prospective purchaser that in his opinion the farm could support 2,000 sheep. This opinion proved to be incorrect but did not amount to a misrepresentation. It was a statement of opinion, honestly held. In the absence of fraud, or a duty of care, such a statement is not actionable. This reflects the idea that it is not reasonable to enter into a contract on the basis of an opinion alone.

But like statements of intention, expressions of opinion can, in the right circumstances, be turned into statements of fact. In *Ritter v North Side Enterprises* (1975), an agent for the vendor said that he believed that a property would be connected to the main sewage system within four months. This was not just a statement of belief. The agent was also saying that he held that belief. Holding a belief is a fact and therefore in saying that he held a belief he could be treated as making a statement of fact. The circumstances in which a statement of opinion is made are important. In *Smith v Land & House* (1884) at 15, Bowen LJ drew this distinction:

> [W]here the facts are equally well known to both parties then what one says to another is a statement of opinion … But if the facts are not equally known to both sides, then a statement of opinion by one who knows the facts best involves very often a statement of a material fact, for he [sic] impliedly states he knows facts which justify his opinion.

If one party has greater knowledge, or has access to greater knowledge, then a statement of fact can be implied. The fact here is that the opinion is based on valid evidence.

18.09   Statements of law

When a contract is entered into as a result of a fraudulent misrepresentation of law, the contract can be rescinded: *Public Trustee v Taylor* (1978). In the absence of fraud, however, statements of law have not traditionally been treated as grounds for rescission, even though someone may be just as likely to be influenced by a statement of law as one of fact. It is sometimes said that everyone can be taken to know the law, but this is unrealistic. Neither party is likely to have greater legal knowledge than the other. But the exclusion of misrepresentations of law can still be justified. It is not unreasonable to expect someone entering into a contract to pay for their own legal advice rather than rely on what they are told by the other party. Nevertheless, English judges have now accepted that a misrepresentation of law, even in the absence of fraud, provides grounds to rescind a contract: *Pankhania v London Borough of Hackney* (2002). One of the reasons used to justify this change was that it was now possible to recover payments made under a mistake of law. To distinguish between the two was said (at [55]) to be a 'quixotic anachronism'.

While this step has not yet been taken in Australia, it seems likely that it will be. In *David Securities v Commonwealth Bank* (1992), the High Court confirmed that a mistake of law is not to be treated differently to a mistake of fact, in the context of a restitutionary action to recover a mistaken payment. The distinction between representations of fact and law has also been abandoned in the doctrine of estoppel: see eg *Commonwealth v Verwayen* (1990). All this suggests that misrepresentations of law that are non-fraudulent will, in time, be regarded as grounds for rescission.

18.10   Conduct and silence

There are a number of examples in contract law where conduct is treated as equivalent to words. Contract formation (see **5.18**, **5.22**) and termination for breach (see **16.12**) provide two examples. In much the same way, misrepresentation can occur through conduct as well as by words. The mode of communication is of less relevance than the fact that a falsehood is communicated. The principle can be illustrated by the English case of *Gordon v Selico* (1985). The vendor of a house covered up dry rot in a property in order to conceal a problem from prospective purchasers and their surveyors. This conduct was held to be a misrepresentation that the property did not suffer from dry rot.[4]

As noted in **4.07**, the law does not usually place a positive duty of disclosure on negotiating parties. Remaining silent does not, at least as a general rule, amount to a misrepresentation. In *W Scott Fell v Lloyd* (1906), the plaintiff agreed to purchase a particular type of coal from the defendant, who was party to a restrictive arrangement concerning the supply of that coal.[5] The plaintiff did not reveal its intention to ship the coal to South Australia, in clear breach of that arrangement, nor that the supplier of the coal had refused to sell to the plaintiff. The High Court held that the plaintiff was under no obligation to disclose this information and the defendant could not avoid its obligations under the agreement.

The failure of the law to impose a duty of disclosure reflects both an individualistic model of contract, and an antipathy towards liability for omissions. There are good practical reasons for adopting this stance. To do otherwise would potentially require everything relating to the transaction to be disclosed, which would damage the security of transactions. A party wishing to escape from a contract could usually identify something that had not been disclosed. Alternatively, it would be necessary to draw a line somewhere between information that could reasonably be required to be disclosed and that which could be withheld. Policing the boundary would be difficult, and would cause uncertainty.[6]

There are, nevertheless, some situations in which a failure to speak may constitute a misrepresentation. For example, a statement of fact may be true, but incomplete. It may carry with it the implication of some additional fact that is not disclosed. In *Dimmock v Hallett*

---

4   See also *Wood v Balfour* (2011).
5   The arrangement might well be unlawful today under Part IV of the *Competition and Consumer Act 2010* (Cth): see **21.30**.
6   As indeed has occurred in the context of statutory liability for misleading and deceptive conduct: see **18.25–18.26**.

(1866), the vendor of an estate stated that the farms on the estate were fully let. This was true, but he omitted to say that the tenants had given notice to quit. The silence about the notices to quit made the statement only partially true, and as such it was a misrepresentation. The same idea underlies a failure to convey a change of circumstances. In *With v O'Flanagan* (1936), negotiations for the sale of a medical practice were begun in January. At this point, the practice was said to be worth £2,000. By May, at the time the contract of sale was entered into, the practice was worth much less. The vendor's ill health meant that most of the patients had moved to other doctors. The vendor ought to have communicated the change in circumstances to the purchaser. When they failed to do so, their silence was a misrepresentation. As Smith J explained in *Jones v Dumbrell* (1981) at 203:

> If a representation which is intended to induce the making of a contract is true when made, but becomes false to the knowledge of the representor before the contract is concluded, and the representor thereafter by conduct continues the representation, he is liable as if the representation had been false to his knowledge when originally made.

There are also a few situations in which the nature of the relationship between the parties, or the nature of the transaction, creates obligations of disclosure. If the contractual parties are in a fiduciary relationship, then there is a duty of disclosure. In *McKenzie v McDonald* (1927), the plaintiff agreed to exchange a property with a real estate agent for less than it was worth, after he failed to disclose a valuation of the farm that was the subject matter of the deal. The agent stood in a fiduciary relationship and therefore the valuation report ought to have been disclosed.

As noted in **4.08**, contracts of insurance have been classified as contracts of 'utmost good faith' for centuries: see eg *Carter v Boehm* (1766). This rule is now contained in statute. All material risks must be disclosed to the insurance company by anyone seeking insurance.[7] A contract of guarantee requires a more limited form of disclosure. Under this arrangement, A acts as guarantor for B's debt to C. If B fails to pay, C can bring a claim for the debt against A. The guarantor can usually expect to make their own inquiries about B's financial position. But in the situation where there are circumstances that are not naturally expected to be found in a transaction between a creditor and debtor, then the creditor is under a duty to disclose them to the guarantor: *Goodwin v National Bank* (1968) at 175; and see further **11.13**.

18.11 The element of inducement

A representation need not be made directly to the victim. It is enough if it was intended that it would be relied on by the plaintiff, or by a class of people of which the plaintiff was one: *Commercial Bank v RH Brown* (1972). But communication on its own is not enough. The representation must also act as a material *inducement* to enter into the contract. Materiality looks at the statement from an objective viewpoint. It is a device for filtering out trivial statements that, objectively, could not have influenced a reasonable person to enter into the contract. The materiality condition does not apply to fraudulent statements: *Nicholas v*

---

7   *Marine Insurance Act 1909* (Cth) s 24; *Insurance Contracts Act 1984* (Cth) s 21.

Thompson (1924). Materiality is necessary for non-fraudulent statements, but it is not sufficient. The party seeking rescission must show that the misrepresentation was an actual inducement to enter into contract. The fact that they have relied upon the statement provides a crucial link between the misrepresentation and the contract.

In *Gould v Vaggelas* (1984), the High Court laid down four principles about inducement:

(1) The representation need not be the sole inducement.

(2) The burden of proving the inducement rests on the representee.

(3) Where the representor intends to induce reliance, a factual inference could be drawn that the representee did rely. This is only an inference, but it makes it easier for the representee to show, on the balance of probabilities, that they did rely.

(4) The burden of proof will not be discharged if the representor can show that 'the plaintiff not only actually knew the true facts but knew them to be the truth, or that the plaintiff, either by his words or conduct, disavowed any reliance on the fraudulent representations' (at 236).

The most obvious absence of inducement occurs when a contract is entered into in ignorance of the false statements, or the representations played no part in the decision because the representee entered into the contract solely for other reasons. A further variation occurs where the statements are disbelieved. *Holmes v Jones* (1907) concerned the sale of a farm during which false statements were made by the vendor. The purchaser, who made their own inspection of the property and discovered that the statements were false, could not be said to have been induced by the misrepresentation when they purchased the farm.

It is usually perfectly sensible, as in *Holmes*, to make inquiries about the accuracy of representations. But the law does not require the truth of a representation to be investigated. In *Redgrave v Hurd* (1881), the prospective buyer of a solicitor's practice queried statements that were made to him by the vendor about the turnover of the practice. He declined the opportunity to examine further documents which he was given, and which would have revealed the true turnover. This did not prevent him from rescinding the contract. Baggallay LJ explained (at 23) that 'the representation once made relieves the party from an investigation … [ordinarily] the mere fact that he does not avail himself of the opportunity of testing the accuracy of the representation made to him will not enable the opposing party to succeed on that ground'.

The position of the parties under the general law of misrepresentation may be modified by a contractual provision between them. The parties are perfectly at liberty to include an exclusion or limitation clause. A representee may agree to a term in the subsequent contract that they did not rely on any statement by the representor. This ensures that any inducement is missing: see eg *Byers v Dorotea* (1986). Alternatively, a clause in the contract could simply exclude liability for misrepresentation altogether. However, there are statutory limits on exclusion clauses in some jurisdictions. In South Australia and the ACT, an exclusion clause is only effective if a court considers it fair and reasonable to allow reliance on it.[8]

---

8   *Misrepresentation Act 1972* (SA) s 8; *Civil Law (Wrongs) Act 2002* (ACT) s 176.

18.12 The nature and effect of rescission

Rescission allows the contract to be set aside and the parties returned to the position that they were in prior to the contract. So, for example, when a contract for the sale of land is rescinded, the land is returned to one party, and the price is returned to the other. Contracts that are capable of being rescinded are *voidable*, rather than void. This means that the contract is valid until it is rescinded. The victim of a misrepresentation who wishes to rescind must elect to do so within a reasonable time, and the election must be communicated to the representor: *Ivanof v Phillip Levy* (1971).

Alati v Kruger (1955) illustrates the way rescission operates. A business selling fruit was conducted on leased premises. Kruger bought the business from Alati after fraudulent misrepresentations by Alati and his agent about the takings of the business. The lease was assigned by Alati to Kruger with the landlord's consent, as part of the sale. Kruger quickly realised that there had been a misrepresentation, and claimed rescission, return of his purchase money and damages from Alati and his agents. Before the trial, Kruger entered into a contract in which the landlord agreed to reassign the lease to Alati if the court ordered rescission. Having accepted that the statement about the takings was a misrepresentation, the difficulty arose over whether rescission was possible. The business had deteriorated further after the sale because a supermarket had opened nearby. As a result, it was argued that if the contract was rescinded Alati could not get back the same business he had sold. It followed that rescission would be barred because *restitutio in integrum* (the restoration of the parties' original position) was not possible.

The High Court explained (at 224) that rescission for misrepresentation is 'always an act of the party'. At the same time, it noted (at 225) that rescission is a discretionary remedy. The fact that rescission may be granted on terms set by the court, or that partial rescission may be available (as discussed below), lends credence to the view that rescission is not *merely* an act of the party rescinding. The court is clearly involved in settling the form that the remedy takes. As the High Court explained (at 224), it has the power in equity:

> to ascertain and provide for the adjustments necessary to be made between the parties in cases where a simple handing back of property or repayment of money would not put them in as good position as before they entered into their transaction.

The Court went on to stress that these flexible equitable rules allowed for an account of profits and the making of allowances for deterioration. Any decline in the value of the business was no fault of Kruger. It would have been different if he had acted unconscionably in closing the business when he did. This was not the case because, once it was clear that the business was to be closed, Alati could have made an offer to take the property back or put it in the hands of a receiver until the rescission issue was settled.

The flexibility of equity's power to impose conditions on the grant of rescission is emphasised by the decision in *Vadasz v Pioneer Concrete* (1995). The defendant was the director of a company that was purchasing concrete on credit from the plaintiff. The defendant agreed to personally guarantee the amounts owing to the plaintiff for both past and future supplies. When the plaintiff attempted to enforce this guarantee, the defendant sought to rescind it for misrepresentation on the basis that he had been misled into thinking the guarantee covered only future debts. To grant such relief would mean allowing the defendant to escape any liability at all, yet retain the benefit of having had the concrete supplied to his company. To achieve 'practical justice', therefore, the High Court granted partial rescission. It set aside only that part of the guarantee that related to debts for previous supplies. That left the plaintiff with the contract that he would have been prepared to make but for the misrepresentation – a guarantee covering future debts only.[9]

18.13   Bars to rescission

The rescission of a contract may be barred, as we have seen, where *restitutio in integrum* is not possible. In *Alati v Kruger*, that bar did not apply. It was still possible to restore the parties to their pre-contractual position, albeit only through the court exercising its equitable power to make orders to help achieve this.

Another potential bar to rescission is *affirmation*. Misrepresentation, as we have noted, renders a contract voidable rather than void. So, after the misrepresentation is discovered, the misled party can elect to rescind or affirm the contract. Affirmation depends on intention, viewed objectively. An explicit statement that the representee is affirming is not required, but some unequivocal sign is still necessary: see *Brown v Smitt* (1924). In order to affirm, it is not enough for the representee to be aware of the facts that give rise to a right to rescind. Knowledge of the existence of a legal right to rescind is required before it can be said that the representee has affirmed the contract: *Coastal Estates v Melevende* (1965).

Another bar, *lapse of time*, overlaps with affirmation. The passage of time may provide evidence that a contract has been affirmed. The position of lapse of time as an independent bar to rescission is uncertain in Australia. It has been described as 'doubtful'.[10] If such a bar *does* exist, then it appears that rescission is barred by a lapse of time even when the representee was completely unaware that they had a legal right to rescind: see eg *Leaf v International Galleries* (1950). The period of time which is required to pass before rescission is barred will depend on the nature of the contract. In a contract for perishable goods, for example, a reasonable period may be quite short.

A contract, once concluded, may subsequently involve a third party. Suppose A is selling a car. As a result of a fraudulent misrepresentation, B induces A to enter into a contract to sell the car. B then sells the car on to C, who is entirely innocent and has paid for the car. Once the subject matter of the contract is purchased in good faith for valuable consideration, the contract cannot be rescinded. This result follows from the fact that the contract is only voidable, and that once the subject matter of the contract has passed out of the hands of the representee, restitution is impossible. So it is important, in a case like this, to rescind before the title to the goods passes. It is enough to show an unambiguous intention to rescind, even if that intention was not actually communicated to B. In *Car and Universal Finance v Caldwell* (1965), a car was sold after a fraudulent misrepresentation. The owner of the car informed the police and

---

9   For a critical analysis of the decision and consideration of how it might be applied in other contexts (including rescission for other reasons), see Robertson 2001.

10   Seddon & Bigwood 2017: 571, citing *Elder's Trustee & Executor v Commonwealth Homes & Investment* (1941) as an example of the lapse of a very long period where rescission was allowed.

the Automobile Association. This was sufficient notice to the fraudster to allow rescission before the property passed to the buyer. The original owner could therefore recover it from an innocent third party. Since the original sale had been rescinded, the fraudster did not have good title to pass on to the third party.

A final bar is the so-called rule in *Seddon's* case.[11] *Seddon v North Eastern Salt* (1905) held that, outside fraudulent misrepresentation, a contract cannot be rescinded when all the obligations under the contract have been performed on both sides – that is, the contract has been fully executed. For a long time, the rule in *Seddon's* case was applied (or assumed to apply) in Australia: see eg *Svanosio v McNamara* (1956). But this restriction has been eroded. In New South Wales, the rule was held not to apply to contracts for the sale of goods in *Leason v Princes Farm* (1983). The same result has now been reached by an amendment to the New South Wales *Sale of Goods Act*.[12] In Victoria, a buyer has a reasonable period after accepting the goods in which they can rescind, even though the contract is fully executed.[13] South Australia and the ACT have removed the rule in *Seddon's* case completely.[14] Within the remaining jurisdictions this restriction on rescission is only likely to cause difficulties when contracts fall outside the ACL provisions discussed later in the chapter, such as a private non-commercial sale.

18.14 Rescission of contracts for the sale of goods

The wording of the various statutes on the sale of goods raises doubts about whether equitable rescission, and hence rescission for non-fraudulent statements, is possible at all with such contracts. The relevant provision states that:

> The rules of the common law … and in particular the rules relating to … and the effect of fraud, misrepresentation, duress, coercion, mistake or other invalidating cause, shall continue to apply to contracts for the sale of goods.[15]

One reading of the statute is to say that, rather than equitable principles, it is the common law that applies to contracts for the sale of goods. As a result, there could be no rescission for non-fraudulent misrepresentation in contracts for the sale of goods. This was the position of the Supreme Court of Victoria in *Watt v Westhoven* (1933). Some later decisions have, nevertheless, allowed rescission for contracts for the sale of goods in the absence of fraud: see eg *Graham v Freer* (1980); *Leason v Princes Farm* (1983). As a result of statutory reform, rescission has been explicitly made available in some States for such contracts.[16]

11   See Macfarlane & Willmott 1998.
12   *Sale of Goods Act 1923* (NSW) ss 4(2A)(b), 38(2).
13   *Australian Consumer Law and Fair Trading Act 2012* (Vic) s 24(1).
14   *Misrepresentation Act 1972* (SA) s 6(1)(b); *Civil Law (Wrongs) Act 2002* (ACT) s 173.
15   *Sale of Goods Act 1923* (NSW) s 4(2); *Sale of Goods Act 1896* (Qld) s 61(2); *Sale of Goods Act 1895* (WA) s 59(2); *Sale of Goods Act 1895* (SA) s 59(2); *Sale of Goods Act 1896* (Tas) s 5(2); *Sale of Goods Act 1954* (ACT) s 62(1); *Sale of Goods Act 1972* (NT) s 4(2).
16   *Sale of Goods Act 1954* (ACT) s 62(2); *Sale of Goods Act 1923* (NSW) s 4(2A). The rule is abrogated for contracts for the supply of goods in Victoria: *Australian Consumer Law and Fair Trading Act 2012* (Vic) s 24(1).

Damages for misrepresentation

18.15   Damages in the law of tort

Statements which are made fraudulently, or negligently, give rise to an action in tort law for damages. In the absence of applicable statutory provisions, the remedy for those statements which are entirely innocent – that is, without fraud or negligence – is confined to rescission.[17] The main purpose of damages in contract law, as noted in **23.06**, is to put the injured party in the position that they would have been in had the misrepresentation been true. This is known as an expectation measure. Tort damages are calculated differently. The aim of such damages in this particular context is to put the plaintiff back in the position that they would have been in had they never entered into the contract. These two measures can give a different outcome, which can be illustrated by a simple example.

Suppose A is selling a car to B. He misrepresents that the car has done 50,000 kilometres. A car which has travelled that far would be worth $50,000. In fact, the car has done 70,000 kilometres and is therefore worth just $40,000. B purchases the car for $45,000. She then discovers that the odometer has been tampered with. If A's statement can be construed as a warranty which has become a term of the contract, the correct measure of damages is the difference between the value of the car purchased and the value of the car promised: that is, $50,000 less $40,000. B therefore recovers $10,000 in damages.

The tort measure produces a different figure. It is calculated by working out how much worse off B is by entering into the contract. She has paid $45,000 for a car that is worth $40,000. Her loss is therefore the lower sum of $5,000.

18.16   The tort of deceit

In order to succeed in the tort of deceit, having established a misrepresentation, it is necessary to show that the misrepresentation was fraudulent. Fraud does not require an evil motive or an intention to deceive: *Krakowski v Eurolynx Properties* (1995) at 580. But it is still difficult to establish. The test for fraud laid down by the House of Lords in *Derry v Peak* (1889) is still used today. It requires the representee to prove, on the balance of probabilities, that the representor made the false statement either: (a) knowing it was false; (b) without belief it was true; or (c) recklessly indifferent as to whether it was true or false. Someone who makes a statement honestly believing it to be true, therefore, is not guilty of fraud. Where fraud can be established, all consequential losses suffered by the plaintiff are recoverable, even if they were not reasonably foreseeable by the defendant: *Palmer Bruyn & Parker v Parsons* (2001) at 407–8.

---

17   In South Australia and the ACT, there is a statutory right to damages for non-fraudulent misrepresentation, but the representor has a defence if they had a reasonable belief in the truth of the misrepresentation: *Misrepresentation Act 1972* (SA) ss 7(1)–(2); *Civil Law (Wrongs) Act 2002* (ACT) s 174; and see eg *Slinger v Southern White* (2005). A court may also exercise a discretion to award a representee damages in lieu of rescission where it is fair and just to do so: *Misrepresentation Act 1972* (SA) ss 7(3)–(5); *Civil Law (Wrongs) Act 2002* (ACT) s 175. The effect of such an award is to restore the contract (if it has already been rescinded) and to bar any later attempt to rescind.

18.17   The tort of negligence

The award of damages for a negligent misrepresentation (usually called 'negligent misstatement'), which causes economic losses, is a comparatively recent development. The law was traditionally reluctant to award damages for pure economic loss, as opposed to property damage or physical injury. Negligent misrepresentation sits within the general tort of negligence. The plaintiff must establish that the defendant owed them a *duty of care* as to the accuracy of a statement which was breached, causing them loss. Following the landmark English decision of *Hedley Byrne v Heller* (1964),[18] the High Court has, in a series of decisions, developed a body of law about such liability.

In *Mutual Life v Evatt* (1968) at 573, Barwick CJ explained that liability comes down to whether advice was given voluntarily, in circumstances where the defendant realises or ought to realise the plaintiff will, and does reasonably, rely on the defendant's statement. The High Court held that a defendant can be liable even in the absence of a special skill or expertise in giving such advice. On appeal, the Privy Council held that a special skill *was* required: *Mutual Life v Evatt* (1971). The requirement might well limit liability in a contractual setting when the representor is making statements about matters on which they lack expertise. But its continued existence may be doubted. In the High Court case of *Shaddock & Associates v Council of the City of Parramatta* (1981) Mason J, with whom Aickin J agreed, stressed that no special skill was needed.[19]

Finding the presence of a duty of care is unlikely to be difficult in a contractual context, especially if no special skill is required on the part of the representor. In *Esanda Finance v Peat Marwick Hungerfords* (1997), various formulas were used to identify a duty, including reasonable reliance, proximity, and assumption of responsibility. McHugh J delivered the most comprehensive judgment, in which he considered (at 282–9) six factors in relation to the existence of a duty. In the context of a report by auditors, which was relied on by a finance company, he explained (at 289) that:

> In the end, the most powerful point for holding that auditors owe a duty of care in cases like the present is that investors and creditors suffer their losses because they have relied, as the auditor knew or ought reasonably to have known they would, on his or her report, and the auditor has made that report carelessly. As against that, however, is the fact that the auditor did not invite or intend them to rely on it and they have paid nothing to the auditor for the preparation of the work. They require the auditor to compensate them for the loss that arose from their self-induced reliance, but they were not prepared to pay for the auditor's work.

Statements made in the course of negotiations for a contract are precisely the sort which invite reliance, and which might be expected to give rise to a duty of care. Given the development of the statutory liability discussed in the next section, there has been no great need to resolve the question of how widely a duty of care can or should be imposed in such a context. Yet

---

18   For a detailed account, see Swain 2015b.
19   As Mason J pointed out (at 248), by this time the High Court was no longer bound by decisions of the Privy Council. See further Luntz et al 2017: 866–88.

negligent misstatement claims are often still pleaded, even in situations that attract the operation of the prohibitions on misleading or deceptive conduct.[20]

Statutory prohibitions on misleading or deceptive conduct

18.18   Introduction

Misrepresentation is a much less important concept than it once was. Many of the older misrepresentation cases would, if they arose today, be brought under the ACL, which is enacted as Schedule 2 of the *Competition and Consumer Act 2010* (Cth). In 2011, the ACL replaced equivalent provisions in Pt V of the *Trade Practices Act 1974* (Cth). The ACL replicates the earlier legislation in many respects, and the older case law remains relevant.

The key provision of the ACL is found in s 18(1), formerly s 52(1) of the 1974 Act. This states that: 'A person must not, in trade or commerce, engage in conduct that is misleading or deceptive or is likely to mislead or deceive.' Misleading or deceptive conduct includes what at common law might be termed a misrepresentation, but also a much broader range of activities. Despite the title of the legislation, s 18 applies even when the victim is a business rather than a consumer. Section 18 and its predecessor have generated a vast body of case law over the past four decades.[21] Allegations of misleading or deceptive conduct are routinely included in the statements of claim in almost any form of commercial litigation, whether or not involving a contract.

Alongside the general prohibition in s 18, the ACL makes special provision in Part 3-1 for certain types of misconduct. These include prohibitions on misleading representations about goods and services (s 37), or land (s 38). Division 1 of Part 4-1 has counterpart provisions which criminalise such conduct, subject to certain defences in Part 4-6 that do not apply to contraventions of the civil prohibitions. But there is no offence in Part 4-1 which replicates the general prohibition in s 18, for which only civil remedies are available.

One of the strengths of the ACL is the suite of remedies for which Part 5-2 provides. As we go on to discuss, this part of the legislation, and especially the correct measure of damages to award, has proved to be the most controversial part of the scheme. One major difference from misrepresentation at common law is that damages can be awarded for misleading or deceptive conduct, even if any representation falls outside the definition of fraud or negligence.

18.19   Scope of the ACL

As noted in **1.15**, the ACL is given effect under both Commonwealth *and* State legislation. As a federal law, it covers conduct by trading, financial or foreign corporations; and also conduct by individuals and other entities in relation to interstate or overseas trade, or in a Territory, or when using postal or telecommunications services.[22] Between them, these situations cover most forms of trading activity, though not quite all. For example, if a sole trader operating only

---

20   See Paterson & Bant 2016.
21   For a detailed account, see Lockhart 2015.
22   *Competition and Consumer Act 2010* (Cth) ss 5, 6, 131.

in Sydney posted a sign that misled their customers, the federal regime would not be engaged. But the ACL would still apply in such a case as a State law, by virtue of Part 3 of the *Fair Trading Act 1987* (NSW).[23] As for government agencies, they are typically covered only to the extent that they are carrying on a business.[24]

The ACL is not the only legislation to prohibit misleading or deceptive conduct. The *Australian Securities and Investments Commission Act 2001* (Cth) contains a range of provisions that prohibit misleading or deceptive conduct in relation to 'financial services', as defined in s 12BAB.[25] The provisions include a general prohibition in s 12DA that is similar to s 18 of the ACL. A further prohibition on misleading and deceptive conduct, in relation to a financial product or a financial service, appears in s 1041H of the *Corporations Act 2001* (Cth). To prevent overlap, s 131A of the *Competition and Consumer Act 2010* (Cth) precludes the ACL applying (at least as a federal law) to the supply of financial services or products. The strange insistence on creating these parallel regimes for financial services, each with their own complex definitions, has created considerable confusion and uncertainty.[26] In *Wingecarribee Shire Council v Lehman Brothers* (2012) at [948], Rares J expressed his exasperation:

> Why does a court have to waste its time wading through this legislative porridge to work out which one or ones of these provisions apply even though it is likely that the end result will be the same?'

For convenience, the discussion below focuses exclusively on the more generally applicable provisions in the ACL, although some of the cases cited were actually brought under the financial services legislation.

18.20   The requirement of conduct 'in trade or commerce'

Section 2 of the ACL states that *trade or commerce* 'includes any business or professional activity (whether or not carried on for a profit)'. The extension to professional activities was new in the ACL, although it had previously appeared in some State laws. It encompasses any activity 'that is unequivocally and distinctly characteristic of the carrying-on of a profession', whether or not of a trading or commercial character, though not 'purely instrumental or mundane activities by which professionals or their staff execute their daily tasks': *Shahid v Australian College of Dermatologists* (2008) at [192]–[193].

Despite the breadth of the definition, some dealings are not caught by the legislation. In particular, a private sale of a non-business asset, such as a house, does not fall within the concept of trade or commerce.[27] In *O'Brien v Smolonogov* (1983), the defendants advertised land for sale in a newspaper. The plaintiff also spoke to the defendant by telephone. Once the sale was complete, the plaintiff argued that false or misleading statements had been made

---

23   For equivalent provisions in the other States, see **1.15**.

24   See eg *Competition and Consumer Act 2010* (Cth) s 2A; *Fair Trading Act 1987* (NSW) s 36; and for discussion, see Healey & Coles 2018.

25   Section 12BAB of the 2001 Act has recently been amended so as to include a 'financial product' in the definition of a 'financial service': see *Treasury Laws Amendment (Australian Consumer Law Review) Act 2018* (Cth) Sch 11.

26   See Klotz 2015.

27   But see Tokeley 2017, discussing this issue from a policy perspective.

about the land. It was held that the sale lacked a commercial character. The land was not used for business activities. The fact that the land was advertised in newspapers and negotiations were conducted over the telephone, which were undoubtedly methods used in commercial activity, did not make a difference. Yet others involved in a private sale may be acting in trade or commerce. For example, a real estate agent making misleading or deceptive statements about the property they are selling can certainly fall within the legislation: see eg *Butcher v Lachlan Elder Realty* (2004), discussed below.

Some situations are less clear cut. In *Williams v Pisano* (2015), the owner of a residential property, having lived in it for several years, renovated the property with a view to selling it at a profit. Conduct in connection with the sale was held not to be 'in trade or commerce'. Yet, the private sale of a rental property was considered to fall on the other side of the line in *Havyn v Webster* (2005). The sale of the principal capital asset of a business, like the beauty clinic in *Bevanere v Lubidineuse* (1985), has also been regarded as being in trade or commerce. Although the business was concerned with beauty treatments, rather than property sales, the sale of the clinic was nevertheless a commercial activity.

In *Concrete Constructions v Nelson* (1990) at 604, a majority of the High Court warned, in relation to s 52 of the 1974 Act, that:

> the section was not intended to impose, by a side-wind, an overlay of Commonwealth law upon every field of legislative control into which a corporation might stray for the purposes of, or in connection with, carrying on its trading or commercial activities.

These remarks arose in a very different context from an ordinary commercial transaction. The instructions of a foreman, which led to the injury of another employee, were not within trade or commerce, even though both were employed as part of a business. Yet, in subsequent cases involving employers and employees, some types of conduct *have* been held to fall within the statutory formula. Employees have often (though not invariably) been permitted to complain about misleading statements made during negotiations over the terms of their employment: see eg *Barto v GPR Management Services* (1991); *Walker v Salomon Smith Barney Securities* (2003); although compare *Martin v Tasmania Development and Resources* (1999).[28]

In the last decade or so, at least in a contractual setting, the courts have tended to favour a broad interpretation of the 'in trade or commerce' requirement. The modern attitude towards the legislation is illustrated by *Houghton v Arms* (2006). The plaintiff engaged WSA Online to design a website for his wine business. Two employees of WSA told the plaintiff that they could set up an online payment system in a particular format. The plaintiff was forced to restructure his business and, for a period, lost money. With WSA now insolvent, the plaintiff sued the employees instead. It is common for those involved in a business, especially as managers or directors, to face personal liability in such a situation as accessories to a contravention by the business. As explained in **18.31**, this requires evidence that they have been *knowingly* involved in the contravention. Here, however, the claim was that the employees themselves were acting in trade or commerce, so that they could be liable even for an innocent

---

28   For discussion of the case law on this point, see Lockhart 2015: 72–5. Section 31 of the ACL is, in any event, specifically directed to employment arrangements. It prohibits an employer from misleading a job-seeker 'as to the availability, nature or terms or conditions of, or any other matter relating to, the employment'.

breach. The High Court agreed that this was the case, even though the employees were plainly not the proprietors of a business.[29]

Uncertainty on the part of the charity, not-for-profit and fundraising sector as to the application of the 'in trade or commerce' requirement to some of their activities emerged as a problem in a recent review of the ACL.[30] As the review noted, it is generally irrelevant whether an entity engaging in conduct is a not-for-profit organisation or obtains a profit from its activities.[31] The focus is rather on the particular activities or transaction in question and whether the nature of the relationship between the parties concerned is of a trading or commercial nature. So, for example, a not-for-profit organisation selling goods for payment as part of its fundraising activities would be engaging in conduct 'in trade or commerce'. Similarly, the fact that such an organisation receives funding from other sources when selling goods or providing services to a consumer is also irrelevant. Thus, a charity providing subsidised gardening services to elderly people would be acting in trade or commerce, as it is still supplying a service to a consumer in exchange for payment. Nonetheless, the review acknowledged that this uncertainty (on the part of both the sector and consumers) was problematic and recommended the immediate drafting of regulator guidance to clarify the position.[32] Guidance of this sort was duly issued in December 2017.[33]

18.21   'Misleading or deceptive'

In order to attract the statutory remedy, conduct need only be misleading *or* deceptive, or be *likely* to mislead or deceive. Conduct need not both mislead and deceive, although the terms are more or less synonymous in any event. Both connote a person being led into error: *Parkdale v Puxu* (1982) at 198. It does not matter whether the conduct in question has induced a person to make a contract. For example, it is enough that a potential consumer may have been misled into considering a possible transaction, even if they would be likely to learn the truth before actually making that transaction: *ACCC v TPG Internet* (2013) at [50].

Liability under s 18 is strict. No intention to mislead or deceive is required: *Hornsby Building Information Centre v Sydney Building Information Centre* (1978). The focus is on the effect or likely effect of the conduct on the audience to whom it is directed. This is a fact-dependent exercise, and the same facts can be interpreted quite differently. Some judges may be more interventionist than others. For example, in *Butcher v Lachlan Elder Realty* (2004), the plaintiffs purchased a waterfront property in Sydney. They argued that the estate agent had included a diagram in the property brochure that gave a misleading impression of the boundary of the property. A disclaimer was also included: 'All information contained herein is gathered from sources we deem to be reliable however we cannot guarantee it's [sic] accuracy and interested persons should rely on their own enquiries.' The majority of the High Court, in finding that there was no misleading or deceptive conduct, stressed that the plaintiffs

---

29   For criticism of this highly dubious ruling, see eg Fetter 2007.

30   See CAANZ 2016: 15–21.

31   Note the phrase 'whether or not carried on profit' in s 2 and see *Monroe Topple & Associates v Institute of Chartered Accountants* (2002) at [47].

32   See CAANZ 2017: 75–6.

33   ACCC et al 2017.

were 'intelligent, shrewd and self-reliant', and they were purchasing an expensive property using professional advisors. The view that the real estate agents were only a conduit for the owners of the property was crucial. The information about the boundary did not come from them, as the disclaimer made clear.

In his dissent, Kirby J pointed out that although one of the plaintiffs was a wealthy and intelligent businessman, he was not a land lawyer. He was also concerned (at [211]) that:

> By holding that the printed disclaimer in this pamphlet was effective to exclude liability under the Act, this court, in my respectful view, strikes a blow at the Act's intended operation. Henceforth, in effect, the Act may not operate to protect the ordinary recipient of the representations of corporations engaged in trade or commerce. Many such corporations will be encouraged by this decision to believe that they can avoid the burdens of the Act by the simple expedient of tucking away in an obscure place in minuscule typeface a disclaimer such as now proves effective. This approach is contrary to the language and purpose of the Parliament.

Despite the force of this point, it seems reasonable to accept that someone who is used to dealing with high-value transactions may be less likely to be misled than the average person, whose only major purchase is likely to be the family home. It is unlikely that, in an ordinary property purchase, a disclaimer of this type would have had the same impact. In this light, Kirby J's concerns may have been overstated.

18.22   The victim(s) of the deception

As *Butcher* illustrates, the outcome of a misleading or deceptive conduct claim may depend on the nature of the parties involved – or, more specifically, the nature of the person(s) said to have been deceived. This is especially true where the relevant conduct is directed at the public at large, or a section of the public, rather than an individual. In *Campomar v Nike International* (2000), the defendant, a Spanish company, began selling and marketing a sport fragrance labelled 'Nike Sport Fragrance'. Nike, the sportswear giant, alleged that the defendant had engaged in misleading or deceptive conduct, by leading consumers to think that the product was connected with them. Where there is no identifiable individual, but a class of people to whom the conduct was directed, it is necessary to isolate their characteristics. The class here was considered by the High Court to be ordinary and reasonable members of the public who were prospective purchasers of the product. It was held that this group would believe that it was a Nike product, or one that had their approval. The labelling was therefore misleading or deceptive, despite the fact that it also made clear that the product was manufactured by Campomar. It was not reasonable to expect prospective purchasers to read the small print of the label.

Nevertheless, there are limits to the legislation. As Gibbs J observed in *Parkdale v Puxu* (1982) at 199:

> Although it is true, as has often been said, that ordinarily a class of consumers may include the inexperienced as well as the experienced, and the gullible as well as the astute, the section must in my opinion by regarded as contemplating the effect of the conduct on reasonable members of the class. The heavy burdens which the section creates cannot have been intended to be imposed for the benefit of persons who fail to take reasonable care of their own interests.

In *Parkdale*, the High Court considered that the purchasers of expensive furniture could reasonably be expected to ascertain whether it was a particular brand or just a copy. In some situations, a lack of care may even be sufficient to argue that the misleading or deceptive conduct did not cause any loss suffered: see eg *O'Hagan v Classic Cars* (2014). The legislation does, however, seek to balance the interests of the parties. Given the paternalistic motivation of the legislation, too much in the way of reasonable care should not be expected of the victims of misleading or deceptive conduct: *Suncoast Pastoral v Coburg* (2012) at [52]–[53]. For example, in *ACCC v TPG Internet* (2013) at [47], the High Court stressed that in assessing the impact of an advertisement for internet services, the targeted consumers were very different to those in *Parkdale*. They were not making a considered purchase 'in the calm of the showroom'. Rather, the advertisement was an intrusion (perhaps an unwelcome one) on their consciousness and it would be understandable if they did not focus on the details. If their attention was perfunctory, that did not mean they had necessarily failed to take care of their interests.

18.23   Puffs

The courts are understandably reluctant to give a precise definition of misleading or deceptive conduct because of the risk that, by identifying certain conduct, it will be easier to evade the legislation. Equally clearly, however, some conduct falls outside the ACL. For example, just as at common law, a degree of exaggerated sales talk in negotiations or advertising is to be expected. There is still a line though that, when crossed, makes such statements misleading or deceptive. In *Byers v Dorotea* (1986), the vendor in the sale of apartments 'off the plan' (that is, before they had been built) released a statement that the apartments would be 'bigger and better' than those close by. Since an objective comparison could be made with actual apartments in the vicinity, the statement was too specific to be a mere puff. If it had been just a general statement that the apartments were the biggest and best, the outcome might have been different.

18.24   Statements of law

While there is a degree of overlap between actionable misrepresentations, and misleading or deceptive conduct, there are also important differences. The legislation is broader in scope: *Demagogue v Ramensky* (1992) at 41. For example, statements of law can, in certain circumstances, amount to misleading and deceptive conduct. The crucial indicator is whether the person making the statement holds themselves out to have expertise. The way that this factor is used can be seen from contrasting two decisions. In the first, *Inn Leisure Industries v DF McCloy* (1991), the purchaser of a property told the vendor that the sale would not attract sales tax. This was no more than an 'untutored opinion'. On the other hand, an incorrect opinion on the law by the State Government Insurance Commission in *SWF Hoists v State Government Insurance Commission* (1990) was held to be misleading: see **18.10**.

18.25   Silence

Outside of a few special situations, it is generally possible to remain silent without committing a misrepresentation at common law. Remaining silent may, however, be misleading or deceptive within the ACL. In *Henjo Investments v Collins Marrickville* (1988), it was said that the legislation had a 'broad reach'. Where there was a 'duty to disclose', remaining silent would be misleading or deceptive. In that case, the vendor of a restaurant failed to reveal to the purchaser that the premises were not licensed to seat as many customers as the restaurant's layout suggested.

More recent decisions, however, have moved away from the idea of a duty to disclose. In *Demagogue v Ramensky* (1992), the plaintiff wished to purchase land from the defendant for the purpose of building home units. When the respondents inspected the site, the defendant's agent indicated that there would be access to the block via a driveway built to the road. The plan attached to the contract also referred to a driveway. In fact, the portion of the plan referred to as a driveway was a public road rather than a private driveway. The defendant and their agents remained silent as to the character of the road. They were found liable for a breach of what was then s 52 of the *Trade Practices Act 1974* (Cth). This was not because there was a duty to disclose the nature of the road, but because, on the facts, there was a 'reasonable expectation' that this information would be disclosed. This approach emphasises that the legislation is not dependent on the general law. As Black CJ observed (at 32):

> There is in truth no such thing as 'mere silence' because the significance of silence always falls to be considered in the context in which it occurs. That context may or may not include facts giving rise to a reasonable expectation, in the circumstances of the case, that if particular matters exist they will be disclosed.

This does not mean that there is an expectation that everything the other party might want to know is revealed. *Miller & Associates v BMW Australia Finance* (2010) concerned two large commercial parties, one of whom supplied the other with what was said to be misleading documentation concerning an insurance premium funding loan. It was held that an expectation of disclosure does not arise simply because one party knows that a particular matter is likely to be important to the other. French CJ and Kiefel J explained (at [22]) that what is now s 18 of the ACL:

> does not require a party in commercial negotiations to volunteer information which will be of assistance to the decision-making of the other party. A fortiori it does not impose on a party an obligation to volunteer information in order to avoid the consequences of the careless disregard, for its own interests, of another party of equal bargaining power and competence.

In the right circumstances, nevertheless, there can be a reasonable expectation of disclosure even in commercial negotiations.[34] *Advance Business Finance v Zip Zap* (2014) involved what was found to be a 'scam' financing arrangement. The plaintiff provided finance to a purchaser of goods, on the faith of an invoice provided by the vendor. The goods covered by the invoice were not supplied, as indeed the vendor knew from the outset would be the case. The plaintiff successfully sued the vendor for misleading and deceptive conduct. It was quite clear that the plaintiff would not have contracted had it known of the true facts, and the vendor's silence was compounded by a series of partially misleading statements. Similarly, in *Skinner v Redmond Family Holdings* (2017), the purchaser of what it thought was a controlling interest in a

---

34   Besides the examples given in the text, including *Demagogue*, see also *CPI Group v Stora Enso* (2007).

company was found to have been deceived by two other shareholders. They had not revealed their right to convert loans to the company into equity, an option which, if exercised, would dilute the plaintiff's shareholding.

In theory, the reasonable expectation test operates in a very different way to the common law of misrepresentation. Yet, as studies have shown, the outcomes of non-disclosure cases brought under the statutory regime tend to parallel what would have been decided at common law.[35] Where silence is found to be deceptive, there is generally a half-truth involved, a failure to correct an earlier statement, or a fiduciary relationship. Conversely, where none of those factors are present, it is unusual for liability to be imposed,[36] although *Skinner* appears to be an exception in this respect.

18.26   Must silence be deliberate?

It is possible to make a conscious choice to remain silent, but silence may also be the result of forgetfulness. The definition of 'conduct' in s 2(2) of the ACL includes doing an act and then goes on to refer to 'refraining (other than inadvertently) from doing that act'. This might suggest that, although there is no general requirement of any intention to mislead or deceive, a failure to act can only breach s 18 if it is deliberate. The authorities have consistently been divided on this point.[37] In *Johnson Tiles v Esso Australia* (1999), Merkel J attempted to reconcile them by distinguishing situations in which silence is combined with other conduct, and those where silence is the only basis for saying that there is misleading or deceptive conduct. In the second category, he thought, non-deliberate silence would not be enough to render conduct misleading or deceptive by itself. That view has received at least qualified support in some later decisions: see eg *Owston Nominees v Clambake* (2011) at [66]. But other courts have resisted the suggestion that silence can only be deceptive if it is deliberate: see eg *CCP Australian Airships v Primus Telecommunications* (2004) at [34].

18.27   Representations as to the future

Section 4 of the ACL is a complex provision which establishes a special rule for representations about any future matter. At the risk of over-simplification, such a representation is deemed to be misleading unless the representor can adduce evidence that they had reasonable grounds for making the representation.

The concept of a 'future matter' has proved surprisingly difficult to define. In *Miba v Nescor Industries* (1996), representations concerning the likely takings of a franchise business the defendant was selling were held not to fall within the section. The fact that the estimation had a future element did not make it a representation 'with respect to future matters'. Rather, it was treated as a statement of present belief, because the letter in question spoke of the defendants believing that the takings would be received, and set out how the projections were made. This approach was rejected, however, in *Digi Tech v Brand* (2004). The fact that a forecast was

---

35   See Gillies 2004; Stewart & McClurg 2007: 52–7. Compare De Wilde 2007.
36   See eg *Clifford v Vegas Enterprises* (2011); *Owston Nominees v Clambake* (2011); *NB2 v PT* (2018).
37   Contrast, for example, *Nagy v Masters Dairy* (1996) with *Costa Vraca v Berrigan Weed & Pest Control* (1998).

expressed as a current statement, and the methods of calculation were set out, did not mean it was not a representation on a future matter.

The way that the section applies can be illustrated with examples. Suppose A makes a representation about a future matter to B. In the absence of reasonable grounds for making the statement, it will be treated as misleading (s 4(1)). The burden shifts to A to provide evidence that the statement was reasonable (s 4(2)). If she provides no evidence, the representation will be deemed to be misleading. If A provides evidence suggesting that she had reasonable grounds for making the representation, B is then required to show that A did not have reasonable grounds for making the statement (s 4(3)(a)).[38] If B discharges this burden the statement will be misleading.[39] A, on the other hand, does not, by showing that she had reasonable grounds for making the statement, necessarily prove that the statement was not misleading or deceptive (s 4(4)).

18.28   Opinions

A simple opinion is not an actionable misrepresentation at common law. But the outcome is different when an opinion can be presented as based on an implied statement of fact: see **18.08**. The case law on the ACL adopts a similar approach, even though this is not required under the legislation: see *Johnson & Johnson v Unilever* (2006). Hence, an opinion or belief is not misleading or deceptive simply because it is incorrect. Where the opinion involves a representation, that the opinion is held and based on some reasonable factual foundations, it may amount to misleading or deceptive conduct: see eg *Global Sportsman v Mirror Newspapers* (1984). In *Havyn v Webster* (2005), the plaintiff purchased a small apartment block. It was claimed in the sale's brochure that each apartment was approximately 63 square metres in size. In fact, this overstated the average size. The size was worked out by pacing the unit rather than measuring it. Because it was not measured properly this was treated as a statement of belief. It was implied that the opinion on the area had reasonable foundations. The fact that reasonable foundations for the statement were missing led to the conclusion that the brochure was misleading or deceptive.

18.29   Promises

Section 2(2)(a) of the ACL specifically contemplates that contractual promises and promises to perform contractual obligations may be treated as 'conduct'. The ACL thus operates in parallel to contractual liability. But not all promises are contractually enforceable. An element of a contract claim may be missing. For example, a promise to perform an existing contract would traditionally have failed for want of consideration: see **13.05**. Other contracts may be unenforceable because of a failure to comply with formality requirements: see eg **5.44–5.46**.

Accounting Systems 2000 v CCH Australia (1993) provides a good example of a promise when an element of contractual liability is missing. Accounting Systems entered into a contract

---

38   Section 4(3) was introduced to resolve competing views about the operation of the equivalent provision (s 51A) in the *Trade Practices Act 1974*: see eg *McGrath v Australian Naturalcare Products* (2008).

39   Note that it does not matter that the statement may actually turn out to be true, if A did not *at the time* have a reasonable basis for making the statement: see eg *ACCC v Dateline Imports* (2015).

with Castle Douglas, under which copyright interests in software were assigned. Accounting Systems gave Castle Douglas a warranty that they owned the copyright. Castle Douglas assigned the licence to use the software to CCH Australia. In fact, Accounting Systems were not the owners of the copyright. CCH argued that the warranties on the contract between Accounting Systems and Castle Douglas were misleading, and sought compensation for the money that they had paid Castle Douglas for the licence. The statement about copyright was a contractual warranty, but it was not part of a contract with the plaintiff. It was held, nevertheless, that a promise about a present state of affairs, if false, could amount to misleading or deceptive conduct, even where the statement was a contractual term.

The promise in *Accounting Systems 2000* concerned a statement of existing fact – the ownership of the copyright. A promise may also relate to future conduct, and therefore fall within s 4 of the ACL, as discussed above. In *Futuretronics v Gadzhis* (1992), the defendant had a bid at auction for the plaintiff's property accepted, and then refused to sign the contract and pay the deposit as required under the conditions of sale. The contract was unenforceable for failure to comply with necessary formalities. The plaintiff argued that, by making a bid, the defendant represented that the bid was genuine, and that they intended to be bound by the auction conditions. By refusing to complete the contract their conduct was misleading or deceptive. This was a representation on a future matter. No evidence was offered that the defendant, in making the promise, had reasonable grounds to represent that they intended to sign the contract. The conduct was therefore misleading or deceptive, although on the facts no loss was suffered.

There is a danger that the ACL could potentially be superimposed on every contract. This move has been resisted. Making a promise which is then unfulfilled is not in itself misleading or deceptive conduct: *Global Sportsman v Mirror Newspapers* (1984); *Body Bronze International v Fehcorp* (2011). In some instances, as in *Futuretronics*, a promisor may be taken to represent an intention to perform the promise, and if they do not have reasonable grounds for making such a representation, such conduct is potentially misleading or deceptive.[40] The same may be true where there is a representation that a party has the *capacity* to perform, when there are no reasonable grounds to believe that: see eg *Pramoko v Grande Enterprises* (2015). But the courts have refused to superimpose on every contractual promise an implied representation that the promisor has the ability (as opposed to intention) to perform. In *Concrete Constructions v Litevale* (2002), it was made clear that it will be much more difficult to argue that a contracting party is implicitly representing a capacity to perform, and that, if there is such a representation, it is misleading or deceptive.

18.30   Relaying information

Questions have arisen over the relaying of information. In *Yorke v Lucas* (1985) at 666, it was said that:

> If the circumstances are such as to make it apparent that [a] corporation is not the source of the information and that it expressly or impliedly disclaims any belief in its truth or falsity, merely passing it on for what it is worth, we very much doubt that the corporation can properly be said to be itself engaging in conduct that is misleading or deceptive.

---

40   See also *Idi Enterprises v Classified Transport* (2011).

The question is whether the relevant section of the public would regard the person passing on the information as adopting or endorsing it: *Gardam v George Wills* (1988); *Google v ACCC* (2013). This is a question of fact.

In *Google*, the High Court was concerned with the use of Google's AdWords program. Advertisers using the program were able to enter a competitor's name as a keyword, with the result that a 'sponsored link' (in the form of an advertisement linking to the advertiser's website) would appear when a member of the public used Google to search for that name. At trial, it was found that the sponsored links were misleading and deceptive, as they represented to ordinary and reasonable members of the relevant public that the advertiser had a commercial association with their competitor. What was at issue on appeal was whether Google had done more than merely pass on the sponsored links. The ACCC argued that Google (and its search engine) did not operate analogously to other intermediaries, so that the principles established in the earlier case law were not applicable. Google was said to have 'produced' the sponsored links because it was Google's technology that was used to display them in response to a search request. It did not matter that the advertisers were the source of the sponsored links or that Google would not be understood to be endorsing the contents of those links. A majority of the High Court rejected these arguments, explaining (at [69]) that:

> The fact that the provision of information via the internet will – because of the nature of the internet – necessarily involve a response to a request made by an internet user does not, without more, disturb the analogy between Google and other intermediaries.

In concluding that Google had neither produced the sponsored links nor endorsed or adopted their contents, the majority highlighted Google's lack of control over the material displayed.

There is also a specific exemption in s 19 of the ACL for anyone carrying on business as an 'information provider'. The predecessor of this provision, s 65A of the *Trade Practices Act 1974* (Cth), was introduced in 1984 to meet concerns about the potential for misleading or deceptive conduct claims against the media for inaccurate reporting. The exemption does not apply, among other things, to advertisements: see eg *ACCC v Turi Foods* (2013). But media outlets may still, in such a case, seek to argue that they have not adopted or endorsed the content of a misleading advertisement.

18.31 Remedies

Part 5-2 of the ACL offers a range of remedies for contraventions of the civil prohibitions on misleading or deceptive conduct. These can generally be pursued not just against the person or organisation primarily responsible, but anyone else 'involved' in their contravention. That term is defined in s 2(1) to cover anyone who has aided, abetted, counselled or procured the contravention, induced it, conspired with others to effect it, or 'been in any way, directly or indirectly, knowingly concerned in, or party to, the contravention'.[41] This language has been interpreted to mean that the person involved must be an *intentional* participant with

---

41   Note that in the case of some of the provisions referred to below, including ss 224 and 232, this language actually appears in the sections themselves, rather than there being a shorthand reference to a person being 'involved' in a contravention.

knowledge of the 'essential elements' of the contravention. But they do not need to have been aware that the law was being breached: *Yorke v Lucas* (1985).

In the case of a breach of the prohibitions in Part 3-1, though *not* s 18, a court may impose a civil penalty (s 224). This power has been used to impose substantial fines on businesses for misleading customers or potential customers; for example, as to the true price of their services or the safety of their products: see eg *ACCC v TPG Internet* (2013); *ACCC v Woolworths* (2016). Following a recommendation from the ACL review, the maximum penalties set by s 224 were substantially increased in September 2018 to ensure an adequate level of deterrence.[42] The maximum penalty applicable to a person or entity other than a corporation is now $500,000. In the case of a corporation, the figure is the greater of $10 million, three times the value of the benefit the corporation obtained from the breach, or (where that value cannot be calculated) 10 per cent of the annual turnover of the corporation in the preceding 12 months.

Sections 232–235 also permit a court to grant an injunction 'in such terms as the court considers appropriate'. As with a traditional injunction, this may be used to stop behaviour that is misleading or deceptive. But it is also possible for so-called 'performance injunctions' to be issued. These are injunctions requiring a person who has breached s 18 or one of the other prohibitions to take positive action, such as to refund money, transfer property, honour a promise, or destroy or dispose of goods: s 232(6). The list of positive actions in s 232(6) is not intended to be exhaustive of the type of mandatory injunctions that can be granted under s 232. In practice, however, most litigation under s 18 involves a claim either for damages under s 236, or for one of the other remedies for which s 237 provides.

18.32   Damages

Section 236 of the ACL gives a victim of misleading or deceptive conduct an action to 'recover the amount of the loss or damage'. A series of High Court decisions have debated the correct measure of damages under this provision or its equivalent (s 82) in the *Trade Practices Act 1974* (Cth). A reliance measure would mean that the legislation mirrored the approach taken at common law for negligent and fraudulent misrepresentation. An expectation measure would replicate the standard measure of damages for breach of contract. Each may give a different outcome, as noted in **18.15**.

In *Gates v City Mutual* (1986), Gibbs CJ said that damages in the legislation are analogous to actions in tort, and therefore a tort measure should be used. Mason, Wilson and Dawson JJ held that courts are not bound to make a definitive choice between the tort or the contract measure of damages, but the measure of damages in tort is appropriate in most cases of misleading or deceptive conduct, especially those involving statements. A decade later, in *Marks v GIO Australia* (1998), some members of the High Court were more sympathetic to damages assessed by the expectation measure, and cautioned about limiting damages by analogy in cases of misleading or deceptive conduct.

In a third case, *Murphy v Overton Investments* (2004), the High Court departed from the reliance measure. The plaintiff took out a 99 year lease over a unit in a retirement village owned and managed by the defendant. Before the lease was entered into, the defendant

---

42   See CAANZ 2017: 88–9; *Treasury Laws Amendment (2018 Measures No 3) Act 2018* (Cth) Sch 1.

provided the plaintiffs with an estimate of the amount that they would be required to contribute towards outgoings and upkeep of the property. It was explained that this was only an estimate, and the amount might vary. The figures used to calculate the estimate were erroneous. They did not take into account all of the types of outgoings that the defendant was entitled to recover. When the defendant began charging for those outgoings that they were entitled to recover under the lease, the plaintiffs alleged misleading or deceptive conduct. Damages were sought to reflect the difference between the value of the lease if contributions were calculated in accordance with the defendant's actual entitlement, and if contributions were charged in accordance with the estimate. The difficulty for the plaintiffs was that the lease was worth what they had paid for it. They paid for a service, namely the upkeep of the property, and they received what they paid for. The High Court accepted that, in cases of purchase of property, the difference between the price paid and the value of the property received will often be important, but that was not the only form of loss. The plaintiffs incurred a loss when the defendant began charging the full amount, even though it was entitled to do so. Their loss lay in the fact that the continuing financial obligations they undertook under the lease were larger than they were led to believe.

Murphy is a difficult decision. The outgoings under the lease were the same whether there was misleading or deceptive conduct or not. The plaintiffs received something worth what they paid for it. On any traditional analysis, there was no loss. In effect, the High Court seems to have said that damages can be awarded where someone enters into a contract which was different to the one they thought they were entering. They have changed their position by entering into a contract on the basis of misleading or deceptive conduct. Applying this approach, it would be possible to recover damages when there is a misleading statement about the profitability of a business being sold, yet the business is worth exactly what the plaintiff paid for it. Some subsequent authorities have awarded damages in just this case: see eg *Dalecoast v Guardian International* (2004). But others have sought to distinguish *Murphy*: see eg *Warwick Entertainment Centre v Alpine Holdings* (2008). In *Jamieson v Westpac* (2014) at [189], Jackson J suggested that the *Murphy* approach over-compensates the plaintiff:

> The reason why that outcome is troubling is that damages calculated on that basis do not compensate the plaintiffs for a wrong done to them by restoring them to the position as if the wrong had not been committed. Instead, it gives them a benefit they could not and would not have obtained if there had been no misleading or deceptive conduct. This can only be justified on the footing that it is better to make the defendant pay on that basis than it is to leave the plaintiffs without a remedy in damages.

Damages under s 236 can be awarded for loss of opportunity. The result of the defendant's misleading and deceptive conduct may result in the loss of an opportunity to continue a contract with a third party, or enter into a contract with a third party. As *Sellars v Adelaide Petroleum* (1994) made clear, it is not necessary to prove on the balance of probabilities that a benefit would actually have been derived from the opportunity, had it not been lost. It is enough to show some prospect of deriving a benefit with reference to the degree of possibilities and probabilities.

Since damages under s 236 must necessarily be compensatory, exemplary damages which punish the defendant cannot be recovered under this provision: *Musca v Astle* (1988). On the other hand, the type of damages that may be awarded are not confined to economic loss. They may, for example, include an award for disappointment or distress suffered as a result of the misleading or deceptive conduct: see eg *New South Wales Lotteries v Kuzmanovski* (2011).

18.33   Other orders to remedy a contravention

Section 237 of the ACL is an equivalent to s 87 of the *Trade Practices Act 1974* (Cth). It confers on a court a broad remedial power to make any order it thinks appropriate either to compensate an injured person, or to prevent or reduce any loss or damage they are likely to suffer.

To the extent that s 237 provides for compensatory orders, there is an obvious overlap with s 236. However, there are also significant differences between the two provisions: *Mayne Nickless v Multigroup Distribution Services* (2001) at [58]. First, orders made under s 237 may clearly go beyond compensation, as is apparent from the non-exhaustive list of possible orders that appears in s 243. They may include a declaration that a contract is void (in whole or part),[43] contractual variation, an order for the refund of money or return of property, or specific performance. Second, while s 236 provides a right to *complete* recovery of loss or damage, an order under s 237 may provide *partial* compensation for loss or damage suffered. Third, whereas s 236 is restricted to loss or damage that has already occurred, s 237 expressly allows for orders in respect of loss or damage that is *likely* to be suffered. Fourth, a plaintiff who proves loss or damage has a right to a remedy under s 236, but an order under s 237 is in the court's discretion. This discretion relates both to whether to make an order and the scope of any such order: *Finucane v NSW Egg Corporation* (1988) at 519. The remedial discretion granted by the provision is very wide, allowing for orders that could not be made at common law or in equity: *I & L Securities v HTW Valuers* (2002) at [106]. Finally, a claim under s 236 must be brought by the party who has suffered the loss or damage. Section 237, in contrast, also allows for the bringing of a claim by the regulator (the ACCC or a State equivalent) on a person's behalf.[44]

18.34   Causation and contribution

Sections 236 and 237 require that the plaintiff suffer, or in the case of s 237 be likely to suffer, 'loss or damage by conduct'. The standard of proof is on the balance of probabilities: *Sellars v Adelaide Petroleum* (1994). The defendant must have caused the loss or damage. In *Wardley v Western Australia* (1992) at 525, Mason CJ, Dawson, Gaudron and McHugh JJ explained that 'by' in the legislation 'clearly expresses the notion of causation without defining or elucidating it'. Causation is a question of fact, and proving causation is not usually difficult. In many instances, the plaintiff will have actually relied upon the misleading or deceptive conduct. The exact approach to linking the conduct and loss, however, is a matter of some uncertainty. In *McCarthy v McIntyre* (1999) at [49], the Full Court of the Federal Court admitted that 'perhaps there is no simple test capable of formulation'. *Wardley* had promoted a 'practical or common sense concept of causation'. Yet, in *Travel Compensation Fund v Tambree* (2005) at [45],

---

43   As to the circumstances in which a court will make such an order, which are not limited by the equitable rules as to rescission discussed earlier in the chapter: see eg *Munchies Management v Belperio* (1988); *Akron Securities v Iliffe* (1997); *Tenji v Henneberry* (2000).

44   Note also the power under ss 239–241 for a court, on application by the regulator, to make orders to redress loss or damage suffered by 'non-party consumers' – that is, persons affected by the relevant conduct, but not party to the enforcement proceedings: see eg *Director of Consumer Affairs v Domain Register* (2018).

Gummow and Hayne JJ doubted whether a 'common sense' approach was really very useful. The 'but for' test which has been used in other contexts may not be the exclusive test under the ACL: *Marks v GIO Australia* (1998) at [42]. The misleading or deceptive conduct is usually only one of a number of factors that explains why a contract was entered into. As with misrepresentation, it need not be the only factor. It need not even be shown that, but for the conduct, the plaintiff would not have suffered the loss. Hence, in *Lockyer Investment v Smallacombe* (1994), as a result of misleading conduct, the plaintiff purchased an irrigation system. The fact that they would have suffered similar losses with other systems did not deprive them of a remedy.

In some situations, the contribution of the plaintiff, by failing to take reasonable care, allows damages to be reduced to the extent that the plaintiff was responsible: see eg *Competition and Consumer Act 2010* (Cth) s 137B. The section only applies to economic loss, or damage to property. The plaintiff's fault only becomes relevant if the defendant did not cause the loss fraudulently or intentionally. Part VIA of the 2010 Act also provides for the apportionment of liability between multiple wrongdoers.[45] But this only applies where two or more parties' independent conduct has contributed to the relevant loss. The apportionment provisions cannot be invoked where, for example, both a company and its director are liable for the same breach: *Robinson v 470 St Kilda Road* (2018).

18.35   Exclusion of liability

Legislation in several States prevents the parties excluding liability under the ACL by contracting out of the statute.[46] But even aside from these provisions, attempts to simply exclude liability are unlikely to succeed: *Bowler v Hilda* (1998) at 207; *IOOF Australia Trustees v Tantipech* (1998). The rights and protections created by provisions such as s 18 are for the benefit of the public and cannot validly be surrendered, even by agreement: see **21.14**.

Disclaimers are different to exclusion clauses. Rather than excluding liability, a disclaimer attempts to ensure that no liability arises in the first place. What made the disclaimer in *Butcher v Lachlan Elder Realty* (2004) effective is that, on the majority's reasoning, it was sufficient to prevent the plaintiffs from ever being deceived: see **18.21**. The same is true of an acknowledgment clause – a common device in which one of the parties to a contract formally acknowledges that they did not rely on representations made by the other. In *Campbell v Backoffice Investments* (2009) at [31], French CJ observed that such clauses might provide evidence of non-reliance, and/or break any causal link between the defendant's conduct and any loss suffered by the plaintiff.

Mistake

18.36   Introduction

Mistake is one of the most conceptually confusing areas of contract law. It sits alongside a test for contract formation which, as we saw in **5.02**, stresses the objective intentions of the parties:

---

45   There are similar provisions in State law: see eg *Civil Liability Act 2002* (NSW) Pt 4. For a critical review of these provisions, as they apply to claims for misleading and deceptive conduct, see Dietrich 2016.

46   *Fair Trading Act 1989* (Qld) s 107; *Fair Trading Act 1987* (SA) s 96; *Fair Trading Act 2010* (WA) s 13.

see *Taylor v Johnson* (1983). Irrespective of the subjective intentions of the parties, where, from the perspective of a reasonable person, the parties are in agreement (or as it is sometimes put there is *consensus ad idem*), then a contract is formed. Equity may nevertheless intervene, in which case the contract becomes voidable. The impact of the objective approach will depend upon the ease by which it is possible to rescind contracts in equity.

Contractual mistakes can occur in several different ways. Some mistakes are closer to misrepresentation. One party either induces the other into making a mistake, or knows that the other party is making a mistake and does nothing to correct the error. Only one party is mistaken. These are known as *unilateral mistakes*. Other mistakes occur without any involvement by the other party. A *mutual mistake* arises when both parties are mistaken, but make different mistakes. *Common mistakes* are much more difficult. In these situations, the parties appear objectively to agree. Yet they have contracted under a misapprehension. Equity may have a particularly important role in this sort of case, but the precise nature of that role remains unsettled.

Two final doctrines are concerned only with written agreements. Rectification is used where the written document does not accurately reflect the intentions of the parties – that is, the intentions are wrongly recorded. Neither party is mistaken as such, it is simply that the written contract does not accord with what they intended. A related principle is the non est factum rule. In a very narrow range of situations, it is possible to argue that a written contract 'is not my deed'.

18.37   Mutual mistake

In a situation of mutual mistake, the parties are at cross purposes when they enter into a contract. Each party believes that they are contracting about something different. For example, A believes he is offering a blue car for sale and B believes that she is offering to buy a red car. Here, there is no meeting of minds. These are best seen as occasions in which no contract is formed. Even on an objective test, the parties are not in agreement. The best example of this sort of mistake is the old case of *Raffles v Wichelhaus* (1864). The plaintiff sold '125 bales of Sarat cotton … to arrive ex Peerless from Bombay' to the defendant. The plaintiff tendered cotton from a ship called Peerless, which had sailed from Bombay in December, but the defendant refused to accept it on the ground that he had intended to buy the cotton from another vessel, also called Peerless, which had sailed from Bombay in October. There was held to be no contract. A case like this is highly unusual. Reference to the perspective of a reasonable person simply doesn't help determine the outcome. It is impossible to say on which terms the contract can be concluded.

18.38   Unilateral mistake

A unilateral mistake occurs where only one party makes a mistake. The other knows of the mistake, which is usually to their advantage. These mistakes may be one of two kinds:

(1) A knows of B's mistake as to a term of the contract and fails to disabuse B of the mistake; or

(2) B makes an offer to A, B being mistaken as to A's identity and A, usually a 'rogue' acting with deliberate intent, purports to accept B's offer.

Cases in the second category are also cases of fraud. The problem in many of these cases is that the rogue has succeeded in getting goods from B, and has then sold the goods to a third party, C. Fraudulent misrepresentation only renders a contract voidable, as we have seen earlier in the chapter. This means that where C is a good faith purchaser, they get to keep the goods, unless the contract was rescinded before the property passed: see **18.13**. A mistake at common law, on the other hand, means the contract is void. In that situation the property in the goods can never pass to C. Therefore, B will have an action in the tort of conversion against C, *if* they can establish no contract was ever made with A.

18.39   Unilateral mistake as to the content of the contract

In *Taylor v Johnson* (1983), a vendor agreed to sell two five-acre plots of land for $15,000. The vendor subsequently refused to proceed with the conveyance on the grounds that she had made a mistake, and that, in fact, the contract price was $15,000 per acre (that is, $150,000 in total). The purchaser sought specific performance. The purchaser knew that the vendor was mistaken and, it was said (at 428), 'deliberately set out to ensure that [the vendor] was not disabused of the mistake or misapprehension under which he believed her to be acting'. *Taylor v Johnson* involves a restrictive explanation of contractual mistake. This was described by Mason ACJ, Murphy and Deane JJ (at 429) as the 'objective theory':

> [T]here is a contract which in conformity [with] the common law, continues to be binding, unless and until it is avoided in accordance with equitable principles which take as their foundation a contract valid at common law but transform it so that it becomes voidable.

Applying an objective test of contract formation, the parties had reached agreement, as reflected in the written document. Nevertheless, a majority of the High Court still thought that the contract was voidable in equity, on the basis that there was 'a serious mistake about its contents in relation to a fundamental term' (at 433). It was stressed that the purchaser had acted unconscionably. He knew or had reason to know that the vendor was mistaken, but deliberately engaged in a course of conduct which was designed to inhibit discovery of the mistake. On the basis of *Taylor v Johnson*, a serious mistake by one party on a term as fundamental as price is not enough to set aside the contract. What makes the difference is some kind of sharp practice on the part of the other party. This may involve a fairly minor act. It is not necessary to deliberately mislead. Actual knowledge of the mistake is not required. It is enough that the other party ought to have known of it: *Re St George Bank* (2011) at [20].

18.40   Unilateral mistake of identity

Ordinarily, the identity of the other contracting party will not matter. In a few rare cases, however, the identity of the other party is more crucial. A unilateral mistake of identity can occur in a number of different ways. Some parties deal at a distance, whereas others deal face-to-face. In one situation, A contracts at a distance with B, believing B to be C. C is only an alias, and not a real person. Such contracts are not void for mistake, though they may be voidable for fraud: see eg *King's Norton Metal Edge v Edridge* (1897). But it is more difficult if C, with whom A believes they are contracting, is a real person. In *Shogun Finance v Hudson* (2003), the House of Lords, by majority, held that a contract with a rogue who pretended to be someone else was void. The buyer's identity here was crucial, because it was a hire purchase agreement. Lords Nicholls and Millett dissented. They thought that the parties had entered into a valid contract, albeit one that was voidable for fraud. Given the prominence of the objective theory in Australia, the minority view is likely to find favour here, with the difference that equity might then intervene on the grounds of mistake as well as fraud. There has been little discussion of *Shogun* in Australia, other than in *Vassallo v Haddad Import & Export* (2004) at [65]. There, Rein DCJ of the New South Wales District Court took *Shogun* to support the view that:

> where two individuals deal with each other and agree terms of a contract, then a contract will be concluded between them notwithstanding that one has deceived the other into thinking that he has the identity of a third party, or at least that there is a strong presumption that each intends to contract with the other.

The law relating to face-to-face dealing is no clearer. The classic authority is *Lewis v Avery* (1972). During a face-to-face meeting, the seller was duped into believing that the buyer was a famous actor. He was in fact a rogue, who left with a car after paying with a worthless cheque, and sold the car to an innocent third party. The contract was held to be voidable for fraud and not void for mistake. An earlier Court of Appeal, in *Ingram v Little* (1961), came to the opposite conclusion by holding a contract void, on very similar facts. In *Shogun*, Lords Millett and Walker thought (at [87], [185]) that *Ingram v Little* was wrongly decided. When contracting, a person deals with the person in front of them, even if that person is a rogue and not the person they purport to be. Lord Walker argued (at [187]) that it is only in 'rare exceptions' that there is no intention to deal with the person who is physically present. Once again, the importance attached to the objective theory in Australia would suggest that the usual position is that a contract is not void for mistake when the parties deal face to face. Support for this view can be found from Doyle CJ in *Papas v Bianca Investments* (2002) at [25]. Yet, in *Porter v Latec Finance* (1964), the two dissenting judges, Kitto and Windeyer JJ, seemed to assume that a mistake of identity arising from a face-to-face contract can render a contract void. The majority held on the facts that there was no mistake, and so the point was not considered.

18.41 Common mistake

A common mistake can be distinguished from a mutual mistake. A common mistake is one shared by both parties. Viewed objectively, the parties to a common mistake are in agreement. Statute provides that, in a contract for the sale of specific goods, when the goods have perished without the knowledge of the seller, then the contract is void.[47] Otherwise, the law makes it extremely difficult to avoid a contract for common mistake. In *McRae v Commonwealth Disposals Commission* (1950), the defendant purported to sell to the plaintiff the wreck of an oil tanker said to be lying on the Jourmaund Reef near New Guinea and containing oil. The plaintiff fitted out an expedition to salvage the tanker. No such tanker had ever existed, nor was there any such reef. The trial judge held that there was no contract because there was no subject matter. The High Court disagreed. Its view was that the defendant had promised that

---

[47]   *Sale of Goods Act 1923* (NSW) s 11; *Goods Act 1958* (Vic) s 11; *Sale of Goods Act 1896* (Qld) s 9; *Sale of Goods Act 1895* (WA) s 6; *Sale of Goods Act 1895* (SA) s 6; *Sale of Goods Act 1896* (Tas) s 11; *Sale of Goods Act 1954* (ACT) s 11; *Sale of Goods Act 1972* (NT) s 11.

there was a tanker, and was therefore liable in damages for breach when it did not exist. It has been said of *McRae* that it 'denies, effectively, any general principle that common mistake, even as to a fundamental fact, will vitiate an otherwise binding contract': *Manna v Manna* (2008) at [29].

An equally narrow view of common mistake is found in *Svanosio v McNamara* (1956). A vendor agreed to sell a piece of land which both parties believed to include the whole of the Bull's Head Hotel – a licensed premises. Some of the hotel in fact stood on Crown land. The purchaser argued that this mistake made the contract void. Although the conveyance could not be challenged, the purchaser was seeking to argue that the contract to sell the land was void, as a means of recovering the purchase money. This argument was dismissed. Dixon CJ and Fullagar J stated (at 195) that 'if one thing in this case is clear, it seems to us to be that neither instrument was or is void'. McTiernan, Williams and Webb JJ stressed (at 208) that a contract for the sale of land was in a 'special category', because the purchaser has a right to investigate the title, and rescind the contract, if the vendor did not have good title.

The role of equity in this area is unclear.[48] It was explicitly excluded from contracts for the sale of land by McTiernan, Williams and Webb JJ in *Svanosio* at 201. In *Great Peace Shipping v Tsavliris* (2003), the English Court of Appeal went further, rejecting any role for equity in cases of common mistake. One of the motivations for this outcome was that otherwise the same facts could engage with a very narrow doctrine of mistake at law, and a much wider one in equity. These issues were considered in more depth by the Queensland Court of Appeal in *Australian Estates v Cairns City Council* (2005). Atkinson J pointed out that Australian courts were not bound to follow the English Court of Appeal, even if home grown authority were lacking. Nevertheless, she was persuaded (at [52]) that *Great Peace Shipping* should be followed. Jerrard JA said (at [25]) that he agreed with this analysis.[49] McMurdo P did not consider it necessary to consider the question, because she did not believe that there was a common mistake on the facts of the case.

As Dawson J put it in *Taylor v Johnson* (1983) at 444, 'mistake is not of itself a ground for rescission of the contract'. If equity does provide a remedy in cases of common mistake, unconscionable behaviour will be required. In *Pacer v Westpac* (1996) at 22, Santow J agreed that there is no general jurisdiction to set aside a contract for common mistake. In order for the contract to be rescinded, the mistake needed to be serious, and the product of unconscionable behaviour. Unconscionability is usually equated with some sort of wrongdoing, as explained (at 31):

> Substantive unconscionability is the basis of equity's jurisdiction to relieve for common mistake. This is because in common mistake, procedural unconscionability is unlikely to be involved. By definition both parties are mistaken, though the fact that one may have contributed more than the other to the joint mistake may also have a bearing. Thus, generally unconscionability in common mistake consists, not in concealment actions by the unmistaken party preceding the contract, but rather the unconscionability of retaining a contractual benefit as a result of upholding an agreement which may never have been entered into, but for the mistake.

---

48   For a detailed discussion, see Swain 2015c.
49   There is far from consensus on this point: see eg the very different analysis in *Hawcroft v Hawcroft General Trading* (2016) at [31]–[67].

18.42   Non est factum

At common law, a person is generally bound by a document that they sign, whether they have read and understood it or not: see **9.04**. However, in relatively rare cases a defence of non est factum (it was not my deed) might be raised. It is of great antiquity, being one of the few defences that could be used against a deed in the action of debt (see **1.10**). It was originally available to those who were illiterate, but now includes anyone who cannot understand a document through no fault of their own. The document must be signed in the belief that it was radically or fundamentally different from its true nature.

Non est factum is difficult to successfully plead. *Petelin v Cullen* (1975) is a rare example. Petelin possessed a poor understanding of English. He granted Cullen an option to purchase his land. Once the option expired, Cullen's agent presented Petelin with an agreement to extend the option and enclosed a cheque. Petelin was told that he was only signing a receipt for the cheque. The option was exercised, and Petelin refused to sell. Cullen sought specific performance. The High Court allowed the defence. Two situations were distinguished. In the first, the party against whom the defence is raised is aware of the circumstances and knows or has reason to suspect that the signer may not understand the true character of the transaction. Here, the law protects the signer who has not truly consented to the contract. There is no countervailing reason to enforce the contract, because the other party has not relied on the signature without any reason to doubt its validity. Whether or not the signer's failure to read the document was the result of carelessness is irrelevant.

A second situation occurs when non est factum is raised against an innocent party, usually a third party. Here there are two innocent parties: the signer and the third party. In *Saunders v Anglia Building Society* (1971), a widow of 78 years of age signed a document, not realising that it created a charge over her property. The bank, as the innocent party, sought possession. Where the defence is raised against an innocent party, it must be shown that a failure to read the document was not due to carelessness. For example, it can be expected that if someone is unable to read the document they sign, then they will have it explained to them.

18.43   Rectification

According to Gageler, Nettle and Gordon JJ in *Simic v New South Wales Land and Housing Corporaiton* (2016) at [103] (with citations omitted):

> Rectification is an equitable remedy, the purpose of which is to make a written instrument 'conform to the true agreement of the parties where the writing by common mistake fails to express that agreement accurately'. For relief by rectification, it must be demonstrated that, at the time of the execution of the written instrument sought to be rectified, there was an 'agreement' between the parties in the sense that the parties had a 'common intention', and that the written instrument was to conform to that agreement. Critically, it must also be demonstrated that the written instrument does not reflect the 'agreement' because of a common mistake.

In *Simic*, performance bonds had been issued by a bank at the request of a construction company. The bonds were supposed to be issued in favour of the New South Wales Land and Housing Corporation to provide security for performance of a contract it had awarded to the company. But owing to what was found to be a common mistake, the bonds named a non-existing entity. They were rectified with retrospective effect to stipulate the Corporation as the beneficiary, allowing it to demand the payment required by each instrument.

A party seeking rectification must provide 'clear and convincing proof' of a common intention: see *Pukallus v Cameron* (1982) at 425. According to the majority in *Simic* (at [104]), the task is to establish 'the actual or true common intention of the parties … viewed objectively from their words or actions'. As Kiefel J noted in the same case, however, statements like this should not be misconstrued. A court is seeking for this purpose to determine the parties' subjective (actual) intentions, rather than those a reasonable person would have inferred.[50] But in conducting that inquiry, the court may be said to 'view the evidence of intention objectively, in the sense that it does not merely accept what a party says was in his or her mind, but instead considers and weighs admissible evidence probative of intention': ibid at [42].

Where the parties have abandoned their original common intentions by the time a contract is reduced into writing, the written contract reflects the true agreement of the parties and will not be rectified: see eg *Winks v WH Heck & Sons* (1986). Nor can rectification be used to overcome a mutual mistake and make an instrument conform to a consensus that the parties never actually reached: see eg *Newey v Westpac* (2014). But, if the necessary common intention can be established, it will not matter that the only agreement reached is the very contract which one of the parties is seeking to have rectified. There is no need to show some sort of an 'antecedent' agreement that existed before the written contract was created: *Maralinga v Major Enterprises* (1973) at 350.

While relatively few contracts are set aside for mistake, it is far more common for rectification to be granted. But there are also many cases in which a claim for the remedy is disputed or indeed denied, on the basis that the applicant is seeking to correct a mistake as to something other than the *recording* of the parties' agreement. In *Pukallus*, a contract for the sale of land described the land as including 'Subdivision 1 of Portion 1154'. The vendor and purchaser both believed that an area containing a bore hole and cultivated land formed part of the subdivision. After the conveyance, it was discovered that the bore and cultivation lay outside the subdivision. The High Court held that the contract could not be rectified so as to include the bore and cultivated area. The mistake, which both parties undoubtedly shared, was not a mistake in the relevant sense. The written contract accurately reflected their intentions. Their mistake related not to the way that their intentions were recorded, but the substance of the transaction. Similarly, a document which accurately reflects an agreement cannot be rectified just because the parties may have misunderstood the effect of that agreement: see eg *Maralinga v Major Enterprises* (1973).[51]

---

50   Compare *Chartbrook v Persimmon Homes* (2009) at [59]–[60], proposing an objective test which, as French CJ observed in *Simic* (at [19]) 'does not represent the common law of Australia as it presently stands'.

51   For an extensive review of the case law on the limits of the remedy, see *CA & CA Ballan v Oliver Hume* (2017).

18.44   Rectification of unilateral mistakes

Cases such as *Simic* speak of rectification being a remedy for common mistake. But there is also authority to suggest that it can be ordered where there is a unilateral mistake, and it would be unconscionable for the non-mistaken party to enforce the contract in the unrectified form. This prevents one of the parties from taking advantage of an error on the part of the other. The requirements for rectification of this kind were set out in *Leibler v Air New Zealand* (1999) at [36]:

> If (i) one party, A, makes an agreement under a misapprehension that the agreement contains a particular provision which the agreement does not in fact contain; and (ii) the other party, B, knows of the omission and that it is due to a mistake on A's part; and (iii) B lets A remain under the misapprehension and concludes the agreement on the mistaken basis in circumstances where equity would require B to take some step or steps, depending on those circumstances, to bring the mistake to A's attention; then (iv) B will be precluded from relying upon A's execution of the agreement to resist A's claim for rectification.

Element (iii) mirrors the way that rescission was ordered for mistake in *Taylor v Johnson* (1983): see **18.39**. In the circumstances in *Leibler*, B ought to have brought the mistake to A's attention. The transaction was a complex one, the term omitted was fundamental, and the omission of the term did not reflect the negotiations. It was not necessary to show that B had deliberately set out to ensure that A was not made aware of the mistake. As with the more conventional use of rectification, however, the party seeking the remedy needs to give convincing proof of the precise mistake which they are seeking to have corrected.

19

UNDUE PRESSURE

19.01   Introduction

The law of contract places a high value on autonomy: see **1.10**, **2.05**. As a result, the parties are able to agree terms as they see fit, subject to statutory constraints or other restrictions such as the rules on illegality and public policy considered in Chapter 21. Autonomy only has any real value, however, if it can be said that the parties were truly autonomous and *freely* entered into a consensual agreement. The law aims to protect a party, often referred to as a 'victim', who has entered into a contract as a result of undue pressure. Pressure is a difficult concept to pin down. It covers a wide range of behaviour. At the extreme end of the spectrum, one party forces another to sign a contract with a gun to their head, or by making threats to their personal safety. But pressure is usually much more subtle. It is more commonly exerted through the ties of love, friendship or common business interests. Because of that continuum, it is difficult for the law to draw a line between pressure that is an acceptable part of everyday life, and pressure which calls for some form of relief.

The way in which the law of contract has addressed undue pressure is a product of its own history and reflects the division between law and equity. The common law dealt with the problem of undue pressure through the doctrine of *duress*. Equity developed a separate doctrine of *undue influence*.[1] A third doctrine, that of *unconscionability*, is discussed separately in Chapter 20. It too is derived from equity and has become more important in Australia than undue influence.

There is a degree of overlap between the three doctrines. The nature of the relationship between them has attracted academic and judicial comment: see **19.15**. Nevertheless, the individual elements that make up duress, undue influence, and unconscionability are quite different. The scope of each are, to varying degrees, contested. The consequences of undue pressure in all three cases, however, are the same. Contracts entered into as a result of undue pressure are voidable rather than void. This means that the standard remedy is rescission, which may be exercised in accordance with the rules discussed in the preceding chapter: see **18.05**, **18.12–18.13**.

Duress

19.02   Types of duress

Until comparatively recently, it was quite difficult to rescind a contract on the grounds of duress. Duress was originally confined to threats to the physical safety of the victim, or to those close to them. *Barton v Armstrong* (1976) is a rare modern example in which a contract was concluded under this kind of *duress to the person*, after a threat was made to murder the victim.

Duress of goods is also long established. It involves taking or keeping someone's goods, or threatening to do so. This type of duress is most likely to occur where one party retains the property of another in an attempt to extract payment. In *Hawker Pacific v Helicopter*

---

1   For a history of the treatment of contractual unfairness during the formative period in the eighteenth and nineteenth centuries, see Swain 2014a. The division is not entirely binary, because equity also developed a doctrine of duress which seems to have been similar in scope: see Ibbetson 1999: 72.

Charter (1991), the plaintiff owned a helicopter which was sent to the defendant for repainting. The quality of the work was disputed. The plaintiff signed a document believing that he needed to do so in order to ensure that the helicopter was released. Under this contract, a fee for the work was agreed and the plaintiff also undertook to release the defendant from any further liability. It was successfully argued that the contract could be rescinded because it was signed under a threat not to release the helicopter, which was required for a charter flight. The threat did not need to be expressly made in order to amount to duress. It was enough that it was reasonable for the plaintiff to believe that the helicopter would be withheld if it failed to sign.

The broader concept of *economic duress* has only fully developed more recently.[2] More is said below about the doctrine. For now, it is sufficient to say that it covers two main situations. In the first, a plaintiff is able to recover a payment made under a threat by the defendant not to perform their obligations under an existing contract: see eg *White Rose Flour Milling v Australian Wheat Board* (1944); *TA Sundell & Sons v Emm Yannoulatos* (1955); and see further **24.04**. A second application allows economic duress to be used to challenge a contract variation: see eg *The Siboen & The Sibotre* (1976). As Chapter 13 has noted, the previously strict rules of consideration for contract variation have been relaxed by the introduction of practical benefit as a form of consideration, following decisions such as *Musumeci v Winadell* (1994). This leaves economic duress with an important role in policing contract variations: see **13.11–13.12**.

The final form of duress is statutory. Under s 50 of the Australian Consumer Law (ACL), 'a person must not use physical force, or undue harassment or coercion' in connection with the supply of goods or services or the sale or grant of an interest in land. Statutory duress has some overlap with common law duress but sits within a different remedial structure: see **19.08**.

19.03   The nature of duress at common law

Duress used to be justified on the grounds that a victim's will was 'overborne' and as a result they had failed to consent. This rationale is unsatisfactory.[3] Where a person enters into a contract as a result of duress, they *do* consent in a very literal sense. The victim knows what they are agreeing to, and they intend to agree to it. A better explanation can be found in the judgment of McHugh JA in *Crescendo Management v Westpac* (1988) at 45–6:

> A person who is the subject of duress knows only too well what he [sic] is doing. But he chooses to submit to the demand or pressure rather than take an alternative course of action.[4]

Rather than seeing consent as being overborne by duress, consent can be seen as the product of undue pressure. This explains why, instead of asking whether the will of the victim is overborne, modern courts have tried to identify whether the pressure is *illegitimate*. Some types of pressure are more obviously illegitimate than others.

---

2   See Stewart 1984.
3   See Atiyah 1982.
4   This statement was approved in *Thorne v Kennedy* (2017) at [26].

19.04   Illegitimate pressure

It is not difficult to recognise that the threat of murder or physical violence is illegitimate: see eg *Barton v Armstrong* (1976). Equally, when goods are seized or retained or property damage is threatened, it is not usually too difficult to regard the pressure as illegitimate. These are all instances of actual or threatened unlawful acts. One category of unlawful conduct has, however, proved particularly problematic. Suppose the victim is threatened with a breach of contract.[5] A breach of contract is plainly unlawful: *Electricity Generation v Woodside Energy* (2013) at [26]. All things being equal, unlawful behaviour is usually illegitimate and therefore amounts to duress. But this is problematic in the context of a threatened breach. It assumes that all threatened breaches are the same. There will be occasions where a threatened breach is a legitimate part of the process of contract negotiation. Many renegotiations will involve at least an implied threat to breach the existing contract. *Musumeci v Winadell* (1994) provides a good example of a legitimate variation: see **13.09**. If the landlord had refused to vary the contract by reducing the rent it was clear that the tenant would be unable to pay and would therefore be in breach. There was a clear implied threat to breach the existing lease. But it was never suggested that to do so amounted to economic duress.

What this suggests is that context is important. Whether a threatened breach amounts to duress depends on whether it is used in an exploitative and possibly opportunistic manner. This is why on a set of facts like those in *Atlas Express v Kafco* (1989), discussed at **13.12**, a court readily found that economic duress had been used. The fact that pressure may have been exercised in good faith will not necessarily preclude a finding of duress: *Electricity Generation* at [30]. The presence or absence of good faith is one of a number of factors, including the commercial context, which may be considered in deciding whether the pressure was illegitimate: *Beerens v Bluescope Distribution* (2012) at [46].

There are some rare instances in which a lawful act may amount to duress. Lord Scarman gave an example in *Universe Tankships v ITWF* (1983) at 401 of a blackmailer who threatens to report a crime to the police. Reporting a crime is lawful. The lawful act becomes blackmail when done with the motive of extracting payment. Such behaviour is also exploitative and capable of amounting to duress, though it probably fits more easily within undue influence. In the same fashion, a threat to commence legal proceedings can, in the right context, amount to economic duress: see eg *J & S Holdings v NRMA Insurance* (1982). But as *Beerens* illustrates, a threat by a party to exercise their legal rights – in that case, to support an application to wind up the plaintiff's company – will not be illegitimate if the party has a genuine belief in their entitlement to act in that way. It is also clear that, at least as a general rule, it is not duress to extract a commercial advantage by threatening not to enter into a contract with the plaintiff: *Smith v William Charlick* (1924).

19.05   The scope of economic duress

Economic duress, especially between two commercial parties, is difficult to establish. Whilst many of the leading authorities have accepted that economic duress can be argued, judges are often reluctant to make a finding of such duress on the facts. A good example of quite strong

---

5   For the debate on this, see Bigwood 2003: 332–40.

pressure which was found to be outside the scope of economic duress can be found in *The Siboen & The Sibotre* (1976). Charterers told the ship owners that they would go into liquidation unless the charter price was significantly reduced. The owners agreed to reduce the price because they were unlikely to find alternative charterers, and any rights they might have had would be rendered worthless if the charterer became insolvent. It was held that, whilst in principle a contract could be set aside for economic duress, on the facts at issue there was no more than commercial pressure.

Crescendo Management v Westpac (1988) arose in quite different circumstances. Westpac held the proceeds from the sale of a property belonging to Mr and Mrs Hilbrink amounting to $31,000. The bank was concerned about the indebtedness of two companies of which Mr Hilbrink was a director. As a result, it refused to release the proceeds of the sale unless certain documents were executed in its favour. These included a mortgage executed upon a property in the name of Crescendo Management. It was argued that the mortgage was a product of duress. The threat to withhold the proceeds was held to be improper and unlawful. The difficulty for the plaintiffs was that the mortgage was already signed before that undue pressure was applied. The judgment of McHugh JA nevertheless contains some important statements of principle (at 45):

> The proper approach in determining whether there has been economic duress is to ask whether: (i) any applied pressure induced the victim to enter the contract; and (ii) the pressure went beyond what the law is prepared to countenance as legitimate. The first requirement establishes a causal connection. The second requirement embodies the illegitimate pressure rationale. Pressure is illegitimate if it consists of unlawful threats or amounts to unconscionable conduct. It is sufficient that illegitimate pressure is one of the reasons for the person entering into the agreement; it need not be the sole reason.

Significantly, McHugh JA was envisaging here that conduct which was lawful but unconscionable might also amount to economic duress. But while many later courts have quoted this passage with approval (see eg *Beerens v Bluescope Distribution* (2012) at [145]), others have not. In *Australia and New Zealand Banking Group v Karam* (2005) at [60], the New South Wales Court of Appeal expressed the view that 'the vagueness inherent in the terms "economic duress" and "illegitimate pressure" can be avoided by treating the concept of "duress" as limited to threatened or actual unlawful conduct'.[6] Unconscionable conduct, the Court considered, should only attract relief if it satisfied the requirements of the separate equitable doctrine discussed in Chapter 20, which generally requires the exploitation of some form of 'special disability'. On this approach, there may (contrary to what has been suggested above) be no such thing as 'lawful act duress'.[7] In *Thorne v Kennedy* (2017), the High Court left open the correctness of this view. But Nettle J was plainly sceptical (at [71]–[72]) of the decision in *Karam*, in so far as it suggests that duress is limited to unlawful pressure.

As this difference of opinion suggests, the courts find economic duress troublesome to deal with. It is certainly difficult to define with any precision. In *Equiticorp Finance v Bank of New Zealand* (1993) at 107, Kirby P said that:

---

6   See also *Electricity Generation v Woodside Energy* (2013) at [159], [176].

7   For critical analysis of this view, see Bigwood 2008.

> The doctrine renders the law uncertain and in an area where certainty is highly desirable. This is illustrated by the instant case. It invites judges (and lawyers advising clients) to substitute their opinions and decisions for those of commercial people who, almost always, will have a better grasp of detail of their relationships and a better appreciation of the economic forces which are at work.

Uncertainty is not the only problem. As Chapter 13 has revealed, contract law has endeavoured to find ways to give effect to variations to existing agreements. But the line between exploitation and legitimate commercial pressure is rather difficult to draw in this context. If renegotiation is made too difficult because variations are struck down for duress, then it runs up against the fundamental principle of freedom of contract embraced in decisions like *Musumeci v Winadell* (1994): see **13.08**. Restricting the ability of parties to vary a contract is an undesirable fetter on freedom of contract. This is likely to be especially important in situations in which the circumstances change after a contract is concluded, yet do not amount to frustration within the meaning of the principles discussed in Chapter 15.

19.06   Causation

In the passage quoted above, McHugh JA noted that the illegitimate pressure must induce the making (or variation) of a contract. Inducement provides the causal link between the illegitimate pressure and the contract. Yet, even in the face of strong duress, there may be other legitimate reasons for entering into a contract. In *Barton v Armstrong* (1976), the Privy Council held that it was enough if the murder threat was *a* reason for entering into the contract, even if the victim might have entered into the contract for other reasons as well, or done so had the threat not been made. There is no requirement for the victim to show that 'but for' the illegitimate pressure they would not have entered into the contract. Once it was apparent that the threat of murder was a reason, amongst others, for entering into the contract, the onus was on the perpetrator to show that the threat 'contributed nothing' to the decision to enter into the contract.

Barton v Armstrong (1976) was a case of serious physical duress and it should not be assumed that there is a universal approach to causation in all types of duress. Some English authorities have adopted a higher threshold for causation in cases of economic duress. It has been said that duress can only be argued if there was no alternative but to enter into the contract, or that the victim needed to demonstrate that 'but for' the pressure they would not have entered into the contract: see eg *Huyton v Peter Cremer* (1999). At the very least, it has been stated that the economic duress must be a 'significant cause': *Dimskal Shipping v ITWF* (1992) at 165. The Australian courts have generally favoured a more relaxed approach, however, which aligns economic duress with other types of duress. In *Crescendo Management* at 46, McHugh JA held that it is enough if the duress was *a* cause of the victim entering into the contract. Once it is shown that the pressure was illegitimate, the onus lies on the person applying the pressure to show that it had made no contribution to the decision to enter into the contract.

On the other hand, it appears that a person may not plead duress to escape a contract, where the threats that caused them to enter into it were made by a third party, without the knowledge or consent of the other party to the contract in question: *Dunwoodie v Teachers Mutual Bank* (2014).

19.07   Remedies

In common with other types of vitiating factor, like misrepresentation, and other kinds of undue pressure, contracts which are the product of duress are rendered voidable rather than void: *The Siboen & The Sibotre* (1976) at 336. Accordingly, the victim may rescind the contract. The usual bars to rescission apply: see **18.13**. Particular care needs to be taken to ensure that the contract is not affirmed despite the duress.

In *North Ocean Shipping v Hyundai Construction* (1979), the defendant agreed to build a ship for the plaintiff with a price specified in US dollars. After entering the contract, the US dollar was devalued by 10 per cent. The defendant threatened not to complete the ship unless the plaintiff paid an additional 10 per cent on top of the contract price. The plaintiff required the ship for a valuable charter and agreed to pay the additional money. Payments were made under the modified contract without any protest. Eight months after the ship was delivered, the plaintiff sought to recover the additional payments. It was held that the pressure had been lifted by this point and the plaintiff had affirmed the contract.[8]

Money paid under duress in the absence of any contract can be recovered in restitution. The same remedy is available in respect of money paid under a contract, but in line with general principles it can only be recovered when the contract is brought to an end: *Pavey & Matthews v Paul* (1987) at 233–6, 256, 266–7; and see **24.04–24.05**. Where the victim of duress refuses to perform and the perpetrator seeks specific performance, that remedy is likely to be refused on the basis of the perpetrator's 'unclean hands': see **22.08**.

It has sometimes been suggested that there is a 'tort' of duress, for which damages might be available as a remedy. But the better view appears to be that there is no such action: *Electricity Generation v Woodside Energy* (2013) at [150]. There *is* a tort of *intimidation*, but this requires both an unlawful threat (whether against the plaintiff or, more usually, a third party) and an intent by the defendant to inflict economic loss on the plaintiff: see eg *Construction, Forestry, Mining and Energy Union v Boral Resources* (2014).

19.08   Statutory duress

Section 50 of the ACL gives a remedy to a victim of a contract entered into as a result of 'physical force, or undue harassment or coercion'. The provision has a broad reach and applies to contracts for the supply of goods or services, the sale or grant of an interest in land, or demands for payment under such contracts. Section 50 has commonly been used by regulatory authorities against debt collection agencies: see eg *ASIC v Accounts Control Management Services* (2012); *ACCC v ACM Group* (2018). But it might also be used by individual victims; for example, those who are victims of high pressure sales tactics. 'Coercion' for this purpose implies a negation of choice, while the broader notion of 'harassment' has been said to cover 'persistent disturbance or torment': *ACCC v Maritime Union of Australia* (2001) at [60]–[61]. Any harassment must also be 'undue', but it appears the same is not required of coercion: see *ACM Group* at [183]–[184]. A wider range of remedies are available under the statute than under common law. In common with other breaches of the ACL (see **18.32**, **20.20**), these remedies may include damages under s 236.

---

8   See also *Bustfree v Llewellyn* (2013).

Undue influence

19.09   Introduction

Undue influence emerged in the nineteenth century out of a group of doctrines in the Court of Chancery which had offered protection to those who had entered into a gift or contract as a result of undue pressure.[9] Undue influence remains important in England and New Zealand as a protection against undue pressure.[10] It is less significant in Australia. Particularly since the High Court's decision in *Commercial Bank of Australia v Amadio* (1983), discussed in **20.04**, the doctrine of unconscionability has been preferred as a means of regulating undue pressure.[11]

19.10   Types of undue influence

Influence is not objectionable as such. It is just part of everyday life and an inevitable feature of many transactions. As Kekewich J observed in *Allcard v Skinner* (1887) at 157:

> Few, if any men, are gifted with characters enabling them to act, or even think, with complete independence of others, which could not largely exist without destroying the foundations of society.

There is no exact definition of undue influence: *Allcard v Skinner* (1887) at 183; *Thorne v Kennedy* (2017) at [30]. This is no bad thing. Although there is a risk of uncertainty, the alternative is worse. It runs the risk that it would exclude behaviour which deserves to be caught as a form of undue pressure. Undue influence does, nevertheless, have a well-established internal structure.

Undue influence divides into two basic categories: actual and presumed: *Johnson v Buttress* (1936) at 119[12]. *Actual undue influence* requires the victim to affirmatively demonstrate that the defendant exerted influence over them when they entered into the transaction. *Presumed undue influence* is more complex. It further divides into two kinds. The first kind is concerned with particular categories or classes of relationship. The law deems certain classes of relationship as ones which are especially vulnerable to one party exercising influence over the other. The relationship between a doctor and patient is one example. The second category is different. Rather than generic types of relationship, the focus is on the particular relationship. Some relationships which fall outside a class that the law identifies as vulnerable are nevertheless, as a matter of fact, ones where there is a high level of dependence. A close friendship falls outside the first category but may nevertheless be one which falls inside the second kind of presumed undue influence. Once it can be shown that the relationship is of a particular type (category one) or is a relationship where influence is exercised (category two), the law presumes undue influence. The burden then falls on the alleged perpetrator to rebut the presumption by showing that the transaction did not arise out of undue influence.

---

9   For the historical background, see Swain 2014a.
10   See Peel 2015: 505–24; Burrows et al 2016: 409–35.
11   See also Mason 1994: 249.
12   But see Bigwood 2018, criticising comments made in *Thorne v Kennedy* (2017), discussed below, for blurring the distinction between these categories.

A contract which is the product of undue influence will usually be disadvantageous to the victim, but it need not necessarily be so. A contract could even benefit both parties, or have a neutral impact on the victim. Some English authorities have suggested that, in order to prove undue influence, it is also necessary to demonstrate that the transaction is 'manifestly disadvantageous' or 'calls for an explanation': see eg *National Westminster Bank v Morgan* (1985); *CIBC Mortgages v Pitt* (1994); *Royal Bank of Scotland v Etridge* (2001). The Australian position is unclear. Any requirement of disadvantage was omitted from the classic definitions of undue influence provided by Dixon J in *Johnson v Buttress* (1936) at 134. The authorities are split on the question.[13] But in practice, because the victim usually suffers a disadvantage, the issue is only likely to be relevant in a small handful of cases.

19.11   Actual undue influence

Actual undue influence includes many situations covered by duress. Both doctrines focus on the nature of the pressure exerted, rather than the nature of the relationship of the parties. Actual undue influence cases are rare. Influence is almost always a by-product of a pre-existing relationship, without which it is difficult to influence someone else. Dixon J described actual undue influence in *Johnson v Buttress* (at 134) when he said that '[the] source of power to practise such a domination may be found in no antecedent relation but in a particular situation, or in the deliberate contrivance of the party'.

Some types of pressure sit more comfortably within undue influence than duress. The old case of *Williams v Bayley* (1866) is a good example. A son forged his father's signature to various notes drawn on a bank. Once this came to the attention of the bank, the father then agreed to take over responsibility for the son's debts and to a charge over his property by way of a mortgage. It was held that the agreement was procured by undue influence. The bank had insinuated that the son would face criminal prosecution and transportation unless the father agreed to take on the debt. As Lord Westbury put it (at 218), the 'only motive to induce [the father] to adopt the debt was the hope that by doing so he would relieve the son from the inevitable consequences of his crime'. The bank did nothing unlawful. Yet, at the same time, the mortgage agreement was a product of undue pressure. The reason that the father entered into the mortgage was the fear that to do otherwise would mean that his son would face criminal prosecution.

Actual undue influence can also be found in a commercial context. In *Maher v Honeysett & Maher* (2007), contracts entered into at the dissolution of a business partnership were treated as a product of undue influence. Barrett J endorsed (at [134]) a description of actual undue influence that was earlier used by the English Court of Appeal in *Bank of Credit and Commercial International v Aboody* (1990) at 967:

> [A] person relying on a plea of actual undue influence must show that (a) the party to the transaction (or someone who induced the transaction for his [sic] own benefit) had the capacity to influence the complainant; (b) the influence was exercised; (c) its exercise was undue; (d) its exercise brought about the transaction.

---

13   Compare *Watkins v Combes* (1922) at 195 and *Farmers' Co-op Executors & Trustees v Perks* (1989) at 404 (disadvantage required) with *Barburin v Barburin* (1990) (disadvantage not required).

This detailed description could, according to Barrett J (at [136]), be reduced to what he called a 'central concept' of 'unfair advantage' on the part of the perpetrator and 'injury' to the victim.

Actual undue influence can also be found in a domestic context, and against the backdrop of an existing relationship. One of the grounds for setting aside a transfer of a property from a wife to a husband in *Farmers' Co-op Executors & Trustees v Perks* (1989) was that the husband had exercised actual undue influence over his wife. In *Thorne v Kennedy* (2017), a wealthy groom was found to have exercised such influence in persuading his foreign bride to sign grossly unreasonable pre- and post-nuptial agreements. The evidence showed that she had no real choice but to sign, since without the marriage she would have no income, no right to stay in Australia, and no place in society.

19.12 Presumed undue influence: special classes of relationship

Where presumed undue influence is available, a victim is always well advised to prefer this option to actual undue influence or duress. Once it is shown that the relationship is one that falls within the presumption, the burden shifts to the other party to show that the transaction did not arise out of undue influence. Discharging that burden may be difficult.

Relationships within certain categories generate an automatic presumption of undue influence. These categories are well established, but the list is not yet closed: *Louth v Diprose* (1992) at 628. Once the relationship falls within one of these categories, influence is automatically presumed. The following relationships have been recognised as giving rise to a presumption:

- solicitor and client – see eg *Westmelton v Archer* (1982);
- doctor and patient – see eg *Bar-Mordecai v Hillston* (2004);
- religious advisor and advisee – see eg *Allcard v Skinner* (1887); *Hartigan v International Society for Krishna Consciousness* (2002);
- trustee and beneficiary – see eg *Jenyns v Public Curator* (1953) at 133;
- guardian and ward – see eg *Powell v Powell* (1900) at 243.

There is also a presumption of undue influence between a parent and child: *Bainbridge v Browne* (1881) at 196. The age at which the presumption ceases to apply depends on the particular relationships and how free the child has become of parental control.[14] It is less likely to apply to mature adult children. This presumption works in one direction. There is no presumption between a child and a parent: *Spong v Spong* (1914). Nor does a presumption arise between fiancé and fiancée: *Thorne v Kennedy* (2017). There is also no presumption of undue influence between spouses on the grounds of marital status: *Yerkey v Jones* (1939) at 675. But this does not mean that a transaction between a husband and wife cannot arise from a relationship of influence. Transactions between spouses may also fall within the separate requirements of the so-called rule in *Yerkey v Jones* (1939), which seeks to protect wives who guarantee debts of their husbands: see **20.08–20.10**.

---

14   So an adult child might still rely on the presumption: *Phillips v Hutchinson* (1946).

19.13   Presumed undue influence: relationship of influence

A relationship which falls outside one of the special categories can still be a relationship of influence. Any type of relationship is potentially one where influence can be exercised. The obvious example is a relationship between close friends. As in this example, a relationship of influence will usually have built up over time. More rarely it may arise in the context of one-off dealings: see eg *Tufton v Sperni* (1952).

Johnson v Buttress (1936), the leading Australian authority on what constitutes a relationship of influence, concerned Buttress, a man of 67 years of age. He was described as illiterate, of low intelligence and without experience of business. The evidence showed him to be 'highly excitable, very stupid and mentally unstable'. He was dependent on Johnson for advice and assistance following the death of his wife. Dixon J described him (at 127) as 'peculiarly dependent upon others'. Johnson had known Buttress for 20 years. Buttress was fond of Johnson because she had been good to his wife. His only asset was his house and land, which he transferred to Johnson three years before his death. The High Court held that there was no actual undue influence. Nevertheless, it found that there was a relationship of influence. Dixon J considered the matter in detail. He emphasised (at 137) that the low intelligence and character of Buttress did not of themselves justify setting the transaction aside, but that these were critical in that they 'provide the foundation of the suggested relation'. The presumption of undue influence was not rebutted. Johnson had failed to show that the transaction was the result of 'the free exercise of the donor's independent will' (at 138).

19.14   Rebutting the presumption of undue influence

As in *Johnson v Buttress*, once a presumption is established, it will not be easy to rebut. It was not enough to show that no undue influence was actually exercised. Rather, in order to rebut the presumption, it is necessary to establish that the contract was both understood and voluntary: *Johnson v Buttress* (1936) at 123. There are no set criteria for rebutting a presumption – it varies from case to case. The nature of the parties, the relationship and the type of transaction are all relevant.

The presence of independent advice is an important factor. In *Badman v Drake* (2008), the defendants befriended a woman of 87 years of age. They fell into financial difficulties and she purchased a house for them in return for which they were supposed to look after her. Solicitors acting for both parties had urged that a number of steps be taken, which because of the conflict of interest included providing the plaintiff with independent advice. The parties, who were in a hurry to finalise the transaction, went ahead without independent legal advice. The result was that once a relationship of influence was established, the defendants were unable to rebut the presumption of undue influence.[15]

Whilst it may be relevant to consider whether the weaker party has obtained advice from an independent source before entering into the relevant transaction, this is not a conclusive factor. In *Westmelton v Archer* (1982), in the context of a relationship between a solicitor and

---

15   As to whether courts are always as willing as they should be to find undue influence in cases involving the elderly, see Burns 2002.

client, it was held that there was no rigid rule that all such transactions required independent legal advice in order to rebut the presumption. Rather, it was said to be critical not to lose sight of what mattered, which was whether or not the supposed victim had acted with their own free will or had been influenced. There may be also situations where a weaker party is independently advised not to go ahead with a transaction, but does so anyway because they believe they have no choice in the matter. Such a transaction may still be set aside: see eg *Thorne v Kennedy* (2017).

Structuring undue pressure

19.15   Rationalising the law?

The law as it stands on undue pressure is messy. Duress, undue influence and unconscionability may cover some of the same factual situations, as the recent case of *Thorne v Kennedy* (2017) demonstrates. Despite a possible overlap in their application, however, the different doctrines focus on slightly different forms of conduct. The scope of that conduct is sometimes contested. Economic duress is particularly unstable. It is certainly tricky to apply. In *Musumeci v Winadell* (1994) at 741, Santow J suggested that 'economic duress has not received unqualified acceptance as a basis for setting aside contracts in Australia'. At the same time, he described it (at 743) as 'a useful weapon'. The most radical solution to the perceived problem of economic duress is found in a judgment of Kirby P in *Equiticorp Finance v Bank of New Zealand* (1993) at 107, where he suggests that it should be abolished altogether. He proposed splitting economic duress between undue influence and unconscionability on the basis that it would 'allow relief in a consistent and principled fashion ... rather than by pretending to economic expertise and judgement which they (judges) will generally lack'. One obvious advantage of his proposal is that it avoids the difficult question of whether the pressure is illegitimate. Another less radical alternative is to limit duress to actual or threatened unlawful conduct, as proposed in *Australian and New Zealand Banking Group v Karam* (2005) (see **19.05**). Lawful act duress is a fairly minor issue. The more serious problem lies in deciding how to deal with one particular kind of unlawful act, an actual or threatened breach of contract.

Rationalising the relationship between undue influence and unconscionability discussed in the following chapter is even more difficult. In *Commercial Bank of Australia v Amadio* (1983) at 474, Deane J provided a solution:

> The equitable principles relating to relief against unconscionable dealing and the principles relating to undue influence are closely related. The two doctrines are, however, distinct. Undue influence, like common law duress, looks to the quality of the consent or assent of the weaker party ... Unconscionable dealing looks to the conduct of the stronger party in attempting to enforce, or retain the benefit of, a dealing with a person under a special disability in circumstances where it is not consistent with equity or good conscience that he [sic] should do so.

His analysis has since been cited with approval: see eg *Louth v Diprose* (1992) at 627; *Bridgewater v Leahy* (1998) at 478. It has also appealed to some academic commentators as providing an explanation for the various doctrines. Birks and Chin (1995) have argued that undue influence is plaintiff (victim)-sided. It focuses on the assent of the victim.

Unconscionability, in contrast, is defendant (perpetrator)-sided. The focus there is on the conduct of the perpetrator in attempting to benefit from a contract with someone who is under a 'special disability'.

Despite high judicial and academic approval, this attempt to impose some welcome coherence on the material is not without difficulty. Contract law is inherently bilateral and the victim and perpetrator operate in a relationship with each other. It is highly artificial to regard these factors as distinct rather than an amalgam of factors – though the emphasis might sometimes be different. For example, Birks and Chin regard economic duress as plaintiff-sided. Yet, if the statement of principle of McHugh JA in *Crescendo Management v Westpac* (1988) (see **19.05**) is taken at face value, it refers to factors that are *both* plaintiff- and defendant-sided. The first element of his definition focuses on the plaintiff's assent. The second element looks at the defendant's use of illegitimate pressure.

As for undue influence, it is certainly true that the influence need not be in any sense morally or legally wrong. In some instances, the alleged victim benefits from an evidential presumption. In these cases, it is quite difficult to say that there is pressure in quite the same way as occurs, for example, in a case of duress. The person exercising influence may be entirely blameless. As was made clear long ago, what matters is whether the party entering into the contract has exercised 'an independent will': *Allcard v Skinner* (1887) at 171. No improper conduct is necessary: *Thorne v Kennedy* (2017) at [30]. This would seem to support a plaintiff-sided analysis. The consent of the victim is impaired in some way by the exercise of influence. But this doesn't tell the whole story. As made clear in *Allcard* (at 171), equity intervenes 'on the ground of public-policy, and to prevent the relations which existed between the parties and the influence arising therefrom being abused'. The key word here is 'abused'. The relationship provides the setting for the trusting relationship to be abused. This is defendant-sided. Seen in this way, undue influence has elements of both 'impaired consent' and 'wicked exploitation'.[16]

Unconscionability is discussed in more detail in the next chapter. It rests on the idea of 'exploitation by one party of another's position of special disadvantage': *Commercial Bank of Australia v Amadio* (1983) at 489. This is more obviously a defendant-sided analysis. But there are parallels with undue influence once the position of special disadvantage is seen as the backdrop against which exploitation takes place. The unconscionable bargain doctrine is wider because it is not, unlike most kinds of undue influence, tied to a pre-existing relationship. This means that the central elements of unconscionability are capable of accommodating undue influence.[17] In this way, it is plaintiff-sided too. The exploitation is only made possible because of the 'special disadvantage'.

---

16   See Bigwood 1996. For an alternative analysis, which rejects the plaintiff-sided notion of undue influence and develops a relational analysis, see Chen-Wishart 2006.

17   See Capper 1998.

20

UNCONSCIONABILITY AND UNFAIRNESS

20.01   Introduction

Courts have traditionally been reluctant to intervene in contracts on the grounds of *substantive unfairness* – that is, unfairness in the terms or substance of a contract. This attitude was most pronounced in the latter part of the nineteenth century, when the classical theory of contract (see **2.05**) was at its height. It explains why it is enough for consideration to be sufficient and that the courts will not inquire into whether it is also adequate: see **5.31**. However, the reluctance to intervene on the grounds of substantive unfairness has endured well beyond that period. As Kirby P explained in *Biotechnology Australia v Pace* (1988) at 132–3:

> The law of contract which underpins the economy does not, even today, operate uniformly upon a principle of fairness. It is the essence of entrepreneurship that parties will sometimes act with selfishness. That motivation may or may not produce fairness to the other party. The law may legitimately insist upon honesty of dealings. However, I doubt that, statute or special cases apart, it does or should enforce a regime of fairness upon the multitude of economic transactions.

This statement reflects the idea that the role of the law of contract is merely to facilitate the parties' private ordering of their own affairs, rather than to achieve any particular goals, such as fair outcomes or distributive justice. However, given the centrality of contract to commercial relations, it has always been considered vital to safeguard the contracting *process* from abuse. This explains the existence of contractual doctrines such as those concerned with undue pressure and misrepresentation discussed elsewhere in this book.

Sitting alongside the doctrines of duress and undue influence considered in Chapter 19 is the equitable doctrine of *unconscionable bargains*. The unconscionable bargain doctrine is largely concerned with whether there was unfairness in the process of contract formation. Yet, the substance of the transaction cannot be entirely divorced from this inquiry. Whether the outcome of the contract is unfair (substantive unfairness) is relevant to supporting a finding that the contract was procedurally unfair. As we will explain, the substantive fairness of the contract may also be raised by way of a defence against a claim that the contract is unconscionable.

Originating long ago in the Court of Chancery, the unconscionable bargain doctrine has featured in a number of High Court decisions in recent decades. Besides its more general application, a distinct and more modern variation has emerged to protect wives from being held to guarantees of their husbands' debts, when given without fully appreciating the nature of the arrangement. Whether it might also protect other parties in close relationships remains unclear.

Supplementing these equitable doctrines is a statutory unconscionable conduct regime now found in the Australian Consumer Law (ACL). This includes a broad prohibition in s 21, which applies to commercial transactions involving goods or services. On its face, this provision appears to permit intervention on the grounds of substantive unfairness alone. But the courts have been reluctant to interpret it in this way. To remedy that, a national unfair contract terms regime, with a test of substantive unfairness at its heart, was introduced in 2010. The regime applies only to standard form contracts. Initially framed to protect consumers from unfair terms, it has since been extended to cover many business-to-business transactions as well. Interestingly, a recent review of the ACL has proposed consideration of the need for a more general 'unfair trading' prohibition of a type found in many other countries. This might potentially sit alongside the specific protections from misleading or deceptive conduct, unconscionable conduct and unfair terms.[1]

Unconscionable bargains

20.02   The role of conscience in modern contract law

One of the features of Australian contract law that distinguishes it from English law, with which it otherwise shares many common features, is that doctrines derived from equity play a more prominent role. This has been especially true since the 1980s and 1990s. This was a time when, as discussed in **1.11**, the High Court was actively seeking to remodel Australian contract law.[2] The idea that the law should concern itself with unconscionable conduct is said to underpin a number of contractual doctrines, including promissory estoppel, discussed in Chapter 7. It is the disapproval of such conduct that prevents a contract from being enforced because of the manner in which the contract was created, as, for example, with unilateral mistake (see **18.38–18.39**), as well as the doctrine of unconscionable bargains discussed below. It may also prevent a forfeiture clause or a penalty from being enforced according to its strict terms: see **17.05**, **22.19–22.24**.

Although unconscionability sounds like a broad idea, it does not operate as a cause of action, or as a general basis for granting relief. A court cannot, for example, grant an injunction to restrain unconscionable conduct, unless the plaintiff can bring their case within an established doctrine or principle: *Australian Broadcasting Corporation v Lenah Game Meats* (2001). Nor is there a general jurisdiction to restrain a person from exercising contractual or other rights unconscionably: *Tenth Vandy v Natwest Markets* (2012).

Terms such as unconscionable (or 'unconscientious', a synonym sometimes used by equity specialists) are said to 'describe in their various applications the formation and instruction of conscience by reference to well developed principles': *Tanwar Enterprises v Cauchi* (2003) at [20].[3] Those principles, as in *Tanwar* itself (see **16.24**), are sometimes expressed in the phrase that equity grants relief against 'fraud, mistake, accident and surprise'. Those terms are not particularly helpful. They are rather archaic, and do not cover the whole field of equitable relief, as Gleeson CJ, McHugh, Gummow, Hayne and Heydon JJ appeared (at [58]) to accept. Precise definitions are difficult. *Mistake* in equity is discussed at some length elsewhere: see **18.41**. *Fraud*, when used in an equitable sense, is distinct from its narrow common law counterpart: see **18.16**. It represents a broader idea of advantage-taking, or exploitation. *Surprise* refers to taking advantage of another's ignorance. And an *accident* for this purpose is something which is outside the control of either of the parties, and therefore outside any agreed allocation of risk.[4]

---

1   See CAANZ 2017: 50–1; and see also the comparative account in Corones et al 2016: Pt 3. The Legislative and Governance Forum on Consumer Affairs (CAF) has directed a research and policy project to commence in 2018–19 on the possible introduction of an unfair trading prohibition in Australia: http://consumerlaw.gov.au/communiques/meeting-9-2/.
2   For an account by one of the leading protagonists, see Mason 1998.
3   For a variety of perspectives on the concepts of conscience and unconscionability, see Chen-Wishart 1989; Bigwood 2000; Dal Pont 2000; Rickett 2005; Havelock 2015.
4   See further Heydon et al 2015: 589–90.

20.03   Relief against unconscionable bargains

The idea that relief may be granted against an unconscionable bargain is an old one. The terminology was found in the seventeenth and eighteenth centuries when the Court of Chancery granted relief against unfair transactions. These included money lending contracts, particularly those involving the sale by a young heir of an expected inheritance, in return for an immediate cash payment at less than full value.[5] During the nineteenth century, equitable relief for contractual unfairness was put on a more systematic footing. One consequence of this was the emergence of the distinct doctrine of undue influence discussed in Chapter 19. Meanwhile, the features of an unconscionable bargain doctrine were elaborated in *Earl of Aylesford v Morris* (1873) at 491. Lord Selbourne explained that, when one party took extortionate advantage of a weakness of the other, a contract would not stand unless the party claiming the benefit of the contract could show that the transaction was 'fair, just and reasonable'. In England, the unconscionable bargain doctrine has since withered. In Australia, by contrast, it has come to play a prominent role in regulating contracts, as well as gifts. A court may rescind a contract, or refuse specific performance, where the transaction is unconscionable. Even in Australia, however, the notion of an unconscionable bargain has waxed and waned. Some decisions can be criticised for pushing the doctrine too far and, in doing so, undermining the security of transactions. But a recent High Court ruling, *Kakavas v Crown Melbourne* (2013), is more cautious than some earlier decisions, as discussed below.

The beginning of the modern Australian law relating to unconscionable bargains can be traced to two High Court decisions nearly 70 years ago. In the first, *Wilton v Farnworth* (1948), a gift of a substantial property was set aside. The donor did not understand the transaction and was of low intelligence. The second transaction was more complex. *Blomley v Ryan* (1956) involved a sale of agricultural land, for which the buyer sought specific performance. The sale was at a significant undervalue and on terms favourable to the buyer, including a very low deposit. The seller was an elderly alcoholic. At the time of entering into the contract he was in the middle of a bout of drinking, and consumed some rum supplied by an agent of the buyer. A majority of the High Court refused to order specific performance on the grounds that it was an unconscionable bargain. The seller was not too drunk to know what he was doing. Had he been so, then the contract would have been voidable on the grounds of incapacity: see **5.43**. His age and drunkenness nevertheless put him at a disadvantage, and the buyer took advantage. The fact that the consideration was inadequate (it did not reflect the real value of the land) was not in itself a ground to treat the contract as unconscionable. However, it was relevant evidence to support the inference that there was a position of disadvantage and that unfair advantage was taken.[6] Fullagar J provided (at 405) a useful summary of situations where equity intervenes:

> The circumstances adversely affecting a party, which may induce a court of equity either to refuse its aid or to set a transaction aside, are of great variety and can hardly be satisfactorily classified. Among them are poverty or need of any kind, sickness, age, sex, infirmity of body or mind, drunkenness, illiteracy or lack of education, lack of assistance

---

5   For this historical background, see Swain 2014a.
6   Compare the dissent of Kitto J, suggesting the seller had made a rational decision to divest himself of the property and retire on the proceeds, but then simply changed his mind.

or explanation where assistance or explanation is necessary. The common characteristic seems to be that they have the effect of placing one party at a serious disadvantage *vis-à-vis* the other. It does not appear to be essential in all cases that the party at a disadvantage should suffer loss or detriment by the bargain.

20.04   The elements of the unconscionable bargain doctrine

The basic elements of the modern unconscionable bargain doctrine were laid down by a majority of the High Court in *Commercial Bank v Amadio* (1983). Two elderly Italian migrants with limited knowledge of English, without independent advice, executed a bank's standard form deed of mortgage and guarantee in respect of all existing and future indebtedness to the bank of their son's building company. The High Court agreed to set aside the transaction. Gibbs CJ decided the case on the basis of misrepresentation. The bank had failed to disclose to the couple that, among other things, it had been allowing their son to write cheques and then selectively dishonour them. But Mason, Wilson and Deane JJ preferred to grant relief on the ground that the Amadios had entered into an unconscionable bargain.

The unconscionable bargain doctrine has a number of elements which are sometimes expressed slightly differently, but are conveniently summarised in *Turner v Windever* (2003) at [105]:

(a)   the weaker party must, at the time of entering into the transaction, suffer from a special disadvantage vis-à-vis the stronger party;

(b)   the special disadvantage must seriously affect the weaker party's capacity to judge or protect his or her own interests;

(c)   the stronger party must know of the special disadvantage (or know of facts which would raise that possibility in the mind of any reasonable person);

(d)   that party must take advantage of the opportunity presented by the disadvantage; and

(e)   the taking of advantage must have been unconscientious.

Once these elements are established, then the evidential onus shifts to the stronger party to show that the contract was not in fact unconscionable. They may do so in two ways. It may be shown that steps were taken to negate the disadvantage or the taking of advantage, most obviously by giving the weaker party access to independent advice. Alternatively, it may be established that the transaction was otherwise fair, just and reasonable.

On the facts of *Amadio* itself, the bank knew that the security would almost inevitably be called upon in the near future. It was also aware of the improvidence of the transaction for the guarantors, taking into account their ages, their limited comprehension of English, and their reliance on their son, who, whilst providing them with advice, stood to gain by the transaction. This created a special disadvantage. The bank was treated as being aware of that disadvantage, or at least of facts which would raise that possibility in the mind of any reasonable person. The onus then lay on the bank to show that it was a fair transaction, a burden which it failed to discharge.

Decisions in this area are very fact-specific. They depend on how the different elements are applied. In many of the leading cases, the High Court has been divided. This is not surprising.

Once the law moves beyond protection of someone like the donor in *Wilton v Farnworth*, prescribing the limits of the unconscionable dealing doctrine is always going to be difficult. No two cases are the same. In the absence of a bright-line rule, the best that can be hoped for is a degree of transparency, consistency and coherence.

20.05   Extending the doctrine

The result in *Amadio* seems reasonable, given that it would have been easy enough for the bank to insist that the plaintiffs received independent advice. But later decisions were more questionable. Certainly, they extended the application of the unconscionable bargain doctrine quite considerably. It is now clear that the reason that one party is at a special disadvantage in relation to another is broader than an inherent disadvantage such as age, an inability to speak English, low intelligence or alcoholism. In *Amadio*, the relationship with the son was just one of the relevant factors which collectively meant that there was a special disadvantage. In other authorities, special disadvantage has been found primarily from the nature of the relationship itself.

In *Louth v Diprose* (1992), Diprose, a solicitor, gave $58,000 to Louth, a woman with whom he was infatuated, to purchase a house for her and the children of a former marriage. The majority of the High Court held that the transaction was unconscionable and should be set aside. The key factor was the nature of the relationship, which was characterised in a very particular way. According to Deane J (at 638):

> The case was not simply one in which the respondent had under the influence of his love for, or infatuation with, the appellant made an imprudent gift in her favour. The case was one in which the appellant deliberately used that love or infatuation and her own deceit to create a situation in which she could unconscientiously manipulate the respondent to part with a large proportion of his property. The intervention of equity is not merely to relieve the plaintiff from the consequences of his own foolishness. It is to prevent his victimization.

This description of the relationship is open to criticism. It was presented in very extreme terms which might have been unfair to the woman, especially in characterising the balance of power in the relationship.[7] Only by describing the relationship in these terms was it easy to conclude that there was a special disadvantage which was the product of an emotional manipulation on the part of the stronger party. The respondent was an experienced solicitor. He might have acted foolishly in love. Many people no doubt do so. There was also an element of choice in his behaviour. The law should be cautious about protecting people from their bad choices.

Louth v Diprose, at least in the way that the facts were presented, was a decision which could be justified on the basis of emotional manipulation. Emotional dependency can take many different forms and, once it is accepted as a form of disadvantage, the doctrine of unconscionable bargains is potentially wide ranging. This is illustrated by *Bridgewater v Leahy* (1998). Bill York, a farmer, died in 1989. In 1985, he had made a will. In 1988, he sold some of his land to his nephew, Neil York. The transaction took the form of a sale for $696,811 (the actual value of the land), with a forgiveness clause for $546,811. As a result the sale was, in

---

7   See eg Sarmas 1994; Sangha & Moles 1997.

effect, for $150,000. Other members of the family sought relief on the basis that the deed for forgiveness should be cancelled and the full price paid. The Supreme Court of Queensland found no undue influence, and that decision was not appealed. However, it was contended that the land transfer was an unconscionable bargain.

The focus of the majority (Gaudron, Gummow and Kirby JJ) and the minority (Gleeson CJ and Callinan J) was quite different. The minority emphasised that Bill quite clearly knew what he was doing. He wanted the farm to continue after his death and transferring it to Neil was the best way to achieve that. The majority stressed that Bill's capacity was not an answer. They considered (at 493) that his intention to preserve his rural interests and his perception that Neil could provide reliable and experienced management were 'significant elements in his emotional attachment to and dependency upon Neil'. In granting relief, this approach took emotional dependence to a new level. It overrode Bill's autonomy to do as he chose with his own property. There was a close relationship between Bill and Neil, which explained why Bill acted as he did. This case was fundamentally a dispute about the distribution of an estate. The rest of the family felt that they had been cheated of their inheritance. Even accepting that there was a level of emotional dependency, it is quite difficult to see how someone can be exploited when they are doing what they genuinely want to do, with their eyes open. There was no emotional manipulation in the manner of *Louth v Diprose* and yet the relationship was still treated as one which created a special disadvantage.

20.06   Restricting the scope of the doctrine

Louth v Diprose and *Bridgewater v Leahy* (1998) may have marked the high-water mark of the doctrine of unconscionable bargains, at least in the High Court. A series of later decisions have suggested there are some limits. In *ACCC v CG Berbatis Holdings* (2003), a case brought under what is now s 20 of the ACL (see **20.13**), it was stressed that inequality of bargaining power alone does not render a bargain unconscionable. Gleeson CJ explained (at [11]):

> A person is not in a position of relevant disadvantage, constitutional, situational, or otherwise, simply because of inequality of bargaining power. Many, perhaps even most, contracts are made between parties of unequal bargaining power, and good conscience does not require parties to contractual negotiations to forfeit their advantages, or neglect their own interests.[8]

In the same vein, it has been held that a pressing need for money does not constitute a special disadvantage in dealing with a lender: see eg *Australia and New Zealand Banking Group v Karam* (2005).[9]

If mere inequality of bargaining power were enough to set aside a contract, it would undermine the security of transactions. The law of contract, having accepted that there will

---

8   As to the idea of a distinction between 'constitutional' and 'situational' disadvantage, see *ACCC v Samton Holdings* (2002) at [48].

9   Compare *Elkofairi v Permanent Trustee* (2002), treating the incapacity to repay a loan as a special disadvantage in dealing with a lender. Later decisions have stressed that 'pure asset lending' will not necessarily be regarded as unconscionable: *Kowalczuk v Accom Finance* (2008) at [96]. But such a transaction may still be regarded as 'unjust' under statutes such as the *Contracts Review Act 1980* (NSW) (see **20.32**): see eg *Fast Fix Loans v Samardzic* (2011); and see further McGill 2014; Rajapaksa 2014.

often be an inequality of bargaining power, seeks to ensure that the relationship is regulated in other ways. It prohibits certain kinds of behaviour – for example, duress or misleading conduct – which tend to be *associated* with inequality of bargaining power, rather than inequality alone.

The High Court's decision in *Kakavas v Crown Melbourne* (2013) suggests further limitations on the unconscionable bargain doctrine.[10] A more limited view of what amounted to a special disadvantage was adopted. The knowledge of any special disadvantage required by the stronger party was also clarified. Harry Kakavas, a property developer, was the subject of a self-exclusion order at the defendant's casino.[11] But after the casino agreed to allow him to return, he began to gamble on a mammoth scale, turning over close to $1.5 billion. Sometimes he won millions of dollars. But more often than not, he lost. In the period concerned, his losses totalled $20.5 million. Before the High Court, he sought to argue that the casino had unconscionably taken advantage of his pathological urge to gamble and consequent inability to make worthwhile decisions in his own interests.

In rejecting his claim, the Court explained (at [20]) that the law would not protect a person 'from the consequences of improvident transactions conducted in the ordinary and undistinguished course of a lawful business'. The fact that the loss arose from multiple transactions did not bar a claim, but made it difficult to prove. The Court noted (at [25]) that 'gambling transactions are a rare, if not unique species of economic activity in a civilised community, in that each party sets out openly to inflict harm on the counterparty'. In these circumstances, there was nothing exploitative about the conduct of the casino. Moreover, the gambler's conduct was characterised (at [23]) as 'voluntary'.

A further ground for rejecting the claim was that even if, contrary to the evidence, Kakavas had suffered from a special disadvantage, the casino was not aware of it.[12] The Court held that actual knowledge of the relevant disadvantage is required. Constructive knowledge, in the sense of what a reasonable person would be expected to know, was insufficient. Although Mason J had appeared to suggest otherwise in *Commercial Bank v Amadio* (1983) at 467, this was rather unconvincingly explained in *Kakavas* (at [155]–[156]) as covering a situation where the stronger party is guilty of 'wilful ignorance' in failing to make inquiries.[13]

Kakavas marked a step change from earlier decisions. The claim failed because the casino had not 'victimised' Kakavas, nor acted in a way that was 'predatory' or 'surreptitious'. The emphasis on the importance of autonomy, and the outcome itself, makes the decision difficult to square with *Bridgewater v Leahy* (1998). Other recent decisions suggest a similarly conservative approach to applying the unconscionable bargain doctrine. Several State courts have, for example, taken care to distinguish *Louth v Diprose* (1992) as an 'extreme' case.[14]

Kakavas is not, however, the last word. *Thorne v Kennedy* (2017) arose in the particular context of prenuptial and postnuptial agreements. The High Court was willing to accept that an

---

10   For detailed analysis of the decision, see Bigwood 2013; Swain 2014b.

11   Under the *Casino Control Act 1991* (Vic) gamblers can self-exclude from certain casinos as a way of avoiding the temptation to gamble.

12   For other examples of an unconscionable bargain claim failing on this ground, see eg *Australia and New Zealand Banking Group v Alirezai* (2004); *ACCC v Radio Rentals* (2005).

13   Compare *Thorne v Kennedy* (2017) at [38], [74], apparently adopting Mason J's broader formulation without any requirement of wilful ignorance. This case is discussed in the text below.

14   See eg *Mackintosh v Johnson* (2013); *Lee v Chai* (2013).

impecunious woman was at a serious disadvantage when presented by her wealthy fiancé with a grossly one-sided pre-nuptial agreement a short time before a marriage to which she was by then completely committed. Nor had that disadvantage sufficiently dissipated by the time she was asked to sign a postnuptial agreement after the wedding. The decision clarified a number of issues. Kiefel CJ, Bell, Gageler, Keane and Edelman JJ explained (at [40]) that the unconscionable bargain doctrine was broader than the concept of undue influence. It was possible to take advantage in such a way as to create an unconscionable bargain where the behaviour fell short of undue influence. However, they added (at [64]), when undue influence was used, as on the facts here, that inevitably showed that there was a special disadvantage.

20.07 Defences to a claim of unconscionability

Even if the elements of unconscionability are made out, that is not the end of the matter. The onus shifts to the defendant, who can still show that the transaction was fair and in doing so establish that no unconscionable advantage was taken. One factor in ensuring that the transaction is more likely to be regarded as fair is that the supposed victim went into the contract with their eyes open, having obtained independent legal advice: see eg *Micarone v Perpetual Trustees* (1999).[15] Many financial institutions have indeed adopted the practice of refusing to deal with potentially vulnerable parties, such as spouses or family members seeking to guarantee or provide security for a loan, unless a lawyer is prepared to certify that the transaction has been fully explained.[16] Had Bill York received independent advice in *Bridgewater*, then the transaction was much more likely to have stood. It may be more difficult to treat a transaction as fair when the victim gains nothing from it at all, like the Amadios. Nevertheless, there have been cases in which what might otherwise have been regarded as an unconscionable transaction has been successfully defended as fair, just and reasonable in its terms: see eg *Rodgers v ANZ Banking Group* (2009). In *Thorne v Kennedy*, by contrast, no amount of independent advice could save what were described by the bride's solicitor as the worst agreements she had ever seen. In the High Court's eyes, the fact that the bride was willing to defy her lawyer's advice and sign them simply underscored the disadvantage at which she was operating.

The 'special equity' for married women

20.08 Background

Amadio shows that a guarantee or security given for the benefit of someone else may be set aside where the creditor has acted unconscionably in obtaining it – at least where the guarantor is known to be under some form of special disadvantage. More commonly, however, it is not the creditor who is guilty of impropriety, but the debtor for whose benefit

---

15   Compare *Aboody v Ryan* (2012), where although advice was obtained from a solicitor, it was found neither to be independent nor adequate. In some cases *legal* advice will be insufficient, and financial advice may be required instead: see eg *Hanna v Raoul* (2018).

16   As to such practices, as well as the role of industry codes, see McGill & Howell 2013.

the guarantee or security is provided. They may, for example, have put pressure on the guarantor, or kept the truth of the contract from them. To deal with this situation, Australian law has adopted two safeguards, both of which were outlined by Dixon J in *Yerkey v Jones* (1939) at 677 and 683.

Under the first of these, a guarantee or security may be set aside where the creditor is aware, or ought to be aware, that the main debtor has used duress or undue influence to procure it: see eg *Bank of NSW v Rogers* (1941); *Wenczel v Commonwealth Bank* (2006).[17]

It is the other rule stated by Dixon J, however, that has come to be better known. It was expressed as a special principle of equity for the protection of married women. When a wife acts as a surety for her husband's debts and the creditor accepts the guarantee, without dealing directly with the wife, she has a prima facie right to have the contract set aside. At the same time, the law recognises that a creditor is giving value by way of the loan, and may be completely unaware that anything was amiss. In these circumstances, a court must consider whether the wife benefited from the loan and whether she was put under undue pressure to enter into the guarantee, or at least did not understand what she was agreeing to. On the facts in *Yerkey*, the creditor believed on reasonable grounds that the wife understood the substantial effect of what she was signing. It was emphasised that a solicitor had explained the effect of the wife's guarantee to her in a way that a person of average intelligence would understand. As a result, the bank could enforce the guarantee.

20.09   The modern position

The application of the (better known) rule in *Yerkey v Jones* was tested in *Garcia v National Australia Bank* (1998). To the surprise of many commentators, the majority of the High Court rejected the suggestion that the rule had been subsumed into the unconscionable bargains doctrine recognised in cases such as *Amadio*. According to Gaudron, McHugh, Gummow and Hayne JJ (at [31]), it will be unconscionable for a creditor to enforce a guarantee against a wife when:

(a)   the wife did not understand the effect of the transaction;

(b)   the transaction was voluntary (in the sense that the wife made no gain from it);

(c)   the creditor is taken to have understood that a wife may place trust in her husband in matters of business, and that he may not have fully and accurately explained the effect of the transaction to her; and

(d)   the creditor failed to explain the transaction to the wife, nor ensured that a third party did so.

The application of these principles was not entirely straightforward on the facts. Mrs Garcia was a director and shareholder of the company which was the recipient of the loan. She was still treated as a volunteer, however, because she had no financial interests in the company, which was totally under the control of her husband. Mrs Garcia understood that there was a

---

17   The English courts have gone much further in fixing lenders with constructive notice of undue influence used to obtain a guarantee. Awareness of the *risk* of such influence is considered to be sufficient for this purpose: see eg *Royal Bank of Scotland v Etridge* (2002).

guarantee, but she thought that it was very limited and, critically, did not understand that it was secured by way of a mortgage over the family home.[18]

20.10   The rationale and scope of the rule in *Yerkey v Jones*

It is easy to see how Kirby J, in his dissenting judgment in *Garcia* (1998), could describe the rule (at [66]]) as an 'historical anachronism'. He saw it as putting a wife in an 'advantageous position that she would not have enjoyed had she not been married to the principal debtor'. The majority sought to provide a rationale, which they claimed was not based on the subservience of women or any vulnerability to exploitation.[19] Rather, the creditor was seeking to enforce a guarantee in a situation where there was, as explained (at [23]), a 'lack of proper information about the purport and effect of the transaction'. The lack of proper information was a product of the 'trust and confidence' that married people have in each other. In *Garcia*, the High Court were careful to say that the doctrine applied in these cases was different from the unconscionable bargain doctrine. Nevertheless, the use of the language of unconscionability still raises the question of where these authorities properly sit. There is no presumption of undue influence between husband and wife, as explained at **19.12**. But in appearance these cases seem to turn on whether something close to undue influence can be shown simply by the fact of being married.[20] This begs the question why a particular type of relationship is singled out for special treatment. It would be more rational to look at all the facts of the relationship between the guarantor and the borrower, rather than limit relief by the way that a relationship is classified. In *Garcia*, Kirby J was hostile to limiting protection to those who are married. Callinan J was equally clear (at [109]) that the principle should *not* be extended beyond marriage. The majority (at [22]) left the question open for future decision.

Subsequent authorities have been inconsistent on the issue.[21] In principle, it is difficult to disagree with the statement of McMurdo P in *Australia and New Zealand Banking Group v Alirezai* (2004) at [39] that:

> Special relationships of sufficient trust and confidence in which one party could abuse that trust and confidence so as to invoke equitable relief for transactions entered into by the other are not a closed category; they could, for example, arise in some parent child relationships or perhaps in the relationship between a disabled person and a carer; many other potential examples can be envisaged.

In *Kranz v National Australia Bank* (2003), the Victorian Court of Appeal likewise thought that a relationship with a brother-in-law might fall within the *Yerkey* rule, though in this instance the bank was not aware of the closeness of the relationship. That was also the case in *Alirezai*,

---

18   For further examples of the special equity being successfully invoked: see eg *Wenczel v Commonwealth Bank* (2006); *Agripay v Byrne* (2011).
19   Compare Haigh & Hepburn 2000, discussing the significance of gender stereotyping in both this case and decisions such as *Louth v Diprose* (1992).
20   For a discussion of the relationship between the two, see Seddon & Bigwood 2017: [14.17].
21   For a review of the authorities and the policy issues involved, see Giancaspro 2017b.

where the guarantor and debtor were lifelong friends, but the lender had no idea of the strength of their bond. But in *Alceon Group v Rose* (2015), the rule was, for example, successfully invoked by a mother to set aside a guarantee.

Other judges, however, have resisted extending protection to the likes of a de facto relationship, or one between an aged parent and a child: see eg *Hillston v Bar-Mordecai* (2003); *Permanent Mortgages v Vandenbergh* (2010). It has also been suggested that any attempt to apply the rule to transactions other than a guarantee, no matter how logical that might seem, would have to be a matter for the High Court to decide: see *Narain v Euroasia* (2009).[22] Underpinning this reluctance to extend the rule may well be the fear that it would unduly expose lenders, and threaten the security of loan transactions.

Statutory prohibitions on unconscionable conduct

20.11   Background

Sitting alongside the two equitable doctrines discussed above – the unconscionable bargains doctrine and the rule in *Yerkey v Jones* – are statutory prohibitions on unconscionable conduct, such as those found in ss 20 and 21 of the ACL. These provisions have their origins in the *Trade Practices Act 1974* (Cth). Initially, that Act prohibited unconscionable conduct only in the context of consumer transactions (s 52A, introduced in 1986, which became s 51AB in 1992). The statutory unconscionable conduct regime was subsequently extended in two ways. A new s 51AA, introduced in 1992, prohibited conduct that was unconscionable within the meaning of 'the unwritten law' (that is, the common law). Section 51AC, added in 1998, extended the prohibition on unconscionable conduct to provide protection in certain business transactions. Supposedly (if inexactly) framed to protect 'small businesses', it initially applied to transactions up to $1 million in value. That cap was eventually lifted to $10 million, then removed in 2008.

The current unconscionable conduct regime retains a prohibition on 'unconscionable conduct within the meaning of the unwritten law', in s 20 of the ACL. Section 21 has a unified prohibition on unconscionable conduct in both consumer and business-related transactions. A statement of interpretative principles is provided in s 22 to assist the courts in applying s 21.[23] As with the treatment of misleading and deceptive conduct (see **18.19**), there are parallel provisions in respect of financial services and products in ss 12CA, 12CB and 12CC of the *Australian Securities and Investments Commission Act 2001* (Cth) (*ASIC Act*). For convenience, the discussion below will focus on the ACL provisions, even when discussing cases that have arisen under the *ASIC Act*.

---

22   Compare the view taken in *Elkofairi v Permanent Trustee* (2002), although it was considered in that case that for the *Yerkey* rule to apply to a mortgage, the lender would need to be aware that the wife might be a volunteer. See further Vrodos 2015.

23   The current versions of ss 21 and 22 were introduced by the *Competition and Consumer Legislation Amendment Act 2011* (Cth) Sch 2. As originally enacted, the two sections dealt separately with consumer (s 21) and business (s 22) dealings.

20.12   The relationship between ss 20 and 21 of the ACL

The s 20 prohibition on conduct that is unconscionable under the common law applies only to conduct not already prohibited by s 21. Section 20 is thus a 'residual' provision. While both provisions apply only to conduct 'in trade and commerce', s 21 is restricted to conduct that occurs in connection with the supply or acquisition (or potential supply or acquisition) of goods or services. But despite that narrower scope, the concept of 'unconscionable conduct' in s 21 is wider than that in s 20. This is confirmed by s 21(4), which expressly provides that s 21 'is not limited to the unwritten law in relation to unconscionable conduct'.

20.13   The relationship between s 20 and unconscionable conduct in equity

Section 20(1) provides that a person 'must not, in trade or commerce, engage in conduct that is unconscionable, within the meaning of the unwritten law from time to time'.[24] Its effect is to expand the remedies available, and allow for the involvement of consumer law regulators, in respect of conduct that is unconscionable in equity. The words 'from time to time' indicate that the scope of such conduct may change and develop over time to mirror shifting judicial conceptions. Conversely, s 20 itself may affect the development of the unwritten law through decisions made in cases in which the provision is invoked: *ACCC v Samton Holdings* (2002) at [43]. In one respect, the s 20 prohibition is narrower than unconscionable conduct in equity, in that it is restricted to conduct 'in trade or commerce'. The ACL notion of 'trade and commerce' was discussed in **18.20** in relation to misleading and deceptive conduct and will not be revisited here.[25]

20.14   'Unconscionable conduct within the meaning of the unwritten law'

The term 'unconscionable' has been left undefined in the ACL. The courts have distinguished two usages in the context of what is now s 20: see *ACCC v CG Berbatis* (2000) at [23]. In its first sense, the term is used to refer, at a generic level, to the fundamental principle which underpins equity's intervention across a range of areas and doctrines. But it is also used in a second, more specific sense to refer to particular categories of case. In *ACCC v CG Berbatis* (2003), the High Court seemed to prefer that narrower interpretation. However, it is yet to be definitively decided what the relevant categories of case are for this purpose.

When the prohibition was first introduced, it was described by its drafters as embodying the equitable concept of unconscionable conduct as recognised by the High Court in *Blomley v*

---

24   As with s 21, discussed below, the reference here to a 'person' must be understood by reference to the constitutional considerations noted in **1.15**. As a State or Territory law, the ACL can apply to any type of person. But as a federal law, it generally applies only to conduct by trading, financial or foreign corporations; and also conduct by individuals and other entities in relation to interstate or overseas trade, or in a Territory, or when using postal or telecommunications services.

25   For an example of a complaint of statutory unconscionability failing (perhaps surprisingly) on this ground, see *ASIC v National Exchange* (2005).

Ryan (1956) and *Commercial Bank v Amadio* (1983).[26] On that basis, it would cover only the unconscionable exploitation of special disadvantage, as discussed earlier in this chapter. However, in *ACCC v Samton Holdings* (2002), the Full Court of the Federal Court considered such an approach unduly restrictive. The Court enumerated (at [48]) at least five categories of 'unconscionable conduct' envisaged by what was then s 51AA:

(i)   setting aside a contract or disposition because of the knowing exploitation by one party of another's special disadvantage;

(ii)   setting aside, under the principle recognised in *Garcia v National Australia Bank* (1998), a transaction entered into as a result of defective comprehension, the influence of another and the lack of any independent explanation;

(iii) equitable estoppel;

(iv) relief against forfeiture and penalties; and

(v)   rescission of contracts entered into under the influence of unilateral mistake.

The Court added that these categories might not be exhaustive and that the content and degree of unconscionable conduct would vary according to the category.

As *Berbatis* was argued on the basis of unconscionable exploitation of special disadvantage, it was unnecessary for the High Court to consider the correctness of the approach in *Samton Holdings*. The precise scope of s 20 therefore remains to be settled. In practice, however, the case law under this provision (and its predecessors) has centred on allegations of unconscionable exploitation of special disadvantage. The difficulties of establishing such conduct are demonstrated by three unsuccessful claims brought by the ACCC.

In *Samton Holdings*, a tenant had inadvertently failed to exercise an option to renew his lease in time. Without a renewal, he could not operate the business he had just acquired. Among other things, he faced the loss of his house, against which a loan of the purchase price of the business had been secured. The landlord demanded $70,000 for an extension of the lease. In practical terms, the tenant had no choice but to pay that price. The Full Court of the Federal Court doubted that this amounted to a situation of 'special disadvantage'. Furthermore, while fair-minded people might condemn the landlord's avaricious and opportunistic conduct in driving a hard bargain, that did not mean it was unconscionable. In *Berbatis*, another landlord demanded from its lessees a release from claims under an existing lease as a condition for the grant of a new lease. The High Court stressed that the lessees' only disadvantage was their inferior bargaining position. This fell far short of what was required – a disadvantage seriously affecting a party's ability to make a judgment about their own interests. Merely taking advantage of a superior bargaining position did not constitute unconscionable conduct.

In *ACCC v Radio Rentals* (2005), the stumbling block lay not in proving special disadvantage on the part of a man with an intellectual disability, but in establishing that it was, or should have been, evident to the Radio Rentals' personnel who had dealt with him. The ACCC argued that, between them, those employees had accumulated sufficient knowledge to be aware of the customer's disability, even though none of them individually may have

---

26   Explanatory Memorandum, Trade Practices Legislation Amendment Bill 1992 (Cth), p 8.

appreciated it. But Finn J rejected the suggestion that it was reasonable to aggregate their individual impressions and experiences. There was nothing here to show that these would have been apparent from a single record or that the business had somehow contrived to keep the relevant records separate.

20.15   The scope of the s 21 prohibition

Section 21(1) prohibits a person from engaging, in trade or commerce, in conduct 'that is, in all the circumstances, unconscionable'. Such conduct must occur in connection with the supply or possible supply, or the acquisition or possible acquisition, of goods or services. The original prohibition excluded any supply or acquisition to or from a 'listed public company' – that is, a public company whose shares are listed on an approved stock exchange. It had been thought that those bodies were sufficiently powerful to look after their own interests. However, in its review of the ACL, CAANZ (2017: 49–50) recommended removing this exclusion, on the basis that public listing is not necessarily a reflection of a trader's ability to withstand unconscionable conduct. Legislation to make this change has recently been enacted.[27]

The reference to 'possible' supplies or acquisitions extends the scope of s 21 to situations where no contract is ultimately entered into. This reflects the fact that it is concerned not merely with the effect of the conduct on identifiable 'victims', but with the regulation and modification of business practices through a focus on the conduct of the dominant party. The inclusion of acquisition (or possible acquisition) of goods or services also recognises that businesses may be just as vulnerable to the unconscionable conduct of stronger business parties when supplying goods or services, as when acquiring them.

20.16   The unconscionability standard under s 21

Section 21(4)(a) confirms that the concept of unconscionable conduct in s 21(1) is wider than that developed by the unwritten law (and, thus, that applicable under s 20).[28] The crucial question is just how far the courts will be prepared to extend the concept as developed by the unwritten law. Certainly, their approach towards earlier provisions proved cautious, particularly where s 51AC of the *Trade Practices Act 1974* (Cth) (involving unconscionability in business transactions) was concerned.[29]

Section 21(4) spells out two specific respects in which the current prohibition is more expansive than under the unwritten law. Firstly, it is not restricted to conduct that can be shown to have resulted in disadvantage to a particular individual or individuals. It can apply to 'a system of conduct' or 'pattern of behaviour', regardless of whether disadvantage results: s 21(4)(b). This goes back to the point made above that s 21 is concerned with regulating and modifying business behaviour. Secondly, in considering unconscionability in relation to a contract, the court is not restricted to consideration of circumstances relating to the formation

---

27   See *Treasury Laws Amendment (Australian Consumer Law Review) Act 2018* (Cth) Sch 2, amending ss 21(1)(a) and (b) of the ACL.

28   Even before this provision was added, the courts had taken that view in relation to previous incarnations of s 21: see eg *ASIC v National Exchange* (2005) at [29]–[30]. For a more detailed discussion of the relationship between the equitable and statutory concepts of unconscionability, see Paterson 2015.

29   See Paterson 2009b: 939; Senate Standing Committee on Economics 2008: [5.6].

of the contract, but may take into account both the terms of the contract and the manner and extent to which the contract is carried out: s 21(4)(c).

The term 'unconscionable' itself has been left undefined. It has been described in this context as an 'open-ended' concept, but also one that is 'value-laden': *ACCC v Seal-A-Fridge* (2010) at [12]; *Paciocco v ANZ Banking Group* (2015) at [262]. The court's task is the 'evaluation of the facts by reference to a normative standard of conscience'. That standard is permeated with 'accepted and acceptable community values', although it is recognised that such values are, in some contexts, contestable: *ACCC v Lux Distributors* (2013) at [23]. It is clear that unconscionable conduct requires something more than mere unfairness or unjustness. But it does not require dishonesty: *Paciocco* (2015) at [262]. It can occur in the absence of any motive, intent, bad faith, or intent to injure: *Video Ezy International v Sedema* (2014) at [96].

In an attempt to delineate the unconscionable from the merely unfair or unjust, it has been said that there must be 'serious misconduct, or something clearly unfair or unreasonable ... actions showing no regard for conscience, or that are irreconcilable with what is right or reasonable': *Hurley v McDonald's* (1999) at [22]. Spigelman CJ described unconscionability as requiring a 'high level of moral obloquy': *Attorney-General v World Best Holdings* (2005) at 583. The observation has been endorsed or echoed in many other cases: see eg *Tonto Home Loans v Tavares* (2011) at [291]; *Director of Consumer Affairs Victoria v Scully* (2013) at [18]; *Ipstar v APS Satellite* (2018) at [193]–[195]. But the Full Court of the Federal Court has warned against attempts to capture the meaning of the statutory language with synonyms such as 'moral taint' or 'moral obloquy', or to introduce any fixed elements or rules: *ACCC v Lux* (2013); *Paciocco* (2015); *NRM v ACCC* (2016). The fear is that the search for moral obloquy will deflect the court from its true task – the evaluation of business conduct by reference to the norms and values considered relevant by parliament.

20.17   Relevant factors

In determining whether an acquirer or supplier of goods or services has been treated unconscionably within the meaning of s 21(1), ss 22(1) and (2) provide that a court *may* have regard to:

- the relative bargaining strengths of the parties;
- whether the acquirer/supplier must comply with conditions not reasonably necessary to protect the legitimate interests of the other party;
- whether the acquirer/supplier was able to understand relevant documents;
- any undue influence or pressure exerted or unfair tactics used against the acquirer/supplier or their agent by the other party (or a person acting on their behalf);
- the amount and circumstances under which equivalent goods or services could have been acquired from or supplied by someone else;
- the extent to which the other party's conduct was consistent with their conduct towards other acquirers or suppliers in similar transactions;
- the requirements of any applicable or apparently relevant industry code;
- the extent to which the other party unreasonably failed to disclose intended conduct on their part potentially affecting the acquirer/supplier's interests, and any risks arising from that conduct that would not have been foreseeably apparent;

- the extent of the other party's willingness to negotiate the terms of any contract, the terms themselves, the parties' compliance with those terms and their conduct after entry into the contract;

- whether the other party has a contractual right to unilaterally vary the terms of the contract; and

- the extent to which each party has acted in good faith.

In *Paciocco v ANZ Banking Group* (2016), the High Court had to consider whether a term in credit card agreements imposing late payment fees of $20 and $35 amounted to unconscionable conduct. At first instance, Gordon J had found that the actual loss suffered by the Bank when the customer failed to make the minimum payment by the due date was no more than $3. The customers' argument focused on the first two factors mentioned above. In finding that the fee did not amount to unconscionable conduct, the High Court considered that the argument took too narrow a view of the Bank's 'legitimate interests', which could extend beyond an interest in recovering the actual loss (in the sense of legally recoverable damages). In any event, these were but two factors to be taken into account, along with all the other circumstances. Indeed, judicial reluctance to be too explicit about the factors underlying determinations of unconscionability is apparent in many of the cases. As such, a straightforward characterisation of any given finding of unconscionable conduct as resting on any particular factor or factors is not always possible. In such cases, we are left to speculate as to the particular factors or mix of factors motivating the court.

20.18 Examples of conduct breaching s 21: consumer transactions

In the consumer context, numerous instances of unconscionable conduct have involved a combination of the targeting of vulnerable customers and high-pressure sales tactics. In *ACCC v Keshow* (2005), women living in indigenous communities were persuaded to sign open-ended periodical payment forms in connection with contracts for the supply of children's educational materials. The materials were commonly not supplied (or not in their entirety) and were not needed or useful, having regard to the age of the children in question. It appears to have been significant that many of the women had limited commercial experience and did not fully understand the nature of the form they were signing.[30] The payments would absorb a large part of their income, which came predominantly from welfare payments. At no stage were the women given a written record of the contract they had entered or specific details of the materials, their cost or the date of delivery. In finding a system of unconscionable conduct, Mansfield J also emphasised the defendant's awareness of certain traits precluding the women from resisting his sales pressure.[31] The use of high-pressure tactics on elderly people, in circumstances where access to their homes to sell vacuum cleaners had been gained by deception,[32] was also held to amount to unconscionable conduct in *ACCC v Lux Distributors* (2013).[33]

---

30   See s 22(1)(c) – ability to understand the relevant document.
31   See s 22(1)(d) – undue influence or pressure or unfair tactics.
32   Although the Court did not expressly label it as such, this deception would presumably amount to 'unfair tactics' under s 22(1)(d), quite apart from the element of undue pressure.
33   The case also involved breaches of the unsolicited consumer agreement provisions in ss 69–95.

In *NRM v ACCC* (2016), the Full Court of the Federal Court upheld a finding of a system of unconscionable conduct in connection with the treatment of male sexual dysfunction. The fears and anxieties of men suffering from dysfunction had been deliberately harnessed for the purposes of selling the medical treatments, conduct which North J had described as 'immoral'.[34] Also significant was the use of high-pressure sales techniques and, in circumstances where the men believed they were consulting a medical practice, the failure to disclose that salespeople were remunerated by commission. In other cases, however, regulators have been less successful in establishing systems of unconscionable conduct. In *Kobelt v ASIC* (2018), a Full Court of the Federal Court overturned a finding that a general store in the APY Lands had acted unconscionably in selling second-hand vehicles to indigenous residents by way of 'book-up' (informal credit). The Court stressed, among other things, that the store had not acted in a 'predatory' fashion, and that its customers understood the arrangements and voluntarily entered into them. A finding of an unconscionable system was also overturned in *Unique International College v ACCC* (2018). The case involved a supplier of online vocational education courses. It was said to have targeted socially disadvantaged people by inducing them to enrol in expensive courses they were unlikely to complete, including by offering gifts of laptops or iPads. But while the ACCC's allegation of systemic wrongdoing was rejected for lack of evidence, the supplier was found to have acted unconscionably in dealing with five particular consumers who gave evidence at trial.

Unconscionable conduct has also arisen in the context of debt collection activity.[35] In *ACCC v Excite Mobile* (2013), unconscionable conduct was found on the part of a telecommunications company which sought to scare debtors into payment of alleged debts by creating a fake complaints handling body and debt collection agency. It also made a number of unfounded statements, including that in court proceedings the debtor's assets would be repossessed and an order made for payment of a certain amount of compensation.[36]

20.19 Examples of conduct breaching s 21: business dealings

In the business-to-business context a number of findings of unconscionable conduct have been made in the franchising sector. A number of these appear to rest on the existence of unequal bargaining power, coupled with conduct which might be characterised as the use of 'unfair tactics'. For example, in *ACCC v Seal-A-Fridge* (2010) at [146] the franchisor had demanded increased weekly franchise fees from franchisees, although it had no contractual authority to do so. The Court stressed that taking advantage of a superior bargaining position was not of itself unconscionable. But the abuse of such a position in conjunction with the use of falsehoods to obtain a price increase to which it had no contractual entitlement, as well as advantageous contractual variations, breached the statutory prohibition. In *ACCC v South East Melbourne Cleaning* (2015), a franchisor had been paid by customers for work performed by its franchisees

---

34   Again, this harnessing of fears and anxieties could presumably have amounted to the use of 'unfair tactics' under s 22(1)(d), although there was no explicit reference to this as a factor.

35   Protection from harassment and coercion, including in connection with the payment for goods, services or an interest in land, is also provided under s 50 of the ACL: see **19.08**.

36   See also *ACCC v ACM Group* (2018).

but failed to pay those franchisees for that work – in one case, for a period of three months. The franchisor had also, during that period of non-payment, demanded a substantial fee to which it was not entitled. In another instance, it told the franchisee that, if he terminated his franchise, it would demand repayment of a loan, despite being not entitled to do so. This franchisee was also threatened with disadvantageous consequences if he refused further work and told that a release from the agreement would only be granted on extremely disadvantageous terms.

In *ACCC v Coles* (2014), the supermarket giant was found to have engaged in unconscionable conduct in relation to an 'Active Retail Collaboration' program implemented with a view to securing over $12 million of 'rebates' from its smaller suppliers. When seeking suppliers' agreement to the incorporation of these rebates into their trading agreements, Coles' representatives had made groundless assertions that the rebates reflected savings the suppliers would make as a result of changes to Coles' supply chain and data sharing. Suppliers were told that their agreement was required and that adverse commercial consequences would follow if it was not forthcoming, and they were repeatedly pressed for a speedy response. In all cases, the business with Coles was a very significant part of the supplier's overall business. Indeed, it appears that this was the very reason why the suppliers had been targeted for inclusion in the program. Thus, the finding of unconscionable conduct in this case might be characterised as resting on the combination of extreme inequality of bargaining power, exertion of undue pressure and the use of unfair tactics.

There have been many instances in which complaints of unconscionable behaviour have been rejected, especially in cases brought by private plaintiffs rather than the ACCC. It has frequently been concluded that defendants have done no more than act in their legitimate interests; for example, in terminating a contract: see eg *Freier v Australian Postal* (2012); *DPN Solutions v Tridant* (2014). There has been a particular resistance to finding unconscionability in dealings between well-advised parties: see eg *Body Bronze International v Febcorp* (2011); *BBB Constructions v Aldi Foods* (2012). But there have been some cases in which businesses have successfully complained of unconscionable treatment, such as *Violet Home Loans v Schmidt* (2013). There, a mortgage manager had failed to investigate irregularities in a fraudulently induced loan application from a naïve and unsophisticated borrower, who wished to invest in what turned out to be a fraudster's business.[37]

20.20   Remedies

A finding of unconscionable conduct under s 20 or s 21 opens up the range of potential remedies under Part 5-2 of the ACL that were discussed in **18.31–18.33**. These include orders to set aside or vary a contract, or for a defendant to pay compensation or take other steps to remedy a contravention. For example, in *Messer v Lotus Securities* (2018), the defendant was ordered to pay $6.6 million to compensate the plaintiff for the amount he had spent in purchasing what were essentially worthless shares (see **4.09**).[38] Civil penalties may also be

---

37   For further examples of successful claims, see *Colin R Price & Associates v Four Oaks* (2017); *Ipstar v APS Satellite* (2018).

38   As for the need for a causal connection between the unconscionable conduct and any loss said to have been suffered by an applicant, see eg *Canon Australia v Patton* (2007); *Allphones Retail v Hoy Mobile* (2009).

imposed under s 224. In *ACCC v Coles*, Gordon J ordered Coles to pay fines of $10 million, but questioned whether a maximum available penalty of $1.1 million per contravention was an adequate response to unconscionable conduct on the part of a corporation with annual revenue in excess of $22 billion. As noted in **18.31**, much higher penalties can now be awarded. Coles also entered into an enforceable undertaking with the ACCC under s 218 to establish a formal process to provide options for redress for the suppliers referred to in the proceedings.

Broader controls on unfair contracts

20.21   Background

It took Australia many years to introduce general legislation to regulate *unfair contract terms*. New South Wales did have the *Contracts Review Act 1980*, which afforded that State's courts a discretion to set aside or vary 'unjust' contracts. But as explained in **20.32**, this was never used as widely as it might have been to control substantively unfair terms. The same was true of the controls on unconscionability in the federal *Trade Practices Act 1974* (Cth). On their face, these appeared capable of providing relief from substantive unfairness alone. But, in practice, the courts and tribunals applying them were reluctant to provide relief in the absence of procedural unfairness.[39]

A more significant development proved to be Victoria's enactment in 2003 of Part 2B of the *Fair Trading Act 1999* (Vic), which was squarely aimed at unfair terms in consumer contracts. In its review of Australia's consumer policy framework, the Productivity Commission (2008) identified the absence of equivalent provisions in other jurisdictions as a significant gap. It considered there were sound economic and ethical rationales for proscribing unfair terms. It accepted that such terms were prevalent in practice, though there was limited information as to the extent of any detriment to consumers from their use. Importantly, the Commission noted that there was no evidence of any unintended consequences or significant business compliance costs either in Victoria or in other countries that had acted to bar unfair terms.

The Productivity Commission ultimately recommended the inclusion of an unfair contract terms regime in the proposed new 'single generic consumer law' that was to become the ACL. The relevant provisions were enacted by the *Trade Practices Amendment (Australian Consumer Law) Act (No 1) 2010* (Cth), taking effect in July 2010 ahead of the rest of the ACL. They are now found in Part 2-3 of the ACL and, as explained below, apply to most contracts concerning goods, services or interests in land. Parallel provisions concerning unfair terms relating to financial products and services can be found in ss 12BF–12BM of the *ASIC Act*. Once again, the discussion below focuses on the ACL provisions alone.

20.22   The scope of the ACL provisions

Both the (now repealed) Victorian regime and the ACL provisions were inspired and heavily influenced by the United Kingdom's *Unfair Terms in Consumer Contracts Regulations 1994*.[40]

---

39   See Howell 2006; Paterson 2009b.
40   Now superseded by the *Consumer Rights Act 2015* (UK).

The ACL provisions were initially limited in their operation to consumer contracts, albeit with an added requirement that those contracts be in 'standard form'. There had been some discussion before their enactment that they should also apply to business-to-business transactions, though the then Labor Government decided against this. Following extensive lobbying by small business advocates,[41] the Abbott Government resolved to extend the provisions to cover standard form 'small business contracts'. The change was introduced by the *Treasury Legislation Amendment (Small Business and Unfair Contract Terms) Act 2015*, with effect from 12 November 2016. It reflects a growing recognition that, just like consumers, small businesses often lack the bargaining power and resources to understand and negotiate contract terms, rendering them vulnerable to the imposition of unfair terms.

20.23 'Standard form contract'

Standard form contracts – also referred to as 'contracts of adhesion' or 'boilerplate contracts' – are characterised by two main features. They come into being without any genuine negotiation between the parties; and they apply to all transactions of a particular type entered into by the stronger party (typically, but not always, a supplier). A standard form contract is normally an indication that one party was in a position to present the terms of the deal to the other on a 'take-it-or-leave-it' basis. Such contracts are typical across the whole spectrum of industries supplying consumers with goods or services.[42] In reducing transaction costs, standard form contracting is undoubtedly advantageous for suppliers and consumers alike. There is, however, a dark side. Such contracting poses challenges to the traditional understanding of contract law, in which notions of freedom of contract are premised on the assumption that the terms of the deal are the freely manifested consent of the parties. The problem is not merely one of inequality of bargaining power. There is also a problem of inequality of information. The length and complexity of standard term contracts are generally such that their recipients (at least those other than well-resourced, legally-advised commercial parties) cannot reasonably be expected to read them, let alone understand them. These features have caused some to suggest that such contracts should be denied the status of contracts.[43] At the very least, they are considered to justify statutory interference, something much harder to contemplate with genuinely negotiated contracts: see *Director of Consumer Affairs Victoria v Craig Langley* (2008) at [66]–[67].

The term 'standard form contract' is not defined in the ACL. Section 27(2) permits a court to 'take into account such matters as it thinks relevant' when determining whether a contract meets the description, but provides a list of matters to which regard *must* be had. These include:

- the relative bargaining power of the parties;
- whether the contract was initially prepared by one party;
- whether the terms (other than those exempted by s 26(1), as discussed below) were presented on a take-it-or-leave-it basis;
- whether there was any effective opportunity to negotiate those terms; and

---

41   See eg Zumbo 2009.
42   See ACCC et al 2016b: 8.
43   See eg Slawson 1971.

- whether the terms take into account the specific characteristics of another party or the particular transaction.

Section 27(1) creates a rebuttable presumption that a contract is a standard form contract. The rationale for placing the onus of proof on the party seeking to uphold the term is that, whereas the other party generally only has information about their own affairs, the former can adduce evidence regarding the nature of the contracts it uses and the way in which it deals with other parties.[44] It has been held that a party cannot rebut the presumption merely by asserting that they are willing to negotiate or 'be flexible' over their standard terms, unless there is evidence to show this actually happens: *Ferme v Kimberley Discovery Cruises* (2015). What is less clear is whether a contract will still be in standard form if some terms are typically negotiated, but others are not. Arguably, it would have made more sense for the legislation to focus on whether the challenged term or terms were in standard form, not the contract as a whole.[45] This is a point to which we return below in discussing the remedies available if unfairness is established.

20.24   'Consumer contract'

A 'consumer contract' is defined in s 23(3) of the ACL to mean a contract for the supply of goods or services, or for the sale or grant of an interest in land,[46] to an individual whose acquisition of the goods, services or interest is wholly or predominantly for personal, domestic or household use or consumption. This differs from (and arguably is much clearer than) the general definition of 'consumer' in s 3 which applies in other contexts, such as the consumer guarantees: see **9.29**. Unlike s 3, s 23(3) requires the acquirer to be an *individual*, which is defined as a 'natural person' by s 2B of the *Acts Interpretation Act* 1901 (Cth). In all cases, the acquisition must be 'wholly or predominantly for personal, domestic or household use or consumption'. It appears that use will be 'personal' for this purpose if it is not for commercial or business use: *Terry Truck Rentals v Haseeb* (2016).[47] It is the *subjective* purpose of the buyer in making the acquisition that matters under s 23(3).[48]

20.25   'Small business contract'

Section 23(4) provides that a contract is a 'small business contract' if it is for the supply of goods or services or the sale or grant of an interest in land and at least one party is a business employing fewer than 20 persons. A 'business' for this purpose includes a business not carried on for profit: s 2(1). The headcount of employees for this purpose is stated to exclude casuals, unless they are employed on a regular and systematic basis: s 23(5). In addition, s 23(4)

---

44   Explanatory Memorandum, Trade Practices Amendment (Australian Consumer Law) Bill (No 2) 2010 (Cth), [5.73]. In the footnotes below, this source is abbreviated as EM 2010.

45   See Harder 2011: 311–13.

46   As to the rationale for including land contracts, and the likely effect of the ACL provisions in this context, see Christensen & Duncan 2012.

47   See further Sise 2017a, discussing the relationship between the definition of 'consumer contract' and the later-added definition of 'small business contract', considered below.

48   Compare s 3, which takes an *objective* approach in focusing on the purposes for which goods of that type are *ordinarily* acquired, where the amount paid for the goods exceeds $40,000.

requires the upfront price of the contract not to exceed $300,000 or, in case of a contract of more than 12 months' duration, $1,000,000. The definition of 'upfront price' is discussed below. These monetary limits were included to delineate transactions in respect of which small businesses cannot reasonably be expected to undertake appropriate due diligence, such as seeking legal advice, from those high-value commercial transactions where such an expectation is entirely reasonable. Whereas a transaction will only be a 'consumer contract' if an individual *acquires* goods, services or an interest in land, s 23(4) covers both acquisition and supply by small businesses. It can also apply not just where one party is a small business, but to dealings between small businesses.

20.26   Excluded contracts and terms

A number of standard form contracts are exempted from the unfair contract terms regime. Section 28 excludes contracts of marine salvage or towage, ship charterparties, contracts for the carriage of goods by ship and contracts amounting to the constitution of a company, managed investment scheme or other kind of body. Insurance contracts regulated under the *Insurance Contracts Act 1984* (Cth) are also currently exempt by virtue of s 15 of that Act, although a review of the ACL recommended that this exemption be removed.[49] Following a recommendation by the Senate Economics References Committee (2017) that the unfair contract terms provisions be extended to insurance contracts, the Treasury issued a proposals paper in June 2018.[50] Its proposed model involves amending the *Insurance Contracts Act 1984* (Cth) to bring insurance contracts within the scope of the unfair contract terms provisions of the *ASIC Act* and the introduction of some tailored provisions to accommodate specific features of insurance contracts.

More generally, s 26(1) excludes from review any terms which:

- define the main subject matter of a contract;
- set the upfront price payable under a contract; or
- are required or expressly permitted by a Commonwealth, State or Territory law.

The first of these categories includes terms defining the goods, services or land being supplied under the contract, as well as terms that are necessary to give effect to the supply or grant, or without which, the supply or grant could not occur.[51] A guide produced by consumer protection agencies gives the example of a customer who buys a product over the internet and agrees to have it delivered by post. In this situation, the customer cannot challenge the delivery term, as it is necessary to effect the supply of the product they have agreed to buy.[52]

Section 26(2) provides that the 'upfront price payable under a contract' is the consideration to be provided for the relevant goods, services or interest in land and which is disclosed at or before entry into the contract: s 26(2). It is not restricted to the cash price payable when the contract is made, but also covers any interest payable under the contract, as well as future

---

49   CAANZ 2017: 52–3. The Rudd Government had previously proposed this change, but its Insurance Contracts Amendment (Unfair Terms) Bill 2013 (Cth) lapsed on the calling of the 2013 federal election.

50   Australian Government 2018a.

51   EM 2010, [5.61].

52   ACCC et al 2016b: 9.

payments.[53] However, any future payments that are not disclosed in a transparent manner at or before entry into the contract are not taken to be part of the 'upfront price'. Nor is any consideration for the supply that is contingent on the occurrence or non-occurrence of a particular event. A fee charged by a bank or other credit provider in the event of its customer failing to make the stipulated minimum monthly credit card payment by the due date is an example of a contingent payment that would be open to challenge. The rationale for excluding both the main subject matter of the contract and the upfront price are that these are matters in respect of which there is seen to be a choice.[54]

20.27   The meaning of 'unfair'

All three requirements of s 24(1) must be satisfied for a term to be considered unfair. These are that the term:

- would cause a significant imbalance in the parties' contractual rights and obligations;
- is not reasonably necessary to protect the legitimate interests of the party seeking to rely on it; and
- would cause detriment (whether financial or otherwise) to a party if relied upon or applied.

It is for the party asserting unfairness to establish the significant imbalance and detriment requirements, but there is a rebuttable presumption that a term is not necessary for the legitimate protection of the party seeking to rely on it: s 24(4).

In *Paciocco v ANZ Banking Group* (2015) at [363], Allsop CJ observed that 'unjustness and unfairness are of a lower moral and ethical standard than unconscionability'. In determining unfairness, the court is expressly instructed by s 24(2) to have regard to both the extent to which the term is 'transparent' and the contract as a whole. A term is considered to be transparent if it is expressed in plain language, legible, presented clearly and readily available: s 24(3). Logically, it is hard to see how the transparency or otherwise of a term can have any relevance to the three requirements set out in s 24(1), other than in very limited situations. It is really a factor that goes to whether an affected consumer or small business is aware of the term and can make a choice whether to accept it, not so much its content or effect.[55] Despite this, a lack of transparency has been used to bolster findings of unfairness in a number of cases to date: see eg *ACCC v Chrisco Hampers* (2015); *NRM v ACCC* (2016); *ACCC v Get Qualified Australia* (2017).

In *ACCC v CLA Trading* (2016) at [54], Gilmour J provided a helpful summary of previous case law on the United Kingdom and Victorian unfair terms regimes (with citations omitted):

(a)   the underlying policy of unfair contract terms legislation respects true freedom of contract and seeks to prevent the abuse of standard form consumer contracts which, by definition, will not have been individually negotiated;

(b)   the requirement of 'significant imbalance' directs attention to the substantive unfairness of the contract;

---

53   EM 2010, [5.64]–[5.65].
54   For an economic analysis of the price exclusion, see eg Atamer 2017.
55   See Harder 2011: 316–19; Sise 2017b.

(c)   it is useful to assess the impact of an impugned term on the parties' rights and obligations by comparing the effect of the contract with the term and the effect it would have without it;

(d)   the 'significant imbalance' requirement is met if a term is so weighted in favour of the supplier as to tilt the parties' rights and obligations under the contract significantly in its favour—this may be by the granting to the supplier of a beneficial option or discretion or power, or by the imposing on the consumer of a disadvantageous burden or risk or duty;

(e)   significant in this context means 'significant in magnitude', or 'sufficiently large to be important', 'being a meaning not too distant from substantial';

(f)   the legislation proceeds on the assumption that some terms in consumer contracts, especially in standard form consumer contracts, may be inherently unfair, regardless of how comprehensively they might be drawn to the customer's attention; and

(g)   in considering 'the contract as a whole', not each and every term of the contract is equally relevant, or necessarily relevant at all. The main requirement is to consider terms that might reasonably be seen as tending to counterbalance the term in question.

In *Chrisco Hampers*, Edelman J adopted a similar approach to the concept of 'significant imbalance' to that quoted above, which is based on the judgment of Lord Bingham in *Director General of Fair Trading v First National Bank* (2001). But he stressed (at [49]) that the focus remains on the terms of s 24. He also considered (at [50]) that any lack of individual negotiation between the parties is not relevant to the question of imbalance.

In *Paciocco v ANZ Banking Group* (2016), the High Court had to consider whether the late payment fees mentioned in **20.17** were unfair. In finding that they were not, Keane J emphasised (at [301]–[303]) the fact that the fees had been clearly disclosed, that they could, in most instances, have been avoided, and that the contracts were terminable at the will of the customer. The 'price' – the amount of the fee – was not determinative. According to Gageler J (at [201]), the mere fact that the effect of a term is to allow one party to obtain a windfall from the other's breach of contract is insufficient to establish 'significant imbalance'.[56]

20.28   The statutory examples of unfair terms

Section 25 provides a non-exhaustive list of the kinds of terms that *may* be unfair. These include terms:

- permitting one party only to avoid or limit their performance, to vary the terms, or to terminate or renew the contract;
- penalising one party only for breach or termination of the contract;
- permitting one party to vary the upfront price without the other being able to terminate;
- allowing one party to vary the characteristics of the goods, services or land being supplied;
- permitting one party to determine the meaning of the contract or whether it has been breached;

---

56   For a further example of a case failing on this ground, see *Turner v MyBudget* (2018).

- limiting a party's vicarious liability for wrongdoing by their agents;
- allowing one party to assign the contract to the other party's detriment, without their consent;
- limiting one party's right to sue the other; or
- limiting the evidence that can be adduced, or imposing an evidential burden, in proceedings relating to the contract.

This list is merely intended as guidance. Section 25 neither prohibits the use of such terms, nor creates a presumption that they are unfair.[57] The overarching question remains whether, in all the circumstances, the three requirements in s 24(1) are satisfied.

20.29 Remedies

The ACL provides only one method for challenging the fairness of a standard form consumer or small business contract. A party to the relevant contract, or the regulator, may seek a declaration under s 250 that a particular term in the contract is unfair. The effect of such a declaration is to render that term 'void', with (apparently) retrospective effect. The rest of the contract may remain in operation, provided it can operate without the unfair term (s 23(2)): see eg *Ferme v Kimberley Discovery Cruises* (2015).[58] Merely *including* an unfair term in a contract is not taken to be a contravention of the ACL, either before or after it has been declared void: s 15. The general remedies in Part 5-2 for contraventions of the ACL are not, therefore, applicable. Where, however, a party applies or relies, or purports to apply or rely, on a term *after* it has been declared unfair under s 250, an injunction (s 232) and a compensation order (s 237) are available. Although the matter is not completely free from doubt,[59] the better view seems to be that damages under s 236 are not available in this situation, as was accepted in *Ferme* at [116]–[118]. Section 239 also permits the regulator to seek redress against a party advantaged by a term that has been declared unfair, on behalf of 'non-party consumers'. The consumers must have been part of a class of persons who have been caused to suffer loss or damage by the term, or who are likely to suffer such loss. A court may make any order it thinks appropriate to redress, prevent or reduce the loss or damage, though *not* an award of damages. In determining whether to make such an order, the court may have regard to any conduct since the declaration, by either the consumers or the party against whom the order is sought: s 240(2).

The precise effect of a declaration granted under s 250 is far from clear. The fact that redress may be sought under s 239 on behalf of a 'class' of consumers makes it clear that a declaration can affect more than just one contract. But what if a slightly different version of the term is used in another contract that is otherwise similar to the one challenged? Does it matter that the differences may be purely cosmetic? What if an identical term is used in a slightly different contract? It may be significant that in a review of the ACL, a proposal to prohibit the use of

---

57   See EM 2010, [5.44].
58   As to the difficulties that may arise where it is only one part or aspect of a term that is unfair, see Harder 2011: 320–2.
59   See Coorey 2015: 363–4.

terms previously declared unfair was rejected. It was considered that this would undermine the nature and intent of the existing provisions in determining unfairness on a case-by-case basis, 'acknowledging that what may be unfair in one context is not necessarily unfair in another'.[60]

20.30   Changing business practice and challenging unfair terms

Fortunately, any uncertainty about the remedial regime has been offset by the proactive approach adopted by the ACCC, as the regulator for the federal version of the ACL.[61] Following the introduction of the new regime, the ACCC conducted a review of standard form consumer contracts in the airline, telecommunications, fitness and vehicle rental industries, as well as terms commonly used by online traders and some travel agents. Many businesses were reported to have deleted or amended terms identified as problematic by the agency.[62] Shortly afterwards, the ACCC commenced its first proceedings under the provisions, against an internet service provider, ByteCard. This resulted in a consent declaration by the Federal Court, invalidating terms enabling the provider to discontinue supply without cause, or to unilaterally vary prices without affording any right to its customers to terminate. Also declared void was a contract requiring customers to indemnify the provider for all losses, even those caused by the provider's own breach of contract.[63]

Further cases have followed. In *ACCC v Chrisco Hampers* (2015), Chrisco supplied customers with Christmas hampers, paid for by advance instalments. The term successfully challenged provided that once the current year's order was fully paid, the customer would (unless they ticked a box) be automatically 'rolled into' a plan for the following year, with direct debit payments continuing accordingly. If the customer did not place an order for the subsequent year, their money would be refunded in full, but without interest. This was considered to create a significant imbalance in the parties' rights. A similar finding was made in *NRM v ACCC* (2016). Patients who elected to terminate their treatment for male sexual dysfunction were required to pay a number of fees and charges, regardless of whether the reason for the termination was a simple change of mind, a severe adverse side effect, or the fact that the medication had proved ineffective. It was significant that there was no cogent evidence of the effectiveness of the medications provided, which were not regarded by the medical profession as the usual form of treatment.

ACCC v CLA Trading (2016) involved Europcar's car rental contracts. One category of term challenged in the case required customers to pay for various kinds of loss or damage up to a

---

60   CAANZ 2017: 56.

61   Having said that, CAANZ noted in its review of the ACL that some regulators (including the ACCC) had been restricted in their ability to investigate compliance and take enforcement action in respect of unfair contract terms. This is because, under the original legislation, their investigative powers were only triggered by 'contraventions' or 'possible contraventions' of the law. As discussed at **20.29**, the inclusion of an unfair term in a contract is neither a 'contravention' nor a 'possible contravention'. CAANZ (2017: 54–5) therefore recommended that regulators be allowed to use existing investigative powers to better assess whether or a not a term may be unfair. Section 155(2)(b) (as well as the equivalent provision of the *ASIC Act*) has been amended to this effect by *Treasury Laws Amendment (Australian Consumer Law Review) Act 2018* (Cth) Sch 7.

62   See ACCC 2013a.

63   See ACCC 2013b.

maximum 'damage liability fee' ($3,650), unless they had purchased insurance. The obligation applied irrespective of any fault on the part of the customer. A second category of term removed the liability cap if the customer had breached the car rental contract, regardless of the triviality of the breach and the extent to which it had contributed to the relevant loss or damage. Both categories of terms were confirmed to be unfair. In *ACCC v Get Qualified Australia* (2017), GQA provided assistance and advice to customers making applications for nationally recognised qualifications from registered training organisations. Under its terms and conditions, any customer whose application was unsuccessful was entitled to a full refund. A term excluding a refund where an applicant withdrew from the process after enrolling with GQA was found to be unfair, since it applied even where the company had incurred no significant costs or would not be out of pocket in relation to a particular customer.

20.31   Tackling unfair terms in small business contracts

The ACCC adopted a similar approach when the ACL was amended to cover unfair terms in small business contracts. This time, a review was conducted of contracts in advertising, telecommunications, retail leasing, independent contracting, franchising, waste management and agriculture. A number of large companies participated, with the agency again reporting a good degree of cooperation in removing or altering certain terms. Particular concern was noted with terms of the type that had featured in the ByteCard matter, involving unilateral powers of variation, unnecessarily broad indemnity provisions and unreasonably wide powers of cancellation.[64] Since then, the first court action has been successfully taken under the small business contract provisions. In *ACCC v JJ Richards* (2017), a series of terms imposed by a waste management company were declared by consent to be unfair. Besides price variation powers and unnecessarily broad indemnities, these included automatic renewal clauses binding customers to subsequent contracts unless they cancelled within 30 days before the end of the contract period. Significantly, there was no requirement for JJ Richards to provide notice of the contract's expiry. Also successfully challenged were terms preventing customers from terminating their contracts if there were payments outstanding and entitling JJ Richards to continue charging them equipment rental, despite the fact that no services would be provided. [65]

In August 2017, it was also announced that the major banks had agreed to make a range of changes to their loan agreements with small business customers, following pressure from ASIC and the Australian Small Business and Family Enterprise Ombudsman.[66]

20.32   Other protections against unfair terms

Besides the ACL (and the *ASIC Act*), a range of other statutes have provisions on unfair terms. Nationally, the most significant of these is s 76 of the National Credit Code.[67] This allows a court to reopen any unjust transaction which gives rise to a credit contract, mortgage or guarantee.

---

64   See ACCC 2016.
65   See also *ACCC v Servcorp* (2018).
66   See Waters 2017. See also the recent developments discussed in a review by the Treasury of unfair
       contract term protections for small business: Australian Government 2018b: [4.4].
67   The Code is found in Schedule 1 to the *National Consumer Credit Protection Act 2009* (Cth).

The term 'unjust' is defined for this purpose in s 204 to include anything that is 'unconscionable, harsh or oppressive'.[68] Part 3 of the *Independent Contractors Act 2006* (Cth) likewise permits the review and variation of harsh or unfair terms in contracts concerning the performance of work by contractors: see **13.20**. There are also many statutes that invalidate specific types of unfair provision, as for instance with exemption clauses: see **11.09**.

At the State level, mention has already been made of the *Contracts Review Act 1980* (NSW). Section 7 provides for the grant of relief in respect of a contract or contractual provision which is 'unjust', though only to the extent necessary to avoid 'an unjust consequence or result'. In determining whether a contract is unjust, s 9 requires that regard be had to the 'public interest', among other listed factors. There is no limitation as such on the type of contract that may be reviewed. But s 6 precludes an application for relief by a corporation, the Crown, or any person in relation to a contract they have entered into in the course of, or for the purpose of, a non-farming business. This last limitation has been construed narrowly, so that, for example, an individual may seek relief against a personal guarantee given in respect of business debts: see eg *West v AGC* (1986), although the claim in this case failed. The Act has indeed been very commonly invoked against financial institutions. In that context in particular, it has been used to resist liability under a loan, guarantee or mortgage, even in the absence of conduct by the lender that would be regarded as unconscionable at common law: see eg *Tonto Home Loans v Tavares* (2011). In general, however, the courts have not been willing to apply the legislation quite as widely as they might have done. It has been notable that in many of the cases where claims have succeeded, there have been elements of both procedural *and* substantive unfairness, even though the statute is plainly drafted broadly enough to cover a contract which is unfair purely in terms of its content.[69]

---

68   In interpreting and applying provisions of this kind, it is common to draw on cases decided under the *Contracts Review Act 1980* (NSW), discussed below: see eg *Fast Funds v Coppola* (2010); *Commonwealth Bank v Stephens* (2017). Section 76 was unsuccessfully invoked against various bank fees in *Paciocco v ANZ Banking Group* (2016).

69   See Carlin 2001; Saunders 2007.

21

ILLEGALITY AND PUBLIC POLICY

Introduction

21.01   The changing impact of illegality

Where a contract involves or is associated with conduct that is in some way *illegal or objectionable*, it may be possible for a party to:

- deny liability for what would otherwise be a breach of contract;
- resist a restitutionary claim for benefits transferred under the contract; or
- resist a claim brought 'independently' of the contract, such as for misrepresentation or wrongful dealings with property.[1]

Historically, the courts developed an elaborate and not always consistent set of rules and exceptions to govern the circumstances in which such a plea might succeed. Many of these rested on the imprecise and changing concept of *public policy*. In recent years, much of the law in this area has effectively been overtaken by a series of High Court decisions, including most recently *Equuscorp v Haxton* (2012) and *Gnych v Polish Club* (2015). These make it clear that where a breach of a statute is involved, a flexible approach to the consequences of that illegality should be adopted.[2] The new approach, which emphasises consistency with the purpose of the relevant statute, is easier to explain and arguably more sensible. Unfortunately, however, there is no guidance as to how much of the older case law is still authoritative where no statute is involved. Accordingly, this chapter summarises some of the older principles, to the extent they might be relevant.

New Zealand presents an interesting contrast in this respect. The situations in which a contract will be treated as illegal are very similar to Australia, but the consequences of illegality are governed by legislation. Section 76 of the *Contract and Commercial Law Act 2017* (NZ) expressly gives the courts a discretion to grant relief to the parties to an illegal transaction in order to reach a just outcome. In the exercise of this discretion, the courts are to consider the conduct of the parties, the object of any legislation breached, and any other matters as the court thinks proper (s 78). Relief will only be granted in the public interest (s 79).[3]

21.02   'Illegal' and 'void'

The term 'illegality' can be misleading, in that it may arise at common law where there is no contravention of any positive law – such as a crime, a tort or a statutory duty – but merely 'immoral' or anti-social behaviour. The same is true of the common statement that an 'illegal contract' is 'void': see eg *A v Hayden* (1984) at 557, 596. It is rare to find a contract whose very existence is forbidden, except in the case of a direct statutory provision to that effect.[4]

---

1   For a more extensive treatment of the subject, on which this account is based, see Stewart 2016.
2   In the United Kingdom, the Supreme Court has also moved towards a more flexible, policy-oriented approach: see eg *Patel v Mirza* (2016); Burrows 2017.
3   These provisions were formerly found in the *Illegal Contracts Act 1970* (NZ): see Burrows et al 2016: 13.6–13.8.
4   As to statutory prohibition, see **21.05** and following. Contracts may be void for other reasons, such as for lack of certainty (see **5.36**). As to the distinction between a void contract and a *voidable* contract, see **5.48**.

In most instances, a court has a series of choices. It may allow one party to enforce some or all of the contract, but not the other. It may reject any possibility of enforcement, yet allow one or both parties to seek restitution. Or it may preclude both enforcement and restitution, yet permit a claim brought 'independently' of the contract to succeed. Which response is chosen will depend upon a variety of factors. These include the nature of the objectionable conduct or purpose; the extent of the parties' knowledge of, or complicity in, that conduct or purpose; the nature of the claim before the court; and – most importantly today – the scope and purpose of any legislation involved. To describe a contract as illegal, therefore, is simply to indicate that the courts have responded in one of these ways, or are likely to do so. In itself, the term 'illegal' says nothing as to which response has been or will be chosen: see *Brooks v Burns Philp Trustee* (1969) at 458.

Just to complicate matters further, the common law has traditionally treated certain provisions or arrangements as being contrary to public policy and therefore 'void' (or, more accurately, unenforceable), but *not* as 'illegal'. The difference, if any, is that while the contract or term in question may be treated as ineffective, the courts are less likely to refuse other forms of relief, such as a claim for restitution: see **24.04**. Three types of agreement in this category are considered in this chapter: those that seek to oust the jurisdiction of the courts, that are prejudicial to the status of marriage, and that operate in *restraint of trade*. The last of these is singled out for special treatment in a section of its own, given its practical significance. Another example of a provision considered unenforceable as contrary to public policy, though not illegal, is a *penalty clause* that seeks to impose an arbitrary or extravagant sanction for not fulfilling a contractual obligation. That too warrants separate treatment: see **22.19–22.24**.

21.03   Raising the issue of illegality

The most common way in which an issue of illegality is raised is for a party in court proceedings to plead it as a defence to an action brought against them. But even if this does not happen, the court may itself take notice of any illegality that appears on the face of the contract or is apparent because of the nature of the claim involved: see eg *Ashton v Pratt* (2012). The most (in)famous example of this occurred in *Everet v Williams* (1725), in which a highwayman took his partner to court to resolve a dispute over the proceeds of their robberies. When the truth emerged, the action was dismissed and the lawyers concerned were fined for contempt. The highwaymen themselves were subsequently hanged!

On the other hand, it is not for a court to 'search out illegality'. As a general rule, any party who seeks to rely on it must establish the 'necessary factual basis' for their contention: see *Venus Adult Shops v Fraserside Holdings* (2006) at 471.

Statutory illegality

21.04   The different forms of statutory illegality

Illegality may arise as a result of a statutory provision in two different ways: see *Miller v Miller* (2011) at [24]–[25]. The statute may expressly or impliedly *prohibit* the making of a contract. Or the contract may be framed or performed in such a way as to involve or facilitate a breach of the statute, even though the statute itself has nothing directly to say about the effect of this breach on the contract.

In the former case, it is the statute itself that determines the efficacy of the contract or of any claim brought under or in association with it. In the latter situation, the statutory breach is simply an unlawful act which may trigger the operation of the common law principles of public policy discussed later in the chapter. In practice, the significance of this distinction, as with the difference between express and implied prohibition, has now all but disappeared. As the High Court has emphasised in recent cases, a process of 'statutory construction' will *always* be required to work out the consequences for a given claim: *Gnych v Polish Club* (2015) at [36].

21.05   Express prohibition

Express prohibition occurs when a statutory provision explicitly forbids the making of a particular type of contract. For example, s 45(2) of the *Competition and Consumer Act 2010* (Cth) provides that a corporation must not make a contract or arrangement that seeks to exclude the supply of goods or services to or from particular persons, or that has the purpose or effect of substantially lessening competition in a market: see **21.30**.

Once it is clear that a contract is expressly prohibited, the court's only task is to determine the consequences of the prohibition. In the absence of any provision to the contrary, the traditional approach was to regard the statute as precluding either party from enforcing the contract, whatever their guilt or innocence in the matter: see eg *Yango Pastoral v First Chicago Australia* (1978) at 430. But it has become more common in recent times for courts to construe statutes as permitting enforcement by a party unaware of or uninvolved with the breach, where that would be consistent with the scope and purpose of the legislation.

For example, in *Gnych v Polish Club* (2015), a lease over a part of licensed premises was granted without the permission of the Independent Liquor and Gaming Authority, in breach of s 92(1)(d) of the *Liquor Act 2007* (NSW). It was held that it would not be consistent with the legislative scheme for the lease to be treated as void or unenforceable by the lessee, whether on the basis of statutory prohibition or public policy. The Act imposed a penalty on the licensee/lessor for the breach, as well as empowering the Authority to cancel their licence. To regard the lease as automatically void would preclude the Authority from exercising its discretion to allow both the lessor's licence and the lease to continue in force. French CJ, Kiefel, Keane and Nettle JJ observed (at [45]) that:

> As a matter of legislative construction, the likelihood of adverse consequences for the 'innocent party' to a bargain has been recognised as a consideration which tends against the attribution of an intention to avoid the bargain to the legislature. That consideration is consistent with the general disinclination on the part of the courts to allow a party to a contract to take advantage of its own wrongdoing. There may be cases where the legislation which creates the illegality is sufficiently clear as to overcome that disinclination; but it is hardly surprising that the courts are not astute to ascribe such an intention to the legislature where it is not made manifest by the statutory language.

21.06   Contracts or provisions declared to be 'void'

Some statutes simply declare a contract of a certain type to be 'void', without directly prohibiting anyone from making such a contract. This is the case, for example, with unauthorised gaming or wagering agreements: see eg *Unlawful Gambling Act 1998* (NSW) s 56. Such a provision is generally taken to mean that the contract is *not* illegal. The same applies where legislation treats a contract as unenforceable if certain formalities are not followed, but does not attach the element of prohibition: see **5.44–5.46**.

Similar care must be taken with statutory provisions stipulating that certain types of contractual term are to be treated as void; for instance, s 64 of the Australian Consumer Law (ACL) (see **11.09**). Unless the statute in question is interpreted as prohibiting the whole contract, its only effect will be to annul the term, or to prevent it operating with the proscribed effect, leaving the rest of the contract intact: see eg *Zurich Australian Insurance v Metals & Minerals Insurance* (2009).

21.07 Implied prohibition

A contract is the subject of *implied prohibition* when some aspect of it contravenes a provision of a statute, and the statute is interpreted to prohibit the making of the contract, even in the absence of an express statement to that effect: see eg *Bradshaw v Gilbert's* (1952). As with express prohibition, implied statutory prohibition has traditionally been taken to mean that the contract cannot in any circumstances be enforced: see eg *SST Consulting Services v Rieson* (2006) at 532. Once again, however, there may be exceptions where the statute is interpreted to permit enforcement: see eg *Bondlake v Owners – Strata Plan No 60285* (2005).

Whether a contract is impliedly prohibited requires an analysis of the relevant legislative scheme. In many cases, as Mason J explained in *Yango Pastoral v First Chicago Australia* (1978) at 426, it will be a question of determining:

> whether the statute intends merely to penalize the person who contravenes the prohibition or whether it intends to go further and prohibit contracts . . . In deciding this question the court will take into account the scope and purpose of the statute and the consequences of the suggested implication with a view to ascertaining whether it would conduce to, or frustrate, the object of the statute.

The High Court held in *Yango* that the plaintiff could recover money lent to the defendant, even if the plaintiff had contravened the *Banking Act 1959* (Cth) by carrying on a banking business without authorisation. There was no express prohibition, as the Act penalised the general activity of carrying on business rather than referring to specific contracts. Nor should the Act be interpreted as impliedly prohibiting contracts entered into by a contravening institution. Such a prohibition would leave innocent depositors with no enforceable rights. This would be at odds with the legislative purpose of protecting the public by ensuring the financial soundness of banking institutions.[5]

21.08 Statutory declarations of validity

In some instances, a statute may expressly declare that a contract is *not* to be taken to be invalidated merely because of a breach of the statute in the course of the contract. Besides precluding any suggestion of implied prohibition, this type of declaration may also be

---

5   For other cases in which the High Court has refused to find implied prohibition, see eg *Fitzgerald v FJ Leonhardt* (1997); *Master Education Services v Ketchell* (2008).

interpreted to exclude the common law principles of public policy that might otherwise apply to claims brought under or in relation to the contract. For example, s 230 of the *Life Insurance Act 1995* (Cth) states that '[a] life company's failure to comply with this Act does not invalidate any policy issued by the company'.

Public policy and the *ex turpi causa* principle

21.09   The principle of denying relief for illegal or immoral conduct

The common law principles governing the denial of relief on *public policy* grounds were formulated by the English courts in the second half of the eighteenth century. The approach that developed was famously summarised by Lord Mansfield in *Holman v Johnson* (1775) at 343:

> No court will lend its aid to a man [sic] who founds his cause of action upon an immoral or illegal act. If, from the plaintiff's own stating or otherwise, the cause of action appears to arise *ex turpi causa* [from a base cause], or the transgression of a positive law of this country, there the Court says he has no right to be assisted.

Over the years, this principle has been used not just to preclude actions for breach of contract, but to reject claims in tort, or for restitution, or for equitable remedies. Among other situations, it may be invoked where a contract requires one or both parties to do something unlawful, or where a contract is performed in such a way that this occurs. For example, in *TP Rich Investments v Calderon* (1964), a lessee undertook not to use premises for any purpose other than as a dance studio. Since this type of use was prohibited by statute, it was held that the lessor could not sue the lessee for unpaid rent.

The *ex turpi causa* principle can also be invoked in relation to a contract which does not directly require or involve any illegal or immoral conduct, but nonetheless has the effect of furthering some kind of objectionable purpose. In *Alexander v Rayson* (1936), the parties entered into a lease arrangement that committed the tenant to make payments under both a 'lease agreement' and a separate 'service agreement'. When the landlord sued for money due under the lease, the tenant successfully raised illegality as a defence. The documentation had been drawn up to facilitate a fraud on the revenue authorities, with the landlord disclosing only one of the documents in order to obtain a lower valuation of the premises.

The mere existence of an objectionable purpose does not mean, however, that a contract associated with that purpose is necessarily invalidated. In *Neal v Ayers* (1940), the plaintiff had bought the lease of a hotel, including the goodwill attached to its business. She sued in the tort of deceit upon finding that the takings from the business did not match the levels represented by the defendant. The trial judge rejected the claim on the basis that the contract tended to further an illegal purpose. The plaintiff had been aware that up to 20 per cent of the takings came from illegal after-hours trading. The High Court overturned that decision and ordered a new trial. Dixon and Evatt JJ emphasised that the after-hours trading was not the main purpose of the transaction and the plaintiff had declared her intention to phase it out.

In other cases, a contract may be entered into with no objectionable purpose in mind, yet still be treated as unenforceable in particular circumstances that would offend public policy.

This may, for example, occur in relation to an insurance contract. It is not inherently unlawful to agree to indemnify a person against liability for certain types of unlawful behaviour, such as negligent driving: see eg *Hardy v Motor Insurers' Bureau* (1964).[6] Nevertheless, an insured may be denied recovery for loss or liability arising in the course of, or as a result of, criminal or antisocial conduct: see eg *Beresford v Royal Insurance* (1938).[7] Whether this is the case will depend on how the court weighs up various factors, including the gravity of the wrongdoing, the offender's state of knowledge, and the likelihood that enforcement would promote the commission of similar wrongs and/or the interests of any victims: see *FAI General Insurance v Sherry* (2002) at [80], [133].

21.10   'Public policy'

There are clearly some agreements, such as a contract to have a person murdered, that the courts would never enforce, even in the absence of a statutory prohibition. There is nothing surprising in the idea of a judge invoking public policy to refuse to enforce such a contract. However, as the *Holman v Johnson* formulation makes clear, the courts have taken the *ex turpi causa* principle beyond such flagrantly unacceptable contracts and into situations where no positive law is being transgressed. This is a role that has worried some judges. As Burrough J observed in *Richardson v Mellish* (1824) at 252, public policy 'is a very unruly horse and when you get astride of it, you never know where it will carry you'.

Part of the difficulty with the concept of public policy is the lack of any clear definition of the term. In *Wilkinson v Osborne* (1915) at 97, Isaacs J did his best, describing it as:

> some definite and governing principle which the community as a whole has already adopted either formally by law or tacitly by its general course of corporate life, and which the Courts of the country can therefore recognize and enforce. The Court is not a legislator: it cannot initiate the principle; it can only state or formulate it if it already exists.

From a legal realist perspective, the final comment may be seen as disingenuous. The notion that judges do not create public policy, but simply 'recognise' standards that already exist, is redolent of the now-discredited view that judges do not make law, but simply 'find' it. Nevertheless, the formulation does highlight the need for judges to look beyond their own personal standards.

It is particularly important that judges resist holding a fixed conception of public policy and be prepared to recognise that it may change over time: see *Stevens v Keogh* (1946) at 28. This has been highlighted in decisions relating to contracts which contemplate unmarried partners living together. In *Andrews v Parker* (1973), the plaintiff agreed to transfer title to his house to the defendant, with whom he was in a de facto relationship. The house would be re-conveyed if she returned to her husband. Four months later, the defendant and her husband reunited and she ejected the plaintiff, who took action to recover title to the house. In upholding the action,

---

6   The same may not, however, apply in relation to liability for *intentionally* unlawful conduct, or liability to pay a fine or penalty: see Derrington & Ashton 2005: 123–7.

7   In *Beresford*, it was held that an insurer could not be required to pay out on a life insurance policy for a death by suicide, which was then a crime. The effect of the decision has since been overturned by statute, although a life policy may still validly exclude coverage for suicide: see *Life Insurance Act 1995* (Cth) s 228.

Stable J rejected the argument that the agreement was immoral and unenforceable. He observed (at 102) that the Court was entitled to have regard to 'modern social standards', not those of the nineteenth century.[8] In *Maxcon Constructions v Vadasz* (2017) at [76], Blue J observed that the idea of sanctioning immoral conduct 'originated in a different era of attitudes to the social contract and before the advent of extensive statutory and regulatory control'. With the waning of this approach, he suggested, new categories of immoral conduct were unlikely to be identified in the future.

On the other hand, in two recent cases it has been suggested that an alleged agreement to pay a sex worker to become a man's mistress would, even if established on the facts, be unenforceable as a 'contract to provide meretricious sexual services': see *Ashton v Pratt* (2012) at [52]; *Leighton Contractors v O'Carrigan* (2016) at [161]. For some judges, it seems, 'living in sin' may still be considered contrary to public policy!

21.11   Unlawful conduct

Conduct that is in breach of Australian law, such as a crime, tort or breach of statute, is necessarily objectionable for the purpose of public policy considerations. As noted later on, however, this does not mean that it will automatically be used as a ground for the denial of a legal action.

Where foreign law is concerned, illegality arising under the law of a country which supplies the proper law of the contract (see **3.23**), or which is the place of performance, will preclude enforcement to the same extent as illegality arising under domestic law: see *Mackender v Feldia* (1967) at 601. Moreover, a contract entered into with the intent of violating the laws of any country in friendly relations with Australia may not be enforced here: see *Fullerton Nominees v Darmago* (2000). However, it appears that a contract is not invalidated merely because it contravenes the public policy of a country in which the contract is performed, if the proper law of the contract is the law of the forum (the place in which the matter is being litigated): see *Apple Corps v Apple Computer* (1992).

The converse situation involves a contract being lawful in the foreign country that supplies its proper law, yet contrary to public policy in Australia. There is some authority to suggest that a court may in this case apply the public policy of the forum to deny relief, despite its legality in the country with which it is most closely connected: see eg *Rousillon v Rousillon* (1880).[9]

21.12   Other agreements contrary to public policy

The most common type of agreement that is considered to be against public policy (though not illegal, as such) is an unreasonable restraint of trade. As noted earlier, this is dealt with separately at the end of this chapter. Other categories cover agreements that involve or are associated with conduct that is:

---

8   See also *Seidler v Schallhofer* (1982). Section 90UN of the *Family Law Act 1975* (Cth) now specifically provides that de facto couples (including same-sex partners) can make financial agreements that deal with the consequences of a breakdown in their relationship.

9   See also *International Arbitration Act 1974* (Cth) s 8(7)(b), which provides that a foreign arbitral award may be denied enforcement in Australia if it is contrary to public policy; and see *TCL Air Conditioner v Castel Electronics* (2014) at [64].

- *injurious to good government.* Behaviour in this category includes, for example, offering someone a financial inducement to refrain from standing for public office, or seeking to purchase honours: see *Taylor v Taylor* (1890). In particular, it is objectionable for a person in public office to use their position for personal gain: see eg *Wilkinson v Osborne* (1915).

- *injurious to foreign relations.* Besides agreements that contravene, or are intended to contravene, the laws of a friendly state (as discussed above), this principally covers trading with nationals of countries against whom Australia has declared war: see eg *Hirsch v Zinc Corporation* (1917).

- *injurious to the proper working of justice.* The most obvious example here is a contract to stifle a prosecution or to compromise legal proceedings for an offence of a public nature: see eg *Clegg v Wilson* (1932). In *A v Hayden* (1984), the High Court refused to enforce a term in the service contracts of Australian Secret Intelligence Service officers requiring their identity to be kept confidential. While this provision would ordinarily have been unobjectionable, the officers were attempting to use it to prevent their names being disclosed to police investigating a controversial mock raid on a hotel. Historically, there was also concern about the practices of 'maintenance' (assisting someone else's litigation without a recognised justification for doing so) and 'champerty' (maintaining litigation in return for a share of the proceeds). But as recent decisions involving commercial litigation funding schemes illustrate, courts today are far less likely to discern any public policy against such arrangements: see eg *Campbells Cash & Carry v Fostif* (2006).

- *sexually immoral.* Conduct involving or promoting any form of sexual activity considered immoral by the judiciary may be regarded as contrary to public policy: see eg *H v H* (1983), concerning a spouse-swapping arrangement. Historically, the courts frowned in particular on any agreement relating to the sex industry. The classic example was *Pearce v Brooks* (1866), where a contract to lease a carriage to a prostitute for use in plying her trade was held to be unenforceable. More recently, the antipathy has been relaxed somewhat, with decisions permitting sex workers to assert rights under employment legislation: see eg *Barac v Farnell* (1994). Nevertheless, as noted in **21.10**, an agreement to provide 'meretricious sexual services' may still be considered to be beyond the pale.

21.13 Ousting the jurisdiction of the courts

At common law, a contract is void (though not illegal) to the extent that it seeks to oust the jurisdiction of a court to determine a question of law, whether arising under the same agreement or affecting the rights of the parties in some other way. For example, it is not permissible for an association founded on agreed contractual rules to preclude its members from challenging the interpretation given to those rules by a governing committee: see eg *Harbottle Brown v Halstead* (1968). Indeed, an agreement that merely *deters* litigation, as opposed to precluding it, may be treated as unlawful. An example here is a requirement that a party pay money into trust as security for the other party's costs, before initiating proceedings under the contract: see *Materials Fabrication v Baulderstone* (2009).

However, the principle that parties cannot agree to exclude the jurisdiction of the courts is subject to a number of qualifications. The making of an agreement binding 'in honour only', and thus preventing recourse to the courts to enforce the promises involved, is not treated as an ouster of jurisdiction: see *Rose & Frank v JR Crompton & Brothers* (1925), discussed in **5.04**. It is also perfectly acceptable for parties to settle a genuine dispute between them by entering into a compromise agreement binding them not to litigate the matter further: see *Lieberman v Morris* (1944) at 80.

In the same vein, the courts have not precluded contracting parties from agreeing on processes for the resolution of disputes. For example, an agreement may validly provide for:

- a certificate given by a third party (such as an engineer under a building contract) to have conclusive effect in determining a question of fact – see *Dobbs v National Bank* (1935);
- a dispute to be taken to arbitration before any litigation is commenced – see *Scott v Avery* (1856);
- a dispute to be resolved by a process of expert determination (see **3.08**), even on questions of law – see *New South Wales v UXC* (2011);
- the submission of a dispute to mediation or conciliation – see *Hooper Bailie v Natcom Group* (1992).

In all but the last case, the effect of the agreement is to authorise a third party to define the parties' rights and liabilities under their contract. The courts' jurisdiction is not excluded, since a court may still be asked to determine whether the decision was made in accordance with the contract. In the case of commercial arbitration agreements, the courts have additional powers to control the arbitration process, under the legislation outlined in **3.09**.

21.14   Surrender of statutory rights

Some statutes make it clear that a party may not contract to surrender certain rights conferred by the legislation: see **11.09**. But in the absence of an explicit direction from the legislation itself, whether such an agreement is effective depends on whether those rights are seen as purely private in nature, or whether they have been created for the benefit of the public: see *Brown v R* (1986) at 208. If they are of the latter kind, any surrender or exclusion is likely to be regarded as contrary to public policy. For example, an agreement may not exclude:

- a spouse's right to claim maintenance – see *Brooks v Burns Philp Trustee* (1969);
- the right of a dependant of a deceased person to seek special provision from the estate – see *Lieberman v Morris* (1944);
- the right to complain of discriminatory treatment – see *Qantas Airways v Gubbins* (1992);
- an employee's right to the benefit of minimum employment standards – see eg *ACE Insurance v Trifunovski* (2011);
- the right of the members of a managed investment scheme to call for the scheme to be wound up – see *Westfield Management v AMP* (2012).

The right to invoke a limitation period, on the other hand, is regarded as a 'private' statutory entitlement that is capable of being surrendered: see *Commonwealth v Verwayen* (1990).

21.15   Agreements prejudicial to the status of marriage

Even in the absence of sexual immorality, a range of contracts prejudicial to the status of marriage were traditionally considered to be 'void', though not illegal. For example, parties could not validly agree to impose a restraint on marriage: see *Lowe v Peers* (1768). Nor could they enter into brokerage contracts, whereby money was paid to procure a marriage: see *Hermann v Charlesworth* (1905). It was also considered unacceptable to make agreements providing for the separation of spouses, unless the separation had already occurred or was imminent: see eg *Money v Money* (1966). That type of agreement is now regulated by Part VIIIA of the *Family Law Act 1975* (Cth). Given the change in the social importance of marriage and the rather different policies of regulation underlying that legislation, it is unclear now how many of the restrictions just mentioned still apply.

21.16   The enforceability of a contract that is contrary to public policy

As noted earlier, courts often describe agreements falling into any of the above categories as being 'illegal' and/or 'void'. But it is clear that a more accurate description would be that such a contract *may* be treated as unenforceable, depending on the nature and scope of the objectionable conduct or purpose.

Until recently, the courts drew a distinction between contracts that were 'illegal as formed', and contracts that merely involved illegality in the course of performance or that furthered an objectionable purpose: see *A v Hayden* (1984) at 544. In the former case, a contract that was framed in such a way as to require one or both parties to break the law was treated as unenforceable by both parties, regardless of their knowledge of any wrongdoing: see eg *JM Allan (Merchandising) v Cloke* (1963). By contrast, a contract that was performed in an illegal manner could still be enforced if the parties had not originally intended to break the law when entering into the agreement: see eg *St John Shipping v Joseph Rank* (1957).[10] Similarly, even where an objectionable purpose existed from the outset, a party innocent of that design could still maintain an action under the contract: see eg *Holidaywise Koala v Queenslodge* (1977). But a 'guilty' party would in the same situation be denied redress: see eg *North v Marra Developments* (1981).

The modern trend, at least where the breach of a statute is concerned, is to take a more flexible approach. The question posed by the courts is whether denying relief, even to a party fully aware of the wrongdoing, would be consistent with the scope and purpose of the legislation in question. For example, in *Yango Pastoral v First Chicago Australia* (1978), the High Court allowed an institution unlawfully trading as a bank to enforce its loan contracts in order to protect the interests of its depositors: see **21.07**. Although the question of knowledge was not discussed, it seems clear that the result would have been the same whatever the plaintiff's guilt in relation to the contravention of the banking legislation.

A similar approach was adopted in *Fitzgerald v FJ Leonhardt* (1997), where it was held a landowner could not use the defence of illegality to resist paying for certain bores, despite the

---

10   For a recent application of this principle, see *Civil and Allied Technical Construction v A1 Quality Concrete Tanks* (2018).

fact that they had been drilled without the permit required by the *Water Act 1992* (NT). McHugh, Gummow and Kirby JJ analysed the legislation and concluded that there was nothing in the statute to warrant the contract being considered unenforceable at the suit of the driller. The breach of the statute was, in any event, incidental rather than being intended from the outset, inadvertent rather than deliberate, and not the fault of the driller (it being the landowner's responsibility to secure the necessary permit).

In *Nelson v Nelson* (1995) at 613, McHugh J went so far as to say that:

> courts should not refuse to enforce legal or equitable rights simply because they arose out of or were associated with an unlawful purpose unless: (a) the statute discloses an intention that those rights should be unenforceable in all circumstances; or (b)(i) the sanction of refusing to enforce those rights is not disproportionate to the seriousness of the unlawful conduct; (ii) the imposition of the sanction is necessary, having regard to the terms of the statute, to protect its objects or policies; and (iii) the statute does not disclose an intention that the sanctions and remedies contained in the statute are to be the only legal consequences of a breach of the statute or the frustration of its policies.[11]

In its most recent pronouncements on this point, the High Court has emphasised that 'the central policy consideration at stake is the coherence of the law': *Miller v Miller* (2011) at [15]; *Equuscorp v Haxton* (2012) at [23].[12]

21.17   Severance of objectionable terms

In appropriate cases, a contractual provision or set of provisions tainted by illegality may be severed from the contract, leaving the remainder enforceable. Two requirements must be satisfied: see *Carney v Herbert* (1985) at 311. The first, as with terms that are considered too uncertain to be enforceable (see **5.40**), involves a process of interpretation. The question is whether the objectionable terms can be excised from the contract in such a way as to leave something that can sensibly stand alone. Where those terms 'are in substance so connected with the others as to form an indivisible whole which cannot be taken to pieces without altering its nature', then severance will not be possible and the whole contract must stand or fall together: *McFarlane v Daniell* (1938) at 345; and see eg *Electric Acceptance v Doug Thorley Caravans* (1981).

Second, the nature of the illegality involved must be considered. In the case of provisions which seek to oust the jurisdiction of the courts, or that operate in unreasonable restraint of trade, the courts are more willing to permit severance: see further **21.28**. If, on the other hand, the illegality stems from a statute which manifests a clear intention to strike down the whole of the transaction, severance cannot be contemplated: see *Day Ford v Sciacca* (1990). Beyond that, much turns on the seriousness or wrongfulness of the conduct in question. In some cases, no amount of severability will suffice, as for example with a contract which contains a term providing for an assassination: see *McFarlane v Daniell* (1938) at 346. But where the wrongdoing is of a less heinous nature, there may be no particular reason to invoke public policy and

---

11   For recent illustrations of this approach, see *Maxcon Constructions v Vadasz* (2017); *REW08 Projects v PNC Lifestyle Investments* (2017).

12   As to the broader issues raised here by the concept of 'coherence', see **1.16**.

deny severance. For instance, in *Thomas Brown & Sons v Deen* (1962), the plaintiff deposited gold and gems with the defendant under a single bailment. The High Court held that the part of the arrangement relating to the gems remained enforceable, despite the fact that the deposit of the gold contravened statutory regulations.

21.18 Restitution of benefits transferred under contracts affected by illegality

Where a contract is found to be unenforceable by reason of some form of illegality, one or other party may seek restitution in respect of benefits transferred under the contract. Historically, this type of claim was also liable to be refused under the *ex turpi causa* principle discussed in **21.09**: see *Lowry v Bourdieu* (1780) at 470, 472. In *Hatcher v White* (1953), Herron J invoked yet another Latin maxim that is much quoted in this context: *in pari delicto potior est conditio possidentis* (where both parties are equally at fault, the possessor is in the better position).[13] As he explained (at 298):

> This maxim is established not for the benefit of defendants, but is founded on the principles of public policy which will not assist a plaintiff who has paid over money or handed over property in pursuance of an illegal or immoral contract to recover it back, for the courts will not assist an illegal transaction in any respect.

Besides barring the recovery of money or property, this principle also prevented a party who had rendered services under an illegal contract from bringing an action for *quantum meruit* to recover reasonable recompense for the work done: see eg *Hagenfelds v Saffron* (1986).

In practice, however, the courts developed a great many exceptions to this rule against restitution. Besides the doctrine of 'statutory protection', which is considered separately below, recovery was permitted where the plaintiff could show they were less at fault than the defendant: see eg *Call & Mirror Newspapers v Humble* (1932); *Radford v Ferguson* (1947). Restitution was also sometimes allowed when a party 'repented' of their wrongdoing and withdrew from the contract while it remained 'executory': see eg *Perpetual Executors & Trustees Association v Wright* (1917).

It is unclear to what extent the *in pari delicto* and repentance principles remain good law today. This is because recent decisions, as explained below, have been more concerned with whether the availability of restitutionary relief would be consistent with the legislative regime under which the relevant illegality has arisen. What those decisions have left unclear is what is to happen if the illegality does *not* arise in a statutory context.

21.19 Effect of legislation on restitutionary claims

Statutes sometimes explicitly permit the recovery of money paid under a prohibited contract or provision. Section 39(3) of the *Retail Shop Leases Act 1994* (Qld), for example, provides that a person paying 'key money' to secure a lease in breach of the statute may recover such a payment.

---

13 A common variant is: *in pari delicto potior est conditio defendentis* (where both parties are equally at fault, the defendant is in the better position). See further Grodecki 1955.

Conversely, legislation may make it clear that restitution is *not* to be awarded. For example, s 42(3) of the *Queensland Building and Construction Commission Act 1991* (Qld) provides that, with certain exceptions, a person who carries out building work without a contractor's licence 'is not entitled to any monetary or other consideration'. In *Sutton v Zullo Enterprises* (2000), this was interpreted to preclude an unlicensed builder not just from recovering the agreed price under a building contract, but from suing on a *quantum meruit* to recover reasonable remuneration for their work.[14]

Even where there is no such express provision one way or the other, restitution may still be awarded if that would be consistent with the statutory scheme. In *Equuscorp v Haxton* (2012) at [34], French CJ, Crennan and Kiefel JJ observed that:

> The outcome of a restitutionary claim for benefits received under a contract which is unenforceable for illegality, will depend upon whether it would be unjust for the recipient of a benefit under the contract to retain that benefit. There is no one-size-fits-all answer to the question of recoverability. As with the question of recoverability under a contract affected by illegality the outcome of the claim will depend upon the scope and purpose of the relevant statute. The central policy consideration at stake ... is the coherence of the law. In that context it will be relevant that the statutory purpose is protective of a class of persons from whom the claimant seeks recovery. Also relevant will be the position of the claimant and whether it is an innocent party or involved in the illegality

The case involved loan agreements made in connection with a failed investment scheme. The scheme breached the 'prescribed interest' provisions in what was then the *Companies Code*, since no valid prospectus was issued to the investors. Accepting that the lender could not recover any money paid as a contractual debt, the issue was whether it could bring an action for money had and received, on the basis that the unenforceability of the agreements meant that there was a total failure of consideration for any payments made. By a 5:1 majority, the High Court held that to permit restitution in this case would be inconsistent with, or 'stultify', the policy underlying the prescribed interest provisions.

The reasoning adopted in *Equuscorp* is not consistent with any 'general rule' against restitution, at least where statutory illegality is involved. Indeed the majority stated (at [38], [103]–[104]) that restitution may be awarded whenever that is 'necessary to prevent unjust enrichment', unless to do so would 'defeat or frustrate the policy of the underlying prohibition'. But at the same time, it appears from the quote above that it is still relevant to consider the kind of factors that had previously led the courts to identify exceptions to the general rule against restitution.

One such factor, as the *Equuscorp* judgments make clear, is whether the purpose of the statutory prohibition is to protect a class of individuals to whom the plaintiff belongs. The origins of the doctrine of *statutory protection*, as it is known, can be traced to the judgment of Lord Mansfield in *Browning v Morris* (1778) at 792:

---

14   Compare *Pavey & Matthews v Paul* (1987), where the High Court had allowed a similar claim in respect of work done under a contract unenforceable under an earlier version of this same legislation: see **24.08**. As Deane J stressed (at 262), however, the statute did not at the time prohibit the making of such a contract, or render it in any way 'illegal'.

> [W]here contracts or transactions are prohibited by positive statutes, for the sake of protecting one set of men [sic] from another set of men; the one, from their situation and condition, being liable to be oppressed or imposed upon by the other; there, the parties are not *in pari delicto*.

Thus, in *Kiriri Cotton v Dewani* (1960), the Privy Council permitted the recovery of a premium paid for the sublease of a flat, the payment being contrary to the provisions of a Ugandan rent restriction Ordinance. The purpose of the Ordinance was held to be the protection of tenants from exploitation by landlords at a time of housing shortage.

The doctrine cannot be invoked, however, where the plaintiff does not belong to some definable class of persons which is narrower than the public at large. In *South Australian Cold Stores v Electricity Trust* (1965), the High Court rejected the plaintiff's attempt to recover charges for the supply of electricity demanded by the defendant in excess of the maximum figure prescribed under the *Prices Act 1948* (SA). According to the Court, that Act was passed not for the protection of electricity consumers as a class, but for the benefit of the general public (the aim being to restrain inflation).

21.20 Claims under collateral or related agreements

A claim may be brought under an agreement that is 'collateral' or connected to a contract tainted by illegality, provided that the plaintiff is innocent of any complicity in the illegality and the collateral agreement does not itself further an objectionable purpose.[15] In *Strongman v Sincock* (1955), an unlicensed builder sued for money due under a contract to perform work for an architect. Although that contract was unenforceable, the builder was able to recover damages for breach of a collateral warranty that the architect would obtain all necessary licences for the work. It was stressed that the action would not have been allowed had the builder been aware of the contravention.

21.21 Tort claims

It used to be common for the *ex turpi causa* principle to be invoked to deny an action in tort where there was a connection to illegal conduct. For example, in *Nicholls v Stanton* (1915), the plaintiff, who had purchased a car on the faith of a fraudulent representation that it was new, was unable to recover damages on the ground that the contract of sale was illegal, having been made on a Sunday. But a plaintiff could still sue if the fraudulent representation of which they complained went to the very legality of a contract they had made. In *Hatcher v White* (1953), the plaintiff, who had been induced to perform work for the defendant after being assured that the defendant had obtained the appropriate permit, recovered damages to cover the cost of the work done.

In *Miller v Miller* (2011) at [13], however, the High Court stressed that the availability of tort claims in relation to illegal conduct is not to be determined by 'simply intoning' the *ex turpi causa* maxim. It is rather a matter, the Court added (at [16]), of considering whether it would be 'incongruous' for the law to prohibit particular conduct and yet allow a plaintiff to recover

---

15   As to the concept of a collateral contract, see **9.16.**

damages for loss sustained while engaged in that conduct. The case involved an action for negligent infliction of personal injury arising from the illegal use of a stolen vehicle. But the principles expressed were clearly intended to be relevant to other types of negligence, and indeed other claims in tort.

21.22   Proprietary claims

A dispute may arise regarding the possession of property that has been the subject of a transaction tainted by illegality. The law in this area is far too complex to be fully traversed in a work of this nature.[16] But in brief, whether an action may be brought to claim such property depends on two issues: the effect of the illegality on the transfer of a proprietary interest; and the extent to which that illegality may prevent a person from asserting a right to possession that would otherwise arise.

As a general rule, the 'execution' of a contract to transfer a proprietary interest will be considered to vest a right to possession in the transferee, even if the contract is somehow tainted by illegality. This principle has been recognised in relation to the transfer of absolute ownership (as with a sale), as well as the conferral of more limited rights; for example, under a lease: see eg *Singh v Ali* (1960); *McKenna v Perecich* (1973).

That, however, is not the end of the story, since the question is still whether a transferee who is entitled to possession should be allowed to assert that right. The same issue can arise where an owner who has conferred a limited right to possession seeks to reclaim their property when that right comes to an end. In *Bowmakers v Barnet Instruments* (1945) at 71, the English Court of Appeal considered that a plaintiff should be entitled to assert a right to possession, provided they did not seek, and were not 'forced', to 'found' their claim on an illegal transaction or plead the illegality of a transaction in order to support their claim. This contentious principle has generated great difficulty in application: see eg *Newcastle District Fishermen's Co-op Society v Neal* (1950); *Thomas Brown & Sons v Deen* (1962).

In *Nelson v Nelson* (1995), however, the High Court took a different approach. The case concerned a house which was acquired with a mother's money, but transferred into the names of her children. The purpose was to allow her to claim a statutory benefit (a subsidy to buy a further property) by falsely declaring that she did not already have a financial interest in a house. She then sought to argue that the proceeds of the sale of the house were subject to a resulting trust in her favour, notwithstanding the illegal purpose of the arrangement.

A majority of the Court took the view that the validity of the claim should not depend on whether or not the mother was 'relying' on the illegality. Rather, just as in *Yango Pastoral v First Chicago Australia* (1978) (see **21.07**), it was a question of looking at the policy underlying the relevant statute – the *Defence Service Homes Act 1918* (Cth) – and determining whether that policy would be better served by granting or withholding relief. The claim was allowed, on the basis that to refuse to allow the mother to assert her beneficial ownership of the proceeds of the sale would impose a penalty far in excess of that contemplated by the statute, although she was required to 'do equity' by repaying the subsidy.

---

16   For more extensive discussion, see eg Stewart 1988, Phang 1996.

While *Nelson* concerned a trust rather than a contract, it seems clear that the same approach would apply to determining the availability of a proprietary interest asserted pursuant to a contract – that is, to consider whether allowing such a claim would be congruent with the purposes of any applicable statute. What is not so apparent is how to proceed when there is no element of statutory illegality. It is possible in such cases that the *Bowmakers* principle might still be applied.

Restraint of trade

21.23   The common law doctrine

The common law doctrine of *restraint of trade* can be dated back many centuries.[17] It involves a balance between two key concerns. The first is that unless limits are placed on the principle of freedom of contract, that very freedom can be used – paradoxically – to stifle the making of contracts. In particular, agreements may be used to limit competition between traders, or to restrict the supply of goods or labour. The second is that there are circumstances in which it may nonetheless be legitimate for a person or organisation to agree – or be asked to agree – not to engage in certain trading activities.

The modern doctrine was memorably encapsulated by Lord Macnaghten in *Nordenfelt v Maxim Nordenfelt* (1894) at 565:

> The public have an interest in every person's carrying on [their] trade freely; so has the individual. All interference with individual liberty of action in trading, and all restraints of trade of themselves, if there is nothing more, are contrary to public policy, and therefore void. That is the general rule. But there are exceptions: restraints of trade and interference with individual liberty of action may be justified by the special circumstances of a particular case. It is a sufficient justification, and indeed it is only the justification, if the restriction is reasonable – reasonable, that is, in reference to the interests of the parties concerned and reasonable in reference to the interests of the public, so framed and so guarded as to afford adequate protection to the party in whose favour it is imposed, while at the same time it is in no way injurious to the public.

The principle, therefore, is that any 'covenant' (or contractual provision) that operates in restraint of trade is presumed to be invalid. If the person for whose benefit the restraint was imposed (the 'covenantee') is to rebut that presumption, they must establish that the restriction is no wider than is reasonably necessary to protect a legitimate interest: see *Buckley v Tutty* (1971) at 376. This assessment is generally made by reference to the circumstances as they stood at the time the relevant restriction was first agreed: see *Lindner v Murdock's Garage* (1950) at 638, 647–8, 653; and see eg *McHugh v Australian Jockey Club* (2014).

In theory, a restraint that is shown to be reasonable as between the parties may nevertheless be invalidated if the party challenging the restraint can establish that it is contrary to the public interest. In practice, 'reasonableness in the public interest' is almost never considered as a distinct issue. But this is not to say that the public interest is irrelevant. Rather, it tends to be channelled into the determination of what constitutes a legitimate interest and what

---

17   See Heydon 2008: ch 1.

should be regarded as a reasonable scope for a restraint: see *Amoco Australia v Rocca Brothers* (1973) at 307–8.

21.24 What constitutes a 'restraint'?

The threshold question of what types of restriction are caught by the doctrine is surprisingly hard to answer. There is clear authority for applying the presumption of invalidity to the following types of promise or arrangement:

* by an employee, as to their post-employment activities (including employment or participation in other businesses) – see eg *Lindner v Murdock's Garage* (1950);
* by an independent contractor, as to their activities after completing the work they have been contracted to perform – see eg *N E Perry v Judge* (2002);
* between two or more employers (such as teams involved in a sporting competition), as to who they will employ – see eg *Buckley v Tutty* (1971);
* by a member of a partnership, as to their business activities after ceasing to be a partner – see eg *Geraghty v Minter* (1979);
* by the seller of a business, as to their business activities after the sale – see eg *Nordenfelt v Maxim Nordenfelt* (1894);
* by a franchisee, as to their business activities after the franchise is terminated – see eg *BB Australia v Karioi* (2010);[18]
* by one trader, to source products exclusively from another – see eg *Queensland Co-operative Milling Association v Pamag* (1973);
* between two traders, as to the territories or sectors in which they will market their products – see eg *Peters (WA) v Petersville* (2001);
* for non-use of confidential information, even after it has reached the public domain – see eg *Maggbury v Hafele* (2001).

This is not an exhaustive list. Indeed, the courts have stressed that the categories of restraint presumed to be contrary to public policy 'are not closed': *Petrofina v Martin* (1966) at 169. But not every restriction on trading activities is caught by the doctrine, not least because just about *every* commercial contract involves something that could be called a restraint. If A agrees to work for B, or to supply an item to B, in most instances that will limit their capacity to do the same for someone else. Perhaps for this reason, some common arrangements have long been treated as immune from challenge, such as restrictions as to the use of land imposed on a purchaser or lessee: see eg *Quadramain v Sevastopol Investments* (1976). But there is no blanket exception for sales and leases. For example, the doctrine may apply to a restraint on the business activities of a lessor: see eg *Specialist Diagnostic Services v Healthscope* (2012). Similarly, restrictions on lessees that go beyond the use of the relevant premises may be reviewed: see eg *Amoco Australia v Rocca Brothers* (1973); *Kosciuszko Thredbo v ThredboNet Marketing* (2014).

---

18   See also *Bodycorp Repairers v Australian Associated Motor Insurers* (2015), where the restraint in question was imposed not by the franchise agreement, but a contract between the franchisor and a third party.

Where the courts have struggled has been to articulate a test that explains which restraints must be justified and which need not.[19] In *Peters (WA) v Petersville* (2001), the High Court canvassed three possibilities, each suggested by different members of the House of Lords in *Esso Petroleum v Harper's Garage* (1968). The first was expressly rejected by the High Court: that the doctrine does not apply to a restriction on trading activities *during* (as opposed to after) the subsistence of a contract, unless the restriction is intended to 'sterilise' rather than 'absorb' the parties' services. The Court noted that a second test – that the doctrine only applies where some pre-existing freedom is given up – had been heavily criticised. Indeed, in the later case of *Maggbury v Hafele* (2001) at 203, it was treated as having been rejected. That leaves a third possibility, which was noted by the High Court in *Peters*, but neither endorsed nor dismissed. This was Lord Wilberforce's suggestion that restrictions will be immune from the operation of the restraint of trade doctrine if they have become an acceptable and necessary part of the 'structure of a trading society': *Esso Petroleum* at 335. In *Australian Capital Territory v Munday* (2000), this test was used to reject a challenge to a provision in a contractual licence, under which a person granted permission to enter a rubbish tip and salvage property was prohibited from soliciting for goods at the entrance to the tip. It has since been applied on a number of occasions by intermediate courts of appeal: see eg *Kosciuszko Thredbo v Thredbo-Net Marketing* (2014).

The difficulties in ascertaining the scope of the restraint of trade doctrine are apparent in the treatment of promises by a person to work exclusively for a particular business. It is often said or assumed that the doctrine cannot be used to attack a commitment of this type in an employment contract, at least in normal circumstances: see eg *Curro v Beyond Productions* (1993) at 341–6. Yet, a contrary view has been taken in recent cases where an employer has sought to send a departing employee home for a lengthy period of 'garden leave' before completing their service: see eg *Tullett Prebon v Purcell* (2008). Songwriters and performers have also been allowed to challenge the validity of publishing or recording contracts which commit them to long-term deals on relatively unfavourable terms: see eg *Schroeder Music Publishing v Macaulay* (1974).[20] It appears then that whenever a restriction is perceived to be either unusual or excessive, a court may choose to treat it as presumptively invalid – unless it falls within a clearly established exception.

21.25   Legitimate interests for a restraint

What constitutes a 'legitimate' reason for a restraint varies according to the context. The most straightforward instances involve the protection of some form of business 'goodwill'. For example, a purchaser of a business can seek to protect their investment from being devalued by competitive activities on the part of the vendor. So too can a group of partners restrain one of their number from drawing off clients after quitting the partnership.

By contrast, the courts have tended to 'take a stricter and less favourable view of covenants entered into between employer and employee': *Geraghty v Minter* (1979) at 185.[21] This reflects

---

19   See Thorpe 2012.
20   For a critique of the economic approach in this case, see Trebilcock 1976.
21   As to whether a similar view should be taken of covenants extracted by franchisors, see *BB Australia v Karioi* (2010) at [61]–[77].

the practical reality that 'there is obviously more freedom of contract between buyer and seller than between ... an employer and a person seeking employment': *Nordenfelt v Maxim Nordenfelt* (1894) at 566. In this context, it is not sufficient that a departing employee may be of value to their current employer, or that the employer's business may suffer if they join a competitor. Traditionally, employers have had to justify any post-employment restraint on one of two grounds: see eg *Herbert Morris v Saxelby* (1916); *Lindner v Murdock's Garage* (1950). These are that the employee has either had access to trade secrets or other confidential information, or developed personal connections with the employer's customers, which they might be able to use to the employer's detriment if working elsewhere. Recent cases have suggested that employers may also legitimately seek to prevent key staff from being recruited or 'poached' by former colleagues: see eg *Cactus Imaging v Peters* (2006).[22] In practice, these categories of protectable interest are broad enough to support a fairly wide range of post-employment restraints, with litigation over their use fairly common, especially in the financial services sector.[23]

The various types of interest recognised in the cases involving employment, partnerships, and sales of business are sometimes said to be 'proprietary' in nature. But it is clear from the modern cases that a merely 'commercial' interest may be sufficient to justify a restraint. Hence, in cases involving 'solus' (exclusive dealing) arrangements for service stations, for instance, it has been recognised that petrol companies have a legitimate interest in obtaining 'secure outlets' that enable the distribution of their products 'in an efficient and economical way': *Amoco Australia v Rocca Brothers* (1973) at 319. Similarly, in sporting cases, a governing body or league is considered to have a legitimate interest in seeking to impose restrictions that are intended to create an 'even' competition: see eg *Buckley v Tutty* (1971) at 377.[24]

21.26 The scope of a restraint

If the covenantee can establish a legitimate interest for having a restraint, the question then turns to its reasonableness. This will turn on the *scope* of the restraint, judged by reference to three dimensions: the range of *activities* it purports to restrict; the *duration* of its operation; and the *area* in which it is to have effect. The scope of a restraint is, in the first instance, a matter of interpretation.[25]

The general rule is that a restraint will be struck down if its scope is not commensurate with the interest that it is intended to protect. The simplest cases here involve covenants that are too broadly expressed in terms of area and/or activity. For example, in *Commercial Plastics v Vincent* (1965), the head of a firm's research and development section agreed not to work in

---

22   See also *Informax v Clarius Group* (2012), permitting a labour hire agency to prevent a worker on its books from being directly employed by a client to which the worker had previously been assigned.

23   See further Arup et al 2013; Jackson 2014; and for a comparative perspective, see van Caenegem 2013; Hyde & Menegatti 2015. In the United States, some States apply a common law approach similar to that in Australia, while others such as California entirely prohibit post-employment restraints. The capacity that such a prohibition allows for employees and their know-how to move from firm to firm is often cited as a reason for the success of the technology businesses in Silicon Valley.

24   This is not to say, however, that arrangements such as zoning rules, drafts or salary caps will necessarily withstand challenge as an unreasonable restraint: see eg *Adamson v NSW Rugby League* (1991); and see further Thorpe et al 2018: 589–607.

25   As to the principles applied in this context, see *Just Group v Peck* (2016) at [38].

the plastics industry for a year after leaving the firm. The employee's access to certain trade secrets gave the firm a legitimate interest to protect. But the restraint was too wide because it was not limited to the United Kingdom, where the firm marketed its products,[26] nor to the particular part of the plastics industry in which it operated. In *Lindner v Murdock's Garage* (1950), a firm of garage proprietors sought to enforce a restrictive covenant that prohibited a leading hand from working for a similar business anywhere in the firm's 'sales territory' for a year after his employment ended. That territory covered Crystal Brook and Wirrabara, two country towns more than 40 kilometres apart. Because the defendant had only ever worked at Crystal Brook, and there was no evidence he had established personal relationships with customers in Wirrabara, the restraint was held to be unreasonably wide. But restraints on partners are treated differently in this respect. In *Bridge v Deacons* (1984), the partner of a Hong Kong law firm covenanted for a period of five years not to work as a lawyer in Hong Kong for anyone who, in the three years preceding his departure, had been a client of the firm. The Privy Council upheld the restraint, despite the fact that the former partner had only had dealings with less than 10 per cent of the firm's clients. It was emphasised that the goodwill being protected here was that attaching to the firm as a whole, not merely the part of it associated with the former partner's clientele.

The question of duration, when not simply tied (as in some exclusive dealing provisions) to the subsistence of a commercial arrangement, tends to be harder to assess. Where the covenantee's interest involves guarding against customers or clients being lured away, a court may consider how long it would reasonably take to 'break the connection' between the covenantor and the persons or firms with whom they used to deal: see eg *N E Perry v Judge* (2002). But more often than not a court will simply make an impressionistic decision as to whether the nominated period appears reasonable. As a general rule, restraints on partners or vendors of businesses may be longer than for employees, for whom a valid restraint will often need to be expressed in months rather than years. But there can be exceptions, especially for key personnel. In *Pearson v HRX Holdings* (2012), for example, a two-year restraint was upheld in relation to the chief operating officer of a human resources firm he had helped to establish. As the 'human face' of the business, his extensive knowledge of both the firm's operations and clients were considered to justify a 'non-compete' arrangement, not merely a restriction on soliciting clients.

21.27   Other factors going to reasonableness

Besides the scope of a covenant, a number of other factors may be considered in assessing its reasonableness. It is relevant, for example, to consider what consideration or other benefits a covenantor can expect to receive in return for agreeing to the restraint: see *Amoco Australia v Rocca Brothers* (1973) at 305–6, 316. In the *Pearson* case mentioned above, for example, what helped to make a two-year restraint reasonable was that the employee was paid for 21 of the 24 months, as well as receiving shares in the company. The courts may also take account of the parties' respective bargaining positions, which helps explain the generally stricter approach to

---

26   The internet now allows products to be sold into a much wider range of markets than at the time this case was decided. As to the impact of this factor on the permissible area of restraints, see Thorpe 2015.

restraints in employment contracts. Even in a commercial setting, the fact that one party may be perceived as unconscionably exploiting a superior economic position may increase the chances of a restraint being struck down: see *Schroeder Music Publishing v Macaulay* (1974) at 1315. Conversely, the courts will give weight to the fact that a restriction has been freely agreed between parties dealing on equal terms, although this is not a conclusive factor. Such a restriction may still be invalidated if it is perceived to go beyond what is reasonably necessary: see *Queensland Co-operative Milling Association v Pamag* (1973) at 268.

21.28   Severance of unreasonable restraints

If a restraint is too wide to be reasonable, the covenantee may seek to argue that it should still be given a more limited operation. As a matter of common law, the courts distinguish here between *severance* and *reading down*.

The concept of severance was discussed earlier in the chapter. In this context, it means putting a line (or, as it is traditionally said, a 'blue pencil') through any clauses, or even parts of a clause, that go too far. If a court is satisfied that what remains is reasonable, and is still consistent with the parties' intent, it may enforce what is left of the restraint: see eg *Stenhouse Australia v Phillips* (1974); *Rentokil v Lee* (1995). But severance only works in certain cases. In *Lindner v Murdock's Garage* (1950), discussed earlier, a restraint expressed to operate within a certain radius of either Crystal Brook or Wirrabara could have been severed so that it applied only in the first of those areas. But because the provision here simply referred to the plaintiff's 'sales territory', there was nothing to sever. To make it enforceable only in Crystal Brook, the court would have had to 'read it down' so that it applied only in that location. But that would effectively have meant rewriting the clause, which is something the courts will not do as a matter of common law.[27] Furthermore, the courts will not enforce a restraint that is deliberately framed in vague terms; for example, by reference to what is 'reasonable', or 'so far as the law allows': see *Ross v IceTV* (2010) at [80]–[81].

To overcome that type of problem, lawyers have taken to drafting restraints in a form that makes severance easier. A 'cascade' (or 'step' or 'ladder') clause contains a series of overlapping restraints, some more extensive than others. For example, a restriction might apply for three months, or six months, or one year; and in Adelaide, or South Australia, or Australia; and for all permutations of the above. Any restraints that are too wide can be severed, leaving the employer free to enforce those that remain. Care has to be taken with the drafting, in case the provision be considered too uncertain to be enforceable: see eg *Austra Tanks v Running* (1982). But the general view taken by the courts is that, provided the drafting is sufficiently precise, there is nothing inherently wrong with a clause containing multiple restraints: see eg *Hanna v OAMPS Insurance Brokers* (2010). This is despite the fact that the covenantor may have no way of knowing in advance which of those restraints are reasonable, and which go too far.

For contracts covered by the law of New South Wales, there is no need to resort to such a device. Section 4(1) of the *Restraints of Trade Act 1976* (NSW) confers an express power on the courts to read down otherwise invalid restraints and enforce them to the extent they are

---

27   For a further example of this reluctance, see *Just Group v Peck* (2016).

reasonable.[28] The proviso in s 4(3) is that the person restrained can apply for a court order invalidating or narrowing the restraint, where there has been a 'manifest failure' by the drafter to attempt to keep it within reasonable bounds. As McLelland J explained in *Orton v Melman* (1981), s 4(1) requires a court to determine whether the restraint in question has been or will be breached; and if so, then to consider whether the restraint would be contrary to public policy in its application to *that breach*. If public policy is not offended, the restraint is enforceable to that extent, subject to s 4(3). Unless there is no legitimate basis for having a restraint at all, a covenantee can generally rely on this statute to obtain at least partial enforcement of a restraint, even if at its outer limits its application would be unreasonable: see eg *Woolworths v Olson* (2004).

21.29   Enforcement of restraints

The usual remedy that a covenantee will seek when enforcing a restraint is an injunction to restrain conduct in breach of the relevant restriction. Particularly in cases involving ex-employees, it is common for a plaintiff to seek an interim injunction, pending a full trial of the claim. In accordance with the general requirements for obtaining such relief (see **22.14**), the plaintiff must show two things: see eg *IceTV v Ross* (2007). The first is that they have a legitimate prospect of establishing that the restraint is valid, and that there is evidence to suggest a breach or imminent breach that will cause the plaintiff harm. The second is that the 'balance of convenience' favours the making of an order. Many restraint cases end at this preliminary stage. If an interim order is obtained, the matter will usually be settled. If the plaintiff fails, the action will often be withdrawn. That said, it is not unknown for plaintiffs to go ahead and seek a final injunction, and/or an award of damages to compensate them for any loss suffered as a result of breaches that have already occurred: see eg *Wilson HTM v Pagliaro* (2012).

There may be a problem where a restraint is contained in a contract that has been brought to an end as a result of a breach or repudiation on the part of the covenantee. In such a case, the covenantee may be considered to have forfeited the right to enforce the restraint: see eg *Kaufman v McGillicuddy* (1914); *Crowe Horwath v Loone* (2017).[29]

21.30   Statutory restrictions on anti-competitive arrangements

The common law doctrine of restraint of trade is complemented by the restrictions in Part IV of the *Competition and Consumer Act 2010* (Cth), or the *Trade Practices Act 1974* as it was formerly known. For example, s 45 prohibits making or giving effect to contracts, arrangements or understandings which either have the purpose or effect of substantially lessening competition, or which contain an 'exclusionary' provision. This and other provisions in Part IV

---

28   The Act was introduced in response to criticism by the New South Wales Law Reform Commission (1970) of the common law's narrow and technical approach to severance.

29   Compare *Richmond v Moore Stephens* (2015) at [210], expressing the view that there is no rule of law to that effect and that each contract must be interpreted to determine whether the restraint is intended to operate in such circumstances.

potentially outlaw a wide range pf anti-competitive behaviour, including price fixing, collective boycotts and market sharing: see eg *Visy Paper v ACCC* (2003).[30]

Section 4M makes it clear that the legislation does not affect 'the law relating to restraint of trade', so far as that law can operate concurrently with the statute's provisions. Furthermore, many of the key provisions in Part IV are rendered inapplicable by s 51(2) to a range of covenants that are commonly caught by the common law doctrine. These include restrictions on the performance of work during or after a contract of employment or a contract for services; on competition between partners or ex-partners; or in contracts for the sale of a business or shares in a business, when intended to protect the purchaser in relation to the goodwill of the business.

---

30   See generally Corones 2014. Following a review of the competition provisions in the 2010 Act (see Harper et al 2015), important changes were introduced by the *Competition and Consumer Amendment (Misuse of Market Power) Act 2017* (Cth) and *Competition and Consumer Amendment (Competition Policy Review) Act 2017* (Cth).

PART **VII**

REMEDIES

22

ENFORCING
A CONTRACT

22.01   Introduction

The standard remedy for breach of contract is damages, as discussed in Chapter 23. An award of damages aims to place the innocent party, so far as money can do so, in the position they would have been in had the contract been performed according to its terms. In other words, damages are a monetary *substitute* for contractual performance. The innocent party may be perfectly satisfied with this substitute performance, but this will not always be the case. The situations in which the court will order actual performance of the contract, in the form of *specific performance*, are, nonetheless, rare. This reflects the fact that specific performance is an equitable remedy originating in the Court of Chancery. Equity was, historically, a supplemental jurisdiction which operated only where the common law was defective or inadequate. The consequence is that, whereas common law damages are available as of right, equitable remedies (such as specific performance) are discretionary and generally available only where common law damages would be inadequate.

An *injunction* is another means of obtaining actual performance of the contract. 'Injunction' means the 'act of enjoining' – that is, an order to someone to do something (a *mandatory* injunction) or to refrain from doing something (a *prohibitory* injunction). In a sense, specific performance can be viewed as a form of mandatory injunction, although a number of writers maintain a distinction between specific performance and an injunction for breach of contract.[1] Courts are generally more ready to award prohibitory injunctions than mandatory ones. In the contractual context, injunctions are usually used to restrain breaches of *negative* stipulations and the courts are astute to ensure that specific performance is not obtained by the back door. As an equitable remedy, the grant of an injunction is discretionary and generally available only where common law damages would be inadequate.

Under some circumstances, a contracting party may be in a position to choose between an action to recover damages for breach of contract and the conceptually distinct action for *debt* (also referred to as an action for a liquidated sum, or money due). Although both claims can be brought concurrently, the plaintiff cannot recover the same sum twice. As will be seen, the action for debt has a number of advantages over an action for damages for breach of contract.

Finally, instead of leaving it to the courts to award damages after the event, the parties may agree the consequences of a breach of contract in advance. Commercial parties commonly include clauses in their contracts stipulating for the payment of a sum of money in the event of a particular breach (or breaches) of contract. Such sums are referred to as *liquidated damages* (as opposed to the 'unliquidated' damages that are assessed and awarded by a court). Allowing the parties to agree the consequences of breach in advance has many advantages, not least of which are commercial certainty and the avoidance of the trouble and expense of litigation. But the courts have not allowed the parties complete freedom in this regard. They continue to review such clauses with a view to distinguishing permissible liquidated damages clauses from impermissible *penalty clauses*. The effect of a clause being found to be a penalty has traditionally been that the sum stipulated as payable on breach is not recoverable. The innocent party is restricted to recovering its actual loss or common law damages. As will be seen, however, the scope and operation of the rule against penalties has been thrown into considerable doubt by two recent High Court decisions.

---

1   See eg Spry 2014: 558–9; Heydon et al 2015: 781; Barnett & Harder 2014: 232.

Specific performance

22.02   Introduction

The term 'specific performance' is used in two senses. Technically speaking, in its 'proper' sense, it is a remedy granted in respect of an *executory* contract. Specific performance in this sense 'presupposes an executory as distinct from an executed agreement, something remaining to be done, such as the execution of a deed or a conveyance, in order to put the parties in the position relative to each other in which by the preliminary agreement they were intended to be placed': *Wolverhampton and Walsall Railway v London and North-Western Railway* (1873) at 439.[2] In a looser sense, specific performance is used to describe the remedy granted to enforce contractual obligations under *executed* contracts as well. The practical significance of the distinction between these two uses of specific performance is debatable.[3]

A prerequisite for a decree of specific performance is a valid, binding contract in respect of which the defendant has no right of rescission on grounds such as misrepresentation, duress or unconscionable conduct. But, since equity (unlike the common law) does not recognise a deed as a substitute for consideration, absence of consideration in a contract made under seal will preclude a decree of specific performance, even though damages for breach would have been available at common law.

Specific performance is possible in some situations where common law damages are unavailable. The first situation is that of a mere *threatened* breach of contract: see eg *Turner v Bladin* (1951); *Hasham v Zenab* (1960). A second is where the contract is unenforceable at law due to non-compliance with formality requirements, but the lack of writing is attributable to equitable fraud on the part of the defendant.[4] A third is where there is non-compliance with formality requirements, but there are sufficient acts of part performance of the contract: see eg *McBride v Sandland* (1918); *Regent v Millett* (1976); and see further **5.45**.

Over the centuries, a significant body of case law has developed on the circumstances in which specific performance will be granted or refused. Traditionally, a distinction was drawn between *jurisdictional* and *discretionary* factors. The former are threshold issues affecting a court's decision whether to even consider granting equitable relief. As discussed below, they include the question of whether common law damages would be inadequate, and other factors such as an element of personal service in the contract, or that an order for specific performance would create a need for constant supervision of the contract by the court. If those threshold criteria are satisfied, the discretionary factors are those that determine whether relief should in fact be granted in the particular circumstances of the case.[5] The modern tendency, however,

---

2   In the Australian context, see *Pakenham Upper Fruit v Crosby* (1924) at 394; *JC Williamson v Lukey* (1931) at 294.

3   Its significance is lessened by judicial statements that both 'types' of specific performance are governed by the same principles: see *Australian Hardwoods v Commissioner for Railways* (1961) at 434. But, for the view that the distinction matters, see Heydon et al 2015: [20-015].

4   See Heydon et al 2015: [20-175].

5   On this distinction, see Spry 2014: 93, also referring to these jurisdictional factors as 'conclusive defences' as opposed to 'discretionary considerations'.

has increasingly been to treat a jurisdictional or threshold analysis as unnecessary. On this view, the whole question is one for the court's discretion, albeit some factors will be more decisive than others.[6]

22.03   Inadequacy of common law damages

Inadequacy of damages was traditionally seen as a threshold or jurisdictional requirement. The crucial question was whether an award of common law damages would leave the plaintiff in as favourable a position, materially speaking, as they would be in if the contract were specifically enforced. If it would, specific performance would be refused.[7]

There were a number of reasons why a court might conclude that damages would be inadequate. First, damages might be difficult to assess: see eg *Wight v Haberdan* (1984). Second, the subject matter of the contract might be unique or in extremely limited supply, making it impossible (or at least very difficult) for the plaintiff to purchase a true substitute with an award of damages. This principle underlies the so-called 'rule' that contracts for the sale of land are specifically enforceable – subject, of course, to any other factors or defences that might apply. Historically, courts have assumed that land has a 'peculiar and special value' (*Adderley v Dixon* (1824) at 610) and that the loss of one piece of land is not substitutable or compensable by the acquisition of any other.[8] This is so even where the land is to be acquired purely for investment or commercial purposes: see eg *Pianta v National Finance & Trustees* (1964); *Sudbrook Trading Estate v Eggleton* (1983).

The principle also explains why most contracts for the sale of goods are not specifically enforceable. At one end of the spectrum are commodities, which are, by definition, readily substitutable on the market.[9] At the other end of the spectrum are unique or rare goods; for example works of art or rare antiques, or the vintage airplane purchased in *Smythe v Thomas* (2007). For such items, an award of damages will be inadequate. *Dougan v Ley* (1946) is an example of a case where damages were held to be inadequate even though the subject matter of the contract (a taxi sold with a taxi licence) was not unique. The Court pointed to the fact that the statutory regulation of taxis had resulted in a restriction on the number of licensed taxis that might be available for sale. A similar distinction is often drawn between contracts for the sale of shares in a public company (which are generally publicly available on the market) and those for the sale of shares in private companies (in which there is no such market): see eg *Nurisvan Investment v Anyoption Holdings* (2017) at [127]–[129].[10] The same principle underlies the 'general rule' that contracts to lend or pay money are not specifically enforceable:

---

6   Spry 2014: 62, 93–4.

7   Note that the same principle can apply to the adequacy of some other form of common law relief, such as an action in debt: see eg *Sino Iron v Mineralogy* (2017).

8   For a modern approach challenging this assumption, see the comments of the majority of the Canadian Supreme Court in *Semelhago v Paramadevan* (1996).

9   But, on the position where a commodity is in scarce supply due to special circumstances, see eg *Howard E Perry v British Railways* (1980).

10   Although specific performance has, in some circumstances, been allowed in respect of sales of shares in public companies: see eg *ANZ Executors and Trustees v Humes* (1990); *Georges v Wieland* (2009).

Larios v Bonany v y Gurety (1873); *South African Territories v Wallington* (1898); *Loan Investment v Bonner* (1970).[11]

Increasingly, the English courts have shifted their focus away from the jurisdictional question of whether damages are an adequate remedy, to the broader question of whether it is 'just in all the circumstances that a plaintiff should be confined to his [sic] remedy in damages': *Evans Marshall v Bertola* (1973) at 379; *Beswick v Beswick* (1968) at 102. There has been some judicial support for such an approach in Australia: see eg *Trident General Insurance v McNiece Brothers* (1988) at 119. But it is far from clear whether it will gain traction here.[12]

22.04   Impossibility and futility

Where it is *impossible* for the defendant to perform the contract or it would be *futile* for the court to order such performance, specific performance will be refused. Specific performance will be refused on the grounds of impossibility, even if caused by the defendant; for example, where the defendant has transferred to an innocent third party property that they had agreed to sell to the plaintiff: see eg *Wenham v Ella* (1972). In cases of futility, performance of the contract is possible but a decree of specific performance is unlikely to achieve the end sought. Futility typically arises in situations where, despite a decree of specific performance, the defendant would be able to avoid its contractual obligations by some means. So, for example, in *Hercy v Birch* (1804) specific performance was refused in respect of an agreement to execute a partnership deed creating a partnership terminable at will. Historically, courts refused specific performance of leases of less than a year on the grounds of futility: see eg *Lavery v Pursell* (1888). But this reluctance is less evident in the more recent case law: see eg *Verrall v Great Yarmouth Borough Council* (1981), where specific performance was granted in respect of a contractual licence of just two days' duration.

22.05   The problem of constant supervision

Traditionally, a decree of specific performance was refused if it would require the court's ongoing involvement in *supervising* the contract and resolving potential future disputes as to whether it was being carried out according to its terms: see eg *Ryan v Mutual Tontine* (1893). In other words, unless the nature of the contract was such that the court could dispose of the case once-and-for–all with a decree of specific performance, the remedy would be refused. The issue of constant supervision has been considered a particular problem in certain specific types of contracts, such as construction contracts and contracts of personal service. However, the constant supervision problem can potentially arise in any contract involving performance of a great number of acts, very complex obligations, performance over an extended period of

---

11   But again, there have been circumstances in which such contracts have been specifically enforced: see eg *McIntosh v Dalwood* (1930); *Beswick v Beswick* (1968); *Coulls v Bagot's Executor and Trustee* (1967); *GE Commercial v Nichols* (2012).

12   See further Wright 2014, discussing the tendency of courts and commentators to speak of there being a 'rule' against equitable relief where common law remedies are adequate, while in practice treating the matter as a discretionary consideration.

time, or in which there is scope for uncertainty as to whether stipulated standards of performance are being met.

J C Williamson v Lukey (1931) provides a good illustration. The contract granted the plaintiff confectioner an exclusive right to sell confectionary, ice-cream and non-alcoholic drinks in the defendant's theatre and a licence to enter the theatre for those purposes. After the defendant repudiated the agreement and revoked the licence, the plaintiff sought specific performance. Concurrent with the defendant's obligation to allow the plaintiff and its employees access to the theatre were certain implied conditions. These governed the character of the goods to be sold by the plaintiff and the time, place and manner of their supply, as well as the appearance, dress and behaviour of the plaintiff's employees. In refusing specific performance it was stressed (at 298) that it would be 'contrary to principle for the court to undertake supervision of the specific fulfilment of these conditions'. In other words, every time the plaintiff's employees entered the theatre to sell the goods, a fresh dispute might arise as to whether these conditions were being complied with and, thus, whether the defendant was entitled to refuse the employees access to the theatre. This might necessitate the parties repeatedly returning to the court for rulings as to whether any order for specific performance was being complied with.[13] More recently, however, a more relaxed approach to the problem of constant supervision has been evident: see eg *Patrick Stevedores v Maritime Union of Australia* (1998). Spry has suggested that this consideration will now prevail only in exceptional cases.[14]

22.06   Lack of mutuality

Spry has formulated the *mutuality* principle as follows:

> The defence of lack of mutuality arises ... where, if the defendant were ordered to perform specifically his [sic] contractual obligations, he would not be himself sufficiently protected in view of the unperformed obligations of the plaintiff (especially where these are not susceptible of subsequent specific enforcement) and an order of specific performance would be unjust in all the circumstances.[15]

This can be contrasted with Fry's earlier formulation of the mutuality principle as requiring that, at the time it was entered into, the contract could have been specifically enforced by either party against the other.[16] That formulation has been criticised on two grounds.[17] Firstly, it flies in the face of decisions where specific performance was granted against a defendant who would not have been able to obtain such a remedy against the plaintiff. In some of these cases, the plaintiff's act of seeking specific performance was seen as a waiver of defences they might have raised in an action by the defendant for specific performance of the plaintiff's obligations: see eg *Halkett v Earl of Dudley* (1907). Although it may seem unfair to order specific performance against a defendant who would be confined to a claim in

---

13   Similar considerations underlay the refusal of specific performance in *Co-operative Insurance v Argyll Stores* (1997).
14   Spry 2014: 108.
15   Spry 2014: 95.
16   Fry 1921: 219.
17   See Spry 2014: 95–107; Heydon et al 2015: [20-150]–[20-160].

damages, considerations of hardship might militate in favour of granting the plaintiff specific performance. Indeed, in *Cannavo v FCD Holdings* (2000), Santow J explained the mutuality principle as a manifestation of the broader, underlying consideration of hardship. Secondly, contrary to Fry's formulation, the better view is surely that the relevant date for assessing mutuality is the date of the hearing, rather than that of entry into the contract: see *Price v Strange* (1978).

22.07 Personal services or relationships

Contracts for *personal services*, or those requiring an ongoing *personal relationship* or co-operation between the parties, are not as a general rule specifically enforceable. As Dixon J explained in *JC Williamson v Lukey* (1931) at 298, specific performance 'is not a form of relief which can be granted if the contract involves the performance by one party of services to the other or requires their continual co-operation'. In *Co-operative Insurance v Argyll Stores* (1997) at 906, the House of Lords voiced its unwillingness, in the context of a covenant requiring the defendant's continued operation of a supermarket business from premises leased from the plaintiff, to 'yoke the parties together in a continuing hostile relationship'. Similarly, a wrong-fully dismissed employee cannot, other than in exceptional circumstances, obtain an order requiring an employer to take them back into employment: *Byrne v Australian Airlines* (1995) at 428; *Visscher v Giudice* (2009) at [54].[18]

22.08 Plaintiff in breach or not ready, willing and able to perform

Self-evidently, a plaintiff who is substantially *in breach* of their own contractual obligations, or *not ready, willing and able* to perform, is in no position to seek equity's discretionary assistance to compel performance by the other party. This has been described as an application of equity's 'clean hands' maxim: see eg *Green v Somerville* (1979). However, as Barwick CJ explained in *Mehmet v Benson* (1965) at 307, the test is not a narrow, technical one requiring strict and literal compliance by the plaintiff, but rather one of substance:

> It is important to bear in mind what is the substantial thing for which the parties contract and what on the part of the plaintiff in a suit for specific performance are his [sic] essential obligations.

Here, what the defendant had bargained for was payment of the price. Time was not of the essence of the contract. The fact that the plaintiff had been in arrears for some years did not, therefore, prevent him obtaining a decree of specific performance. Where time *is* of the essence, even the briefest delay by the plaintiff in compliance will act as a bar to specific performance: see eg *Union Eagle v Golden Achievement* (1997). On the other hand, specific performance may be granted to a plaintiff whose refusal to perform was attributable solely to a genuine misinterpretation of the contract, as in *Green*.

---

18   For examples of exceptional circumstances for this purpose, see *Baker v Salisbury* (1982); *Paras v Public Service Body* (2006).

22.09 Hardship or unfairness in the making of the contract

A defendant may resist a claim for specific performance by showing that the effect of a decree would be to impose *undue hardship* upon them. The threshold is, however, a high one.[19] It has been said that specific performance must be 'highly unreasonable': *Wedgwood v Adams* (1843) at 605. The defendant must establish that 'a hardship amounting to an injustice would be inflicted on him [sic] by holding him to his bargain and that it would not be reasonable to do so': *Suttor v Gundowda* (1950) at 439. Neither financial difficulties on the part of the defendant, nor a subsequent increase in the value of the property that the defendant has contracted to sell, will suffice on their own: see eg *Pasedina v Khouri* (1977); *Fitzgerald v Masters* (1956). Any hardship to the defendant must also be weighed against the hardship the plaintiff would suffer as a result of a refusal of specific performance: *Coles Supermarkets v Australian Retail Freeholds* (1996). Hardship to third parties has been held to be relevant in a number of cases: see eg *Gall v Mitchell* (1924). So too has the public interest: see eg *Patrick Stevedores v Maritime Union of Australia* (1998). Although the matter is not free from doubt, the better view is that hardship should be assessed taking into account all of the circumstances known to exist at the time when the order is made, including those arising after entry into the contract and those likely to occur in the future.[20]

Whereas hardship focuses on the effect of a decree of specific performance on the defendant, *unfairness* in the making of the contract is concerned with some unfair or unconscionable conduct on the part of the *plaintiff* at or prior to entry into the contract. The fact that a contract is substantively unfair is insufficient, although such unfairness may operate as evidence of unfair conduct. Unfair conduct justifying refusal of specific performance may extend beyond the sort of conduct entitling the defendant to rescind the contract on grounds such as undue influence or unconscionable conduct.[21]

22.10 Mistake or misrepresentation

It stands to reason that a court will not decree specific performance of a contract which the defendant would be entitled to rescind on the ground of *mistake* or *misrepresentation*, under the principles discussed in Chapter 18. However, specific performance may also be refused in the event of a mistake or misrepresentation to which no right of rescission would attach.[22] In such cases, the plaintiff is confined to common law damages. Where the defendant's mistake has not been induced or contributed to by the plaintiff, courts are generally reluctant to refuse specific performance in the absence of some other consideration such as hardship to the defendant or unfairness in the making of the contract: see eg *Tamplin v Jones* (1880); *Slee v Warke* (1949); *Fragomeni v Fogliani* (1968).

---

19 In *Longtom v Oberon Shire Council* (1996) at 14,799 it was said that 'the defence of hardship these days very rarely meets with much success'.
20 Spry 2014: 203–4.
21 See Spry 2014: 199.
22 For cases of mistake, see eg *Malins v Freeman* (1837); *Webster v Cecil* (1861); *Nield v Davidson* (1890). For misrepresentation, see eg *Re Terry and White's Contract* (1886) at 29; *Hope v Walter* (1900); *Electronic Industries v Harrison & Crossfield* (1966).

22.11 The equitable defence of laches: delay and acquiescence

Where the plaintiff's unreasonable delay in bringing proceedings would create prejudice or unfairness to the defendant or third parties, specific performance may be refused on the grounds of the general equitable defence of *laches*. The delay may, for example, result in loss of documents or other evidence, prejudicing the defendant's ability to defend the claim. Or it may prejudice third parties who have, in the meantime, acquired the property that was the subject matter of the contract: see eg *Lamshed v Lamshed* (1963). For the purposes of assessing the reasonableness or otherwise of the delay, time generally begins to run from the date when the plaintiff had 'sufficient knowledge of the facts constituting the title to relief': *Lindsay Petroleum v Hurd* (1874) at 241. The question whether the delay is unreasonable is highly context-dependent. Although acquiescence is sometimes seen as separate from delay, in truth the two overlap in the defence of laches, as the delay may lead the defendant to *believe* that the plaintiff has acquiesced: see *Lindsay Petroleum* at 239–40; *No 68 v Eastern Services* (2006) at [56].

22.12 Statutory powers to grant specific performance

The remedy of specific performance itself is not expressly mentioned in the Australian Consumer Law (ACL). However, ss 237, 238 and 239 empower a court to make such orders as it thinks appropriate to compensate for loss or damage or to prevent or reduce loss or damage. It is clear that they are broad enough to encompass orders for specific performance. Indeed, some of the remedies specifically mentioned in s 243 as examples of possible remedies under those provisions are akin to specific performance. These include an order requiring the respondent to repair or provide parts for goods supplied by the respondent to the injured person (s 243(f)), or an order directing the respondent to supply specified services to the injured person (s 243(g)).

22.13 Should specific performance be more widely available?

Whereas specific performance is a discretionary, exceptional remedy in common law systems like Australia, it is a generally available remedy for breach of contract in civilian systems such as Germany and France.[23] Whether common law systems should follow suit in making specific performance more widely available is a question that has received a good deal of academic attention. Those who support the general availability of specific performance point to the fact that damages often undercompensate the plaintiff.[24] They may highlight the moral importance of protecting the performance interest.[25] There are also empirical studies suggesting that, in many situations, parties would prefer a 'coercive' remedy to one offering 'substitutionary performance'.[26]

---

23   See *German Civil Code* art 241; *French Civil Code* art 1221.
24   See eg Schwartz 1979.
25   See Friedmann 1995; Webb 2006.
26   See Berryman & Carroll 2014. As to whether parties can or should be able to expand the availability of coercive remedies by expressing a preference in the contract itself, see Carroll 2012.

The primary argument against expanding the availability of specific performance is the theory of *efficient breach*.[27] This is based on the idea that contract law should promote economic efficiency by maximising overall welfare. According to Posner (2014: 130), the objective of contract remedies is to give the promisor an incentive 'to fulfil his [sic] promise unless the result would be an inefficient use of resources'. In other words, parties should be able to breach their contracts and pay damages where it is economically efficient to do so. Take the following example. A agrees to sell goods to B for $5,000. The goods have a market value of $7,000. Before A delivers the goods, C offers A $10,000 for the same goods. If A breaches their contract, and assuming no money has yet been paid, B can claim damages of $2,000: see **23.10**.[28] In this situation, it will be economically efficient for A to breach the contract, pay B $2,000 by way of damages, and instead supply the goods to C. Both A and C will be better off (the former because they receive more money, the latter because they get the goods they want at a price they are willing to pay), while B will be no worse off. In permitting A to breach their contract and pay damages, the current law is said to promote economic efficiency. Giving B a right to specific performance in this situation would (so the argument runs) result in a loss of efficiency.

However, moral objections to the law encouraging breaches of contract aside, the economic case for or against a more widely available remedy of specific performance is inconclusive.[29] For one thing, the simple model of efficient breach outlined above ignores transaction costs. Which remedy is the more efficient, economically speaking, ultimately hinges on the relative transaction costs in any given situation. This is an empirical question on which there is insufficient data. For another, even ignoring transaction costs, economic efficiency might be equally well served by a rule allowing for specific performance. In the example used above, A would agree to pay B a sum of money somewhere between $2,000 and $5,000 for a release from their contract. Since the goods will be going to the person who values them most, economic efficiency is still being served, albeit the exact wealth distribution will be different.

Injunctions

22.14   The use of injunctions to resolve contractual disputes

Injunctions may be sought either as a *permanent* form of relief, or on an *interlocutory* (temporary) basis, pending a final determination of the parties' rights or obligations. It is not unusual, for example, for one party to seek an order restraining the other from terminating a contract, on the basis that the termination would not be lawful under the contract. Under the ordinary principles applying to the grant of interlocutory relief, the applicant must show that they have a serious case to be tried – that is, some prospect of success if their arguments are ultimately accepted – and that the 'balance of convenience' favours the grant of relief: see eg *Corporate Transport Services v Toll* (2005). An applicant will generally have to give an

---

27   See Posner 2014: 128–31; Kronman 1978; Farnsworth 1979.
28   This ignores any possible claim for consequential loss: see **23.03**. But so long as that loss does not reach or exceed $3,000, the analysis in the text will still hold.
29   See Macneil 1982: 951–7.

undertaking to pay damages to the other party in the event that they are unsuccessful at trial, and may also be required to make any payments that would be due under the contract they are trying to preserve: see eg *Telstra v First Netcom* (1997).

In the contractual context, injunctions are most commonly granted to restrain breaches of *negative* stipulations – that is, stipulations *not* to do a particular act.[30] This reflects the courts' general reluctance to grant mandatory as opposed to prohibitory injunctions and their wariness of effectively granting specific performance by the back door.[31] A good example of these considerations is provided by the seminal case of *Lumley v Wagner* (1852). The defendant, Wagner, a celebrated opera singer, had agreed to sing at the plaintiff's London theatre for a period of three months. The contract provided that Wagner would not, during that period, perform elsewhere without the plaintiff's consent. In breach of that obligation, Wagner subsequently accepted a singing engagement, during the term of the contract, at Covent Garden for a larger fee. Lord St Leonards LC granted the plaintiff an injunction restraining Wagner, during the currency of the contract, from singing at any other theatre or place without the plaintiff's permission. He rejected an argument that to grant the injunction would be to decree specific performance of the parties' agreement by the back door.[32] He stressed that the grant of the injunction in respect of the negative stipulation (not to sing elsewhere without permission) was not tantamount to granting specific performance of the positive obligation to perform at the plaintiff's theatre. In other words, the injunction could be complied with without Wagner actually singing in the plaintiff's theatre.[33]

Distinguishing positive from negative obligations is not always straightforward, as positive obligations can easily be couched in negative language and vice versa. As Lindley LJ explained in *Whitwood Chemical v Hardman* (1891) at 426:

> [E]very agreement to do a particular thing in one sense involves a negative. It involves the negative of not doing that which is inconsistent with the thing you are to do. If I agree with a man to be at a certain place at a certain time, I impliedly agree that I will not be anywhere else at the same times, and so on ad infinitum.

Since negative stipulations may therefore be implied as well as express, it is vital to look at substance rather than form: *Wolverhampton and Walsall Railway v London and North-Western Railway* (1873) at 440; *Ampol Petroleum v Mutton* (1952) at 10. A stipulation is negative in substance if it can be complied with by mere inactivity: *Administrative and Clerical Officers Association v Commonwealth* (1979) at 502.

---

30   Although that is not to say that there are not examples of injunctions being used to enforce positive contractual obligations: see Spry 2014: 557. For an unorthodox (and ultimately unsuccessful) attempt to obtain a mandatory interlocutory injunction to require payment of a disputed debt, see *Sino Iron v Mineralogy* (2017).

31   The distinction between specific performance and injunctions (in the contractual context) is generally said to be that specific performance is only granted in respect of the whole contract, whereas injunctions are granted in respect of individual obligations. However, this is not always borne out in practice: see Spry 2014: 113–17.

32   It was accepted that specific performance of the contract would not have been granted here, presumably on the grounds that this was a contract for personal services and would have given rise to a problem of constant supervision.

33   However, it was acknowledged that the grant of the injunction might *indirectly* cause Wagner to fulfil her positive obligation to sing at the plaintiff's theatre.

In *Doherty v Allman* (1878) at 719–20, Lord Cairns suggested that injunctions in respect of negative stipulations were available *as of right*. This would leave no room for questions about the adequacy of common law damages and the usual equitable discretionary factors discussed above in relation to specific performance, such as hardship, unfairness in the making of the contract, or delay and acquiescence. Despite some judicial support for this position, the better view is that such injunctions remain in the court's discretion: see eg *Dalgety Wine Estates v Rizzon* (1979); *Curro v Beyond Productions* (1993) at 346–7. In an attempt to reconcile this seemingly inconsistent case law, Spry (2014: 610) has suggested that the true position is that:

> Where a party to a contract agrees, expressly or impliedly, not to perform a particular act, and the conditions for the partial enforcement of the contract are satisfied, prima facie he [sic] will be enjoined from performing it, and, save in exceptional cases, damages will not be regarded as an adequate remedy; but the defendant may none-theless be able to establish special circumstances of such a nature that the hardship that the making of the order would cause him would so far outweigh the inconvenience to the plaintiff through denying him specific relief that the court considers that its intervention would be unjust; and further, here as elsewhere other discretionary considerations, such as unfairness or laches, may be found to render the grant of an injunction inappropriate.

22.15   Contracts of personal service

Negative stipulations in contracts of personal service may give rise to particular issues of public policy over and above the considerations relating to personal services discussed in the context of specific performance above. Such contracts commonly contain terms forbidding the employee obtaining employment elsewhere, either during the term of the contract or after-wards. Such a clause may be rendered invalid under the common law doctrine of restraint of trade discussed in Chapter 21. But even where such a negative stipulation is valid, a court may, on discretionary grounds, refuse to enforce it by way of injunction.

Lumley v Wagner is, of course, an example of a case where such a stipulation was enforced.[34] In that case, however, Wagner was only precluded from performing her 'special services' (whether publicly or privately). The clause did not, for example, prevent her giving singing lessons or working in another field. The time period of the prohibition – three months – was also fairly short.[35] *Page One Records v Britton* (1968) involved an attempt by a manager of a pop group (The Troggs) to enforce a clause in his contract with the group that they would employ no one other than him as their manager for a period of five years. His attempt to secure an injunction failed. Aside from an issue of mutuality, such an order would effectively have prevented the group from carrying on its business for a period of five years. Stamp J (at 166) stated the principle to be that:

---

34   See also *Warner Brothers Pictures v Nelson* (1937).
35   For examples of employers being able to restrain departing employees from working elsewhere (or for a particular competitor) until the expiration of their contract or notice period, see *Curro v Beyond Productions* (1993); *BGC Partners v Hickey* (2016).

Where a contract of personal service contains negative covenants the enforcement of which will amount either to a decree of specific performance of the positive covenants of the contract or to the giving of a decree under which the defendant must either remain idle or perform those positive covenants, the court will not enforce those negative covenants.[36]

Recovery of debts

22.16   The action for debt and its advantages

The action for debt is conceptually distinct from an action for breach of contract, although both actions may lie on the same set of facts. In *Young v Queensland Trustees* (1956) at 567, the rationale of the action for debt was explained in the following terms:

> The common law does not and never did conceive of indebtedness in a sum certain for an executed consideration as a mere breach of contract: it is rather the detention of a sum of money.

The action for debt has a number of significant advantages over an action for breach of contract and a plaintiff with a choice may be wise to frame their claim in debt. A plaintiff in an action for breach of contract must prove both breach and loss, but the action of debt requires only proof of an accrued debt that has not been paid. Furthermore, the 'duty' imposed on plaintiffs seeking damages to mitigate their loss does not attach to claims in debt: see *White & Carter v McGregor* (1962) and the discussion at **16.26**. Finally, a plaintiff may be able to recover a debt under a contract even though the defendant has terminated the contract on account of the plaintiff's breach: see **17.04**.

22.17   When is an action for debt available?

A debt is a sum which is definite or ascertainable – hence the alternative terminology, *action for a liquidated sum*. An action for debt is only possible in relation to debts which have *accrued*. A debt accrues where the contractual condition for payment of a sum of money – be it performance of a service, delivery of goods or the happening of a specified event – has been satisfied. In cases where payment is conditional upon the plaintiff's performance, the question whether a debt has accrued depends upon whether, as a matter of construction, payment is conditional on the plaintiff's performance of its *entire* contractual obligations, or merely of a *divisible* part of them. This is the distinction between entire and divisible obligations. There is the further question of whether, despite failure to fully perform the contract, the plaintiff can nonetheless be said to have rendered *substantial performance* of the contract justifying recovery of the contract price. The issues and case law on these points have already been discussed in Chapter 12.

---

36   For examples of a similar attitude to the restraint of employees, see *Bearingpoint v Hillard* (2008); *Network Ten v Seven Network* (2014).

22.18 Contractual sums accruing independently of performance

Contracts commonly provide for the payment of sums of money that accrue independently of any duty of performance of the other party. One example is pre-conveyance instalments payable by the purchaser under a contract for the sale of land, as in *McDonald v Dennys Lascelles* (1933). Dixon J stressed (at 476) that in all such cases:

> the purchase money or such part thereof becomes, on the day so fixed for its payment, a debt immediately recoverable by the vendor irrespective of the question whether a conveyance has been executed and notwithstanding the fact that the purchaser may have repudiated his contract. Notwithstanding such repudiation the vendor is not bound to sue for damages or specific performance, but may recover the agreed purchase money.

However, as discussed at **17.05**, the vendor's right to retain those instalments is conditional upon subsequent completion of the contract. Once the contract is terminated, the purchaser is entitled to recover any instalments paid through a restitutionary claim and the purchaser's obligation in respect of any unpaid instalments is extinguished. In other words, the right to such payments accrues independently of performance but does not survive termination.

Another type of contractual payment accruing independently of performance is a deposit. Deposits are treated quite differently from instalments of the purchase price. They are not conditional upon completion of the sale. A deposit becomes immediately recoverable as a debt from the day fixed for its payment (subject to the principles discussed at **17.06**) and the vendor's right to its payment survives termination: *Bot v Ristevski* (1981). That is not, however, the case in circumstances of termination on account of the *vendor's* breach.

Liquidated damages and penalty clauses

22.19 A brief history of the penalty doctrine

To understand the modern day penalty doctrine and the controversies surrounding it, a brief detour into legal history is necessary.[37] The English Court of Chancery first granted relief in the context of *conditional bonds* in the fourteenth century. The conditional bond developed in medieval times and remained the main contractual device for a number of centuries.[38] It operated as follows. An obligor sealed a bond (a deed) binding them to pay a certain sum of money to the obligee by a given date. The bond would contain one or more conditions. If those conditions were satisfied by that date, the obligation to pay the stipulated sum would become void. So, for example, A might seal and deliver a bond to B obliging A to pay B £100 by 1 January, with the bond to become void if A paid B the lesser sum of £50 by that date. Or C might seal and deliver a bond to D, obliging C to pay D £100 by 1 July, with the bond to become void if C transferred certain goods to D by that date. In the event that the stated conditions were not satisfied by the stipulated date, the sum stipulated in the bond was recoverable by the obligee (B and D in our examples) through an action in debt on the bond.

---

37   See Simpson 1966; Turner 2018.
38   On the early development and later history of the conditional bond, see Ibbetson 1999: 28–30, 150.

Importantly, while the aim of the conditional bond was to secure satisfaction of the underlying condition, it did not create any *obligation* (or *promise*) in respect of that condition. The only obligation undertaken by the obligor was payment of the stipulated sum in the event of non-satisfaction of the condition. This is, of course, quite different from the sort of modern contractual arrangement whereby V *undertakes* to pay X $50, or Y *undertakes* to transfer certain goods to Z, with damages payable in the event of breach of that undertaking.

A common characteristic of conditional bonds was that the *size* of the stipulated sum was usually intended to act as an incentive to satisfaction of the underlying condition. It was on this that the Court of Chancery focused when it began to grant relief from *penal* bonds on the basis that the infliction of a penalty was unconscionable. By the seventeenth century, it was doing this routinely. In the case of a penal money bond – that is, a bond to secure payment of a sum of money, such as in the first example above – relief was granted on terms that the obligor pay the sum mentioned in the condition with interest. In the case of a penal performance bond (as in the second example), relief was granted provided the obligee could be compensated for the actual loss caused by non-satisfaction of the condition. As damages was not a remedy known to equity, the Court of Chancery had to refer the case to the common law courts for assessment of damages by a jury. Unlike equity, the common law, at this stage, set its face against relieving from penal bonds. As a result, an obligor who had been sued in a common law court for a (penal) sum under a conditional bond was forced to go to the Court of Chancery to obtain an injunction restraining the common law proceedings. Ultimately, the common law responded by offering relief from penal bonds on similar terms.[39] This was put on a statutory footing around the turn of the eighteenth century.[40] That development rendered the equitable jurisdiction to relieve against penalties redundant for most practical purposes: *AMEV-UDC Finance v Austin* (1986) at 191; *Cavendish Square Holding v El Makdessi* (2015) at [6].

The conditional bond continued to be widely used as a contractual vehicle well into the eighteenth century.[41] But in the seventeenth century, the action of *assumpsit* became the regular action for breach of contract.[42] Central to this action, and just as in the modern law of contract which developed from it, was the notion of *breach of promise*. As a result, the penalty doctrine, which had first developed in the context of *non-promissory* conditional bonds before the emergence of a generalised notion of breach of contract,[43] now operated primarily in the context of breach of *promissory* obligations.

22.20   The scope of the contemporary penalty doctrine

The vast majority of cases involving the penalty doctrine have concerned stipulations for the payment of a sum of money on the occurrence (or non-occurrence) of a particular event. However, the rule clearly extends to clauses providing for non-monetary benefits as well, such as the reconveyance of property: see eg *Ringrow v BP Australia* (2005).

---

39   This happened from the second half of the seventeenth century: see Simpson 1966: 418–19. However, the existence of a common law penalty doctrine pre-dating the statutory enactments referred to below has been challenged: see eg Turner 2018.

40   *Administration of Justice Act 1696* (UK) s 8; *Administration of Justice Act 1705* (UK) ss 12–13.

41   Ibbetson 1999: 150.

42   Simpson 1975b: 3; and see **1.10**.

43   There had, of course, long existed the notion of breach of *covenant* – that is, a deed.

In England, the penalty doctrine has long been confined to situations where the event upon which the stipulation is conditioned is a breach of contract: *Export Credits v Universal Oil Products* (1983). So, for example, a clause requiring payment of a sum of money by a party on their (rightful) exercise of a contractual right of termination is not reviewable under the English doctrine. The breach of contract requirement was recently reaffirmed by the UK Supreme Court in *Cavendish Square Holding v El Makdessi* (2015). However, it has not been without its critics. In *Bridge v Campbell Discount* (1962) at 629, Lord Denning noted that the effect of the breach requirement was, paradoxically, to 'grant relief to a man [sic] who breaks his contract but [to] penalise the man who keeps it'. There is also the practical consideration that the breach requirement allows for circumvention of the penalty doctrine by clever drafting. For example, the doctrine could be easily avoided by redrafting the clause 'X undertakes not to do Y; if X does Y, X must pay Z $1 million' as 'X may, or may not, do Y; if X does Y, X must pay Z $1 million'. However, the court in *Cavendish* was alive to this problem when it stressed (at [15]) that the classification of terms for these purposes depends on the *substance* of the term, rather than its form or the label attached to it.

Despite conflicting statements on the issue, the balance of earlier Australian authority clearly favoured the English approach: see eg *IAC v Humphrey* (1972) at 143; *O'Dea v Allstates Leasing* (1983) at 390; *AMEV-UDC Finance v Austin* (1986) at 184.[44] This position was followed by the New South Wales Court of Appeal in *Interstar Wholesale Finance v Integral Home Loans* (2008). Central to that decision was the view that the equitable penalty doctrine, originally developed in the context of non-promissory conditional bonds, had been extinguished by absorption into the modern common law doctrine. It was considered noteworthy that all modern formulations of the test for identifying whether a stipulation is penal had been couched in terms of breach of contract: see eg *Dunlop Pneumatic Tyre v New Garage* (1915); *Ringrow v BP Australia* (2005). The Court of Appeal stressed the importance of confining within strict and clearly identifiable limits a doctrine that operates as an exception to the principles of freedom of contract.

Interstar was, however, overruled by the High Court in *Andrews v ANZ Banking Group* (2012). This was a decision given on a preliminary point, arising from a challenge to the validity of certain bank fees. Basing its reasoning primarily on legal historical analysis, the High Court asserted that the equitable doctrine had, from its inception, applied to non-promissory stipulations, and continued to do so. It had not been subsumed into a narrower common law doctrine. In the Court's view, neither the development of the common law doctrine nor the later focus on breach of contract that emerged could have affected the equitable doctrine's scope. This is in stark contrast to the UK Supreme Court's view that, by the end of the eighteenth century, the penalty doctrine had become a common law rule operating almost entirely in the context of agreed damages clauses for breach of contract: see *Cavendish* at [8].

Andrews is problematic on a number of levels.[45] For one thing, it is unclear whether there is now just one (equitable) penalty doctrine, or whether a common law doctrine applicable to breach cases exists alongside an equitable doctrine operating in non-breach cases.[46] This

---

44   For a contrary view, see eg *AMEV-UDC Finance v Austin* (1986) at 197–203.
45   See Carter et al 2013; Gray 2017.
46   And perhaps also, as Gageler J has suggested, in rare cases where the party asserting unenforceability is constrained to seek purely equitable relief: *Paciocco v ANZ Banking Group* (2016) at [126].

confusion is evident in the post-*Andrews* case law.[47] *Paciocco v ANZ Banking Group* (2016), a later decision in the same litigation as *Andrews*, provided the High Court with the opportunity to clear up this confusion. Disappointingly, only Gageler J, who considered that there were two doctrines, saw fit to clearly confront the issue.

Perhaps the greatest problem with *Andrews*, though, is the unacceptable degree of commercial uncertainty it has generated. The High Court formulated the scope of the (equitable) doctrine as follows (at [10]):

> In general terms, a stipulation prima facie imposes a penalty on a party (the first party) if, as a matter of substance, it is collateral (or accessory) to a primary stipulation in favour of a second party and this collateral stipulation, upon the failure of the primary stipulation, imposes upon the first party an additional detriment, the penalty, to the benefit of the second party.

This effectively renders any contingent obligation reviewable. As the UK Supreme Court noted in *Cavendish* (at [42]) in its criticism of *Andrews*, the 'collateral stipulation' formulation exposes to potential challenge a whole raft of terms routinely used in commercial contracts. This point is taken up further below.

22.21   When is a stipulation a penalty?

Until recently, the penalty doctrine was closely tied to the notion of unliquidated damages. That was the approach taken in Lord Dunedin's famous guidance in the leading House of Lords decision, *Dunlop Pneumatic Tyre v New Garage* (1915) at 86–8. Assessing whether the stipulation in question was 'in the nature of a penalty' involved comparing the stipulated sum (or other benefit) with the greatest loss that could conceivably be proved to have followed from the breach. This forward-looking assessment took into account all the 'inherent circumstances' of the contract, reflecting the fact that the parties were estimating the loss at the point of entry into the contract and without the benefit of hindsight. To be valid, the stipulated sum had to be a *genuine pre-estimate* of loss. The threshold was a high one: a party seeking to establish that a stipulation was penal had to show that it was out of all proportion to, or 'extravagant or unconscionable in amount in comparison with', the greatest conceivable loss. There was a presumption that a stipulation was a penalty where a single lump sum was payable on the occurrence of one or more of a number of different breaches, some of which would cause serious, and others only trivial, damage. The fact that the consequences of breach were such as to make precise pre-estimation almost impossible did not prevent the stipulation being a genuine pre-estimate. On the contrary, this was exactly the situation where the stipulation was likely to be a valid liquidated damages clause.

The operation of what we might now call the 'old law of penalties' was exemplified by a series of cases dealing with accelerated payment clauses in leases of goods. The contracts in question provided that if a lessee defaulted in their rental payments, the lessor could repossess

---

47   Compare *Cedar Meats v Five Star Lamb* (2014) and *Australia Capital Financial Management v Linfield Developments* (2017), which assume the existence of two doctrines, with *GWC Property v Higginson* (2014) at [43], where *Andrews* was described as a 'reassertion of the penalty doctrine as a rule of equity *not law*' (emphasis added).

and sell the goods *and* be entitled to immediate payment of all remaining instalments. At the risk of oversimplifying what are very complex cases, the results can be explained in this way. Where the accelerated payment clause made some allowance for any benefits received by the lessor in selling the goods, it might be treated as valid: see eg *Esanda Finance v Plessnig* (1989). But if no such allowance was made, the provision was likely to be a penalty: see eg *O'Dea v Allstates Leasing* (1983); *AMEV-UDC Finance v Austin* (1986).

In *Paciocco v ANZ Banking Group* (2016), however, the High Court radically rewrote the penalty doctrine. While not overruling any of the earlier cases that had followed *Dunlop*, the Court stressed that the words 'loss' in Lord Dunedin's formulation had been read too narrowly. What was required was a comparison of the stipulated sum with the other party's 'interest in performance'. While this certainly included an interest in compensation (in the sense of unliquidated damages), it was broader than that. A party might, for example, have an interest in performance that was intangible or unquantifiable. Only if the stipulation was out of all proportion to that party's interest (in this broader sense) could it be found to be a penalty. This approach aligns closely with the test adopted by the UK Supreme Court the previous year in *Cavendish* (at [32]):

> whether the impugned provision ... imposes a detriment on the contract-breaker out of all proportion to any legitimate interest of the innocent party in the enforcement of the primary obligation.[48]

Despite laying down the broader 'interests test' in *Paciocco*, the High Court recognised that Lord Dunedin's principles would nonetheless remain useful in the many cases where the promisee's interest in performance did not extend beyond an interest in compensation.

22.22   The operation of the new 'interests test'

Both *Cavendish* and *Paciocco* provide excellent illustrations of the breadth of the new 'interests test'. In one of two separate cases considered by the Supreme Court in *Cavendish*, Mr Beavis had been charged a fee of £85 when he overstayed the permitted two hours of free parking in a shopping centre car park. He argued that the fee was a penalty because it was out of all proportion to any loss that ParkingEye, the company that managed the car park, could conceivably have suffered as a result of his breach.[49] The Supreme Court found that the fee, which was part of a 'traffic space maximisation scheme' was not a penalty. It had two legitimate objects: managing the efficient use of parking space in the interests of the retail outlets occupying the shopping centre and their customers; and providing an income stream to enable ParkingEye to cover its costs and make a profit, without which its services would not be available. Significantly, ParkingEye was not paid by the landowners for providing its services; it in fact paid them for the right to operate the scheme. Applying the new test, the Court concluded that there was a legitimate interest in charging overstaying motorists, which extended beyond an interest in compensation. Interestingly, despite the new test's reference

---

48   This test is, however, couched in the language of breach of contract, which is no longer a requirement in Australia because of the decision in *Andrews*.

49   As ParkingEye were not the owners of the car park, it was accepted that they suffered no loss (in the sense of unliquidated damages) at all.

to the 'legitimate interest of the innocent party', their Lordships considered that they were entitled to look beyond the interests of ParkingEye itself and consider those of the landowners as well.

In *Paciocco*, the High Court had to decide whether late payment fees of $20 and $35 imposed by the ANZ Bank as part of credit card agreements were penalties. At first instance, Gordon J had found that the loss (in the sense of unliquidated damages) actually suffered by the bank when the customer failed to make the minimum payment by the due date was no more than $3. The High Court, applying the new 'interests test', concluded that the fees were not penalties. The bank argued that its interests extended beyond recovering compensation for its operational costs, such as writing letters and making telephone calls to defaulting customers. It pointed to two other categories of cost it incurred as a result of late payments, neither of which would have been recoverable as unliquidated damages. The first category was the provision that banks are required to hold in their accounts to reflect the fact that increased risk of future non-payment reduces the value of their assets. The second category of cost arose from the fact that, under regulatory requirements, banks must increase the amount of capital they hold when the risk of future non-payment increases. The effect is to reduce the pool of money available to the bank for profit-generating activities (such as making loans at interest). Gordon J had described these two categories of costs as 'theoretical' or simply part of the general costs of running a bank in Australia. Nonetheless, a majority of the High Court considered that the Bank *did* have an interest in avoiding these wider financial impacts. The fees could not be said to be out of all proportion to that interest.

22.23   The consequences of a stipulation being a penalty

A stipulation covering a number of contingencies may be in the nature of a penalty in respect of some but not all of those contingencies. It is nonetheless treated as a penalty, with the consequences outlined below, for all purposes: *Cooden Engineering v Stanford* (1953) at 94; *Pigram v Attorney-General (NSW)* (1975) at 221.

Historically, the consequences of a stipulation being penal differed between equity and the common law. In equity, a penalty was enforceable up to the amount of the promisee's loss. At common law it was void or unenforceable, with the innocent party thrown back on common law (unliquidated) damages. Until the decision in *Andrews*, the modern understanding, reflecting the common law position, was that a penalty was void or unenforceable: see eg *Citicorp v Hendry* (1985) at 39–40. But in *Andrews*, the High Court stated (at [10]) that a penalty is enforceable up to the amount of the actual loss. This was clearly intended as a statement of the equitable doctrine. What is less clear (as discussed above) is whether the equitable doctrine now covers the entire field, or whether a common law doctrine, applicable in breach cases and with the different consequence of making a provision unenforceable or void, sits alongside the equitable rule.

The full ramifications of the equitable position of enforceability up to the amount of the actual loss remain to be worked out. First, there is the question of how courts should approach the 'scaling down' of the penalty to reflect the promisee's actual loss. As Mason and Wilson JJ noted in *AMEV-UDC Finance v Austin* (1986) at 193, the amount equity considered fair and reasonable recompense for the loss suffered was usually equivalent to common law damages. But this will not necessarily be the case. Second, there is the problem of how courts should go about assessing the promisee's loss in non-breach cases. Finally, there is the difficult question of whether, and how, the equitable position of enforceability up to the amount of the actual loss (as opposed to a penalty being wholly void or unenforceable) might affect the availability or analysis of restitutionary claims in cases where a party seeks to recover sums already paid under a penalty clause.[50]

In circumstances where the amount that would be recoverable by way of damages exceeds the penalty, the question has also arisen whether the penalty, although irrecoverable, operates as an upper limit on damages. Unfortunately, the High Court is yet to determine the issue.[51]

22.24   The new law of penalties in practice

Prior to the thoroughly unhelpful decisions in *Andrews* and *Paciocco*, the law on penalty clauses was fairly clear. A contractual provision that (in substance if not necessarily in form) imposed an extravagant or unconscionable penalty for breaching a contract was invalid. But an agreed damages clause was enforceable, so long as the amount stipulated represented a genuine attempt to pre-estimate loss. The same applied to any other type of provision (such as for accelerated payments or reconveyance of property) that operated in response to a breach.

As matters stand, however, it is unclear whether there are two rules against penalties – one at common law for penalties on breach, the other in equity where no breach of contract is involved – or just one (the equitable doctrine). And on either basis, there are now a number of common provisions in commercial contracts that might in theory be challenged as penalties.[52] These include 'take or pay' clauses in long-term supply contracts,[53] 'termination for convenience' payments, provisions for the loss of incentives or fee rebates in the event of not meeting performance targets, and obligations to transfer property in the event of insolvency or a change of control. The remedial consequences of a penalty that offends the equitable doctrine are also a matter attended by considerable doubt

Since *Andrews*, there have been a number of attempts to challenge provisions that are not in substance penalties for breach, though these have generally failed.[54] It is also notable that courts applying the interests test adopted in *Paciocco*, which should in theory mean that provisions 'will hardly ever be penalties',[55] are still tending to strike down clauses that do

---

50   As was the case in the *Andrews* and *Paciocco* litigation.

51   For the view that it does act as an upper limit, see *Wilbeam v Ashton* (1807); *Lord Elphinstone v Monkland Iron & Coal* (1886) at 346; *Public Works Commissioner v Hills* (1906) at 367. For the contrary view, see *Wall v Rederiaktiebolaget Luggude* (1915); *Watts, Watts v Mitsui* (1917).

52   See Carter et al 2013: 112–13.

53   These permit a customer either to take a certain amount of products from a supplier, or pay a stipulated sum. In *Cedar Meats v Five Star Lamb* (2014), a clause of this type was found to be a penalty, although the Victorian Court of Appeal were plainly not convinced about the trial judge's finding (which had not been challenged on appeal) that the amount to be paid was unconscionable or extravagant. The decision might now be different in any event under the interests test adopted in *Paciocco*.

54   See eg *Love v Brien* (2013); *Australia Capital Financial Management v Linfield Developments* (2017); but compare *Cedar Meats*, discussed above.

55   Carter et al 2017: 40.

not represent a genuine pre-estimate of the loss likely to be suffered from a breach.[56] As Sackville AJA noted in *Arab Bank v Sayde Developments* (2016) at [10], it remains unclear yet whether the High Court's recent decisions have ended up expanding or contracting the scope of the penalties doctrine.[57]

---

56   See eg *Melbourne Linh Son Buddhist Society v Gippsreal* (2017), where a majority of the Victorian Court of Appeal found a provision in a loan agreement to be a penalty, but without (as Maxwell P pointed out in dissent) considering the kind of evidence that the new test would seem to require. A similar point can be made about the penalty finding in *Café Du Liban v Bespoke Garage* (2017). Some courts are simply ignoring the new test: see eg *Zintix v Employsure* (2018), where an acceleration clause was found to be a penalty without reference to *Paciocco*.

57   For further discussion, see Tiverios 2017a, 2017b; Eldridge 2018b.

23

DAMAGES
FOR BREACH
OF CONTRACT

General principles

23.01   Damages as the primary remedy for breach of contract

Following a breach of contract, several different remedies are potentially available. Damages are the primary remedy, and they reflect losses caused by the breach. Even when no loss is actually suffered, a token amount will be awarded by way of *nominal damages*: see *Baum v Commonwealth* (1906) at 116–17; and see eg *Romero v Farstad Shipping* (2017). The award of nominal damages is symbolic. It reflects the fact that a breach has occurred, but it does not necessarily follow that the plaintiff will be awarded costs for succeeding in their action: *Motium v Arrow Electronics* (2011) at [96].

It is sometimes said that damages vindicate or substitute for the contractual right to performance, or what is known as the *performance interest*.[1] Yet, damages will not entirely achieve this aim.[2] This is because damages will not exactly replicate performance, since (as will be explained) the law has rules limiting recovery. The transaction costs of bringing a claim also have to be considered. In fact, if contractual remedies are about protecting the performance interest, then specific performance should be a better fit as a default remedy for breach of contract. Yet other remedies for breach have long been treated as of secondary importance to damages. As explained in Chapter 22, specific performance and injunctions will only be granted when damages cannot provide an adequate remedy. In practice, specific performance has a very marginal role in Australian contract law beyond the context of sales of land. A better view then is that, while remedies like specific performance do protect the performance interest, contract damages are more naturally thought of as *compensatory*.[3]

The reason that damages are treated as the primary remedy for breach is historical. As explained in **1.10**, damages were the remedy given in the medieval action of trespass, which developed into the contractual action of assumpsit. Assumpsit in turn morphed into the modern action for breach of contract in the nineteenth century. This arrangement reflects the division between claims in debt and claims in contract. Debt is based on an entitlement to a fixed sum, as discussed in **22.16–22.17**. Contract is founded on a promised performance. A breach of contract amounts to a failure to do what was promised or agreed, and is a wrong causing a loss to be remedied by an award of damages.

23.02   A right to perform or pay damages?

As early as 1897, the great American jurist Oliver Wendell Holmes Jr said that the duty to keep a contract meant no more than a prediction that damages would be payable if the contract was breached.[4] Building on this basic idea, modern law and economics scholars have promoted an instrumentalist view of contract damages. It is assumed that parties to a contract have a choice. They can either perform the contract, or pay damages. In some situations, it will be more

---

1   See eg Friedmann 1995; Stevens 2009; Winterton 2015; Barnett 2016.
2   See Burrows 2012a.
3   See Webb 2006.
4   Holmes 1897: 462.

economically efficient to breach the contract and pay damages. The concept of efficient breach has been discussed at **22.13**. The theory supports the award of 'expectation damages' (see below), because they give a party an incentive to breach if, and only if, the cost of performance for the promisor exceeds the value of performance for the promisee.[5]

The idea that contract damages have an economic rationale has been criticised. It does not fit with any of the many theories of contract law that regard contracts as based on moral or normative principles of one sort or another (see **2.15**). There are also more practical objections. One serious criticism is that there is no 'all or nothing' choice, either to breach the contract and pay damages or to perform the contract. Rather than breach and pay damages, a contract renegotiation may be more efficient. There may be other stronger incentives to perform a contract than the threat of being asked to pay damages, especially when parties are in a long-term relationship, rather than involved in a one-off transaction. This approach may also underestimate the role of transaction costs in litigation or arbitration. These can be very high and, in many cases, the incentive not to breach a contract is equal to the threat of having to pay expectation damages. In any event, the Australian courts have been lukewarm about the efficient breach theory: see eg *Tabcorp Holdings v Bowen Investments* (2009) at [13].

23.03   The assessment of loss: an overview

The assessment of damages for breach of contract essentially involves settling on a monetary amount that will compensate the plaintiff for the fact that the defendant has failed to perform as promised. When damages are awarded in tort, they seek to restore the plaintiff to the position they would have been in had the tort never happened. But damages for breach of contract are generally forward-looking. As we explain at **23.06**, damages in contract generally seek to put the plaintiff in *the position they expected to be in if the contract had been performed*. The rules that have developed to achieve this objective are discussed in more detail later in the chapter. For now, we simply offer an overview.

Most damages awards in contract cover two broad types of loss: direct and consequential. The first category covers the loss of benefits directly expected from performance. Depending on the type of contract and the type of breach, the common law has developed certain guidelines, or rules of thumb, as to how such benefits should be quantified. So, for example, a failure to deliver goods or convey land will generally be compensated by reference to the extra cost (if any) of finding a substitute – or, to put it another way, the difference between the contract price and the market price, but only if the latter is higher. If a defendant fails to complete work, or to complete it to a required standard, the standard assumption is that they must compensate the plaintiff for the cost of engaging someone else to finish it off or make repairs.

Consequential loss means any other type of loss that is caused by a breach. For example, it might include the loss of profits that the plaintiff hoped to make as a result of goods or work supplied by the defendant. Or it might be personal injury or damage to property suffered as a result of shoddy work or defective goods. Or it could be costs associated with looking for substitute goods, land or services, beyond the direct cost of that substitute.

---

5   The literature on this topic is vast. Some accessible examples include Macneil 1982 and Posner 2003.

Importantly, however, not all losses that flow from a breach will be compensated. For example, damages for *non-pecuniary loss* (such as pain and suffering) caused by a breach are not generally recoverable in contract law. Some types of loss, especially of a consequential nature, are considered too *remote* from the breach to be compensable. And the doctrine of *mitigation* means, among other things, that damages cannot be claimed for loss that the plaintiff could reasonably have avoided. In some situations too, damages may be reduced by reference to any *contributory negligence* on the plaintiff's part.

Although damages may take different forms, they are always designed to compensate and not to punish. Australian courts may sometimes, in limited circumstances, award *punitive damages* in tort: see eg *Gray v Motor Accident Compensation Commission* (1998). But punitive or 'exemplary' damages are never awarded for breach of contract: *Addis v Gramophone* (1909); *Butler v Fairclough* (1917) at 89.[6]

23.04   Damages and termination

In order to claim damages, it is unnecessary for the contract to be terminated. As a matter of common law, only the breach of an essential or intermediate term, or a repudiation, allow the victim to terminate the contract: see **16.05–16.17**. But even the breach of a non-essential term creates a right to claim damages. When the breach is of a kind which potentially gives a right to terminate and yet the contract is affirmed, the right to claim damages is not lost by the act of affirming. However, in practice, a failure to terminate when it is possible to do so may amount to a failure to mitigate, and may reduce the amount of damages that can be awarded: see **23.18**.

Where a plaintiff does elect to terminate, this may open up the possibility of claiming *loss of bargain* damages. This means a claim for the loss of all the benefits that were expected under the contract, not just those immediately caused by the defendant's breach. The fact that the plaintiff has in a sense 'caused' that loss by electing to terminate will not disentitle them from making such a claim: *Sunbird Plaza Pty Ltd v Maloney* (1988) at 260–1. To illustrate the concept, suppose that a tenant is late paying their rent. If the landlord does not or cannot terminate, their only claim for damages is for the loss of the use of the money between the due date and the actual date of payment (see **23.22**), which will likely be very small. But if the landlord can terminate, they can now claim damages for the loss of the whole lease. That will typically mean a claim for rent for the remainder of the lease, less whatever they either have actually received or could reasonably have expected to receive from a substitute tenant over that period, but plus any costs in (for example) advertising for another tenant.[7]

23.05   Contractual provisions on damages

The right to damages for a particular type of breach may always be modified, or even excluded, by a contrary provision in the contract. *Exclusion* or *limitation clauses* of that

---

6   Punitive damages for breach of contracts have been resisted in other common law countries as well. An exception is Canada: see *Whiten v Pilot Insurance* (2002). For an argument that such damages *should* be available, see Coci 2015.

7   As to whether a similar claim could be made if the landlord were exercising an express right to terminate granted by the lease, rather than relying on a breach of essential term or a repudiation, see **16.18**.

kind are subject to the special rules of interpretation and statutory controls discussed in Chapter 11. That chapter also notes the use of *party–party indemnity* provisions that may have the effect of extending a right to damages, by removing the limits that the common law would otherwise place on claiming compensation for consequential loss: see **11.21**. Particularly in contracts between commercial parties, it is common too to find an agreement in advance which fixes a sum to be paid on breach. If the law designates this to be a *liquidated damages* clause, it is enforceable. However, if the clause is classified as a *penalty*, it is either void or, at the very least, can only be enforced up to the amount of the loss suffered: see **22.19–22.24**.

Compensable loss

23.06   Types of compensation: expectation, reliance and restitution

In a seminal article, Fuller and Perdue (1936) identified three types of loss or measures of loss that might occur as a result of a breach of contract. They called these the expectation measure, the reliance measure, and the restitutionary measure. This analysis has been criticised,[8] but the terminology remains useful.

The *expectation measure* describes the standard measure of compensation for breach of contract. Suppose A enters into a contract with B. As a result of the contract, they have an expectation that B will perform. If B fails to perform, damages are designed to put A in the position that they would have occupied had the contract been performed. The expectation measure is reflected in the classic statement of contract damages by Parke B in *Robinson v Harman* (1848) at 855:

> The rule of the common law is, that where a party sustains loss by reason of a breach of contract, he [sic] is so far as money can do it, to be placed in the same situation, with respect to damages, as if the contract had been performed.

This statement has been approved in Australia on numerous occasions, including by the High Court: see eg *Wenham v Ella* (1972) at 471; *Burns v MAN Automotive* (1986) at 667, 672; *Tabcorp Holdings v Bowen Investments* (2009) at [13].

The relationship between the *reliance measure* and expectation measure is often misunderstood. Suppose that A enters into a contract with B, and B fails to perform. Anticipating B's performance, A has spent money or incurred commitments. On a reliance measure, A's damages would *solely* reflect the extent of that detrimental reliance. They would be designed to put A in the position they would have been in, had the contract never happened. A's expenditure, however, can also be analysed as one part of a wider expectation measure. This would reflect the idea that contractual parties expect, in addition to making a profit or reaping certain benefits, to cover the costs of their expenditure.

Sometimes, the expectation and reliance measures give the same result; sometimes not. The point can be illustrated with examples.

---

8   See eg Craswell 2000.

Example 1

A contracts to buy a car from B for $10,000. The market value of a car of this kind is $10,000. The value of the car delivered, which is defective or different to the one promised, is $6,000. The expectation measure is worked out on the basis of what A expected to receive if the contract had been performed; namely, a car worth $10,000. Damages are calculated by deducting the value of the thing contracted for (the market value) from the value of what was actually delivered, which in the example is $10,000 – $6,000 = $4,000.

The reliance measure would be worked out on the basis that the contract was never entered into. A would never have parted with $10,000 and never received a car worth $6,000. Damages would be calculated by deducting what was actually received from what was paid, that is, $10,000 – $6,000 = $4,000. In this example, the result is the same, because the contract price reflects the market price. But often this is not the case.

Example 2

A contracts to buy a car from B for $10,000. A car of the sort promised costs $8,000 in the market. The car delivered is worth $6,000. Expectation damages are calculated by deducting the value of the car received from the market value of a car of the kind promised: $8,000 – $6,000 = $2,000.

Reliance damages would be calculated by deducting the value of the car delivered from the sum paid: $10,000 – $6,000 = $4,000. In this example, the plaintiff, if able to claim reliance damages, could escape from the effects of their own bad bargain in which they have paid over the market value for the item purchased. If contract remedies are about giving the victim of the breach the equivalent of the other party's performance, it looks odd to protect reliance.[9] Reliance damages here would give the victim of a breach more than they were promised or could expect. This apparent paradox may explain why the reliance measure has either been rolled up into expectation damages, or pushed to the margins.

The *restitutionary measure* is quite different from the other two. It is calculated on the basis of a gain, such as a profit, made by the party in breach, rather than a loss suffered by the victim. As a remedy for breach of contract, the restitutionary measure is distinct from the restitutionary remedies discussed in Chapter 24.[10] But the shared terminology captures the idea of stripping the other party of a gain. Suppose A enters into a contract with B, and B fails to perform. In exceptional cases, the English courts at least have accepted that damages are not just compensatory, but may also reflect any gain made by B. That gain might be the profit B makes by breaching their contract with A, and entering into an alternative contract with C.

In practice, the expectation measure is the most important. Damages can only be recovered on the basis of reliance in limited circumstances. The restitutionary measure has no place in Australia thus far. Each measure of damages is examined further below in reverse order of importance.

---

9   See McLauchlan 2007.
10   For analysis of gain-based damages in terms of 'disgorgement' rather than restitution, see eg Edelman 2002; K Barnett 2012.

23.07 Gain-based damages

Gain-based damages are not really damages at all. They reflect a gain made by the party in breach and not a loss suffered. As a result, they fall outside traditional categories of contract damages. A gain-based remedy for breach of contract is closer to the action of *account of profits* that is available in equity for breach of trust or another fiduciary duty than it is to contract damages. It was therefore a surprise when, in *Attorney-General v Blake* (2000), the majority of the House of Lords awarded a gain-based remedy for breach of contract. The facts were unusual. Blake worked for British intelligence, but was also a Soviet spy. He escaped to Russia and had his memoirs published by Jonathan Cape. Having committed to observe the *Official Secrets Act 1911* (UK) as part of his contract of employment, Blake was liable for breach of contract by writing the book. It revealed information that he had originally obtained in confidence, but had since been published by other writers. The government suffered no pecuniary losses by the publication of the book. In the leading speech for the majority, however, Lord Nicholls stressed that gain-based damages could be justified when the plaintiff had a strong interest in ensuring performance. He observed that the undertaking of confidentiality in the contract of employment was similar to a fiduciary duty of confidentiality, which did give rise to a duty to account. The majority held that such damages were exceptional. This outcome has been widely criticised.[11] In England, later judgments have restricted gain-based damages: see eg *Experience Hendrix v PPX Enterprises* (2003). As Lord Hobhouse pointed out in his dissent in *Blake*, this new head of damages introduced uncertainty, and he was not prepared to change the existing position in order to reach an outcome that could be justified by public policy on the particular facts.

Australian judges have shown no appetite for introducing a gain-based remedy for breach of contract. In *Hospitality Group v Australian Rugby Union* (2001) at [159], Hill and Finkelstein JJ observed that:

> The position in Australia is that the loss recoverable for breach of contract is limited to that laid down in *Robinson v Harman*. That is the aggrieved party is entitled only to compensation. If he [sic] has suffered no loss, he is not entitled to compensation. In an appropriate case, the aggrieved party may be able to recover the price paid under an incomplete contract or recover possession of goods sold but not paid for. Presently, however, it would be inconsistent with the current practice laid down by the High Court to confer a windfall on a plaintiff under the guise of damages for breach of contract.

Other authorities have taken a similar position: see eg *Australian Medic-Care v Hamilton Pharmaceutical* (2009). For now at least, there seems little prospect of the Australian courts adopting the restitutionary measure as a remedy for breach of contract.

23.08 Reliance damages

Reliance damages do not fit easily within the law of contract. If contractual liability is founded on the idea of expected performance, then reliance damages are difficult to justify. This may

---

11   See eg Doyle & Wright 2001; Campbell & Wylie 2003.

explain why it is not open to the victim of a breach of contract to choose a reliance measure over the standard expectation measure, when this would give them an advantage. Nor can both losses be recovered at the same time. However, there will be some occasions where it is not possible to award expectation damages, and as a result the reliance measure comes into play. One of these rare cases was *McRae v Commonwealth Disposals Commission* (1951). The plaintiff contracted with the defendant to salvage an oil tanker said to contain oil, claimed to be stranded on the Journmaund Reef. The plaintiff equipped a vessel and sent it from Sydney to where the oil tanker ought to have been. No such tanker or reef existed. As explained in **18.41**, there was a breach of contract because the contract contained an implied term that the tanker existed. The usual expectation measure was not appropriate. Such damages were impossible to quantify. Even if the ship had existed, it was by no means certain that it would have been found and, even if located, that it could have been salvaged at a profit. Damages were accordingly awarded to cover the costs of purchasing the salvage ship and other expenditure undertaken in reliance on the contract. There was no conflict with the rule that, in contract law, damages are awarded for loss of expectation, because there was no quantifiable way here of measuring that expectation.[12]

This limited role for a separate category of reliance damages is consistent with remarks by Toohey J in *Commonwealth v Amann Aviation* (1991) at 137, where he said that, '[r]eliance damages are a means of compensating the plaintiff where there has been no loss of profit, or more likely, where the plaintiff cannot prove loss of profit with any certainty'. As Mason CJ and Dawson J pointed out in the same decision (at 81), in normal commercial dealings the parties will expect to recoup expenditure and secure a profit:

> [E]xpectation damages are often described as damages for loss of profits. Damages recoverable as lost profits are constituted by the combination of expenses justifiably incurred by the plaintiff in the discharge of contractual obligations and any amount by which gross receipts would have exceeded those expenses. The second amount is net profit.

So where damages are awarded in respect of expenditure incurred in reliance on a contract being performed, that is usually as an element within the expectation measure. Suppose, for example, that a builder contracts to do some work for a total fee of $20,000 and spends $8,000 in partially performing the contract. The client then repudiates the contract with the work incomplete. Assuming the builder's obligation is entire, they cannot sue for the contract price as a debt: see **12.08**. The builder's claim for damages will include the $8,000 spent, but it must also take account of any profit or loss the builder expected to make. So if the builder expected to spend $17,000, the total award will be $11,000 (minus any deposit or part-payments the builder has received). But if the builder has made a bad contract and would need to spend $22,000 on the work, the damages claim will fall to $6,000 to reflect that anticipated loss. The builder cannot here insist on recovering their reliance loss alone.[13]

---

12   For a further example, see *World Best Holdings v Sarkar* (2010).
13   The builder may, however, have an alternative claim in restitution for reasonable remuneration: see **17.09**.

23.09 Expectation damages

Amann Aviation remains the fullest statement to date on the nature of contract damages by the High Court.[14] Amann Aviation entered into a contract with the Commonwealth to conduct aerial coastal surveillance for three years. A clause in the contract gave the Secretary for the Department of Transport power to serve a notice and require the company, if they failed to perform the contract satisfactorily, to show cause why the contract should not be terminated. The Commonwealth served a notice that was invalid under the contract. Amann treated the notice as a repudiatory breach, and terminated the contract. Amann had spent a great deal of money on surveillance equipment, including specially adapted aircraft. In consequence of the breach, this expenditure was wasted. The aircraft could be sold, but for much less than had been spent on them, and the company was forced to make redundancy payments to employees. The cost to Amann of all these items was $5.5 million. If the contract had not been terminated, it would have had to incur further operating expenditure of approximately $15.8 million for the rest of the contract, while receipts under the contract would have been $17.1 million. Even allowing for the return of a deposit, and that no redundancy payments would have been made had the contract been performed, the potential profit was still less than the expenditure likely to be incurred. The Commonwealth contended that Amann's damages should be nominal. It argued to restrict damages to the difference between the amount Amann would have spent performing the contract, had no breach occurred, and the agreed payments, plus the redundancy payments which would have been saved had the contract been duly performed.

A majority of the High Court accepted that if the contract had been performed for its full term, then it would not have yielded an overall profit. The payments that Amann would have received had the breach not occurred would not have exceeded further expenditure incurred to earn those payments. They had incurred significant pre-breach expenditure, and that should be included in the calculation. But account also had to be taken of Amann's prospects of securing a renewal of its contract with the Commonwealth. This conclusion reflected the commercial reality of the contract, which involved high set-up costs with the prospect of large profits on renewal of the contract. It flowed from how the damages were characterised. In the absence of a profit, Amann's claim could have been treated as one for reliance damages. On this characterisation, damages would reflect the money expended in preparing to perform the contract that was ultimately wasted. Yet, this was not how the damages were characterised. The majority held that the damages fell within the expectation measure described in *Robinson v Harman* (1848). This result was achieved by a presumption that Amann would at least have recovered its expenditure if the contract had been fully performed. The burden of displacing the presumption fell on the defendant. In order to displace the presumption, the defendant had to establish that Amann's expenditure would have been wasted, even if the contract had been performed. It was held that this burden had not been discharged, even though gross receipts under the contract were some $3.9 million less than the expenses to be incurred by Amann. Stress was placed on the strong prospect of renewal, and the fact that the expenditure loss was within the parties' contemplation as a probable consequence of the breach.

---

14   For a reappraisal of the decision and the approaches adopted by different members of the court, see Winterton 2016.

As already explained, the standard expectation measure of damages for breach of contract reflects the profits that the victim would have received had the contract been performed. *Amann Aviation* was unusual, as the profits contemplated by the parties were calculated on the likelihood that the contract would be renewed. Other types of loss are difficult to fit within the standard expectation measure because they are calculated differently, or because they do not conform to the general economic type of loss usually awarded for breach of contract. Some approaches to damages are context-specific.

23.10   Damages in contracts for the sale of goods and land

Contracts for the sale of goods are governed by legislation in all States and Territories. The statutes lay down rules for the assessment of damages which effectively codify the approach that would be taken at common law. For example, the general rule for assessing damages for non-delivery is that the buyer is entitled to all losses that are a direct and natural result of the seller's breach.[15] This corresponds with the first limb of the general remoteness rule in *Hadley v Baxendale* (1854), discussed below at **23.16**. This will ordinarily be measured as the difference between the contract price and the market price at the time the goods were supposed to be delivered.[16] That measure effectively incorporates the requirements of the doctrine of mitigation, discussed at **23.18**. But when the buyer has already agreed to resell the goods at a price exceeding the market price, then damages are calculated as the difference between the contract price and the resale price: *Joseph v Harvest Grain* (1996). In the absence of an available market, the value of the goods is determined by the court: *Tallerman v Nathan's Merchandise* (1957) at 128. In addition, 'special damages' can be awarded which do not arise as a 'direct and natural result' of a breach, corresponding with the second limb of the general remoteness rule in *Hadley v Baxendale*. Buyers are usually able to buy replacement goods in the market, and hence a cost of correction measure is not usually appropriate, unless no substitute is actually available.[17] The principles that apply for assessing damages for non-delivery also apply when there is no right to reject defective goods or the right is not exercised.

Standard rules also apply to contracts for the sale of land. A breach may occur through a failure to convey the land, late delivery of the land or a failure to provide good title. The same general principles apply as for the sale of goods. The ordinary measure of damages is the difference in value between the contract price of the land and the market value of equivalent land at the time that conveyance was due. This general measure can be supplemented or replaced in some instances. In *Wenham v Ella* (1972), a purchaser was entitled to an additional

---

15   *Sale of Goods Act 1923* (NSW) s 53(2); *Goods Act 1958* (Vic) s 57(2); *Sale of Goods Act 1896* (Qld) s 52(2) ; *Sale of Goods Act 1895* (WA) s 50(2); *Sale of Goods Act 1895* (SA) s 50(2); *Sale of Goods Act 1896* (Tas) s 55(2); *Sale of Goods Act 1954* (ACT) s 56(2); *Sale of Goods Act 1972* (NT) s 53(2).

16   *Sale of Goods Act 1923* (NSW) s 53(3); *Goods Act 1958* (Vic) s 57(3); *Sale of Goods Act 1896* (Qld) s 52(3) ; *Sale of Goods Act 1895* (WA) s 50(3); *Sale of Goods Act 1895* (SA) s 50(3); *Sale of Goods Act 1896* (Tas) s 55(3); *Sale of Goods Act 1954* (ACT) s 54(3); *Sale of Goods Act 1972* (NT) s 53(3).

17   There seems to be no Australian authority on this point, but a recent English case confirms that cost of correction damages can be awarded under the equivalent, and similarly worded English legislation: *Hirtenstein v Hill Dickinson* (2014) at [114]–[122]; Bridge 2017: [17–054].

sum, reflecting the income they would have earned from the property up to the date of judgment. A failure to convey the land will usually be remedied by specific performance rather than damages. There are also a number of special restrictions on damages. For example, what is commonly called the rule in *Bain v Fothergill* (1874) restricts liability in damages for a failure to provide good title to land. The purchaser can generally only claim the expenses they have incurred in investigating title: see eg *Noske v McGinnis* (1932). This rule has been abolished completely in New South Wales, and in Queensland and the Northern Territory it does not apply when the land is registered.[18]

23.11   Cost of correction

The decisions under this head are usually concerned with building contracts, where the work is done badly. One way to measure the property owner's expectation loss would be to calculate the difference between the value of the property as it is following the work, and the value it would have had if the work had been performed correctly. Yet, this market value approach may fail to give proper recognition to the personal preferences of the house owner. If a builder is contracted to build a house in a certain style and fails to do so, the house may have the same market value, so that the owner appears to have suffered no loss – but they have not got what they contracted to receive. The general approach then in this situation is to measure the owner's loss in a different way, by awarding the *cost of correction*.[19] This will reflect what it would cost to remedy the defect by engaging a third party to rectify the work.[20]

In *Bellgrove v Eldridge* (1954), a contract to construct a house set down certain specifications for the cement to be used in the construction. The specifications were not followed. As a result of this breach, the house was unstable. The builder argued that, despite the unsecure foundations, the house could still be sold and damages should reflect the difference between the value of the house as constructed, and the market value of the house had the contract not been breached. The High Court rejected this argument and instead awarded damages by reference to the cost of correction, even though that would exceed what the owner had originally contracted to pay for the work. The Court stressed that such damages would only be awarded when it was 'reasonable' and 'necessary'. On the facts here, the only way to ensure that the performance conformed with the contract was to demolish the house and rebuild it. However, it was stressed that it was unnecessary for the plaintiff to show that they would actually use the money to remedy the defect. A plaintiff was not normally required to show how they planned to spend a damages award, and this case was no different. The High Court gave two examples of claims for cost of correction with different outcomes. In the first, a room was painted a different colour from that specified in the contract. The plaintiff would be entitled to the cost of repainting the room. In a second example, cost of correction damages would not be awarded when the parties contracted to build a house in second-hand bricks,

---

18   *Conveyancing Act 1919* (NSW) s 54B; *Property Law Act 1974* (Qld) s 68; *Law of Property Act 2000* (NT) s 70.

19   For a rationalisation of this approach, see eg Ren 2014.

20   Note that where the process of rectification helps produce something that is more valuable than the plaintiff originally had or contracted to receive, such 'betterment' may, if unjustified, call for an offset to any damages awarded: see eg *Gwam Investments v Outback Health Screenings* (2010); *Walker Group Constructions v Tzaneros Investments* (2017).

and new bricks were used. The first example suggests that personal preference is relevant when determining whether to award cost of correction damages. The second scenario shows that a preference is only allowed to go so far. Sometimes, it would be wholly unreasonable to allow the preference to be reflected in the award of cost of correction damages.

Whether or not cost of correction damages are reasonable and necessary is a question of fact. In *Bellgrove v Eldridge* (1954), it was not too difficult to regard rectification as both reasonable and necessary. A good contrary example can be found in the English House of Lords decision, *Ruxley Electronics and Constructions v Forsyth* (1996). The defendant entered into a contract with the plaintiff to build him a swimming pool. Under the terms of the contract, the pool was to be 7 feet 6 inches at the deep end. The pool actually built was 6 feet 9 inches at that end, a depth that was still safe for diving and swimming. To increase the depth to the contractual agreed amount would cost £21,650. The difference in value between a pool of 7 feet 6 inches and the one actually built was trivial. A claim for cost of correction failed. The reasoning was not entirely clear, but seemed to turn on the view of the House of Lords that the cost of correction was wholly disproportionate to any resulting benefit.[21] Instead, the plaintiff was entitled to a smaller sum for 'loss of amenity'. As explained below, these damages fall within the rare instances where mental distress, in the form of a loss of pleasure from the pool not being the contracted depth, might be awarded.[22]

In *Westpoint Management v Chocolate Factory Apartments* (2007) at [59], it was suggested that, in order to be reasonable, it was relevant to consider whether or not the plaintiff intended to carry out the work.[23] This argument seems to run counter to what was said in *Bellgrove v Eldridge* (1954). In *Tabcorp Holdings v Bowen Investments* (2009), the High Court took a fairly expansive view of cost of correction damages. A lease of some offices contained a covenant (promise) that the lessor was not to alter the office without permission from the landlord. The tenant commenced the work before permission was granted. The difference between the modified and non-modified building was $43,820. The cost of restoring the building to its original condition was $1.38 million. It was held that the landlord was entitled to the cost of restoring the property.[24] French CJ, Gummow, Heydon, Crennan and Kiefel JJ stated (at [13]) that:

> [I]n cases where the contract is not for the sale of marketable commodities, selling the defective item and purchasing an item corresponding with the contract is not possible. In such cases, diminution in value damages will not restore the innocent party to the 'same situation . . . as if the contract had been performed'.

They went on to suggest (at [17]) that it would only be in 'fairly exceptional circumstances', such as those in *Ruxley*, that it would be unreasonable to award cost of correction damages.

---

21   For a further example, see *Stone v Chappel* (2017) (apartment ceiling height 40mm less than the 2700mm specified in the building plans).
22   One way of characterising a damages award of this type is that it reflects the 'consumer surplus' – that is, the personal and subjective value to a promisee of performance, over and above the extent by which their financial position will be improved: see Harris et al 1979; Mullen 2016.
23   See also *Condon Investments v Lesdor Properties* (2012).
24   For further examples, see *Metricon Homes v Softley* (2016); *Walker Group Constructions v Tzaneros Investments* (2017).

An example would be the innocent party 'merely using a technical breach to secure an uncovenanted profit'.

23.12   Loss of a chance

The standard expectation measure is premised on the occurrence of a particular outcome if the contract is performed. Damages are assessed by looking at the difference between the promised outcome and the actual outcome. Sometimes it is impossible to know what the outcome will be, even if the contract had been performed. *McRae v Commonwealth Disposals Commission* (1951), as explained earlier, provides an example. This was a rare case in which it was appropriate to award reliance damages. There are other situations where there is a lower level of uncertainty. A particular outcome cannot be predicted, but the *chance* of a particular outcome is something that can be determined. Instead of proving on the balance of probabilities that a particular outcome would have occurred, the plaintiff is able to show that there was a chance of a particular outcome. The way that loss of chance damages are claimed can be illustrated by two authorities. The first has an unusual set of facts. The second demonstrates the same principles in a commercial context.

The defendant in *Chaplin v Hicks* (1911) ran a beauty contest. The prize for the 12 highest-ranked contestants was to be engaged at a theatre. The plaintiff was selected for the final 50 to be interviewed, out of 6,000 applications. In breach of the contract she had signed when entering the competition, the defendant failed to notify the plaintiff that she had been selected for an interview. She was therefore excluded from the opportunity to reach the final 12. It could not be proved that she would have been one of the final 12. Nevertheless, the defendant's breach deprived the plaintiff of the opportunity of winning the competition. There was no certainty that the plaintiff would win, but she lost the chance to try. This was enough. Damages could be assessed on the basis of her chance of being 1 of the 12. Such a chance was much less than 50 per cent. The probability was just under 25 per cent. Given the numbers involved and the variables at stake, making an estimate of chance was not particularly difficult. Provided that the chance can be calculated, then any loss of a chance can form the basis of a claim.[25]

The second decision, *Sellars v Adelaide Petroleum* (1994), was a claim under the forerunner of the Australian Consumer Law (ACL), the *Trade Practices Act 1974* (Cth). Adelaide Petroleum entered into negotiations with two companies, Poseidon and Pagini Resources NL, for a sale of the directors' shareholding as part of a restructure. At the point that an agreement with Pagini was close, Sellars, a Poseidon executive, made a more favourable offer that was accepted. It then transpired that Sellars had exceeded his authority, and Poseidon would not comply with every aspect of the heads of agreement it had signed. This act was treated as repudiating the contract. Adelaide Petroleum resumed negotiations with Pagini. In a claim under what is now s 18 of the ACL, Adelaide Petroleum argued that, as a result of the contract and breach by Poseidon, they had lost the chance of a better deal with Pagini. The High Court held that the law recognised the loss of a commercial opportunity in the legislation, and observed (at 355) that the same principles would apply to a claim for breach of contract.

---

25   For a further example, see *Howe v Teefy* (1927).

There was a 40 per cent chance that, had it not been for the contract with Poseidon, a better deal would have been brokered with Pagini. This is a two-stage process. Once the loss of commercial opportunity had been shown on the balance of probabilities, as with all types of loss, the value of that loss of opportunity is calculated as a degree of probability.[26]

23.13   Damages for non-pecuniary loss

Almost all contract damages reflect economic loss of some sort. For example, as a result of the breach of contract, one party is denied a profit and therefore suffers a pecuniary loss. A breach of contract may also cause non-pecuniary losses as a result of distress, inconvenience, or anxiety. While non-pecuniary awards are perfectly standard in the law of tort, the law of contract has always resisted giving damages for non-pecuniary loss: see eg *Hamlin v Great Northern Railway* (1856). A number of arguments have been suggested to explain this approach. Non-pecuniary losses are intangible. The extent of someone's distress is incapable of precise proof. It is difficult to assess in monetary terms. Yet, the courts manage to do this in tort law for cases of psychiatric injury. Even in contract law, it is sometimes possible to be awarded damages for non-pecuniary loss. In *Ruxley Electronics and Constructions v Forsyth* (1996), as noted above, damages for loss of amenity were awarded. It is sometimes argued that, if non-pecuniary losses are allowed, all claims for breach of contract will contain an allegation of distress under the head of damages. There may be some truth in this statement, but certainly distress and anxiety would not be relevant where a business was the plaintiff. As with all types of contract damages, non-pecuniary loss would need to be within the reasonable contemplation of the parties. This hurdle may be more difficult in the case of non-pecuniary loss.[27]

In *Baltic Shipping v Dillon* (1993), the High Court reviewed the case law on non-pecuniary losses. The rule that they cannot generally be recovered was confirmed. Mason CJ in particular expressed some misgivings about the rule. He explained that the rule was based on policy, but (at 362) he said that:

> We are then left with a rule which rests on flimsy policy foundations and conceptually is at odds with the fundamental principle governing the recovery of damages, the more so now that the approaches in tort and contract are converging.

The High Court accepted, however, that there were a number of exceptions in which non-pecuniary losses *can* be compensated through an award of damages for breach of contract. Three are quite important. The simplest case occurs when a breach of contract causes a physical injury and emotional distress is consequent on the physical injury: see eg *David Jones v Willis* (1934). A second category covers distress consequent on physical 'inconvenience' occasioned by the defendant's breach. This too can be the subject of an award: see eg *Hobbs v London and South Western Railway* (1875); *Athens-Macdonald Travel v Kazis* (1970); but compare *Thorpe v Lochel* (2005). The mere fact that a plaintiff is put to time and trouble in dealing with the consequences of a breach of contract does not fall within this exception. There has to be an element of *physical* imposition: see eg *Archibald v Powlett* (2017).

---

26   For a further example, see *Mal Owen Consulting v Ashcroft* (2018).
27   For a discussion of these issues, see Enonchong 1996.

The third exception, covering distress which is not consequent on injury or physical inconvenience, is more problematic. An exception to the rule of no recovery, which the High Court endorsed in *Baltic Shipping*, was created by the English Court of Appeal in *Jarvis v Swan Tours* (1973). It covers the situation, as the High Court noted in *Baltic Shipping* (at 363), 'where the very object of the contract has been to provide pleasure, relaxation or freedom from molestation'. This typically applies when a contract to provide a holiday falls short of what was promised. The phrase 'very object of the contract' is, however, ambiguous. The majority of the House of Lords chose to interpret this condition broadly in *Farley v Skinner* (2001) at [23], where it was held to be enough if a 'major or important' object of the contract was to provide 'pleasure, relaxation or freedom from molestation'.[28]

Australian decisions in this area have been rather circumspect. *Falko v James McEwan* (1977) is typical. The plaintiff purchased a heater from the defendant, who was to install it for an agreed amount. When the electrician came to fit it, he demanded an extra $5 for installing a new power point, which the plaintiff refused to pay. The plaintiff instead set up a temporary lead to the heater. The cost of remedying the defect and fitting the heater was $11, yet the Magistrates Court awarded $400 for distress. This award was overturned. Anderson J observed (at 452) that '[n]ot every inconvenienced or disappointed plaintiff or disgruntled customer can recover damages beyond monetary loss for breach of contract. There may be signs of some judicial thaw but spring is yet to come'.

A final exception to the rule of no recovery concerns a breach of contract which damages a plaintiff's reputation. An action in tort for defamation would usually be the remedy in such a case. In *Baltic Shipping* at 370, Brennan J accepted that damages to reputation as a result of a direct breach of contract may in general be awarded. But for employment contracts, there is a special (if much-criticised) rule. A wrongfully dismissed employee cannot claim damages for any damage to their reputation caused by either the fact or manner of their dismissal: *Addis v Gramophone* (1909); *Russell v Archdiocese of Sydney* (2008) at [51]–[57]; although compare *Quinn v Gray* (2009).[29]

In *Baltic Shipping* itself, Ms Dillon was a passenger on a cruise ship. The ship sank part way through the cruise. There was no difficulty in allowing her to recover damages for distress. She had suffered physical injury and inconvenience. The very object of the contract was also undoubtedly to provide relaxation. The accepted exceptions are broad enough, therefore, to considerably undermine the exclusory rule.

The availability of a remedy is tempered, however, by the *Civil Liability Acts* in many jurisdictions, which place limits on damages in cases where the loss is an 'impairment of a person's mental condition'.[30] These provisions have been held to apply to breach of contract claims, not just those in tort: see eg *Insight Vacations v Young* (2010).[31] However, for the legislation to apply, the obligation breached must be one that involves a duty to take reasonable care, as opposed to a strict liability: see *New South Wales v Ibbett* (2005) at [117]; *BGC Residential v Fairwater* (2012).

---

28   For an example of damages being award for breach of a non-molestation covenant, see *Silberman v Silberman* (1910).

29   See further Keesing 2012.

30   See eg *Civil Liability Act 2002* (NSW) s 16.

31   But see Walker & Lewins 2014.

Restrictions on recovery

23.14   Introduction

The fact that a particular type of loss can potentially be recovered for breach of contract doesn't mean that it will actually be recovered. Although many losses may flow from a breach of contract, the law places restrictions around damages that can be awarded. For a start, the plaintiff needs to show, on the balance of probabilities, that the defendant *caused* the loss. Causation is usually not contested. Two further restrictions are more significant. The rules of *remoteness* were developed by the courts to place some sort of limits on the damages that the plaintiff can recover. The classic statement of the rules of remoteness in contract law is found in *Hadley v Baxendale* (1854). It remains influential today, but the courts have struggled with its application. The third major restriction on recovery is contained in the *mitigation* rules. Even if it is accepted that the damage was caused by the breach and was not too remote, the plaintiff is still required to mitigate their loss. Mitigation reduces the amount of damages where, among other things, the plaintiff has failed to act reasonably in response to the breach.

23.15   Causation

Causation has caused the courts great difficulties in the law of tort, but in contract law it is rarely a problem. In most instances, it is clear that the defendant's breach caused the plaintiff's loss. Causation, which is a question of fact, provides the link between breach and loss. Judges may differ, however, on how seriously they take causation. In *Reg Glass v Rivers Locking Systems* (1968), the defendants agreed to supply and install a burglar-proof door. However, the door was not reasonably fit for that purpose. Burglars broke into the premises and stole the plaintiff's stock. The plaintiff brought an action for breach of contract, claiming losses for the stolen stock. Windeyer and Owen JJ pointed out in dissent that it could not be demonstrated that, even if the door had complied with the warranty, the thieves would not have gained entry. On the traditional 'but for' test, which asks, but for the breach would the loss have occurred, the claim failed. The majority judges, Barwick CJ, McTiernan and Menzies JJ, conceded that it could not be proved that burglars would not have gained entry even if the door was fit for purpose. Yet they accepted that the loss was caused by the breach, and therefore the claim succeeded.

Particular difficulties arise when the plaintiff's loss occurs partly as a result of the defendant's breach, and partly as a result of some other factor. One of the concurrent causes may be an act of the plaintiff. Sometimes this may be sufficient to break the chain of causation between the breach and the loss, as in *Lexmead (Basingstoke) v Lewis* (1982). The defendant supplied a defective towing hitch that led to an accident for which the plaintiff was liable to a third party. It was held that the plaintiff could not recover against the defendant in breach of contract, because the plaintiff had become aware, or ought to have been aware, that the coupling mechanism was damaged and had failed to repair it or check it was safe to use.[32]

Causation becomes more difficult when the breach is a cause of loss, but some factor external to the contract was a concurrent cause, as in *Alexander v Cambridge Credit* (1987).

---

32   See also *Chand v Commonwealth Bank* (2015).

In 1971, the auditors of Cambridge Credit failed to note in their annual audit certificates that the balance sheet and other accounts were missing key provisions. Had the appropriate note been made, it was highly probable that a receiver would have been appointed. It was argued that, had an auditor been appointed at that stage, rather than in 1974, the losses of the company would have been lower, and therefore the breach of the auditor's contract caused the loss. There was some agreement about the principles to be applied. It was accepted that the breach did not have to be the cause, or the dominant cause, of the loss. There can be multiple causes. It was enough if the breach was *a* cause of loss. The fact that there were other concurrent causes did not in itself mean the breach did not cause loss. On the facts, the other concurrent causes included the way that the company was run, and economic factors relating to the property market outside the control of the company that impacted on their business in real estate. Glass JA applied the 'but for' test, though he noted (at 315) that it was to be used in a 'practical commonsense' way. McHugh JA agreed with the 'practical commonsense' view, but observed (at 351) that it was ultimately a question of whether the breach 'causally contributed' to the damage. He described (at 358) the 'but for' test as 'only a guide'. Mahoney JA was critical of the 'but for' test. He said (at 335) that there are 'insuperable difficulties in accepting it as the definitive test of causality in the law' and favoured the idea of a 'causal field' instead. This would be a broader inquiry, including matters of policy. In practice, there may be little difference between this formula and the one used by McHugh JA and Glass JA. Nevertheless, on the facts, Glass JA felt that the 'but for' test was satisfied, whereas the majority held that the breach did not cause the losses. The decision suggests that the causal test will be applied flexibly.[33]

23.16   Remoteness: the traditional test

Having shown that the defendant caused loss, the plaintiff is required to show that their losses are not too remote. The modern law is derived from a passage in the judgment of Alderman B in *Hadley v Baxendale* (1854) at 354:

> Where two parties have made a contract which one of them has broken, the damages which the other party ought to receive in respect of such breach of contract, should be such as may fairly and reasonably be considered, either arising naturally, i.e. according to the usual course of things from such breach of contract itself, or such as may reasonably be supposed to have been in the contemplation of both parties, at the time they made the contract as the probable result of the breach of it.

The easiest way to think about this formula is to say that the plaintiff has demonstrated that the loss suffered is not too remote, either because the losses:

(1)   arise naturally or as a result of the usual course of things; or

(2)   were otherwise within the reasonable contemplation of both parties at the time they entered into the contract.

---

33   For a further example, see *BGC Residential v Fairwater* (2012), where, on the balance of probabilities, it was held that a house would not have been destroyed by arson if site security had been provided as required by the parties' contract.

These two 'limbs' are commonly regarded as expressing one principle: see *Commonwealth v Amann Aviation* (1991) at 92; *European Bank v Evans* (2010) at [13]. As was explained in *Victoria Laundry v Newman Industries* (1949), losses that arise naturally are taken to be in the reasonable contemplation of the parties. Losses that do not arise naturally can also be within the reasonable contemplation of the parties, but only when special circumstances are known to both parties when making the contract.

On the facts of *Victoria Laundry*, a delay in providing a working boiler to a laundry business in breach of contract would cause a loss of profits in the ordinary course of events. It was not necessary for the defendant actually to realise that; it was enough that a reasonable person in their position would have reached such a conclusion. But to the extent that the plaintiff's lost profits were exceptional, being derived from some especially lucrative orders from the government, they could not be recovered unless those circumstances were in the reasonable contemplation of the parties. On the facts, the defendant did not have the requisite degree of knowledge to make the exceptional profits recoverable.

In *Hadley* itself, the defendant had agreed to transport a broken crankshaft from the plaintiff's flour mill to be repaired. The defendant was late in delivering the shaft and as a result the mill was closed for five days longer than it should have been. But the plaintiff's claim for damages for the profits lost over that period was rejected. In the Court's opinion, the defendant would not reasonably have expected, and had not been told, that there was no spare shaft and the mill would be unable to operate while the broken one was being repaired.

Reasonable contemplation should not be confused with reasonable foreseeability, which is used as the test for remoteness of loss in the tort of negligence. The degree of likelihood in contract and tort is quite different. In negligence, a 'slight possibility' of loss is enough for the loss not to be considered too remote: *The Wagon Mound* (1967) at 643–4. Slightly different formulas can be found in the contract case law, but all of them require a higher degree of probability. In *The Heron II* (1969) at 389, Lord Reid thought that the test was whether the loss was of a kind which the defendant at the time of the contract ought to have realised was 'not unlikely' to result from the breach. The words 'not unlikely' denoted 'a degree of probability considerably less than an even chance but nevertheless not very unusual and easily foreseeable'. Lord Morris suggested (at 405) that the correct expression was 'liable to result or at least not unlikely to result'; Lord Hodson favoured (at 410–11) 'liable to result'; whereas Lord Pearce (at 415) and Lord Upjohn (at 425) preferred the words 'a serious possibility' and 'real danger' as conveying the appropriate shade of meaning. In Australia, support has been expressed for the phrases 'not unlikely' (*Stuart v Condor Commercial Insulation* (2006) at [98]–[103]), a 'serious possibility' (*Alexander v Cambridge Credit* (1987) at 351, 363–7) and 'near certainty' or 'odds on probability' (*Wenham v Ella* (1972) at 471–2).

It is only necessary for a loss of a particular type to arise naturally or be in the reasonable contemplation of the parties. The extent of the loss need not be foreseen. In *Parsons (Livestock) v Uttley Ingham* (1978), the defendant supplied a hopper for storing pig nuts. In breach of contract, the hopper was not properly ventilated. The food had mould on it, and as a result the pigs became ill and many died. A claim was brought in contract for the loss of the pigs. The majority of the English Court of Appeal held that it was only necessary to see a type of loss as foreseeable, not the extent of the loss. It was foreseeable as a serious possibility that the pigs would become ill as a result of the breach. That was a sufficient degree of foresight. The death of the pigs was treated as a loss of the same type. Death was merely a matter of extent.

However, the division between type and extent is not entirely trouble free. In *Victoria Laundry*, for instance, it could be argued that if loss of profits were a type of loss, the exceptional profits differed only in extent, rather than type.

23.17 Remoteness: assumption of responsibility

Provided it is not treated as a penalty, or contravenes the legislation on unfair terms, the parties can always expressly allocate losses in the event of a breach of contract. But Lord Hoffmann went further in the English case, *The Achilleas* (2008). He argued (at [11]) that, even in the absence of an express provision, an allocation of risk between the parties, whilst not expressly agreed, might reflect 'particular types of contract arising out of general expectations in certain markets', and that these should trump the traditional remoteness test. The appellant chartered the respondent's vessel, The Achilleas, with redelivery to be on 2 May 2004. In April 2004, the ship owner agreed to a follow-on charter of the vessel to another company for $39,500 a day. That company was able to cancel if the vessel was not available on 8 May. The ship was delayed, and it was obvious that it would not be available by that date. The market rate for chartering had fallen, and the owner agreed to extend the cancellation date to 11 May and reduce the follow-on charter rate to $31,500 a day. The appellant did not have notice of this second charter. The respondent claimed damages for breach of contract for late redelivery amounting to $1,364,584, consisting of the $8,000 difference per day between the rate originally agreed for the second charter and the amount eventually received. The appellant argued that the loss was limited to the overrun period.

Lord Hoffmann thought the correct approach to damages flowed from the nature of contractual liability. He explained (at [12]):

> It seems to me logical to found liability for damages upon the intention of the parties (objectively ascertained) because all contractual liability is voluntarily undertaken. It must be in principle wrong to hold someone liable for risks for which the people entering into such a contract in their particular market, would not reasonably be considered to have undertaken.

On this approach, the orthodox remoteness test is just the starting point. Lord Hoffmann retained the test of what was reasonably contemplated (the inclusive principle expressed as two limbs in *Hadley v Baxendale*), but added another limb (an exclusive principle). The Court asks two questions rather than one:

(1) If damages are within the reasonable contemplation of the parties, however large, then they are recoverable.

(2) But a defendant can escape liability if the damages are not of the type for which they assumed responsibility, even if the damages are within the reasonable contemplation of the parties.

There are some unanswered questions. Lord Hoffmann still seemed to regard the orthodox approach as the starting point. But he suggested that there are some cases in which it does not provide a final answer. Such cases were described (at [11]) as 'unusual', because 'particular types of contract arising out of general expectations in certain markets, such as banking and shipping, are likely to be more common'. However, if Lord Hoffmann's approach follows from the nature of contractual liability, it is by no means clear why it should not apply to every type of contract.

Lord Hope agreed with Lord Hoffmann. Applying this test, the charterer had not accepted liability for the loss, because the general understanding in the shipping industry was that the charterer was only liable for loss during the overrun period, and the loss was out of its control and unquantifiable. Lord Rodger and Baroness Hale applied the conventional test and came up with the same outcome. For them, the issue was whether it was reasonably contemplated as a serious possibility at the time of contracting that, in the event of a breach by late delivery, a lucrative follow-on charter might be lost. Their Lordships thought that the answer to this question was 'no'. Although the orthodox test was used, the application is not very convincing. They were both commercial parties, well accustomed to dealing in the notoriously volatile charter market. It is difficult, however, to be certain what the decision stands for, because Lord Walker agreed with both sets of speeches.

The precise impact of *The Achilleas* is still being worked out in England.[34] Its status in Australia is unclear. There was support for Lord Hoffmann's approach by Basten JA in *Russell v Archdiocese of Sydney* (2008) at [61]–[62]. In *Evans & Associates v European Bank* (2009) at [58], Campbell JA referred approvingly to the idea of assumed responsibility, which he thought could be reconciled with the traditional remoteness test:

> It is consonant with A having undertaken a risk construed in that way that, if the event does not occur, A will be liable for those consequences of the breach that arise according to the usual course of things from the breach, and also for those consequences of the breach that would reasonably be supposed to be in the contemplation of both parties at the time they made the contract.

23.18   Mitigation of loss

The plaintiff is free to act as they wish in response to the other's breach. There is, strictly speaking, no enforceable *duty* to mitigate any loss likely to be suffered. But mitigation can still be relevant to the assessment of damages in at least three ways.

In the first place, the court will take into account the extent to which the plaintiff has in fact avoided or reduced the loss inflicted by the defendant's breach; for example, by entering into some form of substitute transaction: see eg *British Westinghouse v Underground Electric Railways* (1912); *Lucy v Commonwealth* (1923).[35] Second, the plaintiff can recover for any costs reasonably incurred in attempting to mitigate their loss; for example, in advertising for or arranging a substitute. Indeed, if reasonable attempts to mitigate inadvertently cause the plaintiff to suffer more loss than they would otherwise have done, the defendant can still be liable for that extra loss: see eg *Simonius Vischer v Holt* (1979).

Third, if the plaintiff fails to take reasonable steps to avoid or mitigate their losses on breach, they will be unable to recover that portion of the loss which is attributable to their

---

34   Peel 2015: [20–111].
35   But compare *Clark v Macourt* (2013), where a doctor who had agreed to purchase frozen sperm for use in her assisted reproductive technology business was able to recover the cost of finding an alternative supply, despite the fact that she was able to recoup that cost by charging her patients. The decision has been much debated: see eg Carter et al 2014a; Winterton 2014.

failure to mitigate. A number of explanations for this principle have been suggested,[36] not all of which are convincing. But the mitigation rule seems to reflect a general idea that the defendant has not caused the loss by their breach. Losses which result from a failure to mitigate can be attributed to the plaintiff.

The burden of showing that the plaintiff has not acted reasonably is placed on the defendant: *Burns v MAN Automotive* (1986) at 673. This burden is difficult to discharge, but there are instances in the case law. Where it is possible to obtain substitute performance, then it will usually be unreasonable not to do so: *Wenham v Ella* (1972) at 461, 464. It may even sometimes be unreasonable to refuse an offer of substitute performance from the defendant: *Castle Construction v Fekala* (2006). Doing nothing in response to a breach may amount to a failure to mitigate: see eg *Ardlethan Options v Easdown* (1915). It may also be unreasonable for a plaintiff not to walk away from a contract, rather than try and carry on despite the breach.

In *Burns*, the plaintiff road haulier bought a truck from the defendant through a hire purchase company. The defendant warranted that its engine had been fully reconditioned. This was not in fact the case, and the engine's faults caused considerable disruption to the buyer's business. A year after the purchase, the plaintiff became aware that the engine had not been fully reconditioned so that it could not be used on interstate routes. He was unable to afford the $8,000 cost of refurbishing it. The plaintiff was forced to limit his business to the less profitable local haulage business until the end of 1979, when the engine completely broke down, and the vehicle was repossessed by the hire purchase company. The plaintiff claimed for loss of profits.

Wilson, Deane, and Dawson JJ stressed that the hire purchase agreement could be terminated at any time and the plaintiff could have limited his losses of profit to the period before he became aware that the engine had not been reconditioned by returning the truck. On this reasoning, mitigation seems to shade into concerns that profits for the whole four years were too remote. Gibbs CJ, more explicitly, thought that the loss of profits was not too remote, but agreed that there was a failure to mitigate. It was not reasonable, he argued, for the plaintiff to carry on his business with the defective vehicle when he should have known that he had no prospect of making a profit. Brennan J, who dissented, held that the plaintiff had acted reasonably – even if in hindsight it turned out to be the wrong decision. As Brennan J pointed out, had he terminated the hire purchase agreement, he would have had considerable debts to the hire purchase company. It was not unreasonable for the plaintiff to use the short-haul business as a way of trading out of debt. By analogy, this decision suggests that, where the breach gives rise to a right to terminate, an unreasonable failure to terminate may amount to a failure to mitigate. Different principles may apply in debt, however, as opposed to damages claims: see **16.26**.

Generally speaking, the courts will not be too quick to find that a plaintiff has acted unreasonably, even if a cheaper option is available. This principle is colourfully demonstrated by *Banco de Portugal v Waterlow* (1932). The defendants contracted to print bank notes for the plaintiff bank. In breach of contract, they delivered a large number of these to a criminal who put them into circulation in Portugal. On discovering the error, the Bank withdrew the issue. It then undertook to exchange all notes illegally circulated for others. The defendants

---

36   See Bridge 1989.

argued that they were only liable for the cost of printing the new notes, rather than the enormous losses incurred by the Bank in exchanging the withdrawn notes for new notes. Lord Macmillan pointed out (at 506) that '[it] is often easy after an emergency has passed to criticise the steps which have been taken to meet it, but such criticism does not come well from those who have themselves created the emergency'.

23.19   Contributory negligence and apportionment

In a standard contract action, the negligence of the plaintiff is irrelevant. It only becomes relevant when the claim is based on a breach of a contractual duty of care, rather than the more usual type of strict liability: see **12.03**. Contractual duties of this sort mirror those in the general tort of negligence, and may be expressly agreed or implied into certain types of contract. For example, when a patient is treated privately, a doctor owes a contractual as well as tortious duty of care.

During the twentieth century, legislation was introduced to permit a reduction in damages to reflect the extent of any contributory negligence on the part of the plaintiff. In *Astley v Austrust* (1999), the High Court held that this legislation did not apply where the plaintiff brought a claim for breach of its solicitors' contractual duty of care. This outcome meant that, where there was concurrent tortious and contractual liability, a negligent plaintiff was well advised to bring a contract claim and avoid a reduction for contributory negligence. The decision has been reversed by subsequent statutes.[37] As a result, contributory negligence will result in a reduction of damages when the claim is based on a breach of a duty of care in either tort or contract.

Each State and Territory also has legislation dealing with the apportionment of loss between multiple wrongdoers.[38] The relevant provisions can apply to actions for breach of contract, but only to the extent that they involve claims for economic loss or damage to property that arise from a failure to take reasonable care. Personal injury claims are not affected. The general effect is that where a plaintiff has sustained economic loss or property damage, for which a defendant's breach of a contractual duty of care is partially responsible, the defendant's liability in damages will be proportionate to their contribution. It will not matter that the plaintiff cannot recover against another wrongdoer; for example, because they have died or are insolvent. There are certain exceptions to the use of proportionate liability, however, including where the defendant has acted fraudulently or intentionally. Some jurisdictions also allow parties to contract out of the proportionate liability regime.[39]

---

37   See *Law Reform (Miscellaneous Provisions) Act 1965* (NSW) ss 8–9; *Wrongs Act 1958* (Vic) ss 25–26; *Law Reform Act 1995* (Qld) ss 5, 10; *Law Reform (Contributory Negligence and Tortfeasors' Contribution) Act 1947* (WA) ss 3A–4; *Law Reform (Contributory Negligence and Apportionment of Liability) Act 2001* (SA) ss 3, 7; *Wrongs Act 1954* (Tas) ss 2, 4; *Civil Law (Wrongs) Act 2002* (ACT) ss 101–102; *Law Reform (Miscellaneous Provisions) Act 1956* (NT) ss 15–16.

38   See *Civil Liability Act 2002* (NSW) Pt 4; *Wrongs Act 1958* (Vic) Pt IVAA; *Civil Liability Act 2003* (Qld) Pt 2; *Civil Liability Act 2002* (WA) Pt 1F; *Law Reform (Contributory Negligence and Apportionment of Liability) Act 2001* (SA) Pt 3; *Civil Liability Act 2002* (Tas) Pt 9A; *Civil Law (Wrongs) Act 2002* (ACT) Ch 7A; *Proportionate Liability Act 2005* (NT).

39   See eg *Civil Liability Act 2002* (NSW) s 3A(2).

Date of assessment

23.20   The breach date rule

Damages are generally assessed at the date the contract was breached: *Wenham v Ella* (1972) at 473; *Johnson v Agnew* (1980) at 400–1. In *Ng v Filmlock* (2014), a vendor terminated a contract for the sale of land for the purchaser's repudiatory breach. The New South Wales Court of Appeal confirmed the general rule that damages for breach of a contract for sale of land are assessed as at the date of breach. This was when the contract was terminated. The damages awarded were the difference between the contract price and the value of the land at the time of breach. The Court rejected the argument of the purchaser that the damages should be calculated with reference to the resale price 13 months later, when the property was actually sold in a falling land market.

The breach date rule stems from the idea that any losses post-breach do not flow from the breach itself. Suppose A has entered into a contract to deliver goods to B on 1 September, and fails to deliver on that date. The market price shifts on 4 September so that the goods are more expensive. B cannot recover the increased cost of goods in the market after that date. These losses are not caused by the breach, but by a shift in the market. This approach fits with the idea that B must mitigate their losses by buying alternative goods once the contract is breached.[40] It has been argued that there is no need for a fixed point in time (the breach date) where damages 'crystallise'.[41] Rather, what the courts are doing in these circumstances is applying the mitigation rules. The breach date rule reflects a norm where there is an available market and it is reasonable to expect the plaintiff to mitigate their loss on breach by going to the market. This analysis would explain why exceptions to the breach date rule have been created.

The rule caused some problems during the 1970s where there were major shifts in the value of currency between the breach and the trial. Applying the rule meant that plaintiffs found themselves seriously under-compensated. The so-called 'breach date rule' was nevertheless reaffirmed by Mason CJ in *Johnson v Perez* (1988) at 355. He also accepted that the rule 'must give way' in particular cases in order to 'most fairly compensate' the plaintiff. The application of these exceptions has proved controversial.

23.21   Exceptions to the breach date rule

There are two standard instances when the courts depart from the breach date rule. The victim of a breach may not know that it has occurred. In this instance, damages are only assessed from the date that the plaintiff could, with reasonable diligence, have discovered the breach had occurred: *Vieira v O'Shea* (2012) at [45]. There will also be situations where the innocent party knows of the breach, but is unable to act on that knowledge and secure substitute performance at that point in time. For example, a buyer may have insufficient resources to purchase an alternative in a rising market.

---

40   The breach date rule is the default rule in the various *Sale of Goods Acts*: see eg *Sale of Goods Act 1923* (NSW) s 52(3).
41   Dyson & Kramer 2014.

Anticipatory breaches (see **16.05**) have caused particular problems. Damages are assessed at the date when the contract was due to be performed, rather than the date that the anticipatory breach is accepted: *Hoffman v Cali* (1985). There may be a considerable period between the anticipatory breach and the time at which performance falls due under the contract. If the action comes to trial before the date due for performance, then the damages awarded will be speculative. However, because of the mitigation rules, it will generally be necessary to find a substitute from the point that the breach is accepted. As a result, in practice the date at which breach is accepted is the point at which damages are calculated, rather than the date at which performance falls due. *The Golden Victory* (2007) suggests that facts that arise subsequent to the acceptance of breach can also be taken into account in assessing damages.[42] A charterparty was repudiated, an act accepted by the claimant shipowner as terminating the contract. The question was whether damages should be awarded for the full remaining period of the charter (four years in December 2001), even though the outbreak of war with Iraq, in March 2003, would have entitled the charterers lawfully to cancel the contract (pursuant to a term in the charterparty) before the four years was up. The House of Lords accepted that the usual date for assessment of damages was the date of breach. However, the majority noted a principle of 'fair compensation', which was taken to mean that the claimant should have been in the position it would have been in but for the breach – *but no better off*. That principle suggested that an exception was necessary when subsequent events, known to the court, had reduced the value of the contractual rights in question. The minority thought that departing from the rule created uncertainty.

The Golden Victory was reaffirmed by the UK Supreme Court in *Bunge v Nidera* (2015). Lord Sumption said (at [23]):

> Commercial certainty is undoubtedly important, although its significance will inevitably vary from one contract to another. But it can rarely be thought to justify an award of substantial damages to someone who has not suffered any.

The Supreme Court held that the same principles applied both in the case of a one-off transaction, and where the contract involved continuing conduct.

Australian judges have long accepted that some departures from the breach date rule are possible. *The Golden Victory* has been cited with approval by some courts: see eg *McCrohon v Harith* (2010) at [54], [57]–[59]; *Janos v Chama Motors* (2011) at [35], [39]–[41].

23.22   Interest and loss of the use of money

There may be a significant period of time between the occurrence of the breach and the award of compensation. The traditional approach was that courts could not award interest on damages (or a debt), up until the date of judgment, in the absence of an agreement to the contrary or a statute: see eg *Hungerfords v Walker* (1989) at 137–8. In most Australian jurisdictions, including the Commonwealth, pre-judgment interest can now be awarded on

---

42   For an economic analysis of the decision, see Zhou 2010.

damages and debts, under express powers granted to the courts.[43] In Tasmania, however, the relevant provision only extends to pre-judgment interest on debts, not damages.[44]

In some cases, the result of a breach of contract is that the plaintiff is deprived of the use of money. This form of consequential loss can most obviously occur where the defendant in breach of contract fails to pay a sum due under the contract. The principle can apply in other situations too. For example, in *Hungerfords*, accountants made a mistake in calculating depreciation under a tax return for a partnership. The plaintiffs therefore overpaid on their tax. As a result, they were deprived of the use of their money. It was held that damages may be awarded to reflect such a loss, provided it was within the reasonable contemplation of the parties. Subject to the plaintiff satisfying the onus of proof, losses may be awarded to reflect the cost incurred by the plaintiff in borrowing money, or even the loss of an opportunity to invest and make greater profits: see eg *Hardie v Shadbolt* (2004) at [57]–[64].[45]

Damages and enforcement

23.23 Damages under *Lord Cairns' Act*

All Australian States and Territories make statutory provision for the award of damages in addition to, or in lieu of, specific performance and injunctions.[46] The statutes are based on, though not identical to, s 2 of earlier English legislation known as *Lord Cairns' Act*.[47] Such damages are not awarded as of right. The power to award them is at the court's discretion. In *Madden v Kevereski* (1983) at 307, it was explained in the context of the New South Wales legislation that:

> That section only applies ... where a plaintiff has made out a case for equitable relief by way of injunction or specific performance, and has either got it, or for some equitable or discretionary reason, been refused.

Where common law damages would give an adequate remedy, a court would not consider specific performance or injunction. Therefore, damages under the statutes would not come into the equation.

When specific performance is ordered against a vendor of land, damages may be awarded in addition, to reflect the fact that a purchaser was kept out of possession for a time: see eg *McGavin v Gerraty* (1911). The award of damages *instead of* specific performance or an injunction is more complicated. The authorities were examined in detail by Palmer J in *Mills v Ruthol* (2004). He concluded (at [61]) that:

---

43   See eg *Federal Court of Australia Act 1976* (Cth) s 51A; *Civil Procedure Act 2005* (NSW) ss 100(1)–(2); *Supreme Court Act 1986* (Vic) ss 58, 60; *Civil Proceedings Act 2011* (Qld) s 58(3); *Supreme Court Act 1935* (WA) s 32(1); *Supreme Court Act 1935* (SA) s 30C(1); *Court Procedures Rules 2006* (ACT) r 1619; *Supreme Court Act 1979* (NT) s 84(1).

44   *Supreme Court Civil Procedure Act 1932* (Tas) s 34.

45   For a more detailed treatment of these issues, see Barnett & Harder 2014: 48–52.

46   *Supreme Court Act 1970* (NSW) s 68; *Supreme Court Act 1986* (Vic) s 38; *Civil Proceedings Act 2011* (Qld) s 8; *Supreme Court Act 1935* (WA) s 25(1); *Supreme Court Act 1935* (SA) s 30; *Supreme Court Civil Procedure Act 1932* (Tas) s 11(13); *Supreme Court Act 1933* (ACT) s 20; *Supreme Court Act 1979* (NT) s 14(1)(b).

47   *Chancery Amendment Act 1858* (UK). See now *Senior Courts Act 1981* (UK) s 50.

> [T]he plaintiff must demonstrate that as at the date of commencement of the proceedings the circumstances were such that the court could, not necessarily would, have granted a final injunction or specific performance. If such circumstances change after the commencement of the proceedings so that specific performance or a final injunction becomes impossible or would be refused on discretionary grounds, the court's power to award damages under s 68 is not thereby lost.

When a grant of specific performance or injunction is impossible, it follows that damages are precluded: *McMahon v Ambrose* (1987). The outcome is different when an injunction or specific performance are possible, but not awarded – for example, because of lapse of time – or because it would cause hardship for a defendant (see **22.09**, **22.11**). These are situations when a court could theoretically have granted relief and awarded damages under the Australian equivalents of *Lord Cairns' Act*. The same discretionary bars to relief also apply to a claim for damages, but need not produce the same outcome on a given set of facts.

In *Johnson v Agnew* (1980) at 400, Lord Wilberforce suggested that the principles governing the calculation of damages under *Lord Cairns' Act* are the same as those at common law. It follows that damages under the legislation ought to be compensatory, and subject to the rules limiting damages awards such as remoteness.[48]

---

48   There is some complexity in the application of this general principle: see Heydon et al 2015: [24-045]– [24-105].

24

RESTITUTIONARY REMEDIES

24.01   Introduction

Restitution is the name given to the body of law which allows one party to recover a gain made by another party at their expense. An action in restitution is quite unlike an action for breach of contract. A damages award in contract reflects loss suffered, rather than gains made by the other party. Attempts to award a gain-based remedy for breach of contract have been resisted by Australian judges: see **23.07**.

Restitutionary remedies are not confined to parties in a contractual relationship, but they belong in a book about contract law because they fill some gaps around contractual liability.[1] Restitution becomes relevant when parties are in pre-contractual relationships, or where a contract is void, terminated or frustrated. The gain conferred may be money, property, or the benefit of work that one party does for the other. Where there *is* a contract between the parties, then the law adopts a rule that restitution is subsidiary to the contract.[2] When one person does work for another under a contract – and the work that they do is worth more than the contract price – they cannot simply ignore the contract and instead seek restitution for the true value of the work done.

Restitution becomes available when the legal relationship of the parties is no longer governed by their contract. Where a contract is discharged because it is terminated or frustrated, the absence of an enforceable contract makes a restitutionary remedy possible. But the contractual setting in which restitution is sought remains critical. Even when the parties are not themselves in a direct contractual relationship, the way that risk has been allocated under a chain of contracts might still preclude a restitutionary claim. This was the position in *Lumbers v W Cook Builders* (2008). A house was built using a subcontractor. When the subcontractor became insolvent, it had not been paid for its work. Rather than proceeding against the head contractor on the subcontract, the subcontractor brought a claim in restitution against the owner of the house. The High Court majority noted that the work was done under a subcontract. It was the head contractor who had a contract with the owner and therefore had a right to payment for any work done. It followed from this that to allow a claim in restitution against the owner would undermine the contractual relationships of the parties. The head contractor had said that it would not bring a claim against the owner, but this did not alter the outcome.

The law has for centuries provided a remedy in the situation where one party makes a gain from another that they are not entitled to, or at least are not entitled to receive without payment in return. Until very recently, this group of remedies lacked a single coherent structure.[3] In the common law, several forms of action were used. Most of these claims were a form of assumpsit, as described in **1.10**. The actions of money had and received, and money paid, were used to recover money which another had no right to retain. *Quantum meruit* was the correct remedy for the value of services rendered and *quantum valebat* played a similar function for the value of goods delivered. In so far as lawyers thought about fitting this diverse range of claims under a single concept, they did so by utilising the notion of *quasi-contract*. Quasi-contract was sometimes equated with the idea of an *implied contract* and, in doing so, confused two different grounds of liability. Liability in these cases had nothing to do with agreement. Quasi-contract was just a convenient label for a jumble of unconnected doctrines,

---

1   For general treatments of the subject in Australia, see Mason et al 2016; Edelman & Bant 2016.
2   For an analysis of the subsidiary doctrine, see Grantham & Rickett 2001.
3   For the history, see Ibbetson 1999: 264–93.

rather than a logical rationalisation. Beginning in America in the interwar years and in England from the 1960s, however, legal writers and then judges began to develop a coherent structure for the subject. The fact that the law provides a remedy is not disputed. The way in which these remedies are conceptualised nevertheless remains controversial, especially the place of the idea of unjust enrichment. This debate is discussed at the end of this chapter. As it was said in *MG Corrosion Consultants v Gilmour* (2012) at [13], restitution 'is an area of the law which often seems in a state of constant refinement'.

Money claims

24.02   The action for money had and received

Money had and received is the most important of the old common law 'money counts'. It is a personal remedy, and involves an order for the recovery of the value of money paid, rather than the physical notes and coins transferred. Where the claim relates to a payment, valuation of the benefit is not usually a problem. The benefit is what the defendant receives – or, at least, that part of the payment that the law deems unjust to retain.

24.03   Mistaken payments

Perhaps the most common and uncontroversial example of restitution occurs when there is a payment by *mistake*.[4] There are many different kinds of mistake that someone can make, but a mistake may easily arise against the backdrop of a contract; for example, a payment may be made under the mistaken belief that it is due under a contract. In *David Securities v Commonwealth Bank* (1992) at 378, Mason CJ, Deane, Toohey, Gaudron and McHugh JJ explained that:

> If the payer has made the payment because of a mistake, his or her intention to transfer the money is vitiated and the recipient has been enriched. There is therefore no place for a further requirement that the causative mistake be fundamental; insistence upon that factor would only serve to focus attention in a non-specific way on the nature of the mistake, rather than the fact of enrichment.

This passage suggests that the courts are relaxed about allowing recovery in restitution for mistaken payments. This was reflected in the way that the High Court confirmed that restitution could be granted when a payment is made under the influence of a mistake of law, and was not confined, as previously thought, to mistakes of fact.[5]

24.04   Payments under contracts that are void, voidable, or unenforceable

A payment may be made under a contract which turns out to be void, voidable, or unenforceable. The availability of restitution will depend upon whether it is unjust to retain the money.

---

4   But see Wilmot-Smith 2017, offering a rare dissenting view on the availability of restitution against a payee in the case of a mistaken payment.

5   As to the defences that may be available to such a claim, including a 'change of position' by the payee, see eg *Australian Financial Services and Leasing v Hills Industries* (2014).

A number of well-established situations exist in which restitution is ordered. The most important general ground beyond mistaken payments occurs when there is a *failure of consideration* (or, as it is sometimes now said, *failure of basis*). This term is used to describe an absence of counter-performance, rather than in the more technical sense of the element needed in the formation of a contract and discussed in Chapter 5. A significant limit on recovery in many contexts is that the failure of consideration must be total rather than partial: that is, the payer must have received no part of what they had bargained to receive in return for the payment. A justification for still requiring a total failure was given by Gummow J in *Roxborough v Rothmans of Pall Mall* (2001) at [105], where he said that, if this condition were relaxed, then restitution would 'cut across the compensatory principle' and allow parties to circumvent contracts.

It may not be too difficult in cases of a void contract to find a total failure of consideration. Nevertheless, the question is whether it is unjust to retain the money. Sometimes, even when a payment is made under a void contract, that element of injustice will be missing. For example, money paid under a loan agreement which was void under the doctrine of non est factum (see **18.42**) could not be recovered in *Ford v Perpetual Trustees* (2009). One factor which weighed with the Court was that the recipient was a wholly innocent party, and the lender, who had failed to make proper inquiries, should therefore bear the risk.

A contract may be voidable for a range of reasons which have been discussed throughout the book. Mistake has already been mentioned. Other grounds on which a contract can be avoided include misrepresentation, duress, undue influence and unconscionability. The grounds for avoiding a contract through rescission also provide the justification for restitution. They explain why retention of the money is unjust. For example, when a payment is made under a contract that is then rescinded because it was entered into as a result of duress, it may be recovered in restitution.

Certain types of contract are subject to formality requirements. If these are not met, then the contract is rendered unenforceable. The requirement of writing in contracts for the sale of land is a case in point: see **5.44**. In *Freedom v AHR Constructions* (1987), for example, a payment made under an unenforceable oral contract for the sale of land could be recovered on the basis of a total failure of consideration.

Special rules apply when a contract is void, or unenforceable, for illegality. Traditionally, the *ex turpi causa* principle was a major obstacle to recovery in restitution, although the impact of the maxim was relaxed somewhat by the creation of numerous exceptions: see **21.18**. Today, most illegality involves the breach of a statute. Whether a restitutionary claim is permitted for a payment made under a contract affected by statutory illegality depends on whether recovery would be consistent with the purposes of the statute: see *Equuscorp v Haxton* (2012), discussed in **21.19**.

24.05   Payments when a contract is discharged

When a contract is terminated for breach (see **17.01**), or becomes frustrated (see **15.14**), the unperformed primary obligations of the parties are generally discharged. Prior to that discharge, payments may have been made under the contract. These are standard situations in which it will be argued that restitution can be used to recover payments on the grounds of a failure of consideration. Not all payments can be recovered. Deposits, for example, are excluded, unless the payee was at fault. But other forms of advance payment can be recovered in restitution, even by a party in breach, provided there has been a total failure of consideration. Prior to termination, more often than not there will be performance on both sides and it will be difficult to argue that any failure of consideration is total. Hence, in *Baltic Shipping v Dillon* (1993), the plaintiff had enjoyed nine days of a cruise, before the ship on which she was sailing sank, and as a result there could be no recovery of the payments made in advance of the holiday: see **17.07**.

The need to demonstrate a total failure following frustration is a major disadvantage of the common law. It means that payments made before the frustrating event cannot be recovered if the other side has rendered some though not all of the agreed counter-performance. In many cases, there will be some performance on both sides before the contract becomes impossible to perform or is otherwise radically affected by a frustrating event. It is one reason why New South Wales, Victoria and South Australia have adopted statutory schemes: see **15.15–15.17**.

Claims for services rendered

24.06   *Quantum meruit* and *quantum valebat*

Where work is performed under a valid contract, the right to be paid for that work will generally depend on the terms of that contract. But even where there is no contractual basis for claiming payment, it may still be possible to seek a restitutionary remedy for the monetary value of the services in question. The action used for this purpose is called a *quantum meruit*. A similar claim can be brought where the plaintiff has delivered goods to the defendant, but there is no contractual basis for the recovery of payment for those goods. A restitutionary claim for the monetary value of goods supplied is called a *quantum valebat*. In the discussion that follows, we concentrate on the particular issues posed by *quantum meruit* claims for services rendered.

Before going on, it should be noted that the action for *quantum meruit* is not always a restitutionary remedy. It can sometimes be used to enforce an implied contractual obligation to pay a reasonable sum for work done. The successful claim in *Steele v Tardiani* (1946), discussed in **12.14**, provides an example.

24.07   Valuing services

If money is received, it is not difficult to value. But non-monetary benefits, like the provision of services, may present more difficulties. In a *quantum meruit* claim, the measure of relief is described as 'reasonable remuneration' for the work done. The starting point for the calculation is the normal market value of services of that kind. Because the remedy is restitutionary, and not contractual, the focus is on the value of the work done, rather than the loss that the plaintiff has suffered. The normal market value can, however, be departed from in some circumstances. In *Pavey & Matthews v Paul* (1987) at 263, Deane J observed that:

> In some categories of case, however, it would be to affront rather than satisfy the requirements of good conscience and justice ... to determine what constitutes fair and just compensation for a benefit accepted by reference only to what would represent a fair remuneration for the work involved or a fair market value of materials supplied.

The price that the parties themselves agreed for the work is one relevant consideration when calculating the value of the benefit received. But this is not conclusive. The same applies to any evidence of the actual costs incurred by the plaintiff in performing the relevant work: *Mann v Paterson Constructions* (2018).

There will be situations where the performer has made a bad bargain. As a result, the contract price is less than the value of the work performed. If the contract no longer exists, typically because it has been terminated, then the performer may bring a claim in restitution – provided that it would be unjust for the defendant to retain the benefit of the work without making payment. This sort of scenario faced the New South Wales Court of Appeal in *Renard Constructions v Minister of Public Works* (1992), as noted at **17.09**. A restitutionary claim for the value of work done of $285,000 was upheld, even though the value of the work agreed under the contract was just $208,950. Meagher JA, with whom Priestley JA and Handley JA agreed, found that where there was a repudiatory breach of contract allowing the innocent party to terminate, then they were entitled in restitution to claim the full value of work done under the contract. The amount that could be recovered was not limited by the contract price. The basis of a claim in contract and restitution was different, and further, as Meagher JA pointed out (at 277–8), it would be anomalous if, having been guilty of a repudiatory breach, the party in breach could then rely on the contract to set a ceiling. All that the contract price does is provide 'strong', but not conclusive, evidence of the reasonableness of the remuneration claimed as a *quantum meruit*.

There is an added problem with claims for the value of services. It is not enough for the defendant to benefit. They need to have been shown to have *chosen* the benefit.[6] This reflects the idea that a benefit cannot be forced on someone that may not want it. A payment of money is seen as an incontrovertible benefit to the payee. Services are different. The hypothetical example that is sometimes given concerns A cleaning B's windows, without having been asked. B may very well, for their own idiosyncratic reasons, not wish to have clean windows. This is an example of what is sometimes called 'subjective devaluation'. B may not value clean windows, whatever the objective value of A's work may be. But it is different if the work has been requested. A request may be express, but can also be implied: see *Lumbers v W Cook Builders* (2008) at [89].[7] Historically, a request was unnecessary. It was enough if a service was *freely accepted*. Free acceptance indicates a choice to receive a benefit. It is more passive than a request. It is possible to freely accept with indifference. However, the view that free acceptance is sufficient has fallen out of favour, on at least one view of what was said in *Lumbers*. That issue is discussed further below. In any event, where the parties are in a contractual relationship, it will not usually be too difficult to identify a request, though precisely what was requested might be contested. As discussed below, work done prior to the formation of a contract may be more difficult to link to a request.

---

6   For a detailed discussion of this issue, see Edelman & Bant 2016: 62–77.
7   Compare *Progressive Pod Properties v A & M Green Investments* (2012) and *Woolcorp v Rodger Constructions* (2017) where, on the facts, no request could be identified.

24.08   Services under contracts that are void, voidable, or unenforceable

As with payments of money, services may be rendered under a contract that is void, voidable, or unenforceable. In *Pavey & Matthews v Paul* (1987) at 256, Deane J explained that:

> In such a case, it is the very fact that there is no genuine agreement or that the genuine agreement is frustrated, avoided or unenforceable that provides the occasion for (and part of the circumstances giving rise to) the imposition by the law of the obligation to make restitution.

As these remarks make clear, the mere fact that the contract is void, voidable, or unenforceable does not mean that restitution becomes available. There must be grounds for saying that the retention of the services, without paying a reasonable charge for them, would be unjust. Typically, it will be unjust not to make recompense for services in this situation, because there is a total failure of consideration.

In *Pavey*, a building contract was unenforceable for failing to meet statutory formality requirements. The builder was nevertheless able to recover for the value of the work done and materials supplied, by bringing a claim in *quantum meruit* against the owner whose home it was renovating. The High Court held that the statutory bar on enforcement of the contract should not be interpreted as precluding a restitutionary claim as well.[8]

24.09   Services rendered when the contract is discharged

Restitution for services when a contract is discharged presents more difficulty than a claim for money paid, at least in some situations. Where the completion of work is wrongfully prevented, the innocent performer can choose between claiming damages or suing in *quantum meruit*: see **17.09**. But it is different if it is the performer's breach or repudiation that has led to the contract being terminated. The general rule has always been that, if no right to payment has accrued under the contract, the performer cannot bring a claim in *quantum meruit* to recover reasonable remuneration: see eg *Sumpter v Hedges* (1898). Traditionally, as noted in the discussion of that case in **17.08**, it was thought that a performer could escape that rule by showing that the recipient of the services had freely chosen to accept them. Some of the observations made by the High Court in *Lumbers v W Cook Builders* (2008), discussed below, might be taken to suggest that free acceptance analysis is no longer to be used, and that if the recipient cannot be said to have 'requested' the partially completed work, there can be no claim in restitution. But in *Lampson v Fortescue Metals Group* (2014) at [56]–[90], Edelman J took the view that, until the High Court makes a definitive ruling on the matter, free acceptance cannot be ruled out as a basis for relief.

As with money payments, the common law relating to services rendered before a frustrating event made it difficult to recover in restitution: see eg *Appleby v Myers* (1867). Claims for non-monetary benefits can be made under the statutory regimes in New South Wales, Victoria

---

8   For a further example of such reasoning, see *CMF Projects v Riggall* (2014); but compare *Sutton v Zullo Enterprises* (2000), discussed at **21.19**.

and South Australia: see **15.15–15.17**. But the various formulae used under the legislation to calculate the value of such benefits can be criticised as unduly complicated.

24.10   Services rendered in anticipation of a contract

As part of the negotiation process, prior to contract formation, the parties may enter into preliminary agreements, as discussed in Chapter 6. They may also carry out work in anticipation that a contract will be concluded. There is always a risk that a contract will never materialise. It may be argued that this risk should be shouldered by the party who chooses to undertake work without any certainty of getting paid. But there also comes a point where the law steps in and makes the other party pay for services rendered in anticipation of a contract, on the basis that it is unjust not to grant such relief. Sometimes this occurs through the medium of estoppel, as in *Waltons Stores v Maher* (1988) (see **7.04–7.06**). But, as noted in **4.12**, there have also been cases in which *quantum meruit* claims have succeeded in this situation: see eg *Sabemo v North Sydney Municipal Council* (1977); *British Steel v Cleveland Bridge and Engineering* (1984).

In *Lumbers* at [82]–[90], Gummow, Hayne, Crennan and Kiefel JJ expressed the view that the mere acceptance of a benefit cannot justify the award of a *quantum meruit*. Rather, there would need to be a request to do the work to establish the requisite element of unconscionability. Reference was made to an earlier South Australian Supreme Court decision, *Angelopoulos v Sabatino* (1995). During negotiations for the lease of a hotel, the plaintiff entered into possession and began restoring the property. Negotiations then broke down. It was held that the plaintiff could recover on a *quantum meruit*, by reference to a series of factors that established the defendant's acceptance of the work. But on the view taken in *Lumbers*, the only question should have been whether the defendant had expressly or impliedly requested the work.[9]

Explaining restitution

24.11   The reconceptualisation of restitution

Modern lawyers no longer think of the remedies that the law provides for recovering payments or obtaining reasonable payment for services as a disconnected series of actions. American lawyers began to develop a law of restitution and craft a principle of *unjust enrichment* to explain that law during the late nineteenth century. This work culminated in the *Restatement of the Law of Restitution* in 1937. The *Restatement* still forms the basis of the law in the United States. Some English lawyers were attracted by similar ideas. In 1966 Robert Goff and Gareth Jones published the first edition of their seminal work, *The Law of Restitution*. Their aim was 'to state in a coherent and rational form, the principles of the English Law of Restitution'.[10] This previously diverse group of claims were brought together in one place, with the prevention of unjust enrichment again as the unifying concept. Further rationalisation followed with the

---

9   See eg *Design Joinery & Doors v IPower* (2015), where a claim for the value of electricity supplied in the absence of a contract succeeded on the basis of a request from the customer, without the need to consider what was described (at [103]) as the 'English doctrine of free acceptance'.

10   Goff & Jones 1966: v.

appearance of Peter Birks' *An Introduction to the Law of Restitution* in 1985. Birks too saw restitution as a response to unjust enrichment.[11] In common with other supporters of the concept, he identified a list of factors that would make it unjust to retain a benefit. These could be regarded as the various grounds for making a restitutionary claim.

The reconceptualisation of the law using unjust enrichment has not gone unchallenged by academic commentators in England,[12] but it certainly has its supporters.[13] Since the House of Lords' decision in *Lipkin Gorman v Karpnale* (1991), the superior English courts have also embraced unjust enrichment as an organising principle for the law of restitution. It is now generally accepted that the basis of liability is that the defendant is unjustly enriched at the expense of the plaintiff. The apotheosis of this approach can be found in the project of some English lawyers to draw up an equivalent of the American *Restatement*.[14] The story in Australia, however, is more complex.

24.12 The rise and fall of unjust enrichment in Australia

Given the current state of the law here, it is no small irony that Australian judges were amongst the first in the Commonwealth to recognise the concept of unjust enrichment. In *Pavey & Matthews v Paul* (1987), discussed at **24.08**, the High Court rejected the traditional analysis based on quasi-contract. The builder's right to recover payment for its work did not depend on identifying an 'implied contract' with the owner. Deane J said (at 255) that:

> The basis of the obligation to make payment for an executed consideration given and received under an unenforceable contract should now be accepted as lying in restitution or unjust enrichment.

Mason and Wilson JJ agreed (at 227) with this view. Other decisions followed which also embraced the idea of unjust enrichment: see eg *Australia and New Zealand Banking Group v Westpac* (1988); *David Securities v Commonwealth Bank* (1992).

In *Roxborough v Rothmans of Pall Mall* (2001), however, Gummow J mounted a sustained assault on the concept. His judgment was built around an analysis of the eighteenth century decision in *Moses v Macferlan* (1760).[15] He contended (at [100]) that liability in restitution was derived from equity, and that it was more accurate to equate restitution with unconscionability rather than unjust enrichment. His objections were not purely historical. Unjust enrichment was also flawed, he argued (at [72]), from a more philosophical perspective. This was because the common law 'is derived from judicial decisions upon particular instances, not the other way around'.

Antipathy towards 'top-down' reasoning reflects the resistance amongst Australian judges to the perceived attempts to impose legal taxonomy on a body of case law. As a criticism of unjust enrichment, scholars may think this is unfair, but it reflects a broader cultural gulf in the way that restitution has developed in England and Australia.[16] A series of subsequent High

---

11   See Birks 1989, 2005.
12   For the arguments of a longstanding and significant critic, see Hedley 2001. See also Stevens 2018.
13   See eg Burrows 2011; Virgo 2015.
14   See Burrows 2012b.
15   For the history, see Swain 2006.
16   For a detailed discussion, see Swain 2013a.

Court cases have preferred to emphasise unconscionable or unconscientious retention over unjust enrichment as an explanation for restitutionary remedies: see eg *Farah Constructions v Say-Dee* (2007); *Lumbers v W Cook Builders* (2008); *Bofinger v Kingsway Group* (2009); *Equuscorp v Haxton* (2012).

As a matter of history, there is some basis in the argument that money had and received had equitable antecedents. But as an appropriate model for the modern law of restitution in Australia, the approach is open to criticism.[17] It has arguably left Australia with a less coherent doctrine of restitution. It certainly lacks the more definitive structure of its English counterpart. That is not to say there is no structure, however, or that Australian restitution is completely uncertain. Perhaps it will mirror the unconscionable bargain doctrine (see **20.04**), and a set of principles will be allowed to emerge. But it is difficult to predict where the law will go next.

In *Australian Financial Services and Leasing v Hills Industries* (2014) at [78], Hayne, Crennan, Kiefel, Bell and Keane JJ were adamant that 'the concept of unjust enrichment is not the basis of restitutionary relief in Australian law'. Nevertheless, even if any normative force is denied to unjust enrichment, it may still serve a useful purpose. In *Lampson v Fortescue Metals Group* (2014) at [52], Edelman J, who has since joined the High Court, suggested that: '[p]rovided that [it] is not applied as a direct source of liability, in Australia the taxonomic category of unjust enrichment has served a useful function and might continue to do so'. Observations such as this suggest that the debate over the conceptual underpinnings of restitutionary relief may still have some way to travel.[18]

---

17   See eg Burrows 2010; Mason 2015.
18   For a useful overview of the evolution of the High Court's approach to restitution over the past few
       decades and a sense of where the current court might take it, see Bant 2017.

GLOSSARY

Note: italics indicates term defined in the glossary

ab initio from the beginning

abandonment describing a situation where each party to a contract acts in such a way that the other is entitled to infer that they are no longer bound by the contract, even though neither party has the right to terminate it

absolute describing a contract or obligation which must be performed no matter what excusing circumstances might exist

acceptance a willingness to enter into a contract on the terms specified in an *offer*

accessorial liability the liability of a person who has knowingly encouraged, assisted or otherwise been involved in someone else's wrongdoing

accord and satisfaction an agreement (the 'accord') to release someone from an obligation, in return for some form of *consideration* (the 'satisfaction')

account of profits an order by a court that a wrongdoer give up the profits they have made as a result of wrongdoing

ACL see *Australian Consumer Law*

ad hoc implication see *implied in fact*

ad idem of the same mind, agreed

adequacy of *consideration*: objective value

affirmation a decision not to exercise a right to *terminate* or *rescind* a contract, but rather to keep the contract alive

agency arrangement whereby one person (the *agent*) has *authority* to act and/or enter into contracts on behalf of another (the *principal*)

agent see *agency*

agreed damages see *liquidated damages*

agreement to agree an agreement under which the parties leave certain matters for further negotiation

aleatory contract a contract (such as of insurance) under which one party's principal obligations are triggered by the occurrence of an event which may or may not happen

anti-suit injunction a court order purporting to restrain another court or adjudicator from dealing with a particular dispute

anticipatory breach a *repudiation* occurring before the time for performance of a contractual obligation has arrived

apparent authority see *ostensible authority*

apportionment legislation statutory provisions that provide for certain kinds of payment obligation to be treated as *divisible*

apportionment of loss see *proportionate liability*

arbitration a quasi-judicial process involving an independent adjudicator (the *arbitrator*) hearing evidence and arguments, and deciding between competing claims

arbitrator see *arbitration*

assignment a transfer, for instance of contractual rights or other property

assumpsit an old *form of action* used to enforce a promise

Australian Consumer Law nationally agreed set of rules and standards for consumer transactions, and also in some instances business-to-business transactions

authority of an *agent*: the power granted by a *principal* to act and/or enter contracts on their behalf, which may be actual or *ostensible*

avoid to *rescind*

award (1) a decision given by an *arbitrator*
(2) a statutory instrument setting minimum wages and conditions for particular types of work performed by employees

bailee see *bailment*

bailment an arrangement, which may be contractual or *gratuitous*, whereby one person (the *bailor*) temporarily leaves property in the care of another (the *bailee*)

bailor see *bailment*

bar to rescission a reason why a right of *rescission (1)* cannot be exercised

battle of the forms a situation where both parties to a potential contract are seeking to use their own standardised terms

beneficiary a person who stands to benefit from a particular arrangement, such as a will or a *trust*

bilateral contract an agreement in which one party exchanges an *executory* promise or set of promises in return for an *executory* promise or set of promises from the other party

bill of exchange a form of *negotiable instrument* requiring payment to a specified person

bill of lading a detailed set of terms issued for the carriage of goods by sea

boilerplate terms standardised terms prepared for use in certain types of contract

breach of confidence a wrongful use or disclosure of confidential information, for which remedies may be sought in *equity*

breach of contract a failure to comply with a contractual obligation

canons of construction established principles of *interpretation*

cascade clause a drafting technique used to impose a series of overlapping restrictions of different scope, commonly used to avoid or minimise the effect of the doctrine of *restraint of trade*

causation the factual link that must exist between a defendant's wrongdoing and the loss which a plaintiff claims to have suffered

caveat emptor 'let the buyer beware' – the traditional principle that the buyer of property assumes the risk for any defect not the subject of a specific promise by the seller

champerty a form of *maintenance* provided in return for a share of the proceeds of the relevant litigation

charter the hire of a vessel

charterparty a contract of *charter*

choice of law the selection of the law of a particular country (or State or Territory, etc) as governing a particular act or transaction

chose in action a right to bring a legal action, itself a form of property

CISG see *Vienna Convention*

Civil Liability Acts statutory reforms by the States and Territories in 2002–2003 to restrict fault-based liability, including for some purposes under contracts

collateral contract an agreement (usually implied) whereby A makes a promise (a *collateral warranty*) to B, in return for B entering into a separate contract with A (2-party version) or with C (3-party version)

collateral warranty see *collateral contract*

common law (1) judge-made (non-statutory) law

                (2) a subset of judge-made law which is not *equity*

common mistake a mistaken assumption or belief shared by two parties

compromise an agreement to settle a disputed claim

conciliation a form of *mediation*, often governed by statutory rules

condition (1) used loosely, any term of a contract (eg 'the conditions of sale')

       (2) a contractual term, any breach of which will permit termination of the contract by the other party – also known as an *essential term (2)*

       (3) a promise which A is obliged to perform or make good before B can be called upon to perform

       (4) a contingency which neither party has promised to bring about, but on the occurrence of which depends the creation or subsistence of a contract

condition precedent something which must be done or which must occur before something else is to happen – can be used to apply to *condition (3)*, *condition (4)* and even sometimes *condition (2)*

condition subsequent something which, if it is done or occurs, will bring all or part of a contract or arrangement to an end

conditional bond an old arrangement whereby a promise of a future payment or benefit is made in a *deed*, with the promise to become *void* if certain conditions are met before the due date

conditional contract a contract containing a *condition (4)*; sometimes used also to mean a contract containing a *condition (3)*

consensus ad idem the state of being in agreement

consequential loss any loss suffered as a result of a *breach of contract*, other than the loss of benefits directly expected from performance of the obligation breached

consideration as a requirement of a valid contract: the element of bargain – that which is received in return for a promise, so that it is not *gratuitous*

construction sometimes used to mean *interpretation*

constructive trust a form of *trust* that, among other situations, may be imposed by a court to require a wrongdoer to deal with certain property on behalf of a person they have wronged

consumer guarantee a requirement or standard for the supply of goods or services to a consumer, imposed by the *ACL*

contingent condition see *condition (4)*

contra proferentem a principle of *interpretation*, whereby any uncertainties in the meaning of certain kinds of contractual term will be resolved against the interests of the *proferens*

contract an agreement between two or more parties, involving one or more promises that are given for something in return, and that the parties intend to be legally enforceable

contributory negligence lack of care on the part of a plaintiff in contributing to loss they have suffered – a potential basis for reducing the *damages* they may claim for that loss

counter-offer a response to an *offer* which is not an *acceptance*, but rather the proposal of a willingness to enter into a contract on different terms

covenant (1) an old *form of action* used to enforce a promise
        (2) a written promise

covenantee the person to whom a *covenant (2)* is made

covenantor the person who makes a *covenant (2)*

creditor the person to whom a debt is owed

damages in its usual sense, an award of compensation to a plaintiff for loss suffered as a result of wrongdoing by a defendant

de minimis principle that insignificant or trivial discrepancies or shortfalls in performance or compliance may be ignored

debt, action for an action to compel a defendant to pay a specified sum of money that is owed to the plaintiff

debtor the person who owes a debt

deceit the *tort* of fraudulent misrepresentation

declaration a formal statement by a court as to the existence, scope or effect of a party's rights or obligations

deed a kind of formal document, promises in which are enforceable even in the absence of *consideration*

dependent describing obligations of A and B which are interrelated, so that either A must perform before B is obligated to do, or A and B are concurrently obliged to perform

deposit money or property advanced by A to B on entering into a contract, to be forfeited if A defaults in performing their obligations

discharge of obligations: to release the *obligor* from any duty to perform

disclaimer an attempt to deny responsibility, such as for a misapprehension that might otherwise arise

divisible describing a contract which can be divided into a number of obligations or set of obligations, each of which stand alone

duress the use of threats to compel entry into a contract

duty of care an obligation, either accepted as part of a contract or recognised by the law as a basis for an action in *negligence*, to take reasonable care not to harm someone else

economic duress a form of *duress*, in which what is threatened is the infliction of economic (financial) loss

election where a party has a right to terminate or *rescind* a contract, the choice that party must exercise between either exercising that right or *affirmation* of the contract; more generally, any choice that must be made between inconsistent remedies or courses of action

Electronic Transactions Acts federal, State and Territory statutes that clarify the operation of certain legal rules, including as to *formalities*, in relation to electronic communications or files

entire agreement clause a provision in a contractual document declaring that the document is a complete record of the contract and denying effect to any terms not recorded in the document

entire contract a contract containing one main *entire obligation*

entire obligation an obligation which must be completely performed before the *obligor* can call for counter-performance (eg, get paid for work they have done)

equitable in the technical sense, used to describe a rule, principle or remedy derived from *equity*

equitable compensation compensation that may be awarded by a court for loss caused by certain *equitable* wrongs, such as breach of a *trust* or a *fiduciary* obligation

equitable estoppel a generic term that covers *proprietary estoppel* and *promissory estoppel*

equity in the technical sense, a body of judge-made rules and principles that originated in the English Court of Chancery

essential term (1) a contractual term which must be agreed in order for a particular type of contract not to be treated as *incomplete*

(2) a contractual term any breach of which will permit termination of the contract by the other party – also known as a *condition (2)*

estop to plead *estoppel* against another party to court proceedings

estoppel a pleading device, used in a variety of contractual and non-contractual situations – a person is estopped when they are precluded by a court from denying the truth of, or of acting inconsistently with, an assumption which another person has been encouraged to adopt

estoppel by acquiescence a form of *proprietary estoppel*

estoppel by conduct compendious term for *estoppel by convention* and *estoppel by representation*

estoppel by convention a form of *estoppel* used to prevent a party from acting inconsistently with a factual assumption which they and another party have jointly adopted as the basis for their dealings

estoppel by deed a form of *estoppel* precluding challenges to an assertion or allegation made by the estopped party in a deed

estoppel by encouragement a form of *proprietary estoppel*

estoppel by judgment compendious term for various forms of *estoppel* that seek to prevent the litigation of matters that have already, or could have, been resolved in earlier proceedings

estoppel by record see *estoppel by judgment*

estoppel by representation a form of *estoppel* used to prevent a party from acting inconsistently with a factual assumption they have induced another party to accept

estoppel *in pais* see *estoppel by conduct*

ex turpi causa an old principle that precludes a party from enforcing a contract or making some other kind of legal claim that arises out of, or is associated with, some form of illegal or objectionable conduct

exclusion clause see *exemption clause*

executed of *consideration*, a promise or a contract: already performed or carried out

executor a person responsible for carrying out the instructions of a *testator*

executory of *consideration*, a promise or a contract: yet to be performed or carried out

exemplary damages special form of *damages* that are punitive rather than compensatory, and signify disapproval of a wrongdoer's conduct

exemption clause a contractual provision narrowing or excluding liability for breach of a contract or for some other wrong

expectation loss the loss suffered as a result of a *breach of contract*, when comparing the innocent party's position at the date of assessment to the position in which they expected to be had the contract been performed

expert determination a process of adjudication between competing claims, conducted by an independent expert who may base their decision on their own knowledge and opinion

express prohibition a statutory provision that explicitly forbids the making of a particular type of contract

express term a contractual term that has explicitly been agreed by the parties or the existence of which can otherwise be inferred from their conduct

factual matrix the background to, or circumstances surrounding, the making of a contract

failure of basis a *failure of consideration*

failure of consideration a situation where A has not received what they bargained to receive from B in return for a payment or some other benefit made or conferred by A

fiduciary describing obligations, or persons having such obligations, which requires that one person act strictly in the best interests of another person

forbearance conduct showing a willingness to dispense with a contractual requirement or modify an obligation

force majeure clause a contractual provision suspending performance, or otherwise excusing non-performance, in the event of a disruption caused by an event outside the parties' control

form of action a set procedure under which, historically, a common law action could be brought

formalities legal requirements as to the recording or physical form of a contract or other legal instrument

forum the country (or State or Territory, etc) in which a legal action is brought

forum non conveniens a plea that a particular *forum* is not the appropriate place in which a dispute should be resolved

franchise a commercial arrangement under which the owner of a business (the *franchisor*) licenses to a *franchisee* the right to market certain goods or services under the name of the business and in accordance with a prescribed format

franchisee see *franchise*

franchisor see *franchise*

free acceptance possible basis for a *restitutionary* claim, where a defendant has chosen to take the benefit of goods or services supplied by the plaintiff

frustration a doctrine whereby a contract automatically terminates when circumstances change in a way not contemplated by the parties and that makes performance impossible or radically alters the benefits expected from performance

fundamental breach a breach of an *intermediate term* by one party that is sufficiently serious to warrant the other party being entitled to terminate the contract

good faith generally understood to mean acting honestly, reasonably and with due regard to another person's interests

gratuitous unobligated, non-contractual, given for nothing in return

guarantee an arrangement whereby one person (the *guarantor* or *surety*) promises to take responsibility for another person's failure to perform their obligations

guarantor see *guarantee*

guarantor indemnity a form of *indemnity*, where A must indemnify B against any loss arising from B's contract with C

heads of agreement a document recording an agreement that may or may not (depending on the context) be intended to have legal effect

Himalaya clause a provision designed to allow a *third party* to enforce an *exemption clause* in a contract to which they are not a party

illusory describing a promise or contract which, while appearing to obligate one party, in fact gives them an unfettered discretion as to whether or not to perform

implied by custom and practice a process by which an *implied term* is identified as being part of a contract made in a particular industry, market or region

implied by law a process by which an *implied term* is identified as being part of all contracts, or all contracts of a particular type

implied by statute a process by which an *implied term* is deemed by legislation to be part of a particular type of contract

implied in fact a process by which an *implied term* is identified as being part of a particular contract, and no other

implied prohibition a statutory provision that is interpreted to forbid the making of a particular type of contract, even without an express statement to that effect

implied term a provision on which the parties have not actually agreed, but which is nonetheless taken to be part of their contract

in pari delicto old principle that where both parties are equally involved in some form of illegal transaction, the defendant or possessor of a benefit may resist any *restitutionary* claim arising out of the transaction

incapacity the inability (whether through age, mental state or otherwise) to make an independent decision to enter into a contract or otherwise assume a legal obligation

incomplete describing a contract which fails to include one or more *essential terms (1)* and is thus unenforceable

indemnity a promise to absolve someone of any responsibility or liability for some kind of loss

independent describing promises or obligations of A and B which are not interrelated, so that each party must perform whether or not the other does so

inferred term a type of *express term*, the parties' agreement to which can reasonably be inferred from their conduct

injunction a court order either restraining a party from acting unlawfully (a *prohibitory injunction*) or, less commonly, directing them to do something they are required to do (a *mandatory injunction*)

innominate term an *intermediate term*

integration clause an *entire agreement clause*

interlocutory of an *injunction* or other order: granted by a court on a temporary basis, pending a full hearing on the relevant matter

intermediate term a contractual term which has not been designated as either an *essential term (2)* or a *non-essential term*; only a *fundamental breach* of such a term will give rise to a right to terminate the contract

interpretation the process of determining the meaning of a term, contract, instrument or statute

invitation to treat an expression of willingness to consider an *offer*

joint and several liability a form of liability in which two or more persons may be sued either collectively or individually for failing to fulfil an obligation

joint promisors/promisees two or more persons who jointly make a contract with someone else

jurisdiction of a court or other adjudicator: the power to deal with a particular matter or dispute

laches an *equitable* principle under which a plaintiff may be refused relief on the ground of unreasonable delay

ladder clause see *cascade clause*

landlord colloquial term for a *lessor* of land

lease an agreement by the owner or possessor of property (the *lessor*) to give a right of exclusive possession for a defined period to another person (the *lessee*)

lessee see *lease*

lessor see *lease*

letter of comfort a letter by a person that indicates that some other person has sufficient assets to meet certain obligations

letter of intent a document recording certain promises that may or may not (depending on the context) be intended to have legal effect

limitation clause a type of *exemption clause* restricting the amount of *damages* recoverable, or other remedies available, in respect of one or more breaches of contract or other wrongs

limitation period the period within which a legal action can be brought, after the right to bring the action first arises

liquidated damages a specified amount of *damages* which the parties to a contract have agreed must be paid in the event of a particular *breach of contract*

Lord Cairns' Act old British statute allowing the award of *damages* in addition to, or in lieu of, *specific performance* or an *injunction*

loss of bargain damages *damages* claimed not just for the loss directly caused by a particular *breach of contract* but, where the plaintiff terminates a contract for breach or *repudiation*, for the loss of all the benefits the plaintiff expected to receive under the contract

maintenance sometimes used to mean assisting someone else's litigation without a recognised justification for doing so

major failure a particular type of breach of a *consumer guarantee*, for which certain kinds of remedy are available

mandatory injunction see *injunction*

mandatory law a law of a particular country (or State or Territory, etc) that necessarily applies to a particular act or transaction

mediation process involving a neutral person (the mediator) assisting parties to identify, discuss and resolve issues

memorandum of understanding a document recording an agreement that may or may not (depending on the context) be intended to have legal effect

merger clause an *entire agreement clause*

minimum equity concept sometimes used to limit the relief granted for *estoppel*

minor, a a young person, often defined as someone under the age of 18

misrepresentation an incorrect *representation* as to a fact or current state of affairs that induces the *representee* to enter into a contract

mitigation a doctrine relevant to the assessment of *damages*, whereby (among other things) a plaintiff is expected to take reasonable steps to minimise any loss suffered as a result of the defendant's wrongdoing

money had and received a *restitutionary* action to reclaim money paid to another person

mutual mistake a situation where parties are at cross-purposes

National Credit Code nationally agreed set of rules and standards for the provision of credit to consumers

necessaries goods or services that are needed for subsistence purposes, such as food, clothing and accommodation

negligence a failure to take due care; more specifically, a *tort* that holds a defendant liable for breach of a *duty of care*

negotiable instrument a document (such as a cheque) guaranteeing the payment of a sum of money which may be passed on or 'negotiated' to a *third party*

nominal damages token amount awarded where a plaintiff has been wronged, but cannot establish that they have suffered any loss as a result of the wrong

non-essential term a contractual term no breach of which will permit termination of the contract by the other party – also known as a *warranty (2)*

non est factum a plea that a document was signed by mistake

non-major failure a particular type of breach of a *consumer guarantee*, for which more limited remedies are available, compared to a *major failure*

non-pecuniary loss loss that cannot be directly conceived or measured in financial terms

novation the agreed substitution of one contract for another, usually (but not always) involving different parties

obligee the person to whom a legal obligation or duty is owed

obligor a person who must perform a legal obligation or duty

offer an expression of willingness to enter into a contract on specified terms

offer and acceptance a mode of analysing the steps leading to the formation of an alleged contract in order to ascertain whether the parties have actually reached agreement, based on identifying an *offer* by one party and *acceptance* by the other

offeree a person to whom an *offer* is made

offeror the person by whom an *offer* is made

option an agreement whereby one party undertakes to enter into a specified contract with another party, if and when that other party expresses a wish to do so

ostensible authority the *authority* that an *agent* reasonably appears to have to act and/or enter contracts on behalf of a *principal*

parol evidence rule principle (a) precluding recourse to extrinsic material for the purpose of interpreting written instruments; and (b) precluding incorporation of extrinsic terms into a contract otherwise recorded in writing

part performance *equitable* doctrine whereby non-compliance with the *Statute of Frauds* or similar *formalities* may be excused

partial failure of consideration a *failure of consideration* where some but not all of the expected performance from B has been received by A

party (1) to a contract: a person who has entered into a contract with someone else
(2) to a dispute: a person involved in a dispute with someone else

party–party indemnity a form of *indemnity*, where A must indemnify B against any breach of A's contractual obligations to B

past consideration purported *consideration* for a promise, consisting of something done before that promise was made

penalties, rule against the doctrine whereby *penalty clauses* are treated as unenforceable

penalty (1) a fine imposed by a court for a breach of the law
(2) the effect or impact of a *penalty clause*

penalty clause a contractual provision providing for A to suffer some kind of sanction or detriment in the event that a stipulation in favour of B is not fulfilled

postal acceptance rule rule which is part of the principles of *offer and acceptance*, dealing with the effect of posted communications

practical benefit the benefit obtained by B as a result of A fulfilling or recommitting to a prior contractual obligation owed to B, treated as good *consideration* for a promise by B to confer an additional benefit on A or to make a concession in A's favour

preliminary agreement an attempt to set out the framework or basic details for a contract, before the final terms have been agreed

pretence a term or set of terms not intended by the parties to have effect, despite being part of what is otherwise a genuine contract

primary obligation an obligation to perform, agreed as part of a contract

principal a person on whose behalf an *agent* is authorised to act and/or enter contracts

prior course of dealing a consistent pattern of previous transactions which may be used to support the argument that certain terms have been accepted by the parties

privity of contract a principle precluding any person who is not a party (or 'not privy') to a contract from either enforcing or being obligated under that contract

procedural unfairness unfairness in the process of making a contract

process contract an implied contract, the effect of which is to require a party considering bids or tenders to comply with the rules announced for that process

proferens a party 'putting forward' a contractual provision, in the sense either that they drafted it, or that they are seeking to rely on it

prohibitory injunction see *injunction*

promisee a person to whom a promise is made

promisor the person by whom a promise is made

promissory estoppel particular variety of *estoppel*, originating in *equity*, whereby a person is precluded from resiling from a promise which they have made and which, technically (eg for lack of *consideration*), they need not keep

promissory note a form of *negotiable instrument* requiring payment to a specified person

proper law of the contract the law of a country (or a State or Territory, etc) that is taken to govern a particular contract

proportionate liability the concept of ensuring that where multiple wrongdoers have contributed to loss suffered by a plaintiff, each wrongdoer should be liable only to the extent of their own contribution

proprietary estoppel particular variety of *estoppel*, originating in *equity*, whereby a person is precluded from resiling from a promise to grant an interest in land

public policy a community norm or standard invoked by a court to justify refusing to enforce a particular obligation, as for example with a *penalty clause* or *restraint of trade*

puff an obviously exaggerated statement not meant to be taken literally or seriously, and having no legal consequences

punitive damages see *exemplary damages*

quantum meruit action, usually *restitutionary* in nature, to recover reasonable remuneration for work performed

quantum valebat action, usually *restitutionary* in nature, to recover the reasonable value of goods sold and delivered

quasi-contractual old name given to certain forms of action now recognised as *restitutionary* in nature

ratification the act of accepting an obligation or approving a prior decision that might not otherwise have been binding

reading down giving a narrow interpretation to a provision, so as to limit its application

rectification an *equitable* remedy, whereby corrections are ordered to a document which contains a mistaken recording of a contract or other legal instrument

reliance loss the loss suffered as a result of a *breach of contract*, when comparing the innocent party's position at the date of assessment to the position in which they would have been had the contract never been made

relief against forfeiture a doctrine allowing a court to restrain the *unconscionable* exercise of (a) a right to terminate a contract that results in the loss of a proprietary interest, or (b) the right to retain contractual payments made by a defaulting party

remoteness of damage the principle that *damages* cannot be recovered for a type of loss that would not have been reasonably contemplated by the parties involved

renunciation a form of *repudiation* that involves an inability or unwillingness to perform one or more contractual obligations that have fallen due for performance

representation a statement or conduct that causes a *representee* to believe something

representee a person to whom a *representation* is made

representor the person by whom a *representation* is made

repudiation a refusal or inability by one party to perform one or more contractual obligations that gives the other party the right to terminate the contract

rescind to exercise a right of *rescission*

rescission (1) the exercise of a right to render a contract *void*, so that it is as if the contract had never existed

(2) sometimes used to mean termination of a contract for breach or *repudiation*

restitutio in integrum complete restoration of the previous position: a precondition of *rescission (1)*

restitution(ary) the purpose of various remedies or actions, being to compel a defendant to give up or pay for a benefit which it would be unjust for them to retain

restraint of trade a doctrine whereby unreasonable restrictions on a person's liberty to trade are rendered unenforceable

restrictive covenant a *covenant (2)* intended to limit the *covenantor's* freedom to do something

reverse indemnity a form of *indemnity*, where A must indemnify B against any breach of B's contractual obligations to A

secondary obligation a remedial obligation to provide redress for the breach of a *primary obligation*

severable (1) describing an invalid term or portion of a contract which can be detached (severed) from the contract, leaving the remainder enforceable

(2) see *divisible*

sham an agreement or transaction not intended to have effect, but rather deliberately constructed to disguise the parties' true intentions

smart contract software which can autonomously verify whether specified conditions are met and then execute a transaction

soft law rules and principles that do not have direct legal effect, but which are nonetheless intended to influence behaviour (such as a voluntary code of practice)

special disadvantage an element of the doctrine of *unconscionable bargains*: a particular condition, weakness or disability that leaves a party vulnerable to exploitation by a stronger party

special equity for married women an *equitable* doctrine allowing a guarantee given by a wife in relation to her husband's debts to be set aside in certain circumstances

specific performance an *equitable* remedy used to compel the performance of (among other things) a contractual obligation

Statute of Frauds old British statutory provision prohibiting enforcement of certain contracts (eg for sale of land) unless evidenced in writing

statutory protection old principle allowing *restitutionary* claims by a party involved in an illegal transaction, where the illegality arose under a statute enacted for the benefit or protection of that party

step clause see *cascade clause*

strict describing an obligation which requires that something be done or achieved, not merely that the *obligor* make reasonable efforts or take due care, but for non-performance of which certain excuses may be available

subcontract where A has a contract with B, an arrangement by B to have someone else (a *subcontractor*) undertake some or all of what B needs to do to fulfil B's obligations to A

subcontractor see *subcontract*

subject to contract a phrase used to indicate that agreement has been reached, but subject to the understanding that the terms will be recorded in a formal document

subject to finance a *condition (4)* relating to the purchase of property, in which the purchase is contingent on the buyer being able to raise or borrow enough money

subject to sale a *condition (4)* relating to the purchase of property, in which the purchase is contingent on the buyer being able to sell existing property of their own

subrogation the right to stand in the legal shoes of someone else and assert the rights and remedies available to that person

substantial performance the principle that near enough is good enough when ascertaining whether an *obligor* has discharged their obligation and earned the right to counter-performance

substantive unfairness unfairness in the terms or substance of a contract

sufficiency of *consideration*: satisfaction of the legal requirements of that doctrine

surety see *guarantee*

tenant a person entitled to exclusive possession of property, most commonly as a *lessee* of land

termination for convenience express power for a party to terminate a contract whenever they choose, without having to have a particular reason, though often only after a period of notice is given

testator a person who makes a will

third party sometimes used to mean a person who is affected by, or stands to benefit from, a contract to which they are not technically a party

third-party indemnity a form of *indemnity*, where A must indemnify B against any claim by a *third party* against B in connection with specified matters or transactions

time is of the essence a phrase used to indicate that a *time stipulation* is an *essential term (2)*

time stipulation a requirement that a contractual obligation be performed within a certain time

tort a civil wrong for which one person (the 'tortfeasor') may be sued by another person (the 'victim') who suffers damage

tortious describing the conduct or liability associated with a *tort*

total failure of consideration a *failure of consideration* where no part of the expected performance from B has been received by A

trade or commerce, in requirement that conduct be of a commercial character, so as to attract the operation of certain prohibitions or controls in the *ACL* or other statutes

trespass on the case an old *form of action* used to seek redress for wrongdoing

trust an arrangement whereby one person (the *trustee*) holds property which they are obliged to use for the benefit of, or at some point transfer to, another person (the *beneficiary*)

trustee see *trust*

trustee in bankruptcy a person appointed to manage the affairs of a person who has been declared bankrupt

uberrimae fidei see *utmost good faith*

uncertain describing a promise or contract which is too *vague* to be enforceable

unconscientious *unconscionable*

unconscionable unreasonably exploiting someone else's vulnerability in a way that is against the requirements of good conscience

unconscionable bargains *equitable* doctrine allowing contracts or other dispositions to be set aside when a stronger party unfairly takes advantage of a weaker party's *special disadvantage*

undue influence an *equitable* doctrine allowing contracts or other dispositions to be set aside when procured by the domination or sway one party has over the other's decision-making

unenforceable describing a contract or term that is not *void*, and thus may have some legal effect, but that nonetheless cannot be enforced by one or both parties by way of court action

UNIDROIT Principles Principles of International Commercial Contracts developed by the International Institute for the Unification of Private Law

unilateral contract a contract in which an *executory* promise or set of promises is exchanged for an act, and only one party is at any stage bound to keep a promise

unilateral mistake a variety of *mutual mistake*, where one party has an erroneous belief and the other is or ought to be aware of that fact

unjust enrichment a concept used to explain the availability of *restitutionary* remedies against a person who is seeking to retain or not pay for a benefit conferred on them

unliquidated damages an award of damages that is calculated by a court or arbitrator after an assessment of the loss suffered by a plaintiff, as opposed to being agreed by the parties in advance under a *liquidated damages* provision

unwritten law the *common law (1)*, including *equity*

utmost good faith requirement of *good faith* imposed, historically, on the parties to certain kinds of contract, notably insurance contracts

vague describing a promise or contract whose meaning cannot be ascertained with sufficient precision for it to be enforceable

Vienna Convention United Nations Convention on the International Sale of Goods

vitiating factor a reason why a contract might not be legally valid or enforceable

void of no legal effect

voidable describing a contract whose formation or content is sufficiently defective as to give one or both parties a right of *rescission (1)*; unless and until such a right is exercised to make the contract *void*, the contract is treated as completely valid

waiver the act of dispensing with a requirement or overlooking a defect: used, confusingly, to denote a number of different but overlapping concepts, including a form of *estoppel* or an *affirmation*

warranty (1) a statement of a promissory nature and thus capable of having contractual force; more generally, any term of a contract

(2) a contractual term no breach of which will permit termination of the contract by the other party – also known as a *non-essential term*

BIBLIOGRAPHY

ACCC (Australian Competition and Consumer Commission) (2013a), *Unfair Contract Terms: Industry Review Outcomes*, ACCC, Canberra

—— (2013b), 'Court declares consumer contract terms unfair', media release, 30 July 2013

—— (2016), *Unfair Terms in Small Business Contracts: A Review of Selected Industries*, ACCC, Canberra

ACCC et al (2016a), *Consumer Guarantees: A Guide for Businesses and Legal Practitioners*, Commonwealth, Canberra

—— (2016b), *Unfair Contract Terms: A Guide for Businesses and Legal Practitioners*, Commonwealth, Canberra

—— (2017), *A Guide to the Australian Consumer Law for Fundraising and Other Activities of Charities, Not-For-Profits and Fundraisers*, Commonwealth, Canberra

Acreman, T J (2016), 'The Long Road to a Wide Ambiguity Gateway' 42 *Australian Bar Review* 12

Adams, J N & Brownsword, R (1987), 'The Ideologies of Contract' 7 *Legal Studies* 205

Aghion, P, Dewatripont, M, Legros, P & Zingales, L (eds) (2016), *The Impact of Incomplete Contracts on Economics*, Oxford University Press, Oxford

Akerlof, G (1970), 'The Market for "Lemons": Quality Uncertainty and the Market Mechanism' 84 *Quarterly Journal of Economics* 488

Alexander, N, Howieson, J & Fox, K (2015), *Negotiation: Strategy Style Skills*, 3rd ed, LexisNexis Butterworths, Sydney

Ali, P, Bourova, E & Ramsay, I (2016), 'The Statutory Right to Seek a Credit Contract Variation on the Grounds of Hardship: A History and Analysis' 44 *Federal Law Review* 77

Allsop, J (2011), 'Good Faith and Australian Contract Law: A Practical Issue and a Question of Theory and Principle' 85 *Australian Law Journal* 341

Ames, J B (1899), 'Two Theories of Consideration' 12 *Harvard Law Review* 515

Anderson, G (2016), 'The *Trendtex* Principle in Australian Law: Context and Recent Developments' 40 *University of Western Australia Law Review* 85

Arup, C, Dent, C, Howe, J & van Caenegem, W (2013), 'Restraints of Trade: The Legal Practice' 36 *University of New South Wales Law Journal* 1

Asprey, M M (2010), *Plain Language for Lawyers*, 4th ed, Federation Press, Sydney

Atamer, Y M (2017), 'Why Judicial Control of Price Terms in Consumer Contracts Might Not Always Be the Right Answer – Insights from behavioural Law and Economics' 80 *Modern Law Review* 624

Atiyah, P S (1979), *The Rise and Fall of Freedom of Contract*, Clarendon Press, Oxford

—— (1982), 'Economic Duress and the Overborne Will' 98 *Law Quarterly Review* 197

Attorney-General's Department (2012), *Improving Australia's Law and Justice Framework: A Discussion Paper to Explore the Scope for Reforming Australian Contract Law*, Attorney-General's Department, Canberra

Austen-Baker, R (2009), 'Comprehensive Contract Theory: A Four-Norm Model of Contract Relations' 25 *Journal of Contract Law* 216

Australian Government (2016), 'Australia's Accession to the Convention on Choice of Court Agreements' National Interest Analysis [2016] ATNIA 7, Australian Government, Canberra

—— (2018a), *Extending Unfair Contract Terms Protections to Insurance Contracts: Proposals Paper*, Commonwealth, Canberra

—— (2018b), *Review of Unfair Contract Term Protections for Small Business: Discussion Paper*, Commonwealth, Canberra

Ayres, I & Braithwaite, J (1992), *Responsive Regulation*, Oxford University Press, New York

Baker, J H (2002), *An Introduction to English Legal History*, 4th ed, Butterworths, London

—— (2012), 'Deeds Speak Louder Than Words: Covenants and the Law of Proof 1290–1321' in S Jenks, J Rose & C Whittick (eds), *Law, Lawyers and Texts: Studies in Medieval Legal History in Honour of Paul Brand*, Brill, Leiden, p 177

Bakos, Y, Marotta-Wurgler, F & Trossen, D R (2014), 'Does Anyone Read the Fine Print? Consumer Attention to Standard-Form Contracts' 43 *Journal of Legal Studies* 1

Baldwin, R, Cave, M & Lodge, M (2012), *Understanding Regulation: Theory, Strategy and Practice*, 2nd ed, Oxford University Press, Oxford

Bant, E (2015), 'Statute and Common Law: Interaction and Influence in Light of the Principle of Coherence' 38 *University of New South Wales Law Journal* 367

—— (2017), 'The Evolution of Unjust Enrichment and Restitution Law in the High Court of Australia' 25 *Restitution Law Review* 121

Bant, E & Bryan, M (2015), 'Fact, Future and Fiction: Risk and Reasonable Reliance in Estoppel' 35 *Oxford Journal of Legal Studies* 427

Barnett, K (2012), *Accounting for Profit for Breach of Contract: Theory and Practice*, Hart Publishing, Oxford

—— (2016), 'Great Expectations: A Dissection of Expectation Damages in Contract in Australia and England' 33 *Journal of Contract Law* 163

Barnett, K & Harder, S (2014), *Remedies in Australian Private Law*, Cambridge University Press, Melbourne

Barnett, R (1986), 'A Consent Theory of Contract' 86 *Columbia Law Review* 269

—— (2012), 'Contract is Not Promise; Contract is Consent' 45 *Suffolk Law Review* 647

Barnhizer, D D (2005), 'Inequality of Bargaining Power' 76 *University of Colorado Law Review* 139

Beale, H & Dugdale, T (1975), 'Contracts Between Businessmen: Planning and the Use of Contractual Remedies' 2 *British Journal of Law and Society* 45

Berger, K P (2010), *The Creeping Codification of the New Lex Mercatoria*, 2nd ed, Wolters Kluwer, Alphen aan den Rijn

Bernstein, L (1992), 'Opting out of the Legal System: Extralegal Contractual Relations in the Diamond Industry' 21 *Journal of Legal Studies* 115

Berryman, J & Carroll, R (2014), 'Coercive Relief – Reflections on Supervision and Enforcement Constraints' 38 *University of Western Australia Law Review* 123

Bevan, C (2009), 'Waiver of Contractual Rights: A Non Sequitur' 83 *Australian Law Journal* 817

Bigwood, R (1996), 'Undue Influence: "Impaired Consent" or "Wicked Exploitation"?' 16 *Oxford Journal of Legal Studies* 503

—— (2000), 'Conscience and the Liberal Conception of Contract: Observing Basic Distinctions' 16 *Journal of Contract Law* 1 (Part I) and 191 (Part II)

—— (2003), *Exploitative Contracts*, Oxford University Press, Oxford

—— (2008), 'Throwing the Baby out with the Bathwater? Four Questions on the Demise of Lawful Act Duress in New South Wales' 27 *University of Queensland Law Journal* 41

—— (2011), 'Circumscribing Election: Reflections on the Taxonomization and Mental Componentry of Affirmation of a Contract by Election' 30 *University of Queensland Law Journal* 235

—— (2013), 'Still Curbing Unconscionability: *Kakavas* in the High Court of Australia' 37 *Melbourne University Law Review* 463

—— (2018), 'The Undue Influence of "Non-Australian" Undue Influence Law on Australian Undue Influence Law: Farewell Johnson v Buttress? Part 1' 35 *Journal of Contract Law* 56

Birks, P (1989), *An Introduction to the Law of Restitution*, rev ed, Oxford University Press, Oxford

—— (1996), 'Equity in the Modern Law: An Exercise in Taxonomy' 26 *University of Western Australia Law Review* 1

—— (2000), 'Three Kinds of Objection to Discretionary Remedialism' 29 *University of Western Australia Law Review* 1

—— (2005), *Unjust Enrichment*, 2nd ed, Oxford University Press, Oxford

Birks, P & Chin N Y (1995), 'On the Nature of Undue Influence' in J Beatson & D Friedmann (eds), *Good Faith and Fault in Contract Law*, Oxford University Press, Oxford, p 57

Black, J (2002), 'Critical Reflections on Regulation' 27 *Australian Journal of Legal Philosophy* 1

Bomball, P (2015), 'Subsequent Conduct, Construction and Characterisation in Employment Contract Law' 32 *Journal of Contract Law* 149

—— (2019), 'Intention, Pretence and the Contract of Employment' *Journal of Contract Law* (forthcoming)

Bowers, S (2011), 'National contract law "well received"' *Australian Financial Review*, 10 June 2011, p 20

Braucher, J, Kidwell, J & Whitford, W C (eds) (2013), *Revisiting the Contracts Scholarship of Stewart Macaulay: On the Empirical and the Lyrical*, Hart Publishing, Oxford

Bridge, M (1989), 'Mitigation of Damages in Contract and the Meaning of Avoidable Loss' 105 *Law Quarterly Review* 398

—— (2017), *Benjamin's Sale of Goods*, 10th ed, Sweet & Maxwell, London

Bright, S, Glover, H & Prassl, J (2013), 'Tenancy Agreements' in E Simpson & M Stewart (eds), *Sham Transactions*, Oxford University Press, Oxford, p 105

Brownsword, R, van Gestel, R A J & Micklitz, H-W (eds) (2017), *Contract and Regulation: A Handbook on New Methods of Law Making in Private Law*, Edward Elgar, Cheltenham/Northampton

Burns, F (2001), '*Giumelli v Giumelli* Revisited: Equitable Estoppel, the Constructive Trust and Discretionary Remedialism' 22 *Adelaide Law Review* 123

—— (2002), 'Undue Influence Inter Vivos and the Elderly' 26 *Melbourne University Law Review* 499

Burrows, A (1998), *Understanding the Law of Obligations*, Hart Publishing, Oxford

—— (2010), 'The Australian Law of Restitution: Has the High Court Lost its Way?' in E Bant & M Harding (eds), *Exploring Private Law*, Cambridge University Press, Cambridge, p 67

—— (2011), *The Law of Restitution*, 3rd ed, Oxford University Press, Oxford

—— (2012a), 'Damages and Rights' in D Nolan & A Robertson (eds), *Rights and Private Law* Hart Publishing, Oxford, p 275

—— (2012b), *A Restatement of the English Law of Unjust Enrichment*, Oxford University Press, Oxford

—— (2017), 'Illegality after *Patel v Mirza*' 70 *Current Legal Problems* 55

Burrows, J, Finn, J & Todd, S (2016), *Law of Contract in New Zealand*, 5th ed, LexisNexis NZ, Wellington

Butt, P (2013), *Modern Legal Drafting: A Guide to Using Clearer Language*, 3rd ed, Cambridge University Press, Melbourne

Byrne, N (2013), 'Contracting for "Contextualism" – How Can Parties Influence the Interpretation Method Applied to Their Agreement?' 13 *Queensland University of Technology Law Review* 52

CAANZ (Consumer Affairs Australia and New Zealand) (2016), *Australian Consumer Law Review: Interim Report*, Commonwealth, Canberra

—— (2017), *Australian Consumer Law Review: Final Report*, Commonwealth, Canberra

—— (2018), *Australian Consumer Law Review: Clarification, Simplification and Modernisation of the Consumer Guarantee Framework*, Consultation Regulation Impact Statement, Commonwealth, Canberra

CAF (Legislative and Governance Forum on Consumer Affairs) (2018), 'Joint Communique: Meeting of Ministers for Consumer Affairs', Melbourne, 26 October 2018

Campbell, D (ed) (2001), *The Relational Theory of Contract: Selected Works of Ian Macneil*, Sweet & Maxwell, London

Campbell, D & Wylie, P (2003), 'Ain't No Telling (Which Circumstances are Exceptional)' 62 *Cambridge Law Journal* 605

Capper, D (1998), 'Undue Influence and Unconscionability: A Rationalisation' 114 *Law Quarterly Review* 479

Carlin, T M (2001), 'The Contracts Review Act 1980 (NSW) – 20 Years On' 23 *Sydney Law Review* 125

Carrigan, F (2013), 'The Trivial Nature of Strict Legalism' 13 *Oxford University Commonwealth Law Journal* 1

Carroll, R (2012), 'Agreements to Specifically Perform Contractual Obligations' 29 *Journal of Contract Law* 155

Carter, J W (1984), 'The Embiricos Principle and the Law of Anticipatory Breach' 47 *Modern Law Review* 422

—— (1990), 'Termination Clauses' 3 *Journal of Contract Law* 90

—— (1995), '"Commercial" Construction and the *Canada SS* Rules' 9 *Journal of Contract Law* 69

—— (1998), 'The Renegotiation of Contracts' 13 *Journal of Contract Law* 185

—— (2009), 'Contractual Indemnities – Are They Worth Having?' 28 *Australian Resources and Energy Law Journal* 169

—— (2010), 'The Commercial Side of Australian Consumer Protection Law' 26 *Journal of Contract Law* 221

—— (2012), 'Discharge as the Basis for Termination for Breach of Contract' 128 *Law Quarterly Review* 283

—— (2013), *The Construction of Commercial Contracts*, Hart Publishing, Oxford

—— (2018), *Contract Law in Australia*, 7th ed, LexisNexis Butterworths, Sydney

—— (2019), *Carter's Breach of Contract*, 2nd ed, Hart Publishing, Oxford

Carter, J W & Courtney, W (2015), 'Implied Terms in Contracts: Australian Law' 43 *Australian Business Law Review* 246

Carter, J W, Courtney, W, Peden, E, Riley, J & Tolhurst, G J (2015), 'Terms Implied in Law: "Trust and Confidence" in the High Court of Australia' 32 *Journal of Contract Law* 203

Carter, J W, Courtney, W, Peden, E, Stewart, A & Tolhurst, G J (2013), 'Contractual Penalties: Resurrecting the Equitable Jurisdiction' 30 *Journal of Contract Law* 99

Carter, J W, Courtney, W & Tolhurst, G J (2014a), 'Issues of Principle in Assessing Contract Damages' 31 *Journal of Contract Law* 171

—— (2014b), '"Reasonable Endeavours" in Contract Construction' 32 *Journal of Contract Law* 36

—— (2017), 'Assessment of Contractual Penalties: *Dunlop* Deflated' 34 *Journal of Contract Law* 4

—— (2018), 'Two Models for Discharge of a Contract by Repudiation' 77 *Cambridge Law Journal* 97

Carter, J W & Furmston, M P (1994), 'Good Faith and Fairness in the Negotiation of Contracts Part I' 8 *Journal of Contract Law* 1

—— (1995), 'Good Faith and Fairness in the Negotiation of Contracts Part II' 8 *Journal of Contract Law* 93

Carter, J W & Peden, E (2003), 'Good Faith in Australian Contract Law' 19 *Journal of Contract Law* 155

Carter, J W, Phang, A & Poole, J (1995), 'Reactions to Williams v Roffey' 8 *Journal of Contract Law* 248

Carter, J W & Stewart, A (1993), 'Commerce and Conscience: The High Court's Developing View of Contract' 23 *University of Western Australia Law Review* 49

—— (2002), 'Interpretation, Good Faith and the "True Meaning" of Contracts: The Royal Botanic Decision' 18 *Journal of Contract Law* 182

Carter, J W & Tilbury, M J (1998), 'Remedial Choice and Contract Drafting' 13 *Journal of Contract Law* 5

Carter, J W & Tolhurst, G J (2009), 'Recovery of Contract Debts Following Termination for Breach' 25 *Journal of Contract Law* 191

Carter, J W & Yates, D (2004), 'Perspectives on Commercial Construction and the *Canada SS* Case' 20 *Journal of Contract Law* 233

Castles, A C (1982), *An Australian Legal History*, Law Book Co, Sydney

Catterwell, R (2012), 'The Indirect Use of Evidence of Prior Negotiations and Subjective Intention: Part of the Surrounding Circumstances' 29 *Journal of Contract Law* 183

—— (2019), 'Striking a Balance in Contract Construction: The Primacy of the Text' 23 *Edinburgh Law Review* 52

Chen-Wishart, M (1989), *Unconscionable Bargains*, Butterworths, Wellington

—— (1995), 'Consideration: Practical Benefit and the Emperor's New Clothes' in J Beatson & D Friedmann (eds), *Good Faith and Fault in Contract Law*, Oxford University Press, Oxford, p 123

—— (2006), 'Undue Influence: Beyond Impaired Consent and Wrong-Doing, Towards a Relational Analysis' in A Burrows A & A Rodger (eds), *Mapping the Law*, Oxford University Press, Oxford, p 201

—— (2013), 'In Defence of Consideration' 13 *Oxford University Commonwealth Law Journal* 209

—— (2016), 'Reforming Consideration: No Greener Pastures' in S Degeling, J Edelman & J Goudkamp (eds), *Contract in Commercial Law*, Lawbook Co, Sydney, p 77

Cherednychenko, O (2004), 'The Constitutionalization of Contract Law: Something New under the Sun?' 8.1 *Electronic Journal of Comparative Law*

Chitty, J (1834), *A Practical Treatise on the Law of Contracts, Not under Seal*, S Sweet, London

Christensen, S & Duncan, W D (2012), Unfair Terms in Residential Land Contracts: Will the Australian Consumer Law Improve a Buyer's Bargaining Position?' 20 *Competition and Consumer Law Journal* 56

Clarke, P & Erbacher, S (2018), *Australian Consumer Law: Commentary and Materials*, 6th ed, Lawbook Co, Sydney

Coci, L (2015), 'It's Time Exemplary Damages Were Part of the Judicial Armory in Contract' 40 *University of Western Australia Law Review* 1

Coggins, J (2011), 'From Disparity to Harmonisation of Construction Industry Payment Legislation in Australia: A Proposal for a Dual Process of Adjudication Based upon Size of Progress Payment Claim' 11 *Australasian Journal of Construction Economics and Building* 34

Coggins, J, Davie, T, Earls, T & Evans, P (2016), *Understanding Construction Law*, LexisNexis Butterworths, Sydney

Collins, H (1999), *Regulating Contracts*, Oxford University Press, Oxford

—— (2014), 'Implied Terms: The Foundation in Good Faith and Fair Dealing' [2014] *Current Legal Problems* 1

—— (2016), 'Is a Relational Contract a Legal Concept?' in S Degeling, J Edelman & J Goudkamp (eds), *Contract in Commercial Law*, Lawbook Co, Sydney, p 37

Cooke, E (1997), 'Estoppel and the Protection of Expectations' 17 *Legal Studies* 258

Coorey, A (2015), *Australian Consumer Law*, LexisNexis Butterworths, Sydney

Coote, B (1964), *Exception Clauses*, Sweet & Maxwell, London

—— (1967), 'The Rise and Fall of Fundamental Breach' 40 *Australian Law Journal* 336

Corcoran, S (2012), 'Good Faith as a Principle of Interpretation: What is the Positive Content of Good Faith?' 36 *Australian Bar Review* 1

Corones, S G (2013), *The Australian Consumer Law*, 2nd ed, Lawbook Co, Sydney

—— (2014), *Competition Law in Australia*, 6th ed, Lawbook Co, Sydney

Corones, S, Christensen, S, Malbon, J, Asher, A & Paterson, J (2016), *Comparative Analysis of Overseas Consumer Policy Frameworks*, Commonwealth, Canberra

Courtney, W (2011), 'The Nature of Contractual Indemnities' 27 *Journal of Contract Law* 1

—— (2014), *Contractual Indemnities*, Hart Publishing, Oxford

Craswell, R (2000), 'Against Fuller and Purdue' 67 *University of Chicago Law Review* 99

Cuniberti, G (2014), 'The International Market for Contracts: The Most Attractive Contract Laws' 14 *Northwestern Journal of International Law & Business* 455

Dagan, H & Heller, M (2017), *The Choice Theory of Contracts*, Cambridge University Press, Cambridge

Dahdal, A (2015), 'Good Faith and Post Repudiation Conduct' 40 *University of Western Australia Law Review* 72

Daintith, T (1979), 'Regulation by Contract: the New Prerogative' 32 *Current Legal Problems* 41

—— (2005), 'Contractual Discretion and Administrative Discretion: A Unified Analysis' 68 *Modern Law Review* 554

Dal Pont, G (2000), 'The Varying Shades of "Unconscionable" Conduct – Same Term, Different Meaning' 19 *Australian Bar Review* 135

—— (2013), *Law of Agency*, 3rd ed, LexisNexis Butterworths, Sydney

—— (2015a), *Equity and Trusts in Australia*, 6th ed, Lawbook Co, Sydney

—— (2015b), *Law of Confidentiality*, LexisNexis Butterworths, Sydney

Dalton, C (1985), 'An Essay in the Deconstruction of Contract Doctrine' 94 *Yale Law Journal* 997

D'Angelo, N (2011), 'Indemnities and Guarantees: A Taxonomic Expedition' 27 *Journal of Contract Law* 35

Davies, A (2013), 'Employment Law' in E Simpson & M Stewart (eds), *Sham Transactions*, Oxford University Press, Oxford, p 176

Davis, J L R (2016), 'Joint and Several Contractual Rights and Obligations' in *The Laws of Australia*, Lawbook Co, Melbourne, vol 7 (Contract — General Principles), Title 7.3, ch 4

Dawson, F (1982), 'Making Representations Good' 1 *Canterbury Law Review* 329

De Wilde, F (2007), 'The Less Said - The Worse: Silence as Misleading or Deceptive Conduct' 15 *Trade Practices Law Journal* 7

Deakin, S (2011), 'Economic Relations' in C Sappideen & P Vines (eds), *Fleming's The Law of Torts*, 10th ed, Lawbook Co, Sydney, p 769

Derrington, D & Ashton, R S (2005), *The Law of Liability Insurance*, 2nd ed, Lexis Nexis, Sydney

Dharmananda, J & Firios, L (2015), 'Interpreting Statutes and Contracts: A Distinction Without a Difference?' 89 *Australian Law Journal* 560

Dietrich, J (2012), 'Service Guarantees and Consequential Loss under the Australian Consumer Law: The Illusion of Uniformity' 20 *Comparative and Consumer Law Journal* 43

—— (2016), 'Misleading Conduct by Multiple Parties and Proportionate Liability' 24 *Competition and Consumer Law Review* 157

Dixon, B (2005), 'Common Law Obligations of Good Faith in Australian Commercial Contracts — A Relational Recipe' 33 *Australian Business Law Review* 87

Dixon, W (2017), 'Termination for Convenience or Not?' 45 *Australian Business Law Review* 229

Donahue, C (2004) 'Medieval and Early Modern *Lex Mercatoria*: An Attempt at the *Probatio Diabolica*' 5 *Chicago Journal of International Law* 21

Douglas, M (2018), 'Choice of Court Agreements under an International Civil Law Act' 34 *Journal of Contract Law* 186

Doyle, S & Wright, D (2001), 'Restitutionary Damages – The Unnecessary Remedy' 25 *Melbourne University Law Review* 1

Drahos, P & Parker, S (1990), 'Critical Contract Law in Australia' 3 *Journal of Contract Law* 30

Duggan, A, Bryan, M & Hanks, F (1994), *Contractual Non-Disclosure*, Longman Professional, Melbourne

Duke, A (2007), 'A Universal Duty of Good Faith: An Economic Perspective' 33 *Monash University Law Review* 182

Dyson, A, Goudkamp, J & Wilmot-Smith, F (eds) (2017), *Defences in Contract Law*, Hart Publishing, Oxford

Dyson, A & Kramer, A (2014), 'There is No "Breach Date Rule": Mitigation, Difference in Value and Date of Assessment' 130 *Law Quarterly Review* 259

Edelman, J (2002), *Gain-Based Damages – Contract, Tort, Equity and Intellectual Property*, Hart Publishing, Oxford

Edelman, J & Bant, E (2016), *Unjust Enrichment*, 2nd ed, Hart Publishing, Oxford

Eldridge, J (2018a), 'Contract Codification and "Certainty"' 35 *Journal of Contract Law* 146

—— (2018b), 'The New Law of Penalties: Mapping the Terrain' [2018] *Journal of Business Law* 637

Ellinghaus, M P, Wright, E W & Karras, M (2005), *Models of Contract Law: An Empirical Evaluation of Their Utility*, Themis Press, Sydney

Enonchong, E (1996), 'Breach of Contract and Damages for Mental Distress' 16 *Oxford Journal of Legal Studies* 617

Enright, W I B & Merkin, R M (2015), *Sutton on Insurance Law*, Lawbook Co, Sydney

Evans, S (2001), 'Defending Discretionary Remedialism' 23 *Sydney Law Review* 463

Evans, W (1806), *A Treatise on the Law of Obligations, or Contracts by M Pothier*, A Strahan, London

Farnsworth, E A (1979), 'Damages and Specific Relief' 27 *American Journal of Comparative Law* 247

Fehlberg, B (1997), *Sexually Transmitted Debt: Surety Experience and English Law*, Clarendon Press, Oxford

Feinman, J M (1983), 'Critical Approaches to Contract Law' 30 *UCLA Law Review* 829

Fell, A (2018), 'The Concept of Coherence in Australian Private Law' 41 *Melbourne University Law Review* 1160

Fetter, J (2007), '*Houghton v Arms*: Employees Strictly Liable for Mistakes at Work' 20 *Australian Journal of Labour Law* 302

Finlay, A (1997), 'Section 68A(2) Trade Practices Act 1974: Cinderella Section' 5 *Competition and Consumer Law Journal* 22

Finn, P D (1985), 'Equitable Estoppel' in P D Finn (ed), *Essays in Equity*, Law Book Co, Sydney, p 59

—— (1989a), 'Contract and the Fiduciary Principle' 12 *University of New South Wales Law Journal* 76

—— (1989b), 'Good Faith and Nondisclosure' in P D Finn (ed), *Essays on Torts*, Law Book Co, Sydney, p 150

—— (2010), 'Internationalisation or Isolation: The Australian *cul de sac*? The Case of Contract Law' in E Bant & M Harding (eds), *Exploring Private Law*, Cambridge University Press, Cambridge, p 41

—— (2014), 'Fiduciary Reflections' 88 *Australian Law Journal* 127

—— (2016), 'Unity, Then Divergence: The Privy Council, the Common Law of England and the Common Laws of Canada, Australia and New Zealand' in A Robertson & M Tilbury (eds), *The Common Law of Obligations: Diversity and Unity*, Hart Publishing, Oxford, p 37

Fisher, R & Ury, W (1981), *Getting to Yes: Negotiating Agreement Without Giving In*, Houghton Mifflin, Boston

Freiberg, A (2017), *Regulation in Australia*, Federation Press, Sydney

Freilich, A & Webb, E (2009), 'The Incorporation of Contractual Terms in Unsigned Documents – Is it Time for a Realistic, Consumer-Friendly Approach?' 34 *University of Western Australia Law Review* 261

Fried, C (2015), *Contract as Promise: A Theory of Contractual Obligation*, 2nd ed, Oxford University Press, New York

Friedmann, D (1995), 'The Performance Interest in Contract Damages' 111 *Law Quarterly Review* 628

Frug, M J (1985), 'Re-Reading Contracts: A Feminist Analysis of a Contracts Casebook' 34 *American University Law Review* 1065

Fry, E (1921), *A Treatise on the Specific Performance of Contracts*, 6th ed, Stevens & Sons, London

Fuller, L L & Perdue, W R (1936), 'The Reliance Interest in Contract Damages' 46 *Yale Law Journal* 52 and 373

Gardner, S (1992), 'Trashing with Trollope: A Deconstruction of the Postal Rules in Contract' 12 *Oxford Journal of Legal Studies* 170

Garnett, R (2017), 'Arbitration of Cross-Border Consumer Transaction in Australia: A Way Forward?' 39 *Sydney Law Review* 569

Gava, J (2006), 'Can Contract Law be Justified on Economic Grounds?' 25 *University of Queensland Law Journal* 253

—— (2013), 'How Should Judges Decide Commercial Contract Cases?' 30 *Journal of Contract Law* 133

Giancaspro, M (2013), 'Practical Benefit: An English Anomaly or a Growing Force in Contract Law?' 30 *Journal of Contract Law* 12

—— (2014a), 'Should the Practical Benefit Principle Extend to Contract Formation?' 42 *Australian Business Law Review* 389

—— (2014b), 'The Rules for Contractual Renegotiation: A Call for Change' 37 *University of Western Australia Law Review* 1

—— (2017a), 'Is a "Smart Contract" Really a Smart Idea? Insights from a Legal Perspective' 33 *Computer Law & Security Review* 825

—— (2017b), '"I Now Pronounce You . . . in a State of Uncertainty": Contemporary Treatment of the Wives' Special Equity and a Plan for the Future' 11 *Journal of Equity* 80

Gillies, P (2004), 'Non-Disclosure: Trade Practices Act, s 52' 78 *Australian Law Journal* 653

Gilmore, G (1974), *The Death of Contract*, Ohio State University Press, Columbus

Goddard, D (2000), 'Security of Contract: Why it Matters and What That Means' 16 *Journal of Contract Law* 123

Goetz, C J & Scott, R E (1990), 'Enforcing Promises: An Examination of the Basis of Contract' 89 *Yale Law Journal* 1261

Goff, R & Jones, G (1966), *The Law of Restitution*, Sweet & Maxwell, London

Goldacre, L (2013), 'The Contract for the Supply of Educational Services and Unfair Contract Terms: Advancing Students' Rights as Consumers' 37 *University of Western Australia Law Review* 176

Golding, G (2015), 'Terms Implied by Law into Employment Contracts: Are They Necessary?' 28 *Australian Journal of Labour Law* 113

—— (2016), 'The Role of Judges in the Regulation of Australian Employment Contracts' 32 *International Journal of Comparative Labour Law & Industrial Relations* 69

Goldwasser, V & Ciro, T (2002), 'Standards of Behaviour in Commercial Contracting' 30 *Australian Business Law Review* 369

Gordley, J (1991), *The Philosophical Origins of Modern Contract Doctrine*, Oxford University Press, Oxford

Grantham, R & Jensen, D (2016), 'Coherence in the Age of Statutes' 42 *Monash University Law Review* 360

Grantham, R & Rickett, C (2001), 'The Subsidiarity of Unjust Enrichment' 117 *Law Quarterly Review* 273

Gray, A (2015), 'Good Faith in Australian Contract Law after Barker' 43 *Australian Business Law Review* 358

—— (2017), 'The Law of Penalties and the Question of Breach' 45 *Australian Business Law Review* 8

Graycar, R & Morgan, J (2002), *The Hidden Gender of Law*, 2nd ed, Federation Press, Sydney

Griggs, L, Freilich, A & Webb, E (2011) 'Challenging the Notion of a Consumer: Time for Change' 19 *Competition and Consumer Law Journal* 52

Grodecki, J K (1955), 'In Pari Delicto Potior Est Conditio Defendentis' 71 *Law Quarterly Review* 254

Haigh, R & Hepburn, S (2000), 'The Bank Manager Always Rings Twice: Stereotyping in Equity after Garcia' 26 *Monash University Law Review* 275

Handford, P (2017), *Limitation of Actions: The Laws of Australia*, 4th ed, Lawbook Co, Sydney

Handley, K R (2016), *Estoppel by Conduct and Election*, 2nd ed, Sweet & Maxwell, London

Harder, S (2011), 'Problems in Interpreting the Unfair Contract Terms Provisions of the Australian Consumer Law' 34 *Australian Bar Review* 306

Harper, I, Anderson, P, McCluskey, S & O'Bryan, M (2015), *Competition Policy Review: Final Report*, Commonwealth, Canberra

Harris, D, Ogus, A & Phillips, J (1979), 'Contract Remedies and the Consumer Surplus' 95 *Law Quarterly Review* 58

Havelock, R (2015), 'Conscience and Unconscionability in Modern Equity' 9 *Journal of Equity* 1

Healey, D & Coles, J (2018), 'From "carries on a business" to "in trade or commerce": Efficiency in Government or Semantic Endeavour?' 26 *Competition & Consumer Law Journal* 47

Hedley, S (2001), *A Critical Introduction to Restitution*, Butterworths, London

Heydon, J D (2008), *The Restraint of Trade Doctrine*, 3rd ed, LexisNexis Butterworths, Sydney

Heydon, J D, Leeming, M J & Turner, P G (2015), *Meagher, Gummow & Lehane's Equity: Doctrines & Remedies*, 5th ed, LexisNexis Butterworths, Sydney

Holmes, O W (1897), 'The Path of the Law' 10 *Harvard Law Review* 457

Horwitz, M (1977), *The Transformation of American Law, 1780–1860*, Harvard University Press, Cambridge

House of Representatives Standing Committee on Finance and Public Administration (1991), *A Pocket Full of Change: Banking and Deregulation*, Australian Government Publishing Service, Canberra

Houston, C & Vedelago, C (2018), 'Real estate body faces massive damages over flawed contracts' *The Age*, 8 July 2018

Howarth, W (1984), 'The Meaning of Objectivity in Contract' 100 *Law Quarterly Review* 265

Howe, J (2006), '"Money and Favours": Government Deployment of Public Wealth as an Instrument of Labour Regulation' in C Arup et al (eds), *Labour Law and Labour Market Regulation* (Federation Press, Sydney), p 167

Howell, N (2006), 'Catching up with Consumer Realities: The Need for Legislation Prohibiting Unfair Terms in Consumer Contracts' 34 *Australian Business Law Review* 447

—— (2015), 'Revisiting the Australian Code of Banking Practice: Is Self-Regulation Still Relevant for Improving Consumer Protection Standards?' 38 *University of New South Wales Law Journal* 544

Hudson, A H (1966), 'Retraction of Letters of Acceptance' 82 *Law Quarterly Review* 169

Hudson, J (2017), 'The Price of Coherence in Estoppels' 39 *Sydney Law Review* 1

Hyde, A & Menegatti, E (2015), 'Legal Protection for Employee Mobility' in M W Finkin & G Mundlak (eds), *Comparative Labor Law*, Edward Elgar, Cheltenham/Northampton, p 195

Ibbetson, D (1999), *A Historical Introduction to the Law of Obligations*, Oxford University Press, Oxford

Ibbetson, D J & Swain, W (2008), 'Third Party Beneficiaries in English Law, 1880–2004' in E Schrage (ed), *Ius Quaesitum Tertio*, Duncker & Humblot, Berlin, p 331

Irving, M (2015), 'Australian and Canadian Approaches to the Assessment of the Length of Reasonable Notice' 28 *Australian Journal of Labour Law* 159

Jackman, I M (2015), 'Some Judicial Fallacies Concerning Entire Agreement Clauses' 89 *ALJ* 791

Jackson, R (2014), *Post-Employment Restraint of Trade*, Federation Press, Sydney

Joint Standing Committee on Treaties (2016), *Implementation Procedures for Airworthiness – USA; Convention on Choice of Courts – Accession; GATT Schedule of Concessions – Amendment; Radio Regulations – Practical Revision*, Report No 166, Parliament of Australia, Canberra

Jones, D (2013), *Commercial Arbitration in Australia*, 2nd ed, Lawbook Co, Sydney

Katz, A W (2014), 'Economic Foundations of Contract Law' in G Klass, G Letsas & P Saprai (eds), *Philosophical Foundations of Contract Law*, Oxford University Press, Oxford, p 171

Keating, A & Andersen, C B (2016), 'A Graphic Contract: Taking Visualisation in Contracting a Step Further' 2 *Journal of Strategic Contracting and Negotiation* 10

Keesing, G (2012), 'Contractual Rights and Remedies for Dismissed Employees of the "Employment Revolution"' 36 *Melbourne University Law Review* 104

Keyes, M (2014), 'The Internationalization of Contract Law' in M Keyes & T Wilson (eds), *Codifying Contract Law*, Taylor & Francis, Aldershot, p 15

Keyes, M & Burns, K (2002), 'Contract and the Family: Whither Intention?' 26 *Melbourne University Law Review* 577

Keyes, M & Wilson, T (eds) (2014), *Codifying Contract Law*, Taylor & Francis, Aldershot

Kincaid, P (1989), 'Privity and the Essence of Contract' 12 *University of New South Wales Law Journal* 59

—— (1997), 'Privity and Private Justice in Contract' 12 *Journal of Contract Law* 47

Klotz, E (2015), 'Misleading or Deceptive Conduct in the Provision of Financial Services: An Empirical and Theoretical Critique of the Corporations Act 2001 (Cth) and the Australian Securities and Investments Commission Act 2001 (Cth)' 33 *Company and Securities Law Journal* 451

Knowler, J & Rickett, C (2011), 'The Fiduciary Duties of Joint Venture Parties – When Do They Arise and What Do They Comprise?' 42 *Victoria University of Wellington Law Review* 117

Knowler, J & Stewart, A (2004), 'When is an Agreement Not a Contract? The Uncertain Status of Heads of Agreement and Other Preliminary Arrangements' 18 *Commercial Law Quarterly* 21

Kronman, A T (1978), 'Specific Performance' 45 *University of Chicago Law Review* 351

Kronman, A T & Posner, R A (eds) (1979), *The Economics of Contract Law, Little*, Brown & Co, Boston

Kull, A (1991), 'Mistake, Frustration and the Windfall Principle of Contract Remedies' 43 *Hastings Law Journal* 1

Law Commission (1996), *Privity of Contract: Contracts for the Benefit of Third Parties*, Report no 242, HMSO, London

Leeming, M (2013), 'Theories and Principles Underlying the Development of the Common Law – The Statutory Elephant in the Room' 36 *University of New South Wales Law Journal* 1002

Lewison, K & Hughes, D (2012), *The Interpretation of Contracts in Australia*, Lawbook Co, Sydney

Lindgren, K (1982), *Time in the Performance of Contracts*, 2nd ed, Butterworths, Sydney

Lockhart, C (2015), *The Law of Misleading or Deceptive Conduct*, 4th ed, LexisNexis Butterworths, Sydney

Lorenzen, E G (1919), 'Causa and Consideration in the Law of Contracts' 28 *Yale Law Journal* 621

Loughlan, P (2003), 'The Historical Role of the Equitable Jurisdiction' in P Parkinson (ed), *The Principles of Equity*, 2nd ed, Lawbook Co, Sydney, p 3

Lovric, J & Millbank, J (2003), *Darling, Please Sign This Form: A Report on the Practice of Third Party Guarantees in New South Wales*, Research Report 11, NSW Law Reform Commission and University of Sydney, Sydney

Lücke, H K (1987), 'Good Faith and Contractual Performance' in P D Finn (ed), *Essays on Contract*, Law Book Co, Sydney, 1987, p 155

—— (1991), 'Non-Contractual Arrangements for the Modification of Performance: Forbearance, Waiver and Equitable Estoppel' *University of Western Australia Law Review* 149

Lunney, M (1994), 'Jorden v Money – A Time for Reappraisal?' 68 *Australian Law Journal* 559

Luntz, H, Hambly, D, Burns, K, Dietrich, J & Foster, N (2017), *Torts: Cases and Commentary*, 8th ed, LexisNexis Butterworths, Sydney

Macaulay, S (1963), 'Non-Contractual Relations in Business: A Preliminary Study' 28 *American Sociological Review* 1

Macdonald, E (2009), 'Exception Clause: Exclusionary or Definitional? It Depends!' 29 *Journal of Contract Law* 47

—— (2011), 'Incorporation of Standard Terms in Website Contracting – Clicking "I Agree"' 27 *Journal of Contract Law* 198

Macfarlane, P & Willmott, L (1998), 'Rescission of an Executed Contract at Common Law for an Innocent Misrepresentation' 10 *Bond Law Review* 58

Macneil, I R (1978), 'Contracts: Adjustment of Long-Term Economic Relations under Classical, Neo-classical, and Relational Contract Law' 72 *Northwestern University Law Review* 854

—— (1982), 'The Efficient Breach of Contract: Circles in the Sky' 68 *Virginia Law Review* 947

—— (2000), 'Contracting Worlds and Essential Contract Theory' 9 *Social & Legal Studies* 431

—— (2003), 'Reflections on Relational Contract Theory after a Neo-classical Seminar' in D Campbell, H Collins & J Wightman (eds), *Implicit Dimensions of Contract: Discrete, Relational and Network Contracts*, Hart Publishing, Oxford, p 207

Malbon, J (2013), 'Online Cross-border Consumer Transactions: A Proposal for Developing Fair Standard Form Contract Terms' 37 *University of Western Australia Law Review* 20

Marshall, B (2018), 'The Hague Choice of Law Principles, CISG, and PICC: A Hard Look at a Choice of Soft Law' 66 *American Journal of Comparative Law* 175

Marshall, B A & Keyes, M (2017), 'Australia's Accession to the *Hague Convention on Choice of Court Agreements*' 41 *Melbourne University Law Review* 246

Martin, K (2013), 'Contractual Construction: Surrounding Circumstances and the Ambiguity Gateway' 37 *Australian Bar Review* 118

Mason, A (1987), 'Future Directions in Australian Law' 13 *Monash University Law Review* 149

—— (1994), 'The Place of Equity and Equitable Remedies in the Contemporary Common Law World' 110 *Law Quarterly Review* 238

—— (1998), 'The Impact of Equitable Doctrine on the Law of Contract' 27 *Anglo-American Law Review* 1

—— (2000), 'Contract, Good Faith and Equitable Standards in Fair Dealing' 116 *Law Quarterly Review* 66

—— (2004), 'The Break with the Privy Council and the Internationalisation of the "Common Law"' in P Cane (ed), *Centenary Essays for the High Court of Australia*, LexisNexis Butterworths, Sydney, p 69

—— (2009), 'Opening Address' 25 *Journal of Contract Law* 1

Mason, K (2015), 'String Coherence, Strong Fusion, Continuing Categorical Confusion: The High Court's Latest Contributions to the Law of Restitution' 39 *Australian Bar Review* 285

Mason, K, Carter, J W & Tolhurst, G J (2016), *Mason & Carter's Restitution Law in Australia*, 3rd ed, LexisNexis Butterworths, Sydney

McCrystal, S (2009), 'Is there a "Public Benefit" in Improving Working Conditions for Independent Contractors? Collective Bargaining and the Trade Practices Act 1974 (Cth)' 37 *Federal Law Review* 263

McFarlane, B & Stevens, R (2002), 'In Defence of *Sumpter v Hedges*' 118 *Law Quarterly Review* 569

McGill, D (2014), 'Asset Lending, Unconscionable Conduct and Intermediaries' 42 *Australian Business Law Review* 146

McGill, D & Howell, N (2013), 'Improving the Ability of Guarantors to Make a Real Choice: Lenders' Practices in Taking Third Party Guarantees' 24 *Journal of Banking and Finance Law and Practice* 182

McGivern, B (2013), 'Coming to the Party: The Evolution of Post-Contractual Duties of Utmost Good Faith under the ICA' 24 *Insurance Law Journal* 159

McKendrick, E (2007), '*Force Majeure* Clauses: The Gap between Doctrine and Practice' in A Burrows and E Peel (eds), *Contract Terms*, Oxford University Press, Oxford, p 233

—— (2017), *Contract Law*, 12th ed, Palgrave, London

McLauchlan, D W (1998), 'Rethinking Agreements to Agree' 18 *New Zealand Universities Law Review* 77

—— (2002), 'Intention, Incompleteness and Uncertainty in the New Zealand Court of Appeal' 18 *Journal of Contract Law* 153

—— (2005a), 'Objectivity in Contract' 24 *University of Queensland Law Journal* 479

—— (2005b), 'In Defence of the Fourth Category of Preliminary Agreements: Or Are There Only Two?' 21 *Journal of Contract Law* 286

—— (2007), 'Reliance Damages for Breach of Contract' [2007] *New Zealand Law Review* 417

—— (2009), 'Contract Interpretation: What is it About?' 31 *Sydney Law Review* 5

—— (2012), 'The Contract That Neither Party Intends' 29 *Journal of Contract Law* 26

—— (2016), 'The *ICS* Principles: A Failed "Revolution" in Contract Interpretation?' 27 *New Zealand Universities Law Review* 263

Menting, M-C (2017), 'Industry Codes of Conduct, the Foundations of Contract Law and Regulation: A Bottom-Up Perspective' in R Brownsword, R A J van Gestel & H-W Micklitz (eds), *Contract and Regulation: A Handbook on New Methods of Law Making in Private Law*, Edward Elgar, Cheltenham/ Northampton, p 39

Mescher, B (1990), 'Promise Enforcement by Common Law or Equity?' 64 *Australian Law Journal* 536

Mik, E (2009), 'The Effectiveness of Acceptances Communicated by Electronic Means' 26 *Journal of Contract Law* 68

—— (2010), '"Updating" the Electronic Transactions Act? Australia's Accession to the UN Convention on the Use of Electronic Communications in International Contracts 2005' 26 *Journal of Contract Law* 184

Mitchell, C (2006), 'Entire Agreement Clauses: Contracting out of Contextualism' 22 *Journal of Contract Law* 222

——— (2013), *Contract Law and Contract Practice: Bridging the Gap between Legal Reasoning and Commercial Expectation*, Hart Publishing, Oxford

Moore, A P, Grattan, S & Griggs, L (2016), *Bradbrook, McCallum and Moore's Australian Real Property Law*, 6th ed, Lawbook Co, Sydney

Morgan, J (2013), *Contract Law Minimalism: A Formalist Restatement of Commercial Contract Law*, Cambridge University Press, Cambridge

Morris, D (2015), 'Restitution sans Rescission: Exposing the Myth of a Fallacy' 89 *Australian Law Journal* 117

Mortensen, R, Garnett, R & Keyes, M (2015), *Private International Law in Australia*, 3rd ed, LexisNexis Butterworths, Sydney

Mouzas, S & Furmston, M (2013), 'A Proposed Taxonomy of Contracts' 30 *Journal of Contract Law* 1

Mulcahy, L & Wheeler, S (eds) (2005), *Feminist Perspectives on Contract Law*, GlassHouse Press, London

Mullen, S (2016), 'Damages for Breach of Contract: Quantifying the Lost Consumer Surplus' 36 *Oxford Journal of Legal Studies* 83

Munro, H (2009), 'The "Good Faith" Controversy in Australian Commercial Law: A Survey of the Spectrum of Academic Legal Opinion' 28 *University of Queensland Law Journal* 167

Murray, Jill (2006), 'Work Choices and the Radical Revision of the Public Realm of Australian Statutory Labour Law' 35 *Industrial Law Journal* 343

Murray, John (2017), *Review of Security of Payments Law: Building Trust and Harmony*, Department of Jobs and Small Business, Canberra

Napier, B (2011), 'Process Contracts in Government Commercial Tendering' 27 *Journal of Contract Law* 171

New South Wales Law Reform Commission (1970), *Report on Covenants in Restraint of Trade*, LRC 9, NSW Law Reform Commission, Sydney

O'Brien, T (2014), 'Breach Ordinarily No Bar to Termination' 86 *Australian Law Journal* 38

OECD (Organisation for Economic Cooperation and Development) (2017), *OECD Digital Economy Outlook 2017*, OECD Publishing, Paris

O'Sullivan, J (2000), 'Rescission as a Self-Help Remedy: A Critical Analysis' 59 *Cambridge Law Journal* 509

O'Sullivan, T (2016), 'The Definition of "Consumer" – Will the Real "Consumer" Please Stand Up?' 24 *Competition and Consumer Law Journal* 24

Parkinson, P (2003), 'The Conscience of Equity' in P Parkinson (ed), *The Principles of Equity*, 2nd ed, Lawbook Co, Sydney, p 29

Paterson, J (1996), 'The Contract to Negotiate in Good Faith: Recognition and Enforcement' 10 *Journal of Contract Law* 120

——— (1998), 'Terms Implied in Fact: The Basis for Implication' 13 *Journal of Contract Law* 103

——— (2009a) 'Implied Fetters on the Exercise of Discretionary Contractual Powers' 35 *Monash University Law Review* 45

——— (2009b), 'The Australian Unfair Contract Terms Law: The Rise of Substantive Unfairness as a Ground for Review of Standard Form Consumer Contracts' 33 *Melbourne University Law Review* 934

—— (2011), 'The New Consumer Guarantee Law and the Reasons for Replacing the Regime of Statutory Implied Terms in Consumer Transactions' 35 *Melbourne University Law Review* 252

—— (2014), 'Good Faith Duties in Contract Performance' 14 *Oxford University Commonwealth Law Journal* 283

—— (2015), 'Unconscionable Bargains in Equity and Under Statute' 9 *Journal of Equity* 189

—— (2016), 'The Consumer Guarantee Remedial Regime: Some Uncertainties and the Role of Common Law Analogy' 33 *Journal of Contract Law* 210

Paterson, J & Bant, E (2016), 'In the Age of Statutes, Why Do We Still Turn to the Common Law Torts? Lessons from the Statutory Prohibitions on Misleading and Deceptive Conduct' 23 *Torts Law Journal* 139

Paterson, J, Robertson, A & Duke, A (2016), *Principles of Contract Law*, 5th ed, Lawbook Co, Sydney

Paterson, J & Smith, R L (2016), 'Why Unilateral Variation Clauses in Consumer Contracts are Unfair' 23 *Competition & Consumer Law Journal* 201

Peden, E (2001), 'Policy Concerns Behind Implications of Terms in Law' 117 *Law Quarterly Reports* 459

—— (2003), *Good Faith in the Performance of Contracts*, Butterworths, Sydney

—— (2005), 'When Common Law Trumps Equity: The Rise of Good Faith and Reasonableness and the Demise of Unconscionability' 21 *Journal of Contract Law* 226

—— (2012), 'Forfeiture of Deposits: Where Law and Equity Collide?' 6 *Journal of Equity* 161

—— (2013), 'Contract Development Through the Looking-Glass of Implied Terms' in J T Gleeson, J A Watson and E Peden (eds), *Historical Foundations of Australian Law*, Federation Press, Sydney, p 201

Peden, E & Carter, J W (2005a), 'Incorporation of Terms by Signature: L'Estrange Rules!' 21 *Journal of Contract Law* 96

—— (2005b), 'Taking Stock: The High Court and Contract Construction' 21 *Journal of Contract Law* 172

—— (2006), 'Entire Agreement — and Similar — Clauses' 22 *Journal of Contract Law* 1

Peel, E, (2015), *Treitel on The Law of Contract*, 14th ed, Sweet & Maxwell, London

Phang, A (1996), 'Of Illegality and Presumptions – Australian Departures and Possible Approaches' 11 *Journal of Contract Law* 53

Phillips, J & O'Donovan, J (2014), *The Modern Contract of Guarantee*, online service, Lawbook Co, Sydney

Posner, E A (2003), 'Economic Analysis of Contract Law After Three Decades: Success or Failure?' 112 *Yale Law Journal* 829

Posner, R A (2014), *Economic Analysis of Law*, 9th ed, Wolters Kluwer Law & Business, New York

Posner, R A & Rosenfield, A M (1977), 'Impossibility and Related Doctrines in Contract Law: An Economic Analysis' 6 *Journal of Legal Studies* 83

Prince, T (2015), 'Defending Orthodoxy: Codelfa and Ambiguity' 89 *Australian Law Journal* 491

Productivity Commission (2008), *Review of Australia's Consumer Policy Framework*, Inquiry Report No 45, Productivity Commission, Canberra

—— (2015), *Workplace Relations Framework*, Inquiry Report No 76, Productivity Commission, Canberra

Provis, C (1996), 'Interests vs Positions: A Critique of the Distinction' 12 *Negotiation Journal* 305

Rabal, E (1947), 'The Statute of Frauds and Comparative Legal History' 63 *Law Quarterly Review* 174

Radin, M J (2013), *Boilerplate: The Fine Print, Vanishing Rights, and the Rule of Law*, Princeton University Press, New Jersey

—— (2017), 'The Deformation of Contract in the Information Society' 37 *Oxford Journal of Legal Studies* 505

Raghavan, K (2016), 'Failure of Consideration as a Basis for *Quantum Meruit* Following a Repudiatory Breach of Contract' 42 *Monash University Law Review* 179

Rajapaksa, P J (2014), 'Unconscionable or Unfair Dealing in Asset-Based lending in Australia' 22 *Competition & Consumer Law Journal* 151

Rakoff, T (1983), 'Contracts of Adhesion: An Essay in Reconstruction' 96 *Harvard Law Review* 1173

Ren, J (2014), 'Measure of Damages for Defective Building Work' 32 *Journal of Contract Law* 69

Richter, R (2015) 'The Role of Law in the New Institutional Economics in Comparison With the Economic Analysis of Law' in *Essays on New Institutional Economics*, Springer, Cham, p 77

Rickett, C (2005), 'Unconscionability and Commercial Law' 24 *University of Queensland Law Journal* 73

Roberts, M (2017), 'Variation Contracts in Australia and New Zealand: Whither Consideration?' 17 *Oxford University Commonwealth Law Journal* 238

Robertson, A (1996), 'Satisfying the Minimum Equity: Equitable Estoppel Remedies after *Verwayen*' 20 *Melbourne University Law Review* 805

—— (1997), 'Situating Equitable Estoppel within the Law of Obligations' 19 *Sydney Law Review* 32

—— (1998), 'Reliance and Expectation in Estoppel Remedies' 18 *Legal Studies* 360

—— (2001), 'Partial Rescission, Causation and Benefit' 17 *Journal of Contract Law* 163

—— (2005), 'The Limits of Voluntariness in Contract' 29 *Melbourne University Law Review* 218

—— (2013), 'Three Models of Promissory Estoppel' 7 *Journal of Equity* 226

—— (2016), 'The Foundations of Implied Terms: Logic, Efficacy and Purpose' in S Degeling, J Edelman & J Goudkamp (eds), *Contract in Commercial Law*, Lawbook Co, Sydney, p 143

Robertson, D (2009), 'Force Majeure Clauses' 25 *Journal of Contract Law* 62

—— (2011), 'International Contract Law and Post-Contractual Risk' 30 *Australian Resources and Energy Law Journal* 59

—— (2012), 'The International Harmonisation of Australian Contract Law' 29 *Journal of Contract Law* 1

Rochford, F (2015), 'The Contract Between the University and the Student' in S Varnham, P Kamvounias & J Squelch (eds), *Higher Education and the Law*, Federation Press, Sydney, p 82

Rogers, A (1995), 'Frustration and Estoppel' in E McKendrick (ed), *Force Majeure and Frustration of Contract*, 2nd ed, Lloyd's of London Press, London, p 245

Rousseau, D M (1995), *Psychological Contracts in Organizations: Understanding Written and Unwritten Agreements*, Sage, Thousand Oaks

Rousseau, J-J (1762), *The Social Contract*, eBooks@Adelaide, 2014 web edition

Rowan, S (2017), 'The New French Law of Contract' 66 *International & Comparative Law Quarterly* 805

Royal Commission into Misconduct in the Banking, Superannuation and Financial Services Industry (2018), *Interim Report*, Commonwealth, Canberra

Sangha, B & Moles, B (1997), 'Gendered Stereotypes and Unconscionability – Can We Trust the Judges to Get It Right?' 1 *Flinders Journal of Law Reform* 145

Sarmas, L (1994) 'Storytelling and the Law: A Case Study of Louth v Diprose' 19 *Melbourne University Law Review* 701

Saunders, H (2007), 'Relief from Unconscionable Contracts: The Contracts Review Act 1980 (NSW) and the "Unwritten Law"' 29 *Australian Bar Review* 290

Schwartz, A (1979), 'The Case for Specific Performance' 89 *Yale Law Journal* 271

Seddon, N (1978), 'A Plea for the Reform of the Rule in Hoyt's Pty Ltd v Spencer' 52 *Australian Law Journal* 372

—— (2018), *Government Contracts: Federal, State and Local*, 6th ed, Federation Press, Sydney

Seddon, N & Bigwood, R (2017), *Cheshire & Fifoot's Law of Contract*, 11th Aust ed, LexisNexis Butterworths, Sydney

Senate Economics References Committee (2017), *Australia's General Insurance Industry: Sapping Consumers of the Will to Compare*, Commonwealth, Canberra

Senate Standing Committee on Economics (2008), *The Need, Scope and Content of a Definition of Unconscionable Conduct for the Purposes of Part IVA of the Trade Practices Act 1974*, Commonwealth, Canberra

Sharkey, J, Bell, M, Jocic, W & Marginean, R (2014), *Standard Forms of Contract in the Australian Construction Industry: Research Report*, University of Melbourne

Silink, A (2011), 'Equitable Estoppel in "Subject to Contract" Negotiations' 5 *Journal of Equity* 252

Simpson, A W B (1966), 'The Penal Bond with Conditional Defeasance' 82 *Law Quarterly Review* 392

—— (1975a), 'Innovation in Nineteenth Century Contract Law' 91 *Law Quarterly Review* 247

—— (1975b), *A History of the Common Law of Contract*, Oxford University Press, Oxford

—— (1979), 'The Horwitz Thesis and the History of Contracts' 46 *University of Chicago Law Review* 533

Sise, P (2017a), 'Is There a Gap in the Unfair Contract Term Provisions Between a "Consumer Contract" and a "Small Business Contract"?' 25 *Australian Journal of Competition and Consumer Law* 14

—— (2017b), 'The Unfair Contract Term Provisions: What's Transparency Got to Do with It?' 17 *QUT Law Review* 160

Skilbeck, J (2017), '*Williams Group Australia v Crocker* and the (Non)Binding Nature of Electronic Signatures' 17 *Macquarie Law Journal* 154

Slawson, W D (1971), 'Standard Form Contracts and Democratic Control of Lawmaking Power' 84 *Harvard Law Review* 529

Smith, S A (1997), 'Contracts for the Benefit of Third Parties: In Defence of the Third-Party Rule' 17 *Oxford Journal of Legal Studies* 643

—— (2004), *Contract Theory*, Oxford University Press, Oxford

Smyth, R (2008), 'Citations of Foreign Decisions in Australian State Supreme Courts Over the Course of the Twentieth Century: An Empirical Analysis' 22 *Temple International and Comparative Law Journal* 409

Sourdin, T (2016), *Alternative Dispute Resolution*, 5th ed, Lawbook Co, Sydney

Spagnolo, L (2009), 'The Last Outpost: CISG Opt Outs, Misapplications and the Costs of Ignoring the Vienna Sales Convention for Australian Lawyers' 10 *Melbourne Journal of International Law* 141

Spence, M (1999), *Protecting Reliance: The Emergent Doctrine of Equitable Estoppel*, Hart Publishing, Oxford

Spencer, D (2015), 'Landing in the Right Class of Subject to Contract Agreements' 26 *Australian Dispute Resolution Journal* 75

Spigelman, J J (2011), 'Contractual Interpretation: A Comparative Perspective' 85 *Australian Law Journal* 412

Spottiswood, S (2018), 'The Use of Foreign Law by the High Court of Australia' 46 *Federal Law Review* 161

Spry, I C F (2014), *The Principles of Equitable Remedies*, 9th ed, Lawbook Co, Sydney

Stephenson, A & Molck, B (2017), 'Alliancing in Australia: Commercial Advantage at the Expense of Legal Certainty?' 33 *Building and Construction Law Journal* 99

Stevens, R (2009), 'Damages and the Right to Performance: A Golden Victory or Not?' in J W Neyers, R Bronaugh & S G A Pitel (eds), *Exploring Contract Law*, Hart Publishing, Oxford, p 171

—— (2018), 'The Unjust Enrichment Disaster' 134 *Law Quarterly Review* 574

Stewart, A (1984), 'Economic Duress – Legal Regulation of Commercial Pressure' 14 *Melbourne University Law Review* 410

—— (1987), 'Oral Promises, Ad Hoc Implication and the Sanctity of Written Agreements' 61 *Australian Law Journal* 119

—— (1988), 'Contractual Illegality and the Recognition of Proprietary Interests' 1 *Journal of Contract Law* 134

—— (1992) 'The South Australian Frustrated Contracts Act' 5 *Journal of Contract Law* 220

—— (2012), 'What's Wrong with the Australian Law of Contract?' 29 *Journal of Contract Law* 74

—— (2016), 'Illegality and Public Policy' in *The Laws of Australia*, Lawbook Co, Melbourne, vol 7 (Contract — General Principles), Title 7.2, ch 4

Stewart, A & Carter J W (1992), 'Frustrated Contracts and Statutory Adjustment: the Case for a Reappraisal' 51 *Cambridge Law Journal* 66

Stewart, A, Forsyth, A, Irving, M, Johnstone, R & McCrystal, S (2016), *Creighton & Stewart's Labour Law*, 6th ed, Federation Press, Sydney

Stewart, A & McClurg, L (2007), 'Playing Your Cards Right: Obligations of Disclosure in Commercial Negotiations' [2007] *AMPLA Yearbook* 36

Stewart, I (1999), 'Why Place Trust in a Promise?: Privity of Contract and Enforcement of Contracts by Third Party Beneficiaries' 73 *Australian Law Journal* 354

Stewart, M (2013), 'The Judicial Doctrine in Australia' in E Simpson & M Stewart (eds), *Sham Transactions*, Oxford University Press, Oxford, p 51

Stoljar, J (2013), 'The Categories of Waiver' 87 *Australian Law Journal* 482

—— (2018), 'The Doctrine of Forbearance' 92 *Australian Law Journal* 195

Sunstein, C R (ed) (2000), *Behavioral Law and Economics*, Cambridge University Press, New York

Svantesson, D J (2008), 'Codifying Australia's Contract Law – Time for a Stocktake in the Common Law Factory' 20 *Bond Law Review* 92

Swadling, W (2016), 'Substance and Procedure in Equity' 10 *Journal of Equity* 1

Swain, W (2006), 'Moses v Macferlan (1760)' in C Mitchell & P Mitchell (eds), *Landmark Cases in the Law of Restitution*, Hart Publishing, Oxford, p 19

—— (2012), 'Codification of Contract Law: Some Lessons from History' 31 *University of Queensland Law Journal* 39

—— (2013a), 'Unjust Enrichment and the Role of Legal History in England and Australia' 36 *New South Wales Law Journal* 1030

—— (2013b), 'Contract as Promise: The Role of Promising in the Law of Contract. An Historical Account' 17 *Edinburgh Law Review* 1

—— (2014a), 'Reshaping Contractual Unfairness in Eighteenth and Nineteenth Century England' 35 *Journal of Legal History* 131

—— (2014b), 'The Unconscionable Dealing Doctrine: In Retreat?' 31 *Journal of Contract Law* 255

—— (2014c), 'Contract Codification in Australia: Is it Necessary, Desirable and Possible?' 36 *Sydney Law Review* 131

—— (2015a), *The Law of Contract 1670–1870*, Cambridge University Press, Cambridge

—— (2015b), 'Hedley Byrne v Heller in Australia: Never Has There Been Such a Judicial Jamboree' in K Barker, R Grantham & W Swain (eds), *The Many Faces of Negligent Misstatement*, Hart Publishing, Oxford, p 29

—— (2015c), 'Common Mistake in Equity: Some Unanswered Questions' 40 *Australian Bar Review* 124

—— (2016), 'AWB Simpson's, "The Horwitz Thesis and the History of Contracts" (1978–1979) 46 University of Chicago Law Review 533' 35 *University of Queensland Law Journal* 115

Swanton, J P (1984) '"Subject to Finance" Clauses in Contracts for the Sale of Land' 58 *Australian Law Journal* 633 and 691

Symes, C & Duns, J (2015), *Australian Insolvency Law*, 3rd ed, LexisNexis Butterworths, Sydney

Tarr, A A, Tarr, J-A & Clarke, M (2009), *Insurance: The Laws of Australia*, Law Book Co, Sydney

Tarrant, J (2006), 'Preliminary Agreements' 3 *University of New England Law Journal* 151

Teubner, G (1993), *Law as an Autopoetic System*, Blackwell, London

Thampapillai, D (2015), 'Practical Benefits and Promises to Pay Lesser Sums: Reconsidering the Relationship Between the Rule in *Foakes v Beer* and the Rule in *Williams v Roffey*' 34 *University of Queensland Law Journal* 301

Thomas, E W (2005), *The Judicial Process*, Cambridge University Press, Cambridge

Thorpe, D (2012), 'Expositions on the Restraints of Trade Threshold' 29 *Journal of Contract Law* 208

—— (2015), 'The Restraint of Trade Doctrine in the Era of Digital Markets' 32 *Journal of Contract Law* 244

Thorpe, D, Buti, A, Davies, C & Jonson, P (2018), *Sports Law*, 3rd ed, Oxford University Press, Melbourne

Tiverios, N (2017a), 'A Restatement of Relief Against Contractual Penalties (I): Underlying Principles in Equity and at Common Law' 11 *Journal of Equity* 1

—— (2017b), 'A Restatement of Relief Against Contractual Penalties (II): A Framework for Applying the Australian and English Approaches' 11 *Journal of Equity* 185

Tokeley, K (2017), 'When Not All Sellers are Traders: Re-evaluating the Scope of Consumer Protection Legislation in the Modern Marketplace' 39 *Sydney Law Review* 59

Tolhurst, G J (2006), *The Assignment of Contractual Rights*, Hart Publishing, Oxford

—— (2008), 'The Nature of an Assignee's Right to Damages for Breach of Contract That Occur Prior to Assignment' 24 *Journal of Contract Law* 77

Tolhurst, G J & Carter, J W (2014), 'Prohibitions on Assignment: A Choice to be Made' 73 *Cambridge Law Journal* 405

Tolhurst, G J, Carter, J W & Peden, E (2011), '*Masters v Cameron* – Again!' 42 *Victoria University of Wellington Law Journal* 49

Trade Practices Commission (1992a), *Guarantors: Problems and Perspectives*, Discussion Paper, Trade Practices Commission, Canberra

—— (1992b), *Protecting Consumer Guarantees in the Australian Code of Banking Practice*, Trade Practices Commission, Canberra

Trebilcock, M (1976), 'The Doctrine of Inequality of Bargaining Power: Post-Benthamite Economics in the House of Lords' 26 *University of Toronto Law Journal* 359

—— (1993), *The Limits of Freedom of Contract*, Harvard University Press, Cambridge

Triantis, G G (1992), 'Contractual Allocations of Unknown Risks: A Critique of the Doctrine of Commercial Impracticability' 42 *University of Toronto Law Journal* 450

Turner, P G (2018), 'Lex Sequitur Equitatem: Fusion and the Penalty Doctrine', https://papers.ssrn.com/sol3/papers.cfm?abstract_id=3105921

Tyree, A (2017), *Banking Law in Australia*, 9th ed, LexisNexis Butterworths, Sydney

van Caenegem, W (2013), 'Employee Know-How, Non-Compete Clauses and Job Mobility Across Civil and Common Law Systems' 29 *International Journal of Comparative Labour Law and Industrial Relations* 219

Victorian Law Reform Commission (1992), *An Australian Contract Code*, Discussion Paper No 27, VLRC, Melbourne

Vincent-Jones, P (2000), 'Contractual Governance: Institutional and Organisational Analysis' 20 *Oxford Journal of Legal Studies* 317

Virgo, G (2015), *The Principles of the Law of Restitution*, 3rd ed, Oxford University Press, Oxford

Vogenauer, S (2013), 'Regulatory Competition Through Choice of Contract Law and Choice of Forum in Europe: Theory and Evidence' 21 *European Review of Private Law* 13

—— (ed) (2015), *Commentary on the UNIDROIT Principles of International Commercial Contracts (PICC)*, 2nd ed, Oxford University Press, Oxford

Von Mehren, A (1982), 'General Limits on the Use of Contract', *International Encylopeadia of Comparative Law*, vol VII, JCB Mohr Paul Siebeck, Tübingen

Vrodos, Y N (2015), 'Revisiting the "Wives' Special Equity": An Exploration of the Volunteer Requirement' 40 *University of Western Australia Law Review* 244

Waddams, S (2007), 'What Were the Principles of Nineteenth-Century Contract Law?' in A Lewis, P Brand & P Mitchell (eds), *Law in the City: Proceedings of the Seventeenth British Legal History Conference, London, 2005*, Four Courts Press, Dublin, p 305

Walker, S & Lewins, K (2014), 'Dashed Expectations? The Impact of Civil Liability Legislation on Contractual Damages for Disappointment and Distress' 42 *Australian Business Law Review* 465

Waters, C (2017), '"Huge win" for small business as banks agree to eliminate unfair terms from contracts' *The Age*, 23 August 2017

Waye, V (2009), 'Who Are Judges Writing For?' 34 *University of Western Australia Law Review* 274

Webb, C (2006), 'Performance and Compensation: An Analysis of Contract Damages and Contractual Obligation' 26 *Oxford Journal of Legal Studies* 41

Whittaker, B (2016), 'Remote Signings under Australian Law' 44 *Australian Business Law Review* 229

Wilkinson-Ryan, T & Hoffman, D A (2015), 'The Common Sense of Contract Formation' 67 *Stanford Law Review* 1269

Williams, G (1945), 'Language and the Law' 61 *Law Quarterly Review* 71, 179, 283 and 384

Williams, G, Brennan, S & Lynch, G (2018), *Blackshield & Williams' Australian Constitutional Law and Theory: Commentary and Materials*, 7th ed, Federation Press, Sydney

Wilmot-Smith, F (2017), 'Should the Payee Pay?' 37 *Oxford Journal of Legal Studies* 844

Winterton, D (2014), '*Clark v Macourt*: Defective Sperm and Performance Substitutes in the High Court of Australia' 38 *Melbourne University Law Review* 755

—— (2015), *Money Awards in Contract Law*, Hart Publishing, Oxford

—— (2016), 'Commonwealth v Amann Aviation Pty Ltd 25 Years On: Re-examining the Problem of Pre-breach Expenditure in Contract Law' in S Degeling, J Edelman & J Goudkamp (eds), *Contract in Commercial Law*, Lawbook Co, Sydney, p 333

Witzleb, N, Bant, E, Degeling, S & Barker, K (2015), *Remedies: Commentary and Materials*, 6th ed, Lawbook Co, Sydney

Wong, D & Michael, B (2012), 'Western Export Services v Jireh International: Ambiguity as the Gateway to Surrounding Circumstances' 86 *Australian Law Journal* 57

World Bank Group (2017), *Measuring and Analyzing the Impact of GVCs on Economic Development*, World Bank, Washington DC

Wright, D (2014), 'Unity in Remedies – Finding the Best Remedy – The Adequacy of Common Law Remedies' 38 *University of Western Australia Law Review* 30

Wright, T, Ellinghaus, M & Kelly, D (2014), 'A Draft Australian Law of Contract', https://papers.ssm.com/sol3/Papers.cfm?abstract_id=2403603

Zhou, Q (2010), 'Damages for Repudiation: An Ex Ante Perspective on the Golden Victory' 32 *Sydney Law Review* 579

—— (2011), 'What Can Contract Lawyers Learn from Law and Economics?' 30 *University of Tasmania Law Review* 157

Zumbo, F (2009), 'The Case for Enhancing the Federal Unfair Contract Terms Framework' 17 *Trade Practices Law Journal* 276

INDEX

penalty doctrine, 22, 227, 323, 409, 434
  consequences of stipulation being a penalty,
    451–2
  contemporary, scope of, 447–9
  history of, 446–7
  new law of, 452–3
  operation of new 'interests test', 450–1
  penalty, test for identifying, 449–50
performance, 227
  breach of contract and its consequences, 227–8
  complete, 227, 232–4, 236, 321–2
  concurrent, 232
  contracts impossible to perform, 277
  contractual sums accruing independently of, 446
  counter-performance, 232, 234, 268, 324, 484
  delay in, termination and, 303–5
  duty of cooperation in, 236–7
  duty of good faith in, 240–6
  fiduciary duties, 237–8
  order and completeness of See order and
    completeness of performance
  pre-existing duties, consideration and, 96–8,
    251–6
  standards and methods of See standards and
    methods of performance
  substantial, 234–5
  temporary impossibility and, 278
  time of See time of performance
  transferring responsibility for, 269–70
  vicarious, 229
  withholding of, 41–2, 227, 231, 301
performance interest, 441, 455
plain English drafting, 63–4
post-employment restraints, 319, 424–30
postal acceptance rule, 86–8
practical benefit, 96, 253–61
pragmatism, 10, 37
pre-contractual statements
  collateral contracts, 167–8
  determining the status of, 163–4
  entire agreement clauses, 166–7
  parol evidence rule, 165–7, 331
  presumption of integration, 166
  warranty or representation, 164–5
pre-existing duties
  consideration and, 96–8, 251–6
preliminary agreements
  agreements to negotiate, 115–17
  intention to form contract, 111–15
  legal issues, 110–11
  prevalence of, 110
preparation of contracts
  common provisions in written contracts, 64–5
  disclosure of information See disclosure of
    information
  drafting styles, 63–4

duty to negotiate in good faith, 69–70
negotiation techniques, 60–1
pre-contractual liability, 68–9
  See also pre-contractual statements
standard form contracts, 62–3
use of agents, 61–2
ways to make a contract, 60
presumed undue influence, 372, 374–6
presumptions of intention
  role of, 76–7
pretence, doctrine of, 169
primary obligations, 319
prior course of dealing, 161–2
private international law, 52–5
privity of contract, 5, 24, 36, 50, 136–52
  agency and, 142–4
  consideration and, 137–8
  doctrine of, 137–8, 140, 149, 151
  insurance contracts, 138–40, 148, 238
  reform to doctrine of, 149–50, 152
  statutory reform, 149–50
  third party benefits See third parties
  third party burdens, 151
process contract, 83
Productivity Commission, 17, 28, 32, 397
professional activity
  conduct in trade and commerce, as, 344
progress payments, 44
prohibitory injunctions, 434, 443
promissory estoppel, 21, 32, 52, 70, 120, 262–3,
    380
  as way around *Foakes v Beer* rule, 263
  development of, 121–2
  See also equitable estoppel
promissory note, 271
promissory theory, 37
proper law of the contract, 54, 414
proportionate liability, 357, 475
proprietary estoppel, 106, 120–2, 124–5, 130–2
  See also equitable estoppel
public policy
  assignment of rights, 269
  ex turpi causa principle, 412–13, 419, 421, 483
  enforceability of a contract contrary to, 413–18
  illegal or immoral conduct and, 413–14
  implication of terms and, 175–6
  penalties See penalty doctrine
  restraint of trade See restraint of trade
puffs, 77, 333, 348
punitive damages, 49, 355, 457

quantum meruit, 48, 71, 234–6, 325–6, 419, 481,
    484, 486–7
quantum valebat, 325, 481, 484
quasi-contractual actions, 23, 48, 51, 481, 488
quiet possession, 177, 180

reading down, 428–9
reasonable notice
  estoppel and, 129
  incorporation of written terms and, 62–3,
    158–63
  termination of contracts by, 42, 100, 173,
    230–1, 265, 308
recovery of debts *See* debt, action for
recreational services, 55, 185, 214
rectification, 21, 48, 163, 167, 264, 330, 358,
    362–4
  common mistake, 362–3
  limited scope of, 264
  unilateral mistake, 364
regulatory theory, 36–7
relational analysis, 38–9, 250
reliance
  estoppel, 126–7
reliance loss, 354, 458–9, 461
relief against forfeiture, 21, 32, 312–14, 322,
    391
remedies
  account of profits, 49, 157, 460
  ACL, 353–7
  anticipated contracts that fail to materialise,
    70–1, 487
  civil penalty, 49–50, 354, 369–70
  constructive trust, 49, 106, 150–1
  consumer guarantees, 185–7
  court-ordered, 46–50
  damages *See* damages
  debt *See* debt, action for
  declaration, 50
  duress, 371
  equitable estoppel and, 129–32
  injunction *See* injunctions
  misinformation, 330–1
  misleading or deceptive conduct, 353–7
  misrepresentation, 338–43
  money had and received, 48, 324, 481–4
  quantum meruit See quantum meruit
  quantum valebat, 325, 481, 484
  rectification *See* rectification
  rescission *See* rescission
  restitution *See* restitution
  self-help, 41–3
  specific performance *See* specific
    performance
  termination *See* termination of contracts
  unconscionable conduct, 396–7
  unfair contract terms, 403–4
remoteness of damage, 470–3
  mitigation and, 474
  party–party indemnities and, 223
renegotiation, 275, 287–8, 368, 370, 456
  See also variation of contracts

renunciation
  repudiation by, 300
  requirement of seriousness, 301
  types of, 300–1
  See also repudiation
representations
  false or misleading consumer guarantees, as to,
    187–8
  warranties, distinguished from, 164–5
  See also estoppel; misleading or deceptive
    conduct; misrepresentation
repudiation, 228, 319–20
  inability to perform, 302–3
  misapprehension, based on, 301–2
  renunciation, 300
rescission, 21, 42–3, 49, 108, 338–9
  bars to, 339–40
  duress, 366, 371
  election, 338–40
  misrepresentation, 338–40
  See also misrepresentation
  termination and, 292–3
  See also remedies
Restatement of the Law of Restitution (US), 487–8
Restatement (Second) of the Law of Contracts
    (US), 35, 137, 240
restitutio in integrum, 338–9
restitution, 48–9, 70, 228, 293, 481–2
  equity and, 488–9
  illegality and, 419–21, 483
  legislation, effect on, 419–21
  money claims *See* money claims
  property supplied, for *See quantum valebat*
  reconceptualisation of, 487–8
  rise and fall of unjust enrichment, 488–9
  services rendered, for *See* services rendered,
    claims for
  termination of contracts and, 323–6
restitutionary claims
  effect of legislation on, 419–21
restitutionary damages, 458–60
restraint of trade, 28, 409
  common law doctrine of, 423–4
  duration of, 426–7
  enforcement of restraints, 429
  legitimate reasons for, 425–6
  other factors going to reasonableness, 427–8
  'restraint', 424–5
  scope of, 426–7
  severance of unreasonable restraints, 428–9
  statutory restrictions on anti-competitive
    arrangements, 429–30
restrictions on damages, 469
  causation, 469–70
  contributory negligence and apportionment,
    357, 475

surrounding circumstances evidence, 194–9
suspension
    contractual obligations, of, 275, 292
    estoppel, effect of, 129, 262–3

tenders, 82–3
termination of contracts
    abandonment, 317
    accrued rights after, 320–1
    conditional contracts, 91–2, 293
    consumer guarantees, for breach of, 186
    damages and, 293, 307, 319, 457
    delay in performance, for, 303–5
    discharge and, 292
    effect of
        ancillary obligations, 319–20
        primary obligations, 319
        secondary obligations, 319
        termination other than for breach, 320
        unperformed primary obligations, 321, 483
    election to affirm, 310–11, 315–16
    election to terminate, 308–10
    express rights of, 305–7
    finding a basis for, 308–9
    for convenience, 304, 314, 320
    frustration, by See frustration
    good faith, 314
    implied rights to, 307–8
    mutual consent to, 316
    non-performance for
        actual breach, 295
        anticipatory breach, 294–5
        common law rights, 228, 294–305
        delay, 303–5
        essential terms, 156, 228, 295–8
        fundamental breach, 156, 228, 295–6,
            298–300, 303, 310
        intermediate terms, 156, 228, 295–6, 298–9
        non-essential terms, 156, 295, 298
        repudiation See repudiation
        time stipulations, 303–5
    reasons for, 293–4
    relief against forfeiture, 312–13
    rescission and, 292–3
    restitutionary claims 323–6
    self-help remedy, as, 42, 293
    statutory rights of, 307
    termination clauses, 305–7
    unconscionable, 313–14
    unfair, 313–14
    unfair affirmation, 315–16
    without cause, 307–8
terms, 27, 31
    electronic, 159
    essential See essential terms

express See express terms
implied See implied terms
inferred, 156, 172
intermediate, 156, 228, 295–6, 298–9
non-essential, 156, 295, 298, 331
onerous or unusual, 161
types of, 156
unfair See unfair terms
written See written terms
terms implied by custom and practice, 156,
        173–4
terms implied by law, 156
    default rules, as, 174–5
    policy or necessity, as basis for, 175–6
    recognition of new terms, 175–6
terms implied by statute, 156, 175, 177
terms implied in fact, 156
    division between implication and
            interpretation, 172–3
    establishing necessity, 171–2
    inferred terms, 172
    test for, 170–1
third parties
    assistance from in dispute resolution,
            43–4
    conferring benefits on
        agency arrangements, 142–4
        collateral contracts, 148
        enforcement by promisee, 140–2
        estoppel and, 148–9
        Himalaya clauses, 144–5
        privity See privity of contract
        Queensland and Northern Territory
            legislation, 150
        statutory reform of privity rule, 149–50
        tort law and, 146–8
        trust, inferring a, 145–6
        Western Australian legislation, 149–50
    duress by, 370–1
    duties owed to in consideration, 98
    imposing a burden on, 151
    meaning of, 5, 134
    non est factum and, 362
    rescission, effect on, 339–40, 359–60
    specific performance and, 142, 437, 440–1
    See also privity of contract
third party claims indemnity, 223–4
ticket cases, 160–1, 206
time is of the essence, 303, 439
time of performance
    delay in See delay
    duration of contracts, 230–1
    order of performance See order and
            completeness of performance
    when performance is required, 230